Color Figure 2 (for Demonstration 2.4)

Cognition

EIGHTH EDITION

MARGARET W. MATLIN
SUNY Geneseo

WILEY

VP & Executive Publisher   Jay O'Callaghan
Executive Editor   Christopher Johnson
Assistant Editor   Brittany Cheetham
Editorial Assistant   Maura Gilligan
Marketing Manager   Margaret Barrett
Photo Editor   Jennifer Atkins
Cover Designer   Joseph Goh
Associate Production Manager   Joyce Poh
Production Editor   Jolene Ling
Covers/Title Page/Chapter Openers Photo   Kaz Chiba/Getty Images, Inc.
Front Endpaper Photo   Courtesy Arnold H. Matlin, M.D. (SIR Norita, El Sauce, Nicaragua)

This book was set in 10/12 JansonText-Roman by Laserwords Private Limited and printed and bound by R. R. Donnelley. The cover was printed by R. R. Donnelley.

This book is printed on acid free paper.

Founded in 1807, John Wiley & Sons, Inc. has been a valued source of knowledge and understanding for more than 200 years, helping people around the world meet their needs and fulfill their aspirations. Our company is built on a foundation of principles that include responsibility to the communities we serve and where we live and work. In 2008, we launched a Corporate Citizenship Initiative, a global effort to address the environmental, social, economic, and ethical challenges we face in our business. Among the issues we are addressing are carbon impact, paper specifications and procurement, ethical conduct within our business and among our vendors, and community and charitable support. For more information, please visit our website: www.wiley.com/go/citizenship.

Evaluation copies are provided to qualified academics and professionals for review purposes only, for use in their courses during the next academic year. These copies are licensed and may not be sold or transferred to a third party. Upon completion of the review period, please return the evaluation copy to Wiley. Return instructions and a free of charge return mailing label are available at www.wiley.com/go/returnlabel. If you have chosen to adopt this textbook for use in your course, please accept this book as your complimentary desk copy. Outside of the United States, please contact your local sales representative.

Library of Congress Cataloging-in-Publication Data

Matlin, Margaret W.
  Cognition / Margaret W. Matlin. -- 8th ed.
    p. cm.
  Includes bibliographical references and index.
  ISBN 978-1-118-14896-9 (cloth)
  1. Cognition. I. Title.
  BF311.M426 2013
  153—dc23
                    2012027798

Printed in the United States of America

10 9 8 7 6 5 4 3 2

This book is dedicated to

Helen and Donald White

and

Clare and Harry Matlin

The first edition of this *Cognition* textbook was published in 1983, three decades ago. As I began to write this eighth edition, I thought about how the book had changed during these 30 years; the first section in this preface discusses these general changes. I will then discuss specific features in this book, and I'll describe the book's organization. The fourth section presents highlights of this eighth edition. The fifth section describes the Test Bank. In the final section, I acknowledge the contributions from the Wiley team, others who have worked on this book, and members of my family.

GENERAL CHANGES IN THIS TEXTBOOK

If you could compare the first edition of this textbook with this current eighth edition, you would recognize the chapter titles. However, you would also notice the expanded coverage in this new version. The first edition featured one chapter titled "Perceptual Processes," whereas the eighth edition includes separate chapters on perceptual recognition and on attention. This earlier edition had a single chapter on language, but the current edition has one chapter on language comprehension and one on language production. The most dramatic comparison focuses on memory. That first, 1983 edition of *Cognition* featured just one chapter, in contrast to three chapters in this current eighth edition: Working Memory (Chapter 4), Long-Term Memory (Chapter 5), and Memory Strategies and Metacognition (Chapter 6).

The field of cognitive psychology is also changing in important ways. Three of these changes are particularly relevant in the current decade: (1) connections with other perspectives; (2) research in biopsychology; and (3) applying cognitive psychology in the "real world." Let's consider these topics in more detail.

Connections with Other Perspectives. John Cacioppo wrote a thought-provoking article in his role as the president of the Association for Psychological Science, the organization that would include the largest number of cognitive psychologists. According to Cacioppo (2007), psychology has long been a discipline with distinctly separate fields. For example, some social psychologists, cognitive psychologists, and biological psychologists might believe that they have little to offer each other. As Cacioppo wrote,

> The important point here is that each perspective has substantive implications for the others in the pursuit of comprehensive psychological explanations. The in-depth study of any one of these perspectives is essential, but a comprehensive understanding of the mind and behavior is likely to be achieved by an integration of what we know and can learn across multiple perspectives. (p. 50)

In particular, Cacioppo described three different levels of organization: (1) neuroscience, (2) cognitive science, and (3) social science. Furthermore, each of these levels could be studied from several different perspectives: (a) abnormal psychology, (b) individual differences, and (c) developmental psychology. Some researchers might argue that cognitive psychologists should study only those topics that are strictly cognitive. This viewpoint suggests that human cognitive processes must be remarkably standardized, a viewpoint that is not consistent with our daily observations about a wide variety of other people.

Cacioppo's article describes my own views, and it also confirmed my decision to continue the individual-differences feature in the eighth edition of *Cognition*. Accordingly, this new edition again includes an individual-differences feature in Chapters 2 through 13. Several of these features focus on abnormal psychology, for example, face identification in people with schizophrenia (Chapter 2), and working memory in people with depression (Chapter 4).

Other individual-differences features focus on demographic variables. For example, Chapter 7 explores gender comparisons in spatial ability. Still others look at the relationship between personality characteristics and cognitive performance. For example, Chapter 11 examines the relationship between intrinsic motivation and Chapter 12 looks at the relationship between decision-making style and psychological well-being.

According to Cacioppo's article, a third psychological perspective is developmental psychology. The final chapter in this textbook focuses on three periods of development: infancy, childhood, and later adulthood. As you'll see, this chapter emphasizes that infants have some remarkable cognitive skills. Furthermore, elderly adults are more competent than many people believe.

Research in Biopsychology. Quite clearly, the research in biopsychology has made enormous contributions to cognitive psychology. For example, the fMRI research demonstrates that the brain responds more quickly to faces presented in the normal, upright position, in comparison to faces presented upside-down. This research is consistent with research showing that people are much more accurate in identifying upright faces, compared to upside-down faces.

For decades, researchers have tried to identify the specific locations in the brain that are relevant in language comprehension. Some of these studies employ new techniques. For example, the "language-localizer task" compensates for individual differences in brain patterns during language processing. This research demonstrates, for example, that the brain is more active when processing actual sentences, instead of jumbled words.

Applied Psychology. Some researchers believe that cognitive psychologists should not emphasize research that focuses on practical applications. However, I'm persuaded by George Miller's perspectives on psychology. As Chapter 4 points out, Miller (1957) was one of the first researchers to emphasize the limited capacity of working memory (short-term memory). As Miller wrote in one of his classic articles, people can typically remember between five and nine items.

Miller's other classic article is called "Psychology as a Means of Promoting Human Welfare" (Miller, 1969). Miller reaffirmed that psychologists have an obligation to conduct scientifically rigorous research. However, Miller's article also emphasized that psychologists have an obligation as citizens. Specifically, when psychologists conduct research that has important practical applications in the real world, they should "give psychology away" (Miller, 1969, p. 1071). Miller pointed out that psychological research should be applied in schools, hospitals, industry, and other institutions.

A textbook in cognitive psychology provides numerous applications for students, especially at the college level. For example, students reading this textbook can easily apply the information about topics such as divided attention (Chapter 3), improving memory (Chapters 4, 5, and 6), how to write a paper (Chapter 10), solving problems (Chapter 11), and making wise decisions (Chapter 12).

Consider some other areas where researchers can give psychology away. For instance, the research on bilingualism (Chapter 10) has practical applications in society. Specifically, bilingual people experience some cognitive advantages, and our culture should value those who can speak two or more different languages. In Chapter 13, the research by Judy DeLoache and her colleagues (2010) shows that infants do not learn vocabulary from commercially produced videos that show a familiar household object, together with its spoken name. However, babies *do* learn vocabulary when a parent shows them an object and talks to them about this object. Furthermore, Chapter 12 has implications for our own everyday decision making, and also for political decisions that will affect the lives of millions. These applications include decisions about healthcare policy and decisions about starting (or continuing) a war.

FEATURES OF THIS TEXTBOOK

I genuinely believe that cognitive psychology can have practical applications. Therefore, students must be able to understand and remember the material. Here are some of the ways in which I consider this textbook to be student-oriented:

1. The writing style is clear and interesting, with frequent examples to make the information more concrete. Over the years, I've received letters and comments from hundreds of students and professors, telling me how much they enjoyed reading this textbook.

2. The text demonstrates how our cognitive processes are relevant in our everyday, real-world experiences.

3. The book frequently examines how cognition can be applied to other disciplines, such as clinical psychology, social psychology, consumer psychology, education, communication, business, medicine, and law.

4. The first chapter introduces five major themes that I emphasize throughout the book. Because the current research in cognitive psychology is so extensive, students need a sense of continuity that helps them appreciate the connections among many diverse topics.

5. An outline and a preview introduce each chapter, providing a helpful framework for understanding the new material.

6. Each new term is presented in **boldface print**. Every term is also accompanied by a concise definition that appears in the same sentence. In addition, I include pronunciation guides for new terms with potentially ambiguous pronunciation. If students are hesitant about pronouncing terms such as *schema* and *saccadic*, they will be reluctant to use these words or ask questions about them.

7. Many easy-to-perform demonstrations illustrate important research in cognition, and they clarify central concepts in the discipline. I designed these demonstrations so that they would require equipment that undergraduate students typically have on hand.

8. Each major section within a chapter concludes with a summary. This feature enables students to review and consolidate material before moving to the next section, rather than waiting until the chapter's end for a single, lengthy summary. When students are preparing for an exam, they can test themselves by reading each section summary and providing additional information about each topic.

9. Each chapter concludes with 10 comprehensive review questions and a list of new terms. After students test themselves, they can consult the detailed subject index if a topic seems unfamiliar.

10. Each chapter concludes with a list of recommended readings, along with a brief description of each resource. This feature should be useful if students are searching for a topic for a literature-review paper. Furthermore, professors can consult these resources if they would like to update a specific topic during class time.

11. A glossary at the end of the book provides a definition of every keyword. I tried to include additional contextual information wherever it might be useful, in order to clarify the terms as much as possible. For example, the word *antecedent* can be used in several different contexts. Accordingly, my definition for *antecedent* begins with the phrase, "In conditional reasoning...."

12. The subject index is comprehensive and detailed. Students can quickly locate the keywords, because they appear in boldface.

THE TEXTBOOK'S ORGANIZATION

A textbook needs to be interesting and helpful. It must also reflect current developments in the discipline, and it should allow instructors to adapt the book's structure to their own teaching plans. The following features should therefore be useful for professors:

1. The eighth edition of *Cognition* offers a comprehensive overview of the field, including chapters on perceptual processes, memory, imagery, general knowledge, language, problem solving and creativity, reasoning and decision making, and cognitive development.

2. Each chapter is a self-contained unit. For example, terms such as *heuristics*, *schema*, and *top-down processing* are defined in every chapter where they are used. This feature allows professors considerable flexibility in the sequence of chapter coverage. Some professors may wish to discuss the topic of imagery (Chapter 7) prior to the three chapters on memory. Others might want to assign the chapter on general knowledge (Chapter 8) during an earlier part of the academic term.

3. Each section within a chapter can stand as a discrete unit, especially because every section concludes with a section summary. Professors may choose to discuss the individual sections in a different order. For example, one professor may want students to read the section on schemas prior to the chapter on long-term memory. Another professor might prefer to subdivide Chapter 13, on cognitive development, so that the first section of this chapter (on memory) follows Chapter 5, the second section (on metacognition) follows Chapter 6, and the third section (on language) follows Chapter 10. In summary, these separate sections provide professors with additional flexibility.

4. Chapters 2 through 13 each include an "In-Depth" feature, which focuses on recent research about a selected topic in cognitive psychology. This feature also provides details about research methods. Five of these features are new to this eighth edition, and the remaining seven have been updated and revised.

5. This eighth edition includes a feature called "Individual Differences." This feature is described in detail in Chapter 1, on pages 27 and 28.

6. In all, the bibliography contains 2,011 references; 690 of them are new to the eighth edition. Furthermore, 51% of these references have been published since the year 2005. As a result, the textbook provides a current overview of cognitive psychology.

HIGHLIGHTS OF THE EIGHTH EDITION

The field of cognitive psychology has made impressive advances since the seventh edition of this textbook was published in 2009. Research in the areas of memory, language, and cognitive development has been especially ambitious. In addition, researchers have refined the details about theoretical approaches to cognitive to psychology. Other researchers have employed neuroscience techniques to provide information about cognitive topics as diverse as face recognition, language comprehension, and memory development during childhood. Here are some important updates for this new edition.

The Individual-Differences Feature

While organizing the material for an earlier edition of *Cognition*, I noticed a substantial increase in the number of research articles that focused on individual differences in cognitive performance. Furthermore, I discovered that my own students' literature-review papers frequently addressed topics such as "The Relationship between Major Depression and Working-Memory Performance."

Chapters 2 through 13 in this eighth edition therefore include an "Individual-Differences Feature." Some of these focus on psychological disorders such as schizophrenia and depression. Others focus on demographic variables—such as gender and profession—that could potentially be related to cognitive performance. In Chapter 1 (pages 27–28), you can read more details about this important feature.

Updated Coverage of Research in Cognitive Psychology

In preparing this eighth edition, I carefully reviewed each chapter. In fact, every page of this textbook has been updated and rewritten. Some of the more substantial changes include the following:

- Chapter 1 has a new structure that highlights neuroscience techniques and explains why individual-differences research is important in cognitive psychology.
- Chapter 2 includes information that describes neuroscience research about object recognition, prosopagnosia, and the face-inversion effect.
- Chapter 3 clarifies the different kinds of attention tasks; it also discusses current research on "multitasking," as well as an individual-differences feature on eating disorders and Stroop test performance.
- Chapter 4 examines new research that uses a technique called Transcranial Magnetic Stimulation to study the phonological loop; this chapter also provides new information about working memory and academic performance.
- Chapter 5 now includes an In-Depth feature about emotions, mood, and memory, and the individual-differences feature explores anxiety disorders and performance on explicit and implicit memory tasks.
- Chapter 6 includes new information about topics such as retrieval practice and embodied cognition, as well as an In-Depth feature on prospective memory.
- Chapter 7 has a revised structure, in which the research on cognitive neuropsychology has been incorporated into the In-Depth feature on visual imagery and rotation. This chapter now includes a new section on auditory imagery, as well as a new discussion of the situated-cognition approach.
- Chapter 8 begins with an informal exercise to make this introduction more accessible. It also includes a new In-Depth feature that includes new research on the prototype approach.
- Chapter 9 now begins with a discussion of sign language, as well as new information about English-centered linguistics and an In-Depth feature about neurolinguistics.

- Chapter 10 examines new information about using gestures and embodied cognition. It also includes expanded coverage of bilingualism, consistent with the increased attention to this important topic.
- Chapter 11 now includes more coverage of embodied cognition, as well as information about changes in event-related brain potentials that occur when a person breaks a mental set.
- Chapter 12 now discusses how dual-process theory can be applied to both deductive reasoning and decision making. This chapter also explores recent cross-cultural research about overconfidence.
- Chapter 13 includes reorganized and updated research on children's source memory and word mastery. This chapter also explores working memory and explicit recall memory in elderly adults.

In preparing this new edition, I made every effort to emphasize current research. I searched for relevant articles in six cognitive psychology journals and five general psychology journals. This investigation was supplemented by numerous specific *PsycINFO* searches. Furthermore, I systematically examined the lists of new books from seven publishers that emphasize cognitive psychology. The research on cognition is expanding at an ever-increasing rate, and I want this textbook to capture the excitement of the current research.

TEST BANK

Professors who teach courses in cognitive psychology consistently emphasize the importance of a high-quality Test Bank. The multiple-choice questions must be clear and unambiguous, and they must not focus on relatively trivial details. Most of the questions should be conceptually rich, rather than requiring brief, obvious answers. Also, the questions should be carefully reviewed and updated with each new edition of the textbook. Furthermore, each chapter in the Test Bank should contain a large number of questions, so that professors can select a different sample every time they create an examination.

I have extensively revised the Test Bank for the eighth edition of *Cognition*. For example, the textbank contains an average of 10 new questions in each chapter. Furthermore, approximately half of the questions that had appeared in the seventh edition have been revised for this new eighth edition.

The Test Bank questions continue to emphasize conceptual knowledge, as well as applications to real-world situations. Furthermore, I have rated each question as "easy," "moderate," and "difficult." These difficulty ratings can help professors to create a test that is appropriate for the students in their classes.

To learn more information, professors should contact their Wiley sales representative about the Test Bank for the eighth edition of *Cognition*. They can also visit the Wiley Web site for this book, www.wiley.com/college/matlin.

ACKNOWLEDGMENTS

I want to thank many individuals at John Wiley & Sons for their substantial contributions to the development and the production of the eighth edition of *Cognition*. I have been fortunate to work with two superb Associate Editors, in preparing the eighth edition of this textbook. Brittany Cheetham and Eileen McKeever were both conscientious about responding quickly to my questions and providing useful information about new developments that were relevant to this textbook. (For example, Brittany's expertise in current copyright rules was especially welcome.) I would also like to acknowledge Chris Johnson (Executive Editor) for his thoughtful responses to my questions and his guidance throughout the planning, writing, and editing phases of this textbook.

Furthermore, the Production Department at Wiley is superb! This eighth edition of *Cognition* is the 25th book I have written, so I've had extensive experience with textbook production. I would especially like to commend several outstanding individuals. Julie Kennedy deserves special praise for her intelligent, careful attention throughout the copy-editing phase. Jolene Ling is clearly one of the best production editors I've ever known! She is well-organized, thoughtful, and knowledgeable. In addition, Joseph Goh designed the elegant cover for this textbook. I also want to praise the individuals at Laserwords, who created a well-organized and user-friendly design for this eighth edition. Professors sometimes adopt a textbook with admirable content and writing style, but they often complain that the textbook's design is simply not consistent with the special features in the book. In contrast, the Laserwords staff are especially skilled in "translating" each feature's function into the appropriate design format! Thanks as well to Wiley's photo editor, Jennifer Atkins, who located the appropriate photos for this eighth edition.

Once more, Linda Webster compiled both the subject index and the author index for the current edition. Linda has worked on all my recent textbooks, and I continue to be impressed with her intelligent, careful work on these important components of this textbook. Both faculty and students will appreciate these useful guides!

In addition, I would like to thank Margaret Barrett, the marketing manager at Wiley, for her creativity, positive feedback, and excellent organizational skills. Thanks are also due to the Wiley sales representatives for their exceptional work and enthusiastic support!

During my undergraduate and graduate training, many professors encouraged my enthusiasm for the growing field of cognition. I would like to thank Leonard Horowitz, Gordon Bower, Albert Hastorf, and Eleanor Maccoby of Stanford University, and Robert Zajonc, Edwin Martin, Arthur Melton, and Richard Pew of the University of Michigan.

Many other people have contributed in important ways to this book. My student assistants on this edition of *Cognition* were Kristina Judge, Heather Henderson, Kristen Kolb, and Olivia Derella. These superb students helped to locate and order references. They also checked to make sure that the chapter citations agreed with the entries in the reference section, and they handled numerous other details connected with writing a textbook. In addition, I'm grateful to Ryan Fraser, for his expert technical support.

Also, Monica Morris and Connie Ellis kept other aspects of my life running smoothly, allowing me more time to work on this writing project.

In addition, I want to acknowledge the helpfulness of Tim Bowersox, who coordinates the Information Delivery Service at Milne Library, SUNY Geneseo. Tim efficiently ordered several hundred books and articles for this eighth edition of *Cognition*. It's difficult to imagine how I could have completed this book without his intelligent and timely assistance!

In addition, a number of students contributed to the book and provided useful suggestions after they had read various editions of *Cognition*: Aspen Ainsworth, Magnus Bakken, Jennifer Balus, Alesya Borisyuk, Mary Jane Brennan, Meredith Cannella, A. Eleanor Chand, Miriam Dowd, Elizabeth Einemann, Michelle Fischer, Sarah Gonnella, Laurie Guarino, Benjamin Griffin, Jessica Hosey, Don Hudson, Jay Kleinman, Jessica Krager, Mary Kroll, Eun Jung Lim, Pamela Mead, Pamela Mino, Kaveh Moghbeli, Jacquilyn Moran, Michelle Morante, Jennifer Niemczyk, Danielle Palermo, Alison Repel, Judith Rickey, Mary Riley, Margery Schemmel, Richard Slocum, John Tanchak, Brenna Terry, Sherri Tkachuk, Dan Vance, Heather Wallach, and Rachelle Yablin. Several students at Stanford University's Casa Zapata provided insights about bilingualism: Laura Aizpuru, Sven Halstenburg, Rodrigo Liong, Jean Lu, Edwardo Martinez, Sally Matlin, Dorin Parasca, and Laura Uribarri.

Other students provided information about useful cognitive psychology articles: Ned Abbott, Angela Capria, Stacey Canavan, Elizabeth Carey, Lindsay Ciancetta, Melissa Conway, Amanda Crandall, Moises Gonzales, Katie Griffin, Hideaki Imai, Peter Kang, Becky Keegan, Maria Korogodsky, Patricia Kramer, Leslie Lauer, JiYun Lee, Sally Matlin, Kristen Merkle, Jill Papke, Christopher Piersante, Heather Quayle, Brooke Schurr, Laura Segovia, Nancy Tomassino, Sara Vonhold, Melissa Waterman, and Lauren Whaley.

Thanks also to colleagues Drew Appleby, Brian Nosek, Ganie DeHart, Thomas Donnan, K. Anders Ericsson, Beverly Evans, Hugh Foley, Mary Ann Foley, Mark Graber, Donald Hall, Elliot D. Hammer, Douglas Herrmann, Eve Higby, Kenneth Kallio, Colin M. MacLeod, Nora Newcombe, Lisbet Nielsen, Matt Pastizzo, Paul Norris, Keith Rayner, Barry Schwartz, Bennett L. Schwartz, Douglas Vipond, Lori Van Wallendael, Julia Wagner, and Alan Welsh for making suggestions about references and improved wording for passages in the text.

Special thanks are also due to Lucinda DeWitt, who has now assisted me in preparing a total of nine textbooks! For example, Lucinda has helped me assemble four editions of the Test Item File for *Cognition*. Her knowledge base, writing style, and computer expertise are superb! Furthermore, Lucinda also created the glossary for this eighth edition. I consider a good glossary to be a work of art; each item requires a precise definition, and enough detail, without overwhelming the reader. Lucinda is also an exceptionally helpful reviewer; she examined this eighth edition of this book (and three earlier editions) for continuity, clarity, and accuracy. She also created the PowerPoint slides and chapter outlines for this edition. Her contributions clearly influence many components of this eighth edition!

I would also like to express my continuing appreciation to the textbook's reviewers. The reviewers who helped on the first edition included: Mark Ashcraft, Cleveland

State University; Randolph Easton, Boston College; Barbara Goldman, University of Michigan, Dearborn; Harold Hawkins, University of Oregon; Joseph Hellige, University of Southern California; Richard High, Lehigh University; James Juola, University of Kansas; Richard Kasschau, University of Houston; and R. A. Kinchla, Princeton University.

The reviewers who provided assistance on the second edition were: Harriett Amster, University of Texas, Arlington; Francis T. Durso, University of Oklahoma; Susan Dutch, Westfield State College; Sallie Gordon, University of Utah; Richard Gottwald, University of Indiana, South Bend; Kenneth R. Graham, Muhlenberg College; Morton A. Heller, Winston-Salem State University; Michael W. O'Boyle, Iowa State University; David G. Payne, SUNY Binghamton; Louisa M. Slowiaczek, Loyola University, Chicago; Donald A. Smith, Northern Illinois University; Patricia Snyder, Albright College; and Richard K. Wagner, Florida State University.

The third-edition reviewers included: Ira Fischler, University of Florida; John Flowers, University of Nebraska; Nancy Franklin, SUNY Stony Brook; Joanne Gallivan, University College of Cape Breton; Margaret Intons-Peterson, Indiana University; Christine Lofgren, University of California, Irvine; Bill McKeachie, University of Michigan; William Oliver, Florida State University; Andrea Richards, University of California, Los Angeles; Jonathan Schooler, University of Pittsburgh; and Jyotsna Vaid, Texas A&M University.

The reviewers of the fourth edition included: Lucinda DeWitt, Concordia College; Susan Dutch, Westfield State College; Kathleen Flannery, Saint Anselm College; Linda Gerard, Michigan State University; Catherine Hale, University of Puget Sound; Timothy Jay, North Adams State College; W. Daniel Phillips, Trenton State College; Dana Plude, University of Maryland; Jonathan Schooler, University of Pittsburgh; Matthew Sharps, California State University, Fresno; Greg Simpson, University of Kansas; Margaret Thompson, University of Central Florida; and Paul Zelhart, East Texas State University.

The following reviewers for the fifth edition were: Lise Abrams, University of Florida; Tom Alley, Clemson University; Kurt Baker, Emporia State University; Richard Block, Montana State University; Kyle Cave, University of Southampton (United Kingdom); Lucinda DeWitt, University of Minnesota; Susan Dutch, Westfield State College; James Enns, University of British Columbia; Philip Higham, University of Northern British Columbia; Mark Hoyert, Indiana University Northwest; Anita Meehan, Kutztown University of Pennsylvania; Joan Piroch, Coastal Carolina University; David Pittenger, Marietta College; and Matthew Sharps, California State University, Fresno.

The reviewers of the sixth edition included: Lise Abrams, University of Florida; Thomas R. Alley, Clemson University; Tim Curran, University of Colorado; Susan Dutch, Westfield State College; Ira Fischler, University of Florida; Kathy E. Johnson, Indiana University–Purdue University Indianapolis; Gretchen Kambe, University of Nevada, Las Vegas; James P. Van Overschelde, University of Maryland; and Thomas B. Ward, University of Alabama.

The following individuals provided perspectives that guided me when I was preparing the seventh edition: Heather Bartfeld, Texas A&M University; James

Bartlett, University of Texas at Dallas; Nancy Franklin, SUNY Stony Brook; Robert J. Hines, University of Arkansas, Little Rock; Joseph Lao, Teachers College, Columbia University; Susan Lima, University of Wisconsin, Milwaukee; Janet Nicol, University of Arizona; Catherine Powright, University of Ottawa; Sara Ransdell, Nova Southeastern University; Tony Ro, Rice University; Michael Root, Ohio University; and David Somers, Boston University.

For the current, eighth edition of *Cognition*, I want to acknowledge the following psychologists who teach courses in cognitive psychology: John Agnew, University of Colorado, Boulder; Stephen Christman, University of Toledo; Mike Dodd, University of Nebraska, Lincoln; Matthew Hunsinger, Mary Baldwin College; Eduardo Mercado, University at Buffalo, SUNY; Mithell Serman, University of Wisconsin, Stout; and Christian Vorstius, Florida State University.

I would also like to acknowledge several cultural resources that continue to inspire me and provide useful perspectives whenever I write my textbooks. These include the Stratford Shakespeare Festival (Ontario, Canada), the Metropolitan Museum of Art and the Metropolitan Opera (New York City), and the Art Institute of Chicago and the Lyric Opera of Chicago. Other sources of inspiration are the National Gallery and the Victoria & Albert Museum (London) and the Hermitage (St. Petersburg). In Rochester, New York, these resources include the Little Theatre, the Dryden Theatre, Pegasus Early Music, and the Eastman School of Music.

The final words of thanks belong to my family members. My husband, Arnie Matlin, encouraged me to write the first edition of this book during the early 1980s. His continuing enthusiasm, superb sense of humor, and loving support always bring joy to my writing, and certainly to my life! Our daughters and their husbands now live in other parts of the United States, but I always value their perspectives. I'd like to thank Sally Matlin and Jay Laefer, who now live in the San Francisco Bay area. Thanks also to Beth Matlin-Heiger, Neil Matlin-Heiger, and our grandchildren, Jacob and Joshua Matlin-Heiger, who live in the Boston area. Their continuing pride in my accomplishments makes it even more rewarding to be an author! Last, I would like to express my gratitude to four other important people who have shaped my life, my parents by birth and my parents by marriage: Helen and Donald White, and Clare and Harry Matlin.

Margaret W. Matlin
Geneseo, New York

Table of Contents

CHAPTER 7   Mental Imagery and Cognitive Maps   **207**

CHAPTER 11 Problem Solving and Creativity   **369**

CHAPTER 12   Deductive Reasoning and Decision Making   **407**

CHAPTER 13   Cognitive Development Throughout the Lifespan   **453**

An Introduction to Cognitive Psychology

Cognition is the area within psychology that examines how we acquire, store, transform, and use knowledge. Human thought processes have intrigued theorists for more than 2,000 years. The contemporary study of cognition can be traced to (1) Wilhelm Wundt's contributions in creating the discipline of psychology, (2) the early research about memory, and (3) William James's theories about cognitive processes. In the early 20th century, the behaviorists emphasized observable behavior, rather than mental processes. However, new research in areas such as memory and language produced disenchantment with behaviorism, and the cognitive approach gained popularity during the 1960s.

Researchers interested in cognitive neuroscience have developed a number of techniques to determine which structures in the brain are activated when people perform specific cognitive tasks. Cognitive psychology is also influenced by research in artificial intelligence. Furthermore, cognitive psychology is part of an active interdisciplinary area known as cognitive science.

This introductory chapter also gives you a preview of the chapters in this book and an overview of five themes in cognitive psychology. The chapter concludes with some tips on how to make the best use of your textbook's special features.

CHAPTER INTRODUCTION

At this exact moment, you are actively performing several cognitive tasks. In order to reach this second sentence of the first paragraph, you used pattern recognition to create words from an assortment of squiggles and lines that form the letters on this page. You also consulted your memory and your knowledge about language to search for word meanings and to link together the ideas in this paragraph into a coherent message. Right now, as you think about these cognitive tasks, you are engaging in another cognitive task called *metacognition*; you were thinking about your thought processes. Perhaps you made an inference such as, "This book may help me study more effectively." You may also have used decision making, for instance, by saying to yourself, "I'll finish this section of the book before I go to lunch."

Cognition, or mental activity, describes the acquisition, storage, transformation, and use of knowledge. If cognition operates every time you acquire some information, place it in storage, transform that information, and use it . . . then cognition definitely includes a wide range of mental processes! This textbook will explore mental processes such as perception, memory, imagery, language, problem solving, reasoning, and decision making.

A related term, **cognitive psychology**, has two meanings: (1) Sometimes it is a synonym for the word *cognition*, and so it refers to the variety of mental activities we just listed. (2) Sometimes it refers to a particular theoretical approach to psychology.

Specifically, the **cognitive approach** is a theoretical orientation that emphasizes people's thought processes and their knowledge. For example, a cognitive explanation of ethnic stereotypes would emphasize topics such as the influence of these stereotypes on the judgments we make about people from different ethnic groups (Whitley & Kite, 2010).

Psychologists often contrast the cognitive approach with several other current theoretical approaches. For example, the behaviorist approach emphasizes our observable behaviors, and the psychodynamic approach focuses on our unconscious emotions. To explain ethnic stereotypes, these two approaches would describe our behaviors or our emotions, rather than our thought processes.

Why should you and other students learn about cognition? One reason is that cognition occupies a major portion of human psychology. In fact, almost everything you have done in the past hour required you to perceive, remember, use language, or think. As you'll soon see, psychologists have discovered some impressive information about every topic in cognitive psychology. Even though cognitive psychology is extraordinarily central in every human's daily life, many college students cannot define this term accurately (Maynard, 2006; Maynard et al., 2004). To demonstrate this point, try Demonstration 1.1.

A second reason to study cognition is that the cognitive approach has widespread influence on other areas of psychology, such as clinical psychology, educational psychology, and social psychology. Let's consider an example from clinical psychology. One cognitive task asks people to recall a specific memory from their past. People who are depressed tend to provide a general summary, such as "visiting my grandmother." In contrast, people who are not depressed tend to describe an extended memory that lasts more than one day, such as "the summer I drove across the country" (Wenzel, 2005). Cognitive psychology also influences interdisciplinary areas. For example, a journal called *Cognitive Neuropsychology* examines specific neurological problems, such as an extreme difficulty in recognizing people's faces, when other cognitive skills are normal (e.g., Wilson et al., 2010).

ⓢ Demonstration 1.1

Awareness About Cognitive Psychology

Locate several friends at your university or college who have not enrolled in any psychology courses. Ask each person the following questions:

1. How would you define the term "cognitive psychology"?
2. Can you list some of the topics that would be included in a course in cognitive psychology?

When Amanda Maynard and her coauthors (2004) asked introductory psychologists to define "cognitive psychology," only 29% provided appropriate definitions. How adequate were the responses that your own friends provided?

The final reason for studying cognition is more personal. Your mind is an impressively sophisticated piece of equipment, and you use this equipment every minute of the day. If you purchase a new phone, you typically receive a brochure that describes its functions. However, no one issued a brochure for your mind when you were born. In a sense, this textbook is like a brochure or owner's manual, describing information about how your mind works. This book—like some owner's manuals—also includes hints on how to improve performance.

This introductory chapter focuses on three topics. First, we'll briefly consider the history of cognitive psychology. Then we'll outline some important techniques used in cognitive neuroscience, followed by two perspectives that are related to cognitive psychology. The final part of the chapter describes this textbook, including its content and major themes; I will also give you some suggestions for using the book effectively.

A BRIEF HISTORY OF COGNITIVE PSYCHOLOGY

The cognitive approach to psychology traces its origins to the classical Greek philosophers and to developments that began in the 19th century. As we will also see in this section, however, the contemporary version of cognitive psychology emerged within the last 60 years.

The Origins of Cognitive Psychology

Philosophers and other theorists have speculated about human thought processes for more than 23 centuries. For example, the Greek philosopher Aristotle (384–322 BCE) examined topics such as perception, memory, and mental imagery. He also discussed how humans acquire knowledge through experience and observation (Barnes, 2004; Sternberg, 1999). Aristotle emphasized the importance of **empirical evidence**, or scientific evidence obtained by careful observation and experimentation. His emphasis on empirical evidence and many of the topics he studied are consistent with 21st-century cognitive psychology. In fact, Aristotle can reasonably be called the first cognitive psychologist (Leahey, 2003). However, psychology as a discipline did not emerge until the late 1800s.

Wilhelm Wundt. Most scholars who study the history of psychology believe that Wilhelm Wundt (pronounced "Voont") should be considered the founder of psychology (Benjamin, 2009; Pickren & Rutherford, 2010). Wundt lived in Leipzig, Germany, between 1832 and 1920. Students traveled from around the world to study with Wundt, who taught about 28,000 students during the course of his lifetime (Bechtel et al., 1998; Benjamin, 2009; Fuchs & Milar, 2003).

Wundt proposed that psychology should study mental processes, using a technique called introspection. In this case, **introspection** meant that carefully trained observers would systematically analyze their own sensations and report them as objectively as possible, under standardized conditions (Blumenthal, 2009; Pickren & Rutherford, 2010; Zangwill, 2004b). For example, observers might be asked to objectively report their reactions to a specific musical chord, without relying on their previous knowledge about music.

Wundt's introspection technique sounds subjective to most current cognitive psychologists. As you'll see throughout this textbook, our introspections are sometimes inaccurate (Wilson, 2009; Zangwill, 2004b). For example, you may introspect that your eyes are moving smoothly across this page of your textbook. However, cognitive psychologists have determined that your eyes actually move in small jumps—as you'll read in Chapter 3.

Early Memory Researchers. Another important German psychologist, Hermann Ebbinghaus (1850–1909), was the first person to scientifically study human memory (Baddeley et al., 2009; Schwartz, 2011). Ebbinghaus examined a variety of factors that might influence performance, such as the amount of time between two presentations of a list of items. He frequently chose nonsense syllables (e.g., DAX), rather than actual words. This precaution reduced people's previous experience with the material (Fuchs & Milar, 2003; Zangwill, 2004a).

Meanwhile, in the United States, similar research was being conducted by psychologists such as Mary Whiton Calkins (1863–1930). For example, Calkins reported a memory phenomenon called the recency effect (Schwartz, 2011). The **recency effect** refers to the observation that our recall is especially accurate for the final items in a series of stimuli. In addition, Calkins emphasized that psychologists should study how real people use their cognitive processes in the real world, as opposed to the psychology laboratory (Samelson, 2009). Calkins was also the first woman to be president of the American Psychological Association. In connection with that role, she developed guidelines for teaching college courses in introductory psychology (Calkins, 1910; McGovern & Brewer, 2003). During her career, Calkins also published four books and more than 100 scholarly papers (Pickren & Rutherford, 2010).

Ebbinghaus, Calkins, and other pioneers inspired hundreds of researchers to examine how selected variables influenced memory. Some of their findings are still considered relevant in contemporary cognitive psychology.

William James. Another central figure in the history of cognitive psychology was an American named William James (1842–1910). James was not impressed with Wundt's introspection technique or Ebbinghaus's research with nonsense syllables. Instead, James preferred to theorize about our everyday psychological experiences (Benjamin, 2009; Hunter, 2004a; Pickren & Rutherford, 2010). He is best known for his textbook *Principles of Psychology*, published in 1890. (Incidentally, try Demonstration 1.2 on page 6 before you read further.)

Principles of Psychology provides clear, detailed descriptions about people's everyday experiences (Benjamin, 2009). It also emphasizes that the human mind is active and inquiring. James's book foreshadows numerous topics that fascinate 21st-century

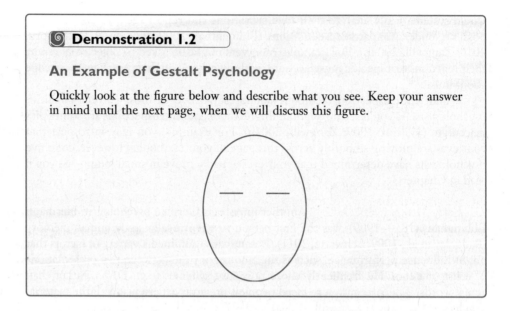

cognitive psychologists, such as perception, attention, memory, understanding, reasoning, and the tip-of-the-tongue phenomenon (Leary, 2009; Pickren & Rutherford, 2010). Consider, for example, James's vivid description of the tip-of-the-tongue experience:

> Suppose we try to recall a forgotten name. The state of our consciousness is peculiar. There is a gap therein but no mere gap. It is a gap that is intensely active. A sort of wraith of the name is in it, beckoning us in a given direction, making us at moments tingle with the sense of our closeness and then letting us sink back without the longed-for term.
> (James, 1890, p. 251)

Behaviorism. During the first half of the 20th century, behaviorism was the most prominent theoretical perspective in the United States. According to the principles of **behaviorism,** psychology must focus on objective, observable reactions to stimuli in the environment, rather than introspection (Benjamin, 2009; O'Boyle, 2006). The most prominent early behaviorist was the U.S. psychologist John B. Watson (1913), who lived from 1878–1958.

Watson and other behaviorists emphasized observable behavior, and they typically studied animals (Benjamin, 2009). Behaviorists also argued that researchers could not objectively study mental representations, such as an image, idea, or thought (Epstein, 2004; Skinner, 2004).

The behaviorists did not conduct research in cognitive psychology, but they did contribute significantly to contemporary research methods. For example, behaviorists emphasized the importance of the **operational definition,** a precise definition that specifies exactly how a concept is to be measured. Similarly, cognitive psychologists in the 21st century need to specify exactly how memory, perception, and other cognitive processes will be measured in an experiment. Behaviorists also valued carefully controlled research, a tradition that is maintained in current cognitive research (Fuchs & Milar, 2003).

We must also acknowledge the important contribution of behaviorists to applied psychology. Their learning principles have been extensively used in psychotherapy, business, organizations, and education (Craske, 2010; O'Boyle, 2006; Rutherford, 2009).

The Gestalt Approach. Behaviorism thrived in the United States for several decades, but it had less influence on European psychology (G. Mandler, 2002). An important development in Europe at the beginning of the 20th century was gestalt (pronounced "geh-*shtahlt*") psychology. **Gestalt psychology** emphasizes that we humans have basic tendencies to actively organize what we see; furthermore, the whole is greater than the sum of its parts (Benjamin, 2009).

Consider, for example, the figure represented in Demonstration 1.2. You probably saw a human face, rather than simply an oval and two straight lines. This figure seems to have unity and organization. It has a **gestalt,** or overall quality that transcends the individual elements, in this case, the oval and the two horizontal lines (Fuchs & Milar, 2003).

Gestalt psychologists valued the unity of psychological phenomena. As a result, they strongly objected to Wundt's introspective technique of analyzing experiences into separate components (Pickren & Rutherford, 2010). They also criticized the behaviorists' emphasis on breaking behavior into observable stimulus-response units and ignoring the context of behavior (Baddeley et al., 2009; Benjamin, 2009). Gestalt psychologists constructed a number of laws that explain why certain components of a pattern seem to belong together. In Chapter 2, we'll consider some of these laws, which help us to quickly recognize visual objects.

Gestalt psychologists also emphasized the importance of insight in problem solving (Fuchs & Milar, 2003; Viney & King, 2003). When you are trying to solve a problem, the parts of the problem may initially seem unrelated to each other. However, with a sudden flash of insight, the parts fit together into a solution. Gestalt psychologists conducted most of the early research in problem solving. In Chapter 11 of this textbook, we will examine their concept of insight, as well as more recent developments.

Frederic Bartlett. In the early 1900s, the behaviorists were dominant in the United States, and the gestalt psychologists were influential in continental Europe. Meanwhile in England, a British psychologist named Frederic Bartlett (1886–1969) conducted his research on human memory. His important book *Remembering: An Experimental and Social Study* (Bartlett, 1932) is considered one of the most influential books in the history of cognitive psychology (Benjamin, 2009). Bartlett rejected the carefully controlled research of Ebbinghaus (Pickford & Gregory, 2004). Instead, he used meaningful materials, such as lengthy stories.

Bartlett discovered that people made systematic errors when trying to recall these stories. He proposed that human memory is an active, constructive process, in which we interpret and transform the information we encounter. We search for meaning, trying to integrate this new information so that it is more consistent with our own personal experiences (Benjamin, 2009; Pickford & Gregory, 2004; Pickren & Rutherford, 2010).

Bartlett's work was largely ignored in the United States during the 1930s, because most U.S. research psychologists were committed to behaviorism. However, about half a century later, U.S. cognitive psychologists discovered Bartlett's work and admired his use of naturalistic material, in contrast to Ebbinghaus's artificial nonsense syllables. Bartlett's emphasis on a schema-based approach to memory foreshadowed some of the research we will explore in Chapters 5 and 8 (Benjamin, 2009; Pickford & Gregory, 2004).

The Emergence of Modern Cognitive Psychology

We have briefly traced the historical roots of cognitive psychology, but when was this new approach actually "born"? Cognitive psychologists generally agree that the birth of cognitive psychology can be listed as 1956 (Eysenck & Keane, 2010; G. Mandler, 2002; Thagard, 2005). During this prolific year, researchers published numerous influential books and articles on attention, memory, language, concept formation, and problem solving. By the 1960s, the methodology, approach, and attitudes had changed substantially (Shiraev, 2011).

This growing support for the cognitive approach has sometimes been called the "cognitive revolution" (Bruner, 1997; Shiraev, 2011). Let's examine some of the factors that contributed to the increased popularity of cognitive psychology. Then we'll consider the information-processing approach, one of the most influential forces in the early development of cognitive psychology.

Factors Contributing to the Rise of Cognitive Psychology. Psychologists were becoming increasingly disappointed with the behaviorist outlook that had dominated U.S. psychology in previous decades. Many researchers interested in memory had shifted from animal learning to human memory (Baddeley et al., 2009; Bower, 2008). It was difficult to explain complex human behavior using only behaviorist concepts such as observable stimuli, responses, and reinforcement (G. Mandler, 2002; Neisser, 1967). The behaviorist approach tells us nothing about numerous psychologically interesting processes, such as the thoughts and strategies that people use when they try to solve a problem (Bechtel et al., 1998).

Research and theory in three content areas also increased the emerging popularity of the cognitive approach. For example, new developments in linguistics increased psychologists' dissatisfaction with behaviorism (Bargh & Ferguson, 2000; Bower, 2008). The most important contributions came from the linguist Noam Chomsky (1957), who emphasized that the structure of language was too complex to be explained in behaviorist terms (Pickren & Rutherford, 2010; Pinker, 2002). Chomsky and other linguists argued that humans have an inborn ability to master all the complicated and varied aspects of language (Chomsky, 2004). This perspective clearly contradicted the behaviorist perspective that language acquisition can be entirely explained by the same kind of learning principles that apply to laboratory animals.

Also, research in human memory began to blossom at the end of the 1950s, further increasing the disenchantment with behaviorism. Psychologists examined the organization of memory, and they proposed memory models. They frequently found that material was altered during memory by people's previous knowledge. Behaviorist principles such as "reinforcement" could not explain these alterations (Bargh & Ferguson, 2000).

Another influential force came from research on children's thought processes. Jean Piaget (pronounced "Pea-ah-*zhay*") was a Swiss theorist who lived from 1896 to 1980. Piaget's books began to attract the attention of U.S. psychologists and educators toward the end of the 1950s, and his perspectives continue to shape developmental psychology (Feist, 2006; Hopkins, 2011; Pickren & Rutherford, 2010). According to Piaget, children actively explore their world in order to understand important concepts (Gregory, 2004b). Children's cognitive strategies change as they mature, and adolescents often use sophisticated strategies in order to conduct experiments about scientific principles.

We have seen that the growth of the cognitive approach was encouraged by research in linguistics, memory, and developmental psychology. By the mid-1970s, the cognitive approach had replaced the behavioral approach as the dominant theory in psychological research (Robins et al., 1999). Let's now consider an additional factor contributing to that growth, which was the enthusiasm about the information-processing approach.

The Information-Processing Approach. Beginning in the 1960s, psychologists created a new theoretical approach to human memory. This **information-processing approach** argued that (a) our mental processes are similar to the operations of a computer, and (b) information progresses through our cognitive system in a series of stages, one step at a time (Gallistel & King, 2009; Leahey, 2003; MacKay, 2004). On pages 17 to 20, we will reconsider this comparison between mental processes and computers. This conceptual breakthrough persuaded many leading researchers (Bower, 2008).

Richard Atkinson and Richard Shiffrin (1968) developed an information-processing model that became extremely popular within the emerging field of cognitive psychology (Baddeley et al., 2009; Rose, 2004). The **Atkinson-Shiffrin model** proposed that memory involves a sequence of separate steps; in each step, information is transferred from one storage area to another. Let's look more closely at this model because it was extremely influential in persuading research psychologists to adopt the cognitive psychology perspective.

Figure 1.1 shows an example of the information-processing approach to memory, with arrows indicating the transfer of information. External stimuli from the environment first enter sensory memory. **Sensory memory** is a storage system that records information from each of the senses with reasonable accuracy (Schwartz, 2011). During the 1960s and 1970s, psychologists frequently studied both visual sensory memory and auditory sensory memory (e.g., Darwin et al., 1972; Parks, 2004; Sperling, 1960).

FIGURE 1.1

Atkinson and Shiffrin's Model of Memory.

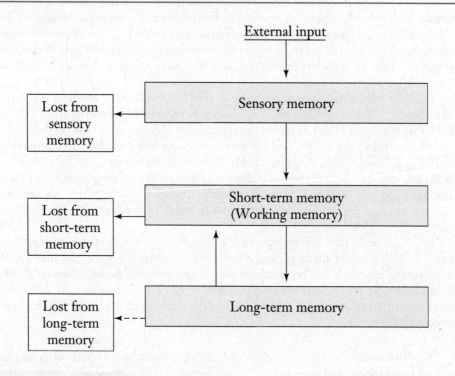

Source: Atkinson, R. C., & Shiffrin, R. M. (1968). Human memory: A processed system and its control process. In K. W. Spence & J. T. Spence (Eds.), *The psychology of learning and motivation: Advances in research and theory* (Vol. 2, pp. 89–105). New York: Academic Press.

The model proposed that information is stored in sensory memory for 2 seconds or less, and then most of it is forgotten. For example, your auditory memory briefly stores the last words of a sentence spoken by your professor, but this memory disappears within about 2 seconds.

Atkinson and Shiffrin's model proposed that some material from sensory memory then passes on to short-term memory. **Short-term memory**—which is now typically called **working memory**—holds only the small amount of information that you are actively using. Memories in short-term memory are fragile—though not as fragile as those in sensory memory (J. Brown, 2004). These memories can be lost within about 30 seconds, unless they are somehow repeated.

According to the model, only a fraction of the information in short-term memory passes on to long-term memory (Leahey, 2003). **Long-term memory** has an enormous capacity because it contains memories that are decades old, in addition to memories of events that occurred several minutes ago. Atkinson and Shiffrin's model proposed that information stored in long-term memory is relatively permanent, compared to the information stored in working memory.

Let's see how the Atkinson-Shiffrin model could account for the task you are working on right now. For instance, the sentences in the previous paragraph served as "external input," and they entered into your sensory memory. Only a fraction of that material passed into your short-term memory, and then only a fraction passed from short-term memory to long-term memory. In fact, without glancing back, can you recall the exact words of any sentence in that previous paragraph?

Atkinson and Shiffrin's (1968) information-processing model dominated memory research for many years. However, its influence is now diminished. For instance, most cognitive psychologists now consider sensory memory to be the very brief storage process that is part of perception, rather than an actual memory (Baddeley et al., 2009).

Many researchers also question Atkinson and Shiffrin's (1968) clear-cut distinction between short-term memory and long-term memory (Baddeley et al., 2009; J. Brown, 2004). In this textbook, the topic of memory is divided into two parts, more for the sake of convenience than a conviction that we have two entirely different kinds of memory. Chapter 4 examines short-term memory, although I use the current, more descriptive term "working memory" as the chapter title. Chapters 5, 6, 7, and 8 examine various components of long-term memory.

The Current Status of Cognitive Psychology

In the previous part of this chapter, we discussed the Atkinson-Shiffrin (1968) model of memory. This model provided an appealing perspective on memory, which is a central part of our cognitive processes. This model is also the best-known example of the information-processing approach. In general, however, enthusiasm for this kind of information-processing model has declined. Many cognitive psychologists still favor the computer metaphor. However, they now acknowledge that we need more complex models to account for human thinking (Gallistel & King, 2009; Leahey, 2003).

Even if psychologists do not endorse a specific model of cognitive processes, cognitive psychology has had an enormous influence on the discipline of psychology. For example, almost all psychologists now recognize the importance of mental representations, a term that behaviorists would have rejected in the 1950s.

In contrast, examples of "pure behaviorism" are now difficult to locate. For instance, the Association of Behavioral Therapy is now known as the Association for Behavioral and Cognitive Therapies. Recent articles in their journal, *Cognitive and Behavioral Practice*, have focused on using cognitive behavioral therapy for a variety of clients, including people with eating disorders, elderly adults with post-traumatic stress disorder, and severely depressed adolescents.

The cognitive approach has also permeated most areas of psychology that had not previously emphasized people's thought processes. Demonstration 1.3 illustrates this point.

---

⑥ Demonstration 1.3

The Widespread Influence of Cognitive Psychology

Locate a psychology textbook used in some other class. An introductory textbook is ideal, but textbooks in developmental psychology, social psychology, abnormal psychology, etc., are all suitable. Glance through the subject index for terms beginning with *cognition* or *cognitive*, and locate the relevant pages. Depending on the nature of the textbook, you may also find entries under terms such as memory, language, and perception.

Cognitive psychology has its critics, however. One common complaint concerns the issue of ecological validity. Studies are high in **ecological validity** if the conditions in which the research is conducted are similar to the natural setting where the results will be applied.

In contrast, consider an experiment in which participants must memorize a list of unrelated English words, presented at 5-second intervals on a white screen in a barren laboratory room. Half of the people are instructed to create a vivid mental image of each word; the other half receive no instructions. The experiment is carefully controlled.

The results of this experiment would tell us something about the way memory operates. However, this task is probably low in ecological validity, because it cannot be applied to the way people learn in the real world (Sharps & Wertheimer, 2000). How often do you try to memorize a list of unrelated words in this fashion, when you study for an upcoming psychology exam?

Most cognitive psychologists prior to the 1980s did indeed conduct research in artificial laboratory environments, often using tasks that differed from daily cognitive activities. However, current researchers frequently study real-life issues. For example, Chapter 3 describes how people are much more likely to make driving errors if they are talking on a handheld cell phone (Folk, 2010). Furthermore, Chapters 5 and 6 discuss numerous methods for improving your memory (e.g., Davies & Wright, 2010a). Chapter 12 provides many suggestions about how to improve your decision-making ability (Kahneman, 2011).

Psychologists are also studying how cognitive processes operate in our everyday social interactions (e.g., Cacioppo & Berntson, 2005a; Easton & Emery, 2005). In general, most cognitive psychologists acknowledge that the discipline must advance by conducting both ecologically valid and laboratory-based research.

⑥ Section Summary: *Chapter Introduction and a Brief History of Cognitive Psychology*

1. The term *cognition* refers to the acquisition, storage, transformation, and use of knowledge; *cognitive psychology* is sometimes used as a synonym for cognition, and sometimes it refers to a theoretical approach to psychology.

2. It's useful to study cognitive psychology because (a) cognitive activities are a major part of human psychology, (b) the cognitive approach influences other important areas of psychology, and (c) you can learn how to use your cognitive processes more effectively.

3. Many historians maintain that Wilhelm Wundt is responsible for creating the discipline of psychology; Wundt also developed the introspection technique.

4. Hermann Ebbinghaus and Mary Whiton Calkins conducted early research on human memory.

5. William James examined numerous everyday psychological processes, and he emphasized the active nature of the human mind.

6. Beginning in the early 20th century, behaviorists such as John B. Watson rejected the study of mental processes; the behaviorists helped to develop the research methods used by current cognitive psychologists.

7. Gestalt psychology emphasized that people use organization to perceive patterns, and they often solve problems by using insight.

8. Frederick C. Bartlett conducted memory research using long stories and other meaningful material.

9. Cognitive psychology began to emerge in the mid-1950s. This new approach was stimulated by disenchantment with behaviorism, as well as a growing interest in linguistics, human memory, developmental psychology, and the information-processing approach.

10. According to the information-processing approach, mental processes operate like a computer, with information flowing through a series of storage areas.

11. The best-known example of the information-processing approach is the Atkinson-Shiffrin (1968) model, which proposes three different memory-storage systems. Enthusiasm has declined for both this model and for the general information-processing approach, because cognitive psychologists now realize that human thinking requires more complex models.

12. Cognitive psychology has had a major influence on the field of psychology. In the current era, cognitive psychologists are more concerned about ecological validity than in previous decades.

COGNITIVE NEUROSCIENCE TECHNIQUES

Cognitive neuroscience combines the research techniques of cognitive psychology with various methods for assessing the structure and function of the brain (Marshall, 2009). In recent decades, researchers have examined which structures in the brain are activated when people perform a variety of cognitive tasks (Gazzaniga et al., 2009).

Furthermore, psychologists now use neuroscience techniques to explore the kind of cognitive processes that we use in our interactions with other people; this new discipline is called **social cognitive neuroscience** (Cacioppo, 2007; Cacioppo & Berntson, 2005a; Easton & Emery, 2005). For example, researchers have identified a variety of brain structures that are active when people look at a photograph of a face and judge whether the person is trustworthy (Winston et al., 2005).

However, neurological explanations for some cognitive processes are elusive. For example, take several seconds to stand up and walk around the room in which you are reading. As you walk, notice what you see in your environment. This visual activity is actually extremely complicated, requiring billions of neurons and more than fifty regions of the surface of your brain (Emery & Easton, 2005).

Because the brain is so complex, we need to be very cautious when we read summaries of cognitive neuroscience research in the popular media. For example, I discovered a newspaper article that claimed "Scientists Find Humor Spot in the Brain." In reality, numerous parts of the brain work together to master the complicated task of appreciating humor.

Let's examine several neuroscience techniques that provide particularly useful information for cognitive psychologists. We will begin with a method that studies individuals who have experienced brain damage. Then we will consider three methods used with humans without brain damage. Positron emission tomography and functional magnetic resonance imaging both provide images of the brain when a participant engages in a cognitive task. In contrast, the event-related potential technique examines the brief electrical changes in the brain during a cognitive task.

Brain Lesions

In humans, the term **brain lesions** refers to the destruction of an area in the brain, most often by strokes, tumors, blows to the head, and accidents. The formal research on lesions began in the 1860s, but major advances came after World War II, when researchers examined the relationship between damaged regions of the brain and cognitive deficits (Farah, 2004; Kolb & Whishaw, 2009). Tragically, neurologists continue to learn more about specific cognitive deficits from the thousands of U.S. soldiers with brain lesions from the Iraq and Afghanistan wars (e.g., Department of Veterans Affairs, 2010; Oakie, 2005).

The study of brain lesions has definitely helped us understand the organization of the brain. However, the results are often difficult to interpret. For example, a brain lesion is not limited to just one specific area. As a result, researchers typically cannot associate a cognitive deficit with a specific brain structure (Gazzaniga et al., 2009; Kalat, 2009).

In this textbook, we will occasionally discuss research on people with brain lesions. However, three neuroscience techniques provide better-controlled information (Hernandez-García et al., 2002).

Positron Emission Tomography (PET Scan)

When you perform a cognitive task, your brain needs chemicals such as oxygen to support the neural activity. The brain does not store oxygen. Instead, the blood flow increases in the activated part of the brain in order to carry oxygen to that site. Brain-imaging techniques measure brain activity indirectly. These techniques are based on the following logic: By measuring certain properties of the blood in different regions of the brain while people perform a cognitive task, we can determine which brain regions are responsible for that cognitive task (Coren et al., 2004; Szpunar, 2010).

In a **positron emission tomography (PET scan)**, researchers measure blood flow in the brain by injecting the participant with a low dose of a radioactive chemical just before this person works on a cognitive task. This chemical travels through the bloodstream to the parts of the brain that are activated during the tasks. While the person works on the task, a special camera makes an image of the accumulated radioactive chemical in various regions of the brain.

For example, the participant might perform two slightly different cognitive tasks. By comparing the two brain images, researchers can determine which parts of the brain are activated when the participant works on each task (Kolb & Whishaw, 2011; Szpunar, 2010). PET scans can be used to study such cognitive processes as attention, memory, and language.

PET scans require several seconds to produce data, so this method is not very precise. If the activity in a specific brain region increases and then decreases within this brief period, the PET scan will record an average of this activity level (Hernandez-García et al., 2002). For example, you can scan an entire room in 2 or 3 seconds, so an average activity level for this entire scene would not be meaningful. Furthermore, in the current era, PET scans are used less often than some other imaging techniques, because they are expensive and they expose people to radioactive chemicals (Kalat, 2009).

Functional Magnetic Resonance Imaging

PET scans and functional magnetic resonance imaging are both based on comparing brain images during cognitive activity. However, fMRIs do not use radioactive material (Bermúdez, 2010; Bernstein & Loftus, 2009).

More specifically, **functional magnetic resonance imaging (fMRI)** is based on the principle that oxygen-rich blood is an index of brain activity (Cacioppo & Berntson, 2005b; Kalat, 2009; Szpunar, 2010). The research participant reclines with his or her head surrounded by a large, doughnut-shaped magnet. This magnetic field produces changes in the oxygen atoms. A scanning device takes a "photo" of these oxygen atoms while the participant performs a cognitive task.

For example, researchers have used the fMRI method to examine regions of the brain that process visual information. They found that specific locations in the brain respond more to letters than to numbers (Polk et al., 2002).

The fMRI technique was developed during the 1990s, based on the magnetic resonance imaging (MRI), which is used in medical settings. In general, an fMRI is preferable to a PET scan because it is less invasive, with no injections and no radioactive material (Gazzaniga et al., 2009). In addition, an fMRI can measure brain activity that occurs fairly quickly—in about 1 second (Frith & Rees, 2004; Huettel et al., 2004; Kalat, 2009).

The fMRI technique is more precise than a PET scan in identifying the exact time sequence of cognitive tasks. The fMRI technique can also detect subtle differences in the way that the brain processes language. For example, Gernsbacher and Robertson (2005) used this technique to discover a different pattern of brain activation when students read sentences like, "The young child played in a backyard," as opposed to "A young child played in a backyard."

Notice the subtle difference in meaning between "A child" and "The child." Would you have thought that your brain responded differently to these almost identical phrases?

However, even the fMRI technique is not precise enough to study the sequence of events in the cognitive tasks that we perform very quickly. In addition, neither PET scans nor fMRIs can tell us precisely what a person is thinking. For instance, some news commentators have suggested using brain scans to identify terrorists. The current technology for this precise kind of identification is clearly inadequate.

Event-Related Potential Technique

As we've seen, PET scans and the fMRI technique are too slow to provide precise information about the timing of brain activity. In contrast, the **event-related potential (ERP) technique** records the very brief fluctuations in the brain's electrical activity, in response to a stimulus such as an auditory tone (Bernstein & Loftus, 2009; Gazzaniga et al., 2009; Kolb & Whishaw, 2011).

To use the event-related potential technique, researchers place electrodes on a person's scalp. Each electrode records the electrical activity generated by a group of neurons located directly underneath the skull. The ERP technique cannot identify the response of a single neuron. However, it can identify electrical changes over a very brief period in a specific region of the brain (Kutas & Federmeier, 2011).

For example, suppose that you are participating in a study that examines how humans respond to facial movement. Specifically, you have been instructed to watch a video that lasts one second. One video shows a woman opening her mouth; a second video shows her closing her mouth. The electrodes are fastened to your scalp, and you watch numerous presentations of both the mouth-opening and the mouth-closing videos. Later, the researchers will average the signal for each of the two conditions, to eliminate random activity in the brain waves (Puce & Perrett, 2005).

The ERP technique provides a reasonably precise picture about changes in the brain's electrical potential while people perform a cognitive task. Consider the research on mouth movement, for example. If you were to participate in this study, your brain would show a change in electrical potential about half of a second after you saw each mouth movement. However, your brain would respond more dramatically when you watch her mouth open than when you watch a mouth close (Puce & Perrett, 2005).

Why does this fine-grained ERP analysis show that your brain responds differently to these two situations? Puce and Perrett propose that a mouth-opening movement is more important, because it signals that a person is about to say something. You therefore need to be attentive, and this exaggerated ERP reflects this attentiveness. In contrast, it's less important to notice that someone has finished talking.

A detailed investigation of cognitive neuroscience techniques is beyond the scope of this book. However, these techniques will be mentioned further in the chapters on perception, memory, and language. You can also obtain more information from other resources (e.g., Gazzaniga et al., 2009; Kalat, 2009; Kolb & Whishaw, 2011). However, it's important to point out that neuroscientists have not developed a detailed explanation for any human cognitive process, despite the claims in the popular media (Gallistel & King, 2009).

⊚ Section Summary: *Cognitive Neuroscience Techniques*

1. The area of cognitive neuroscience combines the research techniques of cognitive psychology with a variety of methods for assessing the brain's structure and function.

2. A brain lesion refers to an area of the brain that has been destroyed by strokes and other forms of damage; it is often difficult to interpret the relationship between brain lesions and cognitive deficits.

3. In the positron emission tomography or PET-scan technique, researchers inject a small dose of radioactive chemical to see what parts of the brain are activated when a person is working on a cognitive task.

4. Functional magnetic resonance imaging (fMRI) tracks oxygen-rich blood to see what parts of the brain are active when a person is working on a cognitive task.

5. The event-related potential technique uses electrodes to track the very brief changes in the brain's electrical activity, in response to specific stimuli.

ADDITIONAL AREAS THAT CONTRIBUTE TO COGNITIVE PSYCHOLOGY

Cognitive neuroscience, the topic that we have just discussed, is clearly the area that contributes most to cognitive psychology. However, we also need to consider two other topics, *artificial intelligence* and the broad field of *cognitive science*.

Artificial Intelligence

Artificial intelligence (AI) is a branch of computer science; it seeks to explore human cognitive processes by creating computer models that show "intelligent behavior" and also accomplish the same tasks that humans do (Bermúdez, 2010; Boden, 2004; Chrisley, 2004). Researchers in artificial intelligence have tried to explain how humans recognize a face, create a mental image, and write a poem, as well as hundreds of additional cognitive accomplishments (Boden, 2004; Farah, 2004; Thagard, 2005).

In this textbook, you'll read about research on artificial intelligence in Chapter 8 (general knowledge), Chapter 9 (language comprehension), and Chapter 11 (problem solving). Let's consider several important topics that are related to artificial intelligence: (1) the computer metaphor, (2) pure AI, (3) computer simulation, and (4) the connectionist approach.

The Computer Metaphor. During recent decades, the computer has been a popular metaphor for the human mind. According to the **computer metaphor**, our cognitive processes work like a computer, that is, a complex, multipurpose machine that processes information quickly and accurately. As we noted earlier, the information-processing approach emphasizes the similarity between human cognitive processes and the operation of a computer.

Of course, researchers acknowledge the obvious differences in physical structure between the computer and the human brain that manages our cognitive processes. However, both the human and the computer may operate according to similar general principles. For example, both humans and computers can compare symbols and can make choices according to the results of the comparison. Furthermore, computers have a processing mechanism with a limited capacity. Humans also have a limited attention capacity. For example, the research in Chapter 3 definitely shows that humans cannot pay attention to numerous tasks at the same time.

Computer models need to describe both the structures and the processes that operate on these structures. Thagard (2005) suggests that a computer model resembles a recipe in cooking. A recipe has two parts: (1) the ingredients, which are somewhat like the *structures*; and (2) the cooking instructions for working with those ingredients, which are somewhat like the *processes*.

Researchers who favor the computer approach try to design the appropriate "software." With the right computer program and sufficient mathematical detail, researchers hope to imitate the flexibility and the efficiency of human cognitive processes (Boden, 2004).

Artificial-intelligence researchers appreciate the analogy between the human mind and the computer because computer programs must be detailed, precise, unambiguous, and logical (Boden, 2004). Researchers can represent the functions of a computer with a flowchart that shows the sequence of stages in processing information. For instance, Figure 1.1 on page 10 is a simplified flowchart. Suppose that the computer and the human show equivalent performance on a particular task. Then the researchers can speculate that the computer program could represent an appropriate theory for describing the human's cognitive processes (Carpenter & Just, 1999).

Every metaphor has its limitations, and the computer cannot precisely duplicate human cognitive processes. For example, no artificial-intelligence system can speak and understand language as well as you do, because your background knowledge is so much more extensive (Boden, 2004). Furthermore, humans have more complex and fluid goals. If you play a game of chess with a friend, you may be concerned about how long the game lasts, whether you are planning to meet someone for dinner, and how you will interact socially with your opponent. In contrast, the computer's goals are simple and rigid: The computer deals only with the *outcome* of the chess game.

Pure Artificial Intelligence. We need to draw a distinction between "pure AI" and computer simulation. **Pure artificial intelligence (pure AI)** is an approach that designs a program to accomplish a cognitive task as efficiently as possible, even if the computer's processes are completely different from the processes used by humans.

For example, the most high-powered computer programs for chess will evaluate as many potential moves as possible in as little time as possible (Michie, 2004). Chess is an extremely complex game, in which both players together can make about 10^{128} possible different moves. This is larger than the total number of atoms contained in our universe. Consider a computer chess program named "Hydra." The top chess players in the world make a slight error about every ten moves. Hydra can identify this error—even though chess experts cannot—and it therefore wins the game (Mueller, 2005).

Researchers have designed pure AI systems that can play chess, speak English, or diagnose an illness. However, as one researcher points out, "I wouldn't want a chess-playing program speculating as to the cause of my chest pain" (Franklin, 1995, p. 11).

Computer Simulation. As we have seen, pure AI tries to achieve the best possible performance. In contrast, **computer simulation** or **computer modeling** attempts to take human limitations into account. The goal of computer simulation is to program a computer to perform a specific cognitive task in the same way that humans actually perform this task. A computer simulation must produce the same number of errors—as well as correct responses—that a human produces (Carpenter & Just, 1999; Thagard, 2005).

Computer-simulation research has been most active in such areas as memory, language processing, problem solving, and logical reasoning (Bower, 2008; Eysenck & Keane, 2010; Thagard, 2005). For example, Carpenter and Just (1999) created a classic computer-simulation model for reading sentences. This model was based on the assumption that humans have a limited capacity to process information. As a result, humans will read a difficult section of a sentence more slowly. Consider the following sentence:

The reporter that the senator attacked admitted the error.

Carpenter and Just (1999) designed their computer simulation so that it took into account the relevant linguistic information contained in sentences like this one. The model predicted that processing speed should be fast for the words at the beginning and the end of the sentence. However, the processing should be slow for the awkward two-verb section, "attacked admitted." In fact, Carpenter and Just demonstrated that the human data matched the computer simulation quite accurately.

Surprisingly, people can accomplish some tasks quite easily, even though these tasks are beyond the capacity of computer simulations. For example, a 10-year-old girl can search a messy bedroom for her watch, find it in her sweatshirt pocket, read the pattern on the face of the watch, and then announce the time. However, no current computer can simulate this task. Computers also cannot match humans' sophistication in learning language, identifying objects in everyday scenes, or solving problems creatively (Jackendoff, 1997; Sobel, 2001).

The Connectionist Approach.   In 1986, James McClelland, David Rumelhart, and their colleagues at the University of California, San Diego, published an influential two-volume book titled *Parallel Distributed Processing* (McClelland & Rumelhart, 1986; Rumelhart et al., 1986). This approach contrasted sharply with the traditional information-processing approach. As we discussed on pages 9 and 10, the information-processing approach emphasizes that a mental process can be represented in terms of information that progresses through the system in a linear series of stages, one step at a time. However, this information-processing approach cannot explain how we manage to perform most of our complex cognitive tasks.

In contrast, the **connectionist approach** argues that cognitive processes can be understood in terms of networks that link together neuron-like units; in addition, many operations can proceed simultaneously—rather than one step at a time. In other words, human cognition is often *parallel*, not strictly linear (Barrett, 2009; Gazzaniga et al., 2009). Two other names that are often used interchangeably with connectionism are the **parallel distributed processing (PDP) approach** and the **neural-network approach**.

The connectionist approach is useful for explaining why we can perform some cognitive tasks very quickly and accurately. This approach grew out of developments in both neuroscience and artificial intelligence—the two topics we have just discussed.

During the 1970s, neuroscientists developed research techniques that could explore the structure of the cerebral cortex. As you'll recall, the **cerebral cortex** is the outer layer of the brain that is essential for your cognitive processes. One important discovery in this research was the numerous connections among neurons, a pattern that resembles many elaborate networks (Bermúdez, 2010; Rolls, 2004; Thagard, 2005).

This network pattern suggests that an item stored in your brain cannot be localized in a specific pinpoint-sized location of your cortex (Barrett, 2009; Fuster, 2003; Woll, 2002). Instead, the neural activity for that item seems to be *distributed* throughout a section of the brain. For example, researchers cannot pinpoint one small portion of your brain that stores the name of your cognitive psychology professor. Instead, that information is probably distributed throughout numerous neurons in a region of your cerebral cortex. Notice that the term "parallel *distributed* processing" captures the distributed characteristic of the neurons in your brain.

The researchers who developed the connectionist approach proposed a model that simulates many important features of the brain (Bermúdez, 2010; Levine, 2002; Woll, 2002). Naturally, the model captures only a fraction of the brain's complexity. However, like the brain, the model includes simplified neuron-like units, numerous interconnections, and neural activity distributed throughout the system.

During the time that some researchers were learning about features of the human brain, other researchers were discovering the limitations of the classical artificial-intelligence approach. This classical approach viewed processing as a series of separate operations; in other words, processing would be serial. During **serial processing**, the system must complete one step before it can proceed to the next step in the flowchart.

This one-step-at-a-time approach may capture the leisurely series of operations you conduct when you are thinking about every step in the process. For example, a classical AI model might be appropriate when you are solving a long-division problem (Leahey, 2003).

In contrast, it is difficult to use classical AI models to explain the kinds of cognitive tasks that humans do very quickly, accurately, and without conscious thought. For example, these AI models cannot explain how you can instantly perceive a visual scene (Bermúdez, 2010; Leahey, 2003). Glance up from your book, and then immediately return to this paragraph. When you looked at this visual scene, your retina presented about one million signals to your cortex—all at the same time. If your visual system had used serial processing in order to interpret these one million signals, you would still be processing that visual scene, rather than reading this sentence!

Many cognitive activities seem to use **parallel processing**—with numerous signals handled at the same time—rather than serial processing. On these tasks, processing seems to be both parallel and distributed, explaining the origin of one label for this theory, the *parallel distributed processing approach*.

Many psychologists welcomed the connectionist approach as a groundbreaking new framework. They have developed models in areas as unrelated to one another as college students' stereotypes about a group of people and children's mastery of irregular verbs (Bermúdez, 2010). Researchers continue to explore whether the PDP approach can adequately account for the broad range of skills demonstrated by our cognitive processes.

Keep in mind that the connectionist approach uses the human brain—rather than the serial-computer—as the basic model (Woll, 2002). This more sophisticated design allows the connectionist approach to achieve greater complexity, flexibility, and accuracy as it attempts to account for human cognitive processes.

Cognitive Science

Cognitive psychology is part of a broad field known as cognitive science. **Cognitive science** is an interdisciplinary field that tries to answer questions about the mind. Cognitive science includes three disciplines we've discussed so far—cognitive psychology, neuroscience, and artificial intelligence. It also includes philosophy, linguistics, anthropology, sociology, and economics. This field emerged when researchers began to notice connections among a variety of disciplines (Bermúdez, 2010; Sobel, 2001; Thagard, 2005).

According to cognitive scientists, thinking requires us to manipulate our internal representations of the external world. Cognitive scientists focus on these internal representations. In contrast, you'll recall, the behaviorists focused only on observable stimuli and responses in the external world.

Cognitive scientists value interdisciplinary studies, and they try to build bridges among the academic areas. Both the theory and the research in cognitive science are so extensive that no one person can possibly master everything (Bermúdez, 2010; Sobel, 2001; Thagard, 2005). However, if all these different fields remain separate, then cognitive scientists won't achieve important insights and relevant connections.

Therefore, cognitive science tries to coordinate the information that researchers have gathered throughout the relevant disciplines.

🌀 Section Summary: *Additional Areas that Contribute to Cognitive Psychology*

1. Theorists who are interested in artificial intelligence (AI) approaches to cognition typically try to design computer models that accomplish the same cognitive tasks that humans do.

2. According to the computer metaphor, human cognitive processes work like a computer that can process information quickly and accurately.

3. The approach called "pure artificial intelligence" attempts to design programs that can accomplish cognitive tasks as efficiently as possible.

4. The approach called "computer simulation" attempts to design programs that accomplish cognitive tasks the way that humans do.

5. According to the connectionist approach, cognitive processes can be represented in terms of networks of neurons; furthermore, many operations can proceed at the same time, in parallel, rather than one step at a time.

6. Cognitive science examines questions about the mind; it includes disciplines such as cognitive psychology, neuroscience, artificial intelligence, philosophy, linguistics, anthropology, sociology, and economics.

AN OVERVIEW OF YOUR TEXTBOOK

This textbook examines many different kinds of mental processes. We'll begin with perception and memory—two processes that contribute to all of the other cognitive tasks. We'll then consider language, which is probably the most challenging cognitive task that humans need to master. Later chapters discuss "higher-order" processes. As the name suggests, these higher-order cognitive processes depend upon the more basic processes introduced in earlier chapters. The final chapter examines cognition across the life span, from infancy to old age. Let's preview Chapters 2 through 13. Then we'll explore five themes that can help you appreciate some general characteristics of cognitive processes. Our final section provides hints on how you can use your book more effectively.

Preview of the Chapters

Visual and auditory recognition (**Chapter 2**) are perceptual processes that use your previous knowledge to interpret the stimuli that are registered by your senses. For example, visual recognition allows you to recognize each letter on this page, whereas auditory recognition allows you to recognize the words you hear when a friend is talking to you.

Another perceptual process is attention (**Chapter 3**). The last time you tried to follow a friend's story—while simultaneously reading your biology textbook—you probably noticed the limits of your attention. This chapter also examines a related topic, called *consciousness*. **Consciousness** is your awareness of the external world, as well as your thoughts and emotions about your internal world. An important characteristic of consciousness is that we sometimes have trouble *avoiding* thoughts about an unpleasant topic.

Memory is the process of maintaining information over time. Memory is such an important part of cognition that it requires several chapters. **Chapter 4** describes working memory (short-term memory). You're certainly aware of the limits of working memory when you forget someone's name that you heard less than a minute earlier.

Chapter 5, the second of the memory chapters, focuses on long-term memory. We'll note that factors such as mood can influence your ability to remember information. We'll also explore memory for everyday life events, as well as people's accuracy during eyewitness testimony.

Chapter 6, the last of the general memory chapters, provides suggestions to help you improve your memory. This chapter also considers **metacognition**, which is your knowledge about your own cognitive processes. For instance, do you know whether you could remember the definition for *metacognition* if you were to be tested tomorrow?

Chapter 7 examines **imagery**, which is the mental representation of things that are not physically present. One important controversy in the research on imagery is whether your mental images truly resemble perceptual images. Another important topic concerns the mental images we have for physical settings. For example, the cognitive map you have developed for your college campus may show several buildings lined up in a straight row, even though their actual positions are much more random.

Chapter 8 concerns general knowledge. One area of general knowledge is **semantic memory**, which includes factual knowledge about the world as well as knowledge about word meanings. General knowledge also includes schemas (pronounced "*skee-mahz*"). **Schemas** are generalized kinds of information about situations. For example, you have a schema for the typical sequence of events that happen during the first day of a new course.

Chapter 9 is the first of two chapters on language, and it examines language *comprehension*. For example, a friend may mumble a sentence, yet you can easily perceive the message. Reading is the second topic in Chapter 9; you'll see that reading is much more complex than you might think! We'll also explore **discourse**, which is a long passage of spoken or written language.

Chapter 10, the second of the language chapters, examines language *production*. One component of speaking is its social context. For example, when you describe an event to some friends, you probably check to make certain that they have the appropriate background knowledge. Writing requires many cognitive processes that are different from speaking, but both of them require working memory and long-term memory. Our final language topic is bilingualism; even though learning a single language is challenging, many people can speak two or more languages fluently.

Chapter 11 considers problem solving. Suppose you want to solve a problem, such as how to complete a course assignment if you do not understand the instructions. You may solve the problem by using a strategy such as dividing the problem into several smaller problems. Chapter 11 also explores creativity. As you'll see, people are often less creative if they have been told that they will be rewarded for their creative efforts.

Chapter 12 addresses deductive reasoning and decision making. Reasoning tasks require you to draw conclusions from several known facts. In many cases, your background knowledge interferes with drawing accurate conclusions. In decision making, you make a judgment about uncertain events. For example, people often cancel an airplane trip after reading about a recent plane accident, even though statistics clearly show that driving is more dangerous.

Chapter 13 examines cognitive processes in infants, children, and elderly adults. People in these three age groups are more competent than you might guess. For example, 6-month-old infants can recall an event that occurred two weeks earlier. Young children are also very accurate in remembering events from a medical procedure in a doctor's office. Furthermore, elderly people are competent on many memory tasks, and they actually perform better than younger adults on some tasks, such as crossword puzzles (Salthouse, 2012). Chapter 13 also encourages you to review your knowledge about three important topics in cognitive psychology: memory, metamemory (or your thoughts about your memory), and language.

Themes in the Book

This book emphasizes certain themes and consistencies in cognitive processes. The themes are designed to guide you and offer you a framework for understanding many of the complexities of our mental abilities. These themes are also listed in abbreviated form inside the front cover; you can consult the list as you read later chapters. The themes are as follows:

Theme 1: *The cognitive processes are active, rather than passive.* The behaviorists viewed humans as passive organisms, who wait until a stimulus arrives from the environment before they respond. In contrast, the cognitive approach proposes that people seek out information. In addition, memory is a lively process that requires you to continually synthesize and transform information. When you read, you actively draw inferences that were never directly stated. In summary, your mind is not a sponge that passively absorbs information leaking out from the environment. Instead, you continually search and synthesize.

Theme 2: *The cognitive processes are remarkably efficient and accurate.* For example, the amount of material in your memory is astonishing. Language development is similarly impressive. For instance, preschoolers can master thousands of new words, in addition to the complex structure of language. Naturally, humans make mistakes. However, these mistakes often occur when people use a strategy that is usually appropriate. For instance, people frequently base their decisions on how easily they can recall relevant examples. This strategy often leads to a correct decision, but it can occasionally produce an error.

Furthermore, many of the limitations in human information processing may actually be helpful. You may wish that your memory could be more accurate. However, if you retained all information forever, your memory would be hopelessly cluttered with facts that are no longer useful. Before you read further, try Demonstration 1.4, which is based on a Demonstration by Hearst (1991).

⊚ Demonstration 1.4

Looking at Unusual Paragraphs

How fast can you spot what is unusual about this paragraph? It looks so ordinary that you might think nothing is wrong with it at all, and, in fact, nothing is. But it is atypical. Why? Study its various parts, think about its curious wording, and you may hit upon a solution. But you must do it without aid; my plan is not to allow any scandalous misconduct in this psychological study. No doubt, if you work hard on this possibly frustrating task, its abnormality will soon dawn upon you. You cannot know until you try. But it is commonly a hard nut to crack. So, good luck!

I trust a solution is conspicuous now. Was it dramatic and fair, although odd? Author's hint: I cannot add my autograph to this communication and maintain its basic harmony.

Theme 3: *The cognitive processes handle positive information better than negative information.* We understand sentences better if they are worded in the affirmative—for example, "Mary is honest," rather than the negative wording, "Mary is not dishonest." In addition, we have trouble noticing when something is missing, as illustrated in Demonstration 1.4 (Hearst, 1991). (See page 31 for the answer to this demonstration, as well as for the credit for this quotation.)

We also tend to perform better on a variety of different tasks if the information is emotionally positive (that is, pleasant), rather than emotionally negative (unpleasant). In short, our cognitive processes are designed to handle *what is*, rather than *what is not* (Hearst,1991; Matlin, 2004).

Theme 4: *The cognitive processes are interrelated with one another; they do not operate in isolation.* This textbook discusses each cognitive process in one or more separate chapters. However, this organizational plan does not imply that every process can function by itself, without input from other processes. For example, decision making typically requires perception, memory, general knowledge, and language. In fact, all higher mental processes require careful integration of our more basic cognitive processes. Consequently, such tasks as problem solving, logical reasoning, and decision making are impressively complex.

Theme 5: *Many cognitive processes rely on both bottom-up and top-down processing.* **Bottom-up processing** emphasizes the importance of information from the stimuli registered on your sensory receptors. Bottom-up processing uses only a low-level sensory analysis of the stimulus. In contrast, **top-down processing** emphasizes how our concepts, expectations, and memory influence our cognitive processes. This top-down processing requires higher-level cognition, for example, the kind of processes we will emphasize in Chapters 5 and 8 of this textbook. Both bottom-up and top-down processing work simultaneously to ensure that our cognitive processes are typically fast and accurate.

Consider pattern recognition. You recognize your aunt partly because of the specific information from the stimulus—information about your aunt's face, height, shape, and so forth. This bottom-up processing is important. At the same time, top-down processing would operate if you went to her house, and you were expecting to see her in this location.

How to Use Your Book Effectively

Your textbook includes several features that are specifically designed to help you understand and remember the material. As you read the list that follows, figure out how to use each feature most effectively. In addition, Chapter 6 focuses on memory-improvement techniques. Turn to Table 6.1 on pages 186 to 187. This table summarizes many memory strategies, and we will explore them in more detail throughout Chapters 5 and 6. However, you may discover some hints to help you right now.

Chapter Outline. Notice that each chapter begins with an outline. When you start to read a new chapter, first examine the outline so that you can appreciate the general structure of a topic. For example, notice that Chapter 1 has four main topics, beginning on page 4 with **A BRIEF HISTORY OF COGNITIVE PSYCHOLOGY**. Each of these headings is in large, boldface print, with all of the letters capitalized. The second-level headings are smaller, with the major words capitalized, as you can see on page 4, for **The Origins of Cognitive Psychology**. The third-level headings are the smallest; they appear at the beginning of a paragraph in italics, for example, *Wilhelm Wundt* at the bottom of page 4.

Chapter Preview. Another feature is the chapter preview, which is a short description of the material to be covered. This preview builds upon the framework provided in each chapter outline, and it also introduces some important new terms.

Opening Paragraph. Each chapter begins with a paragraph that encourages you to think how your own cognitive experiences are related to the material in the chapter. By combining the material from the outline, the preview, and the opening paragraph, you'll be better prepared for the specific information about the research and theories in each chapter. You may be tempted to skip the chapter outline, the chapter preview, and the opening paragraph. However, these three features will all facilitate your top-down processing.

Demonstrations. I designed the demonstrations in this book to make the research more meaningful. The informal experiments in these demonstrations require little or no equipment, and you can perform most of them by yourself. Students have told me that these demonstrations help make the material more memorable, especially when they try to picture themselves performing the tasks in a research setting. As you will see in Chapters 5 and 6, we remember information more accurately when we try to relate the material to ourselves.

Individual Differences Feature. Chapters 2 through 13 each discuss one study that focuses on individual differences in cognitive performance. **Individual differences** refer to the systematic variation in the way that groups of people perform on the same cognitive task. Prior to about 1995, cognitive psychologists rarely studied how individual differences could influence people's thought processes. However, cognitive psychology is changing.

The exploration of individual differences in cognitive performance is consistent with a relatively new approach that makes connections among the various disciplines within psychology. John T. Cacioppo (2007) wrote about this important issue when he was the president of the Association for Psychological Science. APS is an organization that focuses on psychology research in areas such as cognitive psychology, social psychology, and biopsychology.

Cacioppo emphasized that psychology can make major advances by combining each of these areas with one of three specific perspectives. These three perspectives are abnormal psychology, individual differences, and developmental psychology. For instance, a group of researchers could combine one area (e.g., cognitive psychology) with a perspective (e.g., abnormal psychology).

Consider individuals who have major depression. **Major depression** is a psychological disorder in which feelings of sadness, discouragement, and hopelessness interfere with the ability to perform daily mental and physical functions. In an earlier era, psychologists seldom studied whether depressed individuals might differ from other people when performing cognitive tasks. This situation is puzzling, because therapists—and the individuals themselves—frequently noticed these problems on cognitive tasks. Fortunately, many contemporary psychologists now conduct research on the relationship between psychological disorders and cognitive performance. However, psychologists are now examining the relationship between psychological disorders and cognitive performance (e.g., Hertel & Matthews, 2011).

This kind of interdisciplinary research is important, from both practical and theoretical reasons. As you know, Theme 4 emphasizes that our cognitive processes are interrelated. Therefore, cognitive aspects of psychological problems—such as major depression—could certainly be related to attention, memory, and other cognitive processes.

Other researchers who investigate individual differences choose to compare groups of people who differ on a demographic characteristic. In Chapter 7, for example, we'll see that women and men are actually similar in most kinds of spatial abilities.

Here is the list of individual differences that we will explore in this textbook:

Chapter 2 (Perceptual Processes I: Visual and Auditory Recognition):

    Face Identification in People with Schizophrenia

Chapter 3 (Perceptual Processes II: Attention and Consciousness):

    Eating Disorders and the Stroop Task

Chapter 4 (Working Memory):
  Major Depression and Working Memory
Chapter 5 (Long-Term Memory):
  Anxiety Disorders and Performance on Explicit and Implicit Memory Tasks
Chapter 6 (Memory Strategies and Metacognition):
  Attention-Deficit/Hyperactivity Disorder and Metamemory
Chapter 7 (Mental Imagery and Cognitive Maps):
  Gender Comparisons in Spatial Ability
Chapter 8 (General Knowledge):
  Country of Residence and Gender Stereotypes
Chapter 9 (Language I):
  Test Anxiety and Reading Comprehension
Chapter 10 (Language II):
  Simultaneous Interpreters and Working Memory
Chapter 11 (Problem Solving and Creativity):
  The Relationship Between Intrinsic Motivation and Creativity
Chapter 12 (Deductive Reasoning and Decision Making):
  Decision-Making Style and Psychological Well-Being
Chapter 13 (Cognitive Development Throughout the Lifespan):
  Children's Intellectual Abilities and Eyewitness Testimony

Applications. As you read the actual chapters, notice the numerous applications of cognitive psychology. The recent emphasis on ecological validity has inspired many studies that are relevant for our everyday cognitive activity. In addition, research in cognition has important applications in such areas as education, medicine, business, and clinical psychology. These applications provide concrete illustrations of psychological principles.

These examples should also facilitate your understanding. The research on memory demonstrates that people recall information better if it is concrete, rather than abstract, and if they try to determine whether the information applies to themselves (Paivio, 1995; Rogers et al., 1977; Symons & Johnson, 1997).

Keywords. Notice that each new term in this book appears in boldface type (for example, **cognition**) when it is first discussed. I have included the definition in the same sentence as the term, so you do not need to search an entire paragraph to discover the term's meaning. Also notice that phonetic pronunciation is provided for a small number of words that are often mispronounced. Students tell me that they feel more comfortable using a word in class discussion if they are confident that their pronunciation is correct. (I also included pronunciation guides for the names of several prominent theorists and researchers, such as Wundt and Piaget.)

Also, some important terms appear in several different chapters. I will define these terms the first time they occur in each chapter, so that you can read the chapters in any order.

In-Depth Feature. Chapters 2 through 13 each contain an "In Depth" feature, which examines research on an important topic relevant to the chapter. These features focus on the research methodology and the outcome of the studies.

Section Summaries. A special component of this textbook is a summary at the end of each major section in a chapter, rather than at the end of the entire chapter. For example, Chapter 2 includes four section summaries. These summaries allow you to review the material more frequently and to master small, manageable segments before you move on to new material. When you reach the end of a section, cover the section summary and see which important points you remember. Then read the section summary and notice which items you omitted or remembered incorrectly. Finally, test yourself again and recheck your accuracy. Also, you may learn the material more efficiently if you read only one section at a time, rather than an entire chapter.

End-of-Chapter Review Questions. You will find a set of review questions at the end of each chapter. Many review questions ask you to apply your knowledge to an everyday problem. Other review questions encourage you to integrate information from several parts of the chapter.

Keywords List. At the end of each chapter, a new terms list shows these terms in order of their appearance in the chapter. Check each item to see whether you can supply a definition and an example. You can consult the chapter for a discussion of the term; the glossary also has a brief definition for each of the terms.

Recommended Readings. Each chapter features a list of recommended readings. This list can supply you with resources if you want to write a paper on a particular topic or if an area is personally interesting. In general, I tried to locate books, chapters, and articles that provide more than an overview of the subject but are not overly technical.

Glossary. Your textbook includes a glossary at the end of the book. The glossary will be helpful when you need a precise definition for a technical term. It will also be useful when you want to check your accuracy while reviewing the list of new terms in each chapter.

One unusual aspect of cognitive psychology is that you are actually using cognition to learn about cognition! These learning aids, combined with the material on memory improvement in Chapter 6, should help you use your cognitive processes even more efficiently.

CHAPTER REVIEW QUESTIONS

1. Define the terms *cognition* and *cognitive psychology*. Now think about your ideal career, and suggest several ways in which the information from cognitive psychology would be relevant to this career.

2. Compare the following approaches to psychology, with respect to their specific emphasis on human thinking: (a) William James's approach, (b) behaviorism, (c) gestalt psychology, (d) Frederic Bartlett's approach, and (e) the cognitive approach.

3. This chapter addresses the trade-off between ecological validity and carefully controlled research. Define these two concepts. Then compare the following approaches in terms of their emphasis on each concept: (a) Ebbinghaus's approach to memory, (b) James's approach to psychological processes, (c) Bartlett's approach to memory, (d) the behaviorist approach, (e) the cognitive psychology approach from several decades ago, and (f) current cognitive psychology research.

4. List several reasons for the increased interest in cognitive psychology and the decline of the behaviorist approach. In addition, describe the field of cognitive science, noting the disciplines that are included in this field.

5. The section on cognitive neuroscience described four different research techniques. Answer the following questions for each technique: (a) Can it be used with humans? (b) How precise is the information it yields? (c) What kind of research questions can it answer?

6. What is artificial intelligence, and how is the information-processing approach relevant to this topic? Select three specific cognitive processes that might interest researchers in artificial intelligence. Then provide examples of how pure AI and the computer-simulation investigations of these cognitive process would differ in their focus.

7. How does connectionism differ from the classical artificial-intelligence approach? List three characteristics of the PDP approach. In what way is this approach based on discoveries in cognitive neuroscience?

8. Theme 4 emphasizes that your cognitive processes are interrelated. Think about a problem you have solved recently, and point out how the solution to this problem depended upon perceptual processes, memory, and other cognitive activities. Use the description of chapter topics (see pp. 22–24) to help you answer this question.

9. As you'll see in Chapter 6, your long-term memory is more accurate if you carefully think about the material you are reading; it is especially accurate if you try to relate the material to your own life. Review the section called "How to Use Your Book" (pp. 26–29), and describe how you can use each feature to increase your memory for the material in the remaining chapters of this book.

10. Review each of the five themes of this book. Which of them seem consistent with your own experiences, and which seem surprising? From your own life, think of an example of each theme.

KEYWORDS

cognition
cognitive psychology
cognitive approach
empirical evidence
introspection
recency effect
behaviorism
operational definition
gestalt psychology
gestalt
information-processing
   approach
Atkinson-Shiffrin model
sensory memory
short-term memory
working memory
long-term memory
ecological validity
cognitive neuroscience

social cognitive neuroscience
brain lesions
positron emission tomography
   (PET scan)
functional magnetic resonance
   imaging (fMRI)
event-related potential (ERP)
   technique
artificial intelligence
   (AI)
computer metaphor
pure AI
computer simulation
computer modeling
connectionist approach
parallel distributed processing
   (PDP) approach
neural-network approach
cerebral cortex

serial processing
parallel processing
cognitive science
consciousness
memory
metacognition
imagery
semantic memory
schemas
discourse
Theme 1
Theme 2
Theme 3
Theme 4
Theme 5
bottom-up processing
top-down processing
individual differences
major depression

RECOMMENDED READINGS

Bermúdez, J. L. (2010). *Cognitive science: An introduction to the science of the mind*. New York: Cambridge University Press. Because cognitive science is an interdisciplinary area; many psychologists have difficulty understanding some of the less familiar topics. However, this textbook is more accessible than others.

Kalat, J. W. (2009). *Biological psychology* (10th ed.). Belmont, CA: Cengage Wadsworth. Kalat's textbook provides a interesting, clear description of biopsychology and neuropsychology; the illustrations are especially helpful.

Pickren, W. E., & Rutherford, A. (2010). *A history of modern psychology in context*. Hoboken, NJ: Wiley. I highly recommend this clearly written, well-organized overview of the history of psychology.

ENDNOTE

Quotation on page 25 from: Hearst, E. (1991). Psychology and nothing. *American Scientist, 79*, 432–443.

ANSWER TO DEMONSTRATION 1.4

The letter *e* is missing from this entire passage. The letter *e* is the most frequent letter in the English language. Therefore, a long passage—without any use of the letter *e*—is highly unusual. The exercise demonstrates the difficulty of searching for something that is not there (Theme 3).

CHAPTER 2

Perceptual Processes I: Visual and Auditory Recognition

PREVIEW

When you perceive something, you use your previous knowledge to gather and interpret the stimuli registered by your senses. Chapter 2 explores both visual and auditory recognition, two processes that are especially relevant in cognitive psychology. (Chapter 3 will examine two other important topics related to perception: attention and consciousness.)

When you recognize a visual object, you identify a complex arrangement of sensory stimuli, such as several printed letters of the alphabet or a human face. We will briefly discuss the visual system; next we'll explore how the visual system organizes our visual world. Then we'll consider two current theories that are useful in explaining how we recognize object

Theme 5 of this textbook emphasizes the principle of bottom-up and top-down processing. With respect to perception, bottom-up processing focuses on the physical stimuli in the environment. In contrast, top-down processing emphasizes how your concepts, expectations, and memory influence perceptual processing. We will first explore how top-down processing aids reading. Then an in-depth discussion examines how overactive top-down processing can lead to errors when you try to recognize someone or something.

Face perception is vitally important in our social interactions, and we seem to process human faces differently from other visual stimuli. Neuroscience research helps to clarify the biological processes that explain face perception. This section also explores the challenges of recognizing faces from identification cards or security surveillance systems. Then we'll consider whether individuals with schizophrenia encounter difficulties in recognizing faces.

Speech perception is more complicated than it initially seems. For example, you need to figure out where one word stops and another word begins. Speakers also vary in the way they pronounce the basic speech sounds. However, you use context and visual cues to help interpret speech that isn't clear. Although speech is socially important, we apparently process speech in the same way that we process other auditory information.

CHAPTER INTRODUCTION

Take a minute to appreciate your perceptual abilities, and hold your hand directly in front of your eyes. You definitely perceive a solid object that includes distinctive characteristics. For example, you can easily identify its size, shape, and color. You also notice that your hand is a unified object, clearly located in front of a more distant and less clearly defined background.

As you shift your gaze back to this textbook, your eyes perceive a series of squiggles on this page. However, you can instantly identify each squiggle as a letter of the alphabet. If a friend walks by, you can immediately recognize this person's face. Your visual system perceives more than just one shape at a time. In fact, you can quickly and effortlessly identify hundreds of shapes in any natural scene (Geisler, 2008). Your auditory abilities are equally impressive; you can recognize the words spoken by your friend, as well as music, squeaking chairs, and footsteps.

Most of us take perception for granted (Jain & Duin, 2004). *Of course* we can see and hear! Chapters 2 and 3 should persuade you that perception is actually a remarkably complex human ability. Perception may seem to be far easier than other cognitive skills, such as playing chess. However, as we noted in Chapter 1, a computer program can be designed that can outperform a chess master. In contrast, you cannot buy a vision machine that will outperform the visual skills of a preschool child. Furthermore, you can identify a complex scene—such as a baseball game or a wedding—within about one-tenth of a second (Gallistel & King, 2009).

Perceptual processes provide clear evidence for Theme 2 of this textbook. As you'll see in this chapter, our visual and auditory achievements are impressively efficient and accurate (Grill-Spector & Kanwisher, 2005; Lappin & Craft, 2000).

Chapters 2 and 3 explore perception. **Perception** uses previous knowledge to gather and interpret the stimuli registered by the senses. For example, you use perception to interpret each of the letters on this page. Consider how you managed to perceive the letter at the end of the word *perception*. You combined (1) information registered by your eyes, (2) your previous knowledge about the shape of the letters of the alphabet, and (3) your previous knowledge about what to expect when your visual system has already processed the fragment *perceptio-*.

Notice that perception combines aspects of both the outside world (the visual stimuli) and your own inner world (your previous knowledge). You'll notice that this process of pattern recognition is a good example of Theme 5 of this book, because it combines bottom-up and top-down processing.

Many colleges offer an entire course on the topic of perception, so we cannot do justice to this discipline in just two chapters. Other resources can provide information about sensory processes such as the nature of the receptors in the eye and the ear, as well as more details about other areas of perception (Foley & Matlin, 2010; Goldstein, 2010a; Wolfe et al., 2009). These books examine how we perceive important characteristics of visual objects, such as shape, size, color, texture, and depth. These resources also investigate other perceptual systems—audition, touch, taste, and smell.

Our current chapter explores several aspects of perceptual processing. We will begin with some background information on recognizing visual objects. Then we'll examine two important topics in vision: top-down processing and face perception. Finally, we will shift to the perceptual world of audition as we consider speech perception. These perceptual processes are vitally important because they prepare the "raw" sensory information so that it can be used in the more complex mental processes—such as reading—which we'll discuss in later chapters of this book.

This textbook features two chapters about perceptual processes. Chapter 2 examines how we recognize visual and auditory stimuli. In contrast, Chapter 3 discusses attention and consciousness. For example, if you are paying close attention to the sentence that you are reading, can you simultaneously perceive a nearby conversation?

BACKGROUND ON VISUAL OBJECT RECOGNITION

During **object recognition** or **pattern recognition**, you identify a complex arrangement of sensory stimuli, and you perceive that this pattern is separate from its background. When you recognize an object, your sensory processes transform and organize the raw information provided by your sensory receptors. You also compare the sensory stimuli with information in other memory storage. Consistent with Theme 2, we recognize objects quickly and accurately (Gazzaniga et al., 2009; Kersten et al., 2004). This first section of the chapter considers three topics: (a) the visual system, (b) how organization operates in visual perception, and (c) three theories about object recognition.

The Visual System

Psychologists have developed two terms to refer to perceptual stimuli. The **distal stimulus** is the actual object that is "out there" in the environment—for example, the pen on your desk. The **proximal stimulus** is the information registered on your sensory receptors—for example, the image that your pen creates on your retina. Your **retina** covers the inside back portion of your eye; it contains millions of neurons that register and transmit visual information from the outside world.

When we recognize an object, we manage to figure out the identity of the distal stimulus, even when the information available in the proximal stimulus is far from perfect (Kersten et al., 2004; Palmer, 2003; Pasternak et al., 2003). For example, you recognized the human face on page 6, even though the face lacks a nose, mouth, and ears. Gazzaniga and his colleagues (2009) point out that object recognition depends primarily on shape, rather than on color or texture. You recognized this human face, even though it was blue.

Try Demonstration 2.1 to illustrate your skill in identifying the distal stimulus. As this demonstration notes, you can recognize objects in a new scene that

---

Ⓖ Demonstration 2.1

The Immediate Recognition of Objects

Turn on a television set and adjust the sound to "mute." Now change the channel with your eyes closed. Open your eyes and then immediately shut them. Repeat this exercise several times. Notice how you can instantly identify and interpret the image on the TV screen, even though you did not expect that image and have never previously seen it in that exact form. In less than a second—and without major effort—you can identify colors, textures, contours, objects, and people.

This demonstration was originally suggested by Irving Biederman (1995), who noted that people can usually interpret the meaning of a new scene in one-tenth of a second. Consistent with Theme 2, humans are impressively efficient in recognizing patterns.

has been presented for about one-tenth of a second (Biederman, 1995). Does this mean that your visual system manages to take the proximal stimulus, representing perhaps a dozen objects, and recognize all of these objects within one-tenth of a second?

Fortunately, your visual system has some assistance from one of its other components (Gregory, 2004a). As we noted in Chapter 1 (p. 9), your **sensory memory** is a large-capacity storage system that records information from each of the senses with reasonable accuracy. To be specific, **iconic memory**, or **visual sensory memory**, preserves an image of a visual stimulus for a brief period after the stimulus has disappeared (Hollingworth, 2006b; Parks, 2004; Sperling, 1960).

Visual information that is registered on the retina (the proximal stimulus) must make its way through the visual pathway, a set of neurons between the retina and the primary visual cortex. The **primary visual cortex** is located in the occipital lobe of the brain; it is the portion of your cerebral cortex that is concerned with basic processing of visual stimuli. (See Figure 2.1.) It is also the first place where information from your two eyes is combined (Briggs & Usrey, 2010). If you place your hand at the back of your head, just above your neck, the primary visual cortex lies just beneath your skull at that location.

The primary visual cortex is only the first stop within the cortex. For instance, researchers have identified at least 30 additional areas of the cortex that play a role in visual perception (Bruce et al., 2003; Frishman, 2001; Sillito, 2004). These regions beyond the primary visual cortex are activated when we recognize complex objects. Researchers are currently studying the functions of these regions. For example, your ability to recognize a tool—such as a fork or scissors—depends partly on your parietal lobe, as shown on page 38 (Almeida et al., 2010; Mahon et al., 2010).

However, researchers have not yet discovered which brain region is paired with each individual component of object recognition (Pasternak et al., 2003; Purves & Lotto, 2003). Our examination of face recognition, later in this chapter, will emphasize some of these more "sophisticated" regions of the cortex.

Organization in Visual Perception

At the beginning of this chapter, we emphasized that object recognition is a remarkable human achievement. As it happens, our visual system is designed to impose organization on the richly complicated visual world (Geisler & Super, 2000; Palmer, 2003).

In Chapter 1, we introduced a historical approach to psychology called "gestalt psychology." One important principle in **gestalt psychology** is that humans have basic tendencies to organize what they see; without any effort, we see patterns, rather than random arrangements (I. E. Gordon, 2004; Schirillo, 2010). For example, when two areas share a common boundary, the **figure** has a distinct shape with clearly defined edges. In contrast, the **ground** is the region that is "left over," forming the background. As gestalt psychologists pointed out, the figure has a definite shape, whereas the ground simply continues behind the figure. The figure also seems closer

FIGURE 2.1

A Schematic Drawing of the Cerebral Cortex, as Seen from the Left Side, Showing the Four Lobes of the Brain. Notice the primary visual cortex (discussed in this section). The inferotemporal cortex (discussed on p. 55) plays an important role in recognizing complex objects such as faces.

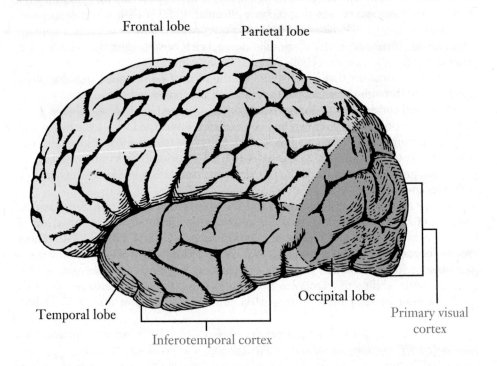

Frontal lobe   Parietal lobe

Occipital lobe

Primary visual cortex

Temporal lobe

Inferotemporal cortex

to us and more dominant than the ground (Kelly & Grossberg, 2000; Palmer, 2003; Rubin, 1915/1958). Even young infants demonstrate some of the gestalt principles of organization (Quinn et al., 2002).

In an **ambiguous figure-ground relationship,** the figure and the ground reverse from time to time, so that the figure becomes the ground and then becomes the figure again. Figure 2.2 illustrates the well-known vase-faces effect. At first, you see a white vase against a blue background, but a moment later, you see two blue faces against a white background. Even in this ambiguous situation, our perceptual system imposes organization on a stimulus, so that one portion stands out and the remainder recedes into the background. We are so accustomed to the certainty of the figure-ground relationship that we are surprised when we encounter a situation where the figure and the ground exchange places (Wolfe et al., 2009).

FIGURE 2.2

The Vase-Faces Effect: An Example of an Ambiguous Figure-Ground Relationship.

The explanation for these figure-ground reversals seems to have two components: (1) The neurons in the visual cortex become adapted to one figure, such as the "faces" version of Figure 2.2, so you are more likely to see the alternative or "vase" version; and (2) furthermore, people try to solve the visual paradox by alternating between two reasonable solutions (Gregory, 2004a; Long & Toppino, 2004; Toppino & Long, 2005).

Surprisingly, we can even perceive a figure-ground relationship when a scene has no clear-cut boundary between the figure and the ground. One category of visual illusions is known as illusory contours. In **illusory contours** (also called **subjective contours**), we see edges even though they are not physically present in the stimulus. In the illusory contour in Figure 2.3, for example, people report that an inverted white triangle seems to loom in front of the outline of a second triangle and three small blue circles. Furthermore, the triangle appears to be brighter than any other part of the stimulus (Grossberg, 2000; Palmer, 2002).

In our everyday life, we typically perceive scenes more accurately if we "fill in the blanks." However, in the case of illusory contours, this rational strategy leads to a perceptual error (Mendola, 2003; Purves & Lotto, 2003). You can see why gestalt psychologists were especially intrigued by ambiguous figure-ground relationships and

FIGURE 2.3

An Example of Illusory Contours.

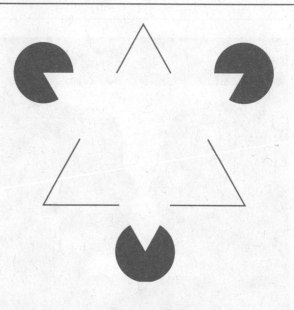

illusory contours (Foley & Matlin, 2010; Wolfe et al., 2009). Human perception is more than the sum of the information in the distal stimulus.

Theories of Visual Object Recognition

Researchers have proposed many different theories of object recognition. According to one early theory, your visual system compares a stimulus with a set of **templates**, or specific patterns that you have stored in memory. Then it notes which template matches the stimulus. However, every day you manage to recognize letters that differ substantially from the classic version of a letter, especially in handwritten text.

For instance, notice in Figure 2.4 that all of the letter C's in the word *Cognitive* are somewhat different. You can see that the letter P's in *Psychology* are also somewhat different. Still, you can recognize each of those letters, even if you view the letters from a different perspective (Palmer, 2003). The template approach fares even worse in recognizing the more complex objects that occupy your visual world. Perception requires a more flexible system than matching a pattern against a specific template (Gordon, 2004; Jain & Duin, 2004; Wolfe et al., 2009).

The two other theories—feature analysis and recognition-by-components—are more sophisticated. As you read about these two current theories, keep in mind that we don't need to decide that one theory is correct and the other is wrong. Human

FIGURE 2.4

An Example of Variability in the Shape of Letters. Notice specifically the difference in the shape of the letter P in Cognitive Psychology.

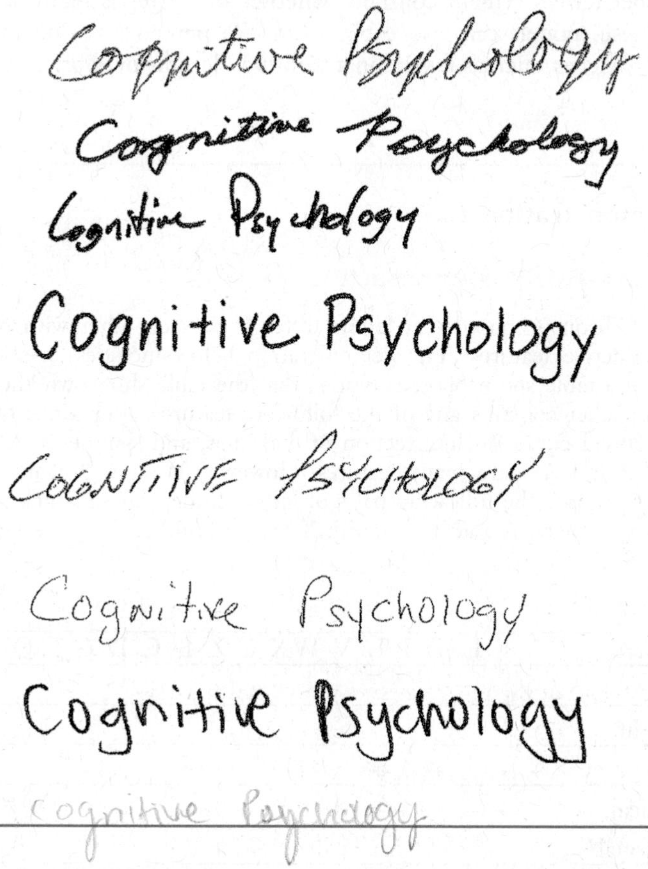

perception is somewhat flexible, and we may use different approaches for different object-recognition tasks (Mather, 2006).

Feature-Analysis Theory. Several **feature-analysis theories** propose a relatively flexible approach, in which a visual stimulus is composed of a small number of characteristics or components (Gordon, 2004). Each visual characteristic is called a **distinctive feature**. Consider, for example, how feature-analysis theorists might explain the way that we recognize letters of the alphabet. They argue that we store a list of distinctive features for each letter. For example, the distinctive features for the letter R include a curved component, a vertical line, and a diagonal line. When you look at a new letter, your visual system notes the presence or absence of the various features. It then compares this list with the features stored in memory for each letter of the alphabet. People's handwriting may differ, but each of their printed R's will include these three features.

Try Demonstration 2.2, which is based on a chart developed by Eleanor Gibson (1969). The feature-analysis theories propose that the distinctive features for each of the alphabet letters remain constant, whether the letter is handwritten, printed, or typed. These models can also explain how we perceive a wide variety of two-dimensional patterns, such as figures in a painting, designs on fabric, and illustrations

---

⊚ Demonstration 2.2

A Feature-Analysis Approach

Eleanor Gibson proposed that letters differ from each other with respect to their distinctive features. The demonstration below includes an abbreviated version of a table she proposed. Notice that the table shows whether a letter of the alphabet contains any of the following features: four kinds of straight lines, a closed curve, an intersection of two lines, and symmetry. As you can see, the P and R share many features. However, W and O share only one feature. Compare the following pairs of letters to determine which distinctive features they share: A and B; E and F; X and Y; I and L.

Features	A	E	F	H	I	L	V	W	X	Y	Z	B	C	D	G	J	O	P	R	Q
Straight																				
horizontal	+	+	+	+		+					+				+					
vertical		+	+	+	+	+						+		+				+	+	
diagonal/	+						+	+	+	+	+									
diagonal\	+						+	+	+	+									+	+
Closed Curve												+		+			+	+	+	+
Intersection	+	+	+	+					+			+						+	+	+
Symmetry	+	+		+	+		+	+	+	+		+	+	+			+			

Source: Gibson, E. J. (1969). *Principles of perceptual learning and development.* New York: Prentice Hall.

in books. However, most research on this topic focuses on our ability to recognize letters and numbers.

Feature-analysis theories are consistent with the psychological research. For example, the psychological research by Eleanor Gibson (1969) demonstrated that people require a relatively long time to decide whether one letter is different from a second letter when those two letters share a large number of critical features. According to the table in Demonstration 2.2, the letters P and R share many critical features; Gibson's research participants made slow decisions about whether these two letters were different. In contrast, O and L do not share any critical features. In this research, people decided relatively quickly whether letter pairs like these were different from each other.

Other psychological research analyzes the letters and numbers in the addresses that people write on envelopes (Jain & Duin, 2004). For example, Larsen and Bundesen (1996) designed a model based on feature analysis that correctly recognized an impressive 95% of the numbers written in street addresses and zip codes.

The feature-analysis theories are also compatible with evidence from neuroscience (Gordon, 2004; Palmer, 2002). The research team of Hubel and Wiesel focused on the primary visual cortex of anesthetized animals (Hubel, 1982; Hubel & Wiesel, 1965, 1979, 2005). They presented a simple visual stimulus—such as a vertical bar of light—directly in front of each animal's eyes. Hubel and Wiesel then recorded how a particular neuron in the primary visual cortex responded to that visual stimulus. They continued to test how a variety of neurons in this region of the cortex responded to visual stimuli.

Hubel and Wiesel's results showed that each neuron responded especially vigorously when the bar was presented to a specific retinal region and when the bar had a particular orientation. For example, suppose that a bar of light is presented to a particular location on the animal's retina. One specific neuron might respond strongly when the bar has a vertical orientation. Another neuron, just a hairbreadth away within the visual cortex, might respond most vigorously when the bar is rotated about 10 degrees from the vertical. The visual system contains feature detectors that are present when we are born (Gordon, 2004). These detectors help us recognize certain features of letters and simple patterns.

However, the feature-analysis approach has several problems. For example, the feature-analysis theories were constructed to explain the relatively simple recognition of letters. In contrast, the shapes that occur in nature are much more complex (Kersten et al., 2004). How can you recognize a horse? Do you analyze the stimulus into features such as its mane, its head, and its hooves? Wouldn't any important perceptual features be distorted as soon as the horse moved—or as soon as you moved? Horses and other objects in our environment contain far too many lines and curved segments. Recognizing these objects is far more complex than recognizing letters (Palmer, 2003; Vecera, 1998).

Let's now consider the recognition-by-components approach to object recognition. This approach is especially important because it specifically addresses how people recognize the complex kinds of stimuli that we find in everyday life.

The Recognition-by-Components Theory. Irving Biederman and his colleagues have developed a theory to explain how humans recognize three-dimensional shapes (Biederman, 1990, 1995; Hayworth & Biederman, 2006; Kayaert et al., 2003). The basic assumption of their **recognition-by-components theory** is that a specific view of an object can be represented as an arrangement of simple 3-D shapes called **geons**. Just as the letters of the alphabet can be combined into words, geons can be combined to form meaningful objects (Vuong, 2010).

You can see five of the proposed geons in Part A of Figure 2.5. Part B of this figure shows six of the objects that can be constructed from the geons. As you know, letters of the alphabet can be combined to form words with different meanings, depending upon the specific arrangements of the letters. For example, *no* has a different meaning from *on*. Similarly, geons 3 and 5 from Figure 2.5 can be combined to form different meaningful objects. A cup is different from a pail, and the recognition-by-components theory emphasizes the specific way in which these two geons are combined.

FIGURE 2.5

Five of the Basic Geons (A) and Representative Objects that Can Be Constructed from the Geons (B).

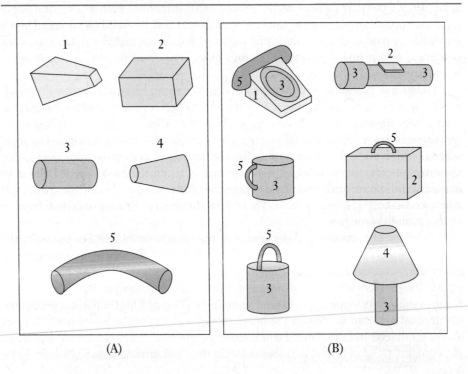

(A) (B)

Source: Biederman, I. (1990). Higher-level vision. In E. N. Osherson, S. M. Kosslyn, & J. M. Hollerback (Eds.), *An invitation to cognitive science* (Vol. 2, pp. 41–72). Cambridge, MA: MIT.

In general, an arrangement of three geons gives people enough information to classify an object. Notice, then, that Biederman's recognition-by-components theory is essentially a feature-analysis theory that explains how we recognize three-dimensional objects.

Biederman and his colleagues have conducted fMRI research with humans, and they also recorded neuronal responses in anesthetized monkeys. Their findings show that areas of the cortex beyond the primary visual cortex respond to geons like those in Figure 2.5A (Hayworth & Biederman, 2006; Kayaert et al., 2003).

Furthermore, computer-modeling research suggests that young children may initially represent each object as an undifferentiated complete object. In contrast, older children and adults can represent an object as a collection of geons (Doumas & Hummel, 2010).

However, the recognition-by-components theory requires an important modification, because people recognize objects more quickly when those objects are seen from a standard viewpoint, rather than a much different viewpoint (Friedman et al., 2005; Graf et al., 2005). Notice, for instance, how your own hand would be somewhat difficult to recognize if you look at it from an unusual perspective.

One modification of the recognition-by-components theory is called the **viewer-centered approach**; this approach proposes that we store a small number of views of three-dimensional objects, rather than just one view (G. Mather, 2006). Suppose that we see an object from an unusual angle, and this object does not match any object shape we have stored in memory. We must then mentally rotate the image of that object until it matches one of the views that is stored in memory (Tarr & Vuong, 2002; Wolfe et al., 2009). This mental rotation may require an additional second or two, and we may not even recognize the object. (Chapter 7 discusses mental rotation in more detail.)

At present, both the feature-analysis theory and the recognition-by-components theory (modified to include the viewer-centered approach) can explain some portion of our remarkable skill in recognizing objects. However, researchers must explore whether these theories can account for our ability to recognize objects that are more complicated than isolated cups and pails. For example, how were you able to immediately identify numerous complex objects in the scene you viewed on your television screen in Demonstration 2.1? The theoretical explanations will become more detailed, as researchers continue to explore how we recognize real-world objects and scenes, using increasingly sophisticated research methods (e.g., Gordon, 2004; Henderson, 2005; Hollingworth, 2006a, 2006b; Wolfe et al., 2009).

◎ Section Summary: *Background on Visual Object Recognition*

1. Perception uses previous knowledge to gather and interpret the stimuli registered by the senses; in object recognition, we identify a complex arrangement of sensory stimuli.

2. Visual information from the retina is transmitted to the primary visual cortex; other regions of the cortex are active when we recognize complex objects.

3. According to gestalt principles, people tend to organize their perceptions, even when they encounter ambiguous figure-ground stimuli and even in illusory-contour stimuli, when no boundary actually separates the figure from the background.

4. Feature-analysis theory is one theory of object recognition; it is supported by research showing that people require more time to make a decision about two letters of the alphabet when those letters share many critical features. This theory is also supported by neuroscience research.

5. The recognition-by-components theory argues that objects are represented in terms of an arrangement of simple 3-D shapes called "geons." Furthermore, according to the viewer-centered approach, we also store several alternate views of these 3-D shapes, as viewed from different angles.

TOP-DOWN PROCESSING AND VISUAL OBJECT RECOGNITION

Our discussion so far has emphasized how people recognize isolated objects. We have not yet considered how our knowledge and expectations can aid recognition. In real life, when you try to decipher a hastily written letter of the alphabet, the surrounding letters of the word might be helpful. Similarly, the context of a coffee shop is useful when you try to identify an object that consists of a narrow, curved geon that is attached to the side of a wider, cylindrical geon.

Theme 5 emphasizes the difference between two kinds of processing. Let's first review that distinction. Then we'll see how these two processes work together in a complementary fashion to help us recognize words during the reading process. Finally, we'll see how we can sometimes make mistakes if our top-down processing is overly active.

The Distinction Between Bottom-Up Processing and Top-Down Processing

So far, this chapter has focused on bottom-up processing. **Bottom-up processing** emphasizes that the stimulus characteristics are important when you recognize an object. Specifically, the physical stimuli from the environment are registered on the sensory receptors. This information is then passed on to higher, more sophisticated levels in the perceptual system (Carlson, 2010; Gordon, 2004).

For example, glance away from your textbook and focus on one specific object that is nearby. Notice its shape, size, color, and other important physical characteristics. When these characteristics are registered on your retina, the object-recognition process begins. This information starts with the most basic (or bottom) level of perception, and it works its way up until it reaches the more "sophisticated"cognitive regions of the brain, beyond your primary visual cortex. The combination of simple, bottom-level features helps you recognize more complex, whole objects.

The very first part of visual processing may be bottom-up (Palmer, 2002). However, an instant later, the second process begins. This second process in object recognition is top-down processing. **Top-down processing** emphasizes how a person's concepts, expectations, and memory can influence object recognition.

In more detail, these higher-level mental processes all help in identifying objects. You expect certain shapes to be found in certain locations, and you expect to encounter these shapes because of your past experiences. These expectations help you recognize objects very rapidly. In other words, your expectations at the higher (or top) level of visual processing will work their way down and guide our early processing of the visual stimulus (Carlson, 2010; Donderi, 2006; Gregory, 2004a).

Think how your top-down processing helped you to quickly recognize the specific nearby object that you selected a moment ago. Your top-down processing made use of your expectations and your memory about objects that are typically nearby. This top-down process then combined together with the specific physical information about the stimulus from bottom-up processing. As a result, you could quickly and seamlessly identify the object (Carlson, 2010). As we noted earlier, object recognition requires both bottom-up and top-down processing (Theme 5). Before you read further, skip to the bottom of this page and try Demonstration 2.3.

As you might imagine, top-down processing is strong when a stimulus is registered for just a fraction of a second. Top-down processing is also strong when stimuli are incomplete or ambiguous (Groome, 1999).

How does top-down processing operate in vision? Researchers have proposed that specific structures along the route between the retina and the visual cortex may play a role. These structures may store information about the relative likelihood of seeing various visual stimuli in a specific context (Kersten et al., 2004).

Cognitive psychologists believe that both bottom-up and top-down processing are necessary to explain the complexities of object recognition (Riddoch & Humphreys, 2001). For example, you recognize a coffee cup because of two almost simultaneous processes: (1) Bottom-up processing forces you to register the component features, such as the curve of the cup's handle; and (2) the context of a coffee shop encourages you to recognize the handle on the cup more quickly, because of top-down processing. Let's now consider how this top-down processing facilitates reading.

🌀 Demonstration 2.3

Context and Pattern Recognition

Can you read the following sentence?

THE MAN RAN.

Top-Down Processing and Reading

As Demonstration 2.3 shows, the same shape—an ambiguous letter—can sometimes be perceived as an H and sometimes as an A. In this demonstration, you began to identify the whole word "THE," and your tentative knowledge of that word helped to identify the second letter as an H. Similarly, your knowledge of the words "MAN" and "RAN" helped you identify that same ambiguous letter as an A in this different context.

Researchers have demonstrated that top-down processing can influence our ability to recognize a variety of objects (e.g., Gregory, 2004a; Hollingworth & Henderson, 2004; Kersten et al., 2004; Kutas & Federmeier, 2011; Rahman & Sommer, 2008). Most of the research on this topic examines how context helps us recognize letters of the alphabet during reading.

Psychologists who study reading have realized for decades that a theory of recognition must include factors other than the information in the stimulus. When you read, suppose that you do identify each letter by analyzing its features. In addition, suppose that each letter contains four distinctive features, a conservative guess. Taking into account the number of letters in an average word—and the average reading rate—this would mean that you would need to analyze about 5,000 features every minute. This estimate is ridiculously high; your perceptual processes couldn't handle that kind of workload (Dahan, 2010).

Furthermore, we can still manage to read a sentence, even if some of the middle letters in a word have been rearranged. For example, Rayner and his colleagues (2006) found that college students could read normal sentences at the rate of about 255 words per minute. They could still read jumbled sentences such as, "The boy cuold not slove the probelm so he aksed for help." However, their reading rate dropped to 227 words per minute.

One of the most widely demonstrated phenomena in the research on recognition is the word superiority effect. According to the **word superiority effect**, we can identify a single letter more accurately and more rapidly when it appears in a meaningful word than when it appears alone by itself or else in a meaningless string of unrelated letters (Dahan, 2010; Palmer, 2002; Vecera & Lee, 2010). For instance, you can recognize the letter *p* more easily if it appears in a word such as *plan* than if it appears in a nonword such as *pnla*.

Dozens of studies have confirmed the importance of top-down processing in letter recognition (e.g., Grainger & Jacobs, 2005; Palmer, 1999; Reicher, 1969; Williams et al., 2006). For example, the letter *s* is quickly recognized in the word *island*, even though the *s* is not pronounced in this word (Krueger, 1992).

Researchers have also shown that the context of a sentence facilitates the recognition of a word in a sentence. For example, people quickly recognize the word *juice* in the sentence, "Mary drank her orange juice" (Forster, 1981; Stanovich & West, 1981, 1983).

Let's discuss a classic study that explored this word-in-a-sentence effect. Rueckl and Oden (1986) demonstrated that both the features of the stimulus and the nature of the context influence word recognition. In other words, both bottom-up and top-down processing operate in a coordinated fashion. These researchers used stimuli that were either letters or letter-like characters. For example, one set of stimuli consisted of a perfectly formed letter *n*, a perfectly formed letter *r*, and three symbols that were intermediate between those two letters. Notice these stimuli arranged along the bottom of Figure 2.6. In each case, this particular stimulus was embedded in the letter sequence "bea-s." As a result, the study included five stimuli that ranged between "beans" and "bears." (In other words, this variable tested the effects of bottom-up processing.)

The nature of the context was also varied by using the sentence frame, "The _____ raised (bears/beans) to supplement his income." The researchers constructed four sentences by filling the blank with a carefully selected term: "lion tamer," "zookeeper," "botanist," and "dairy farmer." You'll notice that a lion tamer and a zookeeper are more likely to raise bears, whereas the botanist and the dairy farmer are

FIGURE 2.6

The Influence of Stimulus Features and Sentence Context on Word Identification.

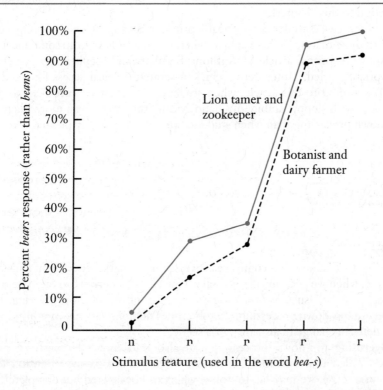

Source: Rueckl, J. G., & Oden, G. C. (1986). The integration of contextual and featural information during word identification. *Journal of Memory and Language, 25*, 445–460.

more likely to raise beans. Other similar ambiguous letters and sentence frames were also constructed, each using four different nouns or noun phrases. (In other words, this second variable tested the effects of top-down processing.)

Figure 2.6 shows the results of Rueckl and Oden's (1986) study. As you can see, people were definitely more likely to choose the "bears" response when the line segment on the right side of the letter was short, rather than long: The features of the stimulus are extremely important because word recognition operates partly in a bottom-up fashion.

However, you'll also notice that people were somewhat more likely to choose the "bears" response in the lion tamer and zookeeper sentences than in the botanist and dairy farmer sentences: The context is important because word recognition also operates partly in a top-down fashion. Specifically, our knowledge about the world leads us to expect that lion tamers and zookeepers would be more likely to raise bears than beans.

Think about how these context effects can influence your reading speed. The previous letters in a word help you identify the remaining letters more quickly. Furthermore, the other words in a sentence help you identify the individual words more quickly. Without context to help you read faster, you might still be reading the introduction to this chapter!

So far, we have considered only neatly printed text; top-down processing certainly operates in this situation. What happens when you read a note from someone with bad handwriting? A journal article by Anthony Barnhart and Stephen Goldinger (2010) is appropriately titled, "Interpreting chicken-scratch: Lexical access for handwritten words." According to this article, when students in this study were reading a hand-written note with sloppy, ambiguous handwriting, they were even more likely to rely on top-down processing than when students were reading neatly printed text.

IN DEPTH

Overactive Top-Down Processing and "Smart Mistakes" in Object Recognition

According to Theme 2, our cognitive processes are remarkably efficient and accurate. However, when we occasionally do make a mistake, that error can often be traced to a "smart mistake," such as overusing the strategy of top-down processing. Because we overuse top-down processing, we sometimes demonstrate **change blindness**; we fail to detect a change in an object or a scene.

Overusing top-down processing can also lead us to demonstrate a second mistake, called **inattentional blindness**; when we are paying attention to some events in a scene, we may fail to notice when an unexpected but completely visible object suddenly appears (Most et al., 2005). Let's now consider these two kinds of visual-processing errors.

Change Blindness. Imagine that you are walking along a sidewalk near your college campus. Then a stranger asks you for directions to a particular building. Right in the middle of this conversation, two people—who are carrying a wooden door sideways—walk between you and this stranger. When they have passed by, the original stranger has been replaced by one of the door-holding strangers. (The door was blocking your vision, so you could not directly see the strangers switching places.) Would you notice that you are no longer talking with the same individual? You may be tempted to reply, "Of course!"

When Daniel Simons and Daniel Levin (1997a, 1997b, 1998) tried this stranger-and-the-door study, only half of the bystanders reported that one stranger had been replaced by a different stranger. Many were still "clueless" when they were explicitly asked, "Did you notice that I'm not the same person who approached you to ask for directions?" (Simons & Levin, 1998, p. 646). Take a moment to try Demonstration 2.4. How quickly can you detect the difference between these two similar scenes?

⊚ Demonstration 2.4

Detecting the Difference Between Two Pictures

Turn to the front of this book, on the right-hand side, where you'll see two color photos of children in a park. Look carefully at these two scenes until you have detected which feature is different. The answer is at the end of the chapter, on p. 67.

This chapter examines how we see objects. When perceiving an entire scene, our top-down processing encourages us to assume that the basic meaning of the scene will remain stable. This assumption is rational, and the mistaken perception makes sense (Carlson, 2010; Rensink, 2010; Saylor & Baldwin, 2004). In the real world, one person does not suddenly morph into a different individual!

Laboratory research provides other examples of change blindness (Moore, 2010). For instance, Rensink and his colleagues (1997) asked participants to look at a photo, which was briefly presented twice. Then a slightly different version of the photo was briefly presented twice. This sequence of alternations was repeated until the participant detected the change.

This result showed that people quickly identified the change when this change was important. For example, when a view of a pilot flying a plane showed a helicopter either nearby or far away, participants required only 4.0 alternations to report the change. In contrast, they required 16.2 alternations to report a change that was unimportant, such as the height of a railing behind two people seated at a table.

Again, these results make sense (Saylor & Baldwin, 2004). The basic meaning of the scene with the pilot is drastically different if the helicopter is nearby, rather than distant. In contrast, the height of the railing doesn't change the actual meaning of the scene at the table.

Additional studies confirm that people are surprisingly blind to fairly obvious changes in the objects that they are perceiving (e.g., Saylor & Baldwin, 2004; Scholl et al., 2004; Simons et al., 2002). In general, when we look at a scene with numerous objects, we typically do not store a detailed representation of every item in that scene (Gillam et al., 2007).

Inattentional Blindness. As we noted on page 50, inattentional blindness occurs when you are paying attention to something, and you fail to notice an unexpected but completely visible object. In general, psychologists use the term *change blindness* when people fail to notice a change in some part of the stimulus. In contrast, they use the term *inattentional blindness* when people fail to notice that a new object has appeared (Moore, 2010). In both cases, however, people are using top-down processing as they concentrate on some objects in a scene. As a result, when an object appears that is not consistent with their concepts, expectations, and memory, people often fail to recognize this changed object (change blindness) or this new object (inattentional blindness).

Let's now consider a dramatic study about inattentional blindness. Simons and Chabris (1999) asked participants to watch a videotape of people playing basketball. These participants were instructed to mentally tally the number of times that members of a specified group made either a bounce pass or an aerial pass. Shortly after the video began, a person dressed in a gorilla suit wandered into the scene and remained there for 5 seconds. Amazingly, 46% of the participants failed to notice the gorilla! Other research confirms that people often fail to notice a new object, if they are paying close attention to something else (Chabris & Simons, 2010; Most et al., 2001; Most et al., 2005). Incidentally, Daniel Simons's Web site contains some interesting demonstrations of his research, including both the "door study," discussed on page 51, as well as the "gorilla study": http://www.simonslab.com./videos.html

As you might imagine, people are more likely to experience inattentional blindness when the primary task is cognitively demanding (Simons & Jensen, 2009). If the primary task in this study had been to monitor moves in a leisurely chess game—rather than moves in basketball—wouldn't people be less likely to experience inattentional blindness?

Reconciling "Smart Mistakes" in Object Recognition. We have just seen that people frequently make two similar perceptual errors, change blindness and inattentional blindness. Theme 2 of this textbook states that our cognitive processes are remarkably efficient and accurate. How can we reconcile the two kinds of errors with this theme? One important point is that many of the visual stimuli that people fail to see are not high in ecological validity (Rachlinski, 2004). Studies are high in **ecological validity** if the conditions in which the research is conducted are similar to the natural setting where the results will be applied. Frankly, I doubt if anyone reading this book has seen someone in a gorilla suit strolling through a basketball game!

Still, you can probably recall a time when you were looking for something and failed to locate it when it was in an unexpected location. Both change blindness and inattentional blindness can also operate in our daily lives.

Simons and Levin (1997a) emphasize that we actually function very well in our normal visual environment. If you are walking along a busy city street, a variety of perceptual representations will rapidly change from one glance to the next. People move their legs, shift a bag to another arm, and disappear behind traffic signs. If you precisely tracked each detail, your visual system would be rapidly overwhelmed by the trivial changes. Instead, your visual system is fairly accurate in creating the "gist," or general interpretation of a scene. You focus only on the information that appears to be important, such as the proximity of an approaching bus as you cross the street, and you ignore unimportant details. Change blindness and inattentional blindness illustrate a point we made in connection with Theme 2: Our cognitive errors can often be traced to a rational strategy.

We have been discussing research that illustrates how we make errors in object recognition if we are not paying close attention to the object. In Chapter 3 (Perceptual Processes II: Attention and Consciousness), we will examine attention in more detail.

So far, we have discussed the visual system, perceptual organization, and theories of object recognition. We have also emphasized the importance of top-down processing in perception. Now let's consider another topic in some detail. One of the most active areas of research on object recognition is the challenging topic of face perception.

🌀 Section Summary: *Top-Down Processing and Visual Object Recognition*

1. Bottom-up processing emphasizes the importance of the stimulus in object recognition; in contrast, top-down processing emphasizes how a person's concepts, expectations, and memory influence object recognition. Both processes work together to allow us to recognize objects.

2. When we read, context can facilitate recognition; for example, the word superiority effect shows that we can identify a single letter more accurately and more rapidly when it appears in a meaningful word than when it appears by itself or in a meaningless string of letters.

3. During reading, the context of a sentence influences how we identify a word in that sentence.

4. Overactive top-down processing can also encourage us to make two kinds of errors: (a) change blindness, or errors in recognizing that an object has changed—for instance, a different man is now carrying a door; and (b) inattentional blindness, or failing to notice that a new object has appeared—for instance, a gorilla suddenly appears in a basketball game.

FACE PERCEPTION

So far, our exploration of visual recognition has primarily focused on how we perceive letters of the alphabet or a variety of objects. Now let's consider the most socially significant kind of recognition (Sinha et al., 2010). How do you manage to recognize a friend, by simply looking at this person's face? The task ought to be challenging, because all faces have the same general shape.

A further complication is that you can recognize the face of your friend Monica—even when you see her face from a different angle, in an unusual setting, and wearing an unexpected frowning expression. Impressively, you manage to overcome all these sources of variation (Esgate & Groome, 2005; McKone, 2004; Styles, 2005). Almost instantly, you perceive that this person is indeed Monica.

We'll consider four areas of research in this section of the chapter. First, we'll examine some laboratory-based research showing that our perceptual system processes human faces differently from other visual stimuli. Next, we'll consider the neuroscience research on face perception. Then we'll explore some applied research on face perception. Our final topic focuses on individual differences, and it demonstrates that people with schizophrenia tend to have difficulty in recognizing faces, as well as facial expressions.

Recognizing Faces Versus Recognizing Other Objects

Researchers emphasize that most people perceive faces in a different fashion from other stimuli. In other words, face perception is somehow "special" (Farah, 2004; McKone, 2004). For example, young infants track the movement of a photographed human face more than any other similar stimuli (Bruce et al., 2003; Johnson & Bolhuis, 2000).

Similarly, Tanaka and Farah (1993) found that research participants were significantly more accurate in recognizing a facial feature when it appeared within the context of a whole face, rather than in isolation. For example, they recognized a nose in the context of a whole face much more accurately than an isolated nose. The same participants also judged parts of a house. In this "house condition," they were equally accurate in recognizing a house feature (such as a window) within the context of a complete house, versus recognizing that window in isolation.

We recognize houses and most other objects by identifying the individualized features that combine together to create these objects. In contrast, faces apparently have a special, privileged status in our perceptual system. We recognize faces on a **holistic** basis—that is, in terms of their overall shape and structure (Richler et al., 2011). In other words, we perceive a face in terms of its **gestalt**, or overall quality that transcends its individual elements. It makes sense that face perception has a special status, given the importance of faces in our social interactions (Fox, 2005; Macrae & Quadflieg, 2010; Styles, 2005).

Neuroscience Research on Face Recognition

Much of the research on face recognition comes from a disability known as prosopagnosia (pronounced "pros-o-pag-*no*-zhe-ah"). People with **prosopagnosia** cannot recognize human faces visually, though they perceive other objects relatively normally (Farah, 2004).

Consider the case of a woman with prosopagnosia who was in her early 30s, and she had recently completed her PhD. She described an experience when she went to pick up her infant son at his daycare center. "I went to the wrong baby at my son's daycare and only realized that he was not my son when the entire daycare staff looked at me in horrified disbelief" (Duchaine & Nakayama, 2006, p. 166).

Many neuroscience case studies show that individuals with prosopagnosia can easily recognize common objects. For example, a man with prosopagnosia may quickly identify a chair, a coffee cup, or a sweater. He may even look at a woman's smiling face and report that she looks happy. However, he may fail to recognize that this woman is his own wife! Furthermore, people with prosopagnosia often report that the various parts of a person's face—such as a nose, a mouth, and two eyes—seem independent of one another, instead of forming a unified, complete face (Farah, 2004; Gazzaniga et al., 2009).

Earlier, we mentioned that the occipital lobe, at the back of your brain, is the location in the part of the cortex that is responsible for the initial, most basic visual processing. Information then travels from the occipital lobe to numerous other locations throughout the brain. The location most responsible for face recognition is the temporal cortex, at the side of your brain (Farah, 2004; Kanwisher et al., 2001; Sinha et al., 2010). The specific location is known as the inferotemporal cortex, in the lower portion of the temporal cortex. (See Figure 2.1 on p. 38.)

Researchers have also tested monkeys, using neuroscience recording techniques. They report that certain cells in the inferotemporal cortex respond especially vigorously to a photo of another monkey's face (Rolls & Tovee, 1995; Wang et al., 1996).

Chapter 1 described the **fMRI** technique, a technique for obtaining images of human brain activity. The fMRI studies have shown that the brain responds more quickly to faces presented in the normal, upright position, in comparison to faces presented upside-down (D'Esposito et al., 1999). Similarly, behavioral research shows that people are much more accurate in identifying upright faces, compared to upside-down faces, a phenomenon called the **face-inversion effect** (Macrae & Quadflieg, 2010; Wilford & Wells, 2010; Wolfe et al., 2009). This research is far from complete, but it may explain why face perception seems to follow different rules, emphasizing holistic processing rather than isolated components.

Applied Research on Face Recognition

As we have noted earlier, many cognitive psychologists now emphasize the importance of ecological validity. The applied research on face recognition focuses on real-life situations that assess our ability to recognize people's faces.

Kemp and his coauthors (1997) studied the accuracy of supermarket cashiers who had been instructed to make judgments about ID photos. Specifically, undergraduate students were given credit cards that showed a 1" × 1" color photo of their faces. Each student was told to select some items at a supermarket and then present his or her credit card to the cashier. The cashier could then decide whether to accept or reject the credit card.

When students carried a credit card that showed their own photo, the cashiers correctly accepted the card 93% of the time. However, when students carried a card that showed a photo of another person—who looked fairly similar—they correctly rejected the photo only 36% of the time. In other words, they let someone with an incorrect photo ID slip past them 64% of the time!

Another applied study on face recognition focused on security surveillance systems. Many banks, businesses, and institutions use a video security system, typically filming people who walk through a door. Burton and his coauthors (1999) asked people to look at video clips of psychology professors walking through the entrance of the department of psychology at the University of Glasgow in Scotland.

First, all of the participants in the study saw a series of video clips of 10 professors. Next, they all saw a series of high-quality photos of 20 professors; 10 of these professors had appeared in a video, and 10 had not. The participants were instructed to rate each photo, using a scale from 1 (indicating certainty that they *had not* seen this person in the video) to 7 (indicating certainty that they *had* seen this person in the video).

Burton and his colleagues (1999) also tested three categories of participants. Twenty of the participants had been taught by all 10 professors in the video clips. Twenty were other students who had never been taught by any of these professors, and 10 were experienced police officers who were not familiar with any of the professors.

Figure 2.7 shows the ratings provided by the three categories of participants. As you can see, the students who were familiar with the professors had highly accurate recognition. These students were very confident in identifying the 10 professors who had actually appeared in the videos, and they were also very confident that the other 10 professors had not appeared in the videos.

However, when students were unfamiliar with the professors, they were only slightly more confident about the professors they had actually seen in the video, compared to the professors whom they had not seen. Unfortunately, the experienced police officers were no more accurate than the second group of students. Additional research confirms that people are much more accurate in identifying familiar faces than unfamiliar faces (Bruce et al., 2001; Henderson et al., 2001). In Chapter 5, we'll examine the related topic of eyewitness testimony in more detail.

These two applied-psychology studies have explored whether people can accurately match two images of a person's face. Other research examines whether people can make accurate judgments about a specific characteristic of a person's face. For example, Matthew Rhodes (2009) reviewed studies in which research participants had tried to guess an unfamiliar person's age. In general, people guessed quite accurately. Notice that this research has an important application when clerks are trying to decide whether a young person is old enough to purchase products such as alcohol or tobacco.

FIGURE 2.7

Participants' Confidence About Having Seen a Target Person in an Earlier Video, as a Function of Kind of Observer and Whether or not the Target Person Actually Appeared in the Video.

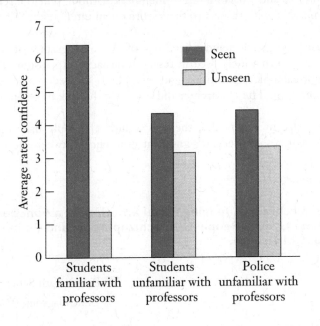

Source: Burton, A. M., Wilson, S., Cowan, M., & Bruce, V. (1999). Face recognition in poor-quality video: Evidence from security surveillance. *Psychological Science*, *10*, 243–248.

Individual Differences: Face Identification in People with Schizophrenia

As we noted in Chapter 1, **individual differences** is a term that refers to the systematic variation in the way that groups of people perform on the same cognitive task. As Chapter 1 also emphasized, many psychologists are now exploring the connections among the varied disciplines of psychology (Cacioppo, 2007). A good example of this interdisciplinary research focuses on the relationship between schizophrenia and face identification.

Schizophrenia is one of the most serious psychological disorders. People with **schizophrenia** typically do not show intense emotions, and they may have hallucinations. For students studying cognitive psychology, an especially important facet is disordered *thinking*. Furthermore, individuals with schizophrenia tend to perform poorly on many cognitive tasks (Reichenberg & Harvey, 2007)

Researchers have also reported that people with schizophrenia seem to have difficulty in perceiving faces and facial expressions (Bediou et al., 2005; Hall et al.,

2004; Martin et al., 2005). However, Edith Pomarol-Clotet and her colleagues (2010) hypothesized that this poor performance in judging faces might be due to more general problems on cognitive tasks, rather than a specific difficulty with faces. These researchers therefore carefully matched their two samples, a group of 22 individuals with schizophrenia and 20 community members without schizophrenia. The two groups were matched with respect to their score on an intelligence test, as well as age and gender.

Each person judged a standardized set of 60 photographs of people's faces; these photos have been widely used in research on facial expression. There were 10 photographs for each of six emotions, and each photo showed a moderate amount of the specified emotion. The researchers did not want the task to be either too easy or too difficult.

As you can see in Figure 2.8, the two groups of people had similar accuracy rates. Further analyses showed no significant difference between the two groups on

FIGURE 2.8

Participants' Accuracy in Judging Facial Emotion, as a Function of Type of Emotion and Group (People with Schizophrenia and People in the Matched Control Group).

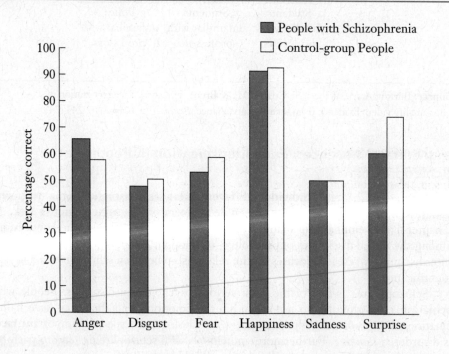

Source: Pomarol-Clotet, E., et al. (2010). Facial emotion processing in schizophrenia: A non-specific neuropsychological deficit? *Psychological Medicine, 40,* 911–919.

any of the six emotions. However, the individuals in the control group responded significantly *faster* than the individuals with schizophrenia, consistent with previous research (Pomarol-Clotet et al., 2010). It's not clear why the two groups had similar scores, but matching for intelligence may be an important factor.

Section Summary: *Face Perception*

1. People can quickly recognize the faces of people they know; we seem to process a face in terms of its gestalt, or its overall shape and structure.

2. A variety of neuroscience methods—including research with people who have prosopagnosia, research with monkeys, and the fMRI technique—have shown that cells in the inferotemporal cortex play a role in perceiving faces.

3. Applied research suggests that people are not very accurate in judging whether a photo matches the face of the cardholder. Furthermore, people are not very accurate in judging whether a photo of an unfamiliar person matches a person in a video that they saw earlier.

4. Individuals with schizophrenia can identify facial emotion as accurately as people in a control group, when the two groups are matched for age, gender, and intelligence, although individuals with schizophrenia typically take longer to make these decisions.

SPEECH PERCEPTION

Speech perception seems perfectly easy and straightforward . . . until you begin to think about everything you must accomplish in order to perceive a spoken sentence. During **speech perception**, your auditory system must record the sound vibrations generated by someone talking; then the system must translate these vibrations into a sequence of sounds that you perceive to be speech. Adults who speak English produce about 15 sounds every second (Kuhl, 1994). Therefore, you must somehow perceive about 900 sounds each minute.

In order to perceive a word, you must distinguish the sound pattern of one word from the tens of thousands of irrelevant words that are stored in your memory. And—as if these tasks are not challenging enough—you must separate the voice of the speaker from the irrelevant background noises. This background typically includes other, simultaneous conversations as well as a wide variety of nonspeech sounds (Brown & Sinnott, 2006; Mattys & Liss, 2008; Plack, 2005). In fact, it's astonishing that we ever manage to perceive spoken language!

Speech perception is extremely complex, and you can locate more details in other textbooks (Foley & Matlin, 2010; Goldstein, 2010b; Wolfe et al., 2009). We'll consider two aspects of speech perception in this section: (1) characteristics of speech perception and (2) theories of speech perception.

Characteristics of Speech Perception

The next time you listen to a radio announcer, pay attention to the sounds you are hearing, rather than the meaning of the words. When describing these speech sounds, psychologists and linguists use the term *phoneme* (pronounced "*foe*-neem"). A **phoneme** is the basic unit of spoken language, such as the sounds *a*, *k*, and *th*. The English language uses between 40 and 45 phonemes, a number that includes both vowels and consonants (Dahan, 2010). When you listen to spoken English, you may think that you hear brief quiet periods throughout this string of sounds. However, most of the words are simply run together in a continuous series.

Let's consider several important characteristics of speech perception:

1. Listeners can impose boundaries between words, even when these words are not separated by silence.
2. Phoneme pronunciation varies tremendously.
3. Context allows listeners to fill in some missing sounds.
4. Visual cues from the speaker's mouth help us interpret ambiguous sounds.

All these characteristics provide further evidence for the Theme 2 of this book. Despite a speech stimulus that is less than perfect, we perceive speech with remarkable accuracy and efficiency.

Word Boundaries. Have you ever heard a conversation in an unfamiliar language? The words may seem to run together in a continuous stream, with no boundaries of silence to separate them. You may think that the boundaries between words seem much more distinct in English—almost as clear-cut as the white spaces that identify the boundaries between any two adjacent words in this textbook. In most cases, however, the actual acoustical stimulus of spoken language shows no clear-cut pauses to mark the boundaries. An actual physical event—such as a pause—marks a word boundary less than 40% of the time (Davis et al., 2002; McQueen, 2005; Sell & Kaschak, 2009).

Impressively, we are rarely conscious that it is difficult to resolve word boundaries. The research shows that our speech recognition system initially considers several different hypotheses about how to divide a phrase into words. This system immediately and effortlessly uses our knowledge about language in order to place the boundaries in appropriate locations (Grossberg et al., 2004; McQueen, 2005; Pitt, 2009; Samuel, 2011). Fortunately, this knowledge usually leads us to the correct conclusions.

Variability in Phoneme Pronunciation. Perceiving phonemes does not initially seem like a challenging task. After all, don't we simply hear a phoneme and instantly perceive it? Actually, phoneme perception is not that easy. For example, speakers vary tremendously in the pitch and tone of their voices, as well as their rate of producing phonemes (McQueen, 2005; Plack, 2005; Uchanski, 2005).

A second source of variability is that speakers often fail to produce phonemes in a precise fashion (Foley & Matlin, 2010; Pitt, 2009; Plack, 2005). Try Demonstration 2.5 to appreciate the problem of sloppy pronunciation that listeners must decode.

⊚ **Demonstration 2.5**

Variability in Phoneme Pronunciation

Turn on the radio and locate a station on which you hear someone talking. After hearing one or two sentences, turn the radio off, and write down the two sentences. Try to determine whether the speaker produced each phoneme in a precise fashion. For instance, did the speaker omit some portion of a word (e.g., *sposed* instead of *supposed*)? Did he or she pronounce consonants such as *k* or *p* precisely? Now try pronouncing the words in each sentence very carefully, so that every phoneme can be clearly identified.

A third source of variability is called **coarticulation**: When you are pronouncing a particular phoneme, your mouth remains in somewhat the same shape it was when you pronounced the previous phoneme; in addition, your mouth is preparing to pronounce the next phoneme. As a result, the phoneme you produce varies slightly from time to time, depending upon the surrounding phonemes (Conway et al., 2010; Diehl et al., 2004; McQueen, 2005). For example, notice that the *d* in *idle* sounds different from the *d* in *don't*.

Despite this remarkable variability in phoneme pronunciation, we still manage to understand the speaker's intended phoneme. Factors such as context and visual cues help us achieve this goal.

Context and Speech Perception. People are active listeners, consistent with Theme 1. Instead of passively receiving speech sounds, we can use context as a cue to help us figure out a sound or a word (Cleary & Pisoni, 2001; Warren, 2006). We saw earlier in this chapter that context and other top-down factors influence visual perception. Top-down factors also influence speech perception (Theme 5), because we use our vast knowledge about language to help us perceive ambiguous words.

For example, when you are listening to your professors' lectures, extraneous noises will sometimes mask a phoneme. People knock books off desks, cough, turn pages, and whisper. Still, without much effort, you can usually reconstruct the missing sound. People tend to show **phonemic restoration**: They can fill in a missing phoneme, using contextual meaning as a cue (Conway et al., 2010).

In a classic study, Warren and Warren (1970) showed that people are skilled at using the meaning of a sentence to select the correct word from several options. They played tape recordings of several sentences for their research participants:

1. It was found that the *eel was on the axle.

2. It was found that the *eel was on the shoe.

3. It was found that the *eel was on the orange.

The researchers inserted a coughing sound in the location indicated by the asterisk. These spoken sentences were identical with one exception: A different word was spliced onto the end of each sentence. The results showed that people typically heard the "word" *eel as *wheel* in the first sentence, *heel* in the second sentence, and *peel* in the third. In this study, then, people were able to reconstruct the missing word on the basis of a context cue at the end of the sentence, which occurred four words later!

Notice that phonemic restoration is a kind of illusion. People think they hear a phoneme, even though the correct sound vibrations never reach their ears. Phonemic restoration is a well-documented phenomenon, and it has been demonstrated in numerous studies (Liederman et al., 2011; Samuel, 2011; Warren, 2006). Our ability to perceive a word on the basis of context also allows us to overcome a speaker's sloppy pronunciations, the problem we mentioned earlier.

One important explanation for the influence of context on perception is top-down processing, although researchers have offered additional explanations (Foley & Matlin, 2010; Grossberg et al., 2004; Plack, 2005). The top-down processing approach argues that we use our knowledge about language to facilitate recognition, whether we are looking at objects or listening to speech.

Perceiving language is not merely a passive process in which words flow into our ears, providing data for bottom-up processing. Instead, we actively use our knowledge about language to create expectations about what we might hear. Consistent with Theme 5 of this textbook, top-down processing influences our cognitive activities.

Visual Cues as an Aid to Speech Perception. Try Demonstration 2.6 when you have the opportunity. This simple exercise illustrates how visual cues contribute to speech perception (Gazzaniga et al., 2009; Smyth et al., 1994). Information from the speaker's lips and face helps to resolve ambiguities from the speech signal. Similarly, you can hear conversation more accurately when you closely watch a speaker's lips, instead of listening to a conversation over the phone (Massaro & Stork, 1998). Even

---

Ⓖ Demonstration 2.6

Visual Cues and Speech Perception

The next time you are in a room with both a television and a radio, try this exercise. Switch the TV set to the news or some other program where someone is talking straight to the camera; keep the volume low. Now turn on your radio and tune it between two stations, so that it produces a hissing noise. Turn the radio's volume up until you have difficulty understanding what the person on television is saying. The radio's "white noise" should nearly mask the speaker's voice. Face the TV screen and close your eyes; try to understand the spoken words. Then open your eyes. Do you find that speech perception is now much easier?

Source: Based on Smyth et al., 1987.

with a superb phone connection, you miss the lip cues that would inform you whether the speaker was discussing *Harry* or *Mary*.

Researchers have demonstrated that we do integrate visual cues with auditory cues during speech perception—even if we don't recognize the usefulness of these visual cues (Nicholls et al., 2004). These results have been replicated for speakers of English, Spanish, Japanese, and Dutch (Massaro, 1998; Massaro et al., 1995).

Research by McGurk and MacDonald (1976) provides a classic illustration of the contribution of visual cues to speech perception. These researchers showed participants a video of a woman whose lips were producing simple syllables, such as "gag." Meanwhile, the researchers presented different auditory information (coming from the same machine), such as "bab."

When the observers were asked to report what they perceived, their responses usually reflected a compromise between these two discrepant sources of information. In this case, the listeners typically reported hearing the word "dad." The **McGurk effect** refers to the influence of visual information on speech perception, when individuals must integrate both visual and auditory information (Beauchamp et al., 2010; Rosenblum, 2005; Samuel, 2011).

Michael Beauchamp and his colleagues (2010) have identified the location within the cerebral cortex that gives rise to the McGurk effect. This region is called the superior temporal sulcus. (In Figure 2.1 on page 38 of this textbook, this region is located in the right side of the horizontal groove along the center of the temporal lobe of the cortex.) This discovery makes sense, because previous research shows that this region is responsible for other tasks where sight and sound must be integrated (Hein & Knight, 2008).

In summary, then, we manage to perceive speech by overcoming the problems of a less-than-ideal speech stimulus. We do so by ignoring the variability in phoneme pronunciation and by using context to resolve ambiguous phonemes. If we can watch the speaker who is producing the stream of speech, the visual information from the speaker's lips provides additional helpful clues.

Theories of Speech Perception

Most current theoretical approaches to speech perception fall into two categories. Some theorists believe that we humans must have a special mechanism in our nervous system that explains our impressive skill in speech perception. Others admire humans' skill in speech perception, but they argue that the same general mechanism that handles other cognitive processes also handles speech perception.

Earlier in this chapter, we examined two theories of visual pattern perception. Unfortunately, researchers have not developed such detailed theories for speech perception. One reason for this problem is that humans are the only species who can understand spoken language. As a result, cognitive neuroscientists have a limited choice of research techniques.

The Special Mechanism Approach. According to the **special mechanism approach** (also called the **speech-is-special approach**), humans are born with a specialized device that allows us to decode speech stimuli (Samuel, 2011). As a result, we process speech sounds more quickly and accurately than other auditory stimuli, such as instrumental music.

Supporters of the special mechanism approach argue that humans possess a **phonetic module** (or **speech module**), a special-purpose neural mechanism that specifically processes all aspects of speech perception; it cannot handle other kinds of auditory perception. This phonetic module would presumably enable listeners to perceive ambiguous phonemes accurately. It would also help you to segment the blurred stream of auditory information that reaches your ears, so that you can perceive distinct phonemes and words (Liberman, 1996; Liberman & Mattingly, 1989; Todd et al., 2006).

The special mechanism approach to speech perception suggests that the brain is organized in an unusual way. Specifically, the module that handles speech perception would *not* rely on the general cognitive functions discussed throughout this book—functions such as recognizing objects, remembering events, and solving problems (Trout, 2001). Notice that this modular approach is not consistent with Theme 4 of this textbook, which argues that the cognitive processes are interrelated and dependent upon one another.

One argument in favor of the phonetic module was thought to be categorical perception. Early researchers asked people to listen to a series of ambiguous sounds, such as a sound halfway between a *b* and a *p*. People who heard these sounds typically showed **categorical perception**; they heard either a clear-cut *b* or a clear-cut *p*, rather than a sound partway between a *b* and a *p* (Liberman & Mattingly, 1989).

When the special mechanism approach was originally proposed, supporters argued that people show categorical perception for speech sounds, but they hear nonspeech sounds as a smooth continuum. However, research shows that humans also exhibit categorical perception for some complex nonspeech sounds (Esgate & Groome, 2005).

The General Mechanism Approaches. Although some still favor the special mechanism approach (Trout, 2001), most theorists now favor one of the general mechanism approaches (e.g., Cleary & Pisoni, 2001; Conway et al., 2010; Wolfe et al., 2009). The **general mechanism approaches** argue that we can explain speech perception without proposing any special phonetic module. People who favor these approaches believe that humans use the same neural mechanisms to process both speech sounds and nonspeech sounds (Foley & Matlin, 2010). Speech perception is therefore a learned ability—indeed, a very impressive learned ability—but it is not really "special."

Current research seems to favor the general mechanism approach. As we just noted, humans exhibit categorical perception for complex nonspeech sounds. Other research supporting the general mechanism viewpoint uses event-related potentials (ERPs), which we discussed on Page 16. This research demonstrates that adults show the same sequence of shifts in the brain's electrical potential, whether they are listening to speech or to music (Patel et al., 1998).

Other evidence against the phonetic module is that people's judgments about phonemes are definitely influenced by visual cues, as we saw in the discussion of the McGurk effect (Beauchamp et al., 2010; Rosenblum, 2005; Samuel, 2011). If speech perception can be influenced by visual information, then we cannot argue that a special phonetic module handles all aspects of speech perception.

Researchers have developed several different general mechanism theories of speech perception (e.g., Fowler & Galantucci, 2005; McQueen, 2005; Todd et al., 2006). These theories tend to argue that speech perception proceeds in stages and that it depends upon familiar cognitive processes such as feature recognition, learning, and decision making.

In summary, our ability to perceive speech sounds is impressive. However, this ability can probably be explained by our general perceptual abilities—combined with our other cognitive abilities—rather than any special, inborn speech mechanism. We manage to distinguish speech sounds in the same way we manage a wide variety of complex cognitive skills.

Section Summary: *Speech Perception*

1. Speech perception is an extremely complicated process; it demonstrates that humans can quickly perform impressively complex cognitive tasks.

2. Even when the acoustical stimulus contains no clear-cut pauses, people are very accurate in determining the boundaries between adjacent words.

3. The pronunciation of a specific phoneme varies greatly, depending upon the vocal characteristics of the speaker, imprecise pronunciation, and the variability caused by coarticulation.

4. When a sound is missing from speech, listeners frequently demonstrate phonemic restoration, using context to help them perceive the missing sound.

5. People use visual cues to facilitate speech perception, as illustrated by the McGurk effect; the superior temporal sulcus is a part of the cortex that integrates sight and sound, and this integration also helps to account for the McGurk effect.

6. According to the special mechanism approach to speech perception, humans have a special brain device (or module) that allows us to perceive phonemes more quickly and accurately than nonspeech sounds.

7. The current evidence supports a general mechanism approach to speech perception, rather than a special mechanism; research suggests that humans perceive speech sounds in the same way we perceive nonspeech sounds.

CHAPTER REVIEW QUESTIONS

1. Think of a person whom you know well, who has never had a course in cognitive psychology. How would you describe perception to this person? As part of your description, provide examples of two visual tasks and two auditory tasks that this person performs frequently. Provide relevant details, using terms from the keylist for this chapter (page 67).

2. Imagine that you are trying to read a sloppily written number that appears in a friend's class notes. You conclude that it is an 8, rather than a 6 or a 3. Why would the feature-analysis approach explain this better than an approach that requires matching the number with a specific template?

3. Look up from your book and notice two nearby objects. Describe the characteristics of each "figure," in contrast to the "ground." How would Biederman's recognition-by-components theory describe how you recognize these objects?

4. Distinguish between bottom-up and top-down processing, with respect to vision. Explain how top-down processing can help you recognize the letters of the alphabet in the word "alphabet." How would the word superiority effect operate if you tried to identify one letter in the word "alphabet," if this printed word were presented very quickly on your computer? If you were trying to read a friend's barely legible handwriting, would your top-down processing increase or decrease, relative to reading a printed word on your computer screen?

5. This chapter emphasizes visual and auditory object recognition, but it can also apply to the other senses. How would top-down processing (e.g., prior knowledge) operate when you smell a certain fragrance and try to identify it? Then answer this question for both taste and touch.

6. According to the material in this chapter, face recognition seems to be "special," and it probably differs from other visual recognition tasks. Discuss this statement, mentioning research about the comparison between faces and other visual stimuli. Be sure to describe material from neuroscience research on this topic.

7. The individual-differences section of this chapter compared people with schizophrenia and without schizophrenia, with respect to identifying facial expressions. What did this study find? Why might the results of this study differ from the results of previous research about schizophrenia?

8. Our visual world and our auditory world are both richly complicated. Describe several ways in which the complexity of the proximal stimuli is challenging, when we try to determine the "true" distal stimuli. How does the gestalt approach help to explain visual perception? What factors help us overcome the difficulties in recognizing everyday speech?

9. What kinds of evidence supports the general mechanism approach to speech perception? Contrast this approach with the special mechanism approach. How could the special mechanism approach be applied to our skill in perceiving faces?

10. Throughout this book, we will emphasize that the research from cognitive psychology can be applied to numerous everyday situations. For example, you learned some practical applications of the research on face perception. Skim through this chapter and describe at least five other practical applications of the research on visual and auditory recognition.

KEYWORDS

perception
object recognition
pattern recognition
distal stimulus
proximal stimulus
retina
sensory memory
iconic memory
visual sensory memory
primary visual cortex
gestalt psychology
figure
ground
ambiguous figure-ground
   relationship
illusory contours

subjective contours
templates
feature-analysis theories
distinctive feature
recognition-by-components
   theory
geons
viewer-centered approach
bottom-up processing
top-down processing
word superiority effect
change blindness
inattentional blindness
ecological validity
holistic (recognition)
gestalt

prosopagnosia
fMRI
face-inversion effect
individual differences
schizophrenia
speech perception
phoneme
coarticulation
phonemic restoration
McGurk effect
special mechanism approach
speech-is-special approach
phonetic module
speech module
categorical perception
general mechanism approaches

RECOMMENDED READINGS

Chabris, C. F., & Simons, D. J. (2010). *The invisible gorilla and other ways our intuitions deceive us*. New York: Crown. This book, written for general audience, provides details on the counterintuitive findings discussed in the in-depth section (pp. 50–53) of this chapter.

Gazzaniga, M. S., Ivry, R. B., & Mangun, G. R. (2009). *Cognitive neuroscience: The biology of the mind* (3rd ed.). New York: Norton. Here's an excellent book that provides many details on the neuroscience related to cognition. The book also includes topics beyond the scope of your textbook, such as emotion and developmental neuroanatomy.

Goldstein, E. B. (Ed.). (2010). *Encyclopedia of perception*. Thousand Oaks, CA: Sage. This two-volume resource examines a wide variety of topics, providing several pages on each entry. The topics include many described in this chapter, but also intriguing topics you might not have considered, such as auditory agnosia, body perception, and phantom-limb sensations.

Henderson, J. M. (Ed.). (2005). *Real-world scene perception*. Hove, UK: Psychology Press. Most of the chapters in your textbook focus on how we perceive isolated objects. This interesting book addresses more complicated questions about how we perceive scenes in the everyday world.

ANSWER TO DEMONSTRATION 2.4

To locate the feature that is different in these two color photos (inside the front cover), look at the little girl with the black top and the orange shorts. In one version, you can see part of a white sock on her left ankle. In the other version, this part of the sock is black.

CHAPTER 3

Perceptual Processes II: Attention and Consciousness

PREVIEW

If you've ever tried to study while someone is shouting into a phone, you know that attention can be limited. Research confirms that performance usually suffers on this kind of *divided-attention task*, where you must perform two or more tasks simultaneously. The chapter also discusses four kinds of selective-attention tasks. (1) If you are paying close attention to one conversation, you usually notice little about another simultaneous conversation in this kind of *dichotic listening task*. (2) On a *Stroop task*, the ink of one color, such as blue, is used for printing the actual name of a different color, such as red; you'll have trouble paying attention to the color of the ink. (3) Some *visual search tasks* are easier than others; for instance, you can easily find a blue X when all other stimuli are red Xs. (4) When you read, you make *saccadic eye movements*, to move your eyes to a new location in the text.

This chapter also discusses some current explanations for attention. According to neuroscience research, the orienting attention network in the brain is responsible for visual search. In contrast, the executive attention network handles conflicting visual or auditory stimuli; it is also crucial for acquiring academic skills. An early theoretical explanation of attention proposed that the brain limits our attention by means of a bottleneck. A current theoretical explanation proposes that we can register some visual features automatically via distributed attention, but more challenging tasks require focused attention and serial processing.

Consciousness is our final major topic in this chapter. One issue related to consciousness is that people sometimes experience "mind wandering." In addition, they are often unaware of the way their cognitive processes operate. They may also have difficulty eliminating some thoughts from consciousness. Finally, in a rare condition called "blindsight," people with a damaged visual cortex can locate an object, even though they claim that they cannot see it.

CHAPTER INTRODUCTION

Take a few minutes to pay attention to your attention. First, look around you and try to take in as many visual objects as possible. If you are reading this book in a room, for instance, try to notice all the objects that surround you. Be sure to notice their shape, size, location, and color. If your room is typical, you'll soon feel that your visual attention is overworked—far beyond its limits—even after a single minute.

Now continue this same exercise, but also try to notice every sound in your environment, such as the hum of a computer, the noise of a clock ticking, and a distant automobile. Next, try to maintain all these visual and auditory stimuli, but also notice your skin senses. Can you feel the pressure that your watch creates on your wrist, and can you sense a slight itch or a subtle pain? If you somehow manage to pay simultaneous attention to your vision, hearing, and skin senses, try expanding your attention to include smell and taste. You'll easily discover that you cannot attend to everything at once (Chun et al., 2011; Cowan, 2005). In other words, "We don't have the brains for it" (Wolfe et al., 2009, p. 189). Interestingly, though, we seldom give much thought to our attention. Instead, attention just "happens," and it seems as natural to us as breathing (LaBerge, 1995).

Attention can be defined as a concentration of mental activity that allows you to take in a limited portion of the vast stream of information available from both your sensory world and your memory (Shomstein, 2010; Styles, 2006; Weierich & Barrett, 2010). Meanwhile the unattended items lose out, and they are not processed in detail. Notice, then, that attention is a vitally important "gatekeeper." If you do not pay attention to a particular item, then this item basically does not exist in your cognitive system!

In Chapter 1, you read about William James (1890), an early pioneer of cognitive psychology. James speculated about the number of ideas that a person could attend to at one time. In contrast, the behaviorists did not study attention. However, cognitive psychologists revived an interest in this topic. In fact, they have always considered attention to be important, from the beginning of the cognitive revolution and increasing during recent years (Chun et al., 2011; Gazzaniga et al., 2009; Wright & Ward, 2008).

Consistent with Theme 4, many of the concepts in this chapter are related to concepts in the previous chapter on perceptual recognition. As you will see, attention tasks use both bottom-up and top-down processing. Specifically, we sometimes concentrate our mental activity because an interesting stimulus in the environment has captured our attention (*bottom-up processing*). For example, an object in your peripheral vision might suddenly move, and you turn your head to see it more clearly. Other times, we concentrate our mental activity because we want to pay attention to some specific stimulus (*top-down processing*). For example, you might be searching for a particular friend in a crowded cafeteria.

Chapter 2 also discussed several visual phenomena that illustrate how shape perception and attention work cooperatively. For instance, consider ambiguous figure-ground relationships (see Figure 2.2 on p. 39). When you pay attention to the central white form, you see a vase; when you shift your attention to the two outer blue forms, you see two faces. Other relevant concepts from Chapter 2 include change blindness (when you fail to notice a change in an object) and inattentional blindness (when you fail to notice that a new object has entered a scene).

Attention also has implications for future topics in this book. For example, attention helps to regulate how many items you can process in working memory (Chapter 4). Attention is also intertwined with your long-term memory (Chapter 5), concepts (Chapter 8), and reading (Chapter 9). Furthermore, as Chapter 11 describes, when you try to solve a problem, you need to pay attention to relevant information, while ignoring trivial details. Also, Chapter 12 explains how you can make incorrect decisions when you pay too much attention to relatively unimportant information.

We will begin our discussion by considering five cognitive tasks: divided attention and four kinds of selective attention. Our second section examines both biological and theoretical explanations for attention. The final topic, consciousness, focuses on our awareness about the external world and our cognitive processes.

SEVERAL KINDS OF ATTENTION PROCESSES

Before you finish reading this chapter, you will perform several kinds of attention tasks. Let's first consider some examples and then define each kind of attention more precisely.

1. You may try to use *divided attention*, for example, concentrating on both your professor's lecture and a nearby whispered conversation between two students. You'll discover, though, that you cannot accurately attend to both categories of stimuli simultaneously. In reality, you are likely to use some form of *selective attention*, by trying to focus your attention. The remaining four items in this list require this selective attention.

2. You may try to avoid this divided-attention situation by focusing your attention on just one category of stimuli. Let's be optimistic and presume that you selectively attend to your professor, screening out almost all of the unattended conversation in this *dichotic listening task*.

3. You will try a demonstration about a kind of selective-attention task called the *Stroop task* (see p. 75). Most people don't encounter the Stroop task in their daily lives; however, you'll see how this task can be applied in clinical psychology.

4. You will definitely perform several *visual searches* by ignoring irrelevant items as you look for your yellow marker, your sweater, or the book that was on your desk a minute ago.

5. Finally, as you read this textbook, you will perform a fourth kind of selective-attention task called *saccadic eye movements*; your eyes will move systematically to the right to take in an appropriate amount of new information.

Divided Attention

In a **divided-attention task**, you try to pay attention to two or more simultaneous messages, responding appropriately to each message. In many cases, both your speed and your accuracy suffer. These problems are especially likely if the tasks are challenging, for instance, if two people are talking quickly to you at the same time (Chabris & Simons, 2010; Folk, 2010; Proctor & Vu, 2010).

When people **multitask**, they try to accomplish two or more tasks at the same time (Salvucci & Taatgen, 2008). When people are multitasking, they strain the limits of attention, as well as the limits of their working memory and their long-term memory (Logie et al., 2011).

Most of the research focuses on people who use their cell phones while they are also engaged in another cognitive task. For example, college students walk more slowly when they are talking on cell phones (Hyman, 2010). Furthermore, the research shows that college students read their textbooks significantly more slowly when they are responding to instant messages.

According to the research, students also earn lower grades when they are tested on the material they had been reading while multitasking (Bowman et al., 2010). They may *believe* that they can multitask, but the research does not support this illusion (Willingham, 2010). A general guideline is that you'll typically perform faster and more accurately if you work on one task at a time (Chabris & Simons, 2010).

This research on divided attention also has specific implications for people who use cell phones while driving. Many U.S. states and Canadian provinces have passed laws prohibiting the use of handheld cell phones and text messaging during driving. The studies show that people make significantly more driving errors when they are having a conversation on a handheld cell phone, compared to driving without conversation (Folk, 2010; Kubose et al., 2006; Strayer & Drews, 2007).

In a representative study, Collet and his coauthors (2009) tested people while they were talking on a handheld cell phone while driving on a simulated-driving task. Their reaction times were about 20% slower than without the cell phone conversation.

Unfortunately, even a hands-free cell phone causes problems with divided attention (Chabris & Simons, 2010; Folk, 2010). For instance, in heavy-traffic conditions, Strayer and his colleagues (2003) found that the people in the hands-free cell phone group took significantly longer to apply the brakes, compared to those in a control group.

In further testing, Strayer and his colleagues discovered that the participants who used cell phones showed a form of inattentional blindness (see pp. 52–53 of Chapter 2). For example, their attention was reduced for information that appeared in the center of their visual field. Even if you use a hands-free cell phone, your attention may wander away from a dangerous situation right in front of you!

Furthermore, if you are the driver, do not allow any passenger to carry on a cell phone conversation. This is even more distracting than a conversation between you and your passenger. Apparently, if you hear half of a conversation, it's less predictable. Therefore, drivers are distracted by trying to guess the content of the other half of the conversation, and it's more difficult to follow (Emberson et al., 2010).

Task switching is closely related to multitasking. If you are deeply engrossed in writing a research paper and your roommate keeps interrupting, you are likely to work more slowly and make more errors during the transitions (Kiesel et al., 2010; Vandierendonck et al., 2010).

As you've just read, a divided-attention task requires people to try to pay *equal* attention to two or more kinds of information. In contrast, a **selective-attention task** requires people to pay attention to certain kinds of information, while ignoring other ongoing information (Gazzaniga et al., 2009; Wolfe et al., 2009).

You might sometimes wish that you could follow two conversations simultaneously. However, imagine the chaos you would experience if you simultaneously paid attention to all the information registered by your senses. You would notice hundreds of simultaneous sights, sounds, tastes, smells, and touch sensations. You could not focus your mental activity enough to respond appropriately to just a few of these sensations. Fortunately, then, selective attention actually simplifies our lives. As Theme 2 suggests, our cognitive apparatus is impressively well designed. Features such as selective attention—which may initially seem to be drawbacks—may actually be beneficial (Gazzaniga et al., 2009; Shomstein, 2010).

We will now consider four different kinds of selective-attention tasks. These include: 1. Dichotic listening; 2. The Stroop Effect; 3. Visual search; and 4. Saccadic eye movements. Selective-attention studies often show that people notice little about the irrelevant task—the one that they are supposed to ignore (McAdams & Drake, 2002).

Dichotic Listening

Now let's consider the specific topic of dichotic listening, the first of the four kinds of selective attention tasks. You've probably held a phone to one ear to hear an important message, while your other ear registers the words from a loud nearby conversation. This situation is known as *dichotic listening* (pronounced "die-*kot*-ick").

In the laboratory, **dichotic listening** is studied by asking people to wear earphones; one message is presented to the left ear, and a different message is presented to the right ear. Typically, the research participants are asked to **shadow** the message in one ear; that is, they listen to that message and repeat it after the speaker. If the listener makes mistakes in shadowing, then the researcher knows that the listener is not paying appropriate attention to that specified message (Styles, 2005).

In the classic research, people noticed very little about the unattended second message (Cherry, 1953; Gazzaniga et al., 2009; McAdams & Drake, 2002). For example, people didn't even notice that the second message was sometimes switched from English words to German words. People did notice, however, when the voice of the unattended message was switched from male to female.

In general, people can process only one message at a time (Cowan, 2005). However, people are more likely to process the unattended message when (1) both messages are presented slowly, (2) the main task is not challenging, and (3) the meaning of the unattended message is immediately relevant (e.g., Duncan, 1999; Harris & Pashler, 2004; Marsh et al., 2007).

In addition, when people perform a dichotic listening task, they sometimes notice when their name is inserted in the unattended message (Clump, 2006; Gazzaniga et al., 2009; Wood & Cowan, 1995). Have you ever attended a social gathering, when you are surrounded by many simultaneous conversations? Even if you are paying close attention to one conversation, you may notice if your name is mentioned in a nearby conversation; this phenomenon is sometimes called the **cocktail party effect**.

In one study, for example, Wood and Cowan (1995) found that about one-third of the participants reported hearing their name in the message that they were supposed to ignore. But why did the participants *ignore* their own name about two-thirds of the time? One possible explanation is that the Wood and Cowan study was conducted in a laboratory, so this research may not have high ecological validity (Baker, 1999). In an unstructured social setting, your attention may easily wander to other intriguing conversations.

Furthermore, the capacity of a person's working memory could help to explain why some people hear their name, but others do not. As we'll see in Chapter 4, **working memory** is the brief, immediate memory for material that we are currently processing. Conway and his coauthors (2001) found that students who had a high working-memory capacity noticed their name only 20% of the time. In contrast, students with a low working-memory capacity noticed their name 65% of the time on the same dichotic-listening task. Apparently, people with a relatively low capacity have difficulty blocking out the irrelevant information such as their name (Cowan, 2005). In other words, they are easily distracted from the task they are supposed to be completing.

In summary, when people's attention is divided, they can sometimes notice characteristics of the unattended message, such as the speaker's gender and whether their own name is mentioned. On the other hand, under more challenging conditions, they may not even notice whether the unattended message is in English or in a foreign language.

The Stroop Effect

So far, we have emphasized a type of selective attention that focuses on hearing, using the dichotic-listening task. The remaining topics in this section focus on vision. Now try Demonstration 3.1, which illustrates the famous Stroop effect.

The Stroop effect is named after James R. Stroop (1935), who created this well-known task. According to the **Stroop effect**, people take a long time to name the ink color when that color is used in printing an incongruent word; in contrast, they can quickly name that same ink color when it appears as a solid patch of color.

In a typical study on the Stroop effect, people may require about 100 seconds to name the ink color of 100 words that are incongruent color names (for example, blue ink used in printing the word YELLOW). In contrast, they require only about 60 seconds to name the ink colors for 100 colored patches (C. M. MacLeod, 2005). Notice why the Stroop effect demonstrates selective attention: People take longer to

---

⑨ Demonstration 3.1

The Stroop Effect

For this demonstration, you will need a watch with a second hand. Turn to Color Figure 3 inside the back cover. Notice the word in the upper-left corner of Part A. This word RED is printed in yellow. Your task is to say out loud the names of the ink colors, ignoring the meaning of the words. Measure the amount of time it takes to go through this list five times. (Keep a tally of the number of repetitions.) Record that time.

Now you will try a second color-naming task. Measure how long it takes to name the colors in the rectangular patches in Part B. Measure the amount of time it takes to go through this list five times. (Again, keep a tally of the number of repetitions.) Record the time.

pay attention to a color when they are distracted by another feature of the stimulus, namely, the meaning of the name itself (Styles, 2006).

Researchers have examined a variety of explanations for the Stroop effect. Some have suggested that it can be explained by the connectionist or parallel distributed processing (PDP) approach, which was discussed on pages 20–21 (e.g., Cohen et al., 1998; C. M. MacLeod, 2005). According to this explanation, the Stroop task activates two pathways at the same time. One pathway is activated by the task of naming the ink color, and the other pathway is activated by the task of reading the word. Interference occurs when two competing pathways are active at the same time. As a result, task performance suffers.

Another explanation is that adults have had much more practice in reading words than in naming colors (T. L. Brown et al., 2002; Cox et al., 2006; Luck & Vecera, 2002). The more automatic process (reading the word) interferes with the less automatic process (naming the color of the ink). As a result, we automatically—and involuntarily—read the words that are printed in Part A of Color Figure 3. In fact, it's difficult to prevent yourself from reading those words, even if you want to! For instance, right now, stop reading this paragraph! Were you successful?

Hundreds of researchers have examined variations of the Stroop effect. For instance, many clinical psychologists have used a related technique called the emotional Stroop task (C. MacLeod, 2005; C. M. MacLeod, 2005). On the **emotional Stroop task**, people are instructed to name the ink color of words that could have strong emotional significance to them. These individuals often require more time to name the color of the stimuli, presumably because they have trouble ignoring their emotional reactions to the words themselves (Most, 2010).

For example, suppose that someone appears to have a **phobic disorder**, which is an excessive fear of a specific object. A person with a fear of spiders would be instructed to name the ink colors of printed words such as *hairy* and *crawl*. People with phobias are significantly slower on these anxiety-arousing words than on control words. In contrast, people without phobias show no difference between the two kinds of words (Williams et al., 1996).

These results suggest that people who have a phobic disorder are hyper-alert to words related to their phobia, and they show an attentional bias to the meaning of these stimuli. An **attentional bias** describes a situation in which people pay extra attention to some stimuli or some features. In the emotional Stroop task, for example, the participants pay *less* attention to the ink color of the words.

In addition, adults who showed an attentional bias toward suicide-related words are more likely than other adults to make a suicide attempt within the following 6 months (Cha et al., 2010). Other research shows that people who are depressed take a long time to report the color of words related to sadness and despair (C. MacLeod, 2005). Also, the Stroop task can be used to assess addiction to alcohol and cigarettes (Cox et al., 2006). In the following individual-differences feature, we will consider how people at risk for eating disorders perform on the Stroop task. As we'll note throughout this book, humans differ widely in the way that they process information

(Hertel & Matthews, 2011). In the following individual-differences feature, we will consider how people at risk for eating disorders perform on the Stroop task.

Individual Differences: Eating Disorders and the Stroop Effect

Let's consider a study by Abbie Pringle and her coauthors (2010), at the University of Oxford in England. These researchers distributed an online screening questionnaire to female dieters who had responded to an earlier advertisement. A total of 82 women met the specified criterion of very frequent dieting.

The researchers had created a set of emotionally relevant words that referred to topics such as body shape, body weight, and eating. Then they matched these words with a control group of neutral words, so that the two groups of stimuli were similar in both word length and word frequency. The women then completed this diet-focused version of the Stroop task.

The women also completed the 26-item Eating Attitudes Test, a standardized test that assesses whether people are at risk for developing eating disorders. According to the results of this study, slow responses to body-shape words predicted women's attitudes about eating. Specifically, when women took much longer to read those words related to shape (as opposed to the control words), they were especially likely to have high scores on the Eating Attitudes Test.

Pringle and her colleagues (2010) point out that these results are consistent with the cognitive-behavioral approach (e.g., Beck, 2011). According to the **cognitive-behavioral approach**, psychological problems arise from inappropriate thinking (cognitive factors) and inappropriate learning (behavioral factors). This study therefore shows a relationship between these women's potential for eating disorders and their thought patterns about words related to body shape.

So far this section on selective attention has examined dichotic listening and the Stroop effect. Next we'll examine the topic of visual search.

Visual Search

Let's now consider visual search, the third topic within our general area of selective attention. In **visual search**, the observer must find a target in a visual display that has numerous distractors. In some cases, our lives may depend on accurate visual searches. For instance, airport security officers search travelers' luggage for possible weapons, and radiologists search a mammogram to detect a tumor that could indicate breast cancer.

Researchers have identified an impressive number of variables that influence visual searches. For example, Jeremy Wolfe and his colleagues (2005) found that people are much more accurate in identifying a target if it appears frequently. If the target appears—in a visually complex background—on 50% of the trials, participants missed the target 7% of the time. When the same target appeared in this same complex background on only 1% of the trials, participants missed the target 30% of the time.

> ⊙ **Demonstration 3.2**
>
> ### The Isolated-Feature/Combined-Feature Effect
>
> After reading this paragraph, turn to Color Figure 4 inside the back cover. First, look at the two figures marked "Part A." In each case, search for a blue X. Notice whether you take about the same amount of time on these two tasks. After trying Part A, return to this page and read the additional instructions.
>
> *Additional instructions*: For the second part of this demonstration, return to Part B inside the back cover. Look for the blue X in each of the two figures in Part B. Notice whether you take the same amount of time on these two tasks or whether one takes slightly longer.

Let's examine two stimulus variables in more detail: (1) whether we are searching for a single, isolated feature or a combined set of features; and (2) whether we are searching for a target in which a particular feature is present or a target in which this feature is absent. As you'll see, two psychologists—Anne Treisman and Jeremy Wolfe—have been especially active in studying visual search. Before you read further, however, try Demonstration 3.2.

1. *The isolated-feature/combined-feature effect.* Demonstration 3.2 is based on classic research by Treisman and Gelade (1980). According to their research, if the target differed from the irrelevant items in the display with respect to a simple feature such as color, observers could quickly detect the target. In fact, people can detect this target just as fast when it is presented in an array of 24 items as when it is presented in an array of only 3 items (Horowitz, 2010; Styles, 2006; Treisman, 1993; Treisman & Gelade, 1980).

When you tried Part A of Demonstration 3.2, you probably found that the blue X seemed to "pop out," whether the display contains 2 or 23 irrelevant items. In contrast, Part B of Demonstration 3.2 required you to search for a target that is a combination (or conjunction) of two properties. When you searched for a blue X among red X's, red O's, and blue O's, you probably found that you had to pay attention to one item at a time, using serial processing. You were distracted by stimuli that resembled the target because they were either blue or X-shaped (Serences et al., 2005).

This second task is more complex, and the time taken to find the target increases dramatically as the number of distractors increases (Wolfe, 2000, 2001; Wolfe et al., 2009). As a result, Figure B2 required a more time-consuming search than Figure B1 did. This demonstration supports the **isolated-feature/combined-feature effect**: People can typically locate an isolated feature more quickly than a combined feature (Quinlan, 2010).

We will return to this area of research when we discuss Anne Treisman's feature-integration theory on pages 86 to 88. Now try Demonstration 3.3 before you read further.

Demonstration 3.3

Searching for Features That Are Present or Absent

In Part A, search for the circle with the line. Then, in Part B, search for the circle without the line.

(A)

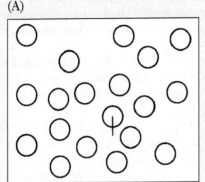

(B)

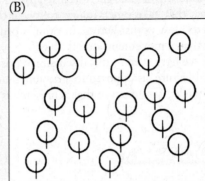

Source: Based on Treisman & Souther, 1985.

---

2. *The feature-present/feature-absent effect.* Theme 3 of this book states that our cognitive processes handle positive information better than negative information. In this case, "positive" means that a feature is present, whereas "negative" means that a feature is missing. Turn back to Demonstration 1.4 on page 25 to remind yourself about this theme.

The research of Treisman and Souther (1985) provides additional support for that theme, as you can see from Demonstration 3.3. This research illustrates the **feature-present/feature-absent effect**: People can typically locate a feature that is present more quickly than a feature that is absent.

Notice in Part A of this demonstration that the circle with the line seems to "pop out" from the display. The search is rapid when we are looking for a particular feature that is *present*. Treisman and Souther (1985) found that people performed rapid searches for a feature that was present (like the circle with the line in Part A), whether the display contained zero irrelevant items or numerous irrelevant items. When people are searching for a feature that is present, the target item in the display usually captures their attention automatically (Franconeri et al., 2005; Matsumoto, 2010; Wolfe, 2000, 2001). In fact, this "pop-out" effect is automatic, and researchers emphasize that locating the target is strictly a bottom-up process (Boot et al., 2005).

In contrast, notice what happens when you are searching for a feature that is *absent* (like the circle without the line in Part B). Treisman and Souther (1985) found that the search time increased dramatically as the number of irrelevant items increased. When people search for a feature that is absent, they typically examine every item, one item at a time. They therefore must use a kind of attention that emphasizes both bottom-up processing and top-down processing. This task is substantially more challenging, as Wolfe has also found in his extensive research on the feature-present/feature-absent effect (Wolfe, 2000, 2001; Wolfe et al., 2009).

Another example of the feature-present/feature-absent effect was discovered by Royden and her coauthors (2001). According to their research, people can quickly locate one moving target when it appears in a group of stationary distractors. In contrast, they take much longer to locate one stationary target when it appears in a group of moving distractors. In other words, it's easier to spot a movement-present object than a movement-absent object.

As we have seen in this discussion of visual search, we search more quickly for an isolated feature, as opposed to a conjunction of two features. Furthermore, we search more quickly for a feature that is present, as opposed to a feature that is absent.

IN DEPTH

Saccadic Eye Movements During Reading

In the first section of this chapter, we considered divided attention, in which we pay attention to two or more simultaneous messages. Then we discussed three kinds of selective attention: (a) dichotic listening, (b) the Stroop effect, and (c) visual search. Now let's consider the final kind of attention task—one that you are performing right now, while moving your eyes forward to read the next words on this page.

Our eye movements provide important information about the way our minds operate when we perform a number of everyday cognitive tasks (Engbert et al., 2005; Radach et al., 2004b; Yang & McConkie, 2004). For example, researchers have studied how our eyes move when we are looking at a scene or searching for a visual target (e.g., Castelhano & Rayner, 2008; Henderson & Ferreira, 2004b; Irwin & Zelinsky, 2002) and when we are driving (Fisher & Pollatsek, 2007). Researchers have also discovered that our eyes move when we are speaking (Griffin, 2004; Meyer, 2004). However, this in-depth section focuses on our eye movements during reading.

We have already considered one perceptual process that is central to reading. In Chapter 2, we examined how people recognize letters of the alphabet (pp. 41–43). In that section, we also discussed how context facilitates the recognition of individual letters, as well as complete words. Eye movement is a second perceptual process that is central to reading. For a moment, pay attention to the way your eyes are moving as you read this paragraph. Your eyes actually make a series of little jumps as they move across the page.

This very rapid movement of the eyes from one spot to the next is known as saccadic (pronounced "suh-*cod*-dik") eye movement. The purpose of a **saccadic eye movement** during reading is to bring the center of your retina into position over the words you want to read. A very small region in the center of the retina, known as the

fovea, has better acuity than other retinal regions. Therefore, the eye must be moved so that new words can be registered on the fovea (Castelhano & Rayner, 2008; Chun et al., 2011; Irwin, 2004). Saccadic eye movement is another example of Theme 1 (active cognitive processes); we actively search for new information, including the material we will be reading (Findlay & Gilchrist, 2001; Radach & Kennedy, 2004).

When you read a passage in English, each saccade moves your eye forward by about 7 to 9 letters (Wolfe et al., 2009). Researchers have estimated that people make between 150,000 and 200,000 saccadic movements every day (Irwin, 2003; Rayner, 2009; Weierich & Barrett, 2010). You cannot process much visual information when your eyes are moving (Irwin, 2003; Radach & Kennedy, 2004; Weierich & Barrett, 2010). However, a fixation occurs during the period between two saccadic movements. During each **fixation**, your visual system pauses briefly in order to acquire information that is useful for reading (Rayner, 2009).

Incidentally, you may think that you have a smooth, continuous view of the material you are processing. However, your eyes are actually alternating between jumps and pauses (Rayner & Liversedge, 2004; Reichle & Laurent, 2006).

What about saccadic eye movements in other languages? As we will emphasize in Chapters 9 and 10, psychological research typically focuses on the English language. We know relatively little about reading and related linguistic processes in other languages. For instance, the modern Chinese language is spoken by 1.2 billion people, which is more than three times as many as the 328 million speakers for the English language (Ethnologue Languages of the World, 2011).

Several decades ago, psychologists knew very little about saccadic eye movements in Chinese. However, some research is now available. For example, researchers have determined that Chinese readers move their eyes only 2 to 3 characters in a saccade. This makes sense because each character in the Chinese written language is more densely packed with information, compared to each letter in written English (Rayner, 2009; Shen et al., 2008; Tsang & Chen, 2008).

The term **perceptual span** refers to the number of letters and spaces that we perceive during a fixation (Rayner & Liversedge, 2004). Researchers have found large individual differences in the size of the perceptual span (Irwin, 2004). When you read English, this perceptual span normally includes letters lying about 4 positions to the left of the letter you are directly looking at, as well as the letters about 15 positions to the right of that central letter (Rayner, 2009).

Notice that this perceptual span for English is definitely lopsided. After all, when we read English, we are looking for reading cues in the text that lies to the right, and these cues provide some general information (Findlay & Gilchrist, 2001; Starr & Inhoff, 2004). For instance, the material in the extreme right side of the perceptual span is useful for noticing the white spaces between words, because these spaces provide information about word length. However, we usually cannot actually identify a word that lies more than 8 spaces to the right of the fixation point (Rayner, 1998).

Other research has demonstrated that saccadic eye movements show several predictable patterns. For example, when the eye jumps forward in a saccadic movement, it usually moves toward the center of a word, rather than to a blank space

FIGURE 3.1

Eye Movement Patterns and Fixations for a Good Reader (top numbers) and a Poor Reader (bottom numbers).

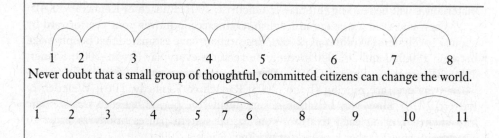

between words or between sentences (Engbert & Krügel, 2010). The eye also jumps past short words, words that appear frequently in a language, and words that are highly predictable in a sentence (Drieghe et al., 2004; Kliegl et al., 2004; White & Liversedge, 2004). In contrast, the size of the saccadic movement is small if the next word in a sentence is misspelled or if it is unusual (Pynte et al., 2004; Rayner et al., 2004; White & Liversedge, 2004). All these strategies make sense, because a large saccadic movement would not be useful if the material is challenging.

Good readers differ from poor readers with respect to their saccadic eye movements. Figure 3.1 shows how two such readers might differ when reading the same sentence. Good readers make larger jumps. They are also less likely to make **regressions,** by moving their eyes backward to earlier material in the sentence. People often make regressions when they realize that they have not understood the passage they are reading (White & Liversedge, 2004). The good reader also has shorter pauses before moving onward (Castelhano & Rayner, 2008).

In summary, the research shows that a wide variety of cognitive factors have an important influence on the pattern and speed of our saccadic eye movements (McDonald & Shillcock, 2003; Reichle et al., 1998). Saccadic eye movements clearly help us become more active, flexible readers (Rayner, 2009; Rayner et al., 2008).

Section Summary: *Several Kinds of Attention Processes*

1. Attention is a concentration of mental activity; it allows our cognitive processes to take in limited portions of our sensory environment and our memory.

2. Research on divided attention shows that performance often suffers when people must attend to several stimuli simultaneously. For example, we cannot talk on a hands-free cell phone and drive carefully at the same time. The remaining attention processes considered in this chapter require selective attention.

3. The dichotic-listening technique is the first of the selective-attention tasks discussed in this section. The research shows that we typically notice little about an irrelevant auditory message. Occasionally, however, we may notice the gender of the speaker or our own name.

4. A second kind of a selective-attention task is the Stroop effect. A variant called the "emotional Stroop task" demonstrates that people with certain disorders have difficulty identifying the ink color of words relevant to their disorder; for example, people with eating disorders take longer than other people to report the ink color of words related to body shape.

5. A third kind of selected-attention task is visual search. For example, we can locate a target faster if it appears frequently, if it differs from irrelevant objects on only one dimension (e.g., color), and if a specific feature of a stimulus (e.g., a line) is present rather than absent.

6. The final kind of selective-attention task is saccadic eye movements, which our visual system makes during reading. Saccadic-movement patterns depend on factors such as the language of the text (e.g., English vs. Chinese), the difficulty of the text, and individual differences in reading skill.

EXPLANATIONS FOR ATTENTION

So far, we've examined several attention processes that help to regulate how much information we take in from our visual and auditory environment. Researchers have tried to account for these components of attention by conducting neuroscience studies and by developing theories to explain the characteristics of attention.

Neuroscience Research on Attention

During recent decades, researchers have developed a variety of sophisticated techniques for examining the biological basis of behavior; Chapter 1 introduced many of these approaches. Research using these techniques has identified a network of areas throughout the brain that accomplish various attention tasks (Posner & Rothbart, 2007b).

Several regions of the brain are responsible for attention. In this discussion, however, we'll focus on structures in the cerebral cortex, as shown in Figure 3.2. Take a moment to compare Figure 3.2 with Figure 2.1 (p. 38), which shows the regions of the cortex that are most relevant in object recognition.

According to Michael Posner and Mary Rothbart, several systems in the cortex process different aspects of attention (Posner & Rothbart, 2007a, 2007b; Rothbart et al., 2011; Tang & Posner, 2009). We will discuss two of them, the orienting attention network and the executive attention network.

The Orienting Attention Network. Imagine that you are searching the area around your bathroom sink for a lost contact lens. When you are selecting information from sensory input, your orienting attention network is activated. The **orienting**

FIGURE 3.2

A Schematic Drawing of the Cerebral Cortex, as Seen from the Left Side, Showing the Four Lobes of the Brain and the Regions that Are Most Important on Attention Tasks.

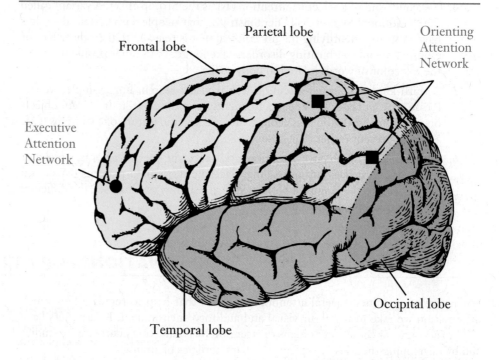

attention network is generally responsible for the kind of attention required for visual search, in which you must shift your attention around to various spatial locations (Chun & Wolfe, 2001; Posner & Rothbart, 2007b). Figure 3.2 shows that two important components of the orienting attention network are located in the region of the cortex known as the parietal lobe (pronounced "pah-*rie*-uh-tul").

How did researchers identify the parietal cortex as the region of the brain that we use in visual searches? Several decades ago, the only clue to the organization of the brain was provided by people with brain lesions (Posner, 2004). The term **brain lesion** refers to specific brain damage caused by strokes, accidents, or other traumas.

People who have brain damage in the parietal region of the right hemisphere of the brain have trouble noticing a visual stimulus that appears on the left side of their visual field. In contrast, people with damage in the left parietal region have trouble noticing a visual stimulus on the right side (Luck & Vecera, 2002; Posner & Rothbart, 2007a, 2007b; Styles, 2005). Neurologists use the term **unilateral spatial neglect** when a person ignores part of his or her visual field (Gazzaniga et al., 2009).

These lesions produce unusual deficits. For instance, a woman with a lesion in the left parietal region may have trouble noticing the food on the right side of her plate. She may eat only the food on the left side of her plate, and she might even complain that she didn't receive enough food (Farah, 2000; Humphreys & Riddoch, 2001). Surprisingly, however, she may seem completely unaware of her deficit. In another study, researchers tested a man with a lesion in his right parietal lobe. They showed him a figure of an ordinary clock and asked him to draw it. His drawing showed only half of the clock, with the other half completely empty (Bloom & Lazerson, 1988).

Some of the more recent research on the orienting attention network has used PET scans. In studies using **positron emission tomography** (abbreviated **PET scan**), the researchers measure blood flow in the brain by injecting the participant with a radioactive chemical just before he or she performs a cognitive task. As discussed in Chapter 1, this chemical travels through the blood to the parts of the brain that are active during the cognitive task. A specialized camera makes an image of the accumulated chemical. According to PET-scan research, the parietal cortex shows increased blood flow when people perform visual searches and when they pay attention to spatial locations (Posner & Rothbart, 2007b).

The orienting network develops during the first year of life. For example, by about 4 months of age, infants can disengage their attention from an overstimulating situation, and they can shift this attention to an object such as a new toy (Posner & Rothbart, 2007a; Rothbart et al., 2011).

The Executive Attention Network. The Stroop task that you tried in Demonstration 3.1 relied primarily on your executive attention network. The **executive attention network** is responsible for the kind of attention we use when a task focuses on conflict (Posner & Rothbart, 2007a, 2007b). On the Stroop task, for example, you need to inhibit your automatic response of reading a word, so that you can name the color of the ink (Fan et al., 2002).

More generally, the executive attention network inhibits your automatic responses to stimuli (Stuss et al., 2002). As you can see in Figure 3.2, the prefrontal portion of the cortex is the region of your brain where the executive attention network is especially active.

The executive attention network is primarily involved during top-down control of attention (Farah, 2000). This network begins to develop at about age 3, much later than the orienting attention network (Posner & Rothbart, 2007a; Rothbart et al., 2011). Posner and Rothbart (2007b) argue that the executive attention network is extremely important when you acquire academic skills in school, for example, when you learned to read. There is also some evidence that adults can enhance their executive attention network by learning meditation, adopted from traditional Chinese techniques (Tang & Posner, 2009).

Executive attention also helps you learn new ideas (Posner & Rothbart, 2007a). For example, as you are reading this passage, your executive attention network has been actively taking in new information. Ideally, you have also been comparing this executive attention network with the orienting attention network. This process of reading and understanding a college-level textbook can be challenging. Not surprisingly, the location of the executive attention network overlaps with the areas of your brain that are related to general intelligence (Duncan et al., 2000; Posner & Rothbart, 2007b).

In summary, PET scans and other neuroscience techniques have identified one brain region that is typically active when we are searching for objects (the orienting attention network). Neuroscience research also show that a different brain region is typically active when we must inhibit an automatic response and produce a less obvious response (the executive attention network); this second network is also active in academic learning.

Theories of Attention

Let us first summarize an approach to attention that was proposed several decades ago, when cognitive psychology was in its infancy. Then we will discuss Anne Treisman's feature-integration theory, which is probably the most influential contemporary explanation of attention (Styles, 2005).

Early Theories of Attention. The first approaches to attention emphasized that people are extremely limited in the amount of information that they can process at any given time. A common metaphor in these theories was the concept of a bottleneck (Gazzaniga et al., 2009). This metaphor was especially appealing because it matches our introspections about attention. The narrow neck of a bottle restricts the flow into or out of the bottle.

Bottleneck theories proposed a similar narrow passageway in human information processing. In other words, this bottleneck limits the quantity of information to which we can pay attention. So, when one message is currently flowing through a bottleneck, the other messages must be left behind. Researchers proposed many variations of this bottleneck theory (e.g., Broadbent, 1958; Treisman, 1964).

However, as you may recall from the discussion of the theories of object recognition (Chapter 2), researchers rejected the template theory because it was not flexible enough. Similarly, researchers rejected the bottleneck theories because those theories underestimate the flexibility of human attention (Luck & Vecera, 2002; Tsang, 2007). Neuroscience research demonstrates that information is not lost at just one phase of the attention process, as the bottleneck theories suggest. Instead, information is lost throughout many phases of attention, from the beginning through later processing (Kanwisher et al., 2001; Luck & Vecera, 2002).

Feature-Integration Theory. Anne Treisman has developed an elaborate theory of attention and perceptual processing. Her original theory was elegantly simple (Treisman & Gelade, 1980). As you might expect, the current version is more complex (Holcombe, 2010; Quinlan, 2010). Let's consider (1) the basic elements of feature-integration theory, (2) research on the theory, and (3) the current status of the theory.

1. *The basic elements:* According to Treisman's **feature-integration theory**, we sometimes look at a scene using distributed attention,* and we process all parts of the scene at the same time; on other occasions, we use focused attention, and we process each item in the scene, one at a time. Treisman also suggested that distributed attention and focused attention form a continuum, rather than two distinctive categories. As a result, you frequently use a kind of attention that is somewhere between those two extremes.

Let's examine these two kinds of processing before considering other components of Treisman's theory (Treisman & Gelade, 1980; Treisman, 1993). One kind of processing uses distributed attention. **Distributed attention** allows you to register features automatically; you use parallel processing across the field, and you register all the features simultaneously. Distributed attention is a relatively low-level kind of processing. In fact, this kind of processing is so effortless that you are not even aware that you're using it.

The second kind of processing in Treisman's theory is called focused attention. **Focused attention** requires slower serial processing, and you identify one object at a time. This more demanding kind of processing is necessary when the objects are more complex. Focused attention identifies which features belong together—for example, a square shape may go with a blue color.

2. *Research on the theory:* Treisman and Gelade (1980) examined distributed attention and focused attention by studying two different stimulus situations. In this study, one situation used isolated features (and therefore it used distributed attention). In contrast, the other situation used combinations of features (and therefore it used focused attention).

Let's first consider the details of the research on *distributed attention*. According to Treisman and Gelade, if you process isolated features in distributed attention, then you should be able to rapidly locate a target among its neighboring, irrelevant items. That target should seem to "pop out" of the display automatically, no matter how many items are in the display.

To test their hypothesis about distributed attention, Treisman and Gelade conducted a series of studies. You already tried Demonstration 3.2A (p. 78), which illustrated part of their study. Remember the results of that demonstration: If the target differed from all the irrelevant items in the display with respect to one simple feature such as color, you could quickly detect this target. In fact, you could detect it just as fast when it appeared in an array of 23 items as when it appeared in an array of only 3 items (Treisman, 1986; Treisman & Gelade, 1980). Distributed attention can operate in a parallel fashion and relatively automatically; the target seemed to "pop out" in Demonstration 3.2A.

---

*In some of her research, Treisman uses the phrase "divided attention," rather than "distributed attention." However, I will use "distributed attention" in this textbook, in order to avoid confusing this concept with the research on divided attention discussed on earlier pages.

In contrast, consider the research on *focused attention*. In Demonstration 3.2B, you searched for a target that was a conjunction (or combination) of properties. When you searched for a blue X buried among red X's, red O's, and blue O's, you needed to use focused attention. In other words, you were forced to focus your attention on one item at a time, using serial processing. This task is more complex. Treisman and Gelade (1980) and other researchers have found that people need more time to find the target when there are a large number of distractors in a focused-attention task (Parasuraman & Greenwood, 2007).

Another effect related to feature-integration theory is called an *illusory conjunction*. Specifically, when we are overwhelmed with too many simultaneous visual tasks, we sometimes form an illusory conjunction (Botella et al., 2011; Treisman & Schmidt, 1982; Treisman & Souther, 1986). An **illusory conjunction** is an inappropriate combination of features, perhaps combining one object's shape with a nearby object's color. Many studies have demonstrated, for example, that a blue N and a green T can produce an illusory conjunction in which the viewer actually perceives either a blue T or a green N (e.g., Ashby et al., 1996; Hazeltine et al., 1997; Holcombe, 2010).

This research on illusory conjunctions confirms a conclusion demonstrated in other perception research. Contrary to our commonsense intuitions, the human visual system actually processes an object's features independently. For example, when you look at a red apple, you actually analyze its red color separately from its round shape. In other words, your visual system sometimes has a **binding problem** because it does not represent the important features of an object as a unified whole (Holcombe, 2010; Quinlan, 2010; Wheeler & Treisman, 2002).

When you use focused attention to look at the apple, you will accurately perceive an integrated figure—a red, round object. Focused attention allows the binding process to operate (Bouvier & Treisman, 2010; Quinlan, 2010; Vu & Rich, 2010). To use a metaphor, focused attention acts like a form of glue, so that an object's color and its shape can stick together.

In contrast, suppose that a researcher shows you two arbitrary figures, for example, a blue N and a green T. Suppose also that your attention is overloaded or distracted, so that you must use distributed attention. In this situation, the blue color from one figure may combine with the T shape from the other figure. As a result, you may perceive the illusory conjunction of a blue T.

Other research shows that our visual system can create an illusory conjunction from verbal material (Treisman, 1990; Wolfe, 2000). For example, suppose that your attention is distracted, and a researcher shows you two nonsense words, *dax* and *kay*. You might report seeing the English word *day*. When we cannot use focused attention, we sometimes form illusory conjunctions that are consistent with our expectations. As Chapter 2 emphasized, top-down processing helps us screen out inappropriate combinations. As a result, we are more likely to perceive familiar combinations (Treisman, 1990).

3. *Current status of the theory:* The basic elements of feature-integration theory were proposed more than 25 years ago. Since that time, researchers have conducted dozens of additional studies, and the original, straightforward theory has been modified.

◎ Demonstration 3.4

Awareness About Automatic Motor Activities

Take a moment to see how aware you are about how you perform one or more of these motor activities. In each case, be as specific as possible about exactly how you perform each step of each activity.

1. Describe in detail how you pick up a pen and write your name.
2. Describe in detail how you stand up from a sitting position.
3. Describe in detail how you walk across the room.
4. Describe in detail how you open one of the doors in the place where you live.

As we will see throughout this textbook, psychologists often propose a theory that initially draws a clear-cut distinction between two or more psychological processes. With extensive research, however, theorists frequently conclude that reality is much more complex. Rather than two clear-cut categories, we find that distributed attention can occasionally resemble focused attention (Bundesen & Habekost, 2005).

Furthermore, your visual system may use distributed attention to quickly gather information about the general gist of a scene. For example, suppose that you are standing near a lake, looking out at the beach. Obviously, you cannot use focused attention to register every pebble on the beach. Treisman and her coauthors suggest that your distributed attention can quickly gather information about the average size of these pebbles. In this fashion, you can form a fairly accurate overall impression of this natural scene (Chong et al., 2008; Emmanouil & Treisman, 2008; Treisman, 2006).

Many questions remain about how visual attention helps us gather relevant information from a real-world scene. However, the current version of feature-integration theory provides an important framework for understanding visual attention (Holcombe, 2010; Müller & Krummenacher, 2006; Quinlan, 2010). Before you read further, try Demonstration 3.4.

◎ Section Summary: *Explanations for Attention*

---

1. According to case studies, some people who have a lesion in the parietal region of the right hemisphere cannot notice visual objects in the left visual field.
2. PET-scan research has also established that the orienting attention network is active when people perform visual searches or when they notice spatial locations.

3. This executive attention network is important in attention tasks that focus on conflict (e.g., the Stroop task), in the top-down control of attention, and in learning new information.

4. Early theories of attention emphasized a "bottleneck" that limits attention at a particular part of processing, but this perspective is now judged too simplistic.

5. Treisman proposed the feature-integration theory, which contains two components: (a) distributed attention, which can be used to register single features automatically, and (b) focused attention, which requires slower serial processing in order to search for combinations of features.

6. In Treisman's theory, illusory conjunctions may arise when attention is overloaded. With some modifications, feature-integration theory still accounts for many important aspects of visual attention.

CONSCIOUSNESS

Our final topic in this chapter—consciousness—is a controversial subject. One reason for the controversy is the variety of different definitions for the term (Baumeister et al., 2011; Dehaene et al., 2006; Velmans, 2009). I prefer a broad definition: **Consciousness** means the awareness that people have about the outside world and about their perceptions, images, thoughts, memories, and feelings (Chalmers, 2007; Revonsuo, 2010; Zeman, 2004).

Notice that the contents of consciousness can include your perceptions of the world around you, your visual imagery, the comments you make silently to yourself, the memory of events in your life, your beliefs about the world, your plans for activities later today, and your attitudes toward other people (Coward & Sun, 2004; Dijksterhuis & Aarts, 2010). As David Barash (2006) writes,

> Thus, consciousness is not only an unfolding story that we tell ourselves, moment by moment, about what we are doing, feeling, and thinking. It also includes our efforts to interpret what other individuals are doing, feeling, and thinking, as well as how those others are likely to perceive one's self. (p. B10)

Consciousness is closely related to attention, but the processes are definitely not identical (Dijksterhuis & Aarts, 2010; Hoffman, 2010; Lavie, 2007). After all, we are frequently not aware or conscious of the tasks we are performing with the automatic, distributed form of attention. For example, when you are driving, you may automatically put your foot on the brake in response to a red light. However, you may not be at all conscious that you performed this motor action—or any of the other motor activities in Demonstration 3.4. In general, consciousness is associated with the kind of controlled, focused attention that is *not* automatic (Dehaene & Naccache, 2001; Dijksterhuis & Aarts, 2010; Weierich & Barrett, 2010).

As Chapter 1 noted, the behaviorists considered topics such as consciousness to be inappropriate for scientific study. However, consciousness edged back into favor when psychologists began to adopt cognitive approaches (Dehaene & Naccache, 2001). In the 21st century, consciousness has become a popular topic for numerous books (e.g., Baruss, 2003; Edelman, 2005; Hassin et al., 2005; Revonsuo, 2010; Velmans, 2009; Velmans & Schneider, 2007; Zeman, 2004).

In recent years, cognitive psychologists have been especially interested in three interrelated issues concerned with consciousness: (1) our inability to bring certain thoughts into consciousness; (2) our inability to let certain thoughts escape from consciousness; and (3) blindsight, which reveals that people with a specific visual disorder can perform quite accurately on a cognitive task, even when they are not conscious of their accuracy. Before you read further, however, try Demonstration 3.5.

To what extent do we have access to our higher mental processes? Consider this situation: You are reading a book, and your eyes are moving over the page. However, you are daydreaming . . . and you aren't actually aware that you are not reading. During **mindless reading**, your eyes may move forward, but you do not process the meaning of the material. In fact, your eyes were moving erratically, rather than using the kind of normal saccadic movements we discussed earlier in this chapter (Reichle et al., 2010). You had no conscious awareness of your higher mental processes, until suddenly you became conscious that you didn't remember any information from the text.

A more general phenomenon, called **mind wandering**, occurs when your thoughts shift from the external environment in favor of internal processing (Barron et al., 2011; McVay & Kane, 2010; Smilek et al., 2010). Again, you may not be conscious that your mind has wandered to another topic.

Here's another example that demonstrates our inability to bring certain thoughts into consciousness. Answer the following question: "What is your mother's maiden name?" Now answer this second question: "How did you arrive at the answer to the first question?" If you are like most people, the answer to the first question appeared swiftly in your consciousness, but you probably cannot explain your thought process. Instead, the name simply seemed to pop into your memory.

In a classic article, Richard Nisbett and Timothy Wilson (1977) argued that we often have little direct access to our thought processes. As they pointed out, you may be fully conscious of the *products* of your thought processes (such as your mother's maiden

---

Ⓢ Demonstration 3.5

Thought Suppression

This demonstration requires you to take a break from your reading and just relax for 5 minutes. Take a sheet of paper and a pen or pencil to record your thoughts as you simply let your mind wander. Your thoughts can include cognitive psychology, but they do not need to. Just jot down a brief note about each topic you think about as your mind wanders. One final instruction:

During this exercise, do not think about a white bear!

name). However, you are usually not conscious of the *processes* that created these products (such as the memory mechanisms that produced her maiden name). Similarly, people may solve a problem correctly; however, when asked to explain how they reached the solution, they may reply, "It just dawned on me" (Nisbett & Wilson, 1977). In Chapter 11 on problem solving, we'll discuss this aspect of consciousness in more detail.

Psychologists currently believe that our verbal reports are somewhat accurate reflections of our cognitive processes (Ericsson & Fox, 2011; Fox et al., 2011; Johansson et al., 2006; Wilson, 1997). As we'll see in Chapter 6, we do have relatively complete access to some thought processes. For example, you can judge—with reasonable accuracy—how well you performed on a simple memory task. However, we have only limited access to other thought processes, such as how well you understand the information in a psychology essay. As Demonstration 3.4 showed, we are not aware of the step-by-step procedures in the motor activities that have become automatic (Diana & Reder, 2004; Levin, 2004).

We need to emphasize this topic of consciousness about thought processes, because it shows that cognitive psychologists should not rely on people's introspections (Johansson et al., 2006; Nisbett & Wilson, 1977; Wegner, 2002). For example, when several people are talking to me at once, it genuinely feels like I am experiencing an "attention bottleneck." However, as we saw earlier in this chapter, humans actually have fairly flexible attention patterns; we really do not experience a rigid bottleneck.

Throughout this book, we'll see that the research findings sometimes do not match our commonsense introspections. This discrepancy emphasizes that objective research is absolutely essential in cognitive psychology.

Thought Suppression

I have a friend who decided to quit smoking, so he tried valiantly to get rid of every idea associated with cigarettes. As soon as he thought of anything remotely associated with smoking, he immediately tried to push that thought out of his consciousness. Ironically, however, this strategy backfired, and he was haunted by numerous thoughts related to cigarettes. Basically, he could not eliminate these undesirable thoughts. When people engage in **thought suppression**, they try to eliminate the thoughts, ideas, and images that are related to an undesirable stimulus.

The research on thought suppression supports my friend's experience (Erskine et al., 2010). How successful were you in suppressing your thoughts in Demonstration 3.5? Did you have any difficulty carrying out the instructions?

The original source for the white bear study is literary, rather than scientific. Apparently, when the Russian novelist Tolstoy was young, his older brother tormented him by instructing him to stand in a corner and not think about a white bear (Wegner, 1996; Wegner et al., 1987). Similarly, if you have ever tried to avoid thinking about food when on a diet, you know that it's difficult to chase these undesired thoughts out of consciousness.

Wegner (1997b, 2002) uses the phrase **ironic effects of mental control** to describe how our efforts can backfire when we attempt to control the contents of our consciousness. Suppose that you try valiantly to banish a particular thought. Ironically, that same thought is especially likely to creep back into consciousness. In other words, you have trouble suppressing certain thoughts.

Wegner and his coauthors (1987) decided to test Tolstoy's "white bear" task scientifically. They instructed one group of students not to think about a white bear during a 5-minute period, and then they were allowed to think about a white bear during a second 5-minute period. These students were very likely to think about a white bear during the second period. In fact, they thought about bears more often than students in a control group. Students in this control group had been instructed to *think freely* about a white bear—without any previous thought-suppression session. In other words, initial suppression of specific thoughts can produce a rebound effect.

Many studies have replicated the rebound effect following thought suppression (e.g., Purdon et al., 2005; Tolin et al., 2002; Wegner, 2002). Furthermore, this rebound effect is not limited to suppressing thoughts about white bears and other relatively trivial ideas. For example, when people are instructed not to notice a painful stimulus, they are likely to become even more aware of the pain. Similar ironic effects—which occur when we try to suppress our thoughts—have been documented when people try to concentrate, avoid movement, or fall asleep (Harvey, 2005; Wegner, 1994).

The topic of thought suppression is highly relevant for clinical psychologists (Clark, 2005; Wegner, 1997a). For example, suppose that a client has severe depression, and the therapist encourages this person to stop thinking about depressing topics. Ironically, this advice may produce an even greater number of depressing thoughts (Wenzlaff, 2005). Thought suppression is also relevant for individuals who experience problems such as post-traumatic stress disorder, generalized anxiety disorder, and obsessive-compulsive disorder (Falsetti et al., 2005; Morrison, 2005; Purdon et al., 2005; Wells, 2005).

Blindsight

According to the first topic related to consciousness, we often have difficulty bringing some thoughts about our cognitive processes into consciousness. According to the second topic, we often have difficulty suppressing some thoughts from consciousness.

The research on a visual condition called *blindsight* reveals a third topic related to consciousness: In some cases, people can perform a cognitive task quite accurately, with no conscious awareness that their performance is accurate (Rasmussen, 2006; Weiskrantz, 2007). Blindsight refers to an unusual kind of vision without awareness. In more detail, **blindsight** is a condition in which an individual with a damaged visual cortex claims not to see an object; however, he or she can accurately report some characteristics of that object, such as its location (Kolb & Whishaw, 2009; Robertson & Treisman, 2010; Weiskrantz, 2007; Zeman, 2004).

Individuals with blindsight believe that they are truly blind in part or all of their visual field. In other words, their consciousness contains the thought, "I cannot see." In a typical study, the researchers present a stimulus in a region of the visual field that had previously corresponded to the damaged cortex. For example, a spot of light might be flashed at a location 10 degrees to the right of center. People with blindsight are then asked to point to the light. Typically, these individuals report that they did not even see the light, so they could only make a guess about its location.

Surprisingly, however, researchers discovered that the participants' performance is significantly better than chance—and often nearly perfect (Robertson & Treisman, 2010; Weiskrantz, 1997, 2007). People with blindsight can report visual attributes such as color, shape, and motion (Zeman, 2004).

Additional research has eliminated several obvious explanations. Furthermore, the individuals do have genuine, complete damage to the primary visual cortex, for example, from a stroke (Farah, 2001; Weiskrantz, 2007).

Here is one possible explanation. Most of the information that is registered on the retina travels to the visual cortex. However, a small portion of this retinal information travels to other locations in the cerebral cortex that are located outside the visual cortex (Weiskrantz, 2007; Zeman, 2004). A person with blindsight can therefore identify some characteristics of the visual stimulus—even with a damaged primary visual cortex—based on information registered in those other cortical locations.

The research on blindsight is especially relevant to the topic of consciousness. In particular, it suggests that visual information must pass through the primary visual cortex in order to be registered in consciousness. However, suppose that some part of this information "takes a detour" and bypasses the primary visual cortex. Then it is possible that the individual will not be *conscious* of the visual experience. However, he or she may indeed *perceive* this stimulus (Farah, 2001; Zeman, 2004). In Chapter 5, we will consider a related phenomenon in our discussion of implicit memory; people can often remember some information, even when they are not aware of this memory.

In summary, this discussion has demonstrated that consciousness is a challenging topic. Our consciousness is not a perfect mirror of our cognitive processes; that is, we often cannot explain how these processes operate. It is also not a blackboard; we cannot simply erase unwanted thoughts from our consciousness. Consciousness is not even an accurate reporter, as the research on blindsight demonstrates. As Wegner (2002) concludes, we usually assume that "How things seem is how they are" (p. 243). However, this convergence between our consciousness and reality is often an illusion.

◉ Section Summary: *Consciousness*

1. Consciousness, or awareness, is different from attention, because we may not be conscious of the tasks we perform when using the automatic, distributed form of attention.

2. Research suggests that people are sometimes unaware of their higher mental processes. For example, they may not be aware when their mind is wandering. Furthermore, they may solve a problem but not be conscious of how they actually reached the solution.

3. Research on thought suppression illustrates the difficulty of eliminating some thoughts from consciousness; ironically, if you try to avoid thinking about an issue, you may actually think about it more frequently. People with psychological problems may have trouble suppressing intrusive thoughts or images that are relevant to their disorder.

4. Individuals with blindsight can identify characteristics of an object, even when their visual cortex is destroyed and they have no conscious awareness of that object.

CHAPTER REVIEW QUESTIONS

1. What is divided attention? Give several examples of divided-attention tasks you have performed within the past 24 hours. What does the research show about the effects of practice on divided attention? Describe some examples of your own experience with practice and divided-attention performance.

2. What is selective attention? Give several examples of selective-attention tasks—both auditory and visual—that you have performed within the past 24 hours. In what kind of circumstances were you able to pick up information about the message you were supposed to ignore? Does this pattern match the research?

3. This chapter discussed the Stroop effect in some detail. Can you think of any academic tasks you routinely perform, where you also need to suppress the most obvious answer in order to provide the correct response? What attentional system in your cortex is especially active during these tasks?

4. Imagine that you are trying to carry on a conversation with a friend at the same time you are reading an interesting article in a magazine. Describe how the bottleneck theories and automatic versus controlled processing would explain your performance. Then describe Treisman's feature-integration theory and think of an example of this theory, based on your previous experiences.

5. Imagine that you are searching the previous pages of this chapter for the term "dichotic listening." What part of your brain is activated during this task? Now suppose that you are trying to learn the meaning of the phrase "dichotic listening." What part of your brain is activated during this task? Describe how research has clarified the biological basis of attention.

6. In what sense do saccadic eye movements represent a kind of attention process? Describe the difference between written English and written Chinese; how do readers differ in these two languages?

7. Define the word "consciousness." Based on the information in this chapter, do people have complete control over the information stored in consciousness? Does this information provide an accurate account of your cognitive processes? How is consciousness different from attention?

8. Cognitive psychology has many practical applications. Based on what you have read in this chapter, what applications can you suggest for driving and highway safety? Describe the research described in this chapter, and then list three or four ways that the material on attention can be applied to a job or a hobby that you have had.

9. Cognitive psychology can also be applied to clinical psychology. Discuss some applications of the Stroop effect and thought suppression to the area of psychological problems and their treatment.

10. Chapters 2 and 3 both examine perception. To help you synthesize part of this information, describe as completely as possible how you are able to perceive the letters in a word, using both bottom-up and top-down processing. Describe how your attention would operate in both a selective-attention situation and a divided-attention situation. How would saccadic eye movements be relevant?

KEYWORDS

attention
divided-attention task
multitask
selective-attention task
dichotic listening
shadow
cocktail party effect
working memory
Stroop effect
emotional Stroop task
phobic disorder
attentional bias
cognitive-behavioral
   approach
visual search

isolated-feature/combined-
   feature effect
feature-present/feature-absent
   effect
saccadic eye movement
fovea
fixation
perceptual span
regressions
orienting attention network
brain lesion
unilateral spatial neglect
positron emission tomography
   (PET scan)
executive attention network

bottleneck theories
feature-integration
   theory
distributed attention
focused attention
illusory conjunction
binding problem
consciousness
mindless reading
mind wandering
thought suppression
ironic effects of mental
   control
blindsight

RECOMMENDED READINGS

Dijksterhuis, A., & Aarts, H. (2010). Goals, attention and (un)consciousness. *Annual Review of Psychology, 61*, 467–490. This interesting article explores a surprising phenomenon that is beyond the scope of your textbook. Specifically, when we want to pursue a goal, we may unconsciously decide to do this before we are consciously aware we would like to do it.

Goldstein, E. B. (Ed.). (2010). *Encyclopedia of perception.* Thousand Oaks, CA: Sage. This excellent two-volume resource examines a wide variety of topics. Because the entries are in alphabetical order, the many entries under the topic of "Attention" provide a useful extension of this current chapter.

Posner, M. I., & Rothbart, M. K. (2007). Research on attention networks as a model for the integration of psychological science. *Annual Review of Psychology, 58*, 1–23. This chapter emphasizes the neuroscience research on attention, and it argues that attention plays a major role in cognitive development and in psychological disorders.

Rayner, K., Shen, D., Bai, X., & Yan, G. (Eds.). (2008). *Cognitive and cultural influences on eye movements.* Tianjin, China: Tianjin People's Publishing House. Here is a wonderful book that appropriately expands cognitive psychology beyond the traditional boundaries of English-speaking research. The book is based on papers presented at a conference in China, and the contributers also include psychologists from Spain, Germany, Finland, and Turkey.

CHAPTER 4
Working Memory

PREVIEW

At this moment, you are using your working memory to remember the beginning of this sentence until you reach the final word in this sentence. Your working memory also helps you remember visual and spatial information. In addition, working memory coordinates your cognitive activities, and it plans strategies.

We'll begin this chapter by examining some influential milestones in the history of working-memory research. The first section starts with George Miller's classic view that our immediate memory can hold approximately seven items. We'll also explore other early research and theories. For example, if you see a series of words from the same semantic category (for example, the category "fruit"), your memory will decline for the later items on this list.

The second part of this chapter explores the working-memory approach, originally proposed by Alan Baddeley. His research showed that people can perform a verbal task and a spatial task at the same time, with little loss of speed or accuracy. This research led Baddeley to propose that working memory has two separate components—the phonological loop and the visuospatial sketchpad—which have independent capacities. We'll examine these two components as well as the central executive, which coordinates your ongoing cognitive activities. We'll also consider the episodic buffer, a temporary storehouse where information from the phonological loop and the visuospatial sketchpad can be combined with information from long-term memory. The various components of working memory are correlated with academic performance. This chapter ends with an individual-differences feature, which shows that people with major depression often experience working-memory problems in several areas.

CHAPTER INTRODUCTION

Imagine yourself in this situation: It's the first day of your summer internship, and you report to the office of the staffperson who had sent you the e-mail. Then he says, "OK, I want you to meet Sharon Anderson, because you'll be working mostly with her this week. She said she would be in the meeting room." You walk down the hall, trying to make pleasant conversation. A few seconds later, you find yourself thinking, "Now what is the woman's name? How could I possibly forget it?"

Unfortunately, some memories are so fragile that they evaporate before you even begin to use them. As you'll soon see, research confirms that your memory is limited in both its duration and its capacity when you must remember new information. In fact, your memory is limited, even when the delay is less than 1 minute (Baddeley et al., 2009; Paas & Kester, 2006).

You may also become aware of these limits when you try mental arithmetic, read a complex sentence, work on a reasoning task, or solve a complicated problem (Gathercole et al., 2006; Schwartz, 2011). Demonstration 4.1 illustrates the limits of our immediate memory for two of these tasks. Try each task before reading further.

---

⑨ **Demonstration 4.1**

The Limits of Short-Term Memory

A. Try each of the following mental multiplication tasks. Be sure not to write down any of your calculations. Do them entirely "in your head."

1. $7 \times 9 =$
2. $74 \times 9 =$
3. $74 \times 96 =$

B. Now read each of the following sentences, and construct a mental image of the action that is being described. (Note: Sentence 3 is technically correct, though it is confusing.)

1. The repairman departed.
2. The librarian that the secretary met departed.
3. The salesperson that the doctor that the nurse despised met departed.

In Demonstration 4.1, you probably had no difficulty with the first mathematics task and the first reading task. The second math and reading tasks were more challenging, but you could still manage. The third tasks probably seemed beyond the limits of your immediate memory.

In the preceding chapter, we saw that attention is limited. For example, you have difficulty dividing your attention between two challenging tasks that you need to complete at the same time. Furthermore, if you are paying selective attention to one task, you typically notice very little about the unattended task. Therefore, your attention processes limit the amount of information that passes on to your memory.

This current chapter also emphasizes the limited capacity of cognitive processes. However, it focuses on *limited memory* instead of *limited attention*. Specifically, this chapter examines working memory. **Working memory** is the brief, immediate memory for the limited amount of material that you are currently processing; part of working memory also actively coordinates your ongoing mental activities. In other words, working memory lets you keep a few items active and accessible, so that you can use them for a wide variety of cognitive tasks (Baddeley, 2007; Baddeley et al., 2009; Hassin, 2005; Pickering, 2006b). In the current research, the term *working memory* is more popular than a similar but older term, **short-term memory** (Schwartz, 2011; Surprenant & Neath, 2009).

In contrast to this chapter on working memory, Chapters 5, 6, 7, and 8 will emphasize various aspects of long-term memory. **Long-term memory** has a large capacity and contains your memory for experiences and information that have accumulated throughout your lifetime. There's no limit to the amount of information in your long-term memory. In fact, as we'll see in future chapters, the more you know about a certain topic, the more new material you can learn about that topic (Schwartz, 2011).

In discussing working memory, we need to repeat a point mentioned in connection with the Atkinson-Shiffrin model of memory in Chapter 1. According to some psychologists, the research suggests that working memory and long-term memory are basically the same (e.g., Eysenck & Keane, 2010; Jonides et al., 2008; Öztekin et al., 2010). Furthermore, even those psychologists who *do* believe in two different systems may not all share the same theoretical explanations (e.g., Atkinson & Shiffrin, 1968; Baddeley et al., 2009; Cowan, 2005; Paas & Kester, 2006; Schwartz, 2011).

Here's another important point. Your performance on everyday tasks is often different from your performance on tasks in the psychology laboratory. In everyday life, for instance, your memory is often much more impressive, especially because you are working on a variety of complex tasks within a short period of time (Miyake & Shah, 1999). Your working memory needs to emphasize the kind of information that is useful to you right now, and it selects this material out of an enormous wealth of information that you possess (Brown, 2004; Cowan, 2005).

At this moment, for example, your working-memory system is rapidly inspecting your extensive knowledge of words, grammar, and concepts, so that you can understand the meaning of this sentence. However, you may soon shift to a completely different memory task. For example, you might contemplate whether you can make a decent meal from the food in your refrigerator.

So let's begin by inspecting some of the classic research on working memory. As you'll notice, this classic research emphasizes the concept of limited memory capacity (Cowan, 2005; Cowan et al., 2005). The other major topic in this chapter is a multicomponent model, originally proposed by Alan Baddeley. This model is currently the most widely accepted theoretical approach to working memory (Eysenck & Keane, 2010). As you'll see, this theory is more flexible than earlier explanations, and it also emphasizes that your memory is active, rather than passive. However, Baddeley's model states clearly that each of the major components of working memory has a limited capacity.

THE CLASSIC RESEARCH ON WORKING MEMORY (SHORT-TERM MEMORY)

We'll begin this section by discussing George Miller's perspective on the limitations of memory, as well as some early studies that attempted to measure these limitations. Then we'll consider how word meaning influences the number of items we can store in short-term memory. We'll end this first section by considering the Atkinson-Shiffrin model of memory.

George Miller's "Magical Number Seven"

In 1956, George Miller wrote a famous article titled "The Magical Number Seven, Plus or Minus Two: Some Limits on Our Capacity for Processing Information." Miller had examined previous research, and he proposed that we can hold only a limited number of items in short-term memory (as this brief memory was called at the time). Specifically, he suggested that people can remember about seven items (give or take two). In other words, we can usually remember between five and nine items.

Miller used the term *chunk* to describe the basic unit in short-term memory. A **chunk** is a memory unit that consists of several components that are strongly associated with one another (Schwartz, 2011). Miller suggested, therefore, that short-term memory holds approximately seven chunks. For example, we could remember a random sequence of about seven numbers or else a random sequence of about seven letters.

However, you can organize several adjacent numbers or letters, so that they form a single chunk. For example, suppose that your area code is 617, and all the office phone numbers at your college begin with the same digits, 346. If 617 forms one chunk and 346 forms another chunk, then the phone number 617-346-3421 really contains only six chunks (that is, $1 + 1 + 4$). The entire number may be within your memory span. Miller's (1956) article received major attention, and the magical number 7 ± 2 became a prominent concept known to almost all psychology students.*

Miller's article was unusual because it was written at a time when behaviorism was very popular. As you know, behaviorism emphasized observable external events. In contrast, Miller's article proposed that people engage in internal mental processes in order to convert stimuli into a manageable number of chunks. This article emphasized that our cognitive processes are active, consistent with Theme 1 of this textbook. We do not focus only on visible stimuli and visible responses (Baddeley, 1994). Miller's work also helped to inspire some of the classic research on short-term memory.

Other Early Research on the Capacity of Short-Term Memory

Between the late 1950s and the 1970s, researchers frequently used two methods to assess how much information our short-term memory could hold. One measure was the Brown/Peterson & Peterson technique, and the other measure was based on the serial-position effect. (Incidentally, here we will use "short-term memory"—the term used during that era—rather than the more current "working memory.") Let's consider these two methods, and then we will consider another factor called "semantic similarity," which can influence short-term-memory capacity.

---

*In more recent research, Nelson Cowan (2005) argues that the magical number is really in the range of four, when we consider the "pure capacity" of short-term memory—without the possibility of chunking.

---

⑨ Demonstration 4.2

A Modified Version of the Brown/Peterson & Peterson Technique

Take out six index cards. On one side of each card, write one of the following groups of three words, one underneath another. On the back of the card, write the three-digit number. Set the cards aside for a few minutes and practice counting backwards by threes from the number 792.

Next, show yourself the first card, with the side containing the words toward you, for about 2 seconds. Then immediately turn over the card and count backward by threes from the three-digit number shown. Go as fast as possible for 20 seconds. (Use a watch with a second hand to keep track of the time.) Then write down as many of the three words as you can remember. Continue this process with the remaining five cards.

1.	appeal		4.	flower	
	simple	687		classic	573
	burden			predict	
2.	sober		5.	silken	
	persuade	254		idle	433
	content			approve	
3.	descend		6.	begin	
	neglect	869		pillow	376
	elsewhere			carton	

The Brown/Peterson & Peterson Technique. Demonstration 4.2 shows a modified version of the Brown/Peterson & Peterson technique, a method that provided much of the original information about short-term memory. John Brown (1958, 2004), a British psychologist, and Lloyd Peterson and Margaret Peterson (1959), two U.S. psychologists, independently demonstrated that material held in memory for less than one minute is frequently forgotten. This technique therefore bears the names of all three researchers. In the standard setup, the **Brown/Peterson & Peterson technique** presented some items that students were instructed to remember; then the students performed a distracting task; and finally they were asked to recall the original items.

Peterson and Peterson (1959), for example, asked the research participants to study three unrelated letters of the alphabet, such as CHJ. Then the participants saw a three-digit number, and they counted backward by threes from this number for a short period. This counting activity prevented them from rehearsing the three-letter sequence during the delay. (**Rehearsal** means repeating the items silently.) Finally, the participants tried to recall the letters they had originally seen. On the first few trials,

FIGURE 4.1

Typical Results for the Percentage Recalled with the Brown/Peterson & Peterson Technique, after Numerous Previous Trials.

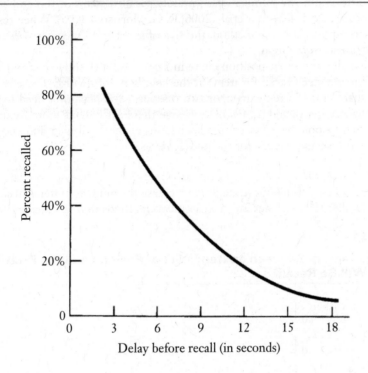

people recalled most of the letters. However, after several trials, the previous letters produced interference, and recall was poor. After a mere 5-second delay—as you can see from Figure 4.1—people forgot approximately half of the letters they had seen.

The early research using the Brown/Peterson & Peterson technique showed that our memory is fragile for material stored for just a few seconds. This technique also inspired hundreds of studies on short-term memory, and it played an important role in increasing the support for the cognitive approach (Bower, 2000; Kintsch et al., 1999).

The Recency Effect. Researchers have also used the serial-position effect to examine short-term memory. The term **serial-position effect** refers to the U-shaped relationship between a word's position in a list and its probability of recall. Figure 4.2 shows a classic illustration of the serial-position effect in research (Rundus, 1971). The U-shaped curve is very common, and it continues to be found in more recent research (e.g., Schwartz, 2011; Thompson & Madigan, 2005; Ward et al., 2005).

As you can see, the curve shows a strong **recency effect**, with better recall for items at the end of the list. Many researchers have argued that this relatively accurate memory for the final words in a list means that these items were still in short-term memory at the time of recall. In addition, the items did not move onward to a more permanent form of memory. Thus, one way of measuring the size of short-term memory is to count the number of accurately recalled items at the end of the list (Davelaar et al., 2005, Davelaar et al., 2006; R. G. Morrison, 2005). When researchers use this serial-position curve method, the size of short-term memory is estimated to be about three to seven items.

Incidentally, the serial-position curve in Figure 4.2 also shows a strong **primacy effect**, with enhanced recall for items at the beginning of the list. These early items are presumably easy to remember for two reasons: (1) They don't need to compete with any earlier items; and (2) People rehearse these early items more frequently. In general, then, people have better recall for items at the beginning and end of a list. They have less accurate recall for the middle items.

Semantic Similarity of the Items in Short-Term Memory. So far, we have considered how the chunking strategy can increase the number of items in short-term memory (Miller, 1956). Then we discussed two methods that researchers can use to

FIGURE 4.2

The Relationship Between an Item's Serial Position and the Probability That It Will Be Recalled.

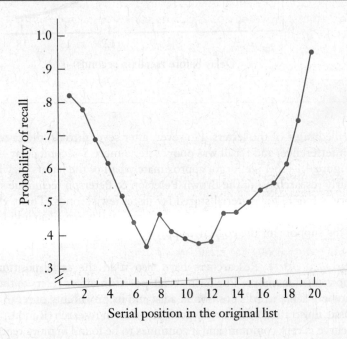

Source: Rundus, D. (1971). Analysis of rehearsal processes in free recall. *Journal of Experimental Psychology, 89,* 63–77.

measure the capacity of short-term memory. One additional factor that can influence short-term memory is **semantics**, or the meaning of words and sentences.

Consider a classic study by Wickens and his colleagues (1976). Their technique uses an important concept from memory research called proactive interference. **Proactive interference (PI)** means that people have trouble learning new material because previously learned material keeps interfering with their new learning.

Consider this example of proactive interference. Suppose you had previously learned three items—XCJ, HBR, and TSV—in a Brown/Peterson & Peterson test of memory. You will then have trouble remembering a fourth item, KRN, because the three previous items keep interfering. However, if the experimenter shifts the category of the fourth item from letters to, say, simple geometric shapes, your memory will improve. You will experience a **release from proactive interference**. In fact, your performance on that new category of items will be almost as high as it had been on the first item, XCJ.

Many experiments have demonstrated release from PI when the category of items is shifted, for example, from letters to numbers. However, Wickens and his coauthors (1976) demonstrated that release from PI could also be obtained when the researchers shifted the *semantic category* of the items. Their study employed five semantic categories, which you can see in Figure 4.3. Wickens and his colleagues initially gave people three trials on the Brown/Peterson & Peterson test. In other words, on each trial they saw a list of three words, followed by a three-digit number. After counting backward from this number for 18 seconds, they tried to recall the three words.

On each trial in this study, participants saw three related words. For example, participants in the Occupations condition might begin with "lawyer, firefighter, teacher" on Trial 1. On Trials 2 and 3, the people in this condition saw lists of additional occupations. Then on Trial 4, they saw a list of three fruits—such as "orange, cherry, pineapple"—as did the people in the other four conditions.

Look through the five conditions shown at the right side of Figure 4.3. Wouldn't you expect the buildup of proactive interference on Trial 4 to be the greatest for those in the fruits (control) condition? After all, people's short-term memory should be filled with the names of other fruits that would interfere with the three new fruits.

How should the people in the other four conditions perform? If meaning really is important in short-term memory, then their recall in these conditions should depend upon the semantic similarity between these items and fruit. For example, people who had seen vegetables on Trials 1 through 3 should do rather poorly on the fruit items, because vegetables and fruit are similar—they are edible and they are produced by plants. People who had seen either flowers or meats should do somewhat better, because flowers and meats each share only one attribute with fruits. However, people who had seen occupations should do the best of all, because occupations are not edible and they are not produced by plants.

Figure 4.3 is an example of the kind of results that every researcher hopes to find. Note that the results match the predictions perfectly. In general, then, semantic factors influence the number of items that we can store in working memory. Specifically, words that we have previously stored can interfere with the recall of new words that are similar in meaning. Furthermore, the degree of semantic similarity is related to the amount of interference.

FIGURE 4.3

Release from Proactive Interference, as a Function of Semantic Similarity. On Trials 1, 2, and 3, each group saw words belonging to the specified category (e.g., occupations). On Trial 4, everyone saw the same list of three fruits.

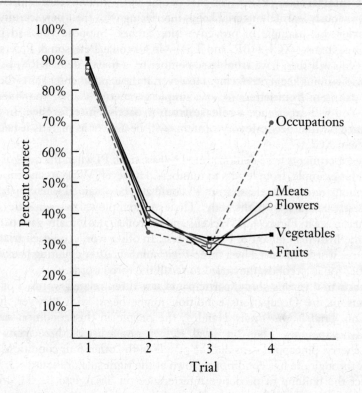

Source: Wickens, D. D., Dalezman, R. E., & Eggemeier, F. T. (1976). Multiple encoding of word attributes in memory. *Memory & Cognition, 4,* 307–310.

The importance of semantic factors in working memory has also been confirmed by other researchers (Cain, 2006; Potter, 1999; Walker & Hulme, 1999). We know, then, that the number of items stored in working memory depends on both chunking strategies and word meaning. Incidentally, for many years, psychologists believed that an additional important factor was the amount of time required to pronounce the words. However, more recent studies have shown that other variables can explain the influence of pronunciation time on recall (e.g., Jalbert et al., 2011; Lovatt et al., 2002).

Atkinson and Shiffrin's Model

During the 1950s and 1960s, many psychologists conducted research on topics related to short-term memory. During that same era, Richard Atkinson and Richard Shiffrin (1968) proposed the classic information-processing model that we discussed in Chapter 1. Turn back to this model, shown in Figure 1.1 on page 10. As you can see, short-term memory (as it was then called) is distinctly separate from long-term memory in this diagram. Atkinson and Shiffrin argued that the items in short-term memory are fragile, and they could be lost within about 30 seconds unless they are repeated.

In addition, Atkinson and Shiffrin proposed **control processes**, which are intentional strategies—such as rehearsal—that people may use to improve their memory (Hassin, 2005; Raaijmakers & Shiffrin, 2002). The original form of this model focused on the role of short-term memory in learning and memory. This model did not explore how short-term memory plays an important role when we perform other cognitive tasks (Roediger et al., 2002).

The Atkinson-Shiffrin model contributed to the growing appeal of cognitive psychology. For instance, researchers conducted numerous studies to determine whether short-term memory really is distinctly different from long-term memory. This is a question that still does not have a clear-cut answer. Let's summarize the discussion of short-term memory, and then we will consider the working-memory approach in the next section of this chapter.

◎ Section Summary: *The Classic Research on Working Memory (Short-Term Memory)*

1. Working memory (originally called short-term memory) is the very brief, immediate memory for material that we are currently processing.

2. In 1956, George Miller proposed that we can hold about seven chunks of information in short-term memory.

3. The Brown/Peterson & Peterson technique, which prevents rehearsal, shows that people have only limited recall for items after a brief delay. The recency effect in a serial-position curve is also used in measuring the limited capacity of short-term memory.

4. Word meaning can also influence the number of items we store in short-term memory; when the semantic category changes between adjacent trials, our recall for the new material increases.

5. According to the Atkinson-Shiffrin (1968) model, the items that we store in short-term memory can be lost within about 30 seconds unless they are repeated; people can use rehearsal and other control processes to improve their short-term memory.

THE WORKING-MEMORY APPROACH

For several years, researchers enthusiastically explored the characteristics of short-term memory. However, no one developed a comprehensive theory for this brief kind of memory until Alan Baddeley and his colleagues proposed the working-memory approach. Now that you are familiar with several factors that influence the capacity of working memory, we can explore this approach in some detail.

During the early 1970s, Alan Baddeley and Graham Hitch were examining the wealth of research on short-term memory. They soon realized that researchers had ignored one very important question: What does short-term memory actually accomplish for our cognitive processes? Eventually, they agreed that its major function is to hold several interrelated bits of information in our mind, all at the same time, so that a person can work with this information and then use it appropriately (Baddeley et al., 2009; Baddeley & Hitch, 1974). In other words, working memory doesn't simply *store* information. Consistent with its name, it actively *works* with that information (Levin et al., 2010; Schmeichel & Hofmann, 2011).

For example, if you are trying to comprehend the sentence that you are reading right now, you need to keep the beginning words in mind until you know how the sentence is going to end. (Think about it: Did you in fact keep those initial words in your memory until you reached the word *end*?) As you'll see in this section of Chapter 4, people also use this kind of working memory for a wide range of cognitive tasks, such as language comprehension, mental arithmetic, reasoning, and problem solving (Baddeley & Hitch, 1974; Logie, 2011).

According to the **working-memory approach** proposed by Baddeley, our immediate memory is a multipart system that temporarily holds and manipulates information while we perform cognitive tasks. Baddeley's model of working memory is different from earlier models because he proposed multiple components for our working memory (Schwartz, 2011). Figure 4.4 illustrates the current design of the model,

FIGURE 4.4

The Working-Memory Approach: A Simplified Version of Alan Baddeley's (2000b) Model of Working Memory.

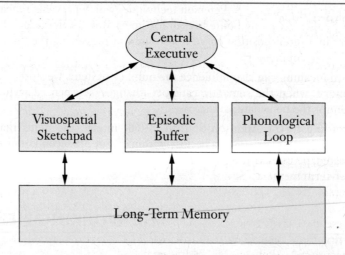

Note: This diagram shows the phonological loop, the visuospatial sketchpad, the central executive, and the episodic buffer—as well as their interactions with long-term memory.

Source: Baddeley, A. D. (2000b). The episodic buffer: A new component of working memory? *Trends in Cognitive Sciences, 4,* 417–423.

featuring the phonological loop, the visuospatial sketchpad, the central executive, and the episodic buffer, which was added more recently (Baddeley, 2000a, 2000b, 2001; Baddeley et al., 2009).

Baddeley's approach emphasizes that working memory is not simply a passive storehouse with a number of shelves to hold partially processed information until it moves on to another location (presumably long-term memory). Instead, Baddeley emphasizes that we manipulate information. As a result, your working memory is more like a workbench where material is constantly being handled, combined, and transformed. Clearly, Baddeley's model is consistent with Theme 1 of this textbook.

Furthermore, this "workbench" holds both new material and old material that you have retrieved from storage (long-term memory). In Figure 4.4, notice that three components of working memory have direct connections with long-term memory.

Let's begin our analysis of the research by first considering why Baddeley felt compelled to conclude that working memory includes several components; it is not simply one box, as the Atkinson-Shiffrin model had suggested. Next we'll consider each of the four components. The first component—the phonological loop—will be considered in depth, and then we'll look at the three other components: the visuospatial sketchpad, the central executive, and the episodic buffer. We'll next consider how the components of working memory are correlated with academic performance. Then the individual-differences feature will focus on the relationship between psychological depression and people's performance on several different kinds of working-memory tasks.

Evidence for Components with Independent Capacities

An important study by Baddeley and Hitch (1974) provided convincing evidence that working memory is not unitary. These researchers presented a string of random numbers to participants, who rehearsed the numbers in order. The string of numbers varied in length from zero to eight items. In other words, the longer list approached the upper limit of short-term memory, according to Miller's (1956) 7 ± 2 proposal.

At the same time, the participants also performed a spatial reasoning task. This reasoning task required them to judge whether certain statements about letter order were correct or incorrect. For example, suppose that the participants see the two letters BA. If they also see the statement, "A follows B," they should respond by pressing a "yes" button. In contrast, suppose that they see the two letters BA, accompanied by the statement, "B follows A." In this case, the participants should press the "no" button.

Imagine yourself performing this task. Wouldn't you think you would take much longer and make many more errors on the reasoning task if you had to keep rehearsing eight numerals, instead of only one? To the surprise of everyone—including the participants in the study—people performed remarkably quickly and accurately on both of these two simultaneous tasks. For example, Baddeley and Hitch (1974) discovered that these participants required less than a second longer on the reasoning task when instructed to rehearse all eight numerals, in contrast to a task that required no rehearsal. Even more impressive, the error rate remained at about 5%, no matter how many numerals the participants rehearsed (Baddeley, 2012; Baddeley et al., 2009).

The data from Baddeley and Hitch's (1974) study clearly contradicted the view that our temporary storage has only about seven slots, as Miller (1956) had proposed. Specifically, this study suggested that people can indeed perform two tasks simultaneously—for instance, one task that requires verbal rehearsal and another task that requires visual or spatial judgments. Incidentally, some other studies actually do suggest that verbal and visual tasks can interfere with each other (Morey & Cowan, 2004, 2005). However, most memory theorists believe that working memory seems to have several components, which can operate somewhat independently of each other (Baddeley et al., 2009; Davelaar et al., 2005; Miyake & Shah, 1999).

As we've already described, Baddeley and his colleagues proposed four components for working memory: a phonological loop, a visuospatial sketchpad, a central executive, and—more recently—an integrative component that Baddeley calls an "episodic buffer" (Baddeley, 2000a, 2000b, 2001, 2006; Baddeley et al., 2009; Gathercole & Baddeley, 1993; Logie, 1995). We'll examine the phonological loop, and then we'll consider the other three components.

IN DEPTH

Phonological Loop

According to the working-memory model, the **phonological loop** can process a limited number of sounds for a short period of time. The phonological loop processes language and other sounds that you hear, as well as the sounds that you make. It is also active during **subvocalization**, for example, when you silently pronounce the words that you are reading. Let's consider the phonological loop in depth, especially because there is more research on this topic than on any other component of working memory (Baddeley, 2012; Baddeley et al., 2009).

Research on Acoustic Confusions. We emphasized earlier that the phonological loop stores information in terms of sounds. Therefore, we would expect to find that people's memory errors can often be traced to **acoustic confusions**; that is, people are likely to confuse similar-sounding stimuli (Baddeley, 2003, 2012; Wickelgren, 1965).

For example, a classic study by Conrad and Hull (1964) showed participants two kinds of lists of letters of the English alphabet. Some lists featured letters that had similar-sounding names, such as the sequence C, T, D, G, V, B. Other lists featured letters with different-sounding names, such as the sequence C, W, Q, K, R, and X. The participants correctly recalled more letters from the second list, where the sounds were different.

Notice an important point: In studies such as Conrad and Hull's, the letters were presented visually. However, people must have been "translating" these visual stimuli into a format based on the acoustic properties of the letters. Other related research examined recall for words. When the words sounded different from one another, people recalled more items than when the words sounded similar (Kintsch & Buschke, 1969).

A study by Dylan Jones and his colleagues (2004) proposes a different explanation for these acoustic confusions. These researchers suggest that people confuse acoustically similar sounds with one another when they are *rehearsing* the items, not when these items are simply stored in the phonological loop. Suppose, for example, that you want to remember the sequence of letters mentioned above: C, T, D, G, V, B. Jones and his colleagues suggest that people try to pronounce these letters in order to repeat them silently to themselves. You may stumble and silently pronounce the wrong sound, just as you might stumble on a rhyming tongue twister such as "She sells seashells." We'll examine this kind of speech-production error in more detail in Chapter 10.

Other Uses for the Phonological Loop. The phonological loop plays a crucial role in our daily lives, beyond its obvious role in working memory (Baddeley, 2006; R. G. Morrison, 2005; Schwartz, 2011). For example, we use the phonological loop on simple counting tasks. Try counting the number of words in the previous sentence, for example. Can you hear your "inner voice" saying the numbers silently? Now try counting the number of words in that same sentence, but rapidly say the word "the" subvocally while you are counting. When our phonological loop is preoccupied with saying "the," we can't even perform a simple counting task!

Theme 4 of this textbook states that our cognitive processes are interrelated with one another; they do not operate in isolation. Let's consider some representative examples of how the phonological loop plays a central role in other cognitive processes:

Chapter 5: Working memory is the "gateway" to long-term memory. For example, think about the wide variety of verbal information that passed through your phonological loop before reaching your long-term memory.

Chapter 6: You use your phonological loop during **self-instruction** when you silently remind yourself about something you need to do in the future or how to use some complicated equipment. In fact, talking to yourself—in moderation!—is a useful cognitive strategy (Gathercole et al., 2006).

Chapter 9: You use your phonological loop when you learn new words in your first language (Baddeley et al., 2009; de Jong, 2006; Knott & Marslen-Wilson, 2001). You also use it when you are reading. Be honest: The first time you see a long word, such as *phonological*, can you read that word without silently pronouncing it?

Chapter 10: The phonological loop plays an important role when you produce language, for example, when you tell a friend about a trip you made last summer (Acheson & MacDonald, 2009) and also when you are learning a new language (Masoura & Gathercole, 2005).

Chapter 11: Mathematical calculations and problem-solving tasks require the phonological loop, so that you can keep track of numbers and other information (Bull & Espy, 2006).

Neuroscience Research on the Phonological Loop. **Researchers** have sometimes used neuroscience techniques to explore the phonological loop. In general, these studies have shown that phonological-loop tasks activate part of the frontal lobe and part of the temporal lobe in the left hemisphere of the brain (Baddeley, 2006; Thompson & Madigan, 2005). This finding makes sense. Compared to the right hemisphere of the brain, the left hemisphere is more likely to process information related to language. (We will explore this topic in more detail in Chapter 9.)

Let's consider a neuroscience study by Leonor Romero Lauro and her colleagues (2010), which provides more specific details. **Transcranial Magnetic Stimulation (TMS)** is a neuroscience technique that uses a magnetic field to briefly stimulate a specific location on the cortex. (No surgery or other invasive procedures are involved.) This stimulation interferes—very briefly—with information processing, but it does not harm the brain. Romero Lauro and her colleagues administered TMS for two parts of the brain, so that they could confirm how the phonological loop processes language.

Figure 2.1, on page 38, shows a diagram of the cortex. One location that Romero Lauro and her colleagues studied was in the left frontal lobe, the part of the brain that might be activated when you *rehearse* verbal material. The other location they studied was in the left parietal lobe, the part of the brain that might be activated when you *store* auditory information. These researchers also included a sham procedure, which resembled each TMS procedure, but without any actual stimulation.

Immediately after either the TMS stimulation or the sham procedure, the participants saw a sentence, accompanied by a sketch. The sentence either matched or did not match the sketch.

For example, a short, simple sentence might be, "The boy is giving the cat to the woman." An *incorrect* match would show the woman giving the cat to the boy. As it happened, this task was so simple that the participants almost always provided the right answer, even with the TMS procedure. In other words, neither the left frontal lobe nor the left parietal lobe is normally responsible for processing short, simple sentences.

A second group of sentences were long, but they had simple syntax. A long but simple sentence might be, "The girl is eating cake and the boy is drinking milk." Participants in this condition made the most errors if the TMS had been administered to the left parietal lobe. Apparently, the stimulation in this area reduced the participants' ability to store all the words in this long sentence, and so they made errors. In other words, it appears that the left parietal lobe is normally responsible for processing long but simple sentences.

A third group of sentences were long, and they also had complex grammar. A long, complex sentence might be, "The cat that the boy is watching is drinking milk." Participants in this condition made many errors if the TMS had been administered to *either* the left parietal lobe or the left frontal lobe. Apparently, the *left frontal lobe* could not effectively rehearse these grammatically complex syntax. Furthermore, the *left parietal lobe* could not effectively store these long sentences immediately following TMS. In other words, both the left frontal lobe and the left parietal lobe are normally responsible for rehearsing and storing complex, lengthy sentences.

Notice, then, that the research on the phonological loop suggests that our working memory is much more sophisticated than just a storehouse of 7 ± 2 items. Even if we focus just on the phonological loop, the findings are complex. Let's now consider a second important component of the working-memory approach, called "the visuospatial sketchpad."

Visuospatial Sketchpad

A second component of Baddeley's model of working memory is the **visuospatial sketchpad**, which processes both visual and spatial information. This kind of working memory allows you to look at a complex scene and gather visual information about objects and landmarks. It also allows you to navigate from one location to another (Logie, 2011; Logie & Della Sala, 2005; Vandierendonck & Szmalec, 2011a). Incidentally, the visuospatial sketchpad has been known by a variety of different names, such as *visuospatial working memory*, and *short-term visual memory*. You may encounter these alternate terms in other discussions of working memory.

The visuospatial sketchpad allows you to store a coherent picture of both the visual appearance of the objects and their relative positions in a scene (Hollingworth, 2004, 2006a; Logie, 2011; Vandierendonck & Szmalec, 2011b). The visuospatial sketchpad also stores visual information that you encode from a verbal description (Baddeley, 2006; Pickering, 2006a). For example, when a friend tells a story, you may find yourself visualizing the scene.

As you begin reading about the visuospatial sketchpad, keep in mind the classic research by Baddeley and Hitch (1974), which we discussed earlier. People can work simultaneously on one phonological task (rehearsing an 8-digit number) and one visuospatial task (making judgments about the spatial location of the letters A and B)—without much alteration in their performance.

Earlier, we saw that the phonological loop has a limited capacity. The visuospatial sketchpad also has a limited capacity (Alvarez & Cavanaugh, 2004; Baddeley, 2006; Hollingworth, 2004). I remember tutoring a high school student in geometry. When working on her own, she often tried to solve her geometry problems on a small scrap of paper. As you might imagine, the limited space caused her to make many errors. Similarly, when too many items enter your visuospatial sketchpad, you cannot represent them accurately enough to recover them successfully.

Alan Baddeley describes a personal experience that made him appreciate how one visuospatial task can interfere with another (Baddeley, 2006; Baddeley et al., 2009). As a British citizen, he became very intrigued with U.S. football while spending a year in the United States. On one occasion, he decided to listen to a football game while driving along a California freeway. In order to understand the game, he tried to form clear, detailed images of the scene and the action. While creating these images, however, he discovered that his car began drifting out of its lane!

Apparently, Baddeley found it impossible to perform one task requiring a mental image—with both visual and spatial components—at the same time that he performed a visuospatial task that required him to keep his car within specified boundaries. In fact, Baddeley found that he actually had to switch the radio to music in order to drive safely.

Let's consider some research on visual coding, as well as some other applications of the visuospatial sketchpad. We'll also briefly consider some relevant brain-imaging research.

Research on the Visuospatial Sketchpad. Baddeley's dual-task experience during driving inspired him to conduct some laboratory studies. This research confirmed that people have trouble performing two visuospatial tasks at the same time (Baddeley, 1999, 2006; Baddeley et al., 1973).

In general, however, psychologists have conducted less research on the visuospatial sketchpad than on the phonological loop (Baddeley et al., 2009). One problem is that we do not have a standardized set of visual stimuli that would be comparable to the words that we process using the phonological loop.

Another problem is that research participants (at least in Western cultures) tend to provide names for stimuli presented in a visual form. Beginning at about age 8, people look at a shape and provide a name, such as "It's a circle inside a square" (Pickering, 2006a). If you use a verbal coding for this form, you'll probably use your phonological loop for further processing, rather than your visuospatial sketchpad.

How can researchers encourage participants to use the visuospatial sketchpad, instead of the phonological loop? Maria Brandimonte and her colleagues (1992) instructed participants to repeat an irrelevant syllable ("la-la-la") while looking at a complex visual stimulus. When the phonological loop was occupied with this repetition task, the participants usually did not provide names for the stimuli. Instead, they were more likely to use visuospatial coding.

Other Uses for the Visuospatial Sketchpad. Students in psychology and other social sciences probably use their phonological loop more often than their visuospatial sketchpad. In contrast, students in disciplines such as engineering, art, and architecture frequently use visual coding and visuospatial sketchpad in their academic studies.

However, we all use our visuospatial sketchpad in everyday life. For example, look at one specific object that is within your reach. Now close your eyes and try to touch this object. Your visuospatial sketchpad presumably allowed you to retain a brief image of that scene while your eyes were closed (Logie, 2003). In addition, your visuospatial sketchpad is activated when you try to find your way from one location to another or when you track a moving object (Coluccia, 2008; Logie, 2003; Wood, 2011). This kind of working memory is also useful in many leisure activities, such as videogames, jigsaw puzzles, and games involving a maze (Pickering, 2006a).

We will examine other uses for visual and spatial memory in Chapter 7. In particular, that chapter explores the mental manipulations we perform on visuospatial information.

Neuroscience Research on the Visuospatial Sketchpad. In general, the neuroscience research suggests that visual and spatial tasks typically activate several regions in the right hemisphere of the cortex, rather than the left hemisphere (Gazzaniga et al., 2009; Logie, 2003; Thompson & Madigan, 2005). Furthermore, working-memory tasks with a strong visual component typically activate the occipital region, a part of the brain that is responsible for visual perception (Baddeley, 2001). (Refer again to Figure 2.1, p. 38.) However, the specific location of brain activity depends on task difficulty and other characteristics of the task (Logie & Della Sala, 2005).

In addition, various regions of the frontal cortex are active when people work on visual and spatial tasks (Logie & Della Sala, 2005; E. E. Smith, 2000). Research on spatial working memory also suggests that people mentally rehearse this material by shifting their selective attention from one location to another in their mental image (Awh et al., 1999). As a result, this kind of mental rehearsal typically activates areas in the frontal and parietal lobes (Olesen et al., 2004; Posner & Rothbart, 2007b). These are the same areas of the cortex that are associated with attention, as we discussed in Chapter 3.

Central Executive

According to the working-memory model, the **central executive** integrates information from the phonological loop, the visuospatial sketchpad, the episodic buffer, and long-term memory. The central executive also plays a major role in focusing attention, selecting strategies, transforming information, and coordinating behavior (Baddeley et al., 2009; Reuter-Lorenz & Jonides, 2007). In addition, Baddeley (2012) argues that the central executive has a wide variety of different functions, such as focusing attention and switching between tasks. The central executive is therefore extremely important and complex. However, it is also the least understood component of working memory (Baddeley, 2006; Bull & Espy, 2006).

In addition, the central executive is responsible for suppressing irrelevant information (Alloway, 2011; Baddeley, 2006, 2012; Hasher et al., 2007). In your everyday activities, your central executive helps you decide what to do next. It also helps you decide what *not* to do, so that you don't become sidetracked from your primary goal.

Characteristics of the Central Executive. **Most** researchers emphasize that the central executive plans and coordinates, but it does not store information (Baddeley, 2000b, 2006; Logie, 2003). As you know, both the phonological loop and the visuospatial sketchpad have specialized storage systems.

Compared to the two systems we've discussed, the central executive is more difficult to study using controlled research techniques. However, the central executive definitely plays a critical role in the overall functions of working memory. Baddeley (1986) provides a literary analogy. Suppose that we were to concentrate on, say, the phonological loop in our analysis of working memory. Then the situation would resemble a critical analysis of Shakespeare's play *Hamlet* that focuses on Polonius—certainly a minor character—and completely ignores the Prince of Denmark!

Baddeley (1999, 2006) proposes that the central executive works like an executive supervisor in an organization. According to this metaphor, an executive decides which topics deserve attention and which should be ignored. An executive also selects strategies and decides how to tackle a problem. Similarly, your own brain's central executive plays an important role when you try to solve mathematical problems (Bull & Espy, 2006). We will examine this issue of strategy selection more completely in Chapter 6 (metacognition) and in Chapter 11 (problem solving).

A good executive also knows not to continue using an ineffective strategy (Baddeley, 2001). Furthermore, like any executive in an organization, the central executive has a limited ability to perform simultaneous tasks. Our cognitive executive cannot make numerous decisions at the same time, and it cannot work effectively on two challenging projects at the same time. Be sure to try Demonstration 4.3, which examines the familiar activity of daydreaming.

---

⑨ Demonstration 4.3

A Task That Requires Central-Executive Resources

Your assignment for this demonstration is to generate a sequence of random numbers. In particular, make sure that your list contains a roughly equal proportion of the numbers 1 through 10. Also, be sure that your list does not show any systematic repetition in the sequence. For example, the number 4 should be followed equally often by each of the numbers 1 through 10.

As quickly as you can, write a series of digits on a piece of paper (at the rate of approximately one digit per second). Keep performing this task for about 5 minutes. If you find yourself daydreaming, check back at the numbers you have generated. During these periods, you'll probably find that your numbers do *not* form a truly random sequence.

The Central Executive and Daydreaming. Let's look at a representative study about the central executive. At this very moment, you may be engaged in the slightly embarrassing activity we typically call "daydreaming." For example, right now you might be thinking about a TV show you saw last night or what you will be doing next weekend, rather than the words that your sensory receptors are currently registering.

Interestingly, daydreaming requires the active participation of your central executive. Consider part of a study by Teasdale and his colleagues (1995), which you tried in Demonstration 4.3. These researchers selected a task that would require a major part of your central executive's limited resources. This task, called the *random-number generation task*, requires the research participants to supply one digit every second, creating the random sequence described in this demonstration. As the demonstration illustrates, the task is challenging. Approximately every 2 minutes, the researcher interrupted the task and asked the participants to write down any thoughts.

The researchers then inspected the trials on which the participants reported that they had been thinking about the numbers. On these trials, the results showed that the participants had been able to successfully generate a random sequence of numbers. In contrast, when the participants reported daydreaming, their number sequences were far from random. Apparently, their daydreaming occupied such a large portion of the resources of the central executive that they could not create a genuinely random sequence of numbers.

Neuroscience Research on the Central Executive. In general, researchers know less about the biological characteristics of the central executive than they know about the phonological loop or the visuospatial sketchpad. However, neuroscientists have gathered data from people with frontal-lobe lesions, as well as from neuroimaging research.

This neuroscience research clearly shows that the frontal region of the cortex is the most active portion of the brain when people work on a wide variety of central-executive tasks (Baddeley, 2006; Derakshan & Eysenck, 2010b; Jonides et al., 2008). Furthermore, both sides of the frontal region play a role in most central-executive activities (Kolb & Whishaw, 2009).

For example, suppose that you are writing a paper for your cognitive psychology course. While you are working on the paper, your central executive may inhibit you from paying attention to some research articles that would distract you from your specific topic. The central executive is also active when you plan the order of topics in your outline. In addition, it guides you as you make decisions about your time frame for writing the paper.

Each of those central-executive tasks seems qualitatively different, though all are clearly challenging. Perhaps we'll have more definitive answers about the biological correlates of the central executive once we have a more clear-cut classification of the kinds of tasks that the central executive performs.

Episodic Buffer

Approximately 25 years after Alan Baddeley proposed his original model of working memory, he added a fourth component of working memory called the *episodic buffer* (Baddeley, 2000a, 2000b, 2006, 2012; Baddeley et al., 2009; Baddeley et al., 2011). You can locate this component in Figure 4.4 on page 108. The **episodic buffer** serves as a temporary storehouse that can hold and combine information from your phonological loop, your visuospatial sketchpad, and long-term memory. (As you'll see in Chapter 5, the term "episodic" refers to your memories about events that happened to you; these memories describe episodes in your life.)

Why did Baddeley feel compelled to propose this episodic buffer? As Baddeley explains, his original theory had proposed that the central executive plans and coordinates various cognitive activities (Baddeley, 2006; Baddeley et al., 2009). However, the theory had also stated that the central executive did not actually *store* any information. Baddeley therefore proposed the episodic buffer as the component of working memory where auditory, visual, and spatial information could all be combined with the information from long-term memory. This arrangement helps to solve the theoretical problem of how working memory integrates information from different modalities (Baddeley et al., 2009, Baddeley et al., 2011; Ketelsen & Welsh, 2010; R. G. Morrison, 2005).

This episodic buffer actively manipulates information so that you can interpret an earlier experience, solve new problems, and plan future activities. For instance, suppose that you are thinking about an unfortunate experience that occurred yesterday, when you unintentionally said something rude to a friend. You might review this event and try to figure out whether your friend seemed offended. For example, you may attempt to recall this person's facial expression, as well as her or his verbal response. Naturally, you'll also need to access some information from your long-term memory about your friend's customary behavior.

The episodic buffer also allows you to bind together some concepts that had not been previously connected (Baddeley et al., 2009). For instance, you might suddenly recall a time when a person had made a rude comment to you. You can then link your friend's reaction with your own personal experiences. The episodic buffer also binds words into meaningful "chunks" or phrases, which you can remember much more accurately than words in random order (Baddeley et al., 2011).

Because the episodic buffer is relatively new, very few journal articles examine the neuroscience research (e.g., Baddeley et al., 2010). However, Baddeley and his colleagues emphasize that the episodic buffer has a limited capacity—just as the capacities of the phonological loop and the visuospatial sketchpad are limited (Baddeley, 2000a, 2006; Baddeley et al., 2011).

Furthermore, this episodic buffer is just a temporary memory system, unlike the relatively permanent long-term memory system. This episodic buffer allows us to create a richer, more complex representation of an event. This complex representation can then be stored in our long-term memory.

We have now examined four components of the working-memory model, as proposed by Alan Baddeley and his colleagues. This model is widely supported. However, other psychologists have devised somewhat different theories about working memory (e.g., Conway et al., 2007; Cowan, 2005, 2010; Ketelsen & Welsh, 2010; Logie & van der Meulen, 2009). Still, all of these theories consistently argue that working memory is complex, flexible, and strategic.

The current perspective on working memory is certainly different from the view held during the 1950s and 1960s that short-term memory is relatively rigid and had a fixed capacity. However, it's interesting that a recent article by Baddeley and his coauthors (2011) specifically used the term "chunk"—the very same term that George Miller (1956) used in his classic article that helped to inspire the cognitive approach to memory.

Working Memory and Academic Performance

During the last decade, psychologists have begun to focus on individual differences in working memory. Their research shows that performance on some working-memory tasks is significantly correlated with academic achievement. Let's consider several of these areas:

1. Scores on working-memory tasks are correlated with overall intelligence and grades in school (Baddeley et al., 2009; Cowan et al., 2007; Levin et al., 2010; Oberauer et al., 2007).

2. Scores on tests of working memory—especially the phonological loop—are usually correlated with reading ability (Bayliss et al., 2005; Swanson, 2005).

3. Scores on central-executive tasks are correlated with verbal fluency, reading comprehension, reasoning ability, and note-taking skills (Jarrold & Bayliss, 2007; Levin et al., 2010; Oberauer et al., 2007).

4. **Attention-Deficit/Hyperactivity Disorder (ADHD)** is a psychological disorder characterized by inattention, hyperactivity, and impulsivity (American Psychiatric Association, 2000). People with ADHD often have more difficulty than others on central-executive tasks, especially when they must inhibit a response, plan a project, or work on two tasks at the same time (Alloway, 2011; Baddeley et al., 2009; Barkley, 2006, 2010; Martinussen et al., 2005; Willcutt et al., 2005).

Individual Differences: Major Depression and Working Memory

For this chapter's individual-differences feature, we will focus on the relationship between psychological depression and working memory. An individual who experiences **major depression** feels sad, discouraged, and hopeless; he or she typically reports feeling fatigued, with little interest in leisure activities (American Psychiatric Association, 2000). Between 10% and 15% of U.S. adults will experience major depression at some point during their lifetime (American Psychiatric Association, 2000). Because major depression is relatively common, it's important to consider how this disorder is related to working memory.

Let's look at a representative study by Gary Christopher and John MacDonald (2005), which compared the working-memory performance of individuals who were either depressed or nondepressed. These researchers tested 35 hospitalized inpatients who met the criteria for major depression, as well as 29 hospital assistants who worked at the same hospital but did not experience depression. The average ages were comparable, 38 for the individuals with depression and 37 for the individuals without depression. The two groups were also comparable in terms of vocabulary skills.

Christopher and MacDonald examined the three major components of Baddeley's model of working memory. For instance, they administered two tests that assessed the phonological loop. One task, for example, asked people to look at a series of similar-sounding letters (such as CDP), while simultaneously repeating the word "the." Then they were instructed to remember the letters in the correct order. The individuals with depression correctly repeated 3.4 letters in a row, in contrast to 5.3 letters for individuals without depression. This difference was statistically significant.

The researchers also administered one test that assessed the visuospatial sketchpad. First, the participants saw a series of visual patterns. Each pattern was arranged in a 3 × 3 display of black and white squares. Each pattern was then presented for 1 second, beginning with two of these patterns and working up to a longer series. Then the participants saw a "probe pattern," and they reported whether this specific pattern matched one of the original patterns in the series. The individuals with depression had an average span of 6.7, in contrast to 7.8 for individuals without depression. Although the difference between the two groups was not as large as on the phonological task, the difference was still statistically significant.

Christopher and MacDonald also administered four tests that assessed the central executive. The two groups of participants had similar scores on two of these tasks, the Brown/Peterson & Peterson task (see pp. 101–103) and a verbal reasoning task.

In contrast, large differences emerged between the two groups on two other tests of central-executive functioning. Specifically, one task required participants to listen to a series of letters and then report them in the reverse order. The individuals with depression had an average span of 2.8, in contrast to an average span of 4.9 for individuals without depression. A final central-executive task required participants to recall the last four letters of a string of letters that varied in length from four to eight letters. The individuals with depression had an average span of 3.2, in contrast to an average span of 7.4 for individuals without depression.

At this point, it's not clear why people with major depression have difficulty with some working-memory tasks, but not others. Still, the general results are consistent with clinical reports: People with depression often comment that they have trouble concentrating. They also tend to have a **ruminative style**; they may worry about all the things that are wrong in their life (De Lissnyder et al., 2010; Nolen-Hoeksema, 2006). These tendencies probably contribute to problems with working memory.

As Christopher and MacDonald (2005) conclude, "These findings emphasize the profound impact that depression has on the day-to-day cognitive activity of people suffering from depression" (p. 397). Poor performance on these daily activities could increase the level of depression even further. Clearly, clinical psychologists and other mental-health professionals need to know about these potential deficits in working memory for people who are clinically depressed.

Section Summary: *The Working-Memory Approach*

1. Alan Baddeley and his colleagues proposed a working-memory approach in which immediate memory is not a passive storehouse; instead, it resembles a workbench where material is continuously being combined and transformed.

2. In a classic study, Baddeley and Hitch (1974) demonstrated that people could perform a verbal task and a spatial task simultaneously, with minimal reduction in speed and accuracy on either task.

3. In the working-memory approach, the phonological loop briefly stores a limited number of sounds; additional research shows that items stored in the loop can be confused with other similar-sounding items.

4. The phonological loop is also used for long-term memory, self-instruction, learning new words, producing language, and solving problems.

5. Neuroscience research reveals that phonological tasks typically activate the left hemisphere, including the frontal lobe (for rehearsal), and the parietal lobe (for storage).

6. A second component of the working-memory approach is the visuospatial sketchpad, which stores visual and spatial information. The capacity of this feature is also limited; two visuospatial tasks will interfere with each other if they are performed simultaneously.

7. Activation of the visuospatial sketchpad is typically associated with the right hemisphere, especially the occipital region (for visual tasks), the frontal region, and the parietal region.

8. The central executive integrates information from the phonological loop, the visuospatial sketchpad, and the episodic buffer—as well as from long-term memory. The central executive is important in such tasks as focusing attention, selecting strategies, and suppressing irrelevant information. However, it does not store information.

9. The central executive cannot perform two complex tasks simultaneously; for example, daydreaming interferes with generating a random-number sequence.

10. According to neuroscience research, the central executive primarily activates various regions within the frontal lobe.

11. A relatively new component in Baddeley's working-memory approach is called the "episodic buffer"; this component temporarily stores material from the phonological loop, the visuospatial sketchpad, and long-term memory. It also binds together stimuli that were not previously connected.

12. Research shows that high scores on working-memory tasks are correlated with intelligence, grades in school, reading ability, and verbal fluency. Also, children with ADHD often have difficulty on central-executive tasks.

13. Adults who experience major depression frequently have difficulty with a variety of tasks involving the phonological loop, the visuospatial sketchpad, and the central executive.

CHAPTER REVIEW QUESTIONS

1. Describe Miller's classic concept about the magical number 7 ± 2. Why are chunks relevant to this concept? Why was Miller's emphasis different from the behaviorist approach? How did the Atkinson-Shiffrin model incorporate the idea of limited memory?

2. What is the serial-position effect? Why is this effect related to short-term memory? Also discuss another classic method of measuring short-term memory.

3. This chapter described an important study by Conrad and Hull (1964), which showed that people recall more letters from the sequence "C, W, Q, K, R, X" than from the sequence "C, T, D, G, V, B." What does this study tell us about working memory? If you rehearsed these letters, what part of your brain would be most active?

4. Suppose that you have just been introduced to five students from another college. Using the information about semantic similarity, why would you find it difficult to remember their names immediately after they have been introduced? How could you increase the likelihood that you would remember their names?

5. According to the discussion of Baddeley's approach, working memory is not just a passive storehouse. Instead, it is like a workbench where material is continually being handled, combined, and transformed. Why is the workbench metaphor more relevant for Baddeley's model than for the Atkinson-Shiffrin model?

6. This chapter describes Baddeley and Hitch's (1974) research on remembering numbers while performing a spatial reasoning task (the "A follows B" task). Why does this research suggest that a model of working memory must have at least two separate stores?

7. Name some tasks that you have performed today that required the use of your phonological loop, the visuospatial sketchpad, the central executive, and the episodic buffer. Can you think of a specific task that uses all four of these working-memory components, as well as long-term memory?

8. What does the central executive do? With respect to its role in working memory, which tasks are similar to those of a business executive?

9. Turn to Figure 2.1 on page 38. Using the descriptions that you have read in the current chapter, point out which parts of the brain are active for tasks that require (a) the phonological loop, (b) the visuospatial sketchpad, and (c) the central executive.

10. For many decades, researchers in the area of human memory primarily studied college students who are enrolled in introductory psychology courses. Why would the research on working memory not be applicable for a group of people who are currently experiencing major depression?

KEYWORDS

working memory
short-term memory
long-term memory
chunk
Brown/Peterson & Peterson
   technique
rehearsal
serial-position effect
recency effect
primacy effect

semantics
proactive interference (PI)
release from proactive
   interference
control processes
working-memory approach
phonological loop
subvocalization
acoustic confusions
self-instruction

Transcranial Magnetic
   Stimulation (TMS)
visuospatial sketchpad
central executive
episodic buffer
Attention-Deficit/Hyperactivity
   Disorder (ADHD)
major depression
ruminative style

RECOMMENDED READINGS

Baddeley, A., Eysenck, M. W., & Anderson, M. C. (2009). *Memory*. New York: Psychology Press. This textbook would be especially useful for students who want more details on Baddeley's approach to working memory.

Derakshan, N., & Eysenck, M. (Eds.). (2010). *Emotional states, attention, and working memory*. New York: Psychology Press. This book includes chapters on how working memory can be influenced by depression, anxiety, and stress, but it also explores how positive emotions can enhance cognitive performance.

Schwartz, B. L. (2011). *Memory: Foundations and applications*. Thousand Oaks, CA: Sage. Here is an excellent, well-balanced book for students who would like additional information about memory. The chapters on memory and the brain and on memory disorders are especially helpful.

Vandierendonck, A., & Szmalec, A. (Eds.). (2011). *Spatial working memory*. New York: Psychology Press. As the title emphasizes, this book focuses on the *spatial* components of the visuospatial sketchpad. The editors argue that this component of the working-memory model has received relatively little attention. The nine chapters in the book explore topics such as memory for spatial sequences and developmental disorders in spatial memory.

PREVIEW

Chapter 5 focuses on long-term memory, in other words, the memories that you've gathered throughout your lifetime. This chapter first examines factors that are relevant when you acquire new information. For example, the research on depth of processing shows that your memory is typically more accurate if you process information in terms of its meaning, rather than more superficial characteristics. If you have ever returned to a once-familiar location and experienced a flood of long-lost memories, you know the importance of another factor, called "encoding specificity." In addition, emotional factors influence your memory in several ways. For example, if you have been watching a violent show on television, your memory will be relatively poor for the advertisements that appear during this show.

The second section of the chapter, on the retrieval of memories, demonstrates that a person's memory accuracy depends on how the researchers measure memory. For example, people with amnesia remember less than other people, in terms of simple recall. However, the two groups are often similar when memory is measured indirectly. This section also looks at the memory abilities of people who have expertise and familiarity in a particular subject area.

Autobiographical memory, the topic of the last section in this chapter, refers to your memory for the everyday events in your life. Your memory is influenced by your general knowledge about objects and events; this general knowledge is usually helpful, but it may create memory errors. This section also examines two kinds of monitoring: (a) In source monitoring, you try to figure out how you learned about some specific information; and (b) in reality monitoring, you try to figure out whether or not a particular event really happened. This discussion points out that our so-called flashbulb memories are typically not very accurate. The chapter also looks at the research about eyewitness testimony, which shows that misleading information can sometimes alter your memory. Finally, we will explore a controversy: Can people forget a traumatic childhood event and then recover this memory many years later?

CHAPTER INTRODUCTION

Take a minute to think about your own long-term memory. Can you remember details about the first day of this current academic term? Now recall the names of your high school science teachers. Can you remember some of the characteristics of your closest friends during fifth grade? Memory is one of our most important cognitive activities. Consistent with Theme 4 of this book, memory is closely connected with numerous other cognitive processes (Einstein & McDaniel, 2004).

As noted in earlier chapters, psychologists often divide memory into two basic categories called **working memory** (the brief, immediate memory for material we are currently processing) and long-term memory. Chapter 4 emphasized that working memory is fragile. As that chapter illustrated, the information that you want to retain can disappear from memory after less than a minute.

In contrast, Chapter 5 demonstrates that your long-term memory can retain material for many decades. **Long-term memory** has a large capacity; it contains your memory for experiences and information that you have accumulated throughout your lifetime.

Like many psychologists, I'm not firmly convinced that working memory and long-term memory are two distinctly different kinds of memory. However, I do believe that the division is a convenient way to partition the enormous amount of research and knowledge about our memory processes.

Psychologists often subdivide long-term memory into more specific categories. Once again, this subdivision reflects convenience, rather than a conviction that the subdivisions represent distinctly different kinds of memory. One popular system subdivides long-term memory into episodic memory, semantic memory, and procedural memory (Herrmann, Yoder, et al., 2006). Let's briefly consider these three components.

Episodic memory focuses on your memories for events that happened to you personally; it allows you to travel backward in subjective time to reminisce about earlier episodes in your life (Gallistel & King, 2009; Surprenant & Neath, 2009). Episodic memory includes your memory for an event that occurred 10 years ago, as well as a conversation you had 10 minutes ago. Episodic memory is the major focus of this current chapter.

In contrast, **semantic memory** describes your organized knowledge about the world, including your knowledge about words and other factual information. For example, you know that the word *semantic* is related to the word *meaning*, and you know that Ottawa is the capital of Canada. Chapter 8 of this textbook focuses on semantic memory and your general knowledge about the world.

Finally, **procedural memory** refers to your knowledge about how to do something. For instance, you know how to ride a bicycle, and you know how to send an e-mail message to a friend. We will mention some aspects of procedural memory in this chapter, in connection with implicit memory (pp. 143–145), and also in Chapter 6, in connection with prospective memory (pp. 183–186).

Within the current chapter, we'll look at three aspects of long-term memory. Our first topic is encoding; during **encoding**, you process information and represent it in your memory (Einstein & McDaniel, 2004). The second topic is retrieval; during **retrieval**, you locate information in storage, and you access that information. Our final topic examines autobiographical memory. Autobiographical memory refers to your memory for experiences and information that are related to yourself (Brewin, 2011). Incidentally, we'll continue to examine long-term memory in Chapter 6, which emphasizes memory-improvement strategies. Now, before you read further, try Demonstration 5.1.

⑨ Demonstration 5.1

Levels of Processing

Read each of the following questions and answer "yes" or "no" with respect to the word that follows.

1. Is the word in capital letters?   BOOK
2. Would the word fit this sentence:
   "I saw a _____ in a pond"?   duck
3. Does the word rhyme with BLUE?   safe
4. Would the word fit this sentence:
   "The girl walked down the _____"?   house
5. Does the word rhyme with FREIGHT?   WEIGHT
6. Is the word in small letters?   snow
7. Would the word fit this sentence:
   "The _____ was reading a book"?   STUDENT
8. Does the word rhyme with TYPE?   color
9. Is the word in capital letters?   flower
10. Would the word fit this sentence:
    "Last spring we saw a _____"?   robin
11. Does the word rhyme with BALL?   HALL
12. Is the word in small letters?   TREE
13. Would the word fit this sentence:
    "My _____ is 6 feet tall"?   TEXTBOOK
14. Does the word rhyme with SAY?   DAY
15. Is the word in capital letters?   FOX

Now, without looking back over the words, try to remember as many of them as you can. Calculate the percentage of items you recalled correctly for each of the three kinds of tasks: physical appearance, rhyming, and meaning.

ENCODING IN LONG-TERM MEMORY

This section explores three important questions about encoding in long-term memory:

1. Are you more likely to remember items that you processed in a deep, meaningful fashion, rather than items processed in a shallow, superficial fashion?

2. Are you more likely to remember items if the context at the time of encoding matches the context at the time of retrieval?

3. How do emotional factors influence memory accuracy?

Before you read further, though, be sure that you have calculated the three percentages for Demonstration 5.1.

Levels of Processing

In 1972, Fergus Craik and Robert Lockhart wrote an extremely influential article about how we encode information. This **levels-of-processing approach** argues that deep, meaningful processing of information leads to more accurate recall than shallow, sensory kinds of processing. (This theory is also called the **depth-of-processing approach**.)

For example, in Demonstration 5.1, you used deep processing when you considered a word's meaning (e.g., whether that word would fit in a sentence). The levels-of-processing approach predicts that your recall will be more accurate when you use a deep level of processing, in terms of meaning. In contrast, you will be less likely to recall a word when you consider its physical appearance (e.g., whether it is typed in capital letters) or its sound (e.g., whether it rhymes with another word).

In general, then, people achieve a deeper level of processing when they extract more meaning from a stimulus. When you analyze for meaning, you may think of other associations, images, and past experiences related to the stimulus. In general, you are more likely to remember a stimulus that you analyzed at a very deep level (Healy et al., 2011; Roediger, Gallo, & Geraci, 2002). As you'll see in Chapter 6, most memory-improvement strategies emphasize deep, meaningful processing.

Let's examine some of the research on the levels-of-processing approach. We'll first consider general material, and then we'll consider an especially deep level of processing called *self-reference*.

Levels of Processing and Memory for General Material. The major hypothesis emerging from Craik and Lockhart's (1972) paper was that deeper levels of processing should produce better recall. For example, in an experiment similar to Demonstration 5.1, Craik and Tulving (1975) found that people were about three times as likely to recall a word if they had originally answered questions about its meaning rather than if they had originally answered questions about the word's physical appearance. Numerous reviews of the research conclude that deep processing of verbal material generally produces better recall than shallow processing (Craik, 1999, 2006; Lockhart, 2001; Roediger & Gallo, 2001).

Deep levels of processing encourage recall because of two factors: distinctiveness and elaboration. **Distinctiveness** means that a stimulus is different from other memory traces. Suppose that you are interviewing for a job. You've just learned that one man is especially important in deciding whether you will be hired, and you want to be sure to remember his name. You'll need to use deep processing and spend extra time processing his name. You'll try to figure out something unusual about his name that makes it different from other similar names you've heard during this interview (Worthen & Hunt, 2011). When you provide a distinctive encoding for a person's name, irrelevant names will be less likely to interfere (Craik, 2006; Schacter & Wiseman, 2006; Surprenant & Neath, 2009).

The second factor that operates with deep levels of processing is **elaboration**, which requires rich processing in terms of meaning and interconnected concepts (Craik, 2006; R. E. Smith, 2006; Worthen & Hunt, 2011). For example, if you want to understand the term *levels of processing*, you'll need to appreciate how this concept is related to both distinctiveness and elaboration. Think about the way you processed the word *duck* in Demonstration 5.1. Perhaps you recalled that you had recently seen ducks on a pond and that a restaurant menu had listed roast duck. This kind of semantic encoding encouraged rich processing. In contrast, suppose that the instructions for this item had simply asked whether the word *duck* was printed in capital letters. You would have simply answered "yes" or "no," without spending time on extensive elaboration.

Let's consider research on the importance of elaboration. Craik and Tulving (1975) asked participants to read sentences and decide whether the words that followed were appropriate to the sentences. Some of the sentence frames were simple, such as "She cooked the _____." Other sentence frames were elaborate, such as "The great bird swooped down and carried off the struggling _____." The word that followed these sentences was either appropriate (for example, rabbit) or inappropriate (for example, rock). You'll notice that both kinds of sentences required deep or semantic processing. However, the more elaborate, more detailed sentence frame produced far more accurate recall.

Other research demonstrates that deep processing also enhances our memory for faces. For instance, people recognize more photos of faces if they had previously judged whether the person looked honest, rather than judging a more superficial characteristic, such as the width of the person's nose (Bloom & Mudd, 1991; Sporer, 1991). People also recall faces better if they have been instructed to pay attention to the distinctions between faces (Mäntylä, 1997).

Levels of Processing and the Self-Reference Effect. According to the **self-reference effect**, you will remember more information if you try to relate that information to yourself (Burns, 2006; Gillihan & Farah, 2005; Schmidt, 2006). Self-reference tasks tend to encourage especially deep processing. Let's look at some representative research on the self-reference effect and then consider a problem with participants who do not follow instructions. Then we'll discuss several factors that help to explain the self-reference effect.

1. *Representative research.* In the classic demonstration of the self-reference effect, T. B. Rogers and his coauthors (1977) asked participants to process each English word according to the specified instruction. They processed words according to (a) their visual characteristics, (b) their acoustic (sound) characteristics, or (c) their semantic (meaning) characteristics. They processed a fourth category of words according to (d) self-reference instructions; the participants were told to decide whether a particular word could be applied to themselves.

The results showed that recall was poor for the two tasks that used shallow processing—that is, processing in terms of visual characteristics or acoustic characteristics. The recall was much better when people had processed in terms of semantic characteristics. However, the self-reference task produced much better recall than all the other three tasks.

Apparently, when we think about a word in connection with ourselves, we develop a particularly memorable coding for that word. For example, suppose that you are trying to decide whether the word *generous* applies to yourself. You might remember how you loaned your notes to a friend who had missed class, and you shared a box of candy with your friends—yes, *generous* does apply. The self-reference task requires organization and elaboration. These mental processes increase the probability of recalling an item.

The research on the self-reference effect also supports Theme 3 of this textbook. Specifically, our cognitive system handles positive instances more effectively than negative instances. In the self-reference studies, people are more likely to recall a word that *does* apply to themselves, rather than a word that *does not* apply (Ganellen & Carver, 1985; Roediger & Gallo, 2001).

Research shows that the self-reference effect is quite powerful (e.g., Howard & Klein, 2011; Kesibir & Oishi, 2010; Rathbone & Moulin, 2010). Symons and Johnson (1997) gathered the results of 129 different studies that had tested the self-reference effect in the research prior to their own article. Then they performed a **meta-analysis**, which is a statistical method for synthesizing numerous studies on a single topic. A meta-analysis computes a statistical index that tells us whether a particular variable has a statistically significant effect, when combining all the studies. Symons and Johnson's meta-analysis confirmed the pattern we have described: People recall significantly more items when they use the self-reference technique, rather than semantic processing or any other processing method.

2. Participants' failure to follow instructions. The self-reference effect is definitely robust. However, Mary Ann Foley and her coauthors (1999) have demonstrated that the research may actually *underestimate* the power of self-reference. Specifically, these investigators speculated that research participants might sometimes "cheat" when they have been instructed to use relatively shallow processing for stimuli. In fact, the participants might actually use the self-reference technique instead.

In one of their studies, Foley and her coauthors (1999) instructed students to listen to a list of familiar, concrete nouns. However, before hearing each word, they were told about the kind of mental image they should form. Let's consider two of the conditions, in which the students were instructed (1) to "visualize the object," or (2) to "imagine yourself using the object."

For the first analysis of the data, Foley and her colleagues classified the results according to the instructions supplied by the experimenter, prior to each word. Notice in Table 5.1 that this first analysis produced identical recall for the two conditions. That is, students recalled 42% of the words, whether they had been instructed to use relatively shallow processing or deep, self-reference processing.

Fortunately, however, Foley and her coauthors had also asked the students to describe their visual image for each word during the learning task. As these researchers

Table 5.1

Percentage of Items Recalled, as a Function of Imagery Condition and Analysis Condition

	Visualize the Object	Imagine Yourself Using the Object
First analysis of data	42%	42%
Second analysis of data	23%	75%

Source: Based on Foley et al., 1999.

had suspected, people in the "visualize the object" condition often inserted themselves into the mental image, so that they had actually used self-reference processing. In a second analysis, the researchers sorted the words according to the processing methods that the students had actually used, rather than the instructions they had received. As you can see, the second analysis revealed that the recall was more than three times as high when the students had used self-reference, rather than visualizing the object.

The research by Foley and her colleagues (1999) has important implications beyond this particular study. This research shows that our cognitive processes are active (Theme 1). People do not just passively follow instructions and obey the researcher precisely. Researchers need to keep in mind that participants are likely to transform the instructions, and this transformation can influence the results of the study.

3. *Factors responsible for the self-reference effect.* Let's now consider another issue: Why should we recall information especially well when we apply it to ourselves? As Tulving and Rosenbaum (2006) emphasize, a cognitive phenomenon typically requires more than just one explanation. Let's consider three cognitive factors that contribute to the self-reference effect.

One factor is that the "self" produces an especially rich set of cues. You can easily link these cues with new information that you are trying to learn. These cues are also distinctive. For example, your trait of honesty seems different from your trait of intelligence (Bellezza, 1984; Bellezza & Hoyt, 1992).

A second factor is that self-reference instructions encourage people to consider how their personal traits are connected with one another. The research shows that this kind of elaboration leads to more accurate retrieval (Burns, 2006; Klein & Kihlstrom, 1986; Thompson et al., 1996).

A third factor is that you rehearse material more frequently if it is associated with yourself. You're also more likely to use rich, complex rehearsal when you associate material with yourself (Thompson et al., 1996). These rehearsal strategies facilitate later recall. In short, several major factors work together to increase your ability to remember material related to yourself.

The Effects of Context: The Encoding-Specificity Principle

Does this scenario sound familiar? You are in the bedroom and realize that you need something from the kitchen. Once you arrive in the kitchen, however, you have no idea why you made the trip. Without the context in which you encoded the item you wanted, you cannot retrieve this memory. You return to the bedroom, which is rich with contextual cues, and you immediately remember what you wanted. Similarly, an isolated question on an exam may look completely unfamiliar, although you might remember the answer in the appropriate context.

These examples illustrate the **encoding-specificity principle**, which states that recall is better if the context during *retrieval* is similar to the context during *encoding* (Baddeley et al., 2009; Surprenant & Neath, 2009; Tulving & Rosenbaum, 2006). When the two contexts do not match, you are more likely to forget the items. Three other similar terms for the encoding-specificity principle are context-dependent memory, transfer-appropriate processing, and reinstatement of context (Craik, 2006; Roediger & Guynn, 1996). Let's now consider this topic of encoding specificity in more detail. We'll begin with some representative research, and then we'll see how the research forces us to modify our earlier conclusions about levels of processing.

Research on Encoding Specificity. In a representative study, Viorica Marian and Caitlin Fausey (2006) tested people living in Chile who were fluent in both English and Spanish. The participants listened to four stories about topics such as chemistry and history. They heard two stories in English and two in Spanish.

After a short delay, the participants listened to questions about each story. Half of the questions were asked in the language that matched the language of the original story (e.g., Spanish-Spanish), and half had a mismatch between the language of the story and the language of the questions (e.g., Spanish-English). The participants were instructed to answer in the same language that was used for the questions.

As you can see on page 134, Figure 5.1 illustrates encoding specificity. In other words, people were relatively accurate if they had heard the story and answered the questions in the same language. However, they were less accurate if they heard the story in one language and answered the questions in a different language. (Incidentally, we will examine bilingualism in more detail in Chapter 10.)

How do these context effects help us to function more competently in our daily lives? Basically, we often forget material that is associated with contexts other than our present context (Bjork, 2011). After all, we don't need to remember numerous details that might have been important in a previous setting but are no longer relevant at the present time (Bjork & Bjork, 1988). For instance, as a college student, you don't want your memory to be cluttered with details about the math textbook you used in fifth grade or the senior trip you took in high school.

Encoding specificity is relatively easy to demonstrate in real life. However, context effects are often inconsistent in the laboratory (e.g., Baddeley, 2004; Nairne, 2005; Roediger & Guynn, 1996). Let's consider two potential explanations.

1. *Different kinds of memory tasks*. One explanation for the discrepancy between real life and the laboratory is that the two situations typically test different kinds of

FIGURE 5.1

Percentage of Items Correctly Recalled, as a Function of Language Used During Encoding and Language Used During Retrieval.

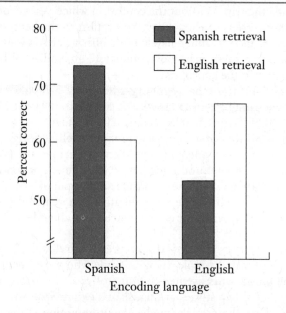

Source: Marian, V., & Fausey, C. M. (2006). Language-dependent memory in bilingual learning. *Applied Cognitive Psychology, 20,* 1025–1047.

memory (Roediger & Guynn, 1996). To explore this point, we need to introduce two important terms: recall and recognition. On a **recall task**, the participants must reproduce the items they learned earlier. (For example, can you recall the definition for *elaboration?*) In contrast, on a **recognition task**, the participants must judge whether they saw a particular item at an earlier time. (For example, did the word *morphology* appear earlier in this chapter?)

Let's return to encoding specificity. Our real-life examples of encoding specificity typically describe a situation in which we *recall* an earlier experience, and that experience occurred many years earlier (Roediger & Guynn, 1996). Encoding specificity is typically strong in these real-life, long-delay situations. For example, when I smell a particular flower called verbena, I am instantly transported back to a childhood scene in my grandmother's garden. I specifically recall walking through the garden with my cousins, an experience that happened decades ago.

In contrast, the laboratory research usually focuses on *recognition*, rather than *recall*: "Did this word appear in the material you saw earlier?" Furthermore, that list was typically presented less than an hour earlier. Encoding specificity is typically weak in these laboratory, short-delay situations.

In summary, then, the encoding-specificity effect is most likely to occur in memory tasks that (a) assess your recall, (b) use real-life incidents, and (c) examine events that happened long ago.

2. *Physical versus mental context.* In the studies on encoding specificity, researchers often manipulate the physical context in which material is encoded and retrieved. However, *physical* context may not be as important as *mental* context. It is possible that physical details—such as the characteristics of the room—are relatively trivial in determining whether the encoding context matches the retrieval context. Instead, the encoding-specificity principle may depend on how similar the two environments *feel*, rather than on how similar they *look* (Eich, 1995).

This point about mental context should remind you of the study by Foley and her colleagues (1999), in which participants' mental activities often did not match the researchers' specific instructions. (See pp. 131–132, earlier in this chapter.) Researchers need to look beyond the variables that they believe they are manipulating. Instead, they must pay attention to the processes going on inside the participants' heads. This importance of mental activities is also crucial to the next topic, which brings us back to the level-of-processing issue.

Levels of Processing and Encoding Specificity. Craik and Lockhart's (1972) original description of the levels-of-processing approach emphasized *encoding*, or how items are placed into memory. It did not mention details about *retrieval*, or how items are recovered from memory. However, according to the encoding-specificity principle, people recall more material if the retrieval conditions match the encoding conditions (Moscovitch & Craik, 1976). Thus, encoding specificity can override level of processing. In fact, shallow processing can actually be more effective than deep processing when the retrieval task emphasizes superficial information. Notice that this point is not consistent with the original formulation of the levels-of-processing approach.

Let's consider a study that demonstrates the importance of the similarity between encoding and retrieval conditions (Bransford et al., 1979). Suppose that you performed the various encoding tasks in Demonstration 5.1 on page 128. Imagine, however, that you were then tested in terms of rhyming patterns, rather than in terms of recalling the words on that list. For example, you might be asked, "Was there a word on the list that rhymed with *toy*?" People usually perform better on this rhyming test if they had originally performed the shallow-encoding task (rhyming), rather than the deep-encoding task (meaning).

This area of research demonstrates that deep, semantic processing is effective only if the retrieval conditions also emphasize these deeper, more meaningful features (Roediger & Guynn, 1996). Henry Roediger (2008) wrote an important article, in which he emphasized that the classic laws of memory have vanished. Consider the levels of processing effect and the encoding-specificity effect. Both of these effects work most of the time. However, when an important variable is changed, then the effect may disappear.

Here is another important issue: Theme 4 of this textbook points out that our cognitive processes are often interrelated. The research on encoding specificity emphasizes that memory often requires problem solving: To determine how to store some information, you'll need to figure out the characteristics of the retrieval task (Phillips, 1995). Consider this question: How would you study the material in this chapter if you knew you would be tested on your recall, by answering essay questions like those at the end of each chapter? Would your study techniques be different if you were tested on your recognition, for instance, by having to answer multiple-choice questions?

Let's review the general conclusions about encoding specificity before we move on to another topic. In summary, memory is sometimes—but not always—enhanced when the retrieval context resembles the encoding context (Nairne, 2005; Surprenant & Neath, 2009). However, the benefits of encoding specificity are more likely when

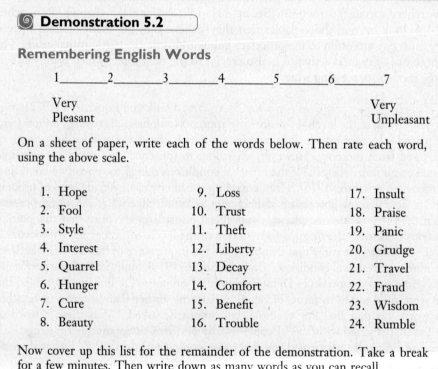

Demonstration 5.2

Remembering English Words

1_____2_____3_____4_____5_____6_____7

Very
Pleasant

Very
Unpleasant

On a sheet of paper, write each of the words below. Then rate each word, using the above scale.

1. Hope	9. Loss	17. Insult
2. Fool	10. Trust	18. Praise
3. Style	11. Theft	19. Panic
4. Interest	12. Liberty	20. Grudge
5. Quarrel	13. Decay	21. Travel
6. Hunger	14. Comfort	22. Fraud
7. Cure	15. Benefit	23. Wisdom
8. Beauty	16. Trouble	24. Rumble

Now cover up this list for the remainder of the demonstration. Take a break for a few minutes. Then write down as many words as you can recall.

Later, count how many of the following words you remembered correctly: Hope, Style, Interest, Cure, Beauty, Trust, Liberty, Comfort, Benefit, Praise, Travel, Wisdom.

Then count how many of the following words you remembered correctly: Fool, Quarrel, Hunger, Loss, Theft, Decay, Trouble, Insult, Panic, Grudge, Fraud, Rumble.

Did you recall more from the first category or the second category?

Source: Balch, W. R. (2006). Introducing psychology students to research methodology: A word-pleasantness experiment. *Teaching of Psychology, 33,* 132–134.

items are tested by recall (rather than recognition), when the stimuli are real-life events, and when the items have been in memory for a long time. In addition, encoding specificity depends on mental context more than physical context.

We've also seen that encoding specificity can modify the levels-of-processing effect; in some cases, the match between encoding and retrieval is even more important than deep processing. As you'll see, context is also relevant when we examine how emotions and mood can influence memory. Before you read further, try Demonstration 5.2.

[**IN DEPTH**]

Emotions, Mood, and Memory

In everyday speech, we often use the terms *emotion* and *mood* interchangeably, and the terms are somewhat similar. However, psychologists define **emotion** as a reaction to a specific stimulus. In contrast, **mood** refers to a more general, long-lasting experience (Bower & Forgas, 2000). For example, you may have a negative emotional reaction to the unpleasant fragrance you just smelled in a locker room, even though you may be in a relatively positive mood today. Let's consider two ways in which emotion and mood can affect our memory:

1. We typically remember pleasant stimuli more accurately than other stimuli.

2. We typically recall material more accurately if our mood matches the emotional nature of the material, an effect called mood congruence.

Memory for Items Differing in Emotion. In 1978, my coauthor and I proposed that the people's enhanced recall of pleasant items is part of a more general Pollyanna Principle (Matlin & Stang, 1978). The **Pollyanna Principle** states that pleasant items are usually processed more efficiently and more accurately than less pleasant items. This principle holds true for a wide variety of phenomena in perception, language, and decision making (Matlin, 2004). However, this current chapter focuses on long-term memory. Let's consider several ways in which the emotional nature of the stimuli can influence long-term memory.

1. *More accurate recall for pleasant items.* For more than a century, psychologists have been interested in the way that emotional tone can influence memory (e.g., Balch, 2006; Hollingworth, 1910; Thompson et al., 1996; Waring & Kensinger, 2011). In a typical study, people learn lists of words that are pleasant, neutral, or unpleasant. Then their recall is tested after a delay of several minutes to several months. In a review of the previous research, we found that pleasant items are often recalled better than negative items, particularly if the delay is long (Matlin, 2004; Matlin & Stang, 1978).

For example, in 39 of the 52 studies that we located on long-term memory, pleasant items were recalled significantly more accurately than unpleasant items.

Incidentally, neutral items are usually recalled least accurately of all, suggesting that the intensity of an item's emotional tone is also important (Bohanek et al., 2005; Talarico et al., 2004). In other words, we typically recall pleasant stimuli better than terrifying stimuli, which are—in turn—recalled better than the blandly boring.

Let's consider Demonstration 5.2, which is a simplified version of a study conducted by William Balch (2006). Check back to page 136, and count how many pleasant words you recalled, compared to the number of unpleasant words. Was your recall more accurate for the pleasant words than for the unpleasant words? When Balch tested introductory psychology students, he found that they recalled significantly more of the pleasant words.

Let's now focus on the neutral stimuli. Jill Waring and Elizabeth Kensinger (2011) explored people's recognition for photos of stimuli that had previously been judged to be (1) very positive, such as candy; (2) very negative, such as a snake; or (3) neutral, such as a postage stamp. Each item was shown with a neutral background, such as a river. About 10 minutes later, participants completed a surprise recognition test. They looked at each of the previous photos (both the stimuli and the backgrounds), as well as some photos that had not been previously presented. In each case, they judged whether they had in fact seen the item.

Table 5.2 shows that people recalled positive stimuli and negative stimuli equally well, perhaps because the delay was short. In contrast, their recall for neutral stimuli was substantially lower. Now look at their recognition of the background setting. Table 5.2 shows that this score was highest for the neutral stimuli. In other words, there is a trade off. When the central stimulus is boring, people explore (and remember) the background more accurately than in other conditions. Notice an additional point: When the stimuli are negative, people do not remember the background very accurately.

How about our memory for real-life events? People generally recall pleasant events more accurately than unpleasant events (Mather, 2006; Matlin, 2004; Walker et al., 1997). A related finding is that drivers quickly forget their near-accidents; in fact, one study showed that they remember only 20% of these accidents just two weeks later (Chapman & Underwood, 2000).

TABLE 5.2

Correct Recognition of Positive, Negative, and Neutral Stimuli, as Well as the Background Setting

	Correct Recognition of the Stimulus	Correct Recognition of the Background
Positive Stimuli	70%	44%
Negative Stimuli	71%	37%
Neutral Stimuli	56%	48%

Source: Based on Waring & Kensinger (2011).

2. *More accurate recall for neutral stimuli associated with pleasant stimuli.* Media violence is an important issue in North American culture. Surveys suggest that about 60% of television programs depict some form of violence. Furthermore, numerous studies have concluded that media violence can have an impact on both children's and college students' aggression (Bushman & Gibson, 2011; Bushman & Huesmann, 2010; Kirsh, 2011). However, let's consider a different aspect of media violence: Do people remember commercials less accurately when they are associated with violent media? To answer this question, Brad Bushman (1998) recorded 15-minute segments of two videos. One video, *Karate Kid III*, showed violent fighting and destruction of property. The other video, *Gorillas in the Mist*, was judged equally exciting by undergraduate students, but it contained no violence. Bushman then inserted two 30-second advertisements for neutral items into each of the two video clips.

College students watched either the violent or the nonviolent film clip. Then they were asked to recall the two brand names that had been featured in the commercials and to list everything they could recall about the commercials. The results showed significantly better recall—on both measures—for commercials that had appeared in the nonviolent film. Additional research confirms that anger and violence typically reduce memory accuracy (Bushman, 2005; Gunter et al., 2005).

People who are concerned about societal violence should be interested in Bushman's research, because they can use this research in persuading advertisers to place their ads during nonviolent programs. Advertisers obviously want viewers to remember their product's name, as well as information about the product. In light of this research, advertisers should be hesitant to sponsor violent television programs.

3. *Over time, unpleasant memories fade more than pleasant memories.* W. Richard Walker and his coauthors (1997) asked undergraduate students to record one personal event each day for about 14 weeks and to rate both the pleasantness and the intensity of the event. Three months later, the participants returned, one at a time, for a second session. A researcher then read each event from the previous list, and the student was instructed to rate the current pleasantness of that event.

In an analysis of the results, the rating did not change for those events that were originally considered to be neutral. However, the events originally considered to be pleasant were now considered to be *slightly* less pleasant. In contrast, the events originally considered to be unpleasant were now considered to be *much* less unpleasant (that is, closer to neutral). This last observation is consistent with the Pollyanna Principle: People tend to rate unpleasant past events more positively with the passage of time, a phenomenon called the **positivity effect**.

In a related study, Walker and his colleagues (2003) tested two groups of students. One group consisted of students who did not have tendencies toward depression, and the other group had depressive tendencies. Those who did not have depressive tendencies showed the usual positivity effect. In contrast, the students with depressive tendencies showed the same amount of fading for unpleasant and pleasant events. In other words, when people at risk for depression look back on their lives, the unpleasant events still remain unpleasant. As you can imagine, this research has important implications for clinical psychologists (Hertel & Matthews, 2011). Therapists must address a depressed client's interpretation of past events, as well as the client's current situation.

So far, we have considered how the pleasantness of the stimuli influences memory. As we've seen, pleasant stimuli usually fare better than less pleasant ones: (1) We often remember them more accurately; (2) we tend to forget information when it is associated with violent, unpleasant stimuli; and (3) over time, pleasant memories become slightly less pleasant, whereas unpleasant memories become much less unpleasant. Let's now see how memory is influenced by the match between your mood and the emotional tone of the stimuli.

Mood Congruence. A second major category of studies about mood and memory is called *mood congruence.* **Mood congruence** means that you recall material more accurately if it is congruent with your current mood (Fiedler et al., 2003; Joorman & Siemer, 2004; Schwarz, 2001). For example, if you are in a pleasant mood, you should remember pleasant material better than unpleasant material, whereas a person in an unpleasant mood, you should remember unpleasant material better.

Consider a study by Laura Murray and her colleagues (1999). Like Walker and his colleagues (2003), these researchers tested one group of students who did not have tendencies toward depression, and one group with depressive tendencies. The participants were instructed to look at a series of 20 positive- and 20 negative-trait words. Later, the participants recalled as many words as possible from this list.

Murray and her colleagues found results that were consistent with earlier research, as well as the research on depression and working memory we considered in Chapter 4. Specifically, the nondepressed individuals recalled a greater overall percentage of the words than did the depression-prone individuals. In addition, as you can see from Table 5.3, the nondepressed students recalled a significantly greater percentage of positive words than negative words. In contrast, the depression-prone students recalled a slightly greater percentage of negative words than positive words.

In these studies about mood congruence, nondepressed people typically recall more positive than negative material. In contrast, depression-prone people tend to

TABLE 5.3

Percentage of Items Recalled, as a Function of Mood and the Nature of the Stimulus

Mood Category	Type of Stimulus	
	Positive	Negative
No depressive tendencies	49%	38%
Depressive tendencies	35%	39%

Source: Murray et al., 1999.

recall more negative material (Fiedler et al., 2003; LeMoult et al., 2010; Mather, 2006; Schwarz, 2001). Like the results of the research by Walker and his colleagues (2003), these findings are important for clinical psychologists. If depressed people tend to forget the positive experiences they have had, then their depression could increase still further (Schacter, 1999).

ⓢ Section Summary: *Encoding in Long-Term Memory*

1. Long-term memory can be subdivided into three categories: episodic memory, semantic memory, and procedural memory; this current chapter focuses on episodic memory.

2. The research on levels of processing shows that people typically remember stimuli more accurately with deep, meaningful processing, rather than with shallow, sensory processing.

3. Deep processing encourages more accurate recall because of distinctiveness and elaboration.

4. Research on the self-reference effect demonstrates that your memory is typically more accurate if you relate the stimuli to your own personal experience.

5. To obtain a valid assessment of the self-reference effect, the stimuli must be classified in terms of the participant's *actual* mental activities, rather than in terms of the experimenter's instructions.

6. The self-reference effect is effective for several reasons: (a) because the self is a rich source of memory cues, (b) because self-reference instructions encourage people to think about how their own characteristics are interrelated, and (c) because self-reference increases people's rich, complex rehearsal.

7. According to the encoding-specificity effect, our recall is more accurate if the context during retrieval is similar to the context during encoding.

8. The encoding-specificity effect is most likely to operate in certain situations: (a) when memory is tested by recall instead of recognition, (b) when real-life events are studied, (c) when the original event happened long ago, and (d) when mental context is emphasized.

9. Encoding specificity can modify the depth-of-processing effect.

10. Research on the influence of emotions and mood on memory shows that (a) people generally recall pleasant stimuli more accurately than unpleasant stimuli; (b) people recall more information if they see the material during a pleasant media presentation, rather than a violent media presentation; and (c) unpleasant memories are more likely than pleasant memories to grow neutral as time passes.

11. Memory is more accurate when the material to be learned is congruent with a person's current mood (mood congruence).

RETRIEVAL IN LONG-TERM MEMORY

So far in this chapter, we have emphasized encoding processes. We examined how your long-term memory could be influenced by the level of processing that you used in encoding the material, by the context at the time of encoding, and by emotional or mood-related factors during encoding.

---

⑨ Demonstration 5.3

Explicit and Implicit Memory Tasks

Take out a piece of paper. Then read the following list of words:

> picture   commerce   motion   village   vessel
> window   number   horse   custom   amount
> fellow   advice   dozen   flower   kitchen   bookstore

Now cover up that list for the remainder of the demonstration. Take a break for a few minutes and then try the following tasks:

A. *Explicit Memory Tasks*

1. *Recall*: On the piece of paper, write down as many of those words as you can recall.

2. *Recognition*: From the list below, circle the words that appeared on the original list:

   > woodpile   fellow   leaflet   fitness   number   butter
   > motion   table   people   dozen   napkin
   > picture   kitchen   bookstore   horse   advice

B. *Implicit Memory Tasks*

1. *Word completion*: From the word fragments below, provide an appropriate, complete word. You may choose any word you wish.

   > v_s_e_   l_t_e_   v_l_a_e   p_a_t_c   m_t_o_   m_n_a_
   > n_t_b_o_   c_m_e_c_   a_v_c_   t_b_e_   f_o_e_   c_r_o_
   > h_m_w_r   b_o_s_o_e

2. Repetition priming: Perform the following tasks:

   - Name three rooms in a typical house.
   - Name three different kinds of animals.
   - Name three different kinds of stores.

Naturally, we cannot discuss encoding without also mentioning retrieval; these two processes cannot be separated (Hintzman, 2011). For instance, psychologists need to test how accurately you can retrieve information in order to examine how effectively you encoded the information. Furthermore, many memory errors can be traced to inadequate retrieval strategies (Einstein & McDaniel, 2004). Take a few minutes to try Demonstration 5.3.

However, retrieval was relatively unimportant in the preceding section of this chapter. Now we'll move retrieval to the center stage. Let's first consider the distinction between two kinds of retrieval, called explicit and implicit memory tasks. Then we'll focus on the two extremes of memory ability by exploring the topics of amnesia and memory expertise.

Throughout this section, keep Theme 1 in mind: Our cognitive processes are active, rather than passive. Yes, sometimes we retrieve material from memory in an effortless fashion; you see a friend, and her name seems to spontaneously appear in your memory. Other times, retrieval requires hard work! For example, you might try to recover someone's name by strategically re-creating the context in which you last encountered this person (Koriat, 2000; Roediger, 2000). Who else was present, how long ago was it, and where did this event take place?

Explicit Versus Implicit Memory Tasks

Imagine this scene: A young woman is walking aimlessly down the street, and she is eventually picked up by the police. She seems to be suffering from an extreme form of amnesia, because she has lost all memory of who she is. She cannot even remember her name, and she is carrying no identification. Then the police have a breakthrough idea: They ask her to begin dialing phone numbers. As it turns out, she dials her mother's number, even though she is not aware whose number she is dialing.

Daniel Schacter tells this story to illustrate the difference between explicit and implicit measures of memory (as cited in Adler, 1991). However, this difference can be demonstrated for people with normal memory, as well as for those who have amnesia. Let's clarify the basic concepts of this distinction and then look at some research.

Definitions and Examples. Demonstration 5.3 provides two examples of explicit memory tasks and two examples of implicit memory tasks. Try this demonstration before you read further.

So far, we have focused on explicit memory tasks. On an **explicit memory task**, a researcher directly asks you to remember some information; you realize that your memory is being tested, and the test requires you to intentionally retrieve some information that you previously learned (Roediger & Amir, 2005; B. L. Schwartz, 2011).

Almost all the studies we have discussed in Chapter 4 and the first section of Chapter 5 have used explicit memory tests. The most common explicit memory test is recall. As we noted earlier, a recall task requires you to reproduce items that you learned earlier. Another explicit memory test is a recognition task, in which you must identify which items on a list had been presented at an earlier time.

In contrast, an implicit memory task assesses your memory indirectly. On an **implicit memory task**, you see the material (usually a series of words or pictures); later, during the test phase, you are instructed to complete a cognitive task that does not directly ask you for either recall or recognition (Roediger & Amir, 2005; B. L. Schwartz, 2011; Whitten, 2011). For example, in Part B1 of Demonstration 5.3, you filled in the blanks in several words. Previous experience with the material—in this case, the words at the beginning of this demonstration—probably facilitated your performance on the task (Roediger & Amir, 2005).

On an implicit memory task, the researchers avoid using words such as *remember* or *recall*. For example, in Schacter's anecdote about the woman with amnesia, dialing a phone number was a test of implicit memory. Implicit memory shows the effects of previous experience that creep out automatically—during your normal behavior—when you are not making any conscious effort to remember the past (De Houwer et al., 2009; Kihlstrom et al., 2007; Roediger & Amir, 2005).

Psychologists initially developed implicit measures so that they could measure attitudes and beliefs in social psychology. However, these techiques soon spread to cognitive psychology, as well as clinical psychology, health psychology, and other applied areas (De Houwer et al., 2009; Lane, Kang, & Banaji, 2007).

Researchers have devised many techniques to assess implicit memory (Amir & Selvig, 2005; Roediger & Amir, 2005; Wiers & Stacy, 2006). You tried two of these in Demonstration 5.3. Look back at Task B1 on page 142. If you stored the words from the original list in your memory, you would be able to complete those words (for example, *commerce* and *village*) faster than the words in Task B1 that had not been on the list (for example, *letter* and *plastic*).

Task B2 illustrates a second measure of implicit memory, called a *repetition priming task*. In a **repetition priming task**, recent exposure to a word increases the likelihood that you'll think of this particular word, when you are given a cue that could evoke many different words. For example, in Task B2, you were likely to supply the words *kitchen*, *horse*, and *bookstore*—words that you had seen at the beginning of the demonstration. In contrast, you were less likely to supply words that you had not seen, such as *dining room*, *cow*, and *drugstore*.

During the last 30 years, implicit memory has become a popular topic in psychology (Roediger & Amir, 2005). For example, we'll see in Chapter 8 that researchers can use implicit memory tasks to assess people's unconscious attitudes about gender, ethnicity, and other social categories (Nosek et al., 2007). However, some researchers argue that implicit memory is not entirely different from explicit memory (Reder et al., 2009; Roediger, 2008).

Representative Research. A variety of studies demonstrate that adults often cannot remember stimuli when they are tested on an explicit memory task. However, they may remember the stimuli when tested on an implicit memory task.

Some of the studies on explicit and implicit memory illustrate a pattern that researchers call a *dissociation*. A **dissociation** occurs when a variable has large effects on Test A, but little or no effects on Test B; a dissociation also occurs when a variable has one kind of effect if measured by Test A, and the opposite effect if measured by

Test B. The term *dissociation* is similar to the concept of a statistical interaction, a term that might sound familiar if you have completed a course in statistics.

Let's consider an illustration of a dissociation based on the research about the level-of-processing effect. As you know from the first section of this chapter, people typically recall more words if they have used deep levels of processing to encode these words. For example, participants recall more words on an *explicit memory test* if they had originally used semantic encoding, rather than encoding physical appearance.

However, on an *implicit memory test*, semantic and perceptual encoding may produce similar memory scores, or people may even score lower if they had used semantic encoding (e.g., Jones, 1999; Richardson-Klavehn & Gardiner, 1998). Notice that these results fit the definition of a dissociation because depth of processing has a large positive effect on memory scores on Test A (an explicit memory task), but depth of processing has no effect or even a negative effect on memory scores on Test B (an implicit memory task).

The research on implicit memory illustrates that people often know more than they can reveal in actual recall. As a result, this research has potential implications for applied areas such as education, clinical psychology, and advertising (Jones, 1999).

Individual Differences: Anxiety Disorders and Performance on Explicit and Implicit Memory Tasks

Kristin Mitte (2008), a professor at the University of Jena in Germany, was interested in memory patterns of people who have anxiety disorders. The broad category called **anxiety disorders** includes psychological problems such as (1) **generalized anxiety disorder**, in which a person experiences at least 6 months of intense, long-lasting anxiety and worry; (2) **post-traumatic stress disorder**, in which a person keeps re-experiencing an extremely traumatic event; and (3) **social phobia**, in which a person becomes extremely anxious in social situations (American Psychiatric Association, 2000). According to Mitte, some of the studies have shown that people with anxiety disorders remember threatening words very accurately, compared to people without these disorders. However, other studies have shown no differences.

Mitte speculated that the results might depend on the nature of the memory task. Therefore, she specifically examined the research about implicit memory tasks, as well as two categories of explicit memory tasks (recognition and recall). She located 165 different research studies that had tested a total of 9,046 participants, most of whom were between the ages of 18 and 60. Then she conducted several meta-analysis. As you saw on page 131, a meta-analysis is a statistical method for synthesizing numerous studies on a single topic. No matter how Mitte analyzed the data for implicit memory tasks, high-anxious and low-anxious people performed similarly.

How about the results for recognition tasks, one of the two categories that assess explicit memory? Mitte analyzed the data for recognition-memory tasks. Once again, high-anxious and low-anxious people performed similarly.

However, the meta-analysis for the recall tasks showed statistically significant differences. Specifically, high-anxious participants were *more likely* than low-anxious participants to recall the negative, anxiety-arousing words. In contrast, high-anxious participants were *less likely* than low-anxious participants to recall both the neutral words and the pleasant words. The high-anxious participants apparently remembered so many of these anxiety-arousing words that they were less likely to remember the other, less disturbing words.

Mitte (2008) points out that this meta-analysis cannot tell us why high-anxious people and low-anxious people differ in their patterns of recall. It may be that anxious individuals pay more attention to the threatening words, and so these words are easier to remember. Alternatively, the recall bias may be linked to a well-developed network of concepts related to the threatening words. When an anxious person recalls a small number of these threatening words, other related words may be easily accessible.

Individuals with Amnesia

In this topic, and the next, we'll consider individuals who have unusual memory abilities. We'll first discuss people with **amnesia**, who have severe deficits in their episodic memory (Buckner, 2010). The second topic examines the impressively accurate performance of memory experts.

One form of amnesia is **retrograde amnesia**, or loss of memory for events that occurred prior to brain damage; the deficit is especially severe for events that occurred during the years just before the damage (Gazzaniga et al., 2009; Meeter et al., 2006; Meeter & Murre, 2004). For example, one woman known by the initials L.T. could not recall events in her life that happened prior to an accident that injured her brain. However, her memory was normal for events after the injury (Conway & Fthenaki, 2000; Riccio et al., 2003).

The other form of amnesia is **anterograde amnesia**, or loss of the ability to form memories for events that have occurred after brain damage (Kalat, 2009). For several decades, researchers had studied a man with anterograde amnesia who was known by his initials, H.M. (James & MacKay, 2001; Milner, 1966). H.M. had such serious epilepsy that neurosurgeons operated on his brain in 1953. Specifically, they removed a portion of his temporal lobe region, as well as his **hippocampus**, a structure underneath the cortex that is important in many learning and memory tasks (Kalat, 2009).

The operation successfully cured H.M.'s epilepsy, but it left him with a severe kind of memory loss. The studies showed that H.M. had normal semantic memory, and he could accurately recall events that occurred before his surgery. However, he could not learn or retain new information. For example, he could not remember meeting certain people, even when he had spoken to them, and they had left the room for just a few minutes (Gazzaniga et al., 2009).

The research demonstrates that people with anterograde amnesia often recall almost nothing on tests of explicit memory, such as recall or recognition. That is, they perform poorly when asked to consciously remember an event that happened after they developed amnesia. They also have trouble imagining events that will occur in the future (Buckner, 2010). After all, you need information about previous events to figure out what you might do in the future!

Let's consider the pioneering work conducted by Elizabeth Warrington and Lawrence Weiskrantz (1970). These researchers presented a list of English words to individuals with anterograde amnesia. Then the researchers administered several recall and recognition tasks. Compared to control-group participants, the individuals with amnesia performed much more poorly on both kinds of explicit memory tasks. So far, then, the results are not surprising.

However, Warrington and Weiskrantz (1970) also administered implicit memory tasks. The tasks were presented as word-guessing games, though they actually assessed people's implicit memory for the words shown earlier. For example, the researchers showed the previously presented English words in a mutilated form that was difficult to read. The participants were told to guess which word was represented. Surprisingly, both the participants with amnesia and the control-group participants were correct 45% of the time. These results have been replicated many times since the original research, using both visual and auditory tasks (e.g., Roediger & Amir, 2005; Schacter et al., 1994), although some researchers have reported exceptions (Reder et al., 2009).

Notice that the research by Warrington and Weiskrantz (1970) is a good example of a dissociation. As we noted on pages 144–145, a dissociation occurs when a variable has a large effect on one kind of test, but little or no effect on another kind of test. In this case, the dissociation was evident because the memory-status variable (amnesic versus control) had a major effect when measured by explicit memory tests. However, this same variable had no effect when measured by implicit memory tests.

The research on individuals with amnesia reminds us that memory is an extremely complex cognitive process. Specifically, some people apparently remember nothing when their memory is tested on a recall task, but they may actually perform quite well when memory is measured in a different fashion.

Expertise

We've seen that people with amnesia experience severe memory deficits. In contrast, people with **expertise** demonstrate impressive memory abilities, as well as consistently exceptional performance on representative tasks in a particular area (Ericsson, 2003a, 2003b, 2006). K. Anders Ericsson is the psychologist who currently has the greatest "expertise" in the area of expertise. As Ericsson and his coauthors emphasize, a key to acquiring expertise is deliberate, intensive practice—on a daily basis (Duckworth et al., 2011; Ericsson, 2003a; Ericsson et al., 2004; Ericsson, Nandagopal, & Roring, 2009).

Our first topic in this discussion illustrates that people's expertise is context specific. Next, we'll examine some of the ways in which memory experts and novices differ. Our final topic—indirectly related to expertise—explores how people can identify individuals from their own ethnic background more accurately than individuals from another ethnic group.

The Context-Specific Nature of Expertise. Researchers have studied memory experts in numerous areas, such as chess, spelling competitions, sports, ballet, maps, musical notation, and memorizing extremely long sequences of numbers. In general, researchers have found a strong positive correlation between knowledge about an area and memory performance in that area (Duckworth et al., 2011; Schraw, 2005).

Surprisingly, however, people who are experts in one area may not display outstanding general memory skills (Kimball & Holyoak, 2000; Wilding & Valentine,

1997). Consider Chao Lu, a 23-year-old graduate student at a Chinese university (Hu et al., 2009). In 2005, he set a new Guinness World Record by correctly reciting the first 67,890 digits of pi. However, his average digit span was 9.3, compared to the digit spans of control students, which ranged between 6.8 and 11.5. His success cannot be traced to innate ability. Instead, Chao Lu was intensely motivated; in fact, he practiced for 7 *years* and developed an elaborate system of encoding and retrieving the numbers.

Other research shows that memory experts typically do not receive exceptional scores on tests of intelligence (Wilding & Valentine, 1997). For example, men who are experts in remembering information at the horse races do not score especially high on standard IQ tests. In fact, one horse race expert had an eighth-grade education and an IQ of 92 (Ceci & Liker, 1986). Again, their expertise tends to be focused on a specific area. Incidentally, in Chapter 11, we'll see that memory expertise for specific areas of knowledge also helps people solve problems in these areas.

How Do Experts and Novices Differ? From the information we've discussed—as well as from other resources—we know that memory experts have several advantages over nonexperts (Ericsson & Kintsch, 1995; Ericsson & Lehmann, 1996; Herrmann, Gruneberg, et al., 2006; Herrmann, Yoder, et al., 2006; Kimball & Holyoak, 2000; McCormick, 2003; Noice & Noice, 1997; Roediger, Marsh, & Lee, 2002; Schraw, 2005; Simon & Gobet, 2000; Van Overschelde et al., 2005; Wilding & Valentine, 1997). Let's consider several ways in which experts tend to have better memory strategies than novices:

1. Experts possess a well-organized, carefully learned knowledge structure, which assists them during both encoding and retrieval. For instance, chess players store a large number of common patterns that they can quickly access.

2. Experts are more likely to reorganize the new material that they must recall, forming meaningful chunks in which related material is grouped together.

3. Experts typically have more vivid visual images for the items they must recall.

4. Experts work hard to emphasize the distinctiveness of each stimulus during encoding. As we saw on pages 129–130, distinctiveness is essential for accurate memory.

5. Experts rehearse in a more strategic fashion. For example, an actor may rehearse her or his lines by focusing on words that are likely to trigger recall.

6. Experts are better at reconstructing missing portions of information from material that they partially remember.

7. Experts are more skilled at predicting the difficulty of a task and at monitoring their progress on this task.

Throughout this book, we have emphasized that our cognitive processes are active, efficient, and accurate (Themes 1 and 2). These cognitive processes also employ both top-down and bottom-up strategies (Theme 5). As we can see from the previous list, these characteristics are especially well developed for someone with memory expertise in a specific area.

Own-Ethnicity Bias. The information on expertise has interesting implications for face recognition. Specifically, you are generally more accurate in identifying members of your own ethnic group than members of another ethnic group, a phenomenon called **own-ethnicity bias** (Brigham et al., 2007; Chiroro et al., 2008; Kovera & Borgida, 2010; Pauker et al., 2010; Walker & Hewstone, 2006). This effect is also known as the *other-ethnicity effect* or the *cross-ethnicity effect.**

Hugenberg and his colleagues (2010) point out that the own-ethnicity bias has stronger research-based support, compared to studies on most other variables related to face recognition. The own-ethnicity bias is related to expertise, because people typically have more opportunities to interact with individuals from their own ethnic group, rather than other ethnic groups (Hugenberg et al., 2010). Expertise can develop with frequent experiences and interactions.

Research in the United States typically shows that both Black and European American individuals are more accurate in recognizing faces of people from their own ethnic group (MacLin & Malpass, 2001; Meissner et al., 2005; Wright et al., 2003). Similar findings are reported for face recognition with European American, East Asian, and Latina/o individuals (Brigham et al., 2007; Gross, 2009; Ng & Lindsay, 1994).

Faces representing your own ethnic group acquire distinctiveness. As you know from previous discussions in this chapter, your memory is most accurate when the stimuli are distinctive. Consistent with this research, Van Wallendael and Kuhn (1997) found that Black students rated Black faces as more distinctive than European American faces. In contrast, European American students rated European American faces as more distinctive than Black faces.

In the United States, Blacks represent about 13% of the population, and Latinas/os represent about 16% of the population (U.S. Census Bureau, 2012b). In many European countries, White residents form the largest ethnic group. However, the second-largest group is not likely to be Black or Latina/o residents. In Germany, for example, many of the residents are from a Turkish background. A study conducted with White and Turkish individuals demonstrated the own-ethnicity bias with each of these groups (Sporer & Horry, 2011).

The largest non-White population in Great Britain is South Asian, a group with origins in countries such as India, Pakistan, and Bangladesh. South Asians represent only about 4% of the British population (Walker & Hewstone, 2006). As a result, White people would have relatively little experience in interacting with South Asian people. In contrast, South Asian people would have relatively extensive experience interacting with White people.

Pamela Walker and Miles Hewstone (2006) studied facial recognition in British high school students who were either White or South Asian. Each student looked at photographs of faces that had been altered. Within each gender category, the faces differed along a continuum. On one end of the continuum, the faces looked clearly

---

*The original phrases used the term *race*; I will substitute the more contemporary term *ethnicity*.

South Asian; at the other end, the faces looked clearly White. Other faces represented intermediate combinations of the two sets of facial features. In each case, the student saw photos of two faces—one after the other—and then judged whether the two faces were the same or different.

As you can see in Figure 5.2, the British White students made more accurate judgments for White faces than for South Asian faces. In contrast, the British South Asian students were equally accurate for both kinds of faces. It would be interesting to see whether British White students also demonstrate more of the own-ethnicity bias in long-term memory for faces, compared to South Asian students.

We would expect to find that the own-ethnicity bias would decrease when people have greater contact with members of other ethnic groups. The research generally shows some support for the contact hypothesis, although the evidence is not strong (Brigham et al., 2007; Meissner & Brigham, 2001; Wright et al., 2003).

How can people work to overcome the other-ethnicity effect? Hugenberg and his coauthors (2010) suggest that people first need to know that they are likely to show the other-ethnicity effect. However, they can become more accurate in identifying people

FIGURE 5.2

Percentage of Accurate Responses in a Discrimination Task, as a Function of the Ethnic Group of the Student and the Ethnic Group of the Faces.

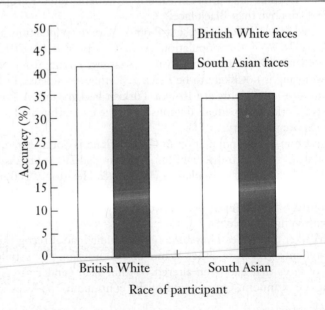

Source: Walker, P. M., & Hewstone, M. (2006). A perceptual discrimination investigation of the own-race effect and intergroup experience. *Applied Cognitive Psychology, 20,* 461–475.

from other ethnic groups if they make a genuine effort to learn facial distinctions that are relevant for other ethnic groups.

Some researchers have explored expertise in social categories other than ethnicity. For example, Anastasi and Rhodes (2003) studied younger-adult and older-adult participants. They found that participants from these two age groups were more accurate in identifying people in their own group. In the next section, we will explore several other important factors that influence accuracy in identifying faces during eyewitness testimony.

⊚ Section Summary: *Retrieval in Long-Term Memory*

1. Explicit-memory tasks instruct participants to recall or recognize information. In contrast, implicit-memory tasks require participants to perform a cognitive task, such as completing a word that has missing letters.

2. Research indicates that depth of processing typically has a major impact on an explicit memory task, but it has no effect on an implicit memory task.

3. People who have anxiety disorders are similar to other people in their memory for high-anxiety words on implicit memory tasks and on explicit recognition tasks; however, they actually *recall* more high-anxiety words than other people.

4. Individuals with retrograde amnesia have difficulty recalling events that occurred prior to brain damage.

5. Individuals with anterograde amnesia have difficulty recalling events that occurred after brain damage. They may recall almost nothing on tests of explicit memory; however, on tests of implicit memory, they typically perform as accurately as people without brain damage.

6. Expertise has an important effect on long-term memory, although expertise is context-specific. Compared to novices, experts have cognitive advantages such as well-organized knowledge structures and vivid visual images.

7. According to the research on the own-ethnicity bias, people are more accurate in recognizing faces from their own ethnic group, in part because their expertise makes these faces more distinctive.

AUTOBIOGRAPHICAL MEMORY

As we noted at the beginning of the chapter, **autobiographical memory** is your memory for events and issues related to yourself. Autobiographical memory usually includes a verbal narrative. It may also include imagery about these events, emotional reactions, and procedural information (Kihlstrom, 2009). In general, the research in this area examines recall for naturally occurring events that happen outside the laboratory. In fact, your autobiographical memory is a vital part of your identity, because it shapes your personal history and your self-concept (Lampinen et al., 2004; Lieberman, 2007; McAdams, 2004).

The previous two sections in this chapter focused on encoding and retrieval in long-term memory, and they primarily examined laboratory research. In general, the dependent variable in those studies is the *number of items* correctly recalled—a *quantity*-oriented approach to memory (Koriat et al., 2000). In contrast, in autobiographical memory, the dependent variable is usually memory *accuracy*; does your recall match the actual events that happened, or does it distort the events?

The studies of autobiographical memory are typically high in ecological validity (Bahrick, 2005; Esgate & Groome, 2005; Lampinen et al., 2004). As we noted in Chapter 1, a study has **ecological validity** if the conditions in which the research is conducted are similar to the natural setting to which the results will be applied.

Our discussion of autobiographical memory first looks at schemas. Schemas can shape your memory for a previous event, so that this memory becomes more consistent with your current viewpoint. Next, we'll examine source monitoring, which shows that you can make mistakes when you try to remember where and when you learned certain information. Then a discussion of the so-called "flashbulb memory" examines some especially vivid memories for important events. Our final topic is eyewitness testimony, an area of research that has obvious applications in the courtroom.

This discussion of autobiographical memory illustrates several important characteristics of our memory for life events:

1. Although we sometimes make errors, our memory is often accurate for a variety of information (Theme 2). For example, adults can recall the names of streets near their childhood home and material from their elementary school textbooks (Read & Connolly, 2007).

2. When people do make mistakes, these mistakes generally concern peripheral details and specific information about commonplace events, rather than central information about important events (Goldsmith et al., 2005; Tuckey & Brewer, 2003). In fact, it's usually helpful *not* to remember numerous small details that would interfere with memory for more important information (Bjork et al., 2005).

3. Our memories often blend together information from a variety of sources; we actively construct a unified memory at the time of retrieval (Davis & Loftus, 2007; Koriat, 2000). Notice that this constructive process is consistent with Theme 1: Our cognitive processes are typically active, rather than passive.

Schemas and Autobiographical Memory

This discussion of schemas emphasizes how you remember common, ordinary events. A **schema** consists of your general knowledge or expectation, which is distilled from your past experiences with someone or something (Davis & Loftus, 2007; Koriat et al., 2000). For example, you have probably developed a schema for "eating lunch." You tend to sit in a particular area with the same group of people. Your conversation topics may also be reasonably standardized. You have also developed a schema for the events that occur during the first day of a class at your university. Because of your personal memories, you have even developed a schema for yourself (Ross & Wang, 2010).

We use schemas to guide our recall. As time passes, we still remember the gist of an event, although we may forget the information that is irrelevant for a particular schema (Davis & Loftus, 2007; Goldsmith et al., 2005). Chapter 8 explores in more detail how schemas influence a variety of our cognitive processes. However, in the present chapter, we'll examine a topic that is especially relevant to autobiographical memory, called the consistency bias.

During recall, we often show a **consistency bias**; that is, we tend to exaggerate the consistency between our past feelings and beliefs and our current viewpoint (Davis & Loftus, 2007; Schacter, 2001). For example, suppose that a researcher asks you today to recall how you felt about feminism when you were a high school student. You would tend to construct your previous emotions and values so that they would be consistent with your current emotions and values. As Schacter (2001) summarizes the consistency bias, "The way we were depends on the way we are" (p. 139). As a result, we underestimate how much we have changed throughout our lives.

The consistency bias suggests that we tell our life stories so that they are consistent with our current schemas about ourselves (Ceballo, 1999). For example, a historian named Emily Honig (1997) interviewed Chicana garment workers who had participated in a strike at a garment manufacturing company in El Paso, Texas. Shortly after the strike, these women viewed the strike as a life-transforming experience that had changed them from timid factory workers into fearless, self-confident activists.

Honig returned to interview these same women several years later. The women recalled that they had always been assertive and nonconforming, even prior to the strike. It's possible that they selectively recalled assertive episodes from their pre-strike lives—episodes that were consistent with their current self-schemas. As Honig argues, these Chicana garment workers are "not inventing nonexistent past experiences, but they are retelling them with the language, perceptions, and mandates of their present" (p. 154). Notice the interdisciplinary nature of research on the consistency bias: It explores the interface of cognitive psychology, personality psychology, social psychology, and history.

We have seen that schemas can influence our memories of the past, so that they seem more similar to our present feelings, beliefs, and actions. Now we will consider source monitoring and reality monitoring. Both of these topics examine whether our memory is consistent with the actual events in our lives.

Source Monitoring and Reality Monitoring

Something like this situation has certainly happened to you. You are trying to recall where you learned some background information about a movie you saw recently. Did a friend tell you this information, or did you learn it from a review of the movie? This process of trying to identify the origin of a particular memory is called **source monitoring** (Johnson, 1997, 2002; Pansky et al., 2005). Unfortunately, we do not spontaneously monitor the source of our memories, although our memory performance would be more accurate if we did so (Higham et al., 2011).

In a typical study, Marsh and his colleagues (1997) asked college students to discuss an open-ended question on a topic such as methods for improving their university.

One week later, the participants returned for a source-monitoring test. Specifically, the participants were told to identify whether each item on a list had been their own idea or someone else's idea. Interestingly, they seldom made source-monitoring mistakes; that is, they seldom claimed that an idea generated by another person had really been their own idea.

Some source-monitoring errors can be puzzling. For example, people may plagiarize inadvertently. In some legal cases, for example, a songwriter believes that he or she has composed a truly new song. However, the melody of the song may actually be based on a melody that another songwriter had composed at an earlier date (Defeldre, 2005; Dunlosky & Metcalfe, 2009).

Earlier in the chapter, we saw that our memory sometimes has a positive bias. Specifically, we tend to remember pleasant events. Furthermore, negative events become more positive as time passes. Similarly, we seem to have a "wishful thinking bias," which sometimes leads us to make errors in source monitoring.

For example, suppose you consulted a number of sources before you bought a new Smartphone made by the Handy Dandy company. A few weeks later, someone asks you what information you consulted before making the decision. You'll tend to recall that the extremely positive review for the Handy Dandy model came from a trustworthy source, such as *Consumer Reports*, rather than a less reliable source, such as an e-mail from a friend (Gordon et al., 2005).

In some cases, the mistakes in source monitoring can have much more serious consequences. Marcia Johnson (1996, 1998, 2002) has emphasized that source-monitoring errors can occur at a societal level, not just at the individual level. The results can be devastating. An important source-monitoring failure occurred in 2003, when President George W. Bush was trying to provide justifications for starting the Iraq War. In his State of the Union address in early 2003, Bush discussed one important reason to justify invading Iraq. Specifically, he announced that Iraq was negotiating with an African country to buy uranium (an ingredient used in making nuclear weapons).

Six months later, the public learned that this claim was based on clearly falsified documents from Niger, a country in west-central Africa. Also, the Central Intelligence Agency claimed that their agents had tried to warn the President that the information from Niger was false. Furthermore, President Bush claimed that this State of the Union address had been cleared by the CIA (Isikoff & Lipper, 2003). Unfortunately, several different errors in source monitoring on "the uranium question" apparently helped to push the United States into an expensive, destructive war that has killed thousands of U.S. troups and hundreds of thousands of Iraqi individuals.

Marcia Johnson (2002) emphasizes that government agencies, the media, and corporation executives need to be meticulous about checking the accuracy of their information. Their goal should be to limit both the frequency and the size of source-monitoring errors.

So far, we have examined a problem called *source-monitoring errors*, in which you make a mistake by thinking that Source A provided some information, when Source B actually provided this information. A related kind of problem is called "reality monitoring." In **reality monitoring**, you try to identify whether an event really occurred, or whether you actually imagined this event (Dunlosky & Metcalfe, 2009;

Reed, 2010; Schwartz, 1991). For example, you might *think* that you told a friend that an upcoming event had been cancelled. However, in reality, you had debated whether to call her or send a message … and you never actually conveyed that message.

In a representative study about reality monitoring, college students saw a series of familiar objects, such as a pencil (Henkel, 2011). For half of the objects, the students performed a specified action, such as breaking a pencil. For the remaining half of the objects, the students were instructed to *imagine* themselves performing a specific action, without actually doing anything to the object. One week later, the students saw photos of some of the completed actions, such as a broken pencil.

One week after that, the students were instructed to indicate whether they had actually performed each action. When they had not seen a photo of the completed action, fewer than 10% were confident that they had completed the action. In contrast, when they had seen the relevant photo three times, 25% were confident that they had actually completed this action.

---

⑥ Demonstration 5.4

Flashbulb Memory

Ask several acquaintances whether they can identify any memories of a very surprising event. Tell them, for example, that many people believe that they can recall—in vivid detail—the circumstances in which they learned about the death of President Kennedy, or the September 11, 2001, terrorist attacks.

Also tell them that other vivid memories focus on more personal important events. Ask them to tell you about one or more memories, particularly noting any small details that they recall.

Flashbulb Memories

At some point in the near future, try Demonstration 5.4. This demonstration illustrates the so-called flashbulb-memory effect. The term **flashbulb memory** refers to your memory for the circumstances in which you first learned about a very surprising and emotionally arousing event. Many people believe that they can accurately recall all the minor details about what they were doing at the time of this event (Brown & Kulik, 1977; Esgate & Groome, 2005).

For example, President John F. Kennedy was shot in 1963, yet many older adults believe that they have accurate recall for the trivial details of that news report (Neisser & Libby, 2000). The classic study by Brown and Kulik (1977) introduced the term "flashbulb memory."

Roger Brown and James Kulik (1977) were the first researchers to study whether various important political events triggered contextually rich memories. They reported that people tended to describe details such as their location when they heard the news and the person who gave them the news. Notice whether your friends included this information in their responses to Demonstration 5.4.

Brown and Kulik (1977) suggested that people's flashbulb memories are more accurate than memories of less surprising events. However, many later studies suggested that people make numerous errors in recalling details of national events, even though they claimed that their memories for these events were very vivid (Roediger, Marsh, & Lee, 2002; Schooler & Eich, 2000; Schwartz, 1991). Furthermore, people's memory for an expected event are just as accurate as their memory for a surprising event (Coluccia et al., 2010; Curci & Luminet, 2009).

Several researchers have studied people's ability to recall details about a tragedy that was especially vivid for many U.S. residents—the terrorist attacks of September 11, 2001. Let's look at an important study by Jennifer Talarico and David Rubin (2003), and then we'll discuss additional observations about people's memory for that particular event.

On September 12, the day after the attacks, Talarico and Rubin asked students at a North Carolina university to report specific details about how they had learned about the attacks. The students also provided similar information for an ordinary event that had occurred at about the same time. This memory about an ordinary event served as a control condition that could be contrasted with the "flashbulb memory" of the attack.

After the initial session, the students were randomly assigned to one of three recall-testing sessions. Some returned to be tested 1 week later, others returned 6 weeks later, and still others returned 32 weeks later. At these recall-testing sessions, Talarico and Rubin asked the students a variety of questions, including the details of their memory for the attack, as well as for the everyday event. These details were checked against the details that the students had supplied on September 12. Then the researchers counted the number of consistent and inconsistent details.

Figure 5.3 shows the results. The number of details provided on September 12 provides the baseline for the number of consistent details. As you can see, the consistency drops over time for each of the three testing sessions. However, notice that the size of the drop was similar for the terrorist-attack memory and for the everyday memory. As the figure shows, the number of inconsistent details increases slightly over time for both kinds of memories. Interestingly, however, the students in all conditions reported that they were highly confident that their recall of the terrorist attacks had been accurate.

Other research about memory for 9/11 shows that students at a college in New York City recalled significantly more factual details about the tragedy, compared to students at colleges in California and Hawaii (Pezdek, 2003). This finding makes sense because the New York City students lived much closer to the World Trade Center at the time they learned about the attack. They were also much more likely than the other students to know people whose lives were impacted by the event. Another study showed that people's memory accuracy for the September 11 tragedy was not related to demographic variables such as gender, age, or education (Conway et al., 2009).

So, what can we conclude from this information about flashbulb memories? It's likely that we do not need to invent any special mechanism to explain them. Yes, these memories can sometimes be more accurate than our memories for ordinary events.

Figure 5.3

Average Number of Consistent and Inconsistent Details Reported for a Flashbulb Event (September 11, 2001, Attacks) and an Ordinary Event, as a Function of the Passage of Time.

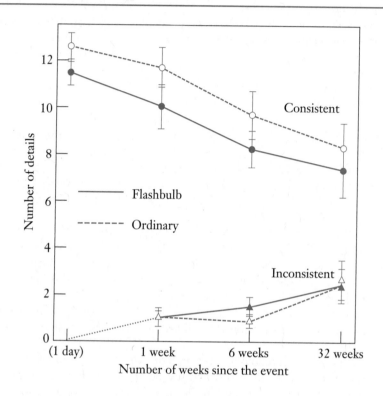

Source: Talarico, J. M., & Rubin, D. C. (2003). Confidence, not consistency, characterizes flashbulb memories. *Psychological Science, 14*, 455–461.

However, these enhanced memories can usually be explained by several standard mechanisms, such as rehearsal frequency, distinctiveness, and elaboration (Neisser, 2003; Read & Connolly, 2007). Furthermore, both flashbulb memories and "ordinary memories" grow less accurate with the passage of time (Kvavilashvili et al., 2003; Read & Connolly, 2007).

Eyewitness Testimony

Let's now consider eyewitness testimony, the most extensively researched topic within the domain of autobiographical memory. We have already discussed three topics that can influence eyewitness testimony. For example, we saw that people have trouble recognizing a person from another ethnic group (pp. 149–150). Furthermore, memory schemas can alter a witness's testimony (pp. 152–153). In addition, faulty source monitoring can lead to errors in eyewitness testimony; people may believe that they really witnessed something, when it had actually been suggested to them in a different situation (pp. 153–154).

We have seen throughout this chapter that people's long-term memory is reasonably accurate, especially if we consider memory for the gist of a message. However, eyewitness testimony requires people to remember specific details about people and events. In these cases, mistakes are more likely (Castelli et al., 2006; Wells & Olson, 2003). When eyewitness testimony is inappropriate, the wrong person may go to jail or—in the worst cases—be put to death (Kovera & Borgida, 2010).

Example of Inappropriate Eyewitness Testimony. **Consider** the case of Gary Graham, who was a suspect in the murder of Bobby Lambert. In truth, there was no convincing evidence for Graham's guilt—nothing like DNA or fingerprint evidence. When Graham came to trial, jury members were informed that Graham had a pistol similar to one that had shot Lambert. They were not told that the Houston police had concluded that it was not the same pistol.

Furthermore, eight eyewitnesses had seen the killer near the store, but only one of them identified Graham as the killer. Graham's fate—the death penalty—was sealed by the eyewitness testimony of one woman. This woman testified that she had seen his face at night for about 3 seconds, from a distance of about 30 feet. Graham's case was never reviewed. Was Gary Graham genuinely guilty? We'll never know, because he was executed on June 22, 2000 (Alter, 2000). Reports like this one have led psychologists to question the validity of eyewitness testimony (Kovera & Borgida, 2010).

Let's examine some psychological research on eyewitness testimony. We will first consider how inaccuracies can arise when people are given misleading information after the event that they had witnessed. Next, we'll discuss several factors that can influence the accuracy of eyewitness testimony. Then we'll see whether witnesses who are confident about their eyewitness testimony are also more accurate about their judgments. Our final topic is the recovered-memory/false-memory debate.

The Post-Event Misinformation Effect. **Many** errors in eyewitness testimony can be traced to incorrect information. In the **post-event misinformation effect**, people first view an event; then they are given misleading information about the event; later on, they mistakenly recall the misleading information, rather than the event they actually saw (Davis & Loftus, 2007; Pansky et al., 2005; Pickrell et al., 2004).

In Chapter 4, we discussed **proactive interference**, which means that people have trouble recalling new material because previously learned, old material keeps interfering with new memories. The misinformation effect resembles a second kind of interference called *retroactive interference*. In **retroactive interference**, people have trouble recalling old material because some recently learned, new material keeps interfering with old memories. For example, suppose that an eyewitness saw a crime, and then a lawyer supplied some misinformation while asking a question. Later on, the eyewitness may have trouble remembering the events that actually occurred at the scene of the crime, because the new misinformation creates retroactive interference.

In the classic experiment on the misinformation effect, Elizabeth Loftus and her coauthors (1978) showed participants a series of slides. In this sequence, a sports car stopped at an intersection, and then it turned and hit a pedestrian. Half the participants saw a slide with a yield sign at the intersection; the other half saw a stop sign.

Twenty minutes to one week after the participants had seen the slides, they answered a questionnaire about the details of the accident. A critical question contained information that was either consistent with a detail in the original slide series, inconsistent with that detail, or neutral (because it did not mention the detail).

For example, the first group of people who had seen the yield sign were asked, "Did another car pass the red Datsun while it was stopped at the yield sign?" (consistent). A second group of people were asked, "Did another car pass the red Datsun while it was stopped at the stop sign?" (inconsistent). For the third group of people, the type of sign was not mentioned (neutral). To answer this question, all participants saw two slides, one with a stop sign and one with a yield sign. They were asked to select which slide they had previously seen.

As Figure 5.4 shows, people who had seen the inconsistent information were much less accurate than people in the other two conditions. They often selected a sign on the basis of the information in the questionnaire, rather than the original slide. Many studies have replicated the detrimental effects of misleading post-event information (e.g., Pickrell et al., 2004; Schacter, 2001; Wade et al., 2002).

The misinformation effect can be at least partly traced to faulty source monitoring (Davis & Loftus, 2007; Schacter et al., 1998; Zhu et al., 2010). For instance, in the study by Loftus and her colleagues (1978), the post-event information in the inconsistent-information condition encouraged people to create a mental image of a stop sign. During testing, they had trouble deciding which of the two images—the stop sign or the yield sign—they had actually seen in the original slide series.

The research on the misinformation effect emphasizes the active, constructive nature of memory. As Theme 1 points out, cognitive processes are active, rather than passive. The **constructivist approach** to memory emphasizes that we construct knowledge by integrating what we know; as a result, our understanding of an event or a topic is coherent, and it makes sense (Davis & Loftus, 2007; Mayer, 2003; Pansky et al., 2005). In the case of the study by Loftus and her colleagues (1978), many people in the inconsistent condition made sense of the event by concluding that the car had probably paused at the stop sign.

Notice, then, that the consistency bias—discussed on page 153—is one component of the constructivist approach. In short, memory does not consist of a list of facts, all stored in intact form and ready to be replayed like a DVD. Instead, we construct a memory by blending information from a variety of sources (Davis & Loftus, 2007; Hyman & Kleinknecht, 1999).

Factors Affecting the Accuracy of Eyewitness Testimony. As you can imagine, a variety of factors influence whether eyewitness testimony is accurate. We have already mentioned three potential problems in eyewitness testimony: (1) People may create

FIGURE 5.4

The Effect of Type of Information and Delay on Proportion of Correct Answers.

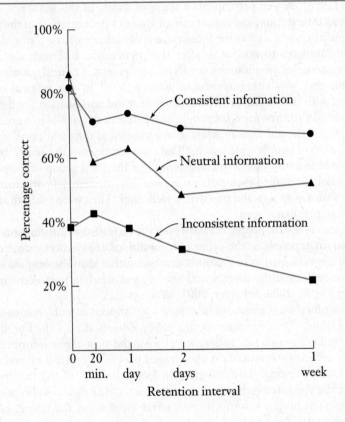

Source: Loftus, E. F., Miller, D. G., & Burns, H. J. (1978). Semantic integration of verbal information into visual memory. *Journal of Experimental Psychology: Human Learning and Memory, 4,* 19–31.

memories that are consistent with their schemas; (2) people may make errors in source monitoring; and (3) post-event misinformation may distort people's recall. Here are several other important variables:

1. Eyewitnesses make more errors if they saw a crime committed during a stressful circumstance, for instance, when someone was carrying a weapon (Kovera & Borgida, 2010). A survey of U.S. law enforcement officers showed that about 85% of the officers were aware of this issue (Wise et al., 2011).

2. Eyewitnesses make more errors when there is a long delay between the original event and the time of the testimony. As time passes, recall accuracy decreases

for most of our ordinary memories. A long delay in eyewitness testimony also allows additional opportunities for "contamination" from post-event misinformation (Dysart & Lindsay, 2007; Kovera & Borgida, 2010; Read & Connolly, 2007).

3. Eyewitnesses make more errors if the misinformation is plausible. For instance, in the classic study by Loftus and her colleagues (1978), a stop sign is just as plausible as a yield sign, so the participants in that study frequently made errors. People are also likely to say that an event occurred in their own life (when

---

⊚ Demonstration 5.5

Remembering Lists of Words

For this demonstration, you must learn and recall two lists of words. Before beginning, take out two pieces of paper. Next, read List 1, then close the book and try to write down as many of the words as possible. Then do the same for List 2. After you have recalled both sets of words, check your accuracy. How many items did you correctly recall?

List 1	List 2
bed	water
rest	stream
awake	lake
tired	Mississippi
dream	boat
wake	tide
snooze	swim
blanket	flow
doze	run
slumber	barge
snore	creek
nap	brook
peace	fish
yawn	bridge
drowsy	winding

it really did not) if the event seems consistent with other similar experiences (Castelli et al., 2006; Davis & Loftus, 2007; Hyman & Loftus, 2002).

4. Eyewitnesses make more errors if there is social pressure (Roebers & Schneider, 2000; Roediger & McDermott, 2000; Smith et al., 2003). People make many errors in eyewitness testimony when someone pressured them to provide a specific answer (for example, "Exactly when did you first see the suspect?"). In contrast, the testimony is more accurate when people are allowed to report an event in their own words, when they are given sufficient time, and when they are allowed to respond, "I don't know" (Koriat et al., 2000; Wells et al., 2000).

5. Eyewitnesses make more errors if someone has provided positive feedback. For instance, they are much more certain about the accuracy of their decision if they had previously been given positive feedback—even a simple "Okay" (Douglass & Steblay, 2006; Semmler & Brewer, 2006). Unfortunately, in real-life lineups, the eyewitnesses often hear this kind of encouragement (Wells & Olson, 2003). Now try Demonstration 5.5, which is located on page 161.

The Relationship Between Memory Confidence and Memory Accuracy. In some studies, researchers ask participants to judge how confident they are about the accuracy of their eyewitness testimony. Interestingly, in many situations, participants are almost as confident about their misinformation-based memories as they are about their genuinely correct memories (Kovera & Borgida, 2010; Wells & Olson, 2003). In other words, people's confidence about their eyewitness testimony is not strongly correlated with the accuracy of their testimony. In fact, the correlations are typically between +.30 and +.50* (Leippe & Eisenstadt, 2007).

This research has practical applications for the legal system. For example, a survey of U.S. law enforcement officers showed that only about 21% of the officers were aware that memory confidence is not strongly correlated with memory accuracy (Wise et al., 2011). Unfortunately, jury members are also much more likely to believe a confident eyewitness than an uncertain one (Brewer et al., 2005; Koriat et al., 2000). However, as you now know, the research shows that a confident eyewitness is not necessarily an accurate eyewitness.

The Recovered-Memory/False-Memory Controversy

If you scan popular magazines, you seldom come across articles about working memory, the encoding-specificity principle, or source monitoring. However, in recent years, one topic from cognitive psychology was especially popular in both the media and professional journals: the controversy about recovered memory versus false memory (e.g., Gallo, 2006; Goodman et al., 2007). For instance, Smith and Gleaves (2007) reported that cognitive psychologists, therapists, and lawyers had published more than 800 books and articles about this topic.

---

*A correlation is a statistical measure of the relationship between two variables, in which .00 represents no relationship and +1.00 represents the strongest positive relationship.

These so-called "memory wars" have not been resolved, though most professionals now seem to favor a compromise position. We will summarize several important components of this issue. Before you read further, however, be sure that you have tried Demonstration 5.5 on page 161.

The Two Contrasting Positions in the Controversy. Most of the discussion about false memory focuses on childhood sexual abuse. One group of researchers argues that these memories can be forgotten for many years and then recovered during adolescence or adulthood.

According to this **recovered-memory perspective**, some individuals who experienced sexual abuse during childhood managed to forget that memory for many years. A child would be especially likely to forget these traumatic events if the abuser was a close relative or a trusted adult. At a later time, this presumably forgotten memory may come flooding back into consciousness (Brewin, 2011; Cromer & Freyd, 2007; Freyd et al., 2005; Freyd et al., 2010; Pezdek & Freyd, 2009; Rubin et al., 2008; Smith & Gleaves, 2007).

A second group of researchers has a different interpretation of phenomena like these. We must emphasize that this second group agrees that childhood sexual abuse is a genuine problem that needs to be addressed. However, these people don't trust the accuracy of many reports about the sudden recovery of early memories. Specifically, the **false-memory perspective** proposes that most of these recovered memories are actually incorrect memories; in other words, they are constructed stories about events that never occurred (Bernstein & Loftus, 2009; Davis & Loftus, 2007; Reyna et al., 2007).

The Potential for Memory Errors. Our discussion throughout this section on autobiographical memory should convince you that memory is less than perfect. For example, people are often guided by schemas, rather than their actual recall of an event. Also, the research on source monitoring shows that people cannot recall with absolute accuracy whether they performed an action or merely imagined performing it. In addition, we noted that flashbulb memories are not as accurate as many people believe. Furthermore, we saw that eyewitness testimony can be flawed, especially when witnesses receive misinformation.

Similar problems arise in recalling memories from childhood. For instance, during therapy, some psychotherapists may repeatedly suggest to clients that they might have been sexually abused during childhood. This suggestion could be blended with reality to create a false memory. These statements encourage clients to invent a false memory, especially because we noted on page 162 that people make more errors when they experience social pressure (Bernstein & Loftus, 2009; Schwartz, 1991; Smith et al., 2003).

We cannot easily determine whether a memory of childhood abuse is correct. After all, the situation is far from controlled, and other independent witnesses are rarely available. Furthermore, the current cognitive neuroscience techniques cannot reliably distinguish between accurate and inaccurate recall of abuse (Bernstein & Loftus, 2009).

However, psychologists have conducted research and created theories that are designed to address the recovered-memory/false-memory issue. Let's first consider laboratory research that demonstrates false memory. Then we'll discuss why sexual abuse during childhood may sometimes require a different kind of explanation, compared to false memory for emotionally neutral material.

Arguments for False Memory. Research in the psychology laboratory clearly demonstrates that people often "recall" seeing a word that was never actually presented. In contrast to the real-life recall of sexual abuse, the laboratory research is very straightforward and unemotional. Researchers simply ask participants to remember a list of words they had seen earlier, and their accuracy can be objectively measured. For example, Demonstration 5.5 asked you to memorize and recall two lists of words, and then you checked your accuracy. Take a moment now to check two other items. On List 1, did you write down the word *sleep*? Did you write *river* on List 2?

If you check the original lists on page 161, you'll discover that neither *sleep* nor *river* was listed. In research with lists of words like these, Roediger and McDermott (1995) found a false-recall rate of 55%. People made intrusion errors by listing words that did not appear on the lists. Intrusions are common on this task, because each word that does appear on a list is commonly associated with a missing word, in this case *sleep* on the first list and *river* on the second list.

This study has been replicated numerous times, using different stimuli and different testing conditions (e.g., Gallo, 2010; Hintzman, 2011; Neuschatz et al., 2007). Many researchers argue that similar intrusions could occur with respect to childhood memories of abuse. People may "recall" events that are related to their actual experiences, but these events never actually occurred.

Other studies have demonstrated that laboratory-research participants can construct false memories for events during childhood that never actually happened. In laboratory research, these false memories include being attacked by a small dog, being lost in a shopping mall, seeing someone possessed by demons, having a skin sample removed by a school nurse, and becoming ill after eating hard-boiled eggs (e.g., Bernstein et al., 2005; Geraerts et al., 2010; Gerrie et al., 2005; Hyman & Kleinknecht, 1999; Mazzoni & Memon, 2003; Pickrell et al., 2004).

However, we need to emphasize that only a relatively small percentage of people actually claim to remember an event that did not occur. For example, researchers tried to implant a false memory that the research participant had attended a wedding at the age of 6. According to this fake story, the 6-year-old had accidentally bumped into a table containing a punch bowl, spilling punch on a parent of the bride. Interestingly, 25% of the participants eventually recalled this false memory—an entire event that did not actually occur (Hyman et al., 1995; Hyman & Loftus, 2002). Notice, however, that 75% of the students refused to "remember" the specific event.

Arguments for Recovered Memory. One problem is that these laboratory studies have little ecological validity with respect to memory for childhood sexual abuse (Freyd & Quina, 2000; Geraerts et al., 2010). Consider the studies on recalling word lists.

There's not much similarity between "remembering" a word that never appeared on a list, compared to a false memory of childhood sexual abuse (Bernstein & Loftus, 2009). Events such as spilling the contents of a punch bowl can be embarrassing. However, these events have no sexual content, and they could be discussed in public. In contrast, the research shows that people cannot be convinced to create false memories for more embarrassing events, such as having had an enema as a child (Pezdek et al., 1997).

Many people have been sexually abused as children, and they continually remember the incidents, even decades later. However, some people may genuinely not recall the abuse. For example, researchers have studied individuals whose sexual abuse had been documented by medical professionals or the legal system. Still, some of these individuals fail to recall the episode when interviewed as adults (Goodman et al., 2003; Pezdek & Taylor, 2002). Indeed, some people can forget about the sexual abuse for many years, but they suddenly recall it decades later.

Jennifer Freyd and her colleagues have proposed an explanation for these cases of recovered memory (DePrince & Freyd, 2004; Freyd et al., 2005; Freyd et al., 2010; Pezdek & Freyd, 2009). These researchers emphasize that childhood sexual abuse is genuinely different from relatively innocent episodes such as spilled wedding punch. In particular, they propose the term **betrayal trauma** to describe how a child may respond adaptively when a trusted parent or caretaker betrays him or her by sexual abuse. The child depends on this adult and must actively inhibit memories of abuse in order to maintain an attachment to this person.

Both Perspectives Are at Least Partially Correct. In reality, both the recovered-memory perspective and the false-memory perspective are at least partially correct. Indeed, some people have truly experienced childhood sexual abuse, and they may forget about the abuse for many decades until a critical event triggers their recall.

In contrast, other people have never experienced childhood sexual abuse. However, a suggestion about abuse may create a false memory of childhood experiences that never really occurred. In still other cases, people can provide quite accurate testimony—even years afterwards—about how they have been abused (Brainerd & Reyna, 2005; Castelli et al., 2006; Goodman & Paz-Alonso, 2006).

We have seen throughout this chapter that human memory is both flexible and complex. These memory processes can account for temporarily forgetting events, they can account for the construction of events that never actually happened, and they can also account for relatively accurate memory, even when the events are terrifying. As Bernstein and Loftus (2009) write,

> In essence, all memory is false to some degree. Memory is inherently a reconstructive process, whereby we piece together the past to form a coherent narrative that becomes our autobiography. In the process of reconstructing the past, we color and shape our life's experiences based on what we know about the world. (p. 373)
> **Source:** Bernstein, D. M., & Loftus, E. F. How to tell if a particular memory is true or false. *Perspectives on Psychological Science, 4,* 370–374. On page 373. Copyright © 2009. Reprinted by permission of Sage Publications.

◎ Section Summary: *Autobiographical Memory*

1. Research on autobiographical memory is typically high in ecological validity; this research shows that our memories are usually accurate, although we may make errors on some details, and we may blend together information from different events.

2. Memory schemas encourage us to make some errors in recalling events; in addition, we may reveal a consistency bias by exaggerating the similarity between our current self-schema and our previous characteristics.

3. The research on source monitoring shows that we may have difficulty deciding where we learned some information.

4. The research on reality monitoring shows that we may have difficulty deciding whether something really happened, instead of imagining it.

5. Flashbulb memories are rich with information, and we are often confident that they are accurate; however, even our memories for national tragedies are not especially accurate.

6. In eyewitness testimony, the post-event misinformation effect can occur if misleading information is introduced after a witness has seen an event. The research is consistent with the constructivist approach to memory.

7. Errors in eyewitness memory are more likely if the crime occurred during stressful circumstances, if the witness observed an event long ago, if the misinformation is plausible, if social pressure was applied, or if positive feedback was supplied to the eyewitness.

8. An eyewitness's self-confidence is not strongly correlated with his or her memory accuracy.

9. Both sides of the recovered-memory/false-memory controversy are at least partially correct. Some people may indeed forget about a painful childhood memory, recalling it years later. Other people apparently construct a memory of abuse that never really occurred, and still other people continue to have accurate memory for abuse, many years afterwards.

CHAPTER REVIEW QUESTIONS

1. Suppose that you are in charge of creating a public service announcement for television. Choose an issue that is important to you, and describe at least five tips from this chapter that would help you make an especially memorable advertisement. Be sure to include depth of processing as one of the tips.

2. What is encoding specificity? Think of a recent example in which encoding specificity could explain why you temporarily forgot something. How strong are the effects of encoding specificity, in real life and in the laboratory?

3. The in-depth section of this chapter examined how emotions and mood can influence your long-term memory. Explain how these two factors might be relevant in your everyday life.

4. Give several examples of explicit and implicit memory tasks you have performed in the past few days. What is dissociation, and how is it relevant in the research that has been conducted with both normal adults and people with amnesia?

5. Although this textbook focuses on cognitive psychology, several topics discussed in this chapter are relevant to other areas, such as social psychology, personality psychology, and abnormal psychology. Summarize this research, discussing topics such as the self-reference effect, emotions and memory, and the consistency bias.

6. Define the term "autobiographical memory," and describe several topics that have been studied in this area. How does research in this area differ from more traditional laboratory research? List the advantages and disadvantages of each approach.

7. Describe how schemas could lead to a distortion in the recall of a flashbulb memory. How might misleading post-event information also influence this recall? In answering the two parts of this question, use the terms *proactive interference* and *retroactive interference*.

8. The constructivist approach to memory emphasizes that we actively revise our memories in the light of new concerns and new information. How would this approach be relevant if a woman were to develop a false memory about her childhood, and she also shows a strong consistency bias? How would this approach be relevant for other topics in the section about autobiographical memory?

9. Chapter 6 emphasizes methods for improving your memory. However, the present chapter also contains some relevant information and hints about memory improvement. Review Chapter 5, and make a list of suggestions about memory improvement that you could use when you study for the next examination in cognitive psychology.

10. Researcher Daniel Schacter (2001) wrote a book describing several kinds of memory errors. He argues, however, that these errors are actually by-products of a memory system that usually functions quite well. What textbook theme is related to his argument? Review this chapter and list some of the memory errors people may commit. Explain why each error is a by-product of a memory system that works well in most everyday experiences.

KEYWORDS

working memory	mood	own-ethnicity bias
long-term memory	Pollyanna Principle	autobiographical memory
episodic memory	positivity effect	ecological validity
semantic memory	mood congruence	schema
procedural memory	explicit memory task	consistency bias
encoding	implicit memory task	source monitoring
retrieval	repetition priming task	reality monitoring
levels-of-processing approach	dissociation	flashbulb memory
depth-of-processing approach	anxiety disorders	post-event misinformation effect
distinctiveness	generalized anxiety disorder	proactive interference
elaboration	post-traumatic stress disorder	retroactive interference
self-reference effect	social phobia	constructivist approach
meta-analysis	amnesia	recovered-memory perspective
encoding-specificity principle	retrograde amnesia	false-memory perspective
recall task	anterograde amnesia	betrayal trauma
recognition task	hippocampus	
emotion	expertise	

RECOMMENDED READINGS

Applied Cognitive Psychology. If you are interested in the topics discussed in Chapter 5, you will enjoy browsing through this journal. Some examples of the research include children's responses to cross-examination, police officers' beliefs about how to interview crime suspects, and adults' memory for children's faces.

Handbook of eyewitness psychology. Memory for people (Vol. 1, Toglia, M. P., et al., Eds.), *Memory for events* (Vol. 2, Lindsay, R. C. L., et al., Eds.) (2007). Mahwah, NJ: Erlbaum. I strongly recommend this two-volume handbook for college libraries, as well as anyone interested in the psychological or legal components of eyewitness testimony. The chapters are clearly written, with numerous references to psychological research and legal cases.

Kovera, K. B., & Borgida, E. (2010). Social psychology and law. In S. T. Fiske, D. T. Gilbert, & G. Lindzey (Eds.), *The handbook of social psychology* (5th ed., Vol. 2, pp. 1343–1385). Hoboken, NJ: Wiley. This excellent chapter provides information about the own-ethnicity bias and eyewitness testimony, and it also includes many additional topics of interest to cognitive psychologists, social psychologists, and people interested in legal issues.

Schwartz, B. L. (2011). *Memory: Foundations and applications.* Thousand Oaks, CA: Sage. Several chapters of this excellent textbook are relevant for Chapter 5, including chapters on memory and the brain, episodic memory, autobiographical memory, and false memory.

CHAPTER 6
Memory Strategies and Metacognition

PREVIEW

Chapter 4 focused on working memory, which is the brief, immediate memory for the material you are currently processing. Chapter 5 explored long-term memory, or memory for events that occurred minutes, days, or even years earlier. Both of those chapters examined theoretical aspects of memory. In contrast, Chapter 6 emphasizes more practical issues concerned with memory strategies and metacognition. (Metacognition focuses on your knowledge and control of your cognitive processes.) The information in this chapter should help you develop more effective memory strategies; it should also help you learn how to monitor both your memory and your reading techniques.

The section on memory strategies begins by reviewing some memory suggestions derived from Chapters 3, 4, and 5. Next, we'll consider how different aspects of practice can enhance your memory. We'll then look at some memory techniques that emphasize imagery and organization. Our final topic in this section explores how you can also enhance your *prospective memory*, or remembering to do something in the future.

The second section of this chapter examines metacognition. We'll begin by exploring several factors that could influence the accuracy of your metamemory. Unfortunately, the research on metamemory suggests that college students are often overconfident when estimating their total score on a memory test. College students with Attention-Deficit/Hyperactivity Disorder are typically as accurate as other college students in predicting their memory performance. In general, however, most college students are not very aware of factors that can affect their memory accuracy. Furthermore, students need to know strategies for deciding which topics need the most study time, when they prepare for an uncoming exam.

The tip-of-the-tongue effect represents another dimension of metacognition. People can frequently supply characteristics of the target word, such as the sound of the target word, even if they cannot recall the precise target word. A related but less powerful phenomenon, the feeling of knowing, may allow you to answer a multiple-choice question correctly.

Our final topic is metacomprehension. Unfortunately, however, the research suggests that students are often overconfident in judging whether they have understood a passage that they have recently read. Throughout this chapter, we will examine techniques to help you learn course material more effectively.

CHAPTER INTRODUCTION

Take a moment to consider the thousands of hours that you spent during high school, listening to lectures, engaging in class discussions, taking notes, and reading textbooks. Most students at my college report that they also spent hundreds of hours—outside of class—studying for examinations and completing other assignments.

Now think about the amount of time your high school teachers spent in teaching you strategies for improving your memory. Perhaps a history teacher urged the class to begin studying early for an upcoming exam, rather than trying to master everything the night before the exam. Maybe a math teacher taught you how to remember the abbreviations for the three basic trigonometry formulas. Possibly a French-language teacher mentioned that you could remember vocabulary more effectively if you used mental imagery. Try to estimate the total amount of time your high school teachers spent helping you learn how to improve your memory.

When my cognitive psychology class begins the chapter on memory strategies and metacognition, we try the exercise I've just described. In contrast to the thousands of hours my students have spent learning in class and studying for exams, most of them estimate that all their high school teachers—combined—spent a grand total of about 1 or 2 hours discussing memory improvement.

Furthermore, some students report that their teachers recommended study strategies that contradict the information that they are learning about human memory. For instance, one student told our class about her history teacher's recommendations: Repeat a sentence out loud three times, and then write it three times, and you'll have it memorized. Pause for a moment, right now. Why should students avoid this particular recommendation?

We'll start this chapter by reviewing some strategy tips you learned about memory improvement, based on the chapters you've already read. Then we'll look at several other useful memory strategies that you can apply to enhance your memory for course material and for everyday memory tasks.

Your choice of memory strategies will typically be guided by your metacognition, which is your knowledge about your cognitive processes, as well as your control of these cognitive processes. The second half of this chapter will encourage you to explore how metacognition can help you use your cognitive processes more effectively.

Throughout this chapter, you'll notice that the research is typically high in ecological validity (Levin et al., 2010). As discussed in Chapters 1 and 5, a study has **ecological validity** if the conditions in which the research is conducted are similar to the natural setting to which the results will be applied. Therefore, when you read about this research, you can generally apply it to your own learning in your classes.

MEMORY STRATEGIES

When you use a **memory strategy**, you perform mental activities that can help to improve your encoding and retrieval. Most memory strategies help you remember something that you learned in the past. For example, when you take an exam in Art History, your professor may ask you to write an essay about the stylistic differences between Renaissance and Baroque paintings. To answer this question, you'll need to remember information from the professor's lectures during the last month and from the Art History chapters that you finished reading last night.

Most of this first part of Chapter 6 explores strategies for remembering something you learned in the *past*. Our last topic in this section is different, however, because it focuses on improving your memory strategies for something you must remember to do in the *future*.

Suggestions from Previous Chapters: A Review

Let's begin the advice about memory by considering information that you learned in earlier chapters. For example, in Chapter 3, you learned that divided attention decreases your ability to process information. This guideline is important when you listen to lectures and read your textbooks (Chabris & Simon, 2010; deWinstanley & Bjork, 2002). Chapter 3 also noted that people may have problems with saccadic eye movements. For instance, their eyes may frequently move backward to an earlier part of a sentence.

Chapter 4 pointed out the limits of working memory. These limits would be relevant when professors speak too quickly or display their detailed PowerPoint slides too briefly. If you encounter this problem, figure out how to respond strategically. You may want to complete the reading assignments before class, to familiarize yourself with the concepts. If the professor makes the slides available before class, study them in advance. When students can use the information for the slides—incorporating additional notes from the lecture—they tend to perform better on examinations (Marsh & Sink, 2010).

Chapter 5 provided much more advice about how to develop effective memory strategies. Let's consider three of these topics: (1) levels of processing, (2) the encoding-specificity principle, and (3) avoiding overconfidence. Before you begin, however, take a minute to describe each of these strategies, and consider how they could help you study more effectively for your next examination.

Levels of Processing. One of the most useful general principles for memory improvement comes from the discussion about levels of processing in Chapter 5. Specifically, the research on **levels of processing** shows that you will generally recall information more accurately if you process it at a deep level, rather than a shallow level (Craik & Lockhart, 1972; Esgate & Groome, 2005; Roediger, 2008).

We noted that deep levels of processing facilitate learning because of two factors, elaboration and distinctiveness. Let's examine elaboration first, and then focus on distinctiveness on page 173.

If you want to emphasize **elaboration,** you will concentrate on the specific meaning of a particular concept; you'll also try to relate this concept to your prior knowledge and to interconnected concepts that you have already mastered. You should emphasize rich, elaborate encoding, for instance, by explaining a concept to yourself (De Koning et al., 2011; Esgate & Groome, 2005; Herrmann et al., 2002). In contrast, if you use simple **rehearsal**, or repeating the information you want to learn, you will be wasting your time.

Here's a specific application of the elaboration factor, which you can use when you need to master a complex topic. Giles Einstein and Mark McDaniel (2004) propose that you can learn and remember complex material more easily if you create and answer "why questions." To answer these questions, you must use deep processing to think about the meaning of the material and connect this new material with the information you already know.

For example, suppose that your American History professor requires you to learn the Ten Amendments in the U.S. Bill of Rights. I recall having trouble remembering the Third Amendment. According to this Amendment, when citizens are asked to provide housing and food for soldiers, these citizens must be paid appropriately. This Amendment is difficult to remember because it is meaningless to most U.S. residents in the 21st century.

Einstein and McDaniel point out that we need to consider why this issue was important enough in American history to deserve one of the Ten Amendments. They suggest that we should think about the citizens of that era. They had little money, and yet they had been forced to house and feed soldiers during the Revolutionary War. Now we can understand why this amendment was so necessary! (Similarly, why did I ask you the "why question" about memory strategies in paragraph 3 on page 171.)

Research specifically shows that deep processing helps students remember more information in their psychology courses. For example, students learned more in a psychology course on personality theories if they had maintained a journal in which they applied various theories to personal friends, political figures, and characters from television programs (Connor-Greene, 2000). In this case, students elaborated on the material and analyzed it in a complex, meaningful fashion, rather than simply rehearsing it.

In Chapter 5, we emphasized that deep levels of processing enhance your memory for two reasons, elaboration and distinctiveness. We've already considered elaboration, so let's discuss **distinctiveness**, which means that one memory trace should be different from all other memory traces. People tend to forget information if it is not distinctly different from the other memory traces in their long-term memory.

Distinctiveness is an especially important factor when we try to learn names. For example, I often need to recall someone's name. Let's say that I have just met a young woman named Kate. I've often made the mistake of telling myself, "That's easy. I'll just remember that she looks like the student in my Cognitive Psychology class named Kate." Later on, I'll realize that I actually have three students in that class named Kate. My encoding had not been sufficiently distinctive. As a result, the face I was trying to recall was extremely vulnerable to interference from other students' faces. With interference from other items, we easily forget the target name (Craik, 2006; Schacter & Wiseman, 2006; Tulving & Rosenbaum, 2006).

As we emphasized in Chapter 5, one especially deep level of processing takes advantage of the **self-reference effect**, in which you enhance long-term memory by relating the material to your own experiences. For example, one of the reasons that I include demonstrations in this textbook is to provide you with personal experiences that focus on some of the important principles of cognitive psychology.

If you read your textbook in a reflective fashion, you'll try to think how to apply major concepts to your own life. I'm hopeful, for instance, that this chapter will encourage you to see how memory strategies and metacognition can be helpful in many other college courses. Now try Demonstration 6.1.

Encoding Specificity. Chapter 5 also discussed the **encoding-specificity principle**, which states that recall is often better if the context at the time of encoding matches the context at the time when your retrieval will be tested. As we noted in Chapter 5, context effects are often inconsistent (e.g., Baddeley, 2004; Nairne, 2005; Wong & Read, 2011). For example, you probably will *not* improve your grade if you decide to study for an upcoming exam by reviewing the material in the specific classroom where you'll be taking this exam.

However, the research on encoding specificity does provide some other more general strategies. For instance, when you are trying to devise study strategies, consider how you will be tested on your next examination (Herrmann, Yoder, et al., 2006; Koriat, 2000). Let's suppose that your exam will contain essays. This format requires you to *recall* information—not simply to *recognize* it. When you are learning the material, make an effort to quiz yourself periodically by closing your notebook and trying to recall the material on the pages you've just read. During studying, try answering the Chapter Review Questions. You can also create some essay questions and then answer them, a strategy that would also increase your deep processing of the material.

Ⓢ **Demonstration 6.1**

Instructions and Memory

Learn the following list of pairs by repeating the members of each pair several times. For example, if the pair were CAT–WINDOW, you would say over and over to yourself, "CAT–WINDOW, CAT–WINDOW, CAT–WINDOW." Just repeat the words, and do not use any other study method. Allow yourself 1 minute to learn this list.

CUSTARD–LUMBER	IVY–MOTHER
JAIL–CLOWN	LIZARD–PAPER
ENVELOPE–SLIPPER	SCISSORS–BEAR
SHEEPSKIN–CANDLE	CANDY–MOUNTAIN
FRECKLES–APPLE	BOOK–PAINT
HAMMER–STAR	TREE–OCEAN

(continued)

Now, cover up the pairs on page 174. Try to recall as many responses as possible:

ENVELOPE _____ JAIL _____

FRECKLES _____ IVY _____

TREE _____ SHEEPSKIN _____

CANDY _____ BOOK _____

SCISSORS _____ LIZARD _____

CUSTARD _____ HAMMER _____

Next, learn the list of pairs below by visualizing a mental picture in which the two objects in each pair are in some kind of vivid interaction. For example, if the pair were CAT–WINDOW, you might make up a picture of a cat jumping through a closed window, with the glass shattering all around. Just make up a mental image and do not use any other study method. Allow yourself 1 minute to learn this list.

SOAP–MERMAID MIRROR–RABBIT

FOOTBALL–LAKE HOUSE–DIAMOND

PENCIL–LETTUCE LAMB–MOON

CAR–HONEY BREAD–GLASS

CANDLE–DANCER LIPS–MONKEY

DANDELION–FLEA DOLLAR–ELEPHANT

Now, cover up the pairs above. Try to recall as many responses as possible:

CANDLE _____ DOLLAR _____

DANDELION _____ CAR _____

BREAD _____ LIPS _____

MIRROR _____ PENCIL _____

LAMB _____ SOAP _____

FOOTBALL _____ HOUSE _____

Finally, count the number of correct responses on each list. Did you recall a greater number of words with the imagery instructions? Incidentally, you may have found it very difficult to avoid using imagery on the first list, because you are reading a section about memory improvement. In that case, your recall scores were probably similar for the two lists. You may wish to test a friend instead. On pages 178–180, we will discuss how imagery can enhance your memory.

Avoiding Overconfidence. **Our** examination of autobiographical memory in Chapter 5 provided a general caution, rather than a specific memory strategy. In that chapter, we saw that people often believe that they have highly accurate memories about their life experiences. However, even their so-called flashbulb memories usually contain some errors. This area of research suggests that we are often overconfident about our memory skills.

If we can make mistakes in remembering important life events, then we can certainly make mistakes in remembering material from a college course. In fact, researchers have documented a foresight bias (E. L. Bjork et al., 2011; R. A. Bjork, 2011). The **foresight bias** occurs when people have been studying for a future exam, and they are overconfident about how they will perform on this exam.

The issue of overconfidence is also an important topic in the second half of the chapter, on metacognition, as well as in future chapters. Now, before reading further, be sure to try Demonstration 6.1.

Strategies Emphasizing Practice

So far, we've considered several memory-improvement suggestions based on concepts discussed in earlier chapters. Let us now turn to some additional suggestions about memory strategies, beginning with those suggestions that focus on practice.

The Total-Time Hypothesis. **The** first of these memory-improvement strategies sounds almost too obvious to mention. According to the **total-time hypothesis**, the amount that you learn depends on the total time you devote to learning. This hypothesis is generally true (Baddeley, 1997; Roediger, 2008).

However, if you simply re-read the material over and over, this additional practice will not be helpful. For instance, researchers have found that the variable "number of hours spent studying" is not a good method of predicting a student's grade-point average. Instead, study time predicts grade-point average only when the researchers also assess the *quality* of study strategies (Plant et al., 2005). For instance, 1 hour spent actively learning the material—using deep levels of processing—will usually be more helpful than 2 hours in which your eyes simply drift across the pages.

The Retrieval-Practice Effect. **To** prepare for an examination, you should also practice retrieving the information from long-term memory. (For example, what are the memory-improvement techniques we have discussed so far in this chapter?) According to the **retrieval-practice effect**, you try to recall important concepts from memory; if retrieval is difficult—and you succeed—your learning is enhanced. The research demonstrates that retrieval practice improves test performance (R. A. Bjork, 2011; deWinstanley & R. A. Bjork, 2002; Herrmann et al., 2002).

The Distributed-Practice Effect. **According** to the **distributed-practice effect**, you will remember more material if you spread your learning trials over time (**spaced learning**). You'll remember less if you try "cramming," by learning the material all at once (**massed learning**). The studies generally support this principle for both recall tasks and recognition tasks (Koriat & Helstrup, 2007; Landauer, 2011; Metcalfe, 2011). Research also confirms the spacing effect with real-life material that can be difficult to master, such as English vocabulary, math knowledge, and people's names (Carpenter & DeLosh, 2005; Kornell, 2009; Pashler et al., 2007; Rohrer & Taylor, 2006).

One reason that distributed practice is helpful for long-term recall is that it introduces **desirable difficulties**, in other words, a learning situation that is somewhat challenging, but not too difficult (R. A. Bjork, 2011; Koriat & Helstrup, 2007; McDaniel & Einstein, 2005). Suppose that you need to learn some key concepts for a biology class. If you test yourself on one concept several times in a row, the concept will seem easy by your third or fourth repetition.

In contrast, if you allow several minutes to pass before the second repetition, you'll pay more attention to that concept. In addition, the task will be slightly more difficult because you will have begun to forget the concept (R. A. Bjork, 2011; Einstein & McDaniel, 2004). As a result, you'll make some mistakes, and you will not be overconfident that you have mastered the concepts. According to the current research, a delay of at least one day between practice sessions is especially effective in boosting long-term retention (Bahrick & Hall, 2005; Cepeda et al., 2006).

I have applied the distributed-practice effect in this textbook. For instance, this chapter begins with an outline, and then the preview foreshadows the topics, including some definitions of terms that may be unfamiliar to you. The introduction provides a review of some concepts you learned in Chapter 5. You will also have another opportunity to review many of these memory concepts in Chapter 13, when we examine memory processes in children and elderly adults.

The Testing Effect. Professors administer tests in an academic course so that they can assess how much you have learned. However, the research demonstrates a second function of tests, called the **testing effect**; taking a test is actually an excellent way to boost your long-term recall for academic material (e.g., Campbell & Mayer, 2009; Roediger et al., 2010; Vojdanoska et al., 2010).

For example, Henry Roediger and Jeffrey Karpicke (2006b) asked students to read short essays on a science-related topic. Then half of the students studied the same essays again. The other half took a test on the contents of the essay. They received a blank sheet of paper and wrote down as much as they could recall from the essay. However, they did not receive feedback about the accuracy of their recall.

During the last step of the study, everyone received a final test in which they wrote down their recall from the essay. Some students received this final test just 5 minutes after the last activity (either studying or taking the first test). Others were tested after a delay of either 2 days or 1 week.

Figure 6.1 shows the results. As you can see, when students took the test only 5 minutes after the last activity, those who had restudied the material performed slightly better than those who had completed a test on the material. However, after a delay of 2 days or 1 week, students earned much higher scores if their last activity had been taking a test—even though they had received no feedback about their accuracy on that test.

FIGURE 6.1

The Effects of Learning Condition (Repeated Study Versus Testing) and Retention Interval on Percentage of Idea Units Correctly Recalled.

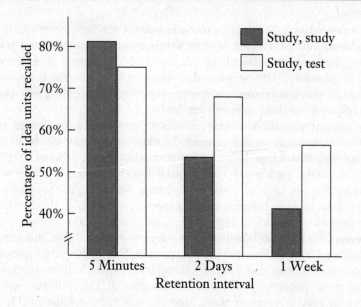

Source: Roediger, H. L., III, & Karpicke, J. D. (2006b). Test enhanced learning: Taking memory tests improves long-term retention. *Psychological Science, 17,* 249–255.

Apparently, when you take a test, this testing provides practice in retrieving the relevant material. Furthermore, that test produces desirable difficulties. When you try to recall the material you had read, you'll see that the task is somewhat challenging, and you will not be overconfident (Pashler et al., 2007; Roediger & Karpicke, 2006a, 2006b; Whitten, 2011). In addition, when students complete a second test, their recall shows greater organization, compared to students who received additional study time (Zaromb & Roediger, 2010). I'm hopeful that Figure 6.1 will encourage you to test yourself on the new terms and the review questions at the end of each chapter in this textbook.

Mnemonics Using Imagery

The preceding discussion emphasized the usefulness of strategies related to practice. This section, as well as the next one on organization, emphasizes the use of mnemonics (pronounced "ni-*mon*-icks," with a silent initial *m*). **Mnemonics** are mental strategies designed to improve your memory (Dunlosky & Bjork, 2008b; Worthen & Hunt,

2011). Some mnemonics emphasize **mental imagery**: We mentally represent objects, actions, or ideas that are not physically present. Chapter 7 examines characteristics of mental images. In the present chapter, however, we'll focus on how imagery can enhance your memory.

Now check your results for Demonstration 6.1 on page 175. This demonstration is a simplified version of a study by Bower and Winzenz (1970), who asked one group of participants to simply repeat pairs of words silently. Other participants tried to construct a mental image of the two words in vivid interaction with each other. Later, the participants saw the first word of each pair, and they were asked to supply the second word. The results showed that people in the imagery condition recalled more than twice as many items, compared with the people in the repetition condition.

Visual imagery can be a powerful strategy for enhancing memory (Davies & Wright, 2010b; Reed, 2010). The research shows that imagery is especially effective when the items that must be recalled are shown interacting with each other (Carney & Levin, 2001; McKelvie et al., 1994). For example, if you want to remember the

FIGURE 6.2

The Keyword Representation for the Pair of Words *Turkey-Chompipe*.

Demonstration 6.2

Remembering Lists of Letters

Read the following list of letters and then cover up the list. Try to recall them as accurately as possible.

YMC AJF KFB ISA TNB CTV

Now read the following list of letters and then cover them up. Try to recall them as accurately as possible.

AMA PHD GPS VCR CIA CBS

---

pair *piano-toast*, try to visualize a piano chewing a large piece of toast. In general, an interacting visual image is especially helpful if the image is bizarre (Davidson, 2006; Worthen, 2006). One reason that visualization mnemonics are effective is that they are motivating and interesting (Herrmann et al., 2002).

For example, if you need to remember unfamiliar vocabulary items, the keyword method is especially helpful. In the **keyword method**, you identify an English word (the keyword) that sounds similar to the new word you want to learn; then you create an image that links the keyword with the meaning of this new word. The research on the keyword method shows that it can help students who are trying to learn new English vocabulary words, vocabulary in another language, or people's names (Carney & Levin, 2001, 2011; Herrmann et al., 2002; Worthen & Hunt, 2011).

One Thanksgiving, our Spanish-speaking guests were from Nicaragua, where the word for *turkey* is *chompipe* (pronounced, "chom-*pea*-pay"). I had trouble remembering this word until I created an image of a turkey chomping down on an enormous pipe, as in Figure 6.2.

Another imagery technique is based on establishing a series of familiar locations, such as the driveway, garage, and front door in a family home. Next you create a mental image of each item that you want to remember. Then you place a mental image of each item in one of those locations. This method is especially useful if you want to remember the items in a specified order (Einstein & McDaniel, 2004; Groninger, 1971; Hunter, 2004b). Incidentally, try Demonstration 6.2 before you read further.

Mnemonics Using Organization

When people use **organization** as a mnemonic strategy, they try to bring systematic order to the material they want to learn. This category of mnemonics makes sense, because you need to use deep processing to sort items into categories (Esgate & Groome, 2005). Furthermore, retrieval is easier when you have constructed a well-organized framework (Wolfe, 2005; Worthen & Hunt, 2011).

When you are examining the four mnemonic strategies that emphasize organization, you may find that some of these may be more helpful than others (Schwartz, 2011). Furthermore, you may find that chunking works well when you try one memory task, but the hierarchy technique might be more effective for a different memory task.

Chunking. Chapter 4 discussed an organizational strategy called **chunking**, in which we combine several small units into larger units. For instance, Demonstration 6.2 on page 180 is a modified version of a study by Bower and Springston (1970). These researchers found that people recalled much more material when a string of letters was grouped according to meaningful, familiar units, rather than in arbitrary groups of three. In Demonstration 6.2, did you recall a larger number of items on the second list, which was organized according to familiar chunks?

Hierarchy Technique. A second effective way to organize material is to construct a hierarchy. A **hierarchy** is a system in which items are arranged in a series of classes, from the most general classes to the most specific. For example, Figure 6.3 shows part of a hierarchy for animals.

Gordon Bower and his colleagues (1969) asked people to learn words that belonged to four hierarchies similar to the one in Figure 6.3. Some people learned the words in an organized fashion, in the format of the upside-down trees you see in Figure 6.3. Others saw the same words, but the words were randomly scattered throughout the different positions in each tree. The group who had learned the organized structure recalled more than three times as many words as the group who learned the random

FIGURE 6.3

An Example of a Hierarchy.

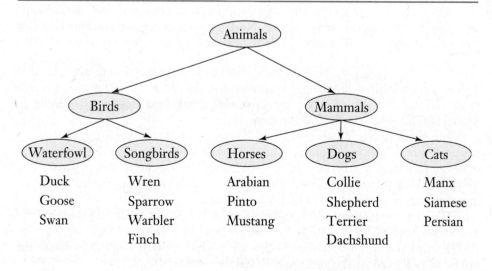

structure. Structure and organization clearly enhance your recall (Baddeley, 1999; Herrmann et al., 2002; Worthen & Hunt, 2011).

An outline is one example of a hierarchy, because an outline is divided into general categories, and each general category is further subdivided. An outline is valuable because it provides organization and structure for concepts that you learn in a particular discipline.

For example, look at the chapter outline on page 169. You'll see that the outline features two general categories: memory strategies and metacognition. When you have finished reading this chapter, see if you can construct—from memory—a hierarchy similar to Figure 6.3. Begin with the two general categories, and then subdivide each category into more specific topics. Then recheck the chapter outline to see whether you omitted anything. If you study the outline of each chapter, you will have an organized structure that can enhance your recall on an examination.

According to a study by Regan Gurung (2003), students in introductory psychology classes report that they seldom use chapter outlines when studying for exams. However, it's possible that students in more advanced courses (such as cognitive psychology!) know that they can learn more effectively if they understand how a topic is organized.

First-Letter Technique. Another popular mnemonic that makes use of organization is the **first-letter technique**; you take the first letter of each word you want to remember, and then you compose a word or a sentence from those letters. Maybe you learned the order of the colors of the rainbow by using the letters ROY G. BIV to recall Red, Orange, Yellow, Green, Blue, Indigo, and Violet. As you may have learned in a statistics class, the nominal, ordinal, interval, and ratio scales conveniently spell *noir*, the French word for "black."

Students frequently use first-letter mnemonics. Unfortunately, however, the laboratory research does not consistently show that this technique is effective (Herrmann et al., 2002). Still, in those cases where it does work, its effectiveness can probably be traced to the fact that these first letters frequently enhance retrieval. For instance, suppose that you are experiencing a memory block for a certain term. If you know the first letter of that term, you'll be more likely to retrieve the item (Herrmann et al., 2002).

Narrative Technique. So far, we have looked at three mnemonic strategies that focus on organization: chunking, hierarchies, and the first-letter technique. A fourth organizational method, called the **narrative technique**, instructs people to make up stories that link a series of words together.

In a classic study, Bower and Clark (1969) told a group of people to make up narrative stories that incorporated a set of English words. People in a control group received no special instructions. In all, each group learned twelve lists of words. The results showed that the people in the narrative-technique group recalled about six times as many words as those in the control group.

The narrative technique is clearly an effective strategy for enhancing memory, and it has also been used successfully with people who have impaired memory (Wilson, 1995). However, techniques such as this are effective only if you can generate the narrative easily and reliably, during both learning and recall.

We have reviewed several categories of memory strategies that can help you study more effectively. However, you cannot improve your performance on exams unless you actually apply these strategies. For example, I recall a student in my introductory psychology course several years ago who provided an unfortunate example of this problem. Dave had earned a low D grade on the first exam in the course, so I wrote a note on his exam, asking him to come to my office to discuss study strategies. Together we talked about several of concepts mentioned in this chapter, including a heavy emphasis on metacognition (the topic we'll address in the second half of this chapter). Eagerly, I inspected Dave's second exam. Another low D. Later, I asked Dave whether he had tried any of the ideas we had discussed. He replied, "No, they would have been too much work, so I studied the same way I always study."

The research suggests that Dave's perspective is fairly common. Students often resist using resources that could help them. For instance, when students enrolled in a Web-based course in introductory psychology course, they seldom used any of the online study material until just two days before their exam (Maki & Maki, 2000). Furthermore, students enrolled in traditional introductory psychology courses sometimes make use of the boldface terms in their textbook. However, they seldom use other helpful features, such as outlines (as we noted earlier), chapter summaries, or practice-test questions (Gurung, 2003, 2004).

The research shows that college students' study habits, study skills, and study attitudes are strong predictors of students' grades in college (Hartwig & Dunlosky, 2012). For example, imagine that you are in charge of the admissions staff at your current college or university. Your major goal is to admit applicants who will earn high grades, once they enroll. Admissions offices typically focus on students' grades in high school and their scores on standardized tests. However, those three factors—study habits, study skills, and study attitudes—are just as important as students' high-school grades and their standardized-test scores, with respect to predicting students grades in college (Credé & Kuncel, 2008).

IN DEPTH

Prospective Memory

So far, Chapters 4, 5, and 6 have focused on **retrospective memory**, or remembering information that you acquired in the *past*. In contrast, we will now focus on **prospective memory**, or remembering that you need to do something in the *future*. Some typical prospective-memory tasks would include remembering to bring your research-methods book to class today, to pick up a friend at work this afternoon, and to keep your office-hour appointment with a professor.

Most people rank prospective-memory errors among the most common memory lapses and also among the most embarrassing (Cook et al., 2005; Einstein & McDaniel, 2004; McDaniel & Einstein, 2007). Students are often relieved to know that this kind of task actually has a name and that other people have similar problems with prospective memory.

Prospective-memory tasks actually include two components. First, you must establish that you intend to accomplish a particular task at some future time. Second, at that future time, you must fulfill your original intention (Einstein & McDaniel, 2004; McDaniel & Einstein, 2007). Occasionally, the primary challenge is to remember the actual *content* of the action. You've probably experienced the feeling that you know you are supposed to do something, but you cannot remember what it is. However, most of the time, the primary challenge is simply to remember to perform an action in the future (McDaniel & Einstein, 2007).

Let's first compare prospective-memory tasks with more standard retrospective-memory tasks, and then we'll consider the related topic of absentmindedness. With this background in mind, we'll consider several specific suggestions about how to improve prospective memory.

Comparing Prospective and Retrospective Memory. Prospective memory typically focuses on action. In contrast, retrospective memory is likely to focus on remembering information and ideas (Einstein & McDaniel, 2004). Furthermore, the research on prospective memory is more likely to emphasize ecological validity. In other words, researchers try to design tasks that resemble the kind of prospective-memory tasks we face in our daily lives.

Despite their differences, prospective memory and retrospective memory are governed by some of the same variables. For example, your memory is more accurate for both kinds of memory tasks if you use both distinctive encoding and effective retrieval cues. In addition, both kinds of memory are more accurate when you have only a short delay prior to retrieval (Einstein & McDaniel, 2004). Also, prospective memory and retrospective memory show similar rates of forgetting, with the passage of time (Tobias, 2009). Finally, prospective memory relies on regions of the frontal lobe that also play a role in retrospective memory (Einstein & McDaniel, 2004).

Absentmindedness and Prospective-Memory Failures. One intriguing component of prospective memory is absentmindedness. Most people do not publicly reveal their absentminded mistakes. You may therefore think that you are the only person who forgets to pick up a quart of milk on your way home from class, who dials Chris's phone number when you wanted to speak to Alex, or who fails to include an important attachment when sending an e-mail. In fact, I recall attending a session at a psychology conference, which focused on the current research about prospective memory. One researcher asked the audience to guess the most frequent kind of prospective-memory error. The clear winner was the "missing attachment mistake."

One problem is that the typical prospective-memory task represents a divided-attention situation. You must focus on your ongoing activity, as well as on the task you need to remember in the future (Marsh et al., 2000; McDaniel et al., 2004). Absentminded behavior is especially likely when the prospective-memory task requires you to disrupt a customary activity. Suppose that this customary activity is

↳ ex: going to the store before going home after work

driving from your college to your home. Now suppose that you have a prospective-memory task that you must perform today, for example, buying milk at the grocery store on your way home. In cases like this, your long-standing habit dominates the more fragile prospective memory, and you fall victim to absentminded behavior.

Prospective-memory errors are more likely in highly familiar surroundings when you are performing a task automatically. For instance, consider people who want to stop smoking. They typically acknowledge that they automatically light up a cigarette in the kitchen, right after breakfast (Tobias, 2009). They will probably need to move directly to a different room, in order to break the smoking habit.

Absentminded behavior is also more likely if you are preoccupied or distracted, or if you are feeling time pressure. In most cases, absentmindedness is simply irritating. However, sometimes these slips can produce airplane collisions, industrial accidents, and other disasters that influence the lives of hundreds of individuals (Finstad et al., 2006). For example, Dismukes and Nowinski (2007) studied the records of 75 airplane crashes that could be attributed to the crew members' memory failures. Out of 75 crashes, 74 could be traced to prospective-memory errors, and only one could be traced to a retrospective-memory error.

Suggestions for Improving Prospective Memory. Earlier in the chapter, we discussed numerous suggestions that you could use to aid your retrospective memory. You can use some of these internal strategies to aid your prospective memory as well. For example, if you create a vivid, interactive mental image of a quart of milk, you might avoid driving past the grocery store in an absentminded fashion (Einstein & McDaniel, 2004).

However, the reminders that you choose must be distinctive if you want to perform a prospective-memory task (Engelkamp, 1998; Guynn et al., 1998). For example, suppose you want to remember to give Tonya a message tomorrow. It won't be helpful just to rehearse her name or just to remind yourself that you have to convey a message. Instead, you must form a strong connection between these two components, linking both Tonya's name and the fact that you must give her a message.

Another problem is that people are often overconfident that they will remember to perform specific prospective memory task. After all, the actual task of buying a quart of milk is extremely simple... but remembering to actually do this task is challenging. Throughout the rest of this book, we will see that people are overconfident on a wide variety of cognitive tasks.

External memory aids are especially helpful on prospective-memory tasks (McDaniel & Einstein, 2007). An **external memory aid** is defined as any device, external to yourself, that facilitates your memory in some way (Herrmann et al., 2002; Worthen & Hunt, 2011). Some examples of external memory aids include a shopping list, a rubber band around your wrist, and the ringing of an alarm clock, to remind you to make an important phone call at a specified time.

The placement of your external memory aid is also important. For example, my nephew sometimes drove to his mother's home for dinner, and she typically told him about some items in the refrigerator that he must remember to take home when he left. After several prospective-memory lapses, he thought of an ideal external memory aid: When he arrives for dinner, he places his car keys in a conspicuous location in the refrigerator (White, 2003). Notice his strategic application of this memory aid. He is highly unlikely to drive home without the refrigerated items.

My students report that they often use informal external mnemonics to aid their prospective memory. When they want to remember to bring a book to class, they place it in a location where they will confront the book on the way to class. They also write reminders on the back of their hands. Other students describe the sea of colored sticky notes that decorate their dormitory rooms.

However, these external memory aids are helpful only if you can use them easily and if they successfully remind you of what you are supposed to remember. Now that you are familiar with the challenges of prospective memory, try Demonstration 6.3. Then review the memory-improvement techniques listed in Table 6.1.

Demonstration 6.3

Prospective Memory

Make a list of five prospective-memory tasks that you need to accomplish within the next day or two. These should be tasks that you must remember to complete on your own, without anyone else providing a reminder.

For each item, first describe the method you would customarily use to remember to do the task. Also note whether this method is typically successful. Then, for each task where you usually make a prospective-memory error, try to figure out a more effective reminder. (Incidentally, one prospective-memory task that you may forget to do is to complete this demonstration!)

TABLE 6.1

Memory-Improvement Strategies

1. Suggestions from previous chapters

   a. Do not divide your attention between several simultaneous tasks.

   b. Keep in mind that your working memory is limited; figure out strategies to overcome this problem.

   c. Process information in terms of its meaning, rather than at a shallow level; emphasize elaborative encodings, distinctiveness, and self-reference.

   d. When you study, apply the encoding-specificity principle by creating questions for yourself that have the same format as the questions on your exam.

   e. Don't be overconfident about the accuracy of your memory for events in your life.

2. **Techniques related to practice**

   a. The amount you learn depends on the total time that you spend practicing.

   b. You'll learn more effectively if you spread your learning trials over time (the distributed-practice effect).

   c. You'll enhance your memory simply by taking tests on the material.

3. **Mnemonics using imagery**

   a. Use imagery, especially imagery that shows an interaction between the items that need to be recalled.

   b. Use the keyword method; for example, if you are learning vocabulary in another language, identify an English word that sounds like the target word, and link the English word with the meaning of that target word.

4. **Mnemonics using organization**

   a. Use chunking by combining isolated items into meaningful units.

   b. Construct a hierarchy by arranging items in a series of categories (e.g., Figure 6.3 on p. 181).

   c. Take the first letter of each item you want to remember, and compose a word or sentence from these letters (first-letter technique).

   d. Create a narrative, or a story that links a series of words together.

5. **Improving prospective memory**

   a. Create a vivid, interactive mental image to prompt future recall.

   b. Create a specific reminder or an external memory aid.

⊚ Section Summary: *Memory Strategies*

1. Chapters 3 and 4 presented several problems that can decrease learning. These include problems with divided attention and limited working memory.

2. Chapter 5 introduced several strategies for improving memory. These include using deep levels of processing (including elaboration, distinctiveness, and the self-reference method). Encoding specificity is sometimes helpful. However, it is important to avoid the dangers of overconfidence.

3. Chapter 6, the current chapter, discusses four general memory-improvement strategies that focus on aspects of practice: the total-time hypothesis, the retrieval-practice effect, the distributed-practice effect, and the testing effect.

4. Some useful mnemonics focus on imagery; these include visualizing the items in vivid interaction and the keyword method.

5. Other useful mnemonics focus on organization; these include chunking, the hierarchy technique, the first-letter technique, and the narrative technique.

6. Most of the research focuses on retrospective memory. In contrast, the in-depth section of this chapter examines prospective memory, or remembering to do something in the future. Although the two kinds of memory have somewhat different focuses, they share some important similarities.

7. People make more errors on prospective-memory tasks when they are in a divided-attention situation, when they need to disrupt a habitual activity to perform the prospective-memory task, and when they are preoccupied.

8. In general, prospective memory is more accurate if people use the same memory strategies they use in retrospective-memory tasks, if they avoid overconfidence, and if they use external memory aids.

METACOGNITION

The first half of this chapter focused on memory strategies, or methods of improving your memory. This second half focuses on the related topic of metacognition. We noted earlier that **metacognition** refers to your knowledge and control of your cognitive processes. One important function of metacognition is to supervise the way you select and use your memory strategies. Consistent with Theme 1, metacognition is an extremely active process. As you'll see, metacognition requires focused thinking and self-assessment (Koriat & Helstrup, 2007).

Think about the different kinds of metacognitive knowledge that you possess. For example, your course in cognitive psychology has probably encouraged you to think about some factors that could influence your own memory. These factors may include the time of day, the type of material, your motivation, and a variety of social factors.

If you have carefully studied the information in this textbook and in your cognitive psychology class, then you already know more than most people about the general factors that can influence your memory (Magnussen et al., 2006). In addition, you probably know how to control or regulate your study strategies. If something looks difficult to remember, you'll typically spend more time trying to commit it to memory.

Metacognition is an intriguing topic because we use our cognitive processes to think about our cognitive processes. This topic is important because your knowledge about your cognitive processes can guide you in selecting strategies to improve your future cognitive performance. Metacognition is also important because a general goal in college should be to learn how to think and how to become a reflective person. As a reflective person, you can consider what you have done and what you plan to do in the future (Dominowski, 2002).

The topic of metacognition belongs to a larger issue in psychology, called **self-knowledge**, or what people believe about themselves (Wilson, 2009). Self-knowledge includes the topics in this chapter, as well as your knowledge about your social behavior and your personality. Furthermore, social psychologists are beginning to study people's metacognition about their attitudes (Rucker et al., 2011). For example, you might wonder to yourself, "Maybe I like Pat and Devon because they look attractive, rather than because they are nice people."

Before we consider the details about metacognition, let's briefly review topics related to metacognition that were described in three previous chapters of this book. For instance, in Chapter 3, you saw that people often have limited consciousness about their higher mental processes. As a result, they may not be able to identify which factors actually helped them solve a problem.

Chapter 4 explored Alan Baddeley's (2007) theory of working memory. According to Baddeley's approach, the central executive plays an important role in planning your cognitive behavior. For example, your central executive is essential in the metacognitive task of planning which topics you'll spend the most time studying when you are preparing for an exam.

Chapter 5 discussed how people may have difficulty on source-monitoring tasks. For instance, you may not be able to recall whether you actually gave a book to a friend—or whether you merely imagined you had done so. We also noted that people are sometimes unaware of the errors they make in flashbulb memory or courtroom testimony.

In this section of the current chapter, we will examine several important kinds of metacognition. Our first topic is **metamemory**, a topic that refers to people's knowledge, monitoring, and control of their memory (Dunlosky & Bjork, 2008a). Metamemory is extremely important when you want to improve your memory. We will therefore explore several components of metamemory. Then we will consider an additional kind of metacognition, which is called *metacomprehension*.

Later chapters of this book also examine aspects of metacognition. For example, in Chapter 11 we will discuss whether people can accurately judge how close they are to solving a cognitively challenging problem. Chapter 12 shows that we are frequently overconfident that we have made a correct decision. Also, Chapter 13 addresses the development of metamemory across the lifespan.

Research on metamemory is more extensive than for all other areas of metacognition. We will examine five questions about metamemory:

1. What factors influence people's metamemory accuracy?
2. How do people with Attention-Deficit/Hyperactivity Disorder perform on metamemory tasks?
3. What are people's beliefs about factors that might influence their memory?
4. What do people know about how to regulate their study strategies?
5. How accurate are people in judging whether they will be able to recall a specific word, for instance, in the tip-of-the-tongue effect?

Factors that Influence People's Metamemory Accuracy

Have you ever been in this situation? You thought that you knew the material for a midterm. In fact, you expected to receive a fairly high grade. However, when the midterms were handed back, you received a C. If this sounds familiar, you already know that your metamemory is not always accurate in predicting your memory performance.

In what circumstances does your metamemory accurately predict your actual memory performance? The answer to this question depends on several important characteristics of the task. Let's start by focusing on people's estimates about their *total score* for a memory test compared to their estimates for *individual items* on a memory test.

Metamemory: Estimating the Accuracy for Total Score Versus the Accuracy for Individual Items. In general, people tend to be overconfident if you ask them to predict their *total score* on a memory test. In contrast, people tend to be accurate if you ask them to predict which *individual* items they will remember and which ones they will forget.

In some of the metamemory studies, students begin by studying a list of paired associates, such as *coat-sandwich*. That is, when they see the word *coat*, they know that they must respond *sandwich*. Then the students are asked to predict the total number of correct responses they will supply on a later test (Koriat, 2007; Koriat & R. A. Bjork, 2005, 2006a, 2006b). In this situation, they are likely to commit the foresight bias; they overestimate the number of answers they will correctly supply on a future test (Koriat et al., 2008).

Another problem here is that the participants are studying those word pairs while the correct responses are visible, so their prediction will probably be overly optimistic. Similarly, students who are reading a chapter in a textbook are often overconfident that they can remember a concept, when they are looking directly at a description of the concept (Gurung & McCann, 2011). Keep this issue in mind if you are learning technical terminology or you are studying vocabulary words in another language. You would be more likely to provide an accurate estimate if you conscientiously used flashcards to assess your learning (Hartwig & Dunlosky, 2012). For example, you might write the English word on one side and the French word on the other side.

Similarly, suppose that you have a psychology exam that will be based on a textbook. A good plan would be to read the material on a page, close the book, and summarize the information on that page. You may have a general idea about the material. However, when your book is closed, you may discover that you cannot provide specific information. In any case, check to see if your answer is correct.

In other studies, students estimate their total scores *after* finishing an exam. For example, Dunning and his coauthors (2003) asked students in a sophomore-level psychology course to estimate the total score that they thought they had earned on an examination they had just completed. Then these researchers graded the test and divided the students into four groups, based on their actual test score.

Figure 6.4 shows the performance for the four groups: the bottom quartile, second quartile, third quartile, and top quartile. Notice that the students in the top quartile estimated their total actual scores very accurately. The students in the third quartile were almost as accurate. However, the less competent students clearly overestimated their performance. Notice, for instance, that the students in the bottom quarter of the class overestimated their performance by about eight items. Ironically, less competent students are often not aware of their limitations (Dunlosky & Metcalfe, 2009). In other words, they do not know that they do not know the material!

FIGURE 6.4

Estimated Total Score Versus Actual Total Score, as a Function of Actual Test Performance.

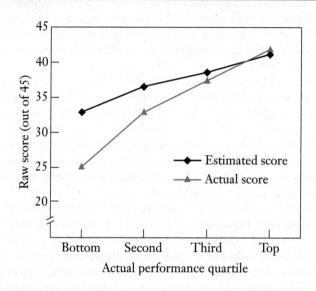

Source: Dunning, D., Johnson, K., Ehrlinger, J., & Kruger, J. (2003). Why people fail to recognize their own incompetence. *Current Directions in Psychological Science, 12,* 83–87. Copyright © 2003. Reprinted by permission of SAGE Publications.

So far, we have seen that people tend to be overconfident when they estimate the *total* number of correct items. However, the situation is more hopeful when we measure metamemory in a different fashion. In fact, the research shows that people's metamemory can be highly accurate when they predict which *individual* items they'll remember and which ones they'll forget (Koriat & Helstrup, 2007; Lovelace, 1984).

Metamemory: Estimating the Score Immediately Versus After a Delay. Researchers have discovered that people do not provide accurate memory estimates for individual items, if they make these estimates immediately after learning the items. In contrast—if they delay their judgments—they are reasonably accurate in predicting which items they will recall (Koriat & Helstrup, 2007; Narens et al., 2008; Roediger et al., 2010; Weaver et al., 2008). These delayed judgments are especially likely to provide accurate assessments of your memory performance because they assess long-term memory (Rhodes & Tauber, 2011). When you actually take the test, you will need to draw the answers from your long-term memory. In contrast, the immediate judgments would assess your working memory, which is less relevant for predicting your actual recall on an examination.

These particular findings suggest an important practical application. Suppose that you are studying your notes for an exam, and you are trying to determine which of the topics need more work. Be sure to wait a few minutes before assessing your memory, because your metamemory is more likely to be accurate.

So far, we've seen that students tend to provide overly optimistic metamemory judgments if they predict their total score on an exam, as opposed to predicting which specific items they will remember. We've also seen that students supply overly optimistic metamemory judgments if they predict their scores immediately after seeing the material, as opposed to predicting their score after some time has passed.

Metamemory: Estimating the Scores on Essay Questions Versus Multiple-Choice Questions. Imagine that you have just finished taking an exam in a psychology course. This exam included both multiple-choice questions and essay questions. As you leave the classroom, you try to assess your performance on each part of the exam. Would your estimate be more accurate on the multiple-choice items or on the essays? Ruth Maki and her colleagues (2009) explored this question. Although the results were complex, students were generally more accurate in estimating their scores on the multiple-choice questions.

So far, we have examined three factors that influence students' metamemory accuracy. We have seen that students' estimates about their memory are generally more accurate under the following conditions: (1) when they predict their accuracy on individual test items, rather than total scores; (2) when they predict their accuracy after a delay, rather than immediately after seeing the items; (3) when they predict their accuracy on multiple-choice questions, rather than on essay questions. Now let's consider whether a specific kind of individual difference could influence metamemory.

Individual Differences: Attention-Deficit/Hyperactivity Disorder and Metamemory

According to estimates, about 3% to 7% of the U.S. population have ADHD. An important cognitive characteristic of people with **Attention-Deficit/Hyperactivity Disorder (ADHD)** is that they have difficulty paying close attention at school, at work, and in other activities (American Psychiatric Association, 2000).

Laura Knouse and her coauthors (2006) studied how people with ADHD performed on a task where metamemory was measured on an item-by-item basis. These researchers located a sample of 28 people from a university and the surrounding community who met the criteria for ADHD. All participants were between the ages of 18 and 60. Then they located 28 people without ADHD, who matched the first group in age, gender, and university versus community status. On the day of the metamemory study, the individuals with ADHD received no medication.

Knouse and her colleagues showed each item pair (e.g., DISEASE-RAILROAD) on a computer screen for 8 seconds. Then the participants were asked to estimate, on a scale from 0 to 100%, the likelihood that they would recall the second word, when given the first word. For 30 pairs, everyone provided metamemory estimates immediately after the initial exposure of each pair. For 30 additional pairs, everyone provided delayed metamemory estimates, after they had seen a random number of intervening items.

Figure 6.5a and 6.5b show the results for individuals with ADHD or without ADHD, for both the immediate judgments (top graph) and delayed judgment (bottom graph), respectively. Notice the diagonal line in solid black. This line represents the performance of people who have perfect calibration. **Calibration** measures people's accuracy in estimating their actual performance. For example, suppose that Robert is perfectly calibrated, and suppose that Robert's estimates average out to be 80%. Because he is perfectly calibrated, he would indeed correctly recall 80% of the items. A perfectly calibrated person would also make accurate predictions for all other levels of item difficulty (Hacker et al., 2008).

Now look at Figure 6.5a. As you can see, people with and without ADHD were similar in the accuracy of their immediate judgments. As Figure 6.5b shows, the two groups were also similar in the accuracy of their delayed judgments. Furthermore, both groups were even more likely to be "well calibrated" in the delayed-judgment condition, consistent with the discussion on pages 191–192.

However, Knouse and her colleagues (2006) point out that their sample of people with ADHD was not representative. People with ADHD who are university students—or who live near a university—are likely to function better than people with ADHD in the general population. Still, this study demonstrates that, in these circumstances, people with ADHD can make highly accurate judgments about an important component of memory.

Metamemory About Factors Affecting Memory Accuracy

According to the research, many college students are not sufficiently aware of strategic factors that can influence their memory performance (Diaz & Benjamin, 2011; Gurung, 2003, 2004; McCabe, 2011). In fact, students who earn low scores on exams are likely to use no specific memory strategies in learning material for an exam (McDougall & Gruneberg, 2002). Furthemore, students may believe that studying for 2 hours is sufficient for a midterm exam (Zinn, 2009). In contrast, their professors might suggest that students need to study for at least 4 hours.

In addition, students' awareness of their memory should help them identify which memory strategies work best for them and which ones are ineffective. However, students tend to believe that "all memory strategies are created equal" (Suzuki-Slakter, 1988). For example, students typically believe that simple repetition is just as effective as the keyword method, which was illustrated in Figure 6.2 on page 179 (Pressley et al., 1984, 1988). However, you already know that repetition is not effective.

This research about study strategies highlights an important point: Try using various study strategies that seem appropriate for you. Then on your next test, identify which methods were indeed most effective. You'll be much more likely to revise your strategies if you can demonstrate that they improve your own performance.

As we've just seen, students may believe that some factors have no effect on memory, although these factors actually *do* have an effect. In contrast, let's consider some research that shows the reverse pattern: Students may believe that some factors do have an effect on memory, although these factors actually *do not* have an effect. For example, students believe that they are more likely to remember a word if it is printed

FIGURE 6.5

Accuracy of Predicting Which Items Will Be Correctly Recalled, When Making Judgments of Learning Immediately After Seeing a Pair (Figure 6.5a) and When Making Delayed Judgments (Figure 6.5b).

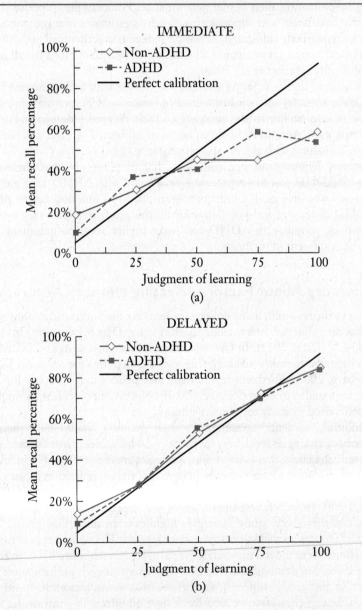

Note: The diagonal straight line (in black) represents perfectly accurate predictions.

Source: Knouse, L. E., Paradise, M. J. & Dunlosky, J. (2006). Does ADHD in adults affect the relative accuracy of metamemory judgments? *Journal of Attention Disorders*, *10*, 160–170. Copyright © 2006. Reprinted by permission of SAGE Publications.

in a large font size, rather than a small font size (Kornell et al., 2011; Rhodes & Castel, 2009). Furthermore, students believe that they are more likely to remember a word if it is spoken at a loud volume, rather than a quiet volume (Rhodes & Castel, 2009).

So, keep in mind that some factors actually have no effect on memory. Let's suppose that a friend has told you about an interesting new study technique. Do not assume that it will work for you. However, you may wish to try it informally, if the technique is consistent with the research described in this chapter.

Metamemory and the Regulation of Study Strategies

You may have developed your metamemory to the point that you know exactly which study strategies work best in which circumstances. However, your exam performance may still be poor unless you effectively regulate your study strategies by spending more time studying the difficult topics. The research on the regulation of study strategies emphasizes that memory tasks require a substantial amount of decision making as you plan how to master the material (Koriat & Helstrup, 2007; Metcalfe, 2000). Consistent with Theme 4, you must often coordinate at least two cognitive processes—in this case, memory and decision making.

Let's examine the way students make decisions about how they will allocate their study time, in preparing for a memory test. As you'll see, in some circumstances, students may spend more time on the difficult items than on the easy items. However, when the material is more challenging and the time is limited, students will spend the most time learning the items that are just within their grasp (Kornell & Metcalfe, 2006).

Allocating Time When the Task Is Easy. In a classic study, Thomas Nelson and R. Jacob Leonesio (1988) examined how students distribute their study time when they can study at their own pace. In this study, students were allowed a reasonable amount of time to study the material.

Nelson and Leonesio found that students allocated somewhat more study time for the items that they believed would be difficult to master. The correlations here averaged about +.30. (A correlation of .00 would indicate no relationship, and a correlation of +1.00 would be a perfect correlation between each item's judged difficulty and its study time.) In other words, the students did not passively review all the material equally. This research on metamemory reveals that people often take an active, strategic approach to this cognitive task, a finding that is consistent with Theme 1 about active processing.

One of my professors in graduate school suggested an interesting strategy for examining research data (Martin, 1967). As he pointed out, whenever you see a number, you should ask yourself, "Why is it so high, and why is it so low?" In this case, the correlation is as *high* as +.30 because students do realize that the difficult items require more time. This general relationship has been replicated in later research (Nelson et al., 1994; Son & Kornell, 2008; Son & Schwartz, 2002).

In contrast, why is this crucial correlation as *low* as +.30? Unfortunately, students are less than ideal in regulating their study strategies. They spend longer than necessary studying items they already know, and not enough time studying the items they have not yet mastered. One possible explanation for these results is that students are not very accurate in judging whether their mastery of material has actually improved when they have spent more time studying it (Townsend & Heit, 2011).

Lisa Son and Janet Metcalfe (2000) reviewed the research on students' allocation of study time. They discovered that 35 out of the 46 published studies demonstrated that these students spend more time on the difficult items. However, they found that all these studies examined relatively easy material, such as learning pairs of English words. In addition, these students typically had enough time to study all of the items. Son and Metcalfe speculated that students might choose a different strategy in other circumstances.

Allocating Time When the Task Is Difficult. Think about the exams you've taken so far this term. In psychology courses, for instance, your exams require you to remember conceptual information about psychology, rather than a simple list of paired words. In addition, students in real-life settings have only a limited time to study for their exams (Kornell & Metcalfe, 2006).

Son and Metcalfe (2000) decided to design a situation that more closely resembles the challenging learning situation that college students often face. Their test material was a series of eight encyclopedia-style biographies. A good reader would need about 60 minutes to read them all completely. However, the researchers increased the time pressure for this task by allowing the students only 30 minutes to read all the material. The students began the study by reading a single paragraph from each biography; they ranked these paragraphs in terms of their perceived difficulty. Then the researchers informed them that they would have 30 minutes to read the material, and they could choose how to spend their time.

The results of this study showed that students spent the majority of their study time on the biographies that they considered easy, rather than those they considered difficult. Notice that this strategy is wise, because they can master more material within the limited time frame.

According to additional studies, when students are facing time pressure, they choose to study material that seems relatively easy to master (Kornell & Metcalfe, 2006; Metcalfe, 2002). Furthermore, Metcalfe (2002) tested students who had expertise in a given area. Compared to novices, these "expert" students chose to concentrate their time on more challenging material.

Conclusions About the Regulation of Study Strategies. As you can see from this discussion, students often regulate their study strategies in a sophisticated fashion. When they have time to master a relatively easy task, they allocate the most time to the difficult items. On a more challenging task—with time pressure—they realistically adjust their study strategies so that they focus on the items they are likely to master in the limited time frame (Kornell & Metcalfe, 2006).

We have seen that students regulate their study strategies. Furthermore, they can also *regulate the regulation* of their study strategies! That is, they choose one style for easy tasks and a different style for difficult tasks. As Metcalfe (2000) concludes, "Rather than simply being passive repositories for knowledge and memories, humans can use their knowledge of what they know to exert control over what they know [and] what they will know" (p. 207).

Let's briefly review the information about metamemory. We have explored how several factors can influence your metamemory accuracy. We also saw that people with ADHD may not differ from other people with respect to their metamemory accuracy. However, people are not sufficiently aware of factors that can influence their metamemory. Finally, students spend somewhat more time studying difficult topics, but their strategies may change when their study time is limited.

Metamemory and the Likelihood of Remembering a Specific Target

At some point during the last week, it's likely that you've had one (or both) of the following memory experiences:

1. The **tip-of-the-tongue effect** describes your subjective experience of knowing the target word for which you are searching, yet you cannot recall it right now (Bacon, 2010; Brown, 2012; Schwartz & Metcalfe, 2011).

2. The **feeling-of-knowing effect** describes the subjective experience of knowing some information, but you cannot recall it right now (Hertzog et al., 2010; Norman et al., 2010).

Tip-of-the-Tongue Effect. The tip-of-the-tongue experience is generally an involuntary effect. In contrast, the feeling of knowing is more conscious. You carefully assess whether you could recognize the answer if you were given several options, as in a multiple-choice question (A. S. Brown, 2012; Koriat & Helstrup, 2007). Both of these effects activate the frontal lobe of the brain, which is also important in other metacognitive tasks (Maril et al., 2005). Both of these effects are clearly related to metacognition because you make judgments about whether you know some information.

Both the tip-of-the-tongue effect and the feeling-of-knowing effect are also related to several other topics in cognitive psychology, including consciousness (Chapter 3), semantic memory (Chapter 8), and language production (Chapter 10). As Theme 4 points out, our cognitive processes are interrelated.

Now try Demonstration 6.4 to see whether any of the definitions encourages a tip-of-the-tongue experience. In our discussion of this topic, we will first consider the classic study by Brown and McNeill (1966). Then we'll examine some of the later research, as well as a related topic, called the "feeling of knowing."

Roger Brown and David McNeill (1966) conducted the first formal investigation in this area. Their description of a man "seized" by a tip-of-the-tongue state may capture the torment you sometimes feel when you fail to retrieve a word from the tip of your tongue:

> The signs of it were unmistakable; he would appear to be in mild torment, something like the brink of a sneeze, and if he found the word his relief was considerable. (p. 326)

🌀 Demonstration 6.4

The Tip-of-the-Tongue Phenomenon

Look at each of the definitions below. For each definition, supply the appropriate word if you know it. Indicate "don't know" for those that you are certain you don't know. Mark "TOT" next to those for which you are reasonably certain you know the word, though you can't recall it now. For these TOT words, supply at least one word that sounds similar to the target word. The answers appear at the end of the chapter. Check to see whether your similar-sounding words actually do resemble the target words.

1. An absolute ruler, a tyrant.
2. A stone having a cavity lined with crystals.
3. A great circle of the earth passing through the geographic poles and any given point on the earth's surface.
4. Worthy of respect or reverence by reason of age and dignity.
5. Shedding leaves each year, as opposed to evergreen.
6. A person appointed to act as a substitute for another.
7. Five offspring born at a single birth.
8. A special quality of leadership that captures the popular imagination and inspires unswerving allegiance.
9. The red coloring matter of the red blood corpuscles.
10. A flying reptile that was extinct at the end of the Mesozoic Era.
11. A spring from which hot water, steam, or mud gushes out at intervals, found in Yellowstone National Park.
12. The second stomach of a bird, which has thick, muscular walls.

In their research, Brown and McNeill produced the tip-of-the-tongue state by giving people the definition for an uncommon English word—such as *sampan*, *ambergris*, or *nepotism*—and asking them to identify the word. Sometimes people supplied the appropriate word immediately, and other times they were confident that they did not know the word. However, in still other cases, the definition produced a tip-of-the-tongue state. In these cases, the researchers asked people to provide words that resembled the target word in terms of sound, but not meaning. For example, when the target word was *sampan*, people provided these similar-sounding responses: *Saipan, Siam, Cheyenne, sarong, sanching,* and *symphoon*.

Think about why the tip-of-the-tongue phenomenon is one kind of metacognition. People are familiar enough with their memory for the target word to say, "This word is on the tip of my tongue." Their knowledge is indeed fairly accurate, because they are likely to identify the first letter and other attributes of the target word. They are also likely to provide similar-sounding words that really do resemble the target word (Brown & McNeill, 1966).

In the decades following the publication of Brown and McNeill's study, researchers have identified more information about the tip-of-the-tongue effect. The studies show, for instance, that young adults report having approximately one tip-of-the-tongue experience each week (Schwartz & Metcalfe, 2011). However, bilingual individuals experience the tip-of-the-tongue effect more frequently than monolinguals. One reason for this difference is that bilinguals have a greater total number of separate words in their semantic memory, compared to monolinguals (Gollan & Acenas, 2004; Gollan et al., 2005).

Researchers have also documented the tip-of-the-tongue phenomenon in non-English languages such as Polish, Japanese, and Italian (A. S. Brown, 2012; B. L. Schwartz, 1999, 2002). Research in these other languages demonstrates that people can retrieve other characteristics of the target word, in addition to its first letter and number of syllables. For example, Italian speakers can often retrieve the grammatical gender of the target word that they are seeking (Caramazza & Miozzo, 1997; Miozzo & Cara-mazza, 1997). Interestingly, the deaf community has a similar term, the **tip-of-the-finger effect**, which refers to the subjective experience of knowing the target sign, but that sign is temporarily inaccessible (A. S. Brown, 2012; Schwartz & Metcalfe, 2011).

People who are captured by a tip-of-the-tongue experience often exhibit various kinds of nonverbal behaviors. If you have the opportunity, try Demonstration 6.4 with some friends. You may notice that your friends make exaggerated facial expression, or they jiggle their feet, or they hold their head in their hands. These physical actions are an example of **embodied cognition**, a perspective that emphasizes how our abstract thoughts are often expressed by our motor behavior (Landau et al., 2010). We will explore embodied cognition in more detail in Chapter 10. In that chapter, we'll consider the hand gestures and other body movements that we use when we talk.

Feeling of Knowing. As defined on page 197, the feeling of knowing is the subjective experience that you know some information, but you cannot recall it right now. So, you contemplate the question, and you judge that you could recognize the answer, for example, if you saw this item on a multiple-choice exam (A. S. Brown, 2012; Hertzog et al., 2010; Koriat & Helstrup, 2007).

People typically have a strong feeling of knowing if they can retrieve a large amount of partial information (Koriat & Helstrup, 2007; Schwartz et al., 1997; Schwartz & Smith, 1997). For example, I was recently thinking about how people can become captivated by reading fiction, and I recalled a wonderful essay that I had read in the *New Yorker* magazine. The author was an Indian woman, and she wrote that she didn't have many books during her early childhood in the United States. This essay described how she became enchanted with books once she started school.

I knew that I had read one of this author's novels and some of her short stories. But what was her name? This name was not on the tip of my tongue, but I definitely had a "feeling of knowing"; I knew that I could recognize her name, if I had several choices. Fortunately, Google came to the rescue: I entered "Indian American women authors," and a website provided a list of 10 possible candidates. Aha! The seventh person on that list was Jhumpa Lahiri!

In reality, the tip-of-the-tongue effect and the feeling-of-knowing effect are fairly similar, though your tip-of-the-tongue experiences may be more extreme and more irritating (A. S. Brown, 2012). The current neuroimaging data suggest that these two effects are associated with somewhat different brain patterns. For example, the right prefrontal region of the cortex is more likely to be associated with the tip-of-the-tongue effect. In contrast, the left prefrontal region is more likely to be associated with the feeling-of-knowing effect (A. S. Brown, 2012; Maril et al., 2005).

Metacomprehension

Did you understand the material on the tip-of-the-tongue phenomenon? Are you aware that you've started reading a new subtopic, which is part of the general discussion of metacognition? How much longer can you read today before you feel that you can't absorb any more? As you think about these issues, you are engaging in metacomprehension.

Metacomprehension refers to your thoughts about language comprehension. Most research on metacomprehension focuses on reading comprehension, rather than on the comprehension of spoken speech (Maki & McGuire, 2002). Remember that the general term, *metacognition*, includes both metamemory (pp. 189–200) and metacomprehension (pp. 200–202), as well as topics related to the tip-of-the-tongue phenomenon and the feeling of knowing (pp. 197–200).

Let's consider two topics in connection with metacomprehension. First, how accurate is the typical college student's metacomprehension? Second, how can you improve your metacomprehension skills?

Metacomprehension Accuracy. In general, college students are not very accurate in their metacomprehension skills. For example, they may not notice that a paragraph contains inconsistencies or missing information. Instead, they think they understand it (Dunlosky & Lipko, 2007; Dunlosky & Metcalfe, 2009; Griffin et al., 2008; McNamara, 2011).

Furthermore, students often believe that they have understood something they have read because they are familiar with its general topic. However, they often fail to retain specific information, and they may overestimate how they will perform when they are tested on the material (Dunlosky & Lipko, 2007; Maki & McGuire, 2002; McNamara, 2011).

Let's consider a classic study about metacomprehension in more detail. Pressley and Ghatala (1988) tested introductory psychology students by assessing their meta-comprehension, as well as their performance on tests of reading ability. Specifically, these researchers selected reading-comprehension tests from the Scholastic Aptitude Test, an earlier form of the current SAT. If you took the SAT, you'll recall that the questions about reading comprehension typically contain between one and three paragraphs, in essay form. The essay remains visible while you answer several multiple-choice questions, so you do not need to rely on your memory. Each question has five possible answers. Therefore, a person who simply guesses on an answer would be correct 20% of the time.

Next, the students in Pressley and Ghatala's study answered the multiple-choice questions, and then they rated how certain they were that they had answered each question correctly. If they were absolutely certain that their answer had been correct, they were told to answer 100%. If they were just guessing, they were told to report 20%. They were also instructed to provide an appropriate intermediate percentage for intermediate levels of confidence. These certainty rating served as the measure of metacomprehension.

Incidentally, you should notice that this task focuses on metacomprehension. The test would have assessed *metamemory*, rather than metacomprehension, if (1) There had been a delay between the reading task and the presentation of the multiple-choice questions and (2) If the essay was no longer present.

Let's examine the results. When a student had answered a reading comprehension question *correctly*, he or she supplied an average certainty rating of 73%. In other words, the students were fairly confident about these items, which is appropriate. However, when a student answered a question *incorrectly*, he or she supplied an average certainty rating of about 64%. Unfortunately, this is about the same level of confidence that the students showed for the items they answered correctly!

Furthermore, these data suggest that students are often highly overconfident. In general, the research shows that readers are not very accurate in estimating whether they have understood the material that they have just read (McDaniel & Butler, 2011).

Other research shows that irrelevant features may lead students to overestimate their understanding of a textbook passage. For example, Serra and Dunlosky (2010) asked students to read a description about lightning storms. Some students read the passage with a photo of lightning accompanying each of six paragraphs. Other students read the same passage without any photos. Students in the six-photos group judged that their comprehension was higher, compared to students in the no-photos group. However, the two groups actually earned similar scores on a short-answer quiz.

When people *are* skilled at metacomprehension, they typically receive high scores on tests of reading comprehension (Maki & McGuire, 2002; Maki et al., 2005). According to research by Maki and her coauthors (1994), for example, readers who were accurate at assessing which sections of a text they had understood were also likely to receive higher scores on a reading-comprehension test. In fact, metacomprehension accuracy and reading-comprehension scores were significantly correlated ($r = +.43$).

Students also become somewhat more accurate in assessing their performance after they gain experience in reading the text and after they receive feedback (Ariel & Dunlosky, 2011; Maki & Serra, 1992; Schooler et al., 2004). However, the improvement is not dramatic. College students clearly need some hints on how to increase their metacomprehension abilities and how to take advantage of their reading experiences.

Improving Metacomprehension. Ideally, students should be accurate in assessing whether they understand what they have read. In other words, their subjective assessments should match their performance on an objective test.

One effective method for improving metacomprehension is to read a passage, wait a few minutes, and then try to explain the passage to yourself, *without* looking at the written passage (Chiang et al., 2010; Dunlosky & Metcalfe, 2009; McDaniel & Butler, 2011). This procedure not only improves your judgment about how well you know the passage, but it should also increase your score on a test about this material (Baker & Dunlosky, 2006; Dunlosky et al., 2005; Thiede et al., 2005). Furthermore, when you use this kind of active reading, you are less likely to "zone out" and fail to notice that you are no longer paying attention to your reading (Schooler et al., 2004).

As we have seen, one component of metacomprehension requires you to accurately assess whether you understand a written passage. However, metacomprehension also requires you to *regulate* your reading, so that you know how to read more effectively (Dunlosky & Metcalfe, 2009). For example, good and poor readers differ in their awareness that certain reading strategies are useful. Good readers are more likely to report that they try to make connections among the ideas they have read. They also try to create visual images, based on descriptions in the text (Kaufman et al., 1985; Pressley, 1996). In addition, good readers outline and summarize material in their own words when they are reading textbooks (McDaniel et al., 1996).

Researchers have pointed out that students may have difficulty applying the more sophisticated metamemory strategies, especially if they have limited working-memory capacity. However, these students can substantially improve their reading comprehension by reading the same material a second time (Chiang et al., 2010; Griffin et al., 2008).

Demonstration 6.5 will help you consider your own metacomprehension skills and think about some strategies for self-management. As researchers emphasize, metacomprehension and strategy use are essential components of skilled reading (McCormick, 2003; Schooler et al., 2004).

⊚ Demonstration 6.5

Assessing Your Metacomprehension Skills

Answer each of the following questions about your own metacomprehension. If you answer "no" to any question, devise a plan for improving metacomprehension, and apply this plan when you read the next assigned chapter in this textbook.

1.　Before beginning to read an assignment, do you try to assess how carefully you should read the material?

2.　In general, are you accurate in predicting your performance on the exam questions that focus on the reading assignments?

3.　After you read a short section (roughly a page in length), do you make yourself summarize what you have just read—using your own words?

4.　After reading a chapter in this textbook, do you test yourself on the list of new terms and on the review questions?

5.　Do you re-read a portion of your textbook when it doesn't make sense or when you realize that you haven't been paying attention?

(continued)

6. Do you try to draw connections among the ideas in your textbook?

7. Do you try to draw connections between the ideas in your textbook and the information you have learned in class?

8. When you read a term you do not know, do you try to determine its meaning by looking it up in a dictionary or in the glossary of your textbook?

9. When you review your textbook prior to a test, do you spend more time reviewing the topics that you consider difficult, compared to the topics that you have already mastered?

10. When reading through several journal articles to see whether they might be relevant for a paper you are writing, do you first try to assess—without reading every word—the general scope or findings of each article?

Section Summary: *Metacognition*

1. Metacognition is your knowledge and control of your cognitive processes; three important components of metacognition are metamemory, the tip-of-the-tongue phenomenon, and metacomprehension.

2. A variety of factors influence people's metamemory accuracy. Specifically, people are more accurate when they are judging individual items, when their judgment is delayed, and when they judge their performance on multiple-choice questions, rather than performance on essays.

3. In a study by Knouse and her coauthors (2006), people with ADHD were similar to people without ADHD in their metamemory judgments, both immediate and delayed.

4. In general, students are not sufficiently aware that some memory strategies are more effective than others.

5. When the task is easy, students spend somewhat more time studying difficult material, rather than easy material. When the task is difficult and time is limited, students typically study the material that they are most likely to master.

6. The research on the tip-of-the-tongue phenomenon shows that—even when people cannot remember the word for which they are searching—they can often identify important attributes such as the sound of the word.

7. The phrase "feeling of knowing" refers to situations in which you think you could select the correct answer from several choices, even though the target isn't actually on the tip of your tongue.

8. Studies on metacomprehension suggest that students are often overconfident in judging whether they understand the material they have read, especially if they have low reading ability.

9. Students' metacomprehension can be improved if they wait a few minutes and then try to summarize the material. Good readers also use a variety of strategies to regulate their reading.

CHAPTER REVIEW QUESTIONS

1. One trend throughout this chapter is that deep levels of processing can enhance your memory. Review the material in the section on memory strategies, and identify which studies use some form of deep processing. Also explain why deep processing would be important in metacognition.

2. In general, your memory is more accurate when you have a small amount of information that you need to remember. Point out why the elaboration strategy doesn't follow this trend. Then choose at least two topics from this chapter, and use elaboration to make the material easier to remember.

3. Review the list of memory-improvement strategies in Table 6.1 (pp. 186–187). Which of these did you already use before you graduated from high school? Which did you discover while studying for exams, after you entered college?

4. Without looking at Table 6.1, describe as many of the memory-improvement techniques from this chapter as you can remember. Which techniques focus on strategies, and which focus on metacognition? In each case, describe how you can use each one to remember some information from this chapter for your next exam in cognitive psychology.

5. How is prospective memory different from retrospective memory? What factors make prospective memory more difficult? Think of a specific person you know who complains about his or her memory. What hints could you provide to this person to encourage better prospective-memory performance?

6. Prior to reading this chapter, did you ever think about the topic of metamemory—even if you didn't know this term? Recall this chapter's discussion about factors that can influence people's metamemory accuracy. Which factors are consistent with your own experiences?

7. What evidence suggests that people can supply information about a target, when they report that a word is on the tip of their tongue? Why is this topic related to metacognition? What other components of the tip-of-the-tongue effect and the feeling-of-knowing effect would be interesting topics for future research?

8. Several parts of this chapter emphasize that people tend to be overconfident about their ability to remember material and to understand written material. Summarize this information. Then describe how you can apply this information when you are reading and studying for your next exam in your course on cognitive psychology.

9. Some parts of the section on metacognition emphasize how people can control and modify their study strategies and reading strategies, in addition to simply knowing about their own cognitive processes. Describe the research on strategy regulation. In what ways has your own strategy regulation changed since you began college? Suppose that you have not changed: What strategies and study techniques would be most useful to modify?

10. What kind of metacomprehension tasks are relevant when you are reading this textbook? List as many different tasks as possible. Why do you suppose that metacomprehension for reading passages of text would be less accurate than people's metamemory for learning pairs of words (for example, the task described in Demonstration 6.1)?

KEYWORDS

ecological validity
memory strategy
levels of processing
elaboration
rehearsal
distinctiveness
self-reference effect
encoding-specificity principle
foresight bias
total-time hypothesis
retrieval-practice effect
distributed-practice effect
spaced learning

massed learning
desirable difficulties
testing effect
mnemonics
mental imagery
keyword method
organization
chunking
hierarchy
first-letter technique
narrative technique
retrospective memory

prospective memory
external memory aid
metacognition
self-knowledge
metamemory
Attention-Deficit/Hyperactivity Disorder (ADHD)
calibration
tip-of-the-tongue effect
feeling-of-knowing effect
tip-of-the-finger effect
embodied cognition
metacomprehension

RECOMMENDED READINGS

Benjamin, A. S. (Ed.). (2011). *Successful remembering and successful forgetting: A festschrift in honor of Robert A. Bjork*. New York: Psychology Press. Although some of the chapters in this book are aimed at graduate students and faculty, the majority of them provide some practical information about academic achievement.

Brown, A. S. (2012). *The tip of the tongue state*. New York: Psychology Press. Here is the definitive book about both the tip-of-the-tongue effect and the feeling-of-knowing effect. In addition to the topics discussed in your textbook, Brown's book examines issues such as the cause of these phenomena and individual differences.

Davies, G. M., & Wright, D. B. (Eds.). (2010). *Current issues in applied memory research*. New York: Psychol-ogy Press. Several chapters in Davies and Wright's book examine how research on memory can be applied to education. Other themes in their book focus on applications to law and to neuroscience.

Dunlosky, J., & Bjork, R. A. (Eds.). (2008). *Handbook of metamemory and memory*. New York: Psychology Press. The chapters in this book are based on research, and most of them would be interesting to motivated undergraduates.

Dunlosky, J., & Metcalfe, J. (2009). *Metacognition*. Los Angeles: Sage. Here is an excellent, well-written summary of information about metamemory, the tip-of-the-tongue effect, and related topics.

ANSWERS TO DEMONSTRATION 6.4

1. despot
2. geode
3. meridian
4. venerable
5. deciduous
6. surrogate
7. quintuplets
8. charisma
9. hemoglobin
10. pterodactyl
11. geyser
12. gizzard

CHAPTER 7

Mental Imagery and Cognitive Maps

PREVIEW

Chapters 4, 5, and 6 emphasized how we remember verbal material. In contrast, Chapter 7 focuses on sights and sounds, as we investigate three components of mental imagery: the characteristics of visual imagery, the characteristics of auditory imagery, and cognitive maps.

Psychologists have devised some creative research techniques to examine the characteristics of mental images. In many ways, mental imagery and the perception of real objects are similar. For example, you can rotate a real object that you are holding in your hands. In a similar fashion, you can mentally rotate an imaginary object. The first section of this chapter also examines a controversy about how we store mental images in memory: Are images stored in a picture-like code or in a more abstract, language-like description? The final topic in this first section explores gender similarities in most kinds of spatial ability.

The second section of this chapter focuses on the characteristics of auditory imagery, a topic that has generated much less research than visual imagery. Still, the research shows that people's imagery about pitch is similar to their actual perception of pitch. Researchers have also explored timbre, which is the quality that makes a flute's sound different from a trumpet's sound. As it happens, people's imagery about timbre is also similar to their perception of timbre.

Our third major topic is cognitive maps. A cognitive map is a mental representation of geographic information, including your visual imagery of the environment that surrounds you. For instance, you have developed a cognitive map for the town or city in which your college is located. Our cognitive maps show certain systematic distortions. For example, you may think that two streets intersect at right angles, even when the angles are far from 90 degrees. Because of these distortions, our mental maps are a more organized and more standardized version of reality.

CHAPTER INTRODUCTION

Take a moment to close your eyes and create a clear mental image of the cover of this textbook. Be sure to include details such as its size, shape, and color, as well as the photo of the nautilus shell. Now try to create an auditory image. Can you hear the voice of a close friend saying your name? Finally, close your eyes again and create a "mental map" of the most direct route between your current location and the nearest store where you can buy a quart of milk.

All three of these tasks require **mental imagery** (also called **imagery**), which is the mental representation of stimuli when those stimuli are not physically present (Kosslyn et al., 2010). You can have a mental image for any sensory experience. However, most of the psychology research examines **visual imagery**, or the mental representation of visual stimuli. Fortunately, during the past decade, the research has increased for **auditory imagery**, which is the mental representation of auditory stimuli.

◎ Demonstration 7.1

The Relevance of Mental Imagery in Earlier Chapters of this Book

Look back at the Table of Contents (just before Chapter 1) to review the outlines for Chapters 2 through 6. How would visual imagery or auditory imagery be relevant in each of these chapters?

Imagery relies exclusively on top-down processing. Consider why this statement must be true: Your sensory receptors do not receive any input when you create a mental image (Kosslyn & Thompson, 2000). We discussed perceptual processes in Chapters 2 and 3 of this book. **Perception** uses previous knowledge to gather and interpret the stimuli registered by the senses. In contrast to imagery, perception requires you to register information through the receptors in your sensory organs, such as your eyes and ears (Kosslyn, Ganis, & Thompson, 2001). As a result, perception requires both bottom-up and top-down processing.

We use mental imagery for a wide variety of everyday cognitive activities (Denis et al., 2004; Tversky, 2005a). Try Demonstration 7.1 to illustrate how imagery is also relevant in the earlier chapters of this book. Imagery is also important in several cognitive processes that we'll discuss later in this textbook. For example, you'll see in Chapter 11 that mental imagery can be helpful when you want to solve a spatial problem, or when you need to work on a task that requires creativity. As you might expect, people who earn high scores on visuospatial working memory are also likely to perform well on tasks that require visual imagery (Gyselinck & Meneghetti, 2011).

What kind of imagery do we use most often? Stephen Kosslyn and his coauthors (1990) asked students to keep diaries about their mental imagery. They reported that about two-thirds of their images were visual. In contrast, images for hearing, touch, taste, and smell were much less common. Psychologists show a similar lopsidedness in their research preferences. Most of the research focuses on visual imagery, though the research on auditory imagery has increased during the last decade. In contrast, psychologists rarely investigate smell, taste, or touch imagery.

Some professions emphasize mental imagery, most often visual imagery (Reed, 2010). Would you want to fly on an airplane if your pilot had weak spatial imagery? Imagery is also important in clinical psychology. Therapists often work with clients who have psychological problems such as post-traumatic stress disorder, depression, or eating disorders. With each of these disorders, individuals sometimes report that they experience intrusive, distressing mental images. Therapists have successfully worked with clients by encouraging them to create alternative, more positive images (Bisby et al., 2010; Brewin et al., 2010).

In addition, spatial ability is extremely important in the **STEM disciplines**, that is, science, technology, engineering, and mathematics (Ganis et al., 2009). For instance, Albert Einstein is well known as one of the geniuses of the last 100 years. Einstein reported that his own thinking processes typically used spatial images, instead of verbal descriptions (Newcombe, 2010).

Unfortunately, elementary school teachers in the United States rarely teach children about spatial skills. In fact, the curriculum may not emphasize spatial skills until students enroll in a geometry class. Psychologist Nora Newcombe (2010) describes some interesting methods for enhancing young children's spatial skills. A typical task might require students to mentally rotate a picture until it resembles one of five options. Many high school and college students believe that they cannot possibly improve their spatial skills. However, training in spatial skills improves spatial performance for students of any age (Ganis et al., 2009; Reed, 2010; Twyman & Newcombe, 2010).

Chapter 1 of this textbook provided an overview of the history of psychology. You may recall that Wilhelm Wundt is often described as the founder of psychology. Wundt and other early psychologists considered imagery to be an important part of the discipline (Palmer, 1999). In contrast, behaviorists such as John Watson strongly opposed research on mental imagery because it could not be connected to observable behavior. In fact, Watson argued that imagery did not exist (Kosslyn et al., 2010).

As a result, North American psychologists seldom studied imagery during the behaviorist period between 1920 and 1960 (Ganis et al., 2009; Kosslyn et al., 2010). For example, I used PsycINFO to search for the term "mental imagery" in any part of every journal article published during the decade from 1950 through 1959. The search identified only 34 articles.

As cognitive psychology gained popularity, however, researchers rediscovered imagery. The topic continues to be important in contemporary cognitive psychology, especially with the development of more sophisticated techniques in cognitive neuroscience (Ganis et al., 2009; Reed, 2010).

This chapter explores three important aspects of imagery that have intrigued contemporary researchers. First, we examine the nature of visual images, with an emphasis on the way that we can transform these images. Then we will consider the nature of auditory images, a relatively new topic in cognitive psychology. Our third topic focuses on cognitive maps, which are mental representations of geographic information, including the environment that surrounds us.

THE CHARACTERISTICS OF VISUAL IMAGERY

As you might expect, research on mental imagery is difficult to conduct, especially because researchers cannot directly observe mental images and because they fade so quickly (Kosslyn et al., 2003; Kosslyn et al., 2006). However, psychologists have modified some research techniques that were originally developed for studying visual perception. These techniques can now be applied to mental images (Allen, 2004). As a result, the investigation of imagery has made impressive advances. Try Demonstration 7.2 on page 211, which illustrates an important research technique that we'll examine shortly.

◎ Demonstration 7.2

Mental Rotation

For the top pair of objects, labeled *A*, look at the object on the left. Try rotating it in any direction you wish. Can you rotate it so that it matches the object on the right? Which of these three pairs of objects are the same, and which are different? Record your answers; we'll discuss this study shortly.

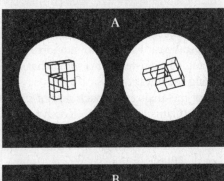

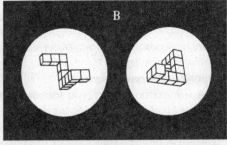

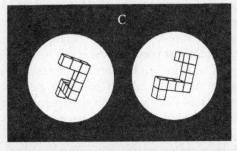

Source: Shepard, R. N., & Metzler, J. (1971). Mental rotation of three-dimensional objects. *Science*, *171*, 701–703. Copyright 1971 American Association for the Advancement of Science.

Stephen Kosslyn and his colleagues (2006) use the term **imagery debate** to refer to an important controversy: Do our mental images resemble perception (using an analog code), or do they resemble language (using a propositional code)? We will introduce that controversy now and return to discuss it in more detail once we've examined the evidence.

The majority of theorists believe that information about a mental image is stored in an analog code (Howes, 2007; Kosslyn et al., 2006; Reisberg et al., 2003). An **analog code** is a representation that closely resembles the physical object. Notice that the word *analog* suggests the word *analogy*, such as the analogy between the real object and the mental image.

According to the analog-code approach, mental imagery is a close relative of perception (Tversky, 2005a). When you look at a sketch of a triangle, the physical features of that triangle are registered in your brain in a form that preserves the physical relationship among the three lines. Those who support analog coding propose that your mental image of a triangle is registered in a somewhat similar fashion, preserving the same relationship among the lines.

However, supporters of the analog approach do not suggest that people literally have a picture in their head (Ganis et al., 2009; Kosslyn et al., 2006). Furthermore, they point out that people often fail to notice precise visual details when they look at an object. These details will also be missing from their mental image of this object (Howes, 2007; Kosslyn et al., 2006).

In contrast to the analog-code position, other theorists argue that we store images in terms of a propositional code (Pylyshyn, 2003, 2006). A **propositional code** is an abstract, language-like representation; storage is neither visual nor spatial, and it does not physically resemble the original stimulus (Ganis et al., 2009; Reed, 2010).

According to the propositional-code approach, mental imagery is a close relative of language, not perception. For example, when you store a mental image of a triangle, your brain will register a language-like description of the lines and angles. Theorists have not specified the precise nature of the verbal description. However, it is abstract, and it does not resemble English or any other natural language. Your brain can then use this verbal description to generate a visual image (Kosslyn et al., 2006; Reed, 2010).

In general, the neuroimaging research shows that the primary visual cortex is activated when people work on tasks that require detailed visual imagery (Ganis et al., 2009). This is the same part of the cortex that is active when we perceive actual visual objects. (See the diagram on page 38.) Furthermore, researchers have studied people who have prosopagnosia. As we noted in Chapter 2, people with **prosopagnosia** cannot recognize human faces visually, though they perceive other objects relatively normally (Farah, 2004). These individuals also have comparable problems in creating visual imagery for faces (Ganis et al., 2009).

The controversy about analog versus propositional coding is difficult to resolve. The majority of people who conduct research on visual imagery support the analog position, perhaps partly because they personally experience vivid, picture-like images (Reisberg et al., 2003). Like most controversies in psychology, both the analog and the propositional approaches are probably at least partially correct, depending on the specific task. As you read the following pages, keep a scorecard of the studies that support each viewpoint. This list will help you appreciate the summary toward the end of this section, on pages 227 to 228.

We noted earlier that mental imagery is a challenging topic to study. Compared with a topic such as verbal memory, the topic of mental imagery is elusive and inaccessible. Researchers have attacked this problem by using the following logic: Suppose that a mental image really *does* resemble a physical object. Then people should be able to make judgments about this mental image in the same way that they make judgments about the corresponding physical object (Hubbard, 2010).

For example, we should be able to rotate a mental image in the same way that we can rotate a physical object. Judgments about distance in a mental image should also be similar, as well as judgments about shape. In addition, a mental image should create interference when we try to perceive a physical object. Furthermore, we should be able to discover two interpretations of a mental image of an ambiguous figure, and we should be able to produce other vision-like effects when we construct a mental image. Let's now consider these potential parallels between visual imagery and visual perception.

IN DEPTH

Visual Imagery and Rotation

Suppose that you are a researcher who wants to study whether people rotate a mental image in the same way that they rotate a physical object. It's tempting to think that you could simply ask people to analyze their mental images and use these reports as a basis for describing mental imagery.

However, think why these introspective reports could be inaccurate and biased. For example, we may not have conscious access to the processes associated with our mental imagery (Anderson, 1998; Pylyshyn, 2006). You may recall the discussion of consciousness in Chapter 3. An important problem is that people's reports about their cognitive processes may not be accurate.

Researchers have explored the mental-rotation issue more than any other topic connected with imagery. Let's begin this in-depth section by considering the original study by Shepard and Metzler (1971), and then we'll examine some more recent research. We will also consider some cognitive neuroscience research about mental rotation.

Shepard and Metzler's Research. Demonstration 7.2 on page 211 illustrates a classic experiment by Roger Shepard and his coauthor Jacqueline Metzler (1971). Here was their reasoning. Suppose that you are holding a physical, geometric object in your hands, and you decide to rotate it. It will take you longer to rotate this physical object by 180 degrees than to rotate it only 90 degrees.

Now suppose that our mental images operate the same way that physical objects operate. Then it will take you longer to rotate this mental image 180 degrees, instead of 90 degrees. Again, remember that this entire question was quite daring during this era. No genuine behaviorist would ever consider research about mental images!

In Demonstration 7.2, notice that, in the top pair of designs (Part A), the left-hand figure can be changed into the right-hand figure by keeping it flat on the page and rotating it clockwise. Suddenly, the two figures match up, and you conclude "same." You can match these two figures by using a two-dimensional rotation.

In contrast, the middle pair (Part B) requires a rotation in a third dimension. You may, for example, take the two-block "arm" that is jutting out toward you and push it over to the left and away from you. Suddenly, the figures match up, and you conclude "same." However, in the case of the bottom pair (Part C), you cannot rotate the figure on the left so that it matches the figure on the right. Therefore, you must conclude "different."

Shepard and Metzler (1971) asked eight extremely dedicated participants to judge 1,600 pairs of line drawings like these. They were instructed to pull a lever with their right hand if they judged the figures to be the same, and to pull a different lever with their left hand if they judged the figures to be different. In each case, the experimenters measured the amount of time required for a decision. Notice, then, that the dependent variable is *reaction time*, in contrast to the dependent variable of *accuracy* used in most of the research we have examined in previous chapters.

Now look at Figure 7.1A, which shows the results for figures like Pair A from Demonstration 7.1. These figures require only a two-dimensional rotation, similar to rotating a flat picture. In contrast, Figure 7.1B shows the results for figures like Pair B in Demonstration 7.1. These figures require a three-dimensional rotation, similar to rotating an object in depth.

As both graphs show, people's decision time was strongly influenced by the amount of mental rotation required to match a figure with its mate. For example, rotating a figure 160 degrees requires much more time than rotating it a mere 20 degrees. Furthermore, notice the similarity between Figures 7.1A and 7.1B. In other words, the participants in this study performed a three-dimensional rotation almost as quickly as a two-dimensional rotation. (Pairs of figures like the two in Pair C in Demonstration 7.1 are based on different shapes, so these data are not included in either Figure 7.1A or 7.1B.)

As you can see, both figures show that the relationship between rotation and reaction time is a straight line. This research supports the analog-code perspective, because you would take much longer to rotate an actual physical object 160 degrees than to rotate it a mere 20 degrees. In contrast, a propositional code would predict similar reaction times for these two conditions; the language-like description for the figure would not vary with the amount of rotation (Howes, 2007).

Subsequent Research on Mental Rotation. The basic findings about mental rotation have been replicated many times. Using a variety of other stimuli, such as letters of the alphabet, researchers have found a clear relationship between angle of rotation and reaction time (e.g., Bauer & Jolicoeur, 1996; Cooper & Lang, 1996; Dahlstrom-Hakki et al., 2008; Kosslyn et al., 2006; Newcombe, 2002). That is, people make judgments more quickly if they need to rotate a mental image just a short distance.

FIGURE 7.1

Reaction Time for Deciding That Pairs of Figures Are the Same, as a Function of the Angle of Rotation and the Nature of Rotation.

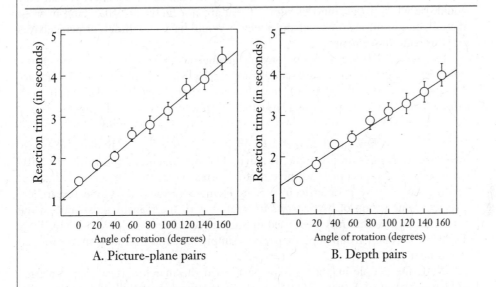

A. Picture-plane pairs

B. Depth pairs

Note: The centers of the circles indicate the means, and the bars on either side provide an index of the variability of those means.

Source: Shepard, R. N., & Metzler, J. (1971). Mental rotation of three-dimensional objects. *Science, 171,* 701–703. Copyright © 1971. American Association for the Advancement of Science.

If you are left-handed, you may wonder if handedness can influence the mental-rotation process. Kotaro Takeda and his coauthors (2010) asked the participants in their study to look at pictures of a human hand and to identify whether they were viewing a left hand or a right hand. Right-handers recognized a right hand faster than a left hand. In contrast, left-handers recognized right and left hands equally quickly. However, both groups recognized upright pictures faster—and more accurately—than upside-down pictures. This particular finding is consistent with the earlier research. After all, people take less time to rotate an image 0 degrees, rather than 180 degrees.

We also know that elderly people perform more slowly than younger people on a mental-rotation task. In contrast, age is not consistently correlated with other imagery skills, such as sense of direction or the ability to scan mental images (Beni et al., 2006; Dror & Kosslyn, 1994).

Other research shows that deaf individuals who are fluent in American Sign Language (ASL) are especially skilled in looking at an arrangement of objects in a scene and mentally rotating that scene by 180 degrees (Emmorey et al., 1998).

Why should deaf people perform so well on these mental rotation tasks? They have an advantage because they have had extensive experience in watching a narrator produce a sign. Then they must mentally rotate this sign 180 degrees. They need to perform this rotation frequently, so that they can match the perspective that they would use when producing this sign. (If you are not fluent in ASL, stand in front of a mirror and notice how you and a viewer would have very different perspectives for your hand movements.)

In general, the research on rotating geometric figures provides some of the strongest support for the analog-coding approach. We seem to treat mental images the same way we treat physical objects when we rotate them through space. In both cases, it takes longer to perform a large mental rotation than a small one.

Cognitive Neuroscience Research on Mental Rotation Tasks. In one of the early neuroscience studies on this topic, Kosslyn, Thompson, and their coauthors (2001) examined whether people use their motor cortex when they imagine themselves rotating one of the geometric figures in Demonstration 7.2. These researchers instructed one group of participants to rotate—with their own hands—one of the geometric figures that had been used in Shepard and Metzler's (1971) study. They instructed a second group of participants to simply watch as an electric motor rotated this same figure.

Next, the people in both groups performed the matching task that you tried in Demonstration 7.2 (page 211), by rotating the figures mentally. Meanwhile, the researchers conducted PET scans to see which areas of the brain the participants were using during the mental-rotation task.

The PET-scan results were clear-cut. Those participants who had originally rotated the original geometric figure with their hands now showed activity in their primary motor cortex—the same part of the brain that had been active when they had rotated the figure with their hands. In contrast, consider the participants who had originally watched the electric motor as it rotated the figure. On the mental-rotation task, these people now showed no activity in the primary motor cortex. Without the "hands on" experience, their primary motor cortex was not active.

The nature of the instructions during the actual mental rotation can also influence the pattern of activation in the cortex. Specifically, when people received the standard instructions to rotate the figure, their right frontal lobes and their parietal lobes were strongly activated (Wraga et al., 2005; Zacks et al., 2003).

However, this pattern of activation was different when researchers modified the instructions. In a second condition, the participants were instructed to imagine rotating themselves so that they could "see" the figure from a different perspective (Kosslyn et al., 2001). These instructions produced increased activity in the left temporal lobe, as well as in a part of the motor cortex (Wraga et al., 2005; Zacks et al., 2003). Notice, then, that a relatively subtle change in wording can make a dramatic change in the way that the brain responds to a mental-imagery task.

The research on mental rotation has practical implications for people who are recovering from a stroke. By watching the rotation of virtual-reality figures, these individuals can provide stimulation to their motor cortex. This form of "exercise" can shorten the time required before they make actual motor movements by themselves (Dijkerman et al., 2010; Ganis et al., 2009).

Visual Imagery and Distance

As we have seen, the first systematic research on imagery demonstrated the similarity between rotating mental images and rotating physical objects. Researchers soon began to examine other attributes of mental images, such as the distance between two points and the shape of the mental image.

Stephen Kosslyn is one of the most important researchers in the field of mental imagery. For example, a classic study by Kosslyn and his colleagues (1978) showed that people took a long time to scan the distance between two widely separated points on a mental image of a map that they had created. In contrast, they quickly scanned the distance between two nearby points on a mental image of that map. Later research confirms that there is a linear relationship between the distance to be scanned in a mental image and the amount of time required to scan this distance (Borst & Kosslyn, 2008; Denis & Kosslyn, 1999b; Kosslyn et al., 2006).

However, some psychologists were concerned about a potential problem with the research methods in these studies. For example, could the results of the research on imagery and distance be explained by experimenter expectancy, rather than a genuine influence from the distance between the two points in the mental image?

In **experimenter expectancy**, the researchers' biases and expectations influence the outcomes of the experiment. For example, when psychologists conduct research about visual imagery, they know that longer distances should require longer scanning times. Perhaps these researchers could somehow transmit these expectations to the participants in the study. These participants might—either consciously or unconsciously—adjust their search speeds according to the researchers' expectations (Denis & Kosslyn, 1999a; Intons-Peterson, 1983).

To answer this potential criticism about experimenter expectancy, Jolicoeur and Kosslyn (1985a, 1985b) repeated the mental-map experiment that we just discussed (Kosslyn et al., 1978). However, these researchers made certain that the two research assistants—who actually administered the new study—were not familiar with the research on mental imagery. Specifically, the assistants did not know about the typical linear relationship found in the previous research. Instead, the assistants were given an elaborate and convincing (but incorrect) explanation about visual imagery. This incorrect explanation described how the participants' results should show a U-shaped relationship between visual-imagery distance and scanning time.

Interestingly, the research assistants did *not* obtain the U-shaped curve that they were told they would find. Instead, their results demonstrated the standard linear relationship: As in the earlier research, participants needed more time to scan a large mental distance, compared to a small mental distance. Experimenter expectancy therefore cannot account for the obtained results (Denis & Kosslyn, 1999b; Kosslyn et al., 2006).

Visual Imagery and Shape

So far, we've seen that our visual images resemble real, physical images in (a) the research on rotation and (b) the research on distance. The research on shape imagery shows the same relationship.

Consider, for example, another classic study on visual imagery. Allan Paivio (1978) asked participants to make judgments about the angle formed by the two hands on an imaginary clock. For instance, try to visualize the two hands on a standard, nondigital clock. Next, create a visual image of the angle formed by the two hands if the time were 3:20. Now create a visual image of the angle between the two hands if the time were 7:25. Which of these two "mental clocks" has the smaller angle between the two hands?

Paivio also gave the participants several standardized tests to assess their visual-imagery ability. As you can see in Figure 7.2, the high-imagery participants made decisions much more quickly than the low-imagery participants. As Figure 7.2 also shows, participants in both groups made decisions very slowly when they compared the angle formed by the hands at 3:20 with the angle of the hands at 7:25. After all, these two angles are quite similar. In contrast, their decisions were relatively fast if the two angles were very different in size, perhaps 3:20 and 7:05.

Think about the implications of this study. With real objects, people take a long time to make decisions when two angles are very similar to each other. When the

FIGURE 7.2

The Influence of Angle Difference on Reaction Time for High-Imagery and Low-Imagery People.

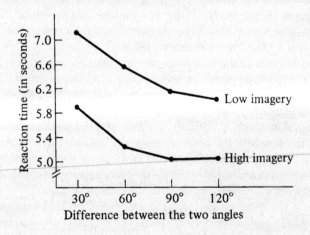

Source: Paivio, A. (1978). Comparison of mental clocks. *Journal of Experimental Psychology: Human Perception and Performance, 4,* 61–71.

two angles are very different, people respond quickly. The research demonstrates that people show the same pattern with their visual images. According to Paivio (1978), this study demonstrates strong support for the proposal that people use analog codes, rather than propositional codes.

Additional support for analog codes comes from research with visual images that represent more complex shapes. Shepard and Chipman (1970) asked participants to construct mental images of the shapes of various U.S. states, such as Colorado and Oregon. Then the participants judged the similarity between the two mental images, with respect to their shapes. For example—without looking at a map—do you think that Colorado and Oregon have similar shapes? How about Colorado and West Virginia?

These same participants also made shape-similarity judgments about pairs of states while they looked at an actual *physical* sketch of each state (rather than only its name). The results showed that the participants' judgments were highly similar in the two conditions. Once again, people's judgments about the shape of *mental* images are similar to their judgments about the shape of physical stimuli.

Let's review our conclusions about the characteristics of visual images, based on the research we have discussed so far:

1. When people rotate a visual image, a large rotation takes them longer, just as they take longer when making a large rotation with a physical stimulus.

2. People make distance judgments in a similar fashion for visual images and for physical stimuli.

3. People make decisions about shape in a similar fashion for visual images and for physical stimuli. This conclusion holds true for both simple shapes (angles formed by hands on a clock) and complex shapes (geographic regions, like Colorado or West Virginia).

Now, let's consider a fourth topic that demonstrates a similarity between mental images and physical stimuli. As you'll see, the research shows how visual images and physical stimuli can interfere with each other.

Visual Imagery and Interference

Many studies show that your mental image can interfere with an actual physical image (e.g., Baddeley & Andrade, 1998; Craver-Lemley & Reeves, 1992; Kosslyn et al., 2006; Richardson, 1999). Let's examine the research related to interference, specifically focusing on visual imagery.

Think about a friend whom you have seen in the last day or two. Next, create a clear mental image of this friend's face. Keep this mental image in mind, and simultaneously let your eyes wander over this page. You will probably find that the task is difficult, because you are trying to "look" at your friend (in a visual image) at the same time that you are trying to look at the words on this page (a physical stimulus). Research has confirmed that visual imagery can interfere with your visual perception.

Consider a classic study about interference, conducted by Segal and Fusella (1970). In part of this study, they asked participants to create a visual image, for example, a

---

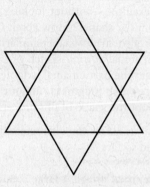

⑨ Demonstration 7.3

Imagery and an Ambiguous Figure

Look at the figure below, and form a clear mental image of the figure. Then turn to the paragraph labeled "Further instructions for Demonstration 7.3" at the bottom of Demonstration 7.4, on page 222.

---

visual image of a tree. As soon as the participant had formed the requested image, the researchers presented a real physical stimulus, for example a small blue arrow. The researchers then measured the participants' ability to detect the physical stimulus.

Segal and Fusella's (1970) results showed that people had more problems detecting the physical stimulus when the mental image was in the same sensory mode. For example, when the participants had been imagining the shape of a tree, they had trouble detecting the small blue arrow. The mental image interfered with the real visual stimulus. In contrast, when they had been imagining the sound of an oboe, they had no trouble reporting that they saw the arrow. After all, the imagined sound and the arrow—a visual stimulus—represented two different sensory modes.

In another study on visual interference, Mast and his colleagues (1999) told participants to create a visual image of a set of narrow parallel lines. Next, they were instructed to rotate their mental image of this set of lines, so that the lines were in a diagonal orientation. Meanwhile, the researchers presented a physical stimulus, a small segment of a line. The participants were told to judge whether this line segment had an exactly vertical orientation. The results showed that the imagined set of lines and the real set of lines produced similar distortions in the participants' judgments about the orientation of that line segment.

Visual Imagery and Ambiguous Figures

Before you read further, try Demonstration 7.3, and note whether you were able to reinterpret the figure. Most people have difficulty with tasks like this. The research suggests that—when people create a mental image of an ambiguous figure—they sometimes use analog codes and sometimes use propositional codes.

In the 1970s, Stephen Reed was concerned that mental imagery might have some limitations (Reed, 1974, 2010). Perhaps language helps us to store visual stimuli on some occasions. Reed's 1974 study tested people's ability to decide whether a specific visual pattern was a portion of a design that they had seen earlier. Specifically, Reed presented a series of paired figures. For example, people might first see a pattern like the Star of David in Demonstration 7.3, and then this figure disappeared. Next, after a brief delay, people saw a second pattern, such as a parallelogram with slanted right and left sides. In half of the trials, the second pattern was truly part of the first one (for example, a parallelogram). In the other half, it was not (for example, a rectangle).

Suppose that people actually do store mental images in their head that correspond to the physical objects they have seen. Then they should be able to draw forth that mental image of the star and quickly discover the parallelogram shape hidden within it. However, the participants in Reed's (1974) study were correct only 14% of the time on the star/parallelogram example. Across all stimuli, they were correct only 55% of the time, hardly better than chance.

Reed (1974) argued that people could not have stored a visual image for figures like the Star of David, given the high error rate on items like this one. Instead, Reed proposed that people sometimes store pictures as descriptions, using the kind of propositional code that we discussed on page 212.

For example, suppose that you stored the description in Demonstration 7.3 as a verbal code, "two triangles, one pointing up and the other pointing down, placed on top of each other." When the instructions asked you whether the figure contained a parallelogram, you may have searched through your verbal description. Your search would locate only triangles, not parallelograms. Notice that Reed's (1974) research supports the verbal propositional-code approach, rather than the analog-code approach.

Similar research explored whether people could provide reinterpretations for a mental image of an ambiguous figure. For example, you can interpret the ambiguous stimulus in Figure 7.3 in two ways: a rabbit facing to the right or a duck facing to the

FIGURE 7.3

An Example of an Ambiguous Figure from Chambers and Reisberg's Study.

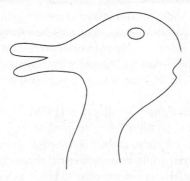

ⓢ Demonstration 7.4

Reinterpreting Ambiguous Stimuli

Imagine the capital letter **H**. Now imagine the capital letter **X** superimposed directly on top of the **H**, so that the four corners of each letter match up exactly. From this mental image, what new shapes and objects do you see in your mind's eye?

(Further instructions for Demonstration 7.3: Without glancing back at the figure in Demonstration 7.3, consult your mental image. Does that mental image contain a parallelogram?)

---

left. Chambers and Reisberg (1985) asked participants to create a clear mental image of this figure. Next, the researchers removed the figure. The participants were then asked to give a second, different interpretation of that particular figure. None of the 15 people could do so. In other words, they apparently could not consult a stored mental image.

Next, the participants were asked to draw the figure from memory. Could they reinterpret this physical stimulus? All of them looked at the figure they had just drawn, and all 15 were able to supply a second interpretation. Chambers and Reisberg's research suggests that a strong verbal propositional code—such as "a duck that is facing left"—can overshadow a relatively weak analog code. Other similar research has replicated these findings. It's often easy to reverse a visual stimulus while you are looking at a physical picture that is ambiguous. In contrast, it's usually more difficult to reverse a *mental* image (Reisberg & Heuer, 2005). Now try Demonstration 7.4 before you read further.

It seems likely that people often use an analog code when they are thinking about fairly simple figures (like the two hands of a clock). In contrast, people may use a propositional code when the figures are more complex, as in the case of the research by Reed (1974) and Chambers and Reisberg (1985). As Kosslyn and his coauthors (2006) point out, our memory has a limited capacity for visual imagery. We may therefore have difficulty storing complex visual information in an analog code and then making accurate judgments about these mental images.

Verbal labels (and a propositional code) may be especially helpful if the visual stimulus is complex. For example, when I work on a jigsaw puzzle, I often find that I've attached a verbal label—such as "angel with outstretched wings"—to aid my search for a missing piece. In the case of these complex shapes, storage may be mostly propositional.

In other research, Finke and his colleagues (1989) asked people to combine two mental images, as in Demonstration 7.4. The participants in this study could indeed create new interpretations for these ambiguous stimuli. In addition to a combined **X** and **H** figure, they reported some new geometric shapes (such as a right triangle), some new letters (such as **M**), and some objects (such as a bow tie). Other research confirms that observers can locate similar, unanticipated shapes in their mental images (Brandimonte & Gerbino, 1996; Kosslyn et al., 2006; Rouw et al., 1997).

In summary, the research on ambiguous figures shows that people can create mental images using both propositional and analog codes. That is, we often use analog codes to provide picture-like representations that capture our mental images. However, when the stimuli or situations make it difficult to use analog codes, we may create a verbal representation, using a propositional code.

Visual Imagery and Other Vision-Like Processes

So far, we have examined a variety of characteristics related to visual imagery. These include rotation, distance, shape, interference, and ambiguous figures. Let's briefly consider another less obvious characteristic of visual perception. We'll see that a relatively unknown visual characteristic has a mental-imagery counterpart.

Research in visual perception shows that people can see a visual target more accurately if the target is presented with vertical lines on each side of this target. Research by Ishai and Sagi (1995) shows that mental imagery produces the same masking effect. That is, people can see a visual target more accurately if they create mental images of vertical lines on each side of the target.

This study on the masking effect is especially important because of a research-methods issue called "demand characteristics." **Demand characteristics** are all the cues that might convey the experimenter's hypothesis to the participant. You already learned about a research-methods concept called "experimenter expectancy." As we noted, researchers may transmit their expectations to participants in an experiment (see pp. 217–218). As it happens, experimenter expectancy is one kind of demand characteristic.

However, experiments provide numerous additional kinds of demand characteristics. Some critics of the analog approach have proposed that the experimental results in imagery experiments might be traceable to one or more of these demand characteristics (Pylyshyn, 2003, 2006). For example, participants may be able to guess the results that the experimenter wants. Perhaps they might guess that a visual mental image is supposed to interfere with visual perception.

In contrast, the masking effect is virtually unknown to people who have not completed a psychology course in perception. The participants in the study by Ishai and Sagi (1995) would not know that visual targets are especially easy to see if they are surrounded by masking stimuli. Therefore, demand characteristics cannot account for the masking effect with mental images. As a result, we can be more confident that *visual imagery* really can produce the masking effect, just as *visual perception* can produce the masking effect. Visual imagery can indeed resemble visual perception.

Researchers have also examined whether mental imagery resembles visual perception in other respects. For example, people have especially good acuity for mental images that are visualized in the center of the retina, rather than in the periphery; visual perception operates the same way (Kosslyn, 1983). Other studies demonstrate additional parallels between mental images and visual perception (Kosslyn, 2001; Kosslyn & Thompson, 2000; Kosslyn et al., 2006).

Explanations for Visual Imagery

Now that you have read about the research on visual imagery, let's reconsider the imagery debate. Then we'll briefly discuss some relevant neuroscience research.

The Imagery Debate. For several decades, cognitive psychologists have debated the potential explanations for mental imagery. At the beginning of this chapter (pages 212 to 213), we introduced the analog and propositional perspectives on imagery. Now that you are familiar with the research, let's reconsider the controversy. The two perspectives definitely differ in their emphasis on the similarity between mental images and physical stimuli. However, the two positions are not completely different from each other, and they may apply to different kinds of tasks.

According to the *analog perspective*, you create a mental image of an object that closely resembles the actual perceptual image on your retina (Ganis et al., 2009; Kosslyn et al., 2006). Take a minute to review pages 213 to 220, and you'll see that your responses to mental images are frequently similar to your responses to physical objects. In fact, the majority of the research supports this position. Of course, no one argues that vision and mental imagery are identical (Kosslyn et al., 2006). After all, you can easily differentiate between your mental image of your textbook's cover and your actual perception of that cover.

According to the *propositional perspective*, mental images are stored in an abstract, language-like form that does not physically resemble the original stimulus. Zenon Pylyshyn (2003, 2004, 2006) has been the strongest supporter of this perspective. Pylyshyn agrees that people do experience mental images; it would be foolish to argue otherwise. However, Pylyshyn says that these images are not a necessary, central component of imagery.

Pylyshyn argues that it would be awkward—and perhaps even unworkable—to store information in terms of mental images. For instance, people would need a huge space to store all the images that they claim to have.

Pylyshyn (2004, 2006) also emphasizes the differences between perceptual experiences and mental images. For example, you can re-examine and re-interpret a real photograph. However, on a task like the rabbit/duck figure, people typically cannot reinterpret a mental image (Chambers & Reisberg, 1985).

At present, the analog code apparently explains most stimuli and most tasks. However, for some kinds of stimuli and several specific tasks, people may use a propositional code.

Neuroscience Research Comparing Visual Imagery and Visual Perception. As part of the in-depth section at the beginning of this chapter, we discussed the neuroscience research on mental-rotation tasks. That research shows that these tasks activate parts of the brain's temporal lobe, as well as the motor cortex.

Now we'll briefly consider the neuroscience research on topics other than mental rotation. Although imagery and perception share many characteristics, they are not identical. After all, mental imagery relies exclusively on top-down processing. In contrast, visual perception activates the rods and cones in your retina. When you create a mental image of the shape of Colorado, no one would suggest that the rods and cones in your retina are registering a Colorado-shaped pattern of stimulation. The subjective experiences for visual imagery and visual perception are obviously different, and it takes about one-tenth of a second longer to create a visual image (Reddy et al., 2010).

Surveying a large number of studies, Kosslyn and his colleagues (2010) conclude that visual imagery activates between about 70% and 90% of the same brain regions that are activated during visual perception. For instance, when people have brain damage in the most basic region of the visual cortex, they have parallel problems in both their visual perception and their visual imagery. Furthermore, some individuals with brain damage cannot distinguish between (1) the colors registered during visual perception and (2) the visual imagery created in a mental image.

As we noted on page 212, people who have prosopagnosia cannot recognize human faces visually, though they perceive other objects relatively normally. The research shows that these individuals also cannot use mental imagery to distinguish between faces (Kosslyn et al., 2010).

This neuroscience evidence about the similarity between visual imagery and visual perception is especially persuasive, because it avoids the demand-characteristics problem that we discussed on page 223. As Farah (2000) pointed out, people seldom know which parts of their brain are typically active during vision. Therefore, when you create a mental image of a bow tie, you cannot voluntarily activate the relevant cells in your visual cortex!

Individual Differences: Gender Comparisons in Spatial Ability

When psychologists conduct research about individual differences in cognition, one of the most popular topics is gender comparisons. Talk-show hosts, politicians—and even university presidents—feel free to speculate about gender differences. However, they rarely consult the extensive psychology research about gender comparisons. As a result, they rarely learn that most gender differences in cognitive abilities are small (Hyde, 2005; Matlin, 2012; Yoder, 2013).

Our Individual Differences Features in Chapters 2 through 6 have all focused on one single study. However, researchers have conducted literally hundreds of studies on gender comparisons in cognitive abilities. If we want to understand gender comparisons in spatial ability, for example, we cannot focus on just one study.

When the research on a topic is abundant, psychologists often use a statistical technique called a meta-analysis. **Meta-analysis** is a statistical method for combining numerous studies on a single topic. Researchers begin by locating all appropriate studies on a topic such as gender comparisons in verbal ability. Then they perform a meta-analysis that combines the results of all these studies.

A meta-analysis yields a number called effect size, or d. For example, suppose that researchers conduct a meta-analysis of 18 studies about gender comparisons in reading comprehension scores. Furthermore, suppose that—on each of the 18 studies—females and males receive very similar scores. In this case, the d would be close to zero.

Psychologists have conducted numerous meta-analyses on cognitive gender comparisons. Janet Hyde (2005) wrote an important article that summarized all of these

TABLE 7.1

The Distribution of Effect Sizes (d) Reported in Meta-Analyses for Three Kinds of Cognitive Skills

	Magnitude of Effect Size			
	Close to Zero (d < 0.10)	Small (d = 0.11 to 0.35)	Moderate (d = 0.36 to 0.65)	Large (d = 0.66 to 1.00)
Verbal Ability	4	1	0	0
Mathematics	4	0	0	0
Spatial Ability	0	4	3	1

Source: Based on Hyde (2005).

previous meta-analyses. Table 7.1 shows a tally of the effect sizes for the meta-analyses that have been conducted in three major areas of cognitive ability.

As you can see in Table 7.1, four meta-analyses on verbal ability showed extremely small gender differences, with *d* values close to zero. One additional meta-analysis produced a *d* value considered to be "small," and no meta-analyses yielded a *d* value considered to be either moderate or large. In other words, these studies show *gender similarities* in verbal ability.

You can also see that all four meta-analyses on mathematics ability produced *d* values that are close to zero, once more showing *gender similarities*. These gender similarities in math ability are extremely important, especially because the headlines in the media usually claim that males are much better than females in their math skills (Hyde, 2005; Matlin, 2012). These math comparisons are consistent with an international study that focused on eighth-grade students in 34 different countries. Interestingly, the boys' average was higher than the girls' average in 16 countries, the girls' average was higher than boys' average in 16 countries, and girls and boys had the same averages in 2 countries (National Center for Education Statistics, 2004).

Let's now consider spatial ability, the topic related to our current discussion. Here, the gender differences are more substantial. Notice, however, that only one meta-analysis yielded a *d* value in the "large" category.

An important point is that spatial ability represents several different skills; it is not unitary (Caplan & Caplan, 2009; Chipman, 2004; Tversky, 2005b). One skill is spatial visualization. A typical task would be to ask people to look at a sketch of a busy street to find hidden drawings of human faces. Gender differences in spatial visualization are small, according to Hyde's (2005) summary of meta-analyses.

The second component of spatial ability is spatial perception. A typical task would be sitting in a dark room and adjusting an illuminated rod so that it is in an exactly vertical position. The two meta-analyses that specifically focused on spatial perception both produced *d* values of 0.44, a moderate gender difference (Hyde, 2005).

The third component of spatial ability is mental rotation. As you know from Demonstration 7.2 on page 211, a typical task would be to look at two geometric figures and then decide whether they would be identical if you rotated one of the figures. Males are more likely than females to respond quickly on this task. The two meta-analyses that specifically focused on mental rotation produced *d* values of 0.56 and 0.73 (Hyde, 2005). For the sake of comparison, however, consider the gender differences in people's height. For height, the *d* is a substantial 2.0.

In other words, mental rotation is the only cognitive skill where a group of males is likely to earn higher scores than a group of females. However, we must emphasize that some studies report no gender differences in mental rotation. Furthermore, some studies report that the gender differences disappear when the task instructions are changed and when people receive training on spatial skills (Matlin, 2012; Newcombe, 2006; Terlecki et al., 2008).

In addition, a large portion of the gender differences in spatial rotation can be traced to the fact that boys typically have more experience with toys and sports that emphasize spatial skills (Voyer et al., 2000). In other words, this one area of cognitive gender differences can be reduced by providing girls with experience and training in spatial activities.

Section Summary: *The Characteristics of Visual Imagery*

1. Spatial ability is important in the STEM disciplines; teachers can provide helpful training in spatial skills.

2. A controversy in cognitive psychology has focused on mental imagery, specifically, whether information is stored in picture-like analog codes or language-like propositional codes. Research on the characteristics of mental images addresses this issue.

3. The amount of time that people take to rotate a mental image depends on the extent of the rotation, just as when we rotate a real, physical object. Deaf people use mental rotation during signing; they also perform well on mental-rotation tasks. The nature of the mental-rotation instructions has an influence on the region of the brain that is activated.

4. People take longer to "travel" a long mental distance, in contrast to a short mental distance. This finding is apparently not due to experimenter expectancy.

5. When judging the shapes of mental images or visual images, people take longer to make decisions when the two stimuli have very similar physical shapes. This conclusion applies to simple shapes (e.g., the hands on a clock), as well as complex shapes (e.g., the shapes of U.S. states).

6. Visual images can interfere with visual perception; this conclusion applies to the perception of figures such as trees, as well as line segments.

7. In several studies, the participants are instructed to create a mental image for an ambiguous figure; they may have difficulty reinterpreting this mental image so that they see a different figure.

8. Another vision-like property of mental images is enhanced acuity when a target is flanked by imaginary masks; this type of research is important because demand characteristics would be minimal.

9. The majority of research supports the analog viewpoint, as described by Stephen Kosslyn and his colleagues, but some people—on some tasks—apparently use a propositional code, as described by Zenon Pylyshyn.

10. According to neuroscience research, visual imagery activates about 70% to 90% of the same brain regions that are activated during visual perception. Furthermore, people with prosopagnosia cannot recognize human faces visually, and they also cannot create a mental image of a face.

11. Meta-analyses on spatial ability show small to moderate gender differences in spatial visualization and spatial perception; gender differences are somewhat larger in mental rotation, but these differences can be reduced by experience in spatial activities.

THE CHARACTERISTICS OF AUDITORY IMAGERY

Up to this point in the chapter, we have considered only visual imagery, which is sometimes called your "mind's eye." However, most people report that they also experience auditory imagery. As we noted at the beginning of this chapter, auditory imagery is our mental representation of sounds when these sounds are not physically present. For example, can you create a vivid auditory image of a close friend's laughter? Can you create a vivid auditory image for the first few bars of a favorite song? What other categories of auditory images can you create in your "mind's ear"?

We can typically identify a variety of "environmental sounds," even though we might not use that particular term. For example, can you create an auditory image of the whining sound made by an almost-dead car battery? In addition, we typically have auditory imagery for the distinctive noises made by a variety of animals (Wu et al., 2006). This section on auditory imagery provides an introduction to the topic.

Psychologists have lamented the relative lack of research on auditory imagery (e.g., Kosslyn et al., 2010; Vuvan & Schmuckler, 2011). For example, Timothy Hubbard (2010) reviewed the research on the topic. The first paragraph of Hubbard's article begins, "Despite the resurgence in imagery research beginning in the late 1960s and early 1970s, auditory forms of imagery have received relatively little interest" (p. 302). Hubbard also discovered that some previous articles had claimed that they had found evidence of auditory imagery, but the evidence was not convincing. As you know from the studies on visual imagery, the research methods need to be carefully designed to demonstrate clear-cut evidence of mental imagery.

Auditory processes clearly play an important role in our cognitive experience. For example, in this textbook, Chapter 2 introduced speech perception. Chapter 3 explored divided attention, for instance when you are hearing two conversations at the same time. Chapter 4 of this textbook examined memory for auditory stimuli, in connection with the phonological loop. Chapters 5 and 6 included memory for auditory information, as well as visual information. Chapters 9 and 10 will explore the role of auditory processes in language comprehension, language production, and bilingualism. In Chapter 13, you'll see that young infants can tell the difference between similar sounds such as "bah" and "pah." Auditory perception is important in all these areas. However, this research typically focuses on the physical stimuli, rather than the auditory images that we create.

Is auditory imagery less vivid than visual imagery? Rubin and Berentsen (2009) asked people in the United States and Denmark to recall an event from their life and rate its vividness. In both countries, people reported higher imagery ratings for visual imagery than for auditory imagery. Even so, the relative lack of research on auditory imagery is puzzling.

Researchers have explored some characteristics of auditory imagery such as loudness (e.g., Hubbard, 2010; Vuvan & Schmuckler, 2011). In this section, we will briefly consider two topics that have clear implications for mental imagery: (1) auditory imagery and pitch, and (2) auditory imagery and timbre.

Auditory Imagery and Pitch

One prominent feature of auditory imagery is pitch. **Pitch** is a characteristic of a sound stimulus that can be arranged on a scale from low to high (Foley & Matlin, 2010; Plack & Oxenham, 2005). One of the classic studies on pitch was conducted by Margaret J. Intons-Peterson, who was one of the creators of the important Brown/Peterson & Peterson technique for assessing short-term memory. (See Chapter 4.) Intons-Peterson and her coauthors (1992) examined how quickly people could "travel" the distance between two auditory stimuli that differ in pitch.

For example, Intons-Peterson and her colleagues asked students to create an auditory image of a cat purring. Then they asked the students to "travel" from the cat-purring image to an image with a slightly higher pitch, such as a slamming door. The participants pressed a button when they reached this slightly higher pitch. The results showed that the students needed about 4 seconds to travel that relatively short auditory distance.

The researchers also asked students to "travel" longer auditory distances, for example, from a cat purring to the sound of a police siren. The participants needed about 6 seconds to travel this relatively long distance. In the case of pitch, the distance between the two actual tones is indeed correlaed with the distance between the two imagined tones.

Auditory Imagery and Timbre

Another important characteristic of a sound is called "timbre" (pronounced "*tam-ber*"). **Timbre** describes the sound quality of a tone. For example, imagine a familiar tune—such as *Happy Birthday*—played on the flute. Now contrast that sound quality with the same song played on a trumpet. Even when the two versions of this song have the same pitch, the flute tune seems relatively pure.

Consider a study by Andrea Halpern and her coauthors (2004), which focused on people's auditory imagery for the timbre of musical instruments. These researchers studied young adults who had completed at least 5 years of formal training in music. This requirement was necessary so that the participants would be familiar with the timbre of eight musical instruments, such as the basoon, flute, trumpet, and violin. Each participant first listened to the sound of every instrument, until he or she could name them all easily.

To assess auditory imagery for timbre, Halpern and her colleagues asked each participant to rate the similarity of timbres in two conditions. In the *perception condition*, the participants listened to a 1.5-second segment of one musical instrument, followed by a 1.5-second segment of another instrument. They heard all possible pairings of the eight different instruments. For every pair, the participants rated the similarity of the two perceptual stimuli. In the *imagined condition*, the participants heard the names of the instruments, rather than their sounds. They heard all possible pairings of the eight names for the different instruments.

The results showed that the ratings for timbre perception and for timbre imagery were highly correlated with each other ($r = .84$). In other words, the participants showed that their cognitive representation for the timbre of an *actual* musical instrument is quite similar to the cognitive representation for the timbre of an *imagined* musical instrument. Clearly, researchers with an interest in imagery can explore many new topics that compare the relationship between auditory perception and auditory imagery.

⊚ Section Summary: *The Characteristics of Auditory Imagery*

1. Researchers have commented on the lack of research on auditory imagery, especially because auditory processes are an important part of human cognition; furthermore, some previous studies did not provide clear-cut evidence for auditory imagery.

2. Research on pitch shows that people can quickly travel the mental distance between two imagined musical tones that are similar in pitch; the "travel time" is longer when the two tones are different in pitch.

3. The word "timbre" refers to the sound quality of a tone. People listened to pairs of tones produced by a variety of musical instruments, and then they rated the perceived similarity of each pair. They also imagined the pairs of tones produced by the same musical instruments, and then they rated their similarity. Timbre perception and timbre imagery were highly correlated.

COGNITIVE MAPS

Have you had an experience like this? You've just arrived in a new environment, perhaps for your first year of college. You ask for directions, let's say, to the library.

You hear the reply, "OK, it's simple. You go up the hill, staying to the right of the Blake Building. Then you take a left, and Newton Hall will be on your right. The library will be over on your left." You struggle to recall some landmarks from the orientation tour. Was Newton Hall next to the College Union, or was it over near Erwin Administration Building? Valiantly, you try to incorporate this new information into your discouragingly hazy mental map.

So far, this chapter has examined the general characteristics of mental images. This discussion primarily focused on a theoretical issue that has intrigued cognitive psychologists: Do our visual and auditory mental images resemble our perception of actual visual and auditory stimuli?

Now we consider cognitive maps, a topic that is clearly related to mental imagery. However, the research on cognitive maps focuses on the way we represent geographic space. More specifically, a **cognitive map** is a mental representation of geographic information, including the environment that surrounds us (Shelton & Yamamoto, 2009; Wagner, 2006). Notice, then, that the first two sections of this chapter emphasize our mental representations of sights and sounds. In contrast, this third section emphasizes our mental images of the *relationships* among objects, such as buildings on your college campus.

Let's discuss some background about cognitive maps, and then we'll see how distance, shape, and relative position are represented in these cognitive maps. We'll conclude this chapter by examining how we create mental maps from verbal descriptions.

Background Information About Cognitive Maps

Try to picture a home that you know quite well. Now picture yourself walking through this home. Does your cognitive map seem fairly accurate, or is this map somewhat fuzzy about the specific size and location of a room? A cognitive map can also represent larger geographic areas, such as a neighborhood, a city, or a country. In general, our cognitive maps represent areas that are too large to be seen in a single glance (Bower, 2008; Poirel et al., 2010; Wagner, 2006). As a result, we create a cognitive map by integrating the information that we have acquired from many successive views (Shelton, 2004; Spence & Feng, 2010). In general, the research on cognitive maps emphasizes real-world settings, as well as high ecological validity.

Research on cognitive maps is part of a larger topic called *spatial cognition*. **Spatial cognition** primarily refers to three cognitive activities: (1) our thoughts about cognitive maps; (2) how we remember the world we navigate; and (3) how we keep track of objects in a spatial array (Shelton, 2004; Spence & Feng, 2010).

Furthermore, spatial cognition is interdisciplinary in its scope. For example, computer scientists create models of spatial knowledge. Linguists analyze how people talk about spatial arrangements. Anthropologists study how different cultures use different frameworks to describe locations. Geographers examine all of these dimensions, with the goal of creating efficient maps. The topic is also relevant when architects design buildings and when urban planners construct new communities (Devlin, 2001; Tversky, 1999, 2000b).

In addition to theoretical issues related to spatial cognition, psychologists study applied topics. These include topics related to entertainment, such as video games (Spence & Feng, 2010). They also study life-and-death topics such as the communication of spatial information between air traffic controllers and airplane flight crews (Barshi & Healy, 2011; Schneider et al., 2011).

As you might expect, individual differences in spatial-cognition skills are quite large (Shelton & McNamara, 2004; Smith & Cohen, 2008; Wagner, 2006). However, people tend to be accurate in judging their ability to find their way to unfamiliar locations (Kitchin & Blades, 2002). In other words, your metacognition about your spatial ability may be reasonably correct.

Furthermore, these individual differences in spatial cognition are correlated with people's scores on tests of the visuospatial sketchpad (Gyselinck & Meneghetti, 2011). Spatial-cognition scores are also correlated with performance on the spatial tasks that we discussed in the first section of this chapter (Newcombe, 2010; Sholl et al., 2006). For example, people who are good at mental rotation (pp. 213–217) are more skilled than others in using maps to find a particular location (Fields & Shelton, 2006; Shelton & Gabrieli, 2004).

Fortunately, people with poor spatial skills can improve their performance. Suppose that you are visiting an unfamiliar college campus (Smith & Cohen, 2008). You park your car, and you set out to find a specific building. You'll increase your

---

⑨ Demonstration 7.5

Learning from a Map

Study the diagram at the bottom of this demonstration for about 30 seconds, and then cover it completely. Now answer the following questions:

1. Imagine that you are standing at Position 3, facing Position 4. Point to Position 1.

2. Now, glance quickly at the diagram and then cover it completely. Imagine that you are now standing at Position 1, facing Position 2. Point to Position 4.

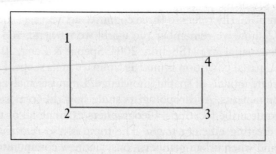

chances of finding your way back to your car if you periodically turn around and study the scene you'll see on your return trip (Heth et al., 2002; Montello, 2005). As you might expect, it's also important to notice specific landmarks along this route (Ruddle et al., 2011). These strategies should improve the accuracy of your cognitive maps.

Try Demonstration 7.5 before you read further. This demonstration is based on research by Roskos-Ewoldsen and her colleagues (1998), which we will discuss shortly.

Our cognitive maps typically include survey knowledge, which is the relationship among locations that we acquire by directly learning a map or by repeatedly exploring an environment. Now look back at Demonstration 7.5. Which of the two tasks was easier? Your cognitive map will be easier to judge and more accurate if you acquire spatial information from a physical map that is oriented in the same direction that you are facing in your cognitive map.

In Question 1 of this demonstration, your mental map and the physical map have the same orientation, so this task should be relatively easy. In contrast, you need to perform a mental rotation in order to answer Question 2, so this task is more difficult. Research confirms that judgments are easier when your mental map and the physical map have matching orientations (Devlin, 2001; Montello, 2005; Montello et al., 2004).

Now we will consider how our cognitive maps represent three geographic attributes: distance, shape, and relative position. Theme 2 of this book states that our cognitive processes are generally accurate. This generalization also applies to cognitive maps. In fact, our mental representations of the environment usually reflect reality with reasonable accuracy, whether these cognitive maps depict college campuses or larger geographic regions.

According to Theme 2, however, when people *do* make cognitive mistakes, these mistakes can often be traced to a rational strategy. The mistakes that people display in their cognitive maps usually "make sense" because they are systematic distortions of reality (Devlin, 2001; Koriat et al., 2000; Tversky, 2000b). These mistakes reflect a tendency to base our judgments on variables that are *usually* relevant. They also reflect a tendency to judge our environment as being more well organized and orderly than it really is.

At this point, we need to introduce a useful term in cognitive psychology, called a "heuristic." A **heuristic** (pronounced "hyoo-*riss*-tick") is a general problem-solving strategy that usually produces a correct solution ... but not always. As you will see, people often use heuristics in making judgments about cognitive maps. As a result, they tend to show systematic distortions in distance, shape, and relative position.

Cognitive Maps and Distance

How far is it from your college library to the classroom in which your cognitive psychology course is taught? How many miles separate the place where you were born from the college or university where you are now studying? People's distance estimates are often distorted by factors such as (1) the number of intervening cities, (2) category membership, and (3) whether their destination is a landmark.

Distance Estimates and Number of Intervening Cities. In one of the first systematic studies about distance in cognitive maps, Thorndyke (1981) constructed a map of a hypothetical geographic region with cities distributed throughout the map. Between any two cities on the map, there were 0, 1, 2, or 3 other cities along the route. Participants studied the map until they could accurately reconstruct it. Then they estimated the distance between specified pairs of cities.

The number of intervening cities had a clear-cut influence on their estimates. For example, when the cities were really 300 miles apart on this map, people estimated that they were only 280 miles apart when there were no intervening cities. In contrast, these target cities were estimated to be 350 miles apart with three intervening cities. Notice that this error is consistent with the concept of heuristics. If cities are randomly distributed throughout a region, two cities are usually closer together when there are no intervening cities between them. In contrast, two cities are likely to be further apart when there are three intervening cities.

Distance Estimates and Category Membership. Research shows that the categories we create can have a large influence on our distance estimates. For example, Hirtle and Mascolo (1986) showed participants a hypothetical map of a town, and they learned the locations on the map. Then the map was removed, and people estimated the distance between pairs of locations. The results showed that people tended to shift each location closer to other sites that belonged to the same category. For example, people typically remembered the courthouse as being close to the police station and other government buildings. However, these shifts did not occur for members of different categories. For instance, people did not move the courthouse closer to the golf course.

People show a similar distortion when they estimate large-scale distances (Tversky, 2009). For instance, Friedman and her colleagues asked college students to estimate the distance between various North American cities (Friedman et al., 2005; Friedman & Montello, 2006). Students from Canada, the United States, and Mexico judged that distances were greater when they were separated by an international border. Specifically, they judged two cities to be an average of only 1,225 miles from each other if the cities were located in the same country. In contrast, they judged two cities to be an average of 1,579 miles from each other if they were located in different countries.

In other words, the estimated difference was 354 miles when the cities were separated by an international border; in reality, the actual difference was only 63 miles (Friedman & Montello, 2006). Students make a similar error when they estimate distances on their own college campus, and there is an invisible border between two parts of the campus (Uttal et al., 2010; Wagner, 2006). They are reluctant to say that two buildings could be near each other if they are on different sides of that invisible border.

According to a phenomenon called **border bias**, people estimate that the distance between two specific locations is larger if they are on *different* sides of a geographic border, compared to two locations on the *same* side of that border. Border bias can have far-reaching consequences. For example, Arul Mishra and Himanshu Mishra (2010) asked participants to imagine that they were thinking about buying a vacation home in the mountains, and their final choices were currently in either Oregon or Washington.

While they were deciding, one group was told that an earthquake had hit Wells, Oregon, in a location 200 miles from both of these vacation homes. Another group received identical instructions, except that the earthquake had hit Wells, Washington. A third group (the control group) received the same initial instructions, but no earthquake was mentioned.

Figure 7.4 shows the results. Even though the epicenter of the earthquake was the same distance from both vacation homes, the participants in the "Oregon earthquake group" were 20% more likely than the control group to choose a Washington home. Similarly, the participants in the "Washington earthquake group" were 25% more likely than the control group to choose an Oregon home.

FIGURE 7.4

An Example of Border Bias: Percentage of Participants Choosing Each Vacation Home, as a Function of Which State Had Experienced an Earthquake. When people hear about an earthquake, they prefer to select a home in a different state, rather than a home that is equally close, but in the same state (Mishra & Mishra, 2010).

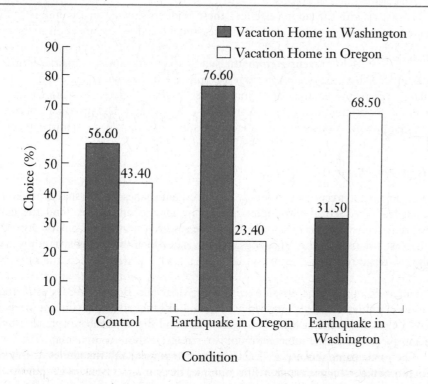

Source: Mishra, A., & Mishra, H. (2010). Border bias: The belief that state borders can protect against disasters. *Psychological Science*, 21, 1582–1586. Copyright © 2010. Reprinted by permission of SAGE Publications.

Notice that this study demonstrates a "same-category heuristic." It's generally a good strategy to guess that two cities are closer together if they are in the same state, rather than in adjacent states.

Distance Estimates and Landmarks. We have some friends who live in Rochester, the major city in our region of upstate New York. We sometimes invite them to come down for a meeting in Geneseo, about 45 minutes away from Rochester. "But it's so far away," they complain. "Why don't you come up here instead?" They are embarrassed when we point out that the distance from Geneseo to Rochester is exactly the same as the distance from Rochester to Geneseo!

The research confirms the **landmark effect**, which is the general tendency to provide shorter estimates when traveling to a landmark—an important geographical location—rather than a nonlandmark (Shelton & Yamamoto, 2009; Tversky, 2005b, 2009; Wagner, 2006). For example, McNamara and Diwadkar (1997) asked students to memorize a map that displayed various pictures of objects. The map included some objects that were described as landmarks, and some objects that were not landmarks. After learning the locations, the students estimated the distance on the map (in inches) between various pairs of objects.

Consistent with the landmark effect, these students showed an asymmetry in their distance estimates. In one study, for instance, students judged distances on an informal map (McNamara & Diwadkar, 1997). They estimated that the distance was an average of 1.7 inches when traveling from the landmark to the nonlandmark. However, the estimated distance was an average of only 1.4 inches when traveling from the nonlandmark to the landmark. Prominent destinations apparently seem closer than less important destinations. This research also demonstrates the importance of context when we make decisions about distances and other features of our cognitive maps.

Cognitive Maps and Shape

Our cognitive maps represent not only distances, but shapes. These shapes are evident in map features such as the angles formed by intersecting streets and the curves illustrating the bends in rivers. Once again, the research shows a systematic distortion. In this case, we tend to construct cognitive maps in which the shapes are more regular than they are in reality.

Angles. Consider the classic research by Moar and Bower (1983), who studied people's cognitive maps of Cambridge, England. All the participants in the study had lived in Cambridge for at least five years. Moar and Bower asked people to estimate the angles formed by the intersection of two streets, without using a map.

The participants showed a clear tendency to "regularize" the angles so that they were more like 90-degree angles. For example, three intersections in Cambridge had "real" angles of 67, 63, and 50 degrees. However, people *estimated* these same angles to be an average of 84, 78, and 88 degrees. As you may recall, the sum of the angles in a triangle should be 180 degrees, but in this study, the sum of the estimated angles was 250 degrees. Furthermore, this study showed that seven of the nine angles were significantly biased in the direction of a 90-degree angle.

What explains this systematic distortion? Moar and Bower (1983) suggest that we employ a heuristic. When two roads meet in most urban areas, they generally form a 90-degree angle. When people use the **90-degree-angle heuristic**, they represent angles in a mental map as being closer to 90 degrees than they really are.

You may recall a similar concept in the discussion of memory schemas in Chapter 5. It is easier to store a schematic version of an event, rather than a precise version of the event that includes all the trivial details. This 90-degree-angle heuristic has also been replicated in other settings (Montello et al., 2004; Tversky, 2005b; Wagner, 2006).

Curves. The New York State Thruway runs in an east-west direction across the state, although it curves somewhat in certain areas. To me, the upward curve south of Rochester seems symmetrical, equally arched on each side of the city. However, when I checked the map, the curve is much steeper on the eastern side.

Research confirms that people tend to use a **symmetry heuristic**; we remember figures as being more symmetrical and regular than they truly are (Montello et al., 2004; Tversky, 2000a; Tversky & Schiano, 1989). Again, these results follow the general pattern: The small inconsistencies of geographic reality are smoothed over, so that our cognitive maps are idealized and standardized.

Cognitive Maps and Relative Position

Which city is farther west—San Diego, California, or Reno, Nevada? If you are like most people—and the participants in a classic study by Stevens and Coupe (1978)—the question seems ludicrously easy. Of course, San Diego would be farther west, because California is west of Nevada. However, if you consult a map, you'll discover that Reno is in fact *west* of San Diego. Which city is farther north—Detroit or its "twin city" across the river, Windsor, in Ontario, Canada? Again, the answer seems obvious; any Canadian city must be north of a U.S. city!

Barbara Tversky (1981, 1998) points out that we use heuristics when we represent relative positions in our mental maps—just as we use heuristics to represent the angles of intersecting streets as being close to 90-degree angles, and just as we represent curves as being symmetrical. Tversky points out that these heuristics encourage two kinds of errors:

1. We remember a slightly tilted geographic structure as being either more vertical or more horizontal than it really is (the rotation heuristic).
2. We remember a series of geographic structures as being arranged in a straighter line than they really are (the alignment heuristic).

The Rotation Heuristic. According to the **rotation heuristic**, a figure that is slightly tilted will be remembered as being either more vertical or more horizontal than it really is (Taylor, 2005; Tversky, 2000b, 2009; Wagner, 2006). For example, Figure 7.5 shows that the coastline of California is obviously slanted. When we use the rotation heuristic for our cognitive map of California, we make the orientation more vertical by rotating the coastline in a clockwise fashion. Therefore, if your

FIGURE 7.5

The Correct Locations of San Diego and Reno. This figure shows that Reno is farther west than San Diego. According to the rotation heuristic, however, we tend to rotate the coastline of California into a more nearly vertical orientation. As a result, we incorrectly conclude that San Diego is farther west than Reno.

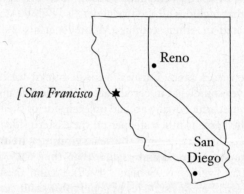

cognitive map reflects the distorting effects of the rotation heuristic, you will conclude (erroneously) that San Diego is west of Reno.

Similarly, the rotation heuristic encourages you to create a horizontal border between the United States and Canada. Therefore, you'll make the wrong decision about Detroit and Windsor. In reality, Windsor, in Canada, is south of Detroit.

Let's look at some research on the rotation heuristic. Barbara Tversky (1981) studied people's mental maps for the geographic region of the San Francisco Bay Area. She found that 69% of the students at a Bay Area university showed evidence of the rotation heuristic. When the students constructed their mental maps, they rotated the California coastline in a more north-south direction than is true on a geographically correct map. However, keep in mind that some students—in fact, 31% of them—were not influenced by this heuristic.

We also have evidence for the rotation heuristic in other cultures. People living in Israel, Japan, and Italy also tend to mentally rotate geographic structures. As a result, these structures appear to have either a more vertical or a more horizontal orientation in a mental map than in reality (Glicksohn, 1994; Tversky et al., 1999).

The Alignment Heuristic. According to the **alignment heuristic**, a series of separate geographic structures will be remembered as being more lined up than they really are (Taylor, 2005; Tversky, 1981, 2000b; 2009). To test the alignment heuristic, Tversky (1981) presented pairs of cities to students, who were asked to select which member of each pair was north (or, in some cases, east).

For example, one pair was Rome and Philadelphia. As Figure 7.6 shows, Rome is actually north of Philadelphia. However, because of the alignment heuristic, people

FIGURE 7.6

The Correct Locations of Philadelphia and Rome. This figure shows that Philadelphia is farther south than Rome. According to the alignment heuristic, however, we tend to line up Europe and the United States. As a result, we incorrectly conclude that Philadelphia is north of Rome.

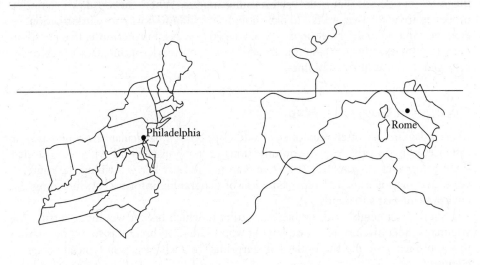

tend to line up the United States and Europe so that they are in the same latitude. We know that Rome is in the southern part of Europe. We also know that Philadelphia is in the northern part of the United States. Therefore, we conclude—incorrectly—that Philadelphia is north of Rome.

Tversky's results indicated that many students showed a consistent tendency to use the alignment heuristic. For example, 78% judged Philadelphia to be north of Rome, and 12% judged that they were at the same latitude. Only 10% correctly answered that Rome is north of Philadelphia. On all eight pairs of items tested by Tversky, an average of 66% of participants supplied the incorrect answer. Other researchers have confirmed that people's cognitive maps are especially likely to be biased when northern cities in North America are compared with southern cities in Europe (Friedman et al., 2002).

The rotation heuristic and the alignment heuristic may initially sound similar. However, the rotation heuristic requires rotating a *single* coastline, country, building, or other figure in a clockwise or counterclockwise fashion so that its border is oriented in a nearly vertical or a nearly horizontal direction.

In contrast, the alignment heuristic requires lining up *several separate* countries, buildings, or other figures in a straight row. Both heuristics are similar, however, because they encourage us to construct cognitive maps that are more orderly and schematic than geographic reality.

The heuristics we have examined in this chapter make sense. For example, our city streets tend to have right-angle intersections. Furthermore, a picture is generally hung on a wall in a vertical orientation, rather than at a slant. In addition, a series of houses is typically lined up so that they are equally far from the street.

However, when our mental maps rely too strongly on these heuristics, we miss the important details that make each stimulus unique. When our top-down cognitive processes are too active, we fail to pay enough attention to bottom-up information. In fact, the angle at an intersection may really be 70 degrees. Furthermore, that coastline may not run exactly north-south. In addition, those two continents are not really arranged in a neat horizontal line.

Creating a Cognitive Map

In everyday life, we often read or hear a description of a particular environment. For instance, a friend calls to give you directions to her house. You have never traveled there before, yet you create a cognitive map as you hear her describing the route. A **cognitive map** is a mental representation of geographic information, including the environment that surrounds us.

Similarly, a neighbor describes the setting in which his car was hit by a truck, or you may read a mystery novel explaining where the dead body was found in relation to the broken vase and the butler's fingerprints. In each case, you typically create a cognitive map.

It's important to emphasize that our cognitive maps are not perfect "map-in-the-head" replicas of geographic reality (Shelton & Yamamoto, 2009). However, they do help us represent the spatial aspects of our environment.

When we encounter a description of a spatial setting, we do not simply store these isolated statements in a passive fashion. Instead—consistent with Theme 1—we actively create a cognitive map that represents the relevant features of a scene (Carr & Roskos-Ewoldsen, 1999; Tversky, 2005a, 2005b). Furthermore, people combine information from separate statements and combine them to form one integrated cognitive map (Newcombe & Huttenlocher, 2000).

Let's examine how people create these cognitive maps, typically based on verbal descriptions. We will begin by considering the classic research on this topic. Then we'll examine the spatial framework model, as well as information about the characteristics of cognitive maps.

Franklin and Tversky's Research. In a classic study, Nancy Franklin and Barbara Tversky (1990) presented verbal descriptions of ten different scenes, such as a barn or a hotel lobby, for example, "You are at the Jefferson Plaza Hotel. . . . " Each description mentioned five objects located in plausible positions in relation to the observer (above, below, in front, in back, to the left side, or to the right side). The description mentioned only five objects, so that the memory load would not be overwhelming.

After the participants had read each description, they were instructed to imagine that they were turning around to face a different object. They were then asked to specify which object was located in each of several directions. (For example, which object is "above your head"?) In all cases, the researchers measured how long the participant took to respond to the question.

Franklin and Tversky were especially interested in discovering whether response time depended upon the location of the object that was being tested. Do we make all those decisions equally quickly?

These researchers found that people could rapidly answer which objects were above or below; their reaction times were short for these judgments. People required somewhat longer to decide which objects were ahead or behind. Furthermore, they took even longer to decide which objects were to the right or to the left. This research has been replicated in additional research (e.g., Bryant & Tversky, 1999). In all these studies, people judged the vertical dimension more quickly than ahead-behind or left-right dimensions. Do these results match your intuitions?

Franklin and Tversky (1990) also asked the participants to describe how they thought they had performed the task. All participants reported that they had constructed images of the environment as they were reading. Most of them also reported that they had constructed imagery that represented their own point of view as an observer of the scene.

The Spatial Framework Model. To explain their results, Franklin and Tversky proposed the spatial framework model (Franklin & Tversky, 1990; Tversky, 1991, 1997, 2005a, 2005b). The **spatial framework model** emphasizes that the above-below spatial dimension is especially important in our thinking, the front-back dimension is moderately important, and the right-left dimension is least important.

When we are in a typical upright position, the vertical (above-below) dimension is especially important for two reasons:

1. The vertical dimension is correlated with gravity, neither of the other two dimensions has this advantage. Gravity has an important asymmetric effect on the world we perceive; objects fall downward, not upward. Because of its association with gravity, the above-below dimension should be particularly important and thus particularly accessible. (Notice, then, that this asymmetry is "good," because we make decisions more quickly.)

2. The vertical dimension on an upright human's body is physically asymmetric. That is, the top (head) and the bottom (feet) are very easy to tell apart, and so we do not confuse them with each other.

These two factors combine to help us make judgments about the above-below dimension very rapidly.

The next most prominent dimension is the front-back dimension. When we are upright, the front-back dimension is not correlated with gravity. However, we usually interact with objects in front of us more easily than with objects in back of us, introducing an asymmetry. Also, a human's front half is not symmetric with the back half, again making it easy to distinguish between front and back. These two characteristics lead to judgment times for the front-back dimension that are fairly fast, although not as fast as for the above-below dimension.

The least prominent dimension is right-left. This dimension is not correlated with gravity, and we usually perceive objects equally well, whether they are on the right or the left. Most of us show minor preferences for our right or left hand when we manipulate objects. However, this dimension does not have the degree of asymmetry we find for the front-back dimension. Finally, your right half is roughly symmetrical with your left half. You can probably remember occasions when you confused your right hand with your left hand, or when you told someone to turn left when you meant right. Apparently, we need additional processing time to ensure that we do not make this error. Therefore, right-left decisions take longer than either above-below or front-back decisions, consistent with other research (Bower, 2008).

In related studies, researchers have examined how people process directions on a physical map. The results demonstrate that people can make north-south (above-below) decisions significantly faster than east-west (right-left) decisions (Newcombe, 2002; Wagner, 2006).

In summary, then, Franklin and Tversky's spatial framework model proposes that the vertical or above-below dimension is most prominent for an upright observer (Franklin & Tversky, 1990; Tversky, 2005a, 2005b). The front-back dimension is next most prominent, and the right-left dimension is least prominent. Our cognitive maps therefore reveal certain biases. These biases are based on our long-term interactions with our bodies and with the physical properties of the external world (Tversky, 2005a, 2005b).

All the research on cognitive maps provides strong testimony for the active nature of human cognitive processes (Theme 1). We take in information, synthesize it, and go beyond the information we have received, so that we create a model to represent our knowledge (Tversky, 2005a, 2005b). As you will see throughout the rest of this textbook, an important general characteristic of our cognitive processes is our tendency to make inferences, so that we can draw conclusions beyond the information that we currently possess.

The Situated Cognition Approach

We have just seen how people make decisions about spatial locations, based on the human body and the world that we inhabit (Tversky, 2009). For example, the context of our bodies helps us make up-down decisions more quickly than front-back decisions, which are easier than right-left decisions.

Some cognitive psychologists point out that the situated cognition approach helps us understand many cognitive tasks. For example, situated cognition is important when we create mental maps (this chapter), form concepts (Chapter 8), and solve problems (Chapter 11). According to the **situated cognition approach**, we make use of helpful information in the immediate environment or situation. Therefore, our knowledge depends on the context that surrounds us (Robbins & Aydede, 2009; Tversky, 2009). As a result, what we know depends on the situation that we are in.

As Barbara Tversky (2009) points out, spatial thinking is vitally important for humans. You need to know where to go to find food, water, and shelter, and you need to find your way back home. One index of the central importance of spatial thinking is the phrases we use. For instance, we say, "Things are looking up," "That was an emotional high," "His spirits are down today," and "I seem to be going around in circles." We also make spatial diagrams to represent relationships. For example, you might create a diagram of your family tree, the roles of people in an organization, and the classification of various world languages. Figure 6.3 on page 181 shows a representative spatial diagram; in this case, it illustrates a memory technique.

In the current chapter, we have emphasized objects and spatial arrangements. We began by considering several important characteristics of our visual images and our auditory images. Then we examined how several factors can lead to systematic biases in our cognitive maps. In Chapter 8, we will move away from geometric and spatial representations to focus on more verbal information, including our concepts and our general knowledge.

Section Summary: *Cognitive Maps*

1. A cognitive map is a mental representation of the surrounding environment; the research on this topic often emphasizes real-world settings, and it is interdisciplinary in scope.

2. Individual differences in spatial cognition are large, and they are correlated with mental-rotation ability.

3. You can make judgments about spatial cognition more easily if your cognitive map matches the orientation of a physical map.

4. Our cognitive maps usually represent reality with reasonable accuracy. However, we make systematic errors in these maps, usually reflecting the tendency to base our judgments on heuristics. We make judgments based on variables that are typically relevant, and we represent our environment as being more regular than it really is.

5. Estimates of distance on cognitive maps can be distorted by the number of intervening cities and by the category membership of the buildings on the cognitive maps. In addition, we estimate that landmarks are closer than a location that is not a landmark.

6. Shapes on cognitive maps can be distorted so that the angles formed by two intersecting streets are closer to 90 degrees than they are in reality, and so that curves are more nearly symmetrical than they are in reality.

7. The relative positions of geographic structures on cognitive maps can be distorted so that a slightly tilted structure will be remembered as being more vertical or more horizontal than it really is (rotation heuristic). Furthermore, a series of geographic structures will be remembered as being more lined up than they really are (alignment heuristic).

8. We often create cognitive maps of an environment that are based on a verbal description. In these maps, the up-down dimension has special prominence, and we make these judgments quickly. We make front-back judgments more

slowly. The right-left dimension is most difficult, and we make these decisions very slowly. Franklin and Tversky (1990) explain these data in terms of the spatial framework model. We also make north-south decisions more quickly than east-west decisions.

9. The situated cognition approach emphasizes that we make use of helpful information in the immediate environment and the context of the situation.

CHAPTER REVIEW QUESTIONS

1. Summarize the two theoretical approaches that focus on the characteristics of mental images: the analog code and the propositional code. Describe the findings about mental rotation, size, shape, reinterpreting ambiguous figures, and any other topics you recall. In each case, note which theory the results support.

2. Most of this chapter deals with visual imagery, with a brief description of auditory imagery. We have little information about imagery in the other senses. How could you design a study on taste imagery that would be conceptually similar to one of the studies mentioned in the sections on visual imagery and auditory imagery?

3. According to the research in cognitive neuroscience, what evidence do we have that visual imagery resembles perception? Why does this research avoid the problem of demand characteristics, which might be relevant in other imagery research?

4. How do the studies on imagery and interference support the viewpoint that visual imagery operates like actual perceptions? Describe how the research on interference supports the analog storage of information about objects.

5. Suppose that you see a newspaper headline, "Males Have Better Spatial Ability, Study Shows." When reading this article, what cautions should you keep in mind, based on the discussion about gender comparisons in spatial ability?

6. The second section of this chapter summarized some of the research on auditory imagery. Discuss this research, and describe why it is more difficult to study than visual imagery. How could researchers study auditory imagery and interference?

7. Cognitive maps sometimes correspond to reality, but sometimes they show systematic deviations. Discuss the factors that seem to produce systematic distortions when people estimate distance on mental maps.

8. What heuristics cause systematic distortions in geographic shape and in relative position represented on cognitive maps? How are these related to two concepts we discussed in earlier chapters—namely, top-down processing (Chapter 2) and schemas (Chapter 5)?

9. According to Franklin and Tversky's spatial framework model, the three dimensions represented in our cognitive maps are not equally important.

Which dimension has special prominence? How does the spatial framework model explain these differences?

10. Cognitive psychologists often ignore individual differences. However, this chapter examined several ways in which individuals differ with respect to mental imagery and spatial cognition. Describe this information, and suggest other areas in which researchers could examine individual differences.

KEYWORDS

mental imagery	prosopagnosia	landmark effect
imagery	experimenter expectancy	90-degree-angle heuristic
visual imagery	demand characteristics	symmetry heuristic
auditory imagery	meta-analysis	rotation heuristic
perception	pitch	alignment heuristic
STEM disciplines	timbre	cognitive map
imagery debate	spatial cognition	spatial framework model
analog code	heuristic	situated cognition approach
propositional code	border bias	

RECOMMENDED READINGS

Brockmole, J. R. (Ed.). (2009). *The visual world in memory*. New York: Psychology Press. Two chapters in Brockmole's book are especially relevant to the discussion of mental imagery, one on visual mental imagery and another on visual memory and navigation. Other chapters focus on memory for faces and real-world scenes.

Hubbard, T. L. (2010). Auditory imagery: Empirical findings. *Psychological Bulletin, 136*, 302–329. This clearly written article discusses many intriguing topics related to imagery for sounds, including harmony, sounds during dreaming, and auditory hallucinations.

Kosslyn, S. M. (2007). *Clear and to the point: 8 psychological principles for compelling PowerPoint® presentations.*

New York: Oxford University Press. You have probably watched some PowerPoint® presentations that were difficult to follow. Stephen Kosslyn's expertise in visual imagery makes him the perfect guide for creating clear presentations!

Reed, S. K. (2010). *Thinking visually*. New York: Psychology Press. Psychologists have written numerous books about language and concepts, but remarkably few about visual imagery. Stephen Reed's book compares images with words, and it also discusses topics such as the production of images and spatial metaphors.

ANSWERS TO DEMONSTRATION 7.1

In Chapter 2, people need to consult some sort of mental image to identify a shape (e.g., a letter of the alphabet) or to identify a sound (e.g., a speech sound). In Chapter 3, when people conduct a search for a target—perhaps for a blue X, as in Demonstration 3.2—they must keep a mental image in mind as they inspect the potential targets. In Chapter 4, the entire discussion of the visuospatial sketchpad is based on visual imagery. In Chapter 5, visual imagery is relevant to the material on face recognition in long-term memory. Chapter 6 discussed visual imagery as a helpful class of mnemonic devices for retrospective memory. In addition, you may use visual imagery in order to prompt your prospective memory for some action that you must perform in the future.

CHAPTER 8

General Knowledge

PREVIEW

This chapter examines our background knowledge, which is the knowledge that informs and influences our memory, spatial cognition, and other cognitive processes. We will explore two major topics: semantic memory and schemas.

Semantic memory refers to our organized knowledge about the world. We will look at three kinds of theories that attempt to explain how all this information could be stored. These theories are partly compatible with one another, but they emphasize different aspects of semantic memory. For example, suppose that you are trying to decide whether an object in the grocery store is an apple. (1) The prototype approach emphasizes that you decide whether this object is an apple by comparing it with an ideal apple, the apple that is most typical of the category. (2) The exemplar approach emphasizes that you decide whether it is an apple by comparing it with several familiar examples of apples—perhaps a McIntosh, an Ida Red, and a Fuji apple.

These first two theories—prototype and exemplar—are primarily concerned about category membership. (3) The network models, in contrast, emphasize the interconnections among related items. For example, an apple may be related to other concepts, such as "red," "seed-bearing," and "pear."

Schemas and scripts apply to larger clusters of knowledge. A schema is a generalized kind of knowledge about situations and events. Schemas are also important in areas such as social psychology and clinical psychology. One kind of schema is called a *script*; scripts describe an expected sequence of events. For example, most people have a well-defined "restaurant script," which specifies all the events that are likely to occur when you dine in a restaurant.

Schemas influence our memories in several ways: (1) selecting the material we want to remember, (2) extending the boundaries for visual scenes, (3) storing the general meaning of a verbal passage, and (4) forming a single, well-integrated representation in memory. Schemas can cause inaccuracies during these stages, but we often represent the information accurately.

CHAPTER INTRODUCTION

Consider the following sentence:

When Lisa was on her way back from the store with the balloon, she fell and the balloon floated away.

Think about all the information that you assume when you are reading this sentence. Now think about all of the inferences that you make. An **inference** refers to the logical interpretations and conclusions that were never part of the original stimulus material. For instance, consider just the word *balloon*. You know that balloons can be made of several lightweight substances, that they can be filled with air or a lightweight gas, and that their shape can resemble an animal or a cartoon character. However, a balloon is unlikely to be created from a hiking boot, it is unlikely to be filled with raspberry yogurt, and it is unlikely to be shaped like the Eiffel Tower.

Now cover all the rest of this page, beginning with the line of asterisks. Then reread that entire sentence about the balloon. Think of five or more additional inferences that you are likely to make.

*   *   *   *   *   *   *

Here are some of the inferences that students in my classes have reported: Lisa is probably a female child, not a 40-year-old man, and she probably bought the balloon in the store. Furthermore, the balloon was attached to a string, but the other end of the string was not firmly attached to Lisa. When Lisa fell, she probably let go of the string. She may have scraped her knee, and it may have bled. As you can see, a sentence that initially seemed simple is immediately enriched by an astonishing amount of general knowledge about objects and events in your world.

To provide a context for Chapter 8, let's briefly review some of the topics we've considered so far in this textbook. In each case, your general knowledge is vitally important.

In Chapter 2 and 3, we examined how your background knowledge can influence several components of perception:

- Knowledge helps you to perceive the stimuli that your visual and auditory systems gathered from the outside world (Chapter 2).
- When you are having trouble paying attention to more than one message at a time, your knowledge may influence which message you choose to process and which one you choose to ignore (Chapter 3).

Chapters 4 through 7 discuss how the stimuli from the outside world are stored in your memory. In many cases, your previous knowledge can influence this memory storage. Here are just a few of the many ways that background knowedge can be influential:

- Knowledge can help you chunk items together to aid your working memory (Chapter 4).
- Knowledge provides the kind of expertise that can enhance your long-term memory for the events in your life (Chapter 5).
- Knowledge can help you organize information more effectively, so that you can recall it more accurately (Chapter 6).
- Knowledge—such as the alignment heuristic—can distort your memories about spatial relationships, making them seem more regular than they actually are (Chapter 7).

All these cognitive processes rely on your general knowledge. Notice that each of these principles demonstrates that our cognitive processes are interrelated (Theme 4).

The first half of this textbook emphasizes how your cognitive system registers and processes information from the outside world. The book notes that this information is influenced by your general knowledge. This general knowledge allows you to go beyond this information in the stimulus in a useful fashion, for example, by making predictions about other similar stimuli (Landauer & Dumais, 1997; Papadopoulos et al., 2011). However, we did not discuss any details about your general knowledge.

This current chapter specifically focuses on two components of general knowledge:

1. First, we'll consider semantic memory. **Semantic memory** refers to our organized knowledge about the world. If you are a typical English-speaking adult, you know the meaning of about 20,000 to 100,000 words (Baddeley et al., 2009; Saffran & Schwartz, 2003). You also know a tremendous amount of information about each word. For example, you know that a cat has fur and that an apple has seeds. You also know that a car is a good example of a vehicle . . . but an elevator is *not* a good example.

2. We will also consider the nature of schemas, or general knowledge about an object or event. A schema allows us to understand much more than just the simple combination of words within a sentence.

Furthermore, this chapter emphasizes our impressive cognitive abilities (Theme 2). We have an enormous amount of information about the world, and we use this information efficiently and accurately. In addition, this chapter confirms the active nature of our cognitive processes (Theme 1).

As we'll see in this current chapter, when people are given one specific piece of information, they can build on this specific information. In fact, they actively retrieve additional stored knowledge about word relationships and other likely inferences. Let's explore the nature of general knowledge as we see how people use both semantic memory and schemas to go beyond the given information.

THE STRUCTURE OF SEMANTIC MEMORY

As we discussed in earlier chapters, **semantic memory** is your organized knowledge about the world (Schwartz, 2011; Wheeler, 2000). We contrasted semantic memory with **episodic memory**, which contains information about events that happen to us. Chapters 4, 5, and 6 emphasized different aspects of episodic memory.

The distinction between semantic and episodic memory is not clear-cut (McNamara & Holbrook, 2003). However, the term *semantic memory* usually refers to knowledge or information; it does not specify how we acquired that information (Barsalou, 2009). An example of semantic memory would be: "Tegucigalpa is the capital of Honduras."

In contrast, episodic memory implies a personal experience, because episodic memory emphasizes when, where, or how this event happened to you (Corballis & Suddendorf, 2010; McNamara & Holbrook, 2003). An example of episodic memory would be: "This morning in my Political Science course, I learned that Tegucigalpa is the capital of Honduras."

Let's discuss some background information about semantic memory before we examine several theoretical models of how it operates.

Background on Semantic Memory

In normal conversation, the term *semantics* refers to the meaning of individual words. However, if you check back to page 248 or the preview, you will see that psychologists use the term *semantic memory* in a much broader sense (McNamara & Holbrook, 2003). For example, semantic memory includes general knowledge (e.g., "Martin Luther King, Jr., was born in Atlanta, Georgia"). It also includes lexical or language knowledge (e.g., "The word *justice* is related to the word *equality*"). In addition, semantic memory includes conceptual knowledge (e.g., "A square has four sides").

Semantic memory influences most of our cognitive activities. For instance, semantic memory helps us determine locations, read sentences, solve problems, and make decisions. Categories and concepts are essential components of semantic memory. In fact, you need to divide up the world into categories in order to make sense of your knowledge (Davis & Love, 2010).

A **category** is a set of objects that belong together. Your cognitive system considers these objects to be at least partly equivalent (Barsalou, 2009; Chin-Parker & Ross, 2004; Markman & Ross, 2003). For example, the category called "fruit" represents a certain category of food items. A category tells us something useful about their members (Close et al., 2010; Murphy, 2010; Ross & Tidwell, 2010). For example, suppose that you hear someone say, "Rambutan is a fruit." You conclude that you should probably eat it in a salad or a dessert, instead of frying it with onions and freshly ground pepper.

Psychologists use the term **concept** to refer to your mental representations of a category (Murphy, 2010; Rips et al., 2012; Wisniewski, 2002). In other words, the physical category called "fruit" is stored as a mental representation within your cerebral cortex. For instance, you have a concept of "fruit," which refers to your mental representation of the objects in that category. Incidentally, I will follow the tradition in cognitive psychology of using italics for the actual word names (e.g., *justice*) and quotation marks for categories and concepts (e.g., "fruit").

Each of your academic courses requires you to form concepts (Barsalou, 2009; Goldstone & Kersten, 2003; Hannon et al., 2010). In an art history course, you may need to create a concept called "15th-century Flemish painting," and in a Spanish course, you learn a concept called "people whom you greet with the 'usted' form of a verb."

In previous chapters, we discussed the situated cognition approach to cognitive psychology. According to the **situated cognition approach**, we make use of information in the immediate environment or situation. As a result, our knowledge often depends on the context that surrounds us (Robbins & Aydede, 2009; Tversky, 2009). With respect to our general knowledge, we tend to code a concept in terms of the context in which we learned this information (Barsalou, 2009). Without these rich resources, it's often difficult to transfer a concept from the classroom to the context of a real-life situation, as you may discover when you enter an art museum or when you try to use your Spanish if you travel to Latin America.

Your semantic memory allows you to organize the objects you encounter. Even though the objects are not identical, you can combine together a wide variety of similar objects by using a single, one-word concept (Milton & Wills, 2004; Wisniewski, 2002; Yamauchi, 2005). This coding process greatly reduces the space required for storage, because many objects can all be stored with the same label.

Your concepts also allow you to make numerous inferences when you encounter new examples from a category (Barsalou, 2009; Davis & Love, 2010; Jones & Ross, 2011). For example, even a young child knows that a member of the category "fruit" has the attribute "you can eat it." When she encounters a new kind of fruit, she makes the inference (usually correctly) that you can eat it.

As we noted earlier, these inferences allow you to go beyond the given information, greatly expanding your knowledge. Otherwise—if you had no concepts—you would need to examine each new chair you encountered, in order to figure out how to use it (Murphy, 2002).

So far, we have been considering terminology, such as categories and concepts, as well as the situated cognition approach to knowledge. Now let's ask an important question: How do we decide which objects are similar? In the following discussion, we'll examine three current approaches to semantic memory. Each of these approaches provides a somewhat different perspective on the nature of similarity. These approaches include (1) the prototype approach, (2) the exemplar approach, and (3) network models.*

According to researchers who study semantic memory, that each model can account for some aspect of semantic memory (Markman, 2002). In fact, it's unlikely that the wide variety of concepts could all be represented in semantic memory in the same fashion (Haberlandt, 1999; Hampton, 1997a). Therefore, as you read about these three approaches, you do not need to choose which approach is correct and which two approaches must therefore be wrong.

> ## IN DEPTH

The Prototype Approach and Semantic Memory

According to a theory proposed by Eleanor Rosch, we organize each category on the basis of a prototype. A **prototype** is the item that is the best, most typical example of a category; a prototype therefore is the ideal representative of this category (Fehr & Sprecher, 2009; Murphy, 2002; Rosch, 1973). According to this **prototype approach**, you decide whether a particular item belongs to a category by comparing this item with a prototype. If the item is similar to the prototype, you

---

*An earlier approach, called the *feature comparison model*, proposed that we store concepts in memory according to a list of necessary characteristics (features). Most cognitive psychologists now believe that this model is not flexible enough to account for the way we create and use real-world categories and concepts.

include that item within this category (Jäkel et al., 2008; Sternberg & Ben-Zeev, 2001; Wisniewski, 2002).

For example, you would conclude that a robin is a bird because it matches your ideal prototype for a bird. Suppose, however, that the item you are judging is quite different from the prototype, for example, a bee. In this case, you place the item in another category (the category "insect"), where it more closely resembles that category's prototype.

Rosch (1973) also emphasizes that members of a category differ in their **prototypicality**, or the degree to which they are representative of their category. A robin and a sparrow are very prototypical birds, whereas an ostrich and a penguin are typically nonprototypes. However, the situated cognition approach emphasizes the importance of context and specific situations. In the context of a zoo, for example, you might consider an ostrich and a penguin to be prototypical (Schwartz, 2011).

To help clarify the concept of prototypes, think of a prototype, or most typical member, for a particular group of students on your campus, perhaps students with a particular academic major. Also think of a nonprototype ("You mean he's an art major? He doesn't seem at all like one!"). Then try Demonstration 8.1 before you read further.

Some classic earlier theories had proposed that an item could belong to a category as long as it possessed the appropriate necessary and sufficient features

---

Demonstration 8.1

Guessing Prototype Ratings

Take a sheet of paper and write the numbers 1 through 12 in a column, beginning at the top left side of the page. Now look at the list of 12 items listed below. Think about which item is the *best* example of the category, "clothing." Write that object's name next to the number 1. Write the name of the second-best example of clothing next to the number 2, and so forth.

Bathing suit; Coat; Dress; Jacket; Pajamas; Pants; Shirt; Shoes; Skirt; Socks; Sweater; Underwear.

When you have completed the ranking, look at Table 8.1 on page 254. As you can see, this table lists the "average prototypicality rating" that students supplied for each of these 12 types of clothing (Rosch & Mervis, 1975). Transfer each prototypicality rating from Table 8.1 to the appropriate item in your own list. For example, a bathing suit has a prototype rating of 11. As an informal method of assessing your responses, calculate a total for the ranks that you supplied for items 1 through 4, then for items 5 through 8, and finally for items 9 through 12.

Does your idea about prototypes match the pattern in Table 8.1? You may find that a few of your rankings differ greatly from those based on the participants in the norms gathered by Rosch and Mervis (1975). If so, can you suggest an explanation?

TABLE 8.1

Prototype Ratings for Words in Three Categories

Item	Clothing	Vehicle	Vegetable
1	Pants	Car	Peas
2	Shirt	Truck	Carrots
3	Dress	Bus	String beans
4	Skirt	Motorcycle	Spinach
5	Jacket	Train	Broccoli
6	Coat	Trolley car	Asparagus
7	Sweater	Bicycle	Corn
8	Underwear	Airplane	Cauliflower
9	Socks	Boat	Brussels sprouts
10	Pajamas	Tractor	Lettuce
11	Bathing suit	Cart	Beets
12	Shoes	Wheelchair	Tomato

Source: Rosch, E. H., & Mervis, C. B. (1975). Family resemblances: Studies in the internal structure of categories. *Cognitive Psychology, 7*, 573–605.

(Markman, 1999; Minda & Smith, 2011). In those theories, category membership is very clear-cut. For example, for the category "bachelor," two defining features would be *male* and *unmarried*.

However, don't you think that your 32-year-old unmarried male cousin would be a much better example of a bachelor than either your 2-year-old nephew or an elderly Catholic priest? All three individuals are indeed male and unmarried. Therefore, a "necessary and sufficient" model would need to conclude that all three deserve to be categorized as "bachelors." That conclusion doesn't seem reasonable. In contrast, the prototype approach would argue that not all members of the category "bachelor" are created equal. Instead, your cousin is a more prototypical bachelor than your nephew or the priest (Lakoff, 1987).

Eleanor Rosch and her coauthors, as well as other researchers, have conducted numerous studies about the characteristics of prototypes. Their research demonstrates that all members of a category are not really equal (Medin & Rips, 2005; Murphy, 2010; Rogers & McClelland, 2004). Instead, a category tends to have a graded structure. A **graded structure** begins with the most representative or prototypical members, and it continues on through the category's nonprototypical members.

Let us examine several important characteristics of prototypes. Then we will discuss another important component of the prototype approach, which focuses on several different levels of categorization. We'll conclude the discussion of prototypes by seeing how this approach helps us understand important aspects of interpersonal relationships.

Characteristics of Prototypes. Prototypes differ from the nonprototypical members of categories in three major respects. As you will see, prototypes have a special, privileged status within a category.

1. *Prototypes are supplied as examples of a category.* Several studies have shown that people judge some items to be better examples of a concept than other items. In a classic study, for example, Mervis and her colleagues (1976) examined some norms. These norms are based on examples that people had provided for categories such as "birds," "fruit," and "sports." Mervis and her coauthors then asked a different group of people to supply prototype ratings for each of these examples.

According to a statistical analysis, the items that were rated most prototypical were the same items that people had supplied most frequently in the category norms. For instance, for the category "bird," people judged a robin to be very prototypical, and *robin* was very frequently listed as an example of the category "bird." In contrast, people rated a penguin as low on the prototype scale, and *penguin* was only rarely listed as an example of the category "bird." In other words, if someone asks you to name a member of a category, you will probably name a prototype.

Furthermore, the prototype approach accounts well for the typicality effect (Murphy, 2002; Rogers & McClelland, 2004). In this procedure, participants are asked whether an item belongs to a particular category. The **typicality effect** occurs when people judge typical items (prototypes) faster than items that are not typical (nonprototypes). For instance, when judging whether items belong to the category "bird," people judge *robin* more quickly than *penguin* (Hampton, 1997b; Heit & Barsalou, 1996). Theorists point out that the typicality effect operates with everyday items, so the results are more useful than research conducted only with artificial concepts (Rips et al., 2012).

Let's summarize this first characteristic of prototypes. The research shows that people often supply prototypes as examples, more frequently than they supply nonprototypes. Furthermore, people make quicker judgments about category membership when assessing prototypes, rather than nonprototypes.

2. *Prototypes are judged more quickly than nonprototypes, after semantic priming.* The **semantic priming effect** means that people respond faster to an item if it was preceded by an item with similar meaning. The semantic priming effect helps cognitive psychologists understand important information about how we retrieve information from memory (McNamara, 2005; McNamara & Holbrook, 2003).

The research shows that semantic priming facilitates people's responses to prototypes significantly more than it facilitates their responses to nonprototypes. Imagine, for example, that you are participating in a study on priming. Your task is to judge pairs of similar colors and to answer whether they are the same. On some occasions, you see the name of the color before you must judge the pair of colors; these are the primed trials. On other occasions, you do not see a color name as a "warning"; these are the unprimed trials. Rosch (1975) tried this priming setup for both prototype colors (for example, a true, bright red) and nonprototype colors (for example, a muddy red).

Rosch's results showed that priming was very helpful when people made judgments about prototypical colors. Specifically, they responded more quickly after primed trials than after nonprimed trials. However, priming actually inhibited the judgments for nonprototypical colors. In other words, if you see the word *red*, you expect to see a true, bright red color. However, if the color is a dark, muddy red, the priming offers no advantage. Instead, you actually need extra time in order to reconcile your image of a bright, vivid color with the muddy color you actually see on the screen.

3. *Prototypes share attributes in a family resemblance category.* Before we examine this issue, let's introduce a new term called family resemblance. **Family resemblance** means that no single attribute is shared by all examples of a concept; however, each example has at least one attribute in common with some other example of the concept (Love & Tomlinson, 2010; Milton & Wills, 2004; Rosch & Mervis,1975).

Rosch and Mervis (1975) examined the role of prototypes in family resemblance categories. They asked a group of students to make prototypicality judgments about members of several categories. As you can see in Table 8.1 on page 254, for example, the students rated a car as being the most prototypical vehicle and a wheelchair as being the least prototypical vehicle on this list.

Then, Rosch and Mervis asked a different group of people to list the attributes possessed by each item. The results showed that the most prototypical item also had the largest number of attributes in common with the other items in the category. For example, a car (the most prototypical vehicle) has wheels, moves horizontally, and uses fuel. In contrast, an elevator has relatively few attributes in common with other items.

Check the categories "vegetable" and "clothing" in Table 8.1. Do the most prototypical items share more attributes with other items, compared to the non-prototypical items? Furthermore, is there any attribute you can identify that is both necessary and sufficient for either of these categories? Alternatively, would you conclude that the items on each list share only a "family resemblance" to one another?

Levels of Categorization. We have just examined three characteristics of prototypes that differentiate them from nonprototypes. The second major portion of prototype theory examines the way that our semantic categories are structured in terms of different levels of categorization.

Consider these examples: Suppose that you are sitting on a wooden structure that faces your desk. You can call that structure by several different names: *furniture*, *chair*, or *desk chair*. You can also refer to your pet as a *dog*, a *spaniel*, or a *cocker spaniel*. You can tighten the mirror on your car with a *tool*, a *screwdriver*, or a *Phillips screwdriver*.

In other words, an object can be categorized at several different levels. Some category levels are called **superordinate-level categories**, which means that they are higher-level or more general categories. "Furniture," "animal," and "tool" are all examples of superordinate-level categories. **Basic-level categories** are moderately specific. "Chair," "dog," and "screwdriver" are examples of basic-level categories. Finally, **subordinate-level categories** refer to lower-level or more specific categories. "Desk chair," "collie," and "Phillips screwdriver" are examples of subordinate categories.

As you continue to read the rest of this description of prototype theory, keep in mind that a prototype is *not* the same as a basic-level category. A prototype is the best example of a category. In contrast, a basic-level category refers to a category that is neither too general nor too specific.

Basic-level categories seem to have special status (Rogers & McClelland, 2004; Rosch et al., 1976; Wisniewski, 2002). In general, they are more useful than either superordinate-level categories or subordinate-level categories. Let's examine how these basic-level categories seem to have special privileges, in contrast to the more general or the more specific category levels.

1. *Basic-level names are used to identify objects.* Try naming some of the objects that you can see around you. You are likely to use basic-level names for these objects. You will mention *pen*, for example, rather than the superordinate term *writing instrument* or the subordinate term *Paper Mate Flair pen*.

Eleanor Rosch and her colleagues (1976) asked people to look at a series of pictures and identify each object. They found that people typically preferred to use basic-level names. Apparently, the basic-level name gives enough information without being overly detailed (Medin et al., 2000; Murphy, 2010; Rogers & McClelland, 2004).

In addition, people produce the basic-level names faster than either the superordinate or the subordinate names (Kosslyn et al., 1995; Rogers & McClelland, 2004). Furthermore, when people see superordinate or subordinate terms, they frequently remember the basic-level version of these terms when they are later tested for recall (Pansky & Koriat, 2004). In other words, the basic level does have special, privileged status.

2. *Basic-level names are more likely to produce the semantic priming effect.* Eleanor Rosch and her colleagues (1976) used a variant of the semantic priming task. In this version, the researchers present the name of an object, followed by two pictures. The participant must decide whether these two pictures are the same as one another. For example, you might hear the word *apple* and see pictures of two identical apples. The priming is effective because the presentation of this word allows you to create a mental representation of this word. This mental representation helps when you make the decision quickly.

Rosch and her coworkers showed that priming with basic-level names was indeed helpful. The participants made faster judgments if they saw a basic-level term like *apple* before judging the apples. However, priming with superordinate names (such as *fruit*) was not helpful. Apparently, when you hear the word *fruit*, you create a general representation of fruit, rather than a specific representation that helps you make a judgment about apples.

3. *Different levels of categorization activate different regions of the brain.* Neuroscience research using PET scans has examined whether different regions of the brain tend to process different category levels (Kosslyn et al., 1995; Rips et al., 2012). On a typical trial, a participant might be asked to judge whether a word (e.g., *toy*, *doll*, or *rag doll*) matched a particular picture.

This research showed that a superordinate term (e.g., *toy*) is more likely than a basic-level term (e.g., *doll*) to activate part of the prefrontal cortex. This finding makes sense, because this part of the cortex processes language and associative memory. If you need to decide whether the picture of the doll qualifies as a toy, you must consult your memory about category membership.

In contrast, the research showed that subordinate terms (e.g., *rag doll*) are more likely than basic-level terms (e.g., *doll*) to activate part of the parietal region of the brain. As Chapter 3 noted, the parietal lobe is active when you perform a visual search. Again, this finding makes sense. To answer the question about a rag doll, you must shift your attention away from the general shape of the object. For example, you need to conduct a visual search, so that you can determine if the fabric and the style of the doll indeed permit it to be categorized as a "rag doll."

Applying the Prototype Approach to Social Relationships. The prototype approach to semantic memory is especially useful when we consider socially relevant concepts such as "bachelor" and "love relationships" (Fehr, 2005; Fehr & Sprecher, 2009). With the increasing interest in cognitive psychology, researchers began to realize that we do not need to restrict cognitive explanations to impersonal concepts such as clothing, vegetables, and birds. For example, your semantic memory also processes your concepts about social interactions. Specifically, the prototype approach helps us understand two kinds of love relationships. As Chapter 1 emphasizes, psychologists are increasingly likely to use an interdisciplinary approach (Cacioppo, 2007). For instance, this particular topic combines cognitive psychology and social psychology.

1. *The Prototype of Compassionate Love.* Beverley Fehr and Susan Sprecher (2009) studied compassionate love, which focuses on providing support to a romantic partner, as well as close friends, and even strangers. Fehr and Sprecher began their research by asking U.S. college students to list characteristics of the concept "compassionate love." The researchers then eliminated any responses that only one person had suggested. Then they combined terms that were similar. Next, they identified the 10 attributes that were listed most often, as well as 10 attributes that were listed a moderate number of times, and 10 attributes that were seldom listed.

In the next step of the study, students at a Canadian university rated each of these 30 attributes on a scale where 1 equaled an extremely poor example of compassionate love, and 9 equaled an extremely good example of compassionate love. The students judged *feeling protective toward the person, sacrifice*, and *pure* to be least prototypical. In contrast, they judged the features of *trust, honesty*, and *caring* to be the three most prototypical characteristics.

Fehr and Sprecher (2009) also gathered other information about these characteristics of compassionate love. For example, students responded very quickly when they were asked whether *trust* was a characteristic of compassionate love. In contrast, they responded signicantly more slowly when they judged the word *pure*. Notice that this is an example of the typicality effect, described on page 255. This effect occurs when people make judgments about typical items (prototypes) more quickly than atypical items (nonprototypes).

2. The Prototype of "Being There" for a Romantic Partner. Other researchers have studied a more specific kind of love relationships. For example, Bulent Turan and Leonard Horowitz focused on a romantic partner being sensitive and supportive, that is, "being there for me" when needed (Horowitz & Turan, 2008; Turan & Horowitz, 2007). These researchers asked U.S. college students to list three attributes that would be relevant when a potential romantic partner could be counted on to "be there" at some future time of major stress. From these responses, Turan and Horowitz identified 55 distinct attributes.

Then a second group of students rated how useful each of these attributes would be in times of stress. For example, these students gave a high rating to the attribute, "Notices changes in my mood and asks if anything is wrong." They gave a low rating to "Doesn't mind being intimate with me in public."

The information from this second group allowed Turan and Horowitz to create a psychological test, which they called the "Knowledge of Indicators Scale." People could earn a high score on this test if they gave *high* ratings for items such as noticing mood changes, as well as *low* ratings for irrelevant items such as being intimate in public. However, these researchers needed to establish the test's **validity**, or its ability to predict a person's performance in another situation, in this case a measure of social sensitivity.

To assess the validity of the Knowledge of Indicators Scale, Turan and Horowitz then tested a third group of students. All of these students had completed this scale earlier in the semester. These students then participated in a study in which they listened to another student. This student was actually a confederate, and she had memorized a specific script that lasted 13 minutes. Her script described a relationship problem that she was having with her boyfriend. For example, this confederate described how her boyfriend had forgotten to ask her about an important job interview that she had recently described to him. As a final task, the "real students" in this third group were asked to summarize the conversation, and the researchers scored how well each student had recalled these specific problems.

The results showed a significant correlation ($r = +.45$) between the two relevant measures. Specifically, those students who had high scores on the Knowledge of Indicators Scale were also more likely to remember the details about this woman's problems with her boyfriend. In other words, those students who understand that a romantic partner should be sensitive and supportive were also likely to remember the specific details about why this woman's boyfriend had not been "there for her."

Conclusions About the Prototype Approach. One advantage of the prototype approach is that it can account for our ability to form concepts about groups that are loosely structured. For example, we can create a concept for stimuli that merely share a family resemblance, when the members of a category have no single characteristic in common.

Another advantage of the prototype approach is that it can be applied to complex social relationships, as well as inanimate objects and nonsocial categories (e.g., Fehr & Sprecher, 2009; Horowitz & Turan, 2008; Turan & Horowitz, 2007). Other research has applied the prototype approach to the personality trait of dominance and to the experience of depression (Horowitz & Turan, 2008).

An ideal model of semantic memory must also acknowledge that concepts can be unstable and variable. For example, our notions about the ideal prototype can shift as time passes and the context changes. In Demonstration 8.1 (page 253), did you notice that the study, published in 1975, listed *dress* as a very prototypical example of clothing?

Consider a related study by Laura Novick (2003) about prototypical vehicles. She found that U.S. college students rated *airplane* as being a prototypical vehicle during the period immediately following the terrorist attack of September 11, 2001. In contrast, *airplane* had been considered a nonprototypical vehicle in studies during the five years prior to this date. Furthermore, when the media coverage decreased after the attack, *airplane* decreased in prototypicality. In fact, $4^1/_2$ months after the attack, *airplane* was no longer a prototypical vehicle.

Another problem with the prototype approach is that we often do store specific information about individual examples of a category. An ideal model of semantic memory would therefore need to include a mechanism for storing this specific information, as well as prototypes (Barsalou, 1990, 1992).

The prototype theory clearly accounts for a number of important phenomena. Let's now examine a second approach to semantic memory, which emphasizes that your concept of a vehicle or an animal or a vegetable also includes information about some of the less obvious members of the category, rather than just the most prototypical member.

The Exemplar Approach and Semantic Memory

The **exemplar approach** argues that we first learn information about some specific examples of a concept; then we classify each new stimulus by deciding how closely it resembles all of those specific examples (Benjamin & Ross, 2011; Love & Tomlinson, 2010; Schwartz, 2011). Each of those examples stored in memory is called an **exemplar**.

The exemplar approach emphasizes that your concept of "dog" would include information about numerous examples of dogs you have known (Benjamin & Ross, 2011; Murphy, 2002). In contrast, the prototype approach would argue that your prototype of a dog would be an *idealized* representation of a dog, with average size for a dog and average other features—but not necessarily like any particular dog you've ever seen.

Consider another example. Suppose that you are taking a course in psychological disorders. Suppose also that you have just read four case studies in your textbook, and each case study described a depressed individual. You then read an article that describes a woman's psychological problems, but the article does not specify her disorder. You decide that she fits into the category "depressed person" because this description closely resembles the characteristics of those four earlier exemplars. Furthermore, this woman's problems do not resemble any exemplars in a set of case studies that you read last week, when you were learning about anxiety disorders.

A Representative Study on the Exemplar Approach. The exemplar approach has successfully predicted people's performance on artificial categories, such as cartoon faces that can be shown with or without glasses, smiling or frowning, and so on (Medin & Rips, 2005; Rehder & Hoffman, 2005). How does this approach work with categories we use in our everyday lives? Before you read further, try Demonstration 8.2, which is based on a study by Evan Heit and Lawrence Barsalou (1996).

Heit and Barsalou (1996) wanted to determine whether the exemplar approach could explain the structure of several superordinate categories, such as "animal." When people make judgments about animals, do they base these judgments on specific exemplars or general prototypes?

Heit and Barsalou (1996) asked a group of undergraduates to supply the first example that came to mind for each of the seven basic-level categories in Part A of Demonstration 8.2. Then a second group of undergraduates rated the typicality of each of those examples, with respect to the superordinate category "animal." For instance, this second group would rate each example—such as *frog* or *salamander*—in terms of whether it was typical of the concept "animal." That second group also rated the seven basic-level categories. (I made this demonstration simpler, though not as well controlled; it includes all three tasks.)

Heit and Barsalou (1996) then assembled all the data. They wanted to see whether they could create an equation that would accurately predict—for the category "animal"—the typicality of the rating of the seven categories ("amphibian," "bird," "fish," and so on), based on the exemplars generated in a task like Task A of Demonstration 8.2. Specifically, they took into account the frequency of each of those exemplars. For example, the basic-level category "insect" frequently produced the exemplar *bee* but rarely produced the exemplar *Japanese beetle*. They also took into account the typicality ratings, similar to those you provided in Task B of the demonstration.

The information about exemplar frequency and exemplar typicality did accurately predict which of the seven categories were most typical for the superordinate category "animal" (Task C). In fact, the correlation between the predicted typicality and the actual typicality was statistically significant ($r = +.92$), indicating an extremely strong relationship. For example, mammals were considered the most typical animals, and microorganisms were the least typical.

> ### 🌀 Demonstration 8.2
>
> ### Exemplars and Typicality
>
> A. For the first part of this demonstration, take out a sheet of paper and write the numbers 1 through 7 in a column. Then, next to the appropriate number, write the first example that comes to mind for each of the following categories:
>
> 1. amphibian
> 2. bird
> 3. fish
> 4. insect
> 5. mammal
> 6. microorganism
> 7. reptile
>
> B. For the second part of the demonstration, look at each of the items you wrote on the sheet of paper. Rate how typical each item is for the category "animal." Use a scale where 1 = not at all typical, and 10 = very typical. For example, if you wrote *barracuda* on the list, supply a number between 1 and 10 to indicate the extent to which a barracuda is typical of an animal.
>
> C. For the final part of this demonstration, rate each of the seven categories in Part A in terms of how typical each category is for the superordinate category "animal." Use the same rating scale as in Part B.
>
> **Source:** Partly based on a study by Heit & Barsalou, 1996.

The prototype approach suggests that our categories consider only the most typical items (Wisniewski, 2002). If this proposal is correct, then we can forget about the less typical items, and our categories would not be substantially changed. In another part of their study, Heit and Barsalou (1996) tried eliminating the less typical exemplars from the equation. The correlation between predicted typicality and actual typicality decreased significantly.

Notice the implications of this study: Suppose that you are asked a question such as, "How typical is an insect, with respect to the category 'animal'?" To make that judgment, you certainly think about a very prototypical insect—perhaps a combination of a bee and a fly. However, you also include some information about a caterpillar, a grasshopper, and maybe even a Japanese beetle.

Comparing the Exemplar Approach with the Prototype Approach. Both of these approaches propose that you make decisions about category membership by comparing a new item against some stored representation of the category (Markman, 1999;

Murphy, 2002). If the similarity is strong enough, you conclude that this new item does indeed belong to the category. In many situations, these two approaches make similar predictions about semantic memory (Rips et al., 2010).

However, the prototype approach proposes that your stored representation is *a typical member of the category*. In contrast, the exemplar approach proposes that your stored representation is *a collection of numerous specific members of the category* (Medin & Rips, 2005; Jäkel et al., 2008; Yang & Lewandowsky, 2004).

Furthermore, the exemplar approach emphasizes that people do not need to perform any kind of abstraction process (Barsalou, 2003; Heit & Barsalou, 1996; Knowlton, 1997). For example, suppose that you had read four case studies about depressed people. You would not need to devise a prototype—an ideal, typical person with depression. The exemplar approach argues that creating a prototypical person would force you to discard useful, specific data about individual cases.

One problem with the exemplar approach, however, is that our semantic memory would quickly become overpopulated with numerous exemplars for numerous categories (Love & Tomlinson, 2010; Nosofsky & Palmeri, 1998; Sternberg & Ben-Zeev, 2001). The exemplar approach may therefore be more suitable when you think about a category that has relatively few members (Knowlton, 1997). For instance, the exemplar approach might operate well for the category "tropical fruit," unless you happen to live in a tropical region of the world.

In contrast, the prototype approach may be more suitable when considering a category that has numerous members. For example, a prototype may be the most efficient approach for a large category such as "fruit" or "animal." Despite the encouraging results from Heit and Barsalou's (1996) study, the exemplar approach may be simply too bulky for some purposes. In many situations, it is not effective to use a classification strategy based purely on exemplars (Erickson & Kruschke, 1998, 2002).

Furthermore, individual differences may be substantial in the way people represent categories. Perhaps some people store information about specific exemplars, especially for categories in which they have expertise. Other people may construct categories that do not include information about specific exemplars (Thomas, 1998). Instead, these individuals may construct categories based on more generic prototypes.

In reality, your semantic memory seems to be quite flexible. The prototype approach and the exemplar approach may both operate, and a concept could include information about both prototypes and specific exemplars (Love & Tomlinson, 2010; Minda & Smith, 2011; Wisniewski, 2002). In fact, one possibility is that the left hemisphere of your brain tends to store prototypes, and the right hemisphere tends to store exemplars (Bruno et al., 2003; Gazzaniga et al., 2009; Laeng et al., 2003). People may in fact use a combination of prototype strategies and exemplar strategies when they form categories in everyday life.

Network Models and Semantic Memory

The prototype approach and the exemplar approach both emphasize whether an item belongs to a category. In contrast, network approaches are more concerned about the interconnections among related items.

Think for a moment about the large number of associations you have to the word *apple*. How can we find an effective way to represent the different aspects of meaning for *apple* that are stored in memory? A number of theorists favor network models. These **network models** of semantic memory propose a netlike organization of concepts in memory, with numerous interconnections.

The meaning of a particular concept, such as "apple" or "psychology," depends on the other concepts to which it is connected. The network models typically represent each concept as a **node**, or one unit located within the network. When you see or hear the name of a concept, the node representing that concept is activated. The activation expands or spreads from that node to other connected nodes, a process called **spreading activation**. The classic network theory was developed by Allan Collins and Elizabeth Loftus (1975). In this chapter, we will consider two relatively recent theories, Anderson's ACT-R Theory and the parallel distributed processing approach.

Anderson's ACT-R Approach.   John Anderson of Carnegie Mellon University and his colleagues have constructed a series of network models, which they now call *ACT-R* (Anderson, 2000, 2009; Anderson & Schooler, 2000; Anderson & Schunn, 2000; Anderson et al., 2004). **ACT-R** is an acronym for "Adaptive Control of Thought-Rational"; this approach attempts to account for a wide variety of tasks (Anderson, 2009; Anderson et al., 2005).

The models that we've considered so far have a limited goal: to explain how we organize our cognitive concepts. In contrast, Anderson created ACT-R and its variants to explain every topic in your textbook. For example, these topics would include memory, learning, spatial cognition, language, reasoning, problem solving, and decision making (Anderson et al., 2004; Morrison & Knowlton, 2012).

Obviously, a theory that attempts to explain all of cognition is extremely complex. However, we will focus on the model's more specific view of **declarative knowledge**, or knowledge about facts and things. As you can see, declarative knowledge is the essence of this current chapter. Important earlier network models focused on networks for individual words (e.g., Collins & Loftus, 1975). Anderson, in contrast, designed a model based on larger units of meaning. According to Anderson (1990, 2009), the meaning of a sentence can be represented by a **propositional network**, which is a pattern of interconnected propositions.

Anderson and his coauthors define a **proposition** as the smallest unit of knowledge that people can judge to be either true or false. For instance, the phrase *white cat* does not qualify as a proposition because we cannot determine whether it is true or false. According to Anderson's model, each of the following three statements qualifies as a proposition:

1. Susan gave a cat to Maria.

2. The cat was white.

3. Maria is the president of the club.

These three propositions can appear by themselves, but they can also be combined into a sentence, such as the following:

Susan gave a white cat to Maria, who is the president of the club.

Figure 8.1 shows how this sentence could be represented by a propositional network. As you can see, each of the three propositions in the sentence is represented by a node, and the links are represented by arrows. Notice, too, that the network represents the important relationships in these three propositions. However, Figure 8.1 does not represent the exact wording of that key sentence. Propositions are abstract; they do not represent a specific set of words.

Furthermore, Anderson suggests that each of the concepts in a proposition can be represented by its own individual network. Figure 8.2 illustrates just a small part of the representation of the word *cat* in memory. Imagine what the propositional network in Figure 8.2 would look like if we could replace each of the concepts in that network with an expanded network representing the richness of meanings you have acquired. (For example, consider just the meaning of the concept *catfood*.) These networks need to be complicated in order to accurately represent the dozens of associations that we have for each item in semantic memory.

Anderson's model of semantic memory makes some additional proposals. For example, the links between nodes become stronger as they are used more often (Anderson, 2000; Anderson & Schunn, 2000; Sternberg & Ben-Zeev, 2001). Practice is vitally important in developing more extensive semantic memory (Anderson & Schooler, 2000).

FIGURE 8.1

A Propositional Network Representing the Sentence "Susan gave a white cat to Maria, who is the president of the club."

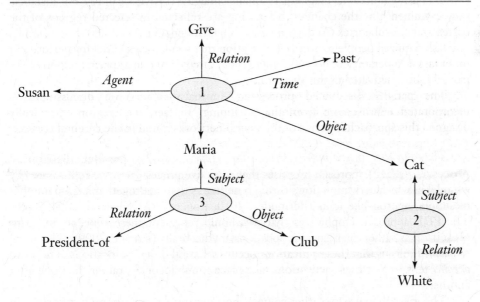

FIGURE 8.2

A Partial Representation of the Word *Cat* in Memory.

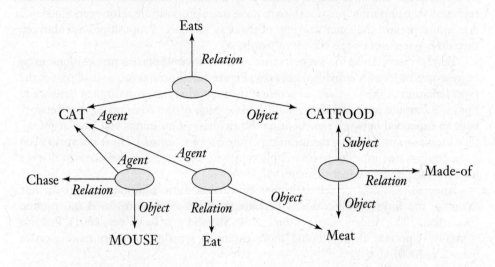

Anderson's model has been highly praised for its skill in integrating cognitive processes and for its scholarship. Anderson and his colleagues have also conducted research, using functional magnetic resonance imaging (fMRI; see p. 15). For instance, they examined how the changes in learning are reflected in selected regions of the cortex and the subcortex (Anderson et al., 2004; Anderson et al., 2005). For example, one task required people to access information that would be essential for performing other tasks. Anderson and his colleagues (2008) discovered that a specific region of the frontal lobe is activated in this situation.

The parallel distributed processing approach—which we discuss next—incorporated neuroscience from the beginning. In fact, the creators specifically designed this approach in terms of the neural networks found in the cerebral cortex.

The Parallel Distributed Processing Approach. The **parallel distributed processing (PDP)** approach proposes that cognitive processes can be represented by a model in which activation flows through networks that link together a large number of simple, neuron-like units (Bermúdez, 2010; Rogers & McClelland, 2004, 2011). The PDP approach emphasizes that we should represent these concepts in terms of networks, rather than specific locations in the brain (Barrett, 2009). The word *distributed* tells us that these activations occur in several different locations. The word *parallel* tells us that these activations take place simultaneously, rather than one after another.

Theorists often use two other names—**connectionism** and **neural networks**—in addition to "the PDP approach." The researchers who designed this approach tried

---

⑨ Demonstration 8.3

Parallel Distributed Processing

For each of the two tasks below, read the set of clues and then guess as quickly as possible what thing is being described.

Task A

1. It is orange.
2. It grows below the ground.
3. It is a vegetable.
4. Rabbits characteristically like this item.

Task B

1. Its name starts with the letter *p*.
2. It inhabits barnyards.
3. It is typically yellow in color.
4. It says, "Oink."

---

to construct their model by taking into account the physiological and structural properties of human neurons (Doumas & Hummel, 2012; Rogers & McClelland, 2011). We briefly introduced the PDP approach in Chapter 1; now let's consider it in more detail. Before you read further, however, try Demonstration 8.3.

The designers of the PDP approach believe that the earlier models based on categorization were too restrictive. Timothy Rogers and James McClelland (2011) point out a representative problem. Suppose that our categories are responsible for guiding how we store knowledge and how we generalize knowledge. How would the various categories manage to interact with one another?

Consider this example: A chicken belongs to the categories of "bird," "animal," and "a food that many people eat." We wouldn't be able to genuinely understand the concept of "chicken" unless those categories could somehow work together. The prototype approach is useful in many situations. However, the PDP approach provides a more flexible account for the richness, flexibility, and subtlety of our knowledge about the world.

Let's now consider four general characteristics of the PDP approach.

1. As suggested by the name *parallel distributed processing*, cognitive processes are based on parallel operations, rather than serial operations. Therefore, many patterns of activation may be proceeding simultaneously.

2. A network contains basic neuron-like units or nodes, which are connected together so that a specific node has many links to other nodes. (Notice that this concept is captured in the alternate name for the theory: *connectionism*.) PDP theorists argue that most cognitive processes can be explained by the activation of these networks (McNamara & Holbrook, 2003; Rogers & McClelland, 2011).

3. As we noted on page 264, this process of spreading information from one node to other nodes is called *spreading activation*. As the name "parallel distributed processing" also suggests, a concept is represented by the pattern of activity distributed throughout a set of nodes (McClelland, 2000; Rogers & McClelland, 2011). Notice that this view is very different from the commonsense idea that all the information you know about a particular person or object is stored in one specific location in your brain.

4. Consistent with the concept of *situated cognition*, the current context often activates only certain components of a concept's meaning (Rogers & McClelland, 2011). If you stroll past the meat department at your grocery store, you won't necessarily connects those plastic-wrapped items with the animal that clucks, pecks for food, and lays eggs.

Each of the clues in Task A of Demonstration 8.3 probably reminded you of several possible candidates. Perhaps you thought of the correct answer after just a few clues, even though the description was not complete. Notice, however, that you did not use a serial search, conducting a complete search of all orange objects before beginning a second search of all below-ground objects, then all vegetables, then all rabbit-endorsed items. As we just noted, you used a parallel search, in which you considered all attributes simultaneously (Rogers & McClelland, 2004, 2011; Sternberg & Ben-Zeev, 2001).

Furthermore, your memory can cope quite well, even if one of the clues is incorrect. For instance, in Task B you searched for a barnyard-dwelling, oink-producing creature whose name starts with the letter *p*. The word *pig* emerged, despite the misleading clue about the yellow color. Similarly, if someone describes a student from Albany who is a tall male in your child development course, you can identify the appropriate student, even if he is actually from Syracuse.

The PDP approach argues that our knowledge about a group of individuals might be stored by connections that link these people with their personal characteristics. James McClelland's (1981) original example portrayed members of two gangs of small-time criminals, the Jets and the Sharks (McClelland, 1981). We'll use a simpler and presumably more familiar example that features five college students. Table 8.2 lists these students, together with their college majors, years in school, and political orientations.

Figure 8.3 shows how this information could be represented in network form. Notice that this figure represents only a fraction of the number of people whom a college student is likely to know and also just a fraction of the characteristics associated with each person. Take a minute to imagine how large a piece of paper you would

TABLE 8.2

Attributes of Representative Individuals Whom a College Student Might Know

Name	Major	Year	Political Orientation
1. Joe	Art	Junior	Liberal
2. Marti	Psychology	Sophomore	Liberal
3. Sam	Engineering	Senior	Conservative
4. Liz	Engineering	Sophomore	Conservative
5. Roberto	Psychology	Senior	Liberal

FIGURE 8.3

A Sample of the Units and Connections That Represent the Individuals in Table 8.2.

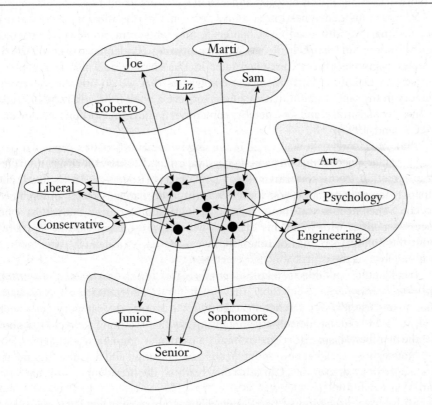

need in order to represent all the people you know, together with their personal characteristics that you consider relevant.

According to the PDP approach, each individual's characteristics are connected in a mutually stimulating network. If the connections among the characteristics are well established through extensive practice, then an appropriate clue allows you to locate the characteristics of a specified individual (McClelland, 1995; McClelland et al., 1986; Rumelhart et al., 1986).

One advantage of the PDP model is that it allows us to explain how human memory can help us when some information is missing. Specifically, people can make a **spontaneous generalization** by using individual cases to draw inferences about general information (Rogers & McClelland, 2004, 2011).

For example, suppose that your memory stores the information in Figure 8.3 and similar information about other college students. Suppose, also, that someone asks you whether engineering students tend to be politically conservative. PDP theory suggests that the clue *engineering student* would activate information about the engineering students you know, including information about their political orientation. You would reply that they do tend to be politically conservative, even though you did not directly store this statement in your memory. (Our ability to make inferences will be discussed in more detail later in this chapter, and also in Chapters 9 and 12.)

Spontaneous generalization accounts for some of the memory errors and distortions that we discussed in Chapter 5, on long-term memory. Spontaneous generalization can also help to explain stereotyping (Bodenhausen et al., 2003), a complex cognitive process discussed later in this chapter and also in Chapter 12, on decision making. The PDP model emphasizes that we do not simply retrieve a memory in the same fashion that we might retrieve a book from a library. Instead, we reconstruct a memory, and this memory sometimes includes inappropriate information (McClelland, 1999).

PDP models also allow us to fill in missing information about a particular person or a particular object by making a best guess; we can make a **default assignment** based on information from other similar people or objects (Rogers & McClelland, 2004). Suppose, for example, that you meet Christina, who happens to be an engineering student. Someone asks you about Christina's political preferences, but you have never discussed politics with her. This question will activate information in the network about the political leanings of other engineers. Based on a default assignment, you would reply that she is probably conservative.

Incidentally, students sometimes confuse the terms *spontaneous generalization* and *default assignment*. Remember that spontaneous generalization means that we draw a conclusion about a general category (for example, the category "engineering students"). In contrast, default assignment means that we draw a conclusion about a specific member of a category (for example, a particular engineering student).

Notice, however, that both spontaneous generalization and default assignment can produce errors. For example, Christina may really be the president of your university's Anti-War Coalition.

So far, our discussion of parallel distributed processing has been concrete and straightforward. In reality, the theory is extremely complex, sophisticated, and abstract (e.g., Gluck & Myers, 2001; Rogers & McClelland, 2011). Let's now consider four theoretical features that are important in the PDP approach:

1. The connections between these neuron-like units are weighted, and these **connection weights** determine how much activation one unit can pass on to another unit (McClelland, 1999). As you learn more information, the values of these weights will change.

2. When a unit reaches a critical level of activation, it may affect another unit, either by exciting it (if the connection weight is positive) or by inhibiting it (if the connection weight is negative). Notice that this design resembles the excitation and inhibition of neurons in the human brain. Incidentally, Figure 8.3 shows only the excitatory connections, but you can imagine additional, inhibitory connections. For example, the characteristic *polite* might have a negative connection weight associated with some of the less civilized students in this figure.

3. Each new experience with a particular item will change the strength of connections among relevant units by adjusting the connection weights (Barsalou, 2003; McNamara & Holbrook, 2003; Rogers & McClelland, 2004, 2011). For example, while you have been reading about the PDP approach, you have been changing the strength of connections between the name *PDP approach* and related terms such as *network* and *spontaneous generalization*. The next time you encounter the term *PDP approach*, all these related terms are likely to be activated.

4. Sometimes we have only partial memory for some information, rather than complete, perfect memory. The brain's ability to provide partial memory is called **graceful degradation**. For example, Chapter 6 discussed the **tip-of-the-tongue phenomenon**, which occurs when you know which target you are seeking, but you cannot retrieve the actual target. Consistent with graceful degradation, you may know the target's first letter and the general sound of the word—even though the word itself refuses to leap into memory. Graceful degradation also explains why the brain continues to work somewhat accurately, even when an accident, stroke, or dementia has destroyed portions of the cortex (Rogers & McClelland, 2004).

We've examined some of the most important characteristics of the PDP approach. Clearly, the PDP approach offers an important perspective in cognitive psychology (Levine, 2002; McNamara & Holbrook, 2003). Some supporters are enthusiastic that the PDP approach seems generally consistent with the neurological design of neurons and the brain (Barrett, 2009; Rogers & McClelland, 2011). Many are therefore hopeful that PDP research may provide important links between psychology and neuroscience.

Theorists emphasize that the PDP approach works better for tasks in which several processes operate simultaneously, as in pattern recognition, categorization, and memory search. However, many other cognitive tasks demand primarily serial processing. Later in this textbook, we will consider sentence production, problem solving, and reasoning. Many components of these cognitive skills require serial processing, rather than parallel operations. For these more linear mental processes, other models may be more effective.

Section Summary: *The Structure of Semantic Memory*

1. Semantic memory includes both general knowledge and knowledge about language.

2. According to prototype theory, people compare new stimuli with prototypes (most typical examples) in order to categorize them. People frequently supply prototypes as examples of a category, and they judge prototypes more quickly after semantic priming. Prototypes also share a large number of attributes with other items in the same family-resemblance category.

3. According to prototype theory, when people discuss a particular item, they use basic-level categories more often than subordinate-level or superordinate-level categories when identifying objects. Basic-level names are more likely to produce the semantic priming effect, and different levels of categorization activate different regions of the brain.

4. Researchers have used the prototype approach to examine social relationships by studying (a) the prototype of compassionate love and (b) the prototype of "being there" for a romantic partner.

5. The exemplar approach proposes that we classify a new stimulus by deciding how closely it resembles specific examples (i.e., exemplars) that we have already learned. The research suggests that our concepts may indeed include information about less typical exemplars. It's possible that people may use both prototypes and exemplars to represent concepts.

6. Anderson's ACT-R model attempts to explain a wide variety of cognitive processes. His model of declarative knowledge represents both sentences and concepts with a propositional-network structure.

7. Another network model is called the parallel distributed processing (PDP) or connectionist approach. It proposes that (a) cognitive processes are based on parallel operations, (b) networks link numerous neuron-like nodes, and (3) a concept is represented by a pattern of activity throughout that set of nodes.

8. The PDP approach also proposes features to explain cognitive phenomena such as spontaneous generalization, default assignment, the strengthening of connections, and graceful degradation.

SCHEMAS AND SCRIPTS

So far, our discussion of general knowledge has focused on words, concepts, and—occasionally—sentences. However, our cognitive processes also depend on much more world knowledge that is much more complex (Traxler, 2012). For example, our knowledge includes information about familiar situations, behavior, and other

---

⑥ Demonstration 8.4

The Nature of Scripts

Read the following paragraph, which is based on a description from Trafimow and Wyer (1993, p. 368):

> After doing this, he found the article. He then walked through the doorway and took a piece of candy out of his pocket. Next, he got some change and saw a person he knew. Subsequently, Joe found a machine. He realized he had developed a slight headache. After he aligned the original, Joe put in the coin and pushed the button. Thus, Joe had copied the piece of paper.

> Now turn to the list of new terms for Chapter 8, on page 293. Look at the first two columns of terms and write out the definition for as many of these terms as you know. Take about 5 minutes on the task. Then look at the paragraph labeled "Further instructions for Demonstration 8.4," which appears at the bottom of Demonstration 8.5, on page 277.

"packages" of things we know. This generalized, well-integrated knowledge about a situation, an event, or a person is called a **schema** (Baddeley et al., 2009). Schemas often influence the way we understand a situation or an event, and we can think of them as the basic building blocks for representing our thoughts about people (Landau et al., 2010).

Consider, for example, the schema you have for the interior of a hardware store. It should have wrenches, cans of paint, garden hoses, and light bulbs. The store certainly should not have psychology textbooks, DVDs of Verdi operas, or birthday cakes.

Schema theories are especially helpful when psychologists try to explain how people process complex situations and events (Davis & Loftus, 2008). In this section of the chapter, we'll consider some background information on schemas and a subcategory called scripts. Then we'll discuss how schemas can influence various components of cognition. First, however, try Demonstration 8.4.

Background on Schemas and Scripts

Schema theories propose that our memories encode "generic" information about a situation (Chi & Ohlsson, 2005; Davis & Loftus, 2008). Then we use this information to understand and remember new examples of the schema. Specifically, schemas guide your recognition and understanding of new examples because you say to yourself, "This is just like what happened when . . ." (Endsley, 2006).

How Schemas Relate to the Themes of This Book. Clearly, schemas emphasize how top-down processing and bottom-up processing work together, a cognitive principle highlighted in Theme 5. Schemas allow us to predict what will happen in a new situation. These predictions are generally correct. Schemas are one kind of **heuristic**, which is a general rule that is typically accurate. You may recall the term "heuristic" from Chapter 7 (p. 233). For example, the *rotation heuristic* describes our tendency to recall the California coastline as being close to vertical, rather than slanted. We will also discuss a variety of decision-making heursitics in Chapter 12.

Schemas also emphasize the active nature of our cognitive processes (Theme 1). An event happens, and we immediately try to think how the event is related to an established schema. If the event is not consistent with a schema, and this event is important to us, we usually feel obligated to reconcile the inconsistency.

However, schemas will sometimes lead us astray, and we can make errors (Baddeley et al., 2009; Davis & Loftus, 2008). Still, these errors usually make sense within the framework of that schema. Consistent with Theme 2, our cognitive processes are generally accurate, and our mistakes are typically rational.

Schemas Throughout Psychology. The concept of schemas has had a long history in psychology. As discussed in Chapter 1, Jean Piaget's work in the 1920s investigated infants' cognitive skills, including schemas. Chapter 1 also mentioned that Frederic Bartlett (1932) tested adults' memory for schemas; we will discuss this research further on pages 285 to 286. In contrast, schemas were not popular during the behaviorist era, because they emphasize unseen cognitive processes. In recent decades, however, cognitive psychologists have conducted numerous studies on this topic, so that *schema* is a standard term in contemporary cognitive psychology.

Schemas are also important in social psychology (Jackson, 2011; Landau et al., 2010; Whitley & Kite, 2010). For instance, Baldwin and Dandeneau (2005) examined how we often have schema-based expectations about what will happen in a social interaction with a specific individual. Furthermore, Hong and her coauthors (2000) examined how bicultural individuals develop a different set of schemas for each of their two cultures. A young boy may see the world through U.S.-based schemas while at school, but he may use Mexican-based schemas when he returns to his home.

Furthermore, clinical psychologists who emphasize cognitive-behavioral approaches may use schema therapy. In **schema therapy**, the clinician and the client may work together in order to explore the client's core beliefs and create appropriate new, more helpful strategies. For example, imagine a female client who says, "My boss praised me, but I didn't deserve it." The therapist can help her modify her interpretation of that praise (Beck, 2011).

Schemas and Scripts. One common kind of schema is called a script. A **script** is a simple, well-structured sequence of events in a specified order; this script is associated with a highly familiar activity (Baddeley et al., 2009; Markman, 2002). A script is an abstraction, in other words, a prototype of a series of events that share an underlying similarity. The terms *schema* and *script* are often used interchangeably. However, *script* is actually a narrower term, referring to a sequence of events that unfold in a specified order (Woll, 2002; Zacks et al., 2001).

Consider a typical script, describing the standard sequence of events that a customer might expect in a traditional restaurant (Shank & Abelson, 1977). The "restaurant script" includes events such as sitting down, looking at the menu, eating the food, and paying the bill. We could also have scripts for visiting a dentist's office, for a trip to the grocery store, and for the first day of class in a college course. In fact, much of our education consists of learning the scripts that we are expected to follow in our culture (Schank & Abelson, 1995).

Several researchers have studied people's life scripts. A **life script** is a list of events that a person believes would be most important throughout his or her lifetime. For example, Erdoğan and his coauthors (2008) studied students in Turkey. These students listed far more positive events than negative events in their life script. This outcome is consistent with Theme 3 of this textbook.

Furthermore, Steve Janssen and David Rubin (2011) discovered that people within a culture often share similar life scripts. They administered a life script questionnaire on the Internet to 595 Dutch participants, 90% of whom were female. The participants were asked to imagine a representative infant growing up in the Netherlands. Then they should list the seven most important events that would take place during this child's life.

Interestingly, the participants' age did not have a significant effect on the listed events. Specifically, participants between the ages of 16–35, 36–55, and 56–75 were all especially likely to create a list that included having children, beginning school, marriage, falling in love, their parents' death, and first full-time job. A related study in Denmark also reported similar life scripts for younger and older individuals (Bohn, 2010).

In contrast, a violation of a familiar script can be both surprising and unsettling. For example, some years ago, several friends and I were watching a Russian movie at another college campus. At the beginning, a young boy rescues a wolf pup. The two grow up together, sharing many adventures. If you have been raised on a diet of U.S films and TV shows about children, you know exactly what happens next: The boy is in great danger, and the wolf rescues him. However, in this particular movie, the wolf kills the boy. At this point, the audience gasped collectively—this violation of a script was simply too devastating!

Identifying the Script in Advance. In general, the research demonstrates that people recall a script significantly more accurately if the script has been clearly identified in advance. For example, Trafimow and Wyer (1993) developed four different scripts, each describing a familiar sequence of actions: photocopying a piece of paper, cashing a check, making tea, and taking the subway. The researchers also added some details that were irrelevant to the script, such as taking a piece of candy out of a pocket. In some cases, the script-identifying event was presented first. In other cases, the script-identifying event was presented last. For instance, in Demonstration 8.4, you saw the information about copying the piece of paper *after* you had read the script.

Five minutes after reading all four descriptions, the participants were asked to recall the events from the four original descriptions. When the script-identifying event had been presented first, participants recalled 23% of those events. In contrast, they recalled only 10% when the script-identifying event had been presented last.

As you might expect, the events in a sequence are much more memorable if you understand—from the very beginning—that these events are all part of a standard script (Davis & Friedman, 2007).

In this second part of the chapter, let's examine four ways in which schemas and scripts can operate during cognitive processing:

1. During the selection of material to be remembered.
2. In boundary extension (when your memory stores a scene).
3. During memory abstraction (when your memory stores the meaning, but not the specific details of the material).
4. During memory integration (when your memory forms a well-integrated representation of the material).

Schemas and Memory Selection

The research on schemas and memory selection has produced some complex findings. Let's look at several studies, and then we will identify some general trends related to this topic.

Be sure to try Demonstration 8.5 when you have the opportunity. This demonstration is based on a classic study by Brewer and Treyens (1981). These authors asked participants in their study to wait, one at a time, in the room pictured in this demonstration. Each time, the experimenter explained that this was his office, and he needed to check the laboratory to see if the previous participant had completed the experiment. After 35 seconds, the experimenter asked the participant to move to a nearby room. Then, the experimenter asked each participant to remember everything in the room in which he or she had waited.

The results showed that people were highly likely to recall objects consistent with the "office schema." Nearly everyone remembered the desk, the chair next to the desk, and the wall. However, only a few recalled the wine bottle and the picnic basket. These items were not consistent with the office schema. When time is very limited—in this case, 35 seconds in that room—people may not have time to process these schema-irrelevant items.

In addition, some people in Brewer and Treyens's (1981) study "remembered" schema-consistent items that were not in the room. For example, several participants said they had remembered books, though none had been visible. Other research has shown that the number of schema-consistent errors is even greater after a two-day delay (Lampinen et al., 2001). This tendency to supply schema-consistent items represents an interesting reconstruction error (Davis & Loftus, 2008; Neuschatz et al., 2007).

Similarly, Neuschatz and his coauthors (2002) instructed students to watch a video of a man giving a lecture. The students were likely to make schema-consistent errors that were consistent with the "lecture schema," such as the lecturer referring to a concept from the previous lecture. The students were not likely to falsely remember events inconsistent with the "lecture schema," such as the lecturer dancing across the floor.

⊚ Demonstration 8.5

Schemas and Memory

After reading these instructions, cover them and the rest of the text in this demonstration so that only the picture shows. Present the picture to a friend, with the instructions, "Look at this picture of a psychology professor's office for a brief time." Half a minute later, close the book and ask your friend to list everything that was in the room.

(Further instructions for Demonstration 8.4: Now without looking back at Demonstration 8.4, write down the story from that demonstration, being as accurate as possible.)

Source: Reprinted from Brewer, W. F. & Treyens, J. C., Role of schemata in memory for places. *Cognitive Pscychology, 13*, Fig. 1., © 1981, with permission from Elsevier.

Demonstration 8.6

Memory for Objects

Look at the objects below for about 15 seconds. Then turn to page 280, just above the rectangle, where you will find further instructions for this demonstration.

Source: From Intraub, H., and Richardson, M. (1989). Wide-angle memories of close-up scenes. *Journal of Experimental Psychology: Learning, Memory and Cognition, 15,* 179–187, Figure 1. © 1989 by the American Psychological Association. Reproduced with permission.

However, we sometimes show *better* recall for material that violates our expectations (e.g., Davis & Loftus, 2008; Lampinen et al., 2000; Neuschatz et al., 2002). Specifically, people are more likely to recall schema-inconsistent material when that material is especially vivid and surprising (Brewer, 2000).

For instance, Davidson (1994) asked participants to read a variety of stories that described well-known schemas such as "going to the movies." The results demonstrated that people were especially likely to recall schema-inconsistent events when those events interrupted the normal, expected story. For example, one story described a woman named Sarah who was going to the movies. The participants were very likely to remember a schema-inconsistent sentence about a child who ran through the movie theater and smashed into Sarah. In contrast, they were less likely to remember a schema-consistent sentence about an usher tearing the movie tickets in half and giving Sarah the stubs. Incidentally, before you read further, try Demonstrations 8.6 and 8.7.

⊚ Demonstration 8.7

Constructive Memory

Part 1

Read each sentence, count to five, answer the question, and go on to the next sentence.

Sentence	Question
The girl broke the window on the porch.	Broke what?
The tree in the front yard shaded the man who was smoking his pipe.	Where?
The cat, running from the barking dog, jumped on the table.	From what?
The tree was tall.	Was what?
The cat running from the dog jumped on the table.	Where?
The girl who lives next door broke the window on the porch.	Lives where?
The scared cat was running from the barking dog.	What was?
The girl lives next door.	Who does?
The tree shaded the man who was smoking his pipe.	What did?
The scared cat jumped on the table.	What did?
The girl who lives next door broke the large window.	Broke what?
The man was smoking his pipe.	Who was?
The large window was on the porch.	Where?
The tall tree was in the front yard.	What was?
The cat jumped on the table.	Where?
The tall tree in the front yard shaded the man.	Did what?
The dog was barking.	Was what?
The window was large.	What was?

Part 2

Cover the preceding sentences. Now read each of the following sentences and decide whether it is a sentence from the list in Part 1.

1. The girl who lives next door broke the window.   (old _____, new _____)

2. The tree was in the front yard.   (old _____, new _____)

3. The scared cat, running from the barking dog, jumped on the table.   (old _____, new _____)

4. The window was on the porch.   (old _____, new _____)

(continued)

🌀 Demonstration 8.7

Constructive Memory   (continued)

5. The tree in the front yard shaded the man. (old _____, new _____)

6. The cat was running from the dog. (old _____, new _____)

7. The tall tree shaded the man who was smoking his pipe. (old _____, new _____)

8. The cat was scared. (old _____, new _____)

9. The girl who lives next door broke the large window on the porch. (old _____, new _____)

10. The tall tree shaded the girl who broke the window. (old _____, new _____)

11. The cat was running from the barking dog. (old _____, new _____)

12. The girl broke the large window. (old _____, new _____)

13. The scared cat ran from the barking dog that jumped on the table. (old _____, new _____)

14. The girl broke the large window on the porch. (old _____, new _____)

15. The scared cat which broke the window on the porch climbed the tree. (old _____, new _____)

16. The tall tree in the front yard shaded the man who was smoking his pipe. (old _____, new _____)

Source: Bransford, J. D., & Franks, J. J. (1971). Abstraction of linguistic ideas. *Cognitive Psychology, 2,* 331–350.

(Further instructions for Demonstration 8.6: In the box below, draw from memory the scene you saw in Demonstration 8.6. Do not look back at that photo!)

These results about schemas and memory may seem inconsistent. However, the outcome may depend on factors such as the details of the study and the length of the specific episode (Davis & Loftus, 2007, 2008; Lampinen et al., 2000). In general, the results show the following trends:

1. If the information describes a minor event—and time is limited—people tend to remember information accurately when it is consistent with a schema (e.g., the desk and the chair in the "office").

2. If the information describes a minor event—and time is limited—people do not remember information that is inconsistent with the schema (e.g., the wine bottle and the picnic basket).

3. People seldom create a completely false memory for a lengthy event that did not occur (e.g., the lecturer did not dance across the room).

4. When the information describes a major event that is inconsistent with the standard schema, people *are* likely to remember that event (e.g., the child who crashes into Sarah).

Schemas and Boundary Extension

Now take a moment to examine the objects you drew on page 278 for Demonstration 8.6, and compare your sketch with the original photo. Does your sketch include the bottom edge of the garbage-can lid, which was not present in the original photo? Compared to the original photo, does your sketch show more background surrounding each garbage can, including the top of the picket fence? If so, you've demonstrated boundary extension.

Boundary extension refers to our tendency to remember having viewed a greater portion of a scene than was actually shown (Munger et al., 2005). We have a schema for a scene like the one depicted in Demonstration 8.6, which we could call "a photo of someone's garbage area," and our cognitive processes fill in the incomplete objects.

Notice that the earlier topics in this discussion of schemas are verbal; in boundary extension, however, the material is visual. Still, our schemas for complete objects help us fill in missing material during a memory task.

Helene Intraub and her colleagues were the first researchers to document the boundary-extension phenomenon (e.g., Intraub, 1997; Intraub & Berkowits, 1996; Intraub et al., 1998). For example, Intraub and Berkowits (1996) showed college students a series of photos like the garbage scene in Demonstration 8.6. Each photo was shown briefly, for 15 seconds or less. Immediately afterward, the students were instructed to draw an exact replica of the original photo. The participants consistently produced a sketch that extended the boundaries beyond the view presented in the original photo. As a result, they drew more of the background that surrounded the central figure, and they also depicted a complete figure, rather than a partial one.

According to Intraub and her coauthors (1998), we comprehend a photograph by activating a perceptual schema. This schema features a complete central figure in the photo, but it also includes a mental representation of visual information that is just outside the boundaries of the photo. We also use perceptual schemas when we look at real-life scenes. Notice why schemas are relevant in boundary extension: Based on our expectations, we create perceptual schemas that extend beyond the edges of the photograph and beyond the scope of our retinas (Munger et al., 2005).

The boundary-extension phenomenon also has important implications for eyewitness testimony, a topic we discussed in Chapter 5. Eyewitnesses may recall having seen some features of a suspect's face, even though these features were not actually visible at the scene of the crime (Foley & Foley, 1998). In addition, after people search for a target in a crowded scene, they recall having viewed a complete target, even if it had been partially blocked by other figures (Foley et al., 2002). Apparently, the incomplete figure activates our imagery processes, so that we "fill in the blanks." Our memory tends to store these idealized, schema-consistent images, rather than partial figures.

Schemas and Memory Abstraction

Abstraction is a memory process that stores the meaning of a message, rather than the exact words. For example, you can probably remember much of the information about the concept "family resemblance" (p. 256), even though you cannot recall any specific sentence in its exact, original form.

Ironically, the term *abstract* is too abstract. Here's one way to remember this word. When you read an article in a psychology journal, the abstract at the beginning of this article will summarize the article. However, you won't find those same exact words elsewhere in the article.

The research shows that people usually have poor word-for-word recall, or **verbatim memory**, even a few minutes after a passage has been presented (e.g., Koriat et al., 2000; Sachs, 1967). However, some professions require accurate verbatim memory. For instance, professional actors must remember the exact words from a Shakespeare play. But do the rest of us need verbatim memory in our everyday lives? Let's consider two approaches to the abstraction issue: the constructive approach and the pragmatic approach.

The Constructive Approach. Be sure that you tried Demonstration 8.7 on pages 279 and 280 before you read further. This is a simpler version of a classic study by Bransford and Franks (1971). How many sentences in Part 2 of the demonstration had you seen before? The answer is at the end of the chapter, on page 293.

Bransford and Franks (1971) asked the participants in their study to listen to sentences from several different stories. Then the participants were given a recognition test that also included some new items, many of which were combinations of the earlier sentences. Nonetheless, people were convinced that they had seen these new items before. This kind of error is called a *false alarm*. In memory research, a **false alarm** occurs when people "remember" an item that was not originally presented.

According to Bransford and Franks's results, people were especially likely to make false alarms when a complex sentence was consistent with the original schema. For instance, they frequently made false alarms for sentences such as, "The tall tree in the front yard shaded the man who was smoking his pipe."

In contrast, the participants seldom made false alarms for sentences that violated the meaning of the earlier sentences. For example, they seldom said that they had heard the sentence, "The scared cat that broke the window on the porch climbed the tree." Subsequent research shows similar findings (Chan & McDermott, 2006; Holmes et al., 1998; Jenkins, 1974).

Bransford and Franks (1971) proposed a constructive model of memory for prose material. According to the **constructive model of memory**, people integrate information from individual sentences in order to construct larger ideas. Later, they believe that they have already seen those complex sentences because they have combined the various facts in memory. Once sentences are fused in memory, we cannot untangle them into their original components and recall those components verbatim.

Notice that the constructive view of memory emphasizes that our cognitive processes are generally accurate, consistent with Theme 1 of this book. Sentences do not passively enter memory, where each is stored separately. Instead, we combine the sentences into a coherent story, fitting the related pieces together. We typically store an *abstract* of the information, rather than a word-for-word representation.

Constructive memory also illustrates Theme 2. Your memory is typically accurate. However, the errors in cognitive processing can often be traced to strategies that are generally useful. In real life, a useful heuristic is to fuse sentences together. However, this heuristic can lead us astray if we apply it inappropriately. As it turns out, the participants in Bransford and Franks's (1971) study used a constructive memory strategy that is useful in real life. However, it is typically inappropriate in a study that tests verbatim memory.

The Pragmatic Approach. Murphy and Shapiro (1994) developed a different view of memory for sentences, which they call the pragmatic view of text memory. The **pragmatic view of memory** proposes that people pay attention to the aspect of a message that is most relevant to their current goals. In other words:

1. People know that they usually need to accurately recall the gist of a sentence.
2. They also know that they usually do not need to remember the specific wording of the sentences.
3. However, in those cases where they *do* need to pay attention to the specific wording, then they know that their verbatim memory needs to be highly accurate.

Murphy and Shapiro (1994) speculated that people are particularly likely to pay attention to the exact wording of a sentence if the words are part of a criticism or an insult. After all, from the pragmatic viewpoint, the exact words *do* matter if someone is insulting you! In this study, participants were reading letters that presumably had been written by a young woman named Samantha. One group read a letter, supposedly written to her cousin Paul. The letter chatted about her new infant in a bland fashion. The letter included a number of neutral sentences such as, "It never occurred to me that I would be a mother so young" (p. 91).

A second group read a letter that was supposedly written by Samantha to her boyfriend, Arthur. Ten of the sentences that had been neutral in the bland letter to cousin Paul now appeared in a sarcastic context, though the exact words were identical. For example, the sentence, "It never occurred to me that I would be a mother so young" now referred to Arthur's infantile behavior.

Murphy and Shapiro then gave both groups a 14-item recognition test that included (a) five of the original sentences, (b) five paraphrased versions of those sentences with a slightly different form, such as, "I never thought I would be a mother at such a young age," and (c) four irrelevant sentences. Table 8.3 shows the results.

As you can see, people rarely made the mistake of falsely "recognizing" the irrelevant sentences. However, correct recognition ("Hits") was higher for the sentences from the sarcastic condition than for the sentences in the bland condition. Furthermore, people made more false alarms for the paraphrases of the bland sentences than for the paraphrases of the sarcastic sentences.

We can compare the overall accuracy for the two conditions by subtracting the false alarms from the correct responses. As you can see, people were much more accurate in their verbatim memory for the sarcastic version (43%) than for the bland version (17%). Similar results have been reported by Schönpflug (2008). Perhaps we are especially sensitive about emotionally threatening material, so we make an effort to recall the exact words of the sentences.

The Current Status of Schemas and Memory Abstraction. In reality, the constructive approach and the pragmatic approach to memory abstraction are actually compatible. Specifically, in many cases, we do integrate information from individual sentences so that we can construct a schema, especially when we don't need to remember the exact words. However, in some cases, we know that the specific words do matter, and so we pay close attention to the precise wording. If you are rehearsing for a play, or you are quarreling with a friend, you will need to remember more than the overall gist of a verbal message.

TABLE 8.3

Percentage of "Old" Judgments Made to Test Items in Murphy and Shapiro's (1994) Study

	Story Condition	
	Bland	Sarcastic
Irrelevant sentences	4%	5%
Hits (original sentences)	71%	86%
False alarms (paraphrases)	54%	43%
Hits minus false alarms	17%	43%

Source: Murphy, G. L., & Shapiro, A. M. (1994). Forgetting of verbatim information in discourse. *Memory & Cognition, 22,* 85–94.

Demonstration 8.8

Using the Implicit Association Test to Assess Implicit Attitudes Toward Social Groups

Log onto the World Wide Web and visit a site sponsored by Harvard University: <https://implicit.harvard.edu/implicit/>

You can examine your own attitudes about gender, ethnicity, sexual orientation, people with disabilities, and elderly people. Be certain to follow the caution to make your responses as quickly as possible. More leisurely responses might assess explicit attitudes, rather than implicit attitudes.

Notice that this conclusion about remembering both general descriptions and specific information is similar to our previous conclusions about semantic memory. As we discussed on page 263, your semantic memory can store both general prototypes and specific exemplar-based information. However, before you read further, try Demonstration 8.8 (above), which we will discuss shortly.

Schemas and Memory Integration

Another important process in memory formation is integration. In **memory integration**, our background knowledge encourages us to take in new information in a schema-consistent fashion (Hamilton, 2005; Hirt et al., 1998; Koriat et al., 2000). As a result, people may remember this schema-consistent information, even though it was not part of the original stimulus material.

Once again, however, schemas do not always operate. For example, suppose that you are tested soon after you learned some new information. Your background knowledge may not alter that new information. In contrast, schema-consistent integration is more likely when there is a delay of a day or two before you are asked to recall the new material (Harris et al., 1989).

The research also suggests that our schemas may not influence memory if we are working on one relatively simple memory task. However, when people work on two simultaneous memory tasks, Sherman and Bessenoff (1999) found that they committed many schema-consistent errors. Specifically, the participants in this study incorrectly remembered that pleasant words had been used to describe a priest, whereas unpleasant words had been used to describe a dangerous person. Let's now examine Bartlett's studies on the integration of culture-consistent information, and then we will consider the more recent work on gender stereotypes.

The Classic Research on Memory Integration. Sir Frederick Bartlett (1932) was an important British researcher who studied people's memory for natural language material. As Chapter 1 noted, Bartlett's theories and techniques foreshadowed the theories of contemporary cognitive psychologists. He also pioneered the research on applied cognition. For example, his laboratory research could be generalized to our everyday patterns of remembering and forgetting (Davies & Wright, 2010b).

Bartlett believed that the most interesting aspect of memory was the complex interaction between the participants' prior knowledge and the material presented during the experiment. In particular, he argued that an individual's unique interests and personal background often shape the contents of memory.

In Bartlett's (1932) best-known series of studies, he asked British students to read a Native American story called "The War of the Ghosts." They were then asked to recall the story 15 minutes later. Bartlett found that the participants tended to omit material that did not make sense from the viewpoint of British students. For example, they often omitted a portion of the story in which a ghost had attacked someone, and this person did not feel the wound. These students also tended to shape the story into a more familiar framework so that it made sense from a British perspective. In many cases, the students' version was more similar to British fairy tales (Brewer, 2000).

Bartlett also asked his participants to recall the story again, after a delay of several days. As time passed after hearing the original story, the participants borrowed more heavily from their previous knowledge and included less information from the original story.

Subsequent research confirms that schemas can influence our memory when we are reading ambiguous or unclear material (Jahn, 2004; Schacter, 2001). As Brewer (2000) emphasizes, the research on schemas demonstrates how our cognitive processes actively work to make sense out of puzzling information (Theme 1). Specifically, our top-down processes often shape our memory for complex material (Theme 5).

The research also shows that schemas can mislead us, so that we make systematic errors and "remember" information that was not actually stated. In our daily lives, however, these schemas are usually helpful, rather than counterproductive. For instance, our background knowledge can help us recall stories from our own culture. Simple stories have definite, regular structures (Schank & Abelson, 1995). We become familiar with the basic structure of stories from experiences in our culture. Then we use this structure to interpret the new stories that we hear. In general, then, this background information helps us draw correct conclusions.

Research About Memory Integration Based on Gender Stereotypes. The research about gender stereotypes provides further information about how schemas can influence our conclusions. **Gender stereotypes** are the beliefs and opinions that we associate with females and males (Jackson, 2011; Whitley & Kite, 2010). Even when a gender stereotype is partially accurate, it cannot be applied to every individual of the specified gender (Eagly & Carli, 2007).

When people know someone's gender, they often draw conclusions about that individual's personal characteristics. For example, people usually rate men as being more competitive than women, and they usually rate women as being more nurturant than men. Some gender stereotypes may be partly true (Matlin, 2012). However, these stereotypes might prevent a corporation from hiring a competitive woman as a senior executive. These stereotypes might also prevent a school from hiring a nurturant man to teach first grade.

In this section, we will examine how the research methods from cognitive psychology can be used to examine people's gender stereotypes. Let's first examine research that employs explicit measures. Then we'll see how implicit measures provide additional information about gender stereotypes.

Dunning and Sherman (1997) assessed gender stereotypes by using a recognition-memory task. They instructed students to read sentences such as, "The women at the office liked to talk around the water cooler." Later, the participants were tested for recognition memory. Specifically, participants saw a series of sentences. They were told to respond "old" if they had previously seen that same exact sentence, earlier in the session. Otherwise, they should respond "new."

Let's look at the results for new sentences that were *consistent* with a widely held gender stereotype about women's conversations: "The women at the office liked to gossip around the water cooler." The participants responded "old" to 29% of these sentences. Other new sentences were *inconsistent* with another widely held stereotype: "The women at the office liked to talk sports around the water cooler." The participants responded "old" to only 18% of these sentences.

Apparently, when people saw the original sentence, they sometimes made the stereotype-consistent inference that the women must have been gossiping. They were less likely to make the gender-inconsistent inference that the women were discussing sports. Oakhill and her colleagues (2005) found similar results.

Dunning and Sherman's (1997) recognition test is an example of an explicit memory task. As you learned in Chapter 5 (p. 143), an **explicit memory task** directly instructs participants to remember information. For example, the participants in this study knew that their memory was being tested when they judged whether the sentences were old or new. People might guess that the researchers could be measuring their gender stereotypes, and they may be aware that it's not appropriate to hold rigid stereotypes (Matlin, 2012; Rudman, 2005).

To reduce this "awareness problem," researchers have designed a variety of implicit memory tasks. The goal of these implicit memory measures is to assess people's gender stereotypes without asking them directly. Implicit memory measures are supposed to discourage people from providing socially desirable answers.

As Chapter 5 described, an **implicit memory task** asks people to perform a cognitive task that does not directly ask for recall or recognition. When researchers use implicit memory tasks to measure gender stereotypes, they assess people's general knowledge about gender in their culture. These implicit memory tasks also measure people's tendency to draw gender-consistent conclusions. Let's consider two different implicit memory tasks that show how gender stereotypes can influence people's implicit memory.

1. *Using neuroscience techniques to assess gender stereotypes.* Osterhout and his coauthors (1997) assessed gender stereotypes by using a neuroscience technique. As you learned in Chapter 1, the **event-related potential (ERP) technique** records tiny fluctuations in the brain's electrical activity, in response to a stimulus. Previous researchers had tested people who were instructed to read sentences such as, "I like my coffee with cream and dog" (p. 273). As you would expect, the ERPs quickly changed in response to the surprising word *dog*.

To examine gender stereotypes, Osterhout and his colleagues (1997) presented some sentences that would be consistent with gender stereotypes, such as, "The nurse prepared herself for the operation." These stereotype-consistent sentences did not elicit a change in the ERPs. Now try Demonstration 8.8 on page 285, unless you have already tried it.

In contrast, the ERPs changed significantly for stereotype-inconsistent sentences such as, "The nurse prepared himself for the operation." In reading the word *nurse*, people had made the gender-stereotyped inference that the nurse must be female. Consequently, the unexpected, stereotype-inconsistent word *himself* produced changes in the ERPs. In a related study, White and her colleagues (2009) found similar results, with greater ERP changes for stereotype-inconsistent pairs of words.

2. *Using the Implicit Association Test to assess gender stereotypes.* Brian Nosek, Mahzarin Banaji, and Anthony Greenwald (2002) used a very different method to assess implicit gender stereotypes. Specifically, they examined the gender stereotypes that mathematics is associated with males and that the arts are associated with females. Suppose that they had asked their research participants (college students at Yale University) an explicit question, such as: "Is math more strongly associated with males than with females?" When research is conducted with college students like these, the students are most likely to answer "No." After all, when students are asked an explicit question like this, they have time to be analytical and to recall that a "Yes" answer would not be socially appropriate.

Instead of an explicit measure, Nosek and his colleagues used the Implicit Association Test (e.g., Greenwald & Nosek, 2001; Greenwald et al., 1998; Nosek et al., 2007). An implicit task asks people to perform a task, but the participants do not know what the task is supposed to measure. The **Implicit Association Test (IAT)** is based on the principle that people can mentally pair two related words together much more easily than they can pair two unrelated words.

Specifically, when participants worked on the IAT, they sat in front of a computer screen that presented a series of words. On a typical trial—where the pairings were consistent with gender stereotypes—the participant would be told to press the key on the left if the word was related to math (e.g., *calculus* or *numbers*) and also if the word was related to males (e.g., *uncle* or *son*). This same participant would be told to press the key on the right if the word was related to the arts (e.g., *poetry* or *dance*) and also if the word was related to females (e.g., *aunt* or *daughter*).

Throughout the study, participants were urged to respond as quickly as possible, so that they would not consciously consider their responses. When completing the IAT, people with strong gender stereotypes would think that math and males fit in the same category, whereas the arts and females would fit in a different category. Therefore, their responses should be quick for this first portion of the task.

Then the instructions shifted so that the pairings were now *inconsistent* with gender stereotypes. Now, on a typical trial, the participant would press the left key if the word was related to math and also if the word was related to females. Also, the participant would press the right key if the word was related to the arts and also if the word was related to males. People with strong gender stereotypes should have difficulty associating math-related terms with women and arts-related terms with men. Their responses should therefore be much slower for this second part of the task.

Nosek and his coauthors (2002) found that the students responded significantly faster to the stereotype-consistent pairings (the first task), compared to the stereotype-inconsistent pairings (the second task). In other words, most of these Yale students believed that math and males seem to go together, whereas the arts and females seem to go together.

Nosek and his coauthors (2002) also analyzed the scores for women who strongly considered themselves to be feminine and strongly associated math with being masculine. These women specifically did *not* associate themselves with mathematics. Sadly, this anti-math tendency was even found with some women who were math majors!

In other words, gender stereotypes are not innocent cognitive tendencies. Instead, these stereotypes can have the power to influence people's self-images and their sense of academic competence.

Psychologists have designed other implicit measures to examine gender stereotypes and other categories such as ethnicity (Ito et al., 2006; Lane, Banaji, & Greenwald, 2007; Reynolds et al., 2006). Furthermore, if you are interested in the connection between social psychology and cognitive psychology, you can find additional information in several useful books (Jackson, 2011; Whitley & Kite, 2010).

Individual Differences: Country of Residence and Gender Stereotypes

The Implicit Association Test (IAT) is extremely popular, but most of the research has been conducted in the United States. You may wonder if the same gender stereotypes are likely to operate in other countries. Fortunately, an impressive cross-cultural study has examined this question. Brian Nosek and his colleagues (2009) worked with researchers in 34 different countries to gather the relevant information.[*]

Specifically, these researchers wanted to determine whether national differences in gender stereotypes would be correlated with national differences in female and male students' scores on a cognitive test. This widely used test is called the "2003 Trends in International Mathematics and Science Study" (TIMS). Fortunately, the average scores on this test were available for 8th grade females and males in 34 different countries. Nosek and his coauthors (2009) used these data to calculate the "male advantage" for each country, specifically, the males' average score on the TIMS test minus the females' average on the TIMS test.

Furthermore, these researchers also recorded the average scores on the Implicit Association Test for each country, because the test is available online in 17 different languages. (In fact, Demonstration 8.8 on page 285 features the online version of the IAT.) About 300,000 people in those 34 countries had completed this test by the time these researchers gathered their data.

---

[*]The Individual Differences Feature in Chapter 7 examined gender comparisons in spatial ability. Here in Chapter 8, we examine whether a variety of countries have different gender stereotypes about math and science, a topic that is related but not the same.

The results showed that the countries with the highest scores on the IAT measure of gender stereotyping were also likely to have the highest "male advantage" scores on both the math and science test (TIMS). Specifically, the correlation was +.34 for math scores and +.39 for science scores. In other words, the countries with the highest measures of gender stereotyping were also more likely to be the countries where males performed better than females in both math and science. Incidentally, the United States and Canada had average scores on both the IAT and the male-advantage measure.

You know from your psychology courses that correlational data can be difficult to interpret. However, Nosek and his coauthors (2009) write that a "likely explanation for the relation is that both the 8th grade test takers and the diverse IAT participants of a given country are influenced by the same socio-cultural context" (p. 10596). The title of this current chapter is "General Knowledge." In this case, people's semantic memory and schemas include information about gender differences, and the strength of this knowledge varies from country to country.

Conclusions About Schemas

In summary, schemas can influence memory (1) in the initial selection of material, (2) in remembering visual scenes, (3) in abstraction, and (4) even in the final process of integration. However, we need to emphasize that our cognitive processes are often accurate, consistent with Theme 2. For instance:

1. We often select material for memory that is not consistent with our schemas.
2. We may sometimes remember that we actually saw only a portion of an object, rather than the complete object.
3. We frequently recall the exact words of a passage as it was originally rather than storing an abstract memory. (Otherwise, chorus directors would have resigned long ago.)
4. We may keep the elements in memory isolated from each other, rather than integrating these memories together.

Yes, schemas clearly can influence memory. However, the influence is far from complete. After all, as Theme 5 states, our cognitive processes are guided by bottom-up processing, as well as top-down processing. Therefore, we select, recall both visual scenes and verbal passages and integrate many unique features of each stimulus, in addition to the schema-consistent features that match our background knowledge.

◎ Section Summary: *Schemas and Scripts*

1. A schema is generalized knowledge about a situation, an event, or a person; schemas are a kind of heuristic, in other words, a general rule that is typically accurate; schemas are important in many areas of psychology.
2. A script is a kind of schema that describes a simple, well-structured sequence of events, for example, a life script about the important events in a person's

life; research shows that we can recall the elements in a script more accurately if the script is identified at the outset.

3. Schemas may operate during memory selection; for example, people recall items consistent with an office schema. However, we often recall schema-*inconsistent* information, for example, when a major event is surprising and inconsistent with the standard schema.

4. When we remember a scene, we often "remember" seeing complete objects, even though we really saw only parts of those objects (boundary extension).

5. According to the constructive model of memory, schemas encourage memory abstraction, so that people tend to remember the general meaning of a message, even if they forget the detail. According to the pragmatic view of memory, people often remember the exact words in a message when the specific words really matter. Both perspectives seem to operate, depending on the circumstances.

6. Schemas also influence memory integration; in Bartlett's classic research, people "recalled" information that never actually appeared in the original material. The tendency is stronger if recall is delayed and if people are performing another memory task at the same time.

7. The research on gender stereotypes shows that people frequently make schema-consistent inferences in explicit memory (e.g., a recognition test) and in implicit memory, for instance with the ERP technique and the IAT task. Cross-cultural research shows that countries with the highest scores on the IAT are also the countries where boys earn higher scores than girls on a test that measures performance in science and mathematics

CHAPTER REVIEW QUESTIONS

1. Think of a prototype for the category "household pet," and contrast it with a nonprototypical household pet. Compare these two animals with respect to (a) whether they would be supplied as examples of the category; (b) how quickly they could be judged after priming; and (c) the attributes that each would share with most other household pets.

2. Consider the basic-level category "dime," in contrast to the superordinate-level category "money" and the subordinate-level category "2005 dime." Describe these three levels, and then explain how the basic level has special status when we want to identify objects. Describe a person who would be most likely to use (a) the superordinate-level name, and (b) the subordinate-level name. Think of an area in which you have more knowledge than the average student; when would you be most likely to use subordinate-level descriptions?

3. Describe the prototype approach and the exemplar approach to semantic memory. How are they similar, and how are they different? Based on the discussion in this chapter, when would you be more likely to use a prototype

approach in trying to categorize an object? When would you be more likely to use the exemplar approach? In each case, give an example from your daily experience.

4. Suppose that you read the following question on a true-false examination: "A script is a kind of schema." Describe how you would process that question in terms of the exemplar approach and network models.

5. Think of some kind of information that could be represented in a diagram similar to the one in Figure 8.3 (for example, popular singers or famous novelists). Then provide examples of how the following terms could apply to this particular diagram: spontaneous generalization, default assignment, and graceful degradation.

6. If you were instructed to describe the characteristics of the PDP approach in a 5-minute overview, what would you say? Include examples, and also be sure to describe why the approach is called "parallel distributed processing." Chapter 5 discussed the topic of expertise (pp. 147–151). Think about a specific area in which you have more expertise than a friend who is a novice. How might the two of you differ with respect to the kind of network you have developed?

7. Describe three scripts with which you are very familiar. How would these scripts be considered heuristics, rather than exact predictors of what will happen the next time you find yourself in one of the situations described in the script?

8. You probably have a fairly clear schema of the concept "dentist's office." Focus on the discussion titled "Schemas and Memory Selection" (pp. 276–281) and point out the circumstances in which you would be likely to remember (a) schema-consistent material and (b) schema-inconsistent material. How might boundary extension operate when you try to reconstruct the scene that you see from the dentist's chair?

9. What evidence do we have from explicit memory tasks that gender stereotypes encourage us to draw inferences that are consistent with those stereotypes? How would the demand characteristics mentioned in Chapter 7 (p. 223) be relevant to explicit memory tasks? Then discuss the two implicit memory tasks described in the discussion about inferences, and explain why they may be more effective than explicit tasks in assessing people's stereotypes.

10. Think of a schema or a script that occurs frequently in your life. Explain how that schema or script might influence your memory during four different processes: memory selection, boundary extension, memory abstraction, and memory integration. Be sure to consider how memory sometimes favors schema-consistent information and sometimes favors schema-inconsistent information, as well as the cases when memory accurately reflects bottom-up processing.

KEYWORDS

inference
semantic memory
episodic memory
category
concept
situated cognition approach
prototype
prototype approach
prototypicality
graded structure
typicality effect
semantic priming effect
family resemblance
superordinate-level categories
basic-level categories
subordinate-level categories
validity
exemplar approach

exemplar
network models
node
spreading activation
ACT-R
declarative knowledge
propositional network
proposition
parallel distributed processing
  (PDP) approach
connectionism
neural networks
spontaneous generalization
default assignment
connection weights
graceful degradation
tip-of-the-tongue phenomenon
schema

heuristic
schema therapy
script
life script
boundary extension
abstraction
verbatim memory
false alarm
constructive model of memory
pragmatic view of memory
memory integration
gender stereotypes
explicit memory task
implicit memory task
event-related potential (ERP)
  technique
Implicit Association Test (IAT)

RECOMMENDED READINGS

Davis, D., & Loftus, E. F. (2008). Expectancies, emotion, and memory reports for visual events. In J. R. Brockmole (Ed.), *The visual world in memory* (pp. 178–214). New York: Psychology Press. Here is a clear and interesting chapter that describes how schemas can influence eyewitness testimony for visual events. An especially important focus is the research about how ethnicity can create biases in eyewitness testimony.

Mareschal, D., Quinn, P. C. & Lea, S. E. G. (Eds.). (2010). *The making of human concepts.* New York: Oxford University Press. Much of the research on concepts is abstract and difficult to apply to everyday life. This book is well written, especially because the editors include an introduction at the beginning of each chapter. The content focuses on concepts in adults, children, and animals

Murphy, G. L. (2002). *The big book of concepts.* Cambridge, MA: MIT Press. Topics in this book include theories of concepts, the development of conceptual knowledge, and word meaning. The tongue-in-cheek title of this book is consistent with the author's sense of humor throughout the chapters.

Whitley, B. E., Jr., & Kite, M. E. (2010). *The psychology of prejudice and discrimination* (2nd ed.). Belmont, CA: Wadsworth Cengage. Bernard Whitley and Mary Kite are well known for their research about biases based on gender, age, and sexual orientation. Two chapters in their book specifically focus on stereotypes.

ANSWER TO DEMONSTRATION 8.7

Every sentence in Part 2 is new.

CHAPTER 9

Language I: Introduction to Language and Language Comprehension

PREVIEW

Chapters 9 and 10 examine how we process language. Specifically, Chapter 9 emphasizes language comprehension in the form of listening and reading. In contrast, Chapter 10 will emphasize language production (speaking and writing), as well as bilingualism—a topic that encompasses both language comprehension and language production.

We'll begin Chapter 9 by exploring the nature of language. As it happens, most of the research in psycholinguistics studies English speakers and readers. In this first section, we'll look at the structure of language, a brief history of psycholinguistics, and several factors that influence comprehension. In addition, we will discuss how people may not manage to comprehend every component of the language they hear or read; instead, they manage to acquire a "good enough" understanding. Our final topic in this section is the in-depth discussion of neuroscience research on language.

Next, we'll examine basic reading processes, beginning with a comparison of written and spoken language. This section also examines some theoretical approaches to word recognition. In addition, we'll consider some implications for teaching reading; teachers face an especially challenging task, given the irregularities of the English language.

The final part of Chapter 9 moves beyond small linguistic units to consider discourse, or language units that are larger than a sentence. Some important components of discourse comprehension include the following topics: forming a cohesive representation of a passage, drawing inferences that were not actually stated in the passage, and teaching metacomprehension skills. We'll also consider the relationship between test anxiety and reading comprehension. In addition, we'll look at artificial intelligence programs that focus on comprehending written language.

CHAPTER INTRODUCTION

Try to imagine a world without language. In fact, think how your life would change if you woke up tomorrow and language were forbidden. Even nonverbal gestures and sign language would be prohibited, because they are alternate forms of language. Phones, televisions, radios, newspapers, books, and electronic communication would be virtually useless. Almost all college courses would disappear. You couldn't even talk to yourself, so it would be impossible to reminisce, remind yourself about a task you must complete, or make plans for the future. Your interactions with other people would be minimal, because language is such an important part of these interactions (Fiedler et al., 2011; Heine, 2010).

In fact, society could not function without language. As Steffensen (2011) remarks, "Language functions as airborne synapses; it contributes to inter-human coordination, thus allowing us to be smarter, more creative and more flexible, just like the brain is smarter and more flexible than a pile of neurons" (p. 205).

Like many cognitive skills, language rarely receives the credit it deserves (Harley, 2008). After all, you simply listen to someone with a moving mouth and vocal equipment, and you understand the message that this person is trying to convey. Equally effortlessly, you open your own mouth and sentences emerge almost instantaneously—an impressive testimony to the efficiency of our cognitive processes (Theme 2). Furthermore, you may know people who use sign language. People from the Deaf Community can converse fluently, even when they are at opposite ends of a large room (Tomasello, 2008; Traxler, 2012).

Another equally impressive characteristic of our language skills is our extraordinary ability to master thousands of words. In Chapter 8, we noted that the average North American has an estimated vocabulary of 20,000 to 100,000 words (Baddeley et al., 2009; Harley, 2008; Saffran & Schwartz, 2003).

Cognitive psychologists emphasize that human language is one of the most complex processes to be found anywhere on our planet (Tomasello, 2008). The domain of language includes an impressive diversity of skills. Consider just a few of the abilities that you need in order to understand a spoken sentence: (1) encoding the sound of a speaker's voice, (2) encoding the visual features of printed language, (3) accessing the meaning of words, (4) understanding the rules that determine word order, and (5) appreciating whether a sentence is a question or a statement, based only on the speaker's intonation.

Furthermore, you manage to accomplish all of these linguistic tasks while listening to a speaker who is probably producing three words each *second* (Vigliocco & Hartsuiker, 2002). In fact, talking is so difficult that it should be an Olympic event—except that most humans have mastered this athletic skill (Bock & Garnsey, 1998; Tomasello, 2008). Now try Demonstration 9.1.

⊚ **Demonstration 9.1**

How Other Cognitive Processes Contribute to Language

Look below at the list of chapters you have read so far. For each chapter, list at least one topic that is connected to language. The answers appear at the end of this chapter, on page 333.

Chapter 2: Perceptual Processes I: Visual and Auditory Recognition

Chapter 3: Perceptual Processes II: Attention and Consciousness

Chapter 4: Working Memory

Chapter 5: Long-Term Memory

Chapter 6: Memory Strategies and Metacognition

Chapter 7: Mental Imagery and Cognitive Maps

Chapter 8: General Knowledge

In addition, the productivity of language is unlimited. For example, consider only the number of 20-word sentences that you could potentially generate in the English language. You would need about 10,000,000,000,000 years—or 2,000 times the age of the earth—to say them all (Miller, 1967; Pinker, 1993).

In Chapters 9 and 10, we will discuss **psycholinguistics**, an interdisciplinary field that examines how people use language to communicate ideas (Corballis, 2006; Harley, 2008). We use language in thousands of different settings, from courtrooms to cartoons. Furthermore, language provides an excellent example of Theme 4 of this textbook, the interrelatedness of the cognitive processes. In fact, virtually every topic we have discussed so far in this book makes some contribution to language processing. To illustrate this point, be sure that you have tried Demonstration 9.1.

The two chapters on language should also convince you that humans are active information processors (Theme 1). Rather than passively listening to language, we actively consult our previous knowledge, use various strategies, create expectations, and draw conclusions. When we speak, we can easily convey complex messages. Language is not only our most remarkable cognitive achievement, but it is also the most social of our cognitive processes (Fiedler et al., 2011).

The first of our two chapters on language focuses on language comprehension. After an introductory discussion about the nature of language, we will examine basic reading, as well as the more complex process of understanding spoken discourse. In Chapter 10, we will switch our focus from understanding to the production of language. Chapter 10 considers two production tasks: speaking and writing. With a background in both language comprehension and language production, we can then consider bilingualism, the third topic in Chapter 10. Bilinguals—certainly the winners in any Olympic language contest—manage to communicate easily in two or more languages.

THE NATURE OF LANGUAGE

Psycholinguists have developed a specialized vocabulary for language terms; let's now consider these terms. A **phoneme** (pronounced "*foe*-neem") is the basic unit of spoken language, such as the sounds *a*, *k*, and *th*. The English language has about 40 phonemes (Mayer, 2004; Traxler, 2012). If you change just one phoneme in a word, you change the meaning of that word (Harley, 2008). For example, *kiss* has a very different meaning from *this*.

In contrast, a **morpheme** (pronounced "*more*-feem") is the basic unit of meaning. For example, the word *reactivated* actually contains four morphemes: *re-*, *active,-ate*, and *-ed*. Each of those segments conveys meaning. Many morphemes can stand on their own (like *giraffe*). In contrast, some morphemes must be attached to other morphemes in order to convey their meaning. For instance, *re-* indicates a repeated action. As you might guess, the term **morphology** refers to the study of morphemes; morphology therefore examines how we create words by combining morphemes (Harley, 2008).

Another major component of psycholinguistics is syntax. **Syntax** refers to the grammatical rules that govern how we organize words into sentences (Owens, 2001; Harley, 2008). A more inclusive and familiar term, **grammar**, encompasses both morphology and syntax; it therefore examines both word structure and sentence structure (Evans & Green, 2006).

Semantics is the area of psycholinguistics that examines the meanings of words and sentences (Carroll, 2004). A related term, **semantic memory**, refers to our organized knowledge about the world. We have discussed semantic memory throughout earlier chapters of this book, but especially in Chapter 8.

Pragmatics—another important term—refers to our knowledge of the social rules that underlie language use; pragmatics takes into account the listener's perspective (Bardovi-Harlig, 2010; Harley, 2008). For example, think how you would define the word *syntax* to a 12-year-old child, as opposed to a college classmate. Pragmatics is the discipline within linguistics that focuses most on social interactions (Holtgraves, 2010). Pragmatics is an especially important topic when we consider the production of language (Chapter 10), but pragmatic factors also influence comprehension.

As you can see from reviewing the terms introduced in the first part of Chapter 9, psycholinguistics encompasses a broad range of topics, including sounds, several levels of meaning, grammar, and social factors. We will begin by noting a problem with the current research in psycholinguistics. Then we'll consider additional aspects of the nature of language: a brief history of psycholinguistics, factors affecting comprehension, information about less-than-perfect language, and neurolinguistics.

A Caution: Psycholinguistics Is English-Centered

Several psychologists and linguists point out an important bias that operates in research about psycholinguistics. Specifically, most researchers in this discipline focus on how people understand and use English. As a result, some of the findings may apply only to English speakers, rather than to all humans (Harley, 2008; Kaplan, 2010b; Share, 2008). Current linguists estimate that about 7,000 languages are spoken throughout the world. Therefore, it's unfortunate that so much of the research emphasizes just one of these world languages (Harley, 2008; Ku, 2006; Lupyan & Dale, 2010; Tomasello, 2008).

If your own first language is English, your ideas about language are probably English-centered. Therefore, you may react with surprise if you travel to another language community. For instance, I recall visiting Grenada, Spain, and hearing the tour guide (who appeared to be Spanish) describing the sights both in Spanish and in Japanese to the tourists in her group. I'm embarrassed to report that I was startled to hear her translating Spanish into Japanese, without first passing through English.

The emphasis on English is especially unfortunate because English is an "outlier language" for two important reasons:

1. English has relatively simple grammar, partly because there is a negative correlation between a language's number of speakers and the complexity of its language (Lupyan & Dale, 2010).

2. English has many more irregular pronunciations than other major world languages (Share, 2008; Traxler, 2012; Ziegler et al., 2010). As we'll emphasize in the discussion of basic reading (pp. 316–323), a sequence of letters in English can have variable pronunciations. For example, the first six letters of the words *though* and *thought* are identical. However, these two words are pronounced differently, and they also have very different meanings.

In addition, English word meaning does not depend on the relative pitch of the syllables in a word. However, in Mandarin Chinese, *ma* means "mother" when the word is spoken at a single pitch. In contrast, *ma* means "horse" when spoken in a tone that initially falls and then rises (Field, 2004). A child can create a yes-no question in English by using a rising intonation, such as "I going outside?" However, young children in Finland cannot use this option, because Finnish does not use this method for asking a question (Harley, 2008).

Another example of linguistic differences is that Sesotho—a language spoken in southern Africa—uses the passive voice more than English does (Bornkessel & Schlesewsky, 2006). Also, you probably know at least one European language in which the nouns have a grammatical gender, even though English nouns do not.

Brain processing even differs as a function of a person's language. For example, one specific region in the frontal lobe is activated when English speakers listen to certain complex sentences. However, this same region does not respond when German speakers listen to the translated versions of those sentences (Bornkessel & Schlesewsky, 2006).

In summary, languages differ widely from one another on numerous dimensions (Share, 2008; Tomasello, 2003). Clearly, psycholinguists will need to conduct extensive research in many other languages if they want to determine which linguistic principles apply universally.

A Brief History of Psycholinguistics

Let's consider some highlights in the history of psycholinguistics. Early philosophers in Greece and India debated the nature of language (Chomsky, 2000). Centuries later, both Wilhelm Wundt and William James also speculated about our impressive abilities in this area (Carroll, 2004; Levelt, 1998).

However, the current discipline of psycholinguistics can be traced to the 1960s, when psycholinguists began to test whether psychological research could support the theories of a linguist named Noam Chomsky (Harley, 2008; McKoon & Ratcliff, 1998). We'll briefly consider Chomsky's theory, the reactions to his theory, and a more recent approach that emphasizes meaning.

Chomsky's Approach. People usually think of a sentence as an orderly sequence of words that are lined up in a row on a sheet of paper. Noam Chomsky (1957) created great enthusiasm among psychologists and linguists, because he proposed that there is more to a sentence than meets the eye (or the ear).

Chapter 1 of this textbook discussed Chomsky's work on the psychology of language. In fact, Chomsky's approach contributed to the decline of behaviorism. The behaviorists emphasized the *observable* aspects of language behavior (Harley, 2008). In contrast, Chomsky argued that your impressive language abilities must be explained in terms of a complex system of rules and principles that are represented in your mind (Chomsky, 2006). Chomsky is clearly one of the most influential theorists in modern linguistics (N. Smith, 2000; Harley, 2008).

Chomsky proposed that humans have innate language skills. That is, we have an inborn understanding of the abstract principles of language. As a result, children do not need to learn the basic, generalizable concepts that are universal to all languages (Chomsky, 2006; Field, 2004).

Of course, children need to learn many superficial characteristics of the language spoken in their community. For instance, children in Spanish-speaking communities will need to learn the difference between *ser* and *estar*. Spanish linguistic space is carved up somewhat differently from that of English, where children learn only one form of the verb *to be*. Still, Chomsky argues that all children have a substantial, inborn language ability. This ability allows them to produce and understand sentences they have never heard before (Chomsky, 2006).

Chomsky (1975) also proposed that language is **modular**; people have a set of specific linguistic abilities that is separated from our other cognitive processes, such as memory and decision making (Harley, 2008; Nusbaum & Small, 2006). We discussed a related concept, the "phonetic module," in connection with speech perception on page 64. Because language is modular, Chomsky (2002, 2006) argues, young children learn complex linguistic structures many years before they master other, simpler tasks, such as mental arithmetic.

In contrast to Chomsky's theory, the standard cognitive approach argues that language is not modular. Instead, it is interconnected with other cognitive processes such as working memory (Harley, 2008). According to this alternative approach, we are skilled at language because our powerful brains can master many cognitive tasks. Language is just one of those tasks, and it has the same status as tasks such as memory and problem solving (Carroll, 2004; Harley, 2008; Tomasello, 2003).

In addition, Chomsky (1957, 2006) pointed out the difference between the deep structure and the surface structure of a sentence. The **surface structure** is represented by the words that are actually spoken or written. In contrast, the **deep structure** is the underlying, more abstract meaning of a sentence (Garnham, 2005; Harley, 2008). People use **transformational rules** to convert deep structure into a surface structure that they can speak or write.

Two sentences may have very different surface structures, but very similar deep structures. For example, consider these two sentences: (1) "Sara threw the ball" and (2) "The ball was thrown by Sara."

Notice how these two surface structures differ. None of the words occupies the same position in both sentences. In addition, three of the words in the second sentence do not even appear in the first sentence. However, "deep down," speakers of English feel that the sentences have identical core meanings (Harley, 2008). In fact, 40 minutes after seeing a sentence such as, "The ball was thrown by Sara," people are likely to report that they had seen a semantically similar sentence, such as "Sara threw the ball" (Radvansky, 2008).

Chomsky (1957, 2006) also pointed out that two sentences may have identical surface structures but very different deep structures; these are called **ambiguous sentences**. For example, I live near the small town of York in rural upstate New York. One day I drove past the announcement board outside the York Town Hall, and the message said: "POP CAN DRIVE." I was puzzled: Whose father is now allowed to drive, and why had he previously been prohibited from driving? To be honest, the alternate meaning (focusing on a community fundraiser) did not occur to me until the next day.

We will discuss ambiguity in more detail later in the chapter. However, context usually helps us resolve these ambiguities. Here are three additional ambiguous sentences, each of which has two meanings:

The shooting of the hunters was terrible.

They are cooking apples.

The lamb is too hot to eat.

Reactions to Chomsky's Theory.   Initially, psychologists responded enthusiastically to Chomsky's ideas about grammar (Bock et al., 1992; Williams, 2005). However, some of the research did not support his theories. For example, the research failed to support Chomsky's prediction that people would take longer to process sentences that required numerous transformations (Carroll, 2004). Furthermore, Chomsky's theories argue that all languages share the same universal patterns of grammar (Juffs, 2010). However, research has demonstrated that many non-European languages do not show these patterns (Everett, 2005, 2007; Tomasello, 2008).

Chomsky's more recent theories have provided more sophisticated linguistic analyses. For example, Chomsky later proposed that young language learners make only a limited number of hypotheses about the structure of their language (Chomsky, 1981, 2000; Harley, 2001). Chomsky's newer approach also emphasizes the information contained in the individual words of a sentence. For example, the word *discuss* conveys information about the word's meaning. However, *discuss* also specifies the requirement that *discuss* must include a noun later in the phrase (Ratner & Gleason, 1993). Consider a sentence that begins, "Rita discussed. . . ." The remainder of the sentence must include a noun phrase such as ". . . the novel."

Psycholinguistic Theories that Emphasize Meaning.   Beginning in the 1970s, many psychologists became discouraged with Chomsky's emphasis on the grammatical aspects of language (Harley, 2008; Herriot, 2004). These psychologists began to develop theories that emphasized the human mind and semantics, rather than the structure of language (Tanenhaus, 2004; Treiman et al., 2003).

Several psychologists have developed theories that emphasize meaning (e.g., Kintsch, 1998; Newmeyer, 1998; Tomasello, 2003). Here, we will briefly describe one

---

⑨ **Demonstration 9.2**

The Cognitive-Functional Approach to Language

Imagine that you recently saw an event in which a man named Fred broke a window, using a rock. A person who was not present at the time asks you for information about the event. For each of the sentences below, construct a question that this person might have asked that would prompt you to reply with that specific wording for the sentence. For example, the brief response, "Fred broke the window" might have been prompted by the question, "What did Fred do?"

1. Fred broke the window with a rock.
2. The rock broke the window.
3. The window got broken.
4. It was Fred who broke the window.
5. It was the window that Fred broke.
6. What Fred did was to break the window.

Source: Based on Tomasello, 1998a, p. 483.

---

representative theory, the cognitive-functional approach to language. The **cognitive-functional approach** emphasizes that the function of human language in everyday life is to communicate meaning to other individuals. As this name suggests, the cognitive-functional approach also emphasizes that our cognitive processes—such as attention and memory—are intertwined with our language comprehension and language production.

Michael Tomasello (2003, 2008) points out that young children have extremely powerful cognitive skills and social-learning skills. During the years when they are mastering language, they will hear several million adult sentences. As we'll see in Chapter 13, children analyze these sentences, and they use flexible strategies to create increasingly complex language (Kuhl, 2006).

Tomasello (1998a, 1998b) also emphasizes that adults use language strategically. Specifically, we structure our language in order to focus our listeners' attention on the information we want to emphasize. Be sure to try Demonstration 9.2, which illustrates a concrete example of the cognitive-functional approach (Tomasello, 1998a).

Notice how each of the sentences in this demonstration emphasizes a somewhat different perspective on the same event. Therefore, each of your questions will focus on a slightly different point of view. In short, the cognitive-functional approach argues that people can use language creatively, in order to communicate subtle shades of meaning. We'll explore the social use of language more thoroughly in Chapter 10.

Factors Affecting Comprehension

Beginning in the 1960s, psychologists began to study how several linguistic factors can influence language comprehension. In general, people have difficulty understanding sentences in these four conditions:

1. If they contain negatives, such as *not*.
2. If they are in the passive rather than the active voice.
3. If they have complex syntax.
4. If they are ambiguous.

Negatives. A sentence in a newspaper column reads. "Georgia rejected a challenge to a referendum that had barred same-sex unions." This sentence requires several readings to understand the basic message: Will the state of Georgia prohibit same-sex unions? The research on negatives is clear-cut. If a sentence contains a negative word, such as *no* or *not*, or an implied negative (such as rejected), the sentence almost always requires more processing time than a similar, affirmative sentence (Williams, 2005).

In a classic study, Clark and Chase (1972) showed a picture of a star above a plus sign. Then they asked people to verify statements, such as the following:

$$\text{Star is above plus.}\begin{array}{c}+\\ *\end{array}$$

The participants responded quickly in this case, when the sentence was affirmative. They responded more slowly if the sentence contained the negative form isn't (for example, "Plus isn't above star"). The participants also made fewer errors with affirmative sentences than with negative sentences. Notice that these results are consistent with Theme 3 of this textbook: Our cognitive processes handle positive information better than negative information.

As you can imagine, readers' understanding decreases as the number of negative terms increases. For example, people perform only slightly better than chance when they judge sentences such as, "Few people strongly deny that the world is not flat" (Sherman, 1976, p. 145). These findings have clear-cut practical applications in numerous areas, such as education, advertisements, and surveys (Kifner, 1994; Lenzner et al., 2010).

The Passive Voice. As we discussed earlier, Chomsky (1957, 1965) pointed out that the active and passive forms of a sentence may differ in their surface structure, even though they have similar deep structures. However, the active form is more basic. For example, we need to add extra words we want to create the passive form of a sentence. As you might guess, the English language uses the active voice much more often than the passive voice (Fiedler et al., 2011).

The active form is also easier to understand (Christianson et al., 2010; Garnham, 2005; Williams, 2005). For example, Ferreira and her coauthors (2002) asked participants to determine whether each sentence in a series was plausible. The participants were highly accurate in responding "No" to sentences in the active voice, such as, "The man bit the dog." In contrast, their accuracy dropped to about 75% when the same sentences were converted to the passive voice, for example, "The dog was bitten by the man" (p. 13).

Most current writing-style manuals recommend using the active voice. For example, the current manual of the American Psychological Association (2010) points out that it's relatively easy to understand an active-voice sentence such as "Nuñez (2009) designed the experiment." In contrast, it's more difficult to understand the passive-voice sentence, "The experiment was designed by Nuñez (2009)."

Complex Syntax. As you might expect, people have trouble understanding complex syntax, such as a sentence with a nested structure. In a **nested structure**, one phrase is embedded within another phrase. Readers often experience a memory overload when they try to read a sentence that has a nested structure (Lenzner et al., 2010; Rayner & Clifton, 2002).

For example, consider the following sentence, which appeared in a review of a Japanese film called "The Makioka Sisters":

> These are somewhat diagrammatically opposed in that the former seems a paragon of virtue and reticence, struggling in her delicate way through several prospective husbands arranged by her sisters—being in her early thirties she is considered past her prime, and her natural shyness inhibits proceedings further—while the latter reflects a rapidly modernizing world in which formal marriages and absolute filial piety are becoming outmoded concepts. (Bingham, 2011, p. 65)
>
> Source: Bingham, A. (2011). "The Makioka sisters." *Cineaste, 36* (4), 65–66.

Notice the nested phrase that appears between the two dashes. Your working memory needs to maintain the first part of this sentence, while you navigate the nested phrase. Then you must relate the last part of this sentence to the first part.

The next time you write a paper, remember how these three factors can influence comprehension. Whenever possible, follow these guidelines: (1) Use linguistically positive sentences, rather than negative ones; (2) use active sentences, rather than passive ones; and (3) use relatively simple sentences, rather than sentences with complex syntax.

Ambiguity. Suppose that you saw the following headline in your local newspaper: "Swedish Queen Silvia hurt evading New York photographer." You might wonder initially wonder why the queen of a relatively peaceful nation would try to harm a photographer. Later, you realize that Queen Silvia was actually the person who was hurt. As you might imagine, sentences are difficult to understand if they contain an ambiguous word or an ambiguous sentence structure (Harley, 2010; Lenzner et al., 2010). In fact, we discussed ambiguous sentences in connection with Chomsky's approach to language. Now let's consider how people manage to understand these sentences.

Psychologists have designed several methods of measuring the difficulty of understanding a sentence with an ambiguous word or phrase (Harley, 2010; MacDonald, 1999; Rodd et al., 2002). For example, one method measures the amount of time that the reader pauses on a word before moving his or her eyes to the next words in the sentence (Pexman et al., 2004; Rayner et al., 2005). People typically pause longer when they are processing an ambiguous word, for example, when they are completing a questionnaire (Lenzner et al., 2010).

Psychologists have proposed many theories to explain how listeners process an ambiguous word (Traxler, 2012; Van Orden & Kloos, 2005). Current research supports the following explanation: When people encounter a potential ambiguity, the activation builds up for all the well-known meanings of the ambiguous item. Furthermore, people are likely to select one particular meaning (1) if that meaning is more common than the alternate meaning and (2) if the rest of the sentence is consistent with that meaning (Hurley, 2011; Morris & Binder, 2001; Sereno et al., 2003).

Consider this potentially ambiguous sentence: *Pat took the money to the bank.* Here, the "financial institution" interpretation of *bank* would receive the most activation. After all, this is the most common interpretation of *bank*, and the context of money also suggests this meaning. Some minimal activation may also build up for other meanings of *bank* (as in *riverbank* and *blood bank*). However, just a fraction of a second later, these alternative meanings are suppressed, and they are no longer active (Fetzer & Oishi, 2011; Traxler, 2012).

◉ Demonstration 9.3

Searching for Ambiguous Language

Ambiguity occurs quite often in the English language (Rodd et al., 2002). Perhaps the best source of ambiguous words and phrases is newspaper headlines. After all, these headlines must be very brief, so they often omit the auxiliary words that could resolve the ambiguity. Here are some actual newspaper headlines that colleagues, students, and I have seen:

1. "Eye drops off shelf"
2. "Squad helps dog bite victims"
3. "British left waffles on Falkland Islands"
4. "Bombing Rocks Hope for Peace"
5. "Clinton wins budget; more lies ahead"
6. "Miners refuse to work after death"
7. "Kids make nutritious snacks"
8. "Local high school dropouts cut in half"
9. "Iraqi head seeks arms"
10. "Oklahoma is among places where tongues are disappearing"

For the next few weeks, search the newspapers you normally read, looking for ambiguous headlines. Try to notice whether your first interpretation of the ambiguous portion was a correct or incorrect understanding of the phrase. If you find any particularly intriguing ambiguities, please send them to me! My address is: Department of Psychology, SUNY Geneseo, Geneseo, NY 14454.

So far, we have considered ambiguous words. However, sometimes a sentence structure is ambiguous, especially if it contains no punctuation (Rayner et al., 2003). Try reading this sentence:

1. "After the Martians invaded the town that the city bordered was evacuated." (Tabor & Hutchins, 2004, p. 432).

Did you find yourself reading along quickly, and then you were suddenly lost? You had wandered down the wrong path. An ambiguous sentence is especially difficult if you read a long string of words that seem consistent with your initial interpretation. In contrast, you can correct your initial mistake more quickly with a shorter string of words. If Sentence 1 is still unclear, see if you can understand this shorter sentence:

2. "After the Martians invaded the town was evacuated." (Tabor & Hutchins, 2004, p. 432).

As Rueckl (1995) observes, "Ambiguity is a fact of life. Happily, the human cognitive system is well-equipped to deal with it" (p. 501). In fact, we can usually understand ambiguous sentences, just as we can usually understand negative sentences, sentences using the passive voice, and sentences with complex syntax. However, we typically respond more quickly and more accurately when the language we encounter is straightforward. Now that you are familiar with the concept of ambiguity, try Demonstration 9.3.

The "Good-Enough" Approach to Language Comprehension

Psychologists have written literally thousands of articles about language comprehension. In general, these articles show that people typically manage to read quite rapidly. For example, read the following sentence:

The authorities needed to decide where to bury the survivors.

When most people read this sentence quickly, they initially think that it sounds perfectly fine. If you read the sentence more carefully, you will notice the problem. Fernanda Ferreira and her colleagues suggest that we process language by using the "good-enough approach" (e.g., Christianson et al., 2010; Ferreira et al., 2002; Swets et al., 2008). According to **the good-enough approach** to language comprehension, we frequently process only part of a sentence. Consistent with Theme 2, this strategy usually works well for us. For instance, when I first saw this sentence about the burial, it seemed perfectly correct. However, I had not paid sufficient attention to bottom-up processing, so I missed the meaning of the specific word "survivor."

Ferreira and her coauthors emphasize that people usually do not work hard to create the most accurate, detailed interpretation of every sentence they read or hear. As Chapter 2 pointed out, college students can read normal sentences at the rate of about

255 words per minute (Rayner et al., 2006). If you paused to think about the true meaning of every word in every sentence, you would never complete any reading assignment!

In Chapters 7 and 8, we discussed the term **heuristic**, which is a general rule that is typically accurate. Notice that the good-enough approach to language comprehension is another example of a heuristic (Ferreira & Patson, 2007). In many cases, we read quickly, and we try to grasp the general meaning of a sentence. Our knowledge of language typically leads us to an accurate interpretation. However, this strategy can sometimes lead to errors in language comprehension (Harley, 2008).

[**IN DEPTH**]

Neurolinguistics

Neurolinguistics is the discipline that examines how the brain processes language. Research in this area has become increasingly active in recent years, and it demonstrates that the neurological basis of language is very complicated. Unfortunately, however, the popular press typically oversimplifies the complex results reported by neurolinguists (Borst et al., 2011; Schumann, 2010). In this part of the chapter, we will consider four topics: (a) people with aphasia, (b) hemispheric specialization in language processing, (c) neuroimaging research with individuals who do not have language disorders, and (d) research on the mirror system, which may facilitate communication.

Individuals with Aphasia. The initial investigations in neurolinguistics began in the 1800s, when early researchers studied individuals who had language disorders. In fact, before the early 1970s, almost all the scientific information about neurolinguistics was based on people with aphasia. A person with **aphasia** has difficulty communicating, caused by damage to the speech areas of the brain. This damage is typically caused by a stroke or a tumor (Gazzaniga et al., 2009; Saffran & Schwartz, 2003). Figure 9.1 illustrates two especially relevant regions of the brain.

Broca's area is located toward the front of the brain. Damage to **Broca's area** typically leads to hesitant speech that primarily uses isolated words and short phrases (Dick et al., 2001; Gazzaniga et al., 2009). For example, one person with Broca's aphasia tried to describe the circumstances of his stroke:

> Alright...Uh...stroke and uh...I...huh tawanna guy...h...h...hot tub and...And the...two days when uh...Hos...uh...huh hospital and uh...amet...am...ambulance. (Dick et al., 2001, p. 760)

Broca's aphasia is primarily characterized by an expressive-language deficit—or trouble producing language. These symptoms make sense. Broca's area is one of the locations of the brain that manages motor movement. To produce speech, you must move your lips and tongue. Therefore, it makes sense that these individuals have trouble with speech production.

FIGURE 9.1

Broca's Area and Wernicke's Area: Two Regions of the Brain that Are Commonly Associated with Aphasia.

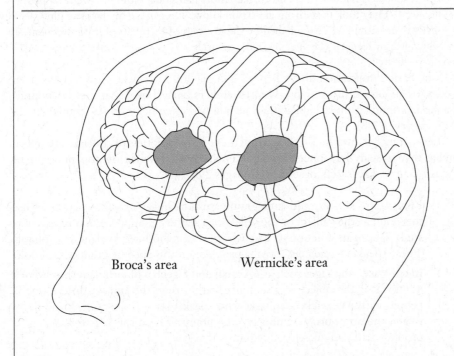

Broca's area   Wernicke's area

However, people with Broca's aphasia may also have some trouble with language comprehension (Dick et al., 2001; Martin & Wu, 2005). For example, they may be unable understand the difference between "He showed her baby the pictures" and "He showed her the baby pictures" (Jackendoff, 1994, p. 149).

A second area that processes language is known as Wernicke's area. Wernicke's area is located toward the back of the brain. ("Wernicke" is pronounced either "*Ver*-nih-kee" or "*Wer*-nih-kee.") Damage to **Wernicke's area** typically produces serious difficulties understanding language (Gazzaniga et al., 2009; Harley, 2001). In fact, people with **Wernicke's aphasia** often have such severe problems with language comprehension that they cannot understand basic instructions such as, "Point to the telephone" or "Show me the picture of the watch."

However, many people with Wernicke's aphasia also have problems with language production, as well as language comprehension. Specifically, their spoken language is often wordy and confused. They usually have relatively few pauses, compared to someone with Broca's aphasia (Gazzaniga et al., 2009; Harley, 2001).

Here's how a person with Wernicke's aphasia tried to describe the circumstances of his stroke:

> It just suddenly had a feffert and all the feffort had gone with it. It even stepped my horn. They took them from earth you know. They make my favorite nine to severed and now I'm a been habed by the uh stam of fortment of my annulment which is now forever. (Dick et al., 2001, p. 761)

The basic information about Broca's aphasia and Wernicke's aphasia has been known for about a century. However, researchers have shown that these two kinds of aphasia are much more similar than people had once believed (Gazzaniga et al., 2009; Harley, 2008).

Let's consider another reason why these two varieties of aphasia are more similar than researchers once thought. This reason focuses on the problem of English-centered research, described on pages 299–300.

1. English speakers use the same grammatical form for a noun, whether we use this noun as the subject or the object of a sentence. Suppose that researchers study speech production in English speakers who have Wernicke's aphasia. These speakers *would not* reveal a problem on this specific grammatical task.

2. In contrast, languages such as German and Czech add letters to the end of a noun if it is the object of a sentence, rather than the subject. Interestingly, people with Wernicke's aphasia who speak German and Czech often fail to add the appropriate endings to the nouns. These speakers *would reveal* a problem with language production.

In short, we see that the two kinds of aphasia can create difficulties for both language comprehension and language production. These difficulties are even more likely when we examine some languages other than English (Dick et al., 2001).

Hemispheric Specialization. We noted at the beginning of this section that the early researchers examined people with aphasia. These scientists also noticed that individuals with speech disorders typically had more severe damage in the left hemisphere of the brain, rather than the right hemisphere. During the mid-1900s, researchers began a more systematic study of lateralization. **Lateralization** means that each hemisphere of the brain has somewhat different functions.

If you've read about lateralization in a popular magazine or Web site—rather than an academic resource—you may have seen a statement such as, "Language is localized in the left hemisphere of the brain." However, this statement is too strong. Yes, most neurolinguistic studies find greater activation in the left hemisphere than in the right (Borst et al., 2011; Gazzaniga et al., 2009; Traxler, 2012). Still, for about 5% of right-handers and about 50% of left-handers, language is either localized in the right hemisphere or is processed equally by both hemispheres (Kinsbourne, 1998).

The left hemisphere does indeed perform most of the work in language processing, for the majority of people. The left hemisphere is especially active during speech perception; it quickly selects the most likely interpretation of a sound (Gernsbacher & Kaschak, 2003; Scott, 2005). It is also very active when you are reading or trying to understand the meaning of a statement (Gernsbacher & Kaschak, 2003). In addition, high-imagery sentences activate the left hemisphere (Just et al., 2004).

For many years, people thought that the right hemisphere did not play a major role in language processing. However, we now know that this hemisphere does perform some tasks. For example, the right hemisphere is active when you are paying attention to the emotional tone of a message (Gernsbacher & Kaschak, 2003; Vingerhoets et al., 2003). It also plays a role in appreciating humor (Harley, 2010). In general, then, the right hemisphere is responsible for more abstract language tasks (Gernsbacher & Kaschak, 2003).

The left and right hemispheres often work together on tasks such as interpreting subtle word meanings, resolving ambiguities, and combining the meaning of several sentences (Beeman et al., 2000; Grodzinsky, 2006). For example, suppose that you are one of the majority of individuals for whom the left hemisphere is dominant for language. Imagine that you see the following ambiguous message, which I once spotted on a bumper sticker:

SOMETIMES I WAKE UP GRUMPY.
OTHER TIMES I LET HIM SLEEP IN.

On seeing the phrase, "SOMETIMES I WAKE UP GRUMPY," your left hemisphere is active in constructing a meaning in which GRUMPY refers to "I" (that is, the owner of the car). After reading the next sentence, "OTHER TIMES I LET HIM SLEEP IN," your right hemisphere is activated when you search for a less obvious interpretation, in which GRUMPY refers to another person. Fortunately, for people have normal brain functions, both hemispheres work together in a complementary fashion (Gazzaniga et al., 2009).

Neuroimaging Research in Adults Without Aphasia. During the past decade, researchers have increasingly used the fMRI technique to investigate language in humans. As we noted in Chapter 1, **functional magnetic resonance imaging (fMRI)** is based on the principle that oxygen-rich blood is an index of brain activity in a particular region (Cacioppo & Berntson, 2005b; Kalat, 2009; Mason & Just, 2006).

An fMRI is superior to a PET scan because it can detect changes that occur very quickly. An fMRI is also safer than a PET scan, because a PET scan requires an injection of radioactive material. However, one disadvantage is that fMRI values can be inaccurate when participants move their heads even slightly (Saffran & Schwartz, 2003). You can guess, therefore, that fMRIs are more suitable for language comprehension than for language production. (Try talking without moving your mouth, your tongue, or any other portion of your head!)

Research using the fMRI technique shows that several regions of both hemispheres process semantic information; language comprehension is not confined to just a small region of the cortex. Let's examine two areas of research using the fMRI method, first with language tasks that are typically associated with the left hemisphere and second with a language task typically associated with the right hemisphere.

1. *Using the fMRI method to study language in the left hemisphere.*
For many decades, researchers have speculated about the specific brain locations associated with language (Kanwisher, 2010). As you saw in Chapter 2, researchers have identified a specific region that is responsible for face recognition. This region is the inferotemporal cortex, located in the lower portion of the temporal cortex (see p. 38).

However, neurolinguists have been less successful in identifying specific areas responsible for a variety of language-comprehension tasks. Nancy Kanwisher (2010) explains an important reason for this problem. As it happens, there are large individual differences in the anatomical structure of the language-related regions of brain. Suppose that researchers give 40 participants a very specific language task, and these reseachers gather fMRI data while the participants perform this task. The researchers then combine these data, across all participants. Unfortunately, the individual differences are so strong that the fMRIs would not be able to identify one specific region of the brain that performs this specific language task.

Several researchers at Massachusetts Institute of Technology have devised a new technique, called the **language-localizer task**, which compensates for the problem of individual differences. For example, Evelina Fedorenko, Michael Behr, and Nancy Kanwisher (2011) began their study of each person with several relatively complex language tasks that lasted 10 to 15 minutes. The researchers gathered fMRI data during this period, and this information allowed them to create a "linguistic map" that applied only to this specific person.

Later, the researchers tested each person on a variety of language and nonlanguage tests. Then they tried to figure out whether certain parts of each person's brain might respond only to language tasks. Using this technique, Fedorenko, Behr, and Kanwisher (2011) were able to identify specific regions of the left frontal lobe that responded only to language tasks, but not to other kinds of cognitive tasks such as performing mathematical problems or using spatial working memory.

In further research using this individual-differences approach, Evelina Fedorenko, Alfonso Nieto-Castañón, and Nancy Kanwisher (2011) were able to locate portions of the left hemisphere that process specific linguistic information. For example, one location responded more vigorously to sentences than to "nonwords" consisting of jumbled letters. This new approach to neurolinguistics will pinpoint additional portions of the brain that each correspond to a specific language task.

2. *Using the fMRI method to study language in the right hemisphere.*
Try Demonstration 9.4 before you read further. The discussion of hemispheric specialization (on pp. 310–311) emphasized that the right hemisphere plays an

important role in language comprehension, even though the left hemisphere receives most of the media publicity. Morton Ann Gernsbacher and David Robertson (2005) provide a good example of the subtlety of right-hemisphere processing. Specifically, they created several sets of sentences, such as those shown in Demonstration 9.4.

The first set of sentences in this demonstration began with "A." The second set of sentences were identical, except that they began with "The." Would you expect such a subtle change to make a difference in the fMRI patterns? Gernsbacher and Robertson (2005) found that the two sets of sentences produced virtually identical patterns of activation in the left hemisphere. In contrast, the right hemisphere responded very differently to the two sets.

Demonstration 9.4

Reading Two Sets of Sentences

A. Read the following set of sentences:

> A grandmother sat at a table.
> A young child played in a backyard.
> A mother talked on a telephone.
> A husband drove a tractor.
> A grandchild walked up to a door.
> A little boy pouted and acted bored.
> A grandmother promised to bake cookies.
> A wife looked out at a field.
> A family was worried about some crops.

B. Now read the following set of sentences:

> The grandmother sat at a table.
> The young child played in a backyard.
> The mother talked on a telephone.
> The husband drove a tractor.
> The grandchild walked up to a door.
> The little boy pouted and acted bored.
> The grandmother promised to bake cookies.
> The wife looked out at a field.
> The family was worried about some crops.

Now answer this question: The first set and the second set differ only with respect to the first word in each sentence. However, did you have a general feeling that the two sets differed in the overall meaning that they conveyed?

Source: Gernsbacher, M. A., & Robertson, D. A. (2005). Watching the brain comprehend discourse. In A. F. Healy (Ed.), *Experimental cognitive psychology and its applications* (pp. 157–167). Washington, DC: American Psychological Association.

As Gernsbacher and Robertson emphasize, when a series of sentences uses the word "The," these sentences seem to create a cohesive story in which the grandmother, the child, and other family members are connected with each other. In contrast, the string of sentences with the word "A" seems disconnected; the characters don't seem like a cohesive unit. Impressively, the right hemisphere manages to respond differently to connected language than to disconnected language.

How the Mirror System Can Facilitate Communication. A relatively recent topic in neurolinguistics focuses on the *mirror system*. The **mirror system** is a network of neurons in the brain's motor cortex; these neurons are activated when you watch someone perform an action (Gallese et al., 2011; Gazzaniga et al., 2009; Glenberg, 2011a). This concept was initially reported by Giacomo Rizzolatti and his colleagues (Rizzolatti & Craighero, 2009; Rizzolatti et al., 1996). These researchers recorded the responses of single neurons in the motor cortex of several monkeys, as they watched a researcher breaking open a peanut; this was an action that the monkeys had frequently done. Surprisingly, each monkey's neurons responded vigorously to this particular action. In fact, these responses were very similar to the response pattern when the monkeys *themselves* broke open a peanut.

Additional research focuses on the mirror system in humans. For example, Beatriz Calvo-Merino and her colleagues (2005) gathered fMRI data for individuals who were experts in classical ballet, while they watched (a) videos of classical ballet and (b) videos of a Brazilian form of martial arts, called *capoeira*. Their fMRIs showed significantly greater activation in the motor-cortex areas relevant to ballet movements, and relatively little activation in the areas relevant to capoeira. In contrast, individuals who were experts in capoeira showed the reverse activation pattern. In other words, experts can grasp meaning by *watching* another person, when they have fully developed the appropriate motor "vocabulary."

Rizzolatti and Craighero (2009) discuss another important point. Language is not limited to spoken and written messages; physical actions are also important. Specifically, these authors emphasize that sound-based language is *not* the only way that people can communicate with one another. They emphasize that sign language, based on gestures, represents a fully structured system of communication.

At this point, you might wonder how the topic of mirror neurons might be relevant to your own language. Neurolinguists do not agree about the details of this process (Gallese et al., 2011; Glenberg, 2011b). However, it appears that communication goes beyond hearing auditory stimuli and reading written material, because mirror neurons also play a role in language comprehension (Glenberg, 2011a, 2011b). Mirror neurons may be especially active when we try to listen to someone talking in a noisy setting—a setting where we really need assistance (Glenberg, 2011b). Apparently, we can also comprehend messages from the actions of other people.

In summary, the neurolinguistics research highlights the complexity of our language skills. We've considered (a) studies about individuals with aphasia,

(b) information about hemispheric specialization, (c) fMRI research, and (d) studies focusing on the mirror system. Neurolinguists still have a long distance to travel, but they have identified some important information about the coordinated brain regions that allow us to understand language.

In the first section of this chapter, we examined the basic structure of language, the history of psycholinguistics, factors affecting comprehension, and neurolinguistics. Let's summarize this background knowledge and then turn our attention to the important topic of reading.

ⓢ Section Summary: *The Nature of Language*

1. Some of the central concepts in psycholinguistics are the phoneme, the morpheme, morphology, syntax, grammar, semantics, semantic memory, and pragmatics.

2. Most psycholinguistics research focuses on English, which has simpler grammar and more variable pronunciation than most other languages. Therefore, we do not know whether the findings from English speakers can be applied to other languages.

3. According to Noam Chomsky, (a) language skills are innate in humans, (b) language is modular, and (c) the deep structure of a sentence captures its core meaning.

4. Many current psychologists emphasize the meaning of language, rather than linguistic structure. For example, the cognitive-functional approach to language emphasizes that we design our language so that listeners will pay attention to the information we want to emphasize.

5. Sentences are more difficult to understand if they (a) contain negatives, (b) use the passive voice, (c) use complex syntax, and (d) are ambiguous.

6. People typically read quite rapidly; this "good-enough heuristic" usually—but not always—leads us to accurate comprehension.

7. Neurolinguistic research on adults with aphasia suggests that damage in Broca's area usually leads to difficulty in producing language, whereas damage in Wernicke's area usually leads to difficulty in understanding language; however, the distinction is not clear-cut.

8. In general, the left hemisphere performs most components of language processing, such as speech perception and understanding meaning. However, the right hemisphere performs abstract language task such as creating a cohesive story.

9. Recent research using fMRIs highlights some specific brain regions in the left hemisphere that are responsible for well-defined language tasks such as

distinguishing between sentences and nonwords. Also, fMRI research confirms that the right hemisphere processes subtle distinctions in meaning.

10. Recent research on mirror neurons—in the brain's motor cortex—provides information about some nonverbal aspects of communication.

BASIC READING PROCESSES

Reading seems so simple to most adults that we forget how challenging the task is for most children, as well as for some adults (Traxler, 2012). Take a minute to think about the impressive variety of cognitive tasks you perform when reading a paragraph like this one. Reading requires you to use many cognitive processes that we have discussed in previous chapters. For example, you must recognize letters (Chapter 2), move your eyes across the page (Chapter 3), use working memory to remember material from the sentence you are currently processing (Chapter 4), and recall earlier material that is stored in long-term memory (Chapter 5).

Reading also requires more sophisticated cognitive activites. For example, you need to use metamemory and metacomprehension to think about your memory for earlier material in this book, as well as your comprehension of the paragraph you are reading right now (Chapter 6). In some cases, you must also construct a mental image to represent the scene of the action in the passage you are reading (Chapter 7). In addition, you should consult your semantic memory, your schemas, and your scripts when you try to understand a paragraph (Chapter 8).

In Demonstration 9.1 and throughout this book, we emphasize that the cognitive processes are interrelated (Theme 4). Reading is an important activity that requires virtually every cognitive process discussed in this textbook. Despite the complexity of the reading process, however, adults typically don't think about the cognitive effort that is required when we read (Gorrell, 1999). For example, we can silently identify an isolated word in about 200 milliseconds, which is 1/5 of a second. In addition, we manage to read quickly, typically at the rate of about 255 words per minute (Rayner et al., 2006). Consistent with Theme 2, reading is remarkably efficient and accurate.

Here's an additional reason to admire your reading skills: In English, we do not have a one-to-one correspondence between letters of the alphabet and speech sounds. These irregular pronunciations make English more challenging than languages with consistent pronunciations, such as Spanish or Russian (Rayner et al., 2003; Traxler, 2012). In fact, try Demonstration 9.5 to illustrate this point. As we noted at the beginning of this chapter, most of the psycholinguistic research examines people whose language is English. Furthermore, we cannot generalize this research to Chinese readers, because their language uses symbols to represent complete words (Qu et al., 2011; Rayner et al., 2008; Traxler, 2012).

Let's begin this second section of the chapter—on basic reading processes—by comparing written language with spoken language. Then we'll consider the two pathways we can use when recognizing words. This second section provides you with

---

🌀 Demonstration 9.5

Noticing that Letters of the Alphabet Do Not Have a One-to-One Correspondence with Speech Sounds

Each of the words below has a somewhat different pronunciation for the two-letter sequence "ea." Read each word aloud and notice the variety of phonemes that can be produced with those two letters.

beauty	deal	react
bread	great	séance
clear	heard	bear
create	knowledgeable	dealt

As you have demonstrated, this two-letter sequence can be pronounced in twelve different ways. Furthermore, each phoneme in the English language can be spelled in a variety of ways. Go back over this list of words and try to think of another word that has a different spelling for that particular sound. For example, the *eau* phoneme in *beauty* is like the *iew* phoneme in *view*.

Source: Based on Underwood & Batt, 1996.

---

a background for the third section in this chapter. This third section examines how we understand larger units of language—such as stories—in both written and spoken language.

Comparing Written and Spoken Language

In Chapter 2, we explored several components of spoken language comprehension. In this section on written language comprehension, we encounter a somewhat different set of challenges. Reading differs in many important ways from the comprehension of spoken language (Ainsworth & Greenberg, 2006; Dahan & Magnuson, 2006; Gaskell, 2009b; Nelson et al., 2005; Saffran & Schwartz, 2003; Traxler, 2012; Treiman & Kessler, 2009):

1. Reading is visual and is spread out across space, whereas speech is auditory and is spread out across time.
2. Readers can control the rate of input, whereas listeners usually cannot.
3. Readers can re-scan the written input, whereas listeners must rely much more heavily on their working memory.
4. Readers usually encounter standardized, error-free input, whereas listeners often need to cope with variability, gramatical errors, sloppy pronunciation, and interfering stimuli.

5. Readers can see discrete boundaries between words, whereas listeners often encounter unclear boundaries in spoken language, as you saw on page 60 in Chapter 2.

6. Readers encounter only the stimuli on a page, whereas listeners encounter both nonverbal cues and auditory cues, such as emphasized words and variations in pace. Researchers are just beginning to appreciate the importance of these additional cues (Glenberg, 2011a, 2011b).

7. Children require elaborate teaching to master some written languages—such as written English—but they learn spoken languages much more easily.

8. Adult readers typically learn new words more quickly when they appear in a written form, rather than a spoken form.

As you can imagine, these eight characteristics of written language have important implications for our cognitive processes. For example, we can consult the words on a page when we want to make sense out of a passage in a book; in contrast, we seldom have this luxury with spoken language.

Despite the differences between written and spoken language, however, both processes require us to understand words and appreciate the meaning of sentences. In fact, the research on individual differences highlights the similarity between the two comprehension processes. For adults, scores on reading comprehension tests are strongly correlated with scores on oral comprehension tests; typically, the correlation is about +.90 (Rayner et al., 2001).

Reading Words: Theoretical Approaches

So far, our examination of reading in this textbook has emphasized how we identify alphabetical letters (Chapter 2), how our saccadic eye movements scan a line of text (Chapter 3), and how working memory plays a role in reading (Chapter 4). Now we'll address an important question about reading: How do we look at a pattern of letters and actually recognize that word? For example, how do you manage to look at the eleven letters in the fourth word in this paragraph and realize that it says *examination*? How about a word with an unusual spelling, such as *choir* or *aisle*?

Researchers have debated whether readers actually "sound out" words while reading a passage. Some researchers conclude that readers always sound out the words, and other researchers conclude that they never sound them out. In the current era, the debate is mostly resolved (Coltheart, 2005). You have probably completed enough psychology courses to guess the answer: Sometimes readers sound out the words, and sometimes they do not. In fact, the **dual-route approach to reading** specifies that skilled readers employ both (1) a direct-access route and (2) an indirect-access route (Coltheart, 2005; Harley, 2008; Treiman & Kessler, 2009).

1. Sometimes you read a word by a **direct-access route**; you recognize this word *directly* through vision, without "sounding out" the words. For example, you look at the word *choir* and the visual pattern is sufficient to access the word and

its meaning. You are especially likely to use direct access if the word has an irregular spelling and cannot be "sounded out"—for example, the words *one* or *through*.

2. Other times, you read a word by an **indirect-access route**; as soon as you see a word, you translate the ink marks on the page into some form of sound, before you can access a word and its meaning (Harley, 2010; Treiman et al., 2003). You are especially likely to use indirect access if the word has a regular spelling and can be sounded out—for example, the words *ten* and *cabinet*.

Notice why this second kind of process is indirect. According to this explanation, you must go through the intermediate step of converting the visual stimulus into a phonological (sound) stimulus. Think about whether you seem to use this intermediate step when you read. As you read this sentence, for example, do you have a speech-like representation of the words? You probably don't actually move your lips or say the words out loud when you read. But do you seem to have an auditory image for some of the words that you are reading? Let's now discuss the research.

The Direct-Access Route. A classic study demonstrates that people can recognize a word visually, without paying attention to the sound of that word. Bradshaw and Nettleton (1974) showed people pairs of words that were similar in spelling, but different in sound, such as *mown–down, horse–worse*, and *quart–part*. In one condition, the participants were instructed to read the first word silently and then pronounce the second word out loud. Now, if they had been translating the first member of a pair into sound, the sound of *mown* would interfere with pronouncing *down* out loud.

However, the results showed that the participants experienced no hesitation in pronouncing the second word. This finding—and other similar studies—suggests that we can go directly to the word; we do not silently pronounce every word during normal reading (Coltheart, 2005).

The Indirect-Access Route. Now let's shift to some research that supports the indirect-access approach. Many studies suggest that we often translate visual stimuli into sound during reading (Coltheart, 2005). Furthermore, the sound coding may enhance working memory, providing an auditory image to assist the visual image during reading (Harley, 2008; Rayner et al., 2003).

A study by Luo and his coauthors (1998) provides evidence for the indirect-access approach in college students. These researchers instructed the students to read a series of pairs of words and decide whether the two words were related or unrelated in meaning. A typical pair in the experimental condition was LION–BARE. As you know, the word BARE sounds the same as the word BEAR, which is indeed semantically related to LION.

The students frequently made errors on these pairs, because they incorrectly judged the two words as being semantically related. This error pattern suggests that they were silently pronouncing the word pairs when they made the judgments. In contrast, they made relatively few errors on control-condition word pairs, such as

> ## 🌀 Demonstration 9.6
>
> ### Reading Tongue Twisters
>
> Read each of the following tongue twisters silently to yourself:
>
> 1. The seasick sailor staggered as he zigzagged sideways.
> 2. Peter Piper picked a peck of pickled peppers. A peck of pickled peppers Peter Piper picked.
> 3. She sells seashells down by the seashore.
> 4. Congressional caucus questions controversial CIA-Contra-Crack connection.
> 5. Sheila and Celia slyly shave the cedar shingle splinter.
>
> Now be honest. Could you "hear" yourself pronouncing these words as you were reading? Did you have to read them more slowly than other sentences in this book?

LION–BEAN. In this word pair, the second word looked like the word BEAR, although it did not sound the same.

Word sounds may be especially important when children begin to read. Numerous studies demonstrate that children with high phonological awareness have superior reading skills. That is, the children who are able to identify sound patterns in a word also receive higher scores on reading achievement tests (Levy, 1999; Share, 2008; Wagner & Stanovich, 1996; Ziegler et al., 2010).

Perhaps you're thinking that children may need to translate the printed word into sound. After all, children even move their lips when they read, but adults usually do not. Try Demonstration 9.6 and see whether you change your mind. Adults read "tongue twisters" very slowly, which indicates that—at least in some circumstances—they are indeed translating the printed words into sounds (Harley, 2008; Keller et al., 2003).

As we noted earlier, the dual-route approach has the definite advantage of flexibility. This approach argues that the characteristics of the reading material determine whether access is indirect or direct. For instance, you may use indirect access the first time you see a long, uncommon word; you may use direct access for a common word (Bernstein & Carr, 1996; Harley, 2008).

The dual-route approach also argues that people's reading skills can determine whether they use indirect or direct access. Beginning readers would be especially likely to sound out the words, using indirect access. More advanced young readers would be especially likely to recognize the words directly from print. Adults also vary in their reading styles. People who are relatively poor readers primarily use indirect access. In contrast, people who are good readers primarily use direct access (Harley, 2008; Jared et al., 1999).

At present, the dual-route approach seems like a useful compromise. The dual-route approach is also consistent with brain-imaging research (Harley, 2008; Jobard et al., 2003). Readers can identify words either directly or indirectly, depending on their own reading skills and the characteristics of the text.

Implications for Teaching Reading to Children

Throughout this chapter, we have noted that English is an "outlier language," because of the numerous irregular pronunciations for English words. Unfortunately, irregular pronunciation has important implications for teaching children to read in English.

Consider, for example, a study that measured children's reading skills in 14 different European countries; this standardized test was administered at the end of first grade. Languages such as Spanish and German have extremely predictable pronunciation, and children learning to read these languages had close to 100% reading-accuracy scores on a standardized test. Languages such as French and Portuguese are less predictable, and these children achieved reading-accuracy scores of about 80%. English was the least predictable of the languages, and these children achieved reading-accuracy scores of only 34% (Seymour et al., 2003; Ziegler et al., 2010).

So, how should children be taught to read English? For many years, reading teachers and reading researchers debated about the most effective way to teach reading. In general, those who favored the direct-access approach also favored the whole-word approach. The **whole-word approach** argues that readers can directly connect the written word—as an entire unit—with the meaning that this word represents (Rayner et al., 2001).

The whole-word approach emphasizes that the correspondence between the written and spoken codes in English is notoriously complex, as we saw in Demonstration 9.5. Supporters therefore argue that children should not learn to emphasize the way a word sounds. Instead, the whole-word approach encourages children to identify a word in terms of its context within a sentence. One problem, however, is that even skilled adult readers achieve only about 25% accuracy when they look at an incomplete sentence and guess which word is missing (Perfetti, 2003; Snow & Juel, 2005).

In contrast, people who favor the indirect-access hypothesis typically support the phonics approach. The **phonics approach** states that readers recognize words by trying to pronounce the individual letters in the word. If your grade school teachers told you to "sound it out" when you stumbled on a new word, they championed the phonics approach.

The phonics approach argues that speech sound is a necessary intermediate step in reading. It also emphasizes developing young children's awareness of phonemes. According to the research, it's clear that phonics training helps children who have reading problems (Harley, 2008; Perfetti, 2011; Traxler, 2012). For example, a meta-analysis of 34 studies showed that phonological training programs had a major impact on children's reading skills (Bus & van IJzendoorn, 1999).

For many years, the debate between the whole-word supporters and the phonics supporters was feverish (McGuinness, 2004; Traxler, 2012). In the current decade, however, most educators and researchers support some form of a compromise: Children should be taught to use phonics to access the pronunciation of a word; they should also use context as a backup to confirm their initial hypothesis. Even the strongest phonics supporters would also agree that teachers should encourage children to recognize some words by sight alone. Teachers should also emphasize oral language throughout the curriculum (Hulme & Snowling, 2011).

Furthermore, educators typically favor some components of an approach called the whole-language approach (as opposed to the whole-*word* approach). According to the **whole-language approach**, reading instruction should emphasize meaning, and it should be enjoyable, to increase children's enthusiasm about learning to read. Children should read interesting stories and experiment with writing before they are expert spellers. They also need to use reading throughout their classroom experiences (Luria, 2006; McGuinness, 2004; Snow & Juel, 2005). An additional benefit is this: When children improve their reading skills, they also improve their ability in mathmatics (Glenberg et al., 2011).

In addition, children need to have books that they can read outside of school, because even children with limited reading skills can benefit from leisure reading (Mol & Bus, 2011). There's even a social benefit when children have early experiences with reading. Specifically, preschool children become more socially aware, when their parents read to them. According to research by Raymond Mar and his colleagues, children whose parents frequently read to them are especially aware of other people's thoughts and feelings (Mar, 2011; Mar et al., 2010). This effect held true, even after the researchers eliminated several other potential explanations.

Before we leave this section on basic reading, however, we need to emphasize an important point. Our discussion assumes that children and adults have had the opportunity to learn how to read. In Canada and the United States, about 98% of adults achieve basic literacy (Luria, 2006). However, the reality is that more than 800 million adults throughout the world are illiterate. Approximately two-thirds of these individuals are women. Clearly, a person who cannot read will face tremendous disadvantages with respect to employment, health care, and everyday communication.

Section Summary: *Basic Reading Processes*

1. Reading is a challenging cognitive task that differs from understanding spoken language in many respects. For example, readers can control the rate of input and they can re-scan the text; furthermore, there are clear-cut boundaries between words.

2. The dual-route approach to reading argues that readers sometimes recognize a word directly from the printed letters (by direct access), and sometimes they convert the printed letters into a phonological code to access the word and its meaning (by indirect access).

3. Skilled adult readers are especially likely to use direct access. In contrast, beginning readers and less skilled adult readers are likely to sound out the words and understand meaning by indirect access.

4. According to research conducted in 14 European countries, when children learn to read languages like Spanish and German, they achieve almost perfect reading accuracy on a standardized test by the end of first grade, in contrast to only 34% of children learning to read English.

5. In teaching young students to read, the whole-word approach emphasizes visual recognition of words, whereas the phonics approach emphasizes sounding out the word. Most educators and researchers favor a combination of these approaches.

6. The whole-language approach emphasizes language meaning, as well as integrating reading throughout the curriculum and reading books at home.

7. Children with poor reading skills can benefit from early exposure to reading; another benefit is that preschoolers are more aware of other people's feelings if their parents read to them. Unfortunately, close to one billion adults throughout the world are illiterate.

UNDERSTANDING DISCOURSE

We began this chapter with an overview of the nature of language; that overview considered both linguistic theory and the biological basis of language. Then we explored basic reading processes. You'll notice that all these topics focus on the way we process small units of language, such as a phoneme, a letter, a word, or an isolated sentence. In your daily life, however, you are continually processing **discourse**, that is, interrelated units of language that are larger than a sentence (Traxler, 2012; Treiman et al., 2003). You listen to the news on the radio, you hear a friend telling a story, you follow the instructions for assembling a bookcase . . . and you read your cognitive psychology textbook.

In Chapters 1 and 8, we considered Frederic Bartlett's (1932) research, which focused on these larger linguistic units. Specifically, Bartlett demonstrated that people's recall of stories becomes more consistent with their schemas after a long delay. However, for the next four decades, psychologists and linguists primarily studied words and isolated sentences. In fact, the topic of discourse processing was not revived until the mid-1970s (Butcher & Kintsch, 2003; Graesser et al., 2003). Fortunately, research on discourse comprehension is now an active topic in psycholinguistics (Lynch, 2010; Traxler, 2012).

So far in this chapter, we've emphasized how context can help us understand sounds, letters, and words. Now we'll see that context also helps us comprehend larger linguistic units. As Chapter 8 pointed out, general background knowledge and expertise help to facilitate our conceptual understanding. Research on discourse comprehension also emphasizes the importance of scripts, schemas, and expertise (e.g., Harley, 2008; Mayer, 2004; Zwaan & Rapp, 2006).

At all levels of language comprehension, we see additional evidence of Theme 5. That is, the processing of the physical stimuli (bottom-up processing) interacts with the context provided by our expectations and previous knowledge (top-down processing). This interaction is especially prominent when we form an integrated, cohesive representation of the text and when we draw **inferences**, which are conclusions that go beyond the isolated phrase or sentence (Harley, 2010).

Our exploration of discourse comprehension in this section focuses on the following selected topics: (1) forming an integrated representation of the text, (2) drawing inferences during reading, (3) teaching metacomprehension skills, (4) individual differences in test anxiety and discourse comprehension, and (5) a technique that can assess the semantic content of discourse.

Forming an Integrated Representation of the Text

Reading comprehension is much more complicated than simply combining words and phrases. Readers must also gather information together and remember the various concepts, so that this information is both cohesive and memorable (Traxler, 2012; Zwaan & Rapp, 2006). In everyday life, we try to figure out the mental state of other people in our lives, a concept called **theory of mind** (Mar, 2011). For example, we might say, "Judith is usually very kind, but she really was mean to Kathy. Maybe she is worried about her final exams." Similarly, readers often try to figure out the mental states of the people they read about in a story or a book.

Listeners—as well as readers—form integrated representations when they hear spoken language. They also remember information and draw inferences when they are listening (e.g., Butcher & Kintsch, 2003; Lynch, 2010; Marslen-Wilson et al., 1993; Poole & Samraj, 2010). However, almost all the research examines discourse processing during reading, rather than during listening.

The research on reading shows that skilled readers frequently organize and integrate information into a cohesive story (Zwaan & Rapp, 2006). For example, look back at Demonstration 9.4 and the description of Gernsbacher and Robertson's (2005) study, on page 313. These researchers demonstrated that readers are attuned to subtle linguistic evidence. Specifically, readers realize that a series of sentences forms a cohesive story if all the sentences begin with the word *the*, but not when the sentences begin with *a*.

Furthermore, when we form a cohesive representation, we often construct a mental model of the material we are reading (Long et al., 2006; Traxler, 2012; Zwaan & Rapp, 2006). In Chapter 7, for example, we saw that readers create cognitive maps, based on a written description of various locations (pp. 239–240).

Readers also construct internal representations that include descriptions of the characters in a story. This descriptive information may include the characters' occupations, relationships, emotional states, personal traits, goals, and actions (Carpenter et al., 1995; Trabasso et al., 1995). In fact, by middle school, some children can monitor events in the stories they are reading, noting twists in a story's plot or a character's unusual behaviors (Bohn-Gettler et al., 2011). However, some novelists can strain even an adult reader's working memory and long-term memory. For example, one of the sentences in James Joyce's *Ulysses* is 12,931 words long (Harley, 2010).

Readers often need to maintain these internal representations in long-term memory for many pages of a novel (Butcher & Kintsch, 2003; Gerrig & McKoon,

2001). In addition, readers often make inferences that go beyond the information supplied by the writer. Let's consider this topic in more detail.

Drawing Inferences During Reading

One of my favorite novels is called *The Kite Runner*. The novel follows two young boys growing up in Kabul, Afghanistan. Amir, the protagonist, is the son of a wealthy, influential man named Baba. Amir's friend, Hassan, lives nearby in the home of Baba's servant. Readers do not need to have a sophisticated knowledge about either social class in Afghanistan or the series of tragic political wars in this country. Even before we finish the first chapter, we know that the friendship between Amir and Hassan must have an unhappy ending. Whenever we read, we activate important mental processes by making inferences that go beyond the information presented on the printed page.

When we make an inference during reading, we use our world knowledge in order to access information that is not explicitly stated in a written passage (Harley, 2008; Lea et al., 2005; Traxler, 2012). We discussed inferences in Chapter 8 in connection with the influence of schemas on memory. Inferences are also important in reading. People combine the information they are reading, together with the information presented in a passage. Then they draw a reasonable conclusion based on that combination. Consistent with Theme 1, people are active information processors.

Let's explore several issues that researchers have explored, in connection with inferences during reading. First, we'll consider the constructionist view of inferences. Then we'll discuss factors that encourage inferences. Our final topic is higher-level inferences. Before you read further, try Demonstration 9.7.

---

⑨ Demonstration 9.7

Reading a Passage of Text

Read the following passage, and notice whether it seems to flow smoothly and logically:

1. Dick had a week's vacation due
2. and he wanted to go to a place
3. where he could swim and sunbathe.
4. He bought a book on travel.
5. Then he looked at the ads
6. in the travel section of the Sunday newspaper.
7. He went to his local travel agent
8. and asked for a plane ticket to Alaska.
9. He paid for it with his charge card.

Source: Huitema, J. S., Dopkins, S., Klin, C. M., & Myers, J. L. (1993). Connecting goals and actions during reading. *Journal of Experimental Psychology: Learning, Memory, and Cognition, 19*, 1054.

The Constructionist View of Inferences. According to the **constructionist view of inferences**, readers usually draw inferences about the causes of events and the relationships between events. When you read a novel, for instance, you construct inferences about a character's motivations, personality, and emotions. You develop expectations about new plot developments, about the writer's point of view, and so forth (Sternberg & Ben-Zeev, 2001; Zwaan & Rapp, 2006).

This perspective is called a "constructionist view" because readers actively construct cohesive explanations when they integrate the current information with all the relevant information from the previous parts of the text, as well as their background knowledge (Harley, 2008; Traxler, 2012; Zwaan & Singer, 2003). The constructionist view argues that people typically draw inferences, even when the related topics are separated by several irrelevant paragraphs.

Let's consider a classic study by John Huitema and his coauthors (1993), who studied brief stories like the one you read in Demonstration 9.7. The introductory material in this demonstration led you to believe that Dick will soon be lounging on a sunny beach. You drew this inference on line 3, and this inference is contradicted five lines later, rather than in the very next sentence. The dependent variable here was the amount of time that participants had taken to read the crucial line about Dick's travel destination (line 8).

Huitema and his colleagues (1993) tested four conditions. You saw the far/inconsistent version of the story in Demonstration 9.7. In this version, several lines of text came between the first sentence, which stated the goal, and the inconsistent statement about Alaska. In the near/inconsistent version, the goal and the inconsistent statement were in adjacent sentences. In the far/consistent version, several lines of text separated the goal and a consistent statement (in which Dick asked for a plane ticket to Florida—a place consistent with swimming). In the near/consistent version, the goal and the consistent statement were in adjacent sentences.

As you can see from Figure 9.2, participants in the *near* condition read the consistent version significantly more quickly than the inconsistent version. This finding is not surprising. However, you'll notice that participants in the *far* condition also read the consistent version significantly more quickly than the inconsistent version in the far condition ... even though the relevant portions of the task were separated by four intervening lines.

The data from Huitema and his colleagues (1993) support the constructionist view. Readers clearly try to connect material within a text passage, and they consult information stored in long-term memory, in this case, the enthusiasm and sunbathing. During discourse processing, we try to construct a representation of the text that is internally consistent, even when irrelevant material intervenes (Klin et al., 1999; Rayner & Clifton, 2002; Underwood & Batt, 1996).

In other research, readers talked out loud about the text passages that they were reading (Suh & Trabasso, 1993; Trabasso & Suh, 1993). In some of these stories, the main character had an initial goal that was blocked but later fulfilled. About 90% of the participants specifically mentioned the initial goal during their comments about the last line. Suh and Trabasso emphasized that readers create causal inferences in order to integrate discourse and construct a well-organized story.

FIGURE 9.2

Amount of Time Taken to Read the Crucial Line in the Study by Huitema and His Colleagues (1993), as a Function of the Amount of Separation Between the Goal and the Crucial Line and the Compatibility Between the Goal and the Crucial Line (Consistent vs. Inconsistent).

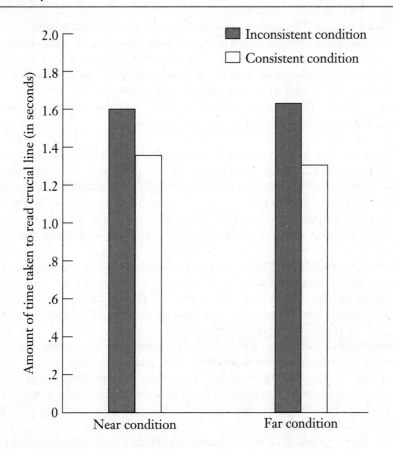

Source: Huitema, J. S., Dopkins, S., Klin, C. M., & Myers, J. L. (1993). Connecting goals and actions during reading. *Journal of Experimental Psychology: Learning, Memory, and Cognition, 19,* 1053–1060.

Factors That Encourage Inferences. Naturally, we do not always draw inferences when we read a passage. For instance, some readers fail to activate information that appeared much earlier in the passage (Harley, 2008; Zwaan & Rapp, 2006). As you might expect, people are more likely to draw inferences if they have a large working-memory capacity (Butcher & Kintsch, 2003; Long et al., 2006). They are also likely to draw inferences if they have excellent metacomprehension skills. These individuals are aware that they need to search for connections between two seemingly unrelated sentences (Ehrlich, 1998; Mayer, 2004).

People are also likely to draw inferences if they have expertise about the topic described in the text (Long et al., 2006). In fact, expertise in an area can compensate for a relatively small working-memory capacity (Butcher & Kintsch, 2003). Other research shows that people are not likely to construct inferences when they are reading scientific texts (Mayer, 2004; Millis & Graesser, 1994).

This part of our discussion has focused on factors that affect inferences, and we have seen that some inferences are more probable than others. In explaining these factors, however, let's recall an important point from Chapter 8: In some cases, we remember our inferences as often as the statements that actually occurred in the text. Our inferences blend with the text, forming a cohesive story. We often retain the gist or general meaning of a passage, forgetting that we constructed some elements that did not actually appear in the story.

Higher-Level Inferences.   Researchers are now exploring higher-level inferences, beyond the level of the paragraph (Harley, 2008; Leavitt & Christenfeld, 2011). For example, some genres of books are especially likely to activate different expectations. Fans of the Harry Potter series—and other magical stories—know that they must suspend their everyday schemas. Of course, Hermione can arrange to be in two locations at the exact same time, and of course, Harry can understand conversations between snakes.

One kind of higher-level inference is based on our own preferences about the way we want a story to turn out. Perhaps you've turned the pages of a fast-paced spy novel and mentally shouted to your favorite character, "Watch out!" In fact, the research shows that readers who are involved in a story do develop strong mental preferences for a particular outcome (Rapp & Gerrig, 2006).

These mental preferences can be so strong that they can actually interfere with readers' ability to judge how the story turned out, making us pause as we try to decide whether that unhappy ending really did occur (Gerrig, 1998; Zwaan & Rapp, 2006). You may even find yourself so hopeful about a happy ending you've constructed that you need to read the final sentences several times, trying to convince yourself that the hero or heroine didn't die!

In summary, people often draw inferences when they read. They integrate material into a cohesive unit, and they are puzzled if they encounter something that contradicts the inferences they drew. People are especially likely to draw inferences if they have a large working-memory capacity or expertise. Inferences may be relatively rare in scientific texts and relatively common in novels. In novels, our own preferences may interfere with text comprehension.

Teaching Metacomprehension Skills

In the second section of this chapter, our discussion of reading examined how educators can teach basic reading skills to young children. Let's now briefly consider how educators can teach older students some important metacomprehension skills.

Chapter 6 focused on the general topic of **metacognition**, which is your knowledge about your cognitive processes, as well as your control of these cognitive processes. An important part of metacognition is **metacomprehension**, a term that refers to your thoughts about comprehension.

Most young children do not have the appropriate cognitive skills for metacomprehension; it's challenging enough to read individual words and sentences (Baker, 2005; Griffith & Ruan, 2005). Furthermore, some aspects of children's reading are counterintuitive. For example, doesn't it seem logical that reading skills would improve if children tried to relate the text to nearby photos? Surprisingly, however, pictures actually *reduce* reading skills (Torcasio & Sweller, 2010).

However, older children, teenagers, and adults can think about their reading and listening strategies (Lynch, 2010). For instance, when you read a book, you know that you should think about your relevant background knowledge. In addition, you consider whether you should read every sentence or else skim through the details. You also know that you should monitor whether you understand the material you have just read (Griffith & Ruan, 2005; Perfetti et al., 2005). Furthermore, you sometimes become aware that your mind has wandered away from the material you are reading (Smallwood & Schooler, 2006).

In the past, educators seldom trained students to develop their metacomprehension skills (Randi et al., 2005). However, educators are currently developing some helpful strategies. For instance, teachers can instruct students in middle school to think out loud, so that they can summarize passages, make predictions about possible outcomes, and describe puzzling sections (Israel & Massey, 2005; Schreiber, 2005; Wolfe & Goldman, 2005).

Individual Differences: Test Anxiety and Reading Comprehension

We've been discussing reading comprehension, a topic that is very important in academic settings. According to numerous studies, people who are high in test anxiety often perform poorly on examinations (Cassady, 2004). Psychologists have usually attributed this poor performance to high levels of worry. The traditional explanation is that worry intrudes on people's consciousness, blocking them from retrieving the correct answers on a test. However, Jerrell Cassady (2004) proposes that test anxiety also decreases students' skills in understanding the information in their textbooks.

Cassady examined the link between anxiety and discourse comprehension by instructing 277 undergraduate students to read several paragraphs from a textbook, and then to read it a second time. Next, everyone completed a measure called the Cognitive Test Anxiety Scale, followed by a multiple-choice test on the earlier textbook material. The students then repeated this procedure with a comparable passage from a different textbook. Then they completed a study-skills survey prior to the multiple-choice test.

Cassady found that scores on the Cognitive Test Anxiety Scale were strongly correlated ($r = -.55$) with performance on the multiple-choice tests. In other words, people who are highly anxious tend to perform poorly on a reading-comprehension test. Scores on the Cognitive Test Anxiety Scale were also strongly correlated ($r = -.66$) with scores on the study-skills survey. In other words, people who are highly anxious tend to report poorer study skills. Surprisingly, however, study skills were not strongly correlated with recall on the multiple-choice test ($r = +.24$).

In a second, similar study, Cassady (2004) found that people with high scores on the Cognitive Test Anxiety Scale also made more errors in summarizing the textbook material. These people also made more errors on a test that assessed their ability to make correct inferences, based on the textbook material. In summary, when people are highly anxious about taking tests, they may experience interference from high levels of worry. In addition, they perform poorly on a variety of tasks related to reading comprehension.

Language Comprehension and Latent Semantic Analysis

Cognitive scientists have developed a variety of computer programs designed to understand language (e.g., Burstein & Chodorow, 2010; Moore & Wiemer-Hastings, 2003; Wolfe et al., 2005). For example, Thomas Landauer and his colleagues created a useful artificial intelligence program (Foltz, 2003; Landauer et al., 2007). Their program, called **latent semantic analysis** (**LSA**), can perform many fairly sophisticated language tasks. For example, LSA can assess creative writing (Davenport & Coulson, 2011).

Furthermore, Arvidsson and his colleagues (2011) used LSA to analyze young adults' self-descriptions, before and after psychotherapy. Their self-descriptions showed significantly greater change than the self-descriptions supplied by people in a control group.

LSA can also assess the amount of semantic similarity between two discourse segments. In fact, LSA can be used to grade essays written by college students (Graesser et al., 2007). For example, suppose that a cognitive psychology textbook contains the following sentence: "The phonological loop responds to the phonetic characteristics of speech but does not evaluate speech for semantic content" (Butcher & Kintsch, 2003, p. 551).

Now imagine that two students are writing a short essay on working memory, for a cognitive psychology exam. With reference to that passage about the phonological loop, Chris writes, "The rehearsal loop that practices speech sounds does not pick up meaning in words. Rather, it just reacts whenever it hears something that sounds like language." On the same exam, Pat writes, "The loop that listens to the words does not understand anything about the phonetic noises that it hears. All it does is listen for noise and then respond by practicing that noise."

LSA's analysis of those two essays concluded that Chris's essay is a more accurate summary of the original text than Pat's essay (Graesser et al., 2007). If you recall the relevant information from Chapter 4, you'll agree with LSA's conclusion.

LSA is indeed impressive, but even its developers note that it cannot match a human grader. Furthermore, all the current programs master just a small component of language comprehension. For example, LSA typically ignores syntax, whereas humans can easily detect syntax errors. In addition, LSA learns only from written text, whereas humans learn from spoken language, facial expressions, and physical gestures (Butcher & Kintsch, 2003). Once again, the artificial intelligence approach to language illustrates humans' tremendous breadth of knowledge, cognitive flexibility, understanding of syntax, and sources of information.

Section Summary: *Understanding Discourse*

1. Psycholinguists are increasingly focusing on discourse processing, or language units that are larger than a sentence.

2. Readers try to form integrated representations of discourse by using subtle cues, mental models, long-term memory, and inferences.

3. According to the constructionist view, people actively draw inferences that connect parts of the text, even though the parts may be widely separated.

4. Inferences are especially likely when people have large working-memory capacity, excellent metacomprehension skills, and expertise in the area. People also draw higher-level inferences, beyond the level of the paragraph.

5. Educators are beginning to emphasize teaching metacomprehension skills to older children and teenagers.

6. Compared to people who are low in test anxiety, people who are high in test anxiety typically make more errors on multiple-choice tests, in summarizing textbook material, and in drawing inferences from a textbook.

7. Latent semantic analysis (LSA) is an artificial intelligence program that was designed to understand language, and it can perform some useful analyses. However, the relatively narrow scope of LSA highlights humans' competence on a wide variety of reading tasks.

CHAPTER REVIEW QUESTIONS

1. Why is language one of the most impressive human accomplishments? Describe at least six cognitive processes that you are using while you are reading this sentence.

2. According to the discussion of factors affecting comprehension, we have more difficulty understanding a sentence if it is in the passive voice, instead of the active voice. Referring to the cognitive-functional approach, why would we occasionally choose to create a sentence such as, "The window was broken by Fred"?

3. Suppose that you are reading a story in which Sam is described as a "left-brain person." Suggest at least three reasons why this phrase is not consistent with the research.

4. Context is an important concept throughout this chapter. Explain how context is important in (a) processing an ambiguous word, (b) discovering the meaning of an unfamiliar word, and (c) background knowledge in understanding discourse.

5. This chapter emphasizes that memory contributes to language comprehension. Using the chapter outline as your guide, specify how both working memory and long-term memory are essential when you try to understand language.

6. This chapter emphasized that English is an "outlier language." Explain this term, and describe why the English-language research about psycholinguistics may not apply to other languages. If you speak another language, how might the research show a different pattern?

7. Describe the constructionist view of inferences discussed in the last section of this chapter. Think about several kinds of reading tasks you have performed in the last two days. Be sure to include examples other than reading your textbook. Point out how the constructionist perspective would be relevant during each discourse-processing task.

8. Describe the research on metacomprehension skills. How could you apply these strategies to improve your own reading skills for a course other than cognitive psychology?

9. Summarize the parts of this chapter that describe individual differences. How might individual differences also be relevant in other aspects of language comprehension?

10. This chapter discussed both listening and reading. Which processes are similar, and which are different? In preparation for Chapter 10, compare speech production and writing in a similar fashion.

KEYWORDS

psycholinguistics
phoneme
morpheme
morphology
syntax
grammar
semantics
semantic memory
pragmatics
modular
surface structure
deep structure
transformational rules
ambiguous sentences
cognitive-functional approach

nested structure
the good-enough approach
heuristic
neurolinguistics
aphasia
Broca's area
Broca's aphasia
Wernicke's area
Wernicke's aphasia
lateralization
functional magnetic resonance
    imaging (fMRI)
language-localizer task
mirror system

dual-route approach to reading
direct-access route
indirect-access route
whole-word approach
phonics approach
whole-language approach
discourse
inferences
theory of mind
constructionist view of
    inferences
metacognition
metacomprehension
latent semantic analysis LSA

RECOMMENDED READINGS

Gaskell, M. G. (Ed.). (2009a). *The Oxford handbook of psycholinguistics*. New York: Oxford University Press. This excellent resource includes several chapters on each of seven topics such as word recognition, comprehension, and language development; this book emphasizes theoretical aspects of language.

Harley, T. A. (2010). *Talking the talk: Language, psychology and science*. New York: Psychology Press. Trevor Harley wrote this book for a general audience, and it includes wonderful examples of language comprehension, as well as a chapter on animal communication.

Kaplan, R. B. (Ed.). (2010a). *The Oxford handbook of applied linguistics* (2nd ed.). New York: Oxford University Press. As the book's title suggests, Kaplan's handbook focuses on more practical aspects of language, such as reading and technology.

Traxler, M. J. (2012). *Introduction to psycholinguistics: Understanding language science*. Chichester, England: John Wiley & Sons. Traxler's textbook provides an excellent, current background on a variety of topics, including reading, sign language, and cognitive neuroscience.

ANSWERS TO DEMONSTRATION 9.1

Chapter 2: Visual recognition allows you to see letters and words, and auditory recognition allows you to hear phonemes and words. Chapter 3: Divided attention can permit you to take in information about two simultaneous verbal messages, whereas selective attention encourages you to pay attention to one message and ignore the other; saccadic eye movements are important in reading. Chapter 4: Working memory helps you store the stimuli (either visual or auditory) long enough to process and interpret them. Chapter 5: Long-term memory allows you to retrieve information you processed long ago. Chapter 6: The tip-of-the-tongue phenomenon means that you will sometimes be unable to access certain words, whereas metacomprehension allows you to determine whether you understand a verbal message. Chapter 7: You create mental models when you process a description about a spatial layout. Chapter 8: Semantic memory stores the meaning of words and the relationships between concepts, whereas schemas and scripts provide background knowledge for processing language. Note: Additional answers are also possible for many of these chapters.

PREVIEW

Chapter 9 examined language comprehension, with an emphasis on listening and reading. In contrast, Chapter 10 focuses on language production, with an emphasis on speaking, writing, and bilingualism.

Our ability to produce spoken words is an impressive accomplishment, although we sometimes make slips-of-the-tongue and other speech errors. We also arrange the words in an orderly sequence within a sentence. When we tell a story, the narrative typically follows a specific structure. The social context of speech is also crucial; for example, speakers must be certain that their conversational partners share the same background knowledge. Speakers must also consider how the listener may interpret a statement and whether the listener shares our own conceptual framework. When we speak, we must also consider how to make strategic requests; we also need to realize that others may not share the same conceptual framework.

Writing is an important activity for college students and many professionals. Writing requires the three major components of working memory, as well as long-term memory. Writing also requires planning, sentence generation, and revision. Expert writers are more likely than novice writers to emphasize organization during writing.

Bilingualism is a topic that demonstrates how humans can master listening, reading, speaking, and writing in two or more languages. Therefore, the topic of bilingualism is an appropriate conclusion to our two-chapter exploration of language. U.S. schools may not value a child's fluency in a language other than English. As you can imagine, social factors are relevant when people want to become fluent in another language.

Bilingual people seem to have a number of advantages over those who are monolingual. For example, they may be especially skilled on tasks where they must ignore an obvious response and focus on more subtle information. Adults and children are similar in acquiring both grammar and vocabulary in a second language. However, people who learn a second language during adulthood often speak with a more pronounced accent, compared to those who learn a second language during childhood. Finally, people who work as simultaneous interpreters are likely to have outstanding working-memory skills.

CHAPTER INTRODUCTION

Consider the language that you have produced today. Unless you are reading this chapter very early in the morning, you may have greeted a friend, talked to someone at breakfast, spoken on the phone, taken notes on a reading assignment, sent a text message, or written a reminder to yourself.

Language is probably the most social of all our cognitive processes (Cowley, 2011; Holtgraves, 2010; Tomasello, 2008). This social aspect is especially obvious when we use language to inform or influence other people (Guerin, 2003). Chapter 1 emphasized that psychologists often create artificial boundaries between areas of psychology. These boundaries encourage us to believe that cognitive psychology belongs to a different category than social psychology (Cacioppo, 2007). In reality, these two areas are intertwined, as you'll see in several parts of this chapter.

Here's another feature of language production: Every sentence that you *comprehend* is a sentence that somebody *produced*. If psychologists distributed their research equitably, we would know just as much about language production as we know about language comprehension. Furthermore, Chapter 10 would be just as long as Chapter 9, rather than six pages shorter.

In reality, psychologists are much more likely to study language comprehension, compared to language production (Costa et al., 2009; Garrett, 2009; Harley, 2008). One reason researchers ignore language production is that they typically cannot manipulate the ideas that an individual wishes to say or write. In contrast, they can easily manipulate the text that a person hears or reads (Carroll, 2004).

We will begin by examining spoken language, and then we'll consider written language. Keep in mind, however, that listening, reading, speaking, and writing are all intertwined with one another. Furthermore, our final topic, bilingualism, employs all four of these skills. Bilingualism will therefore serve as the final section of these two chapters on language.

SPEAKING

Each day, most of us spend several hours telling stories, chatting, quarreling, talking on the phone, and speaking to ourselves. Even when we listen to a friend, we produce supportive comments such as "yeah" and "mm hm." Indeed, speaking is one of our most complex cognitive and motor skills (Bock & Griffin, 2000; Dell, 2005).

Let's begin this first section of the chapter by discussing how we produce an individual word. Then we'll consider some common speech errors, as well as the gestures we make when talking. Then we'll examine how we create a sentence, and how we create discourse (language units that are larger than sentences). Our final topic in this section is an in-depth examination of the social context of speech.

Producing a Word

Like many cognitive processes, word production does not initially seem remarkable. After all, you simply open your mouth and a word emerges effortlessly. Word production becomes impressive, however, once we analyze the dimensions of the task (Traxler, 2012). As noted in Chapter 9, you can produce about three words each second (Vigliocco & Hartsuiker, 2002). Furthermore, the average college-educated North American has a speaking vocabulary of at least 75,000 words (Bock & Garnsey, 1998; Wingfield, 1993). Already, the task of word production looks challenging!

You also need to choose each word carefully, so that its grammatical, semantic, and phonological information are all correct (Meyer & Belke, 2009; Rapp & Goldrick, 2000). As Bock and Griffin (2000) point out, many factors "complicate the journey from mind to mouth" (p. 39).

Psychologists who study language production often examine how we retrieve grammatical, semantic, and phonological information. Some researchers argue that speakers retrieve all three kinds of information at the same time (Damian & Martin, 1999; Saffran & Schwartz, 2003). According to this approach, for example, you look at an apple and simultaneously access the grammatical properties of *apple*, the meaning of *apple*, and the phonemes in the word *apple*. Other researchers argue that we access each kind of information independently, with little interaction among these three components (Ferreira & Slevc, 2009; Meyer & Belke, 2009; Roelofs & Baayen, 2002).

Evidence of the "independent access" perspective comes from Miranda van Turennout and her colleagues (1998), who conducted research with Dutch-speaking individuals. Dutch resembles languages such as Spanish, French, and German, because Dutch nouns have a grammatical gender. These researchers presented pictures of objects and animals, and the participants tried to name the object as quickly as possible.

Using the event-related potential technique (see p. 16), these researchers demonstrated that speakers access the grammatical gender of the word about 40 milliseconds before they access the word's phonological properties. These results suggest that we do not acquire all the different kinds of information at the exact same moment. Instead, we literally use split-second timing.

Speech Errors

The speech that most people produce is generally accurate and well formed, consistent with Theme 2. In spontaneous language samples, people make an error less than once every 500 sentences (Dell, Burger, & Svec, 1997; Vigliocco & Hartsuiker, 2002). However, some high-status speakers—including former U.S. presidents—often make speech errors.

Researchers have been particularly interested in the kind of speech errors called slips-of-the-tongue. **Slips-of-the-tongue** are errors in which sounds or entire words are rearranged between two or more different words. These slips of the tongue are informative because they reveal our extensive knowledge about the sounds, structure, and meaning of the language we are speaking (Dell et al., 2008; Traxler, 2012).

Types of Slip-of-the-Tongue Errors. Gary Dell and his coauthors propose that three kinds of slips-of-the-tongue are especially common in English (Dell, 1995; Dell et al., 2008):

1. Sound errors, which occur when sounds in nearby words are exchanged—for example, *snow flurries → flow snurries*.

2. Morpheme errors, which occur when **morphemes** (the smallest meaningful units in language, such as *-ly* or *in-*) are exchanged in nearby words—for example, *self-destruct instruction → self-instruct destruction*.

3. Word errors, which occur when words are exchanged—for example, *writing a letter to my mother → writing a mother to my letter*.

Furthermore, we are likely to create a word (e.g., *leading*), rather than a nonword (e.g., *londing*) when we make a slip-of-the-tongue error (Griffin & Ferreira, 2006; Rapp & Goldrick, 2000). Finally, we seldom create a word that begins with an unlikely letter sequence. For example, English speakers rarely create a slip-of-the-tongue such as *dlorm* when trying to say *dorm* (Dell et al., 2000). These two principles reflect the importance of our knowledge about the English language and Theme 5's emphasis on top-down processing (Dell et al., 2008).

In almost all cases, the errors occur across items from the same category (Clark & Van Der Wege, 2002; Fowler, 2003; Traxler, 2012). For instance, in sound errors, initial consonants interchange with other initial consonants (as in the *flow snurries* example). The pattern of these errors suggests that the words we are currently pronouncing are influenced by both the words we have already spoken and the words we are planning to speak (Dell, Burger, & Svec, 1997).

Explanations for Speech Errors. Dell and his colleagues propose a comprehensive theory for speech errors that is similar to the connectionist approach and includes the concept of spreading activation (Dell, 1986, 1995, 2005; Dell, Burger, & Svec, 1997; Dell et al., 1997; Dell et al., 2008). Let us consider a brief overview of how you might produce a sound error. When you are about to speak, each element of the word you are planning to say will activate the sound elements to which it is linked. For example, Figure 10.1 shows how the words in the tongue twister "She sells seashells" might activate each of the six sounds in the last word, *seashells*.

FIGURE 10.1

An Example of Dell's Model of Sound Processing in Sentence Production (simplified). See text for explanation.

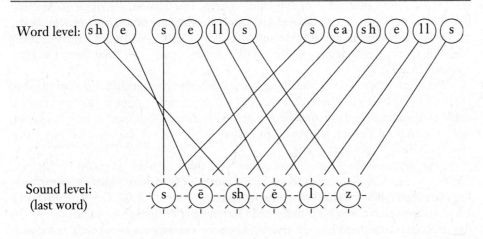

---

⑤ Demonstration 10.1

Slips-of-the-Tongue

Keep a record of all the slips-of-the-tongue that you either hear or make yourself in the next two days. Classify each slip as a sound error, morpheme error, or word error. Does this slip-of-the-tongue produce an actual word? Also note whether the mistake occurs across items from the same category. Finally, see if you can determine why the mistake occurred, using an analysis similar to Dell's.

Usually, we utter the sounds that are most highly activated, and usually these sounds are the appropriate ones. However, each sound can be activated by several different words. Notice, for example, that the *sh* sound in the sound-level representation of *seashells* (that is, *seshelz*) is highly "charged" because it receives activation from the first word in the sentence, *she*, as well as the *sh* in *seashells*.

As Dell (1995) emphasizes, incorrect items sometimes have activation levels that are just as high as (or higher than) the correct items. For example, in Figure 10.1, the activation level for *sh* is just as high as the level for *s*. By mistake, a speaker may select an incorrect sound in a sentence, such as "She sells sheashells." Try Demonstration 10.1 to determine the form and function of the slips-of-the-tongue that you typically make or hear from other speakers.

Using Gestures: Embodied Cognition

When we produce a word, we execute elaborate motor movements of the mouth, the tongue, and other parts of the vocal system. In addition, we often accompany our speech with gestures. **Gestures** are visible movements of any part of your body, which you use to communicate (Hostetter & Alibali, 2008; Jacobs & Garnham, 2007; McNeill, 2005). As Geneviéve Calbris (2011) writes, a gesture is "the mental image's witness" (p. 293).

The same intentional gestures may convey different meanings in different cultures (Ambady & Weisbuch, 2010; Calbris, 2011). For example, suppose that you make a circle with your thumb and your first finger. This gesture signifies "money" in Japan, and "perfect!" in France. However, in Malta—an island off the coast of Italy—this same gesture is an obscene insult.

Your gestures can also influence how you think (Goldin-Meadow & Beilock, 2010). For example, the spontaneous motor movements of your hands can sometimes help you remember the word you want to produce (Carroll, 2004; Griffin, 2004). In a representative study, Frick-Horbury and Guttentag (1998) read the definitions for 50 low-frequency, concrete English nouns. Then the researchers asked each participant to identify the target word. For example, the definition "a pendulum-like instrument designed to mark exact time by regular ticking" (p. 59) was supposed to suggest the

---

⑨ **Demonstration 10.2**

Using Gestures to Communicate Information

Answer each of the following questions, using only words and no body movements. Hold this book in both hands while you try this exercise.

1. Define the word "spiral."
2. Give directions on how to walk from your current location to another location about 10 minutes away.
3. Describe the shape of the steps in a staircase.
4. Describe how you peel a carrot.
5. If you have recent experience in driving a car, give instructions for how to insert the key into the door of a locked car, and then open the door.
6. If you have recent experience in riding a bicycle, give instructions about how you get on a bike and begin to ride.

Which of these items was the most difficult to describe without using any gestures?

---

noun *metronome*. Notice, then, that this technique resembles the tip-of-the-tongue research described in Chapter 6.

In Frick-Horbury and Guttentag's (1998) study, however, half of the participants were instructed to hold a rod with both hands; therefore, their hand movements were restricted. The average score for these individuals was 19 words out of 50. In contrast, the participants with unrestricted hand movements earned an average score of 24 words out of 50. Other research has confirmed this finding. According to these researchers, when our verbal system cannot retrieve a word, a gesture can sometimes activate the relevant information (Brown, 2012).

We frequently produce gestures when we speak, especially when we want to discuss a concept that is easier to describe with body movements than with words (Ambady & Weisbuch, 2010). Try Demonstration 10.2 to illustrate this point. We are also more likely to produce a gesture when we have had previous experience with the relevant physical activity (Hostetter & Alibali, 2010).

In recent years, cognitive psychologists have become increasingly interested in a concept called embodied cognition. **Embodied cognition** emphasizes that people use their bodies to express their knowledge (Hostetter & Alibali, 2008). In other words, there is an ongoing connection between your motor system and the way we process spoken language, for example, when you make gestures or indicate some kind of motion (Hostetter & Alibali, 2008; Tomasello, 2008). Notice that the embodied cognition approach focuses on concrete physical actions, rather than the abstract meaning of language (Holtgraves, 2010).

During the behaviorist era, psychologists emphasized visible motor activity. As the cognitive psychology approach grew in popularity, psychologists could read entire issues of a relevant journal, without any mention of motor actions. However, the recent attention to embodied cognition has convinced many psychologists that we frequently think nonverbally (Ambady & Weisbuch, 2010).

Do gestures actually help us in communicating a message? Amber Hostetter (2011) conducted a meta-analysis of the 63 studies that addressed this question. She found that gestures actually do increase the listener's understanding, especially when the speaker is describing concrete actions.

Producing a Sentence

Every time you speak a sentence, you must overcome the limits of your memory and attention in order to plan and deliver that sentence (Griffin, 2004; Harley, 2008). Speech production requires a series of stages. During the first stage, we mentally plan the **gist**, or the overall meaning of the message we intend to generate. In other words, we begin by producing speech in a top-down fashion (Clark & Van Der Wege, 2002; Griffin & Ferreira, 2006).

During the second stage, we devise the general structure of the sentence, without selecting the exact words. In general, we tend to use the same sentence structure that was used in a previous sentence (Harley, 2008; Kaschak et al., 2011; Pickering & Ferreira, 2008).

During the third stage, we select the specific words we want, abandoning other semantically similar words (Griffin & Ferreira, 2006). We also select the appropriate grammatical form, such as *eating*, rather than *eat*. In the fourth stage, we convert these intentions into speech by articulating the phonemes (Carroll, 2004; Treiman et al., 2003).

As you might expect, the stages of sentence production typically overlap in time. We often begin to plan the final part of a sentence before we have pronounced the first part of that sentence (Fowler, 2003; Treiman et al., 2003). Under ideal circumstances, a speaker moves rapidly through these four stages. For instance, Griffin and Bock (2000) showed college students a simple cartoon. In less than 2 seconds, the students began to produce a description such as, "The turtle is squirting the mouse with water."

However, we sometimes confront an important problem when we are planning a sentence. We may have a general thought or a mental image that we want to express. These rather shapeless thoughts and images must be translated into a statement that has a disciplined, linear shape, with the words following one another in time. This challenge of arranging words in an ordered, linear sequence is called the **linearization problem** (Fox Tree, 2000; Griffin, 2004).

The speech-production process is more complex than most people imagine. For example, you must also plan the **prosody** of an utterance, or the "melody" of its intonation, rhythm, and emphasis (Keating, 2006; Plack, 2005; Speer & Blodgett, 2006). A speaker can use prosody to clarify an ambiguous message. For example, read the following two sentences out loud: (a) "What's that ahead in the road?" and (b) "What's that, a head in the road?" (Speer & Blodgett, 2006, p. 505). Notice how the prosody differs for these two examples. Let's now consider how we produce longer passages of speech.

Producing Discourse

When we speak, we typically produce **discourse,** or language units that are larger than a sentence (Harley, 2008). Unfortunately, most of the research on language production focuses on isolated words and sentences (Griffin & Ferreira, 2006).

One category of discourse is the **narrative,** the type of discourse in which someone describes a series of actual or fictional events (Griffin & Ferreira, 2006). The events in a narrative are conveyed in a time-related sequence, and they are often emotionally involving (Guerin, 2003; Strömqvist & Verhoeven, 2004).

Storytellers usually have a specific goal that they want to convey. However, they do not completely preplan the organization at the beginning of the story (H. H. Clark, 1994). Storytellers typically choose their words carefully, presenting their own actions in a favorable light (Berger, 1997; Edwards, 1997). They also try to make the story more entertaining (Dudukovic et al., 2004; Marsh & Tversky, 2004).

The format of a narrative is unusual, because it allows the speaker to "hold the floor" for an extended period. During that time, the speaker usually conveys six parts of the narrative: (1) a brief overview of the story, (2) a summary of the characters and setting, (3) an action that made the situation complicated, (4) the point of the story, (5) the resolution of the story, and (6) the final signal that the narrative is complete (for example, "...and so that's why I decided that I had to learn Japanese"). These features tend to make the story cohesive and well organized (H. H. Clark, 1994). Now that you know something about the function and structure of narratives, try Demonstration 10.3.

🌀 Demonstration 10.3

The Structure of Narratives

During the next few weeks, try to notice your daily conversations. What happens when someone you know begins to tell a story? First, how does the storyteller announce that she or he is about to begin the narrative? Does the structure of the narrative match the six-part sequence we discussed? Does the storyteller attempt to check whether the listeners have the appropriate background knowledge? What other characteristics do you notice that distinguish this kind of discourse from a normal conversation in which people take turns speaking?

IN DEPTH

The Social Context of Language Production

When you speak, you need to plan the content of your message. You must produce relatively error-free speech, and you must also plan your message. In addition to these challenging assignments, however, you also need to be attuned to the social context of speech. Notice, then, that cognitive processes and social factors are intertwined (Cacioppo, 2007).

Language is definitely a social instrument (Fiedler et al., 2011; Holtgraves, 2010; Segalowitz, 2010). In fact, conversation is like a complicated dance (Clark, 1985, 1994). Speakers cannot simply utter words aloud and expect to be understood. Instead, these speakers must consider their conversation partners, make numerous assumptions about those partners, and design appropriate utterances (Tomasello, 2008).

This complicated dance requires precise coordination. When two people enter a doorway simultaneously, they need to coordinate their motor actions. Similarly, two speakers must coordinate turn taking, they must agree on the meaning of ambiguous terms, and they must understand each other's intentions (Clark & Van Der Wege, 2002; Harley, 2008; Holtgraves, 2010). When Helen tells Sam, "The Smithsons are on their way," both participants in the conversation need to understand that this is an indirect invitation for Sam to start dinner, rather than to call the police for protection (Clark, 1985).

This example of language use is called *pragmatics*. **Pragmatics** focuses on the social rules and world knowledge that allow speakers to successfully communicate messages to other people (De Groot, 2011; Flores Salgado, 2011; Goldenberg & Coleman, 2010; Holtgraves, 2010). Two important topics in the research on pragmatics are common ground and an understanding of directives. We will also consider a concept called *framing*, which examines why we sometimes have trouble communicating with people who have different perspectives.

Common Ground. Suppose that a young man named Andy asks his friend Lisa, "How was your weekend?" and Lisa answers, "It was like being in Conshohocken again." Andy will understand this reply only if they share a similar understanding about the characteristics or events that took place in Conshohocken. In fact, we would expect Lisa to make this remark only if she is certain that she and Andy share the appropriate common ground (Clark & Van Der Wege, 2002; Stone, 2005).

Common ground occurs when conversationalists share the similar background knowledge, schemas, and perspectives that are necessary for mutual understanding (Harley, 2008; Holtgraves, 2010; Traxler, 2012). In fact, the speakers need to collaborate to make certain that they share common ground with their conversational partners (Tomasello, 2008).

For example, speakers should make certain that their listeners are paying attention and they have the appropriate background knowledge. If their listeners

🌀 Demonstration 10.4

Collaborating to Establish Common Ground

For this demonstration, you need to make two photocopies of the figures below. Then cut the figures apart, keeping each sheet's figures in a separate pile and making certain the dot is at the top of each figure. Now locate two volunteers and a watch that can measure time in seconds. Your volunteers should sit across from each other or at separate tables, with their figures in front of them. Neither person should be able to see the other's figures.

Appoint one person to be the "director" and the other the "matcher." The director should arrange the figures in random order, in two rows of six figures each. This person's task is to describe the first figure in enough detail so that the "matcher" is able to identify that figure and place it in Position 1 in front of him or her. The goal is for the matcher to place all twelve figures in the same order as the director's figures. They may use any kind of verbal descriptions they choose, but no gestures or imitation of body position. Record how long it takes them to reach their goal, and then make sure that the figures do match.

Ask them to try the game two more times, with the same person serving as director. Record the times again, and note whether the time decreases on the second and third trials; are these volunteers increasingly efficient in establishing common ground? Do they tend to develop a standard vocabulary (for example, "the ice skater") to refer to a given figure?

look puzzled, speakers need to clarify any misunderstandings (Haywood et al., 2005; Holtgraves, 2010). Unfortunately, however, speakers often think that they are communicating effectively, even when their listeners cannot understand their message (Fay et al., 2008).

Have you ever had difficulty explaining some object or procedure to another person, in a phone conversation? Clark and Wilkes-Gibbs (1986) conducted a classic study on the collaboration process that we use when trying to establish common ground. Try Demonstration 10.4, which is a modification of this study.

The participants in Clark and Wilkes-Gibbs's (1986) study played this game for six trials; each trial consisted of arranging all twelve figures in order. On the first trial, Person 1 required an average of nearly four turns to describe each figure and make certain that Person 2 understood the reference. (A typical "turn" consisted of a statement from Person 1, followed by a question or a guess from Person 2.)

As Figure 10.2 shows, however, the director and the matcher soon developed a mutual shorthand, and the number of required turns decreased rapidly over trials. Just as two dancers become more skilled as they practice together at coordinating their movements, conversational partners become more skilled in communicating efficiently (Barr & Keysar, 2006).

Additional research confirms that people who work together collaboratively can quickly and efficiently develop common ground (Barr & Keysar, 2006; Schober & Brennan, 2003). For example, physicians often adjust their conversations according to the medical sophistication of each patient. If a patient with diabetes initially uses the term "blood sugar level," the physician is less likely to use the technical term, "blood glucose concentration" (Bromme et al., 2005).

We have been discussing how people can establish common ground, even with strangers. However, this process is far from perfect. For example, speakers often overestimate their listeners' ability to understand a message (Barr & Keysar, 2006; Holtgraves, 2010; Schober & Brennan, 2003). Now let's consider how people make requests.

Directives. A **directive** is a sentence that asks someone to do something. For example, suppose that a man named Bob is driving. A police officer stops him, and Bob clearly knows that he has been speeding. Of course, most of us would automatically accept the speeding ticket.

However, let's suppose that Bob is considering giving a bribe to the officer. One possibility is that Bob might make a direct request. As the name suggests, a **direct request** resolves the interpersonal problem in a very obvious fashion. In this situation, an example of a direct request would be, "How much money should I pay you to *not* get a ticket?" Basically, if Bob is considering a bribe like this one, he needs to figure out the consequences of a bribe. Does this officer seem to be honest? If so, a direct bribe would probably lead to Bob being arrested for bribing an officer—the worst possible outcome.

In contrast, an **indirect request** uses subtle suggestions to resolve an interpersonal problem, rather than stating the request in a straightforward manner. In this

FIGURE 10.2

Average Number of Turns that Directors in Clark and Wilkes-Gibb's Study Required for Each Figure, as a Function of Trial Number.

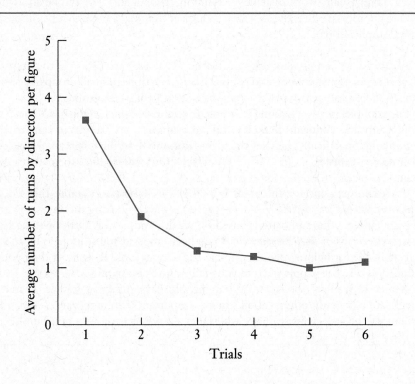

Source: Clark, H. H., & Wilkes-Gibbs, D. (1986). Referring as a collaborative process. *Cognition, 22,* 1–39.

situation, some people might say, "Well, officer, maybe it would be easier if we can take care of the ticket right now, without going through all that paperwork." Linguists have argued that we typically state a request in a relatively brief but clear manner (Grice, 1989; Traxler, 2012). So why should we use all these extra words to make an indirect request?

According to a group of researchers at Harvard, people need to be strategic decision makers in their social interactions (Lee & Pinker, 2010; Pinker et al., 2008). In this case, if the officer is *dishonest*, Bob's indirect request will lead to Bob not getting a ticket. If the officer is *honest*, Bob's indirect request will lead to Bob getting a ticket—not a great outcome, but certainly better than being arrested for bribing a police officer. Notice how this study about requests is an example of Theme 4 of this textbook. In this case, the language we choose (Chapter 10) is related to our decision-making strategies (Chapter 12).

So far, we've seen that speakers are typically attuned to the social context of speech. They usually work to achieve common ground, and they can be strategic in selecting appropriate directives. Now let's look at framing, a topic that has important political implications.

Framing. When psychologists study the social aspects of speech, they typically look at conversations between two people or conversations in small groups. However, linguists and sociologists typically study how large groups use language.

For example, George Lakoff is a cognitive scientist in the Linguistics Department at University of California Berkeley. Lakoff examines how language can structure our thinking. Specifically, he uses the term **frame** to describe our mental structures that simplify reality (Lakoff, 2007, 2009, 2011). Our frames tend to structure what "counts" as facts.

For example, consider the word *responsibility*. Some peole frame this word in terms of *individual responsibility*: You are responsible for making money for yourself and your family; your authority is based on wealth and power. Other people frame this word in terms of *social responsibility*. You have empathy for other people, and you are responsible for helping people who have less money and less power than you do. You need to care for people beyond your family and community.

Notice a problem, however. When people have different frames, it may be difficult to talk with others about many important contemporary issues. This problem will be especially dramatic when they do not share common ground.

◎ Section Summary: *Speaking*

1. Researchers conduct relatively little research on language production, compared to the research on language comprehension.

2. Word production is an impressive accomplishment; researchers disagree about whether grammatical, semantic, and phonological information about a word is accessed simultaneously or at different times.

3. According to Dell and other researchers, slip-of-the-tongue errors occur because a speech sound other than the intended one is highly activated; researchers explain these errors in terms of a parallel distributed processing model with spreading activation.

4. Gestures can sometimes help us remember a specific term; this topic is related to embodied cognition.

5. Four stages in producing a sentence include working out the gist, formulating the general structure of the sentence, making the word choice, and articulating the phonemes; these processes overlap in time.

6. Speaking also requires speakers to overcome the linearization problem and to plan the prosody of their messages.

7. A narrative is a kind of discourse that typically includes certain specified story components.

8. The social context of language production (pragmatics) includes the skilled use of common ground, directives, and framing.

WRITING

Writing is a task that requires almost every cognitive process described in this textbook (Theme 4). Students spend a major portion of their daily life taking notes on lectures and reading assignments, writing papers, and writing essays on exams. Think about the last major writing project that you finished, perhaps a review of the research on a particular topic. This project probably required letter recognition, attention, memory, imagery, background knowledge, metacognition, reading, problem solving, creativity, reasoning, and decision making.

Researchers seldom study writing in college students, though they have conducted studies on children's writing (e.g., Martins et al., 2010; Robins & Treiman, 2009; Treiman & Kessler, 2009). We noted earlier in this chapter that research on under-standing speech is more prevalent than research on speech production. The contrast is even more dramatic when we compare the research on written language. Reading inspires hundreds of books and research articles each year, whereas writing inspires only several dozen (Harley, 2008). For example, researchers seldom study everyday activities such as composing an e-mail (Biorge, 2007; Oberlander & Gill, 2006).

Most adults write fairly often. For example, a large-scale study asked adults in three regions of the United States to keep a diary for two days, recording how frequently they wrote (Cohen et al., 2011). The participants reported writing an average of two hours each day. Several factors—gender, ethnicity, education, and age—were not related to time spent writing. However, employed people spent more time writing than nonemployed people.

Writing and speaking share many cognitive components. However, you are more likely to write in isolation. Writing also takes more time, especially because writing uses more complex syntax. In addition, people revise their writing far more often than their talking (Biber & Vásquez, 2008; Harley, 2001; Treiman et al., 2003).

Writing and speaking also differ with respect to social factors. When you speak, you are more likely to refer to yourself. When speaking, you also interact more with your listeners, and you have a better opportunity to establish common ground with them (Chafe & Danielewicz, 1987; Gibbs, 1998; Harley, 2008).

Writing consists of three phases: planning, sentence generation, and revising (Mayer, 2004). However—like the similar stages we discussed in connection with spoken language—these tasks often overlap in time (Kellogg, 1994, 1996; Ransdell & Levy, 1999). For example, you may be planning your overall writing strategy while you generate parts of several sentences.

All components of the writing task are complex, and they strain the limits of attention (Kellogg, 1994, 1998; Torrance & Jeffery, 1999). In fact, a classic article about writing emphasizes that a person working on a writing assignment is "a thinker on full-time cognitive overload" (Flower & Hayes, 1980, p. 33). However, college students can learn to write more skillfully if they have extensive practice in academic writing and if the assignments emphasize high-quality writing (Beauvais et al., 2011; Engle, 2011; Kellogg & Whiteford, 2009). Furthermore, college students—and professors—often report that they can write more coherent, refined papers if they read a draft out loud (Engle, 2011).

Let's begin by considering the cognitive aspects of writing. After that, we'll examine three phases of writing: planning, sentence generation, and revising. Then we'll emphasize the importance of metacognition throughout the writing process. Finally, we'll discuss several examples of writing in real-world settings.

The Cognitive Components of Writing

Several leading researchers have developed models of writing that emphasize the importance of cognitive processes (Chenoweth & Hayes, 2001; Hayes, 1996; Kellogg, 1994, 2001a, 2001b; McCutchen et al., 2008). We'll emphasize working memory and long-term memory.

Working Memory. Working memory plays a central role in writing (Kellogg et al., 2007; Raulerson et al., 2010). We'll discuss working memory's contributions in some detail, because they may not be as obvious as the contributions from long-term memory.

In Chapter 4, we discussed Alan Baddeley's model of working memory (e.g., Baddeley, 2007). **Working memory** refers to the brief, immediate memory for material that you are currently processing; working memory also coordinates your ongoing mental activities.

Let's look at a study by Ronald Kellogg and his colleagues (2007), who examined which components of working memory might be active during the writing process. These researchers asked college students to write definitions for words, while they worked on a secondary task at the same time. There were three different kinds of secondary tasks, each focusing on a specific component of working memory. If the students responded more slowly on a particular secondary task, Kellogg and his coauthors reasoned that this particular skill would be an important component of writing.

One component of working memory, called the **phonological loop,** stores a limited number of sounds for a short period of time. To test whether the phonological loop is active during writing, Kellogg and his colleagues included a specific secondary task. This task required students to remember a spoken syllable. The results showed that—when the students were writing—they required significantly longer to remember the syllables. Therefore, the phonological loop seems to be an important factor when we write.

Another component of working memory, called the **visuospatial sketchpad**, processes both visual and spatial information. Let's first consider how Kellogg and his coauthors examined the "visual information" component. To test whether the *visual* part of the sketchpad is active during writing, another secondary task required students to remember the visual shape of the item. The results showed that, when students were writing about *concrete* nouns, they required significantly longer to remember the item's visual shape. However, when they wrote about *abstract* nouns, they showed no delay in remembering the item's visual shape. As we might expect, visual information is relevant when you are trying to definite a concrete word, because you are likely to create a mental image. In contrast, visual activity is minimal when you are trying to define an abstract word.

To examine the *spatial* part of the sketchpad, Kellogg and his coauthors included a different secondary task. This task required the students to remember a particular location, while they were writing definitions. In this case, the students' reaction times were not affected by the writing task. In general, then, writing does not require us to emphasize locations.

Let's now shift away from the phonological loop and the visuospatial sketchpad; the most important component of Baddeley's model of working memory is the central executive. The **central executive** integrates information from the phonological loop, the visuospatial sketchpad, and the episodic buffer (see pp. 115–117). The central executive also plays a role in attention, planning, and coordinating other cognitive activities.

Because writing is such a complex task, the central executive is active in virtually every phase of the writing process (Kellogg, 1996, 1998, 2001a). For example, it coordinates the planning phase, and it is also essential when we generate sentences. In addition, the central executive oversees the revision process. We'll discuss these three phases shortly. Because the central executive has a limited capacity, many people report that formal writing is a stressful task.

Long-Term Memory. So far, we've only considered working memory. However, long-term memory is also vitally important during writing. Several important factors that influence long-term memory include the following: the writer's semantic memory, specific expertise about the topic, general schemas, and knowledge about the writing style to be used for the particular assignment (Kellogg, 2001b; McCutchen et al., 2008). As you can see, our summary of the cognitive approach to writing provides an opportunity to review practically every topic we have discussed in the earlier chapters of this textbook!

Planning a Formal Writing Assignment

So far, we have discussed how memory can influence a variety of writing tasks. However, most people begin a formal writing project by generating a list of ideas; this process called **prewriting**. Prewriting is difficult and strategic—very different from many relatively automatic language tasks (Collins, 1998; Torrance et al., 1996).

As you can imagine, students differ enormously in the quality of the ideas they generate during this phase (Bruning et al., 1999). According to the research, good writers are more likely than poor writers to spend high-quality time in planning during prewriting (Hayes, 1989).

Some people prefer to outline a paper before they begin to write (Kellogg, 1998; McCutchen et al., 2008). An outline may help you avoid overloaded attention. It may also help you resolve the linearization problem, which occurs in writing as well as in speaking. You've probably had the experience of beginning to write a paper, only to find that each of several interrelated ideas needs to be placed first! An outline can help you sort these ideas into an orderly, linear sequence. Nevertheless, some writers find that an outline is not helpful (Engle, 2011).

Sentence Generation During Writing

Before you read further, try Demonstration 10.5, which requires you to generate some sentences. During sentence generation, the writer must translate the general ideas developed during planning, thus creating the actual sentences of the text (Mayer, 2004).

During sentence generation, your fluent phases tend to alternate with your hesitant phases (Chenoweth & Hayes, 2001). Think about your own pattern when you were writing the sentences in Demonstration 10.4. Did you show a similar pattern of pauses alternating with fluent writing?

Students often believe that their writing will sound more sophisticated if they use lengthy words. However, according to research by Oppenheimer (2006), people actually judge writers to be more intelligent if their essay uses shorter words.

---

⑥ Demonstration 10.5

Producing Written Sentences

For this exercise, you should be alone in a room, with no one else present to inhibit your spontaneity. Take a piece of paper on which you will write two sentences as requested below. For this writing task, however, say out loud the thoughts you are considering while you write each sentence. Then read the next section, on sentence generation.

1. Write one sentence to answer the question, "What are the most important characteristics that a good student should have?"

2. Write one sentence to answer the question, "What do you consider to be your strongest personality characteristics—the ones that you most admire in yourself?"

Earlier in this chapter, we discussed slips-of-the-tongue. People also make errors when they write, whether they use a keyboard or a pen. However, writing errors are usually confined to a spelling error within a single word, whereas speaking errors often reflect switches between words (Berg, 2002).

The Revision Phase of Writing

Remember that writing is a cognitively challenging task. When writing their first draft, writers have numerous opportunities to make mistakes (Kellogg, 1998). We cannot manage to generate new sentences and revise them at the same time (Silvia, 2007). During the revision phase of writing, you should therefore emphasize the importance of organization and coherence, so that the parts of your paper are interrelated (Britton, 1996). You'll also need to reconsider whether your paper accomplishes the goals of the assignment. In fact, the revision task should be time consuming.

The most effective writers use flexible revision strategies, and they make substantial changes if their paper doesn't accomplish its goal (Harley, 2001). However, college students typically devote little time to revising a paper (Mayer, 2004). For instance, college students in one study estimated that they had spent 30% of their writing time on revising their papers, but observation of their actual writing behavior showed that they consistently spent less than 10% of their time on revisions (Levy & Ransdell, 1995). Chapter 6 pointed out that students' metacognitions about reading comprehension are not very accurate (Chapter 6). In Levy and Ransdell's study, we see that students' metacognitions about the writing process are also inaccurate.

As you can imagine, expert writers are especially skilled at making appropriate revisions. Hayes and his colleagues (1987) conducted a classic study, comparing how first-year college students and expert writers revised a poorly written two-page letter. Most first-year students revised the text one sentence at a time. They fixed relatively minor problems with spelling and grammar, but they ignored problems of organization, focus, and transition between ideas.

The college students in this study were also more likely to say that some defective sentences were appropriate. For example, several students found no fault with the sentence, "In sports like fencing for a long time many of our varsity team members had no previous experience anyway." Furthermore, the students were less likely than the expert writers to identify the source of a problem in a sentence. A student might say, "This sentence just doesn't sound right," whereas an expert might say, "The subject and the verb don't agree here."

One final caution about the revision process focuses on the proofreading stage. Daneman and Stainton (1993) confirmed what many people already suspected: You can proofread someone else's writing more accurately than your own. When you are very familiar with a paper that you've just written, you often overlook the errors in the text. Top-down processing (Theme 5) triumphs again! Furthermore, you've probably found that you cannot proofread your paper for spelling when you are focusing on the paper's content. If you wait at least one day, you'll be more likely to detect those errors.

⦿ Section Summary: *Writing*

1. Writing is a frequent activity for most people, but research on this topic is limited.

2. The cognitive model of writing emphasizes the three major components of working memory, as well as long-term memory.

3. Good writers spend high-quality time in planning; outlining can be helpful in relieving overloaded attention.

4. When people generate sentences during writing, their fluent phases alternate with hesitant phases.

5. During revision, writers should emphasize organization and coherence, making appropriate revisions and diagnosing defective sentences; students also overestimate the amount of time that they spend on revisions.

BILINGUALISM AND SECOND-LANGUAGE ACQUISITION

So far, Chapters 9 and 10 have described four impressively complicated language tasks: understanding spoken language, reading, speaking, and writing. When we need to perform one of these tasks, we must coordinate our cognitive skills and social knowledge. We can marvel that human beings can manage all these tasks in one language. But then we must remind ourselves that many people throughout the world can speak two or more languages (Schwartz & Kroll, 2006).

A **bilingual speaker** is someone who is fluent in two different languages (Harley, 2008; Schwartz & Kroll, 2006). Technically, we should use the term **multilingual speaker** to refer to someone who speaks more than two languages, but psycholinguists often use the term *bilingual* to include multilinguals as well (De Groot, 2011).

Some bilinguals learn two languages simultaneously during childhood, an arrangement called **simultaneous bilingualism**. Other bilinguals experience **sequential bilingualism**; their native language is referred to as their **first language**, and the non-native language that they acquire is their **second language** (De Groot, 2011).

We noted in Chapter 9 that most research in psycholinguistics is English-centered. When we examine bilingualism, we must emphasize that the world has between 6,000 and 7,000 languages (Ku, 2006; Lupyan & Dale, 2010; Segalowitz, 2010). Even so, almost all of the research on bilingualism includes English as one of the two languages (Bassetti & Cook, 2011).

In this section on bilingualism, we will first discuss some background information, as well as the social context of bilingualism. Then we'll note some advantages that people experience when they are bilingual. Our next topic explores the relationship between age of acquisition of a second language and proficiency in that second language. Finally, the Individual Differences feature will focus on simultaneous interpreters, people who have outstanding expertise in two or more languages.

Background on Bilingualism

More than half of the people in the world are at least somewhat bilingual (Luna, 2011; Schwartz & Kroll, 2006). Some people live in countries where at least two languages are commonly used. These countries include Canada, Belgium, Spain, and Switzerland.

Other people become bilingual because their home language is different from the language used for school and business. For example, Zulu speakers in South Africa typically learn English. People also become bilingual because colonization has imposed another language upon them. Still others become bilingual because they have studied another language in school, or because they grew up in homes where family members routinely used two languages. In addition, immigrants moving to a new country usually need to master the language of that culture (Bialystok, 2001; Fishman, 2006; Parry, 2006).

English is the most common language in both Canada and the United States, but many other languages are also widely used in these countries. Table 10.1 shows the ten languages most frequently "spoken at home" in the United States. Table 10.2 shows the ten languages most frequently listed as a person's "mother tongue" in Canada.

TABLE 10.1

Ten Languages Most Frequently Spoken at Home in the United States, Based on the U.S. Census Bureau (2012) for People Aged 5 and Older

Language	Estimated Number of Speakers[1]
English	228,700,000
Spanish	35,500,000
Chinese	2,600,000
Tagalog[2]	1,500,000
French	1,300,000
Vietnamese	1,300,000
German	1,100,000
Korean	1,000,000
Russian	900,000
Arabic	800,000

(1) The number of speakers is rounded to the nearest 100,000. In case of a tie, the language with the larger number of speakers is placed first.
(2) Tagalog is a language spoken in the Philippines.
Source: U.S. Census Bureau (2012). Table 53. Languages spoken at home: 2009.

TABLE 10.2

Ten Languages Most Frequently Identified as the "Mother Tongue" in Canada, Based on 2006 Census

Language	Estimated Number of Speakers[1]
English	17,900,000
French	6,800,000
Chinese	1,000,000
Italian	500,000
German	500,000
Punjabi[2]	400,000
Spanish	300,000
Arabic	300,000
Tagalog	200,000
Portuguese	200,000

(1) The number of speakers is rounded to the nearest 100,000. In case of a tie, the language with the larger number of speakers is placed first.
(2) Punjabi is a language spoken in India and Pakistan.
Source: Statistics Canada, 2006.

Bilingualism is important in the lives of many residents of Canada and the United States, and many people speak a language other than English in their homes.

In the last decade, bilingualism has become an increasingly popular topic in psychology and linguistics. For instance, this interdisciplinary area now has its own journal, *Bilingualism: Language & Culture*. Several recent books also focus on bilingualism (Cook & Bassetti, 2011; De Groot, 2011; Flores Salgado, 2011; Gaskell, 2009a; Kaplan, 2010a; Kroll & De Groot, 2005; Segalowitz, 2010).

Let's begin our discussion by looking at the social context of bilingualism. Then we will consider the advantages of bilingualism, as well as the relationship between age of acquisition and language mastery.

The Social Context of Bilingualism

Many children in the United States and in Canada speak a language other than English in their homes. Unfortunately, the educational system frequently does not value this other language. For example, one of my students described an incident that she had observed in a kindergarten class at a school where many children speak both English and Spanish. Two boys were playing together, and they spoke several sentences to each other in Spanish. The teacher rushed toward them and shouted, "I don't want to hear another word from either of you in that language!" Language is a defining characteristic of every cultural group (Gardner, 2010). Don't you wonder how these two children—and their classmates—interpreted their teacher's response?

Unfortunately, many schools do not appreciate the value of keeping a child fluent in a first language such as Korean, Arabic, or Spanish (Fishman, 2006; Pita & Utakis, 2006; Zentella, 2006). However, if a school values a child's first language, he or she may actually become more fluent in English (Atkinson & Connor, 2008; De Groot, 2011). Caring teachers and administrators can provide a schoolwide culture that supports children who are learning English as a second language (Goldenberg & Coleman, 2010).

As you can imagine, the topic of bilingualism has important political and social implications. This topic is especially important when educators and politicians make biased statements about various ethnic groups (Genesee & Gándara, 1999; Phillipson, 2000).

Social forces are also important when an individual wants to become bilingual. Two important predictors of success in acquiring a second language are a person's motivation and her or his attitude toward the people who speak that language (Harley, 2008; Segalowitz, 2010; Tokuhama-Espinosa, 2001).

In fact, researchers have tried to predict how well English Canadian high school students would learn French. The research shows that the students' *attitude* toward French Canadians was just as important as their cognitive, language-learning *aptitude* (Gardner & Lambert, 1959; Lambert, 1992). Other researchers have found the same relationship between attitudes and mastery of English, for people who come from Hungary, Japan, China, and Iran (Segalowitz, 2010; Taguchi et al., 2009).

As you might expect, the relationship between attitudes and language proficiency also works in the reverse direction. In other words, language proficiency can influence attitudes. For example, when English Canadians learn French in elementary school, they are more likely to develop positive attitudes toward French Canadians, compared to children in a monolingual control group of English Canadian children (Genesee & Gándara, 1999; Lambert, 1987).

Here's further evidence that language can influence students' attitudes. Danziger and Ward (2010) studied Arab Israeli students who were enrolled at Ben-Gurian University. This university is located in Israel, and classes are taught in Hebrew. However, all of the participants were fluent in both Arabic and Hebrew.

Danziger and Ward used the Implicit Association Test, an instrument that assesses people's attitudes. As you saw in Chapter 8, the **Implicit Association Test (IAT)** is based on the principle that people can mentally pair related words together much more easily than they can pair unrelated words. Take a moment to review this technique, discussed in pages 287 to 289. Using the IAT, Danziger and Ward found that these Arab students were more positive about Jewish individuals when the fluently bilingual researcher was speaking Hebrew than when she was speaking Arabic.

Advantages (and Minor Disadvantages) of Bilingualism

During the early 1900s, theorists proposed that bilingualism produced cognitive deficits because the brain must store two linguistic systems (Erwin-Tripp, 2011; De Groot, 2011). However, in the 1960s, researchers controlled for factors such as age and social class. They discovered that bilingual children actually scored higher than monolinguals on a variety of tasks. In one of the best-known studies, for example, bilingual children were more advanced in school. They also scored better on tests of first-language skills, and they showed greater mental flexibility (Lambert, 1990; Peal & Lambert, 1962).

Bilingual people have one tremendous advantage over monolinguals: They can communicate in two languages. Even 10-year-olds can translate spoken and written language with impressive accuracy (Bialystok, 2001).

In addition to gaining fluency in a second language, bilinguals seem to have a number of other advantages over monolinguals. In fact, De Groot (2011) draws a general conclusion about ethnic minority children who also become fluent in English as their second language. These bilingual children tend to perform better than monolingual children on a variety of cognitive tasks. This conclusion even holds true if the monolingual children come from families with higher incomes. Let's look at some of these cognitive comparisons in more detail.

1. Bilinguals actually acquire more expertise in their native (first) language (De Groot, 2011; Rhodes et al., 2005; van Hell & Dijkstra, 2002). For example, English-speaking Canadian children whose classes are taught in French gain greater understanding of English-language structure (Diaz, 1985; Lambert et al., 1991). Bilingual children are also more likely to realize that a word such as *rainbow* can be divided into two morphemes, *rain* and *bow* (Campbell & Sais, 1995).

2. Bilinguals are more aware that the names assigned to concepts are arbitrary (Cromdal, 1999; De Groot, 2011; Hakuta, 1986). For example, many monolingual children cannot imagine that a cow could just as easily have been assigned the name *dog*. A number of studies have examined **metalinguistics**, or knowledge about the form and structure of language. On many measures of metalinguistic skill—but not all of them—bilinguals outperform monolinguals (Bialystok, 1988, 1992, 2001; Campbell & Sais, 1995; De Groot, 2011; Galambos & Goldin-Meadow, 1990).

3. Bilinguals excel at paying selective attention to relatively subtle aspects of a language task, while ignoring more obvious linguistic characteristics (Bialystok, 2001, 2005, 2010; Bialystok & Feng, 2009; Bialystok & Viswanathan, 2009; De Groot, 2011). For example, Bialystok and Majumder (1998) gave third-grade children some sentences that were grammatically correct but semantically incorrect (for example, "Apples grow on noses"). The bilingual children were more likely than the monolingual children to recognize that the sentence was grammatically correct.

Bialystok (2009) also reported that bilingual individuals perform better on the Stroop Test, a task that requires people to emphasize an item's color and ignore its meaning. (See pages 75 to 77.) Bialystok (2005) proposes that these experiences with selective attention may facilitate the development of a portion of the frontal lobe, labeled "executive attention network" in Figure 3.2 on page 84.

4. Bilingual children are better at following complicated instructions and per-forming tasks where the instructions change from one trial to the next (Bialystok, 2005, 2009; Bialystok & Martin, 2004). For example, Bialystok and Martin (2004) asked preschoolers to sort some cards that featured either a blue circle, a red circle, a blue square, or a red square. The researchers first instructed them to sort the cards on one dimension (e.g., shape). Later, the researchers instructed them to sort the cards on the other dimension (e.g., color). Bilingual children were much faster than monolingual children in switching to the new dimension.

5. Bilinguals perform better on concept-formation tasks and on tests of non-verbal intelligence that require reorganization of visual patterns (Peal & Lambert, 1962). Bilinguals also score higher on problem-solving tasks that require them to ignore irrelevant information (Bialystok, 2001; Bialystok & Codd, 1997; Bialystok & Majumder, 1998).

6. Bilingual children are more sensitive to some pragmatic aspects of language (Comeau & Genesee, 2001). For example, English-speaking children whose classes are taught in French are more aware than monolinguals that—when you speak to a blind-folded child—you may need to supply additional information (Genesee et al., 1975).

7. Bilingual adults who have dementia typically develop signs of dementia *later* than monolingual adults with dementia (Bialystok, 2009; Bialystok et al., 2007). As you may know, **dementia** is an acquired, persistent syndrome of cognitive deficits (Kolb & Whishaw, 2011). For example, Bialystok and her coauthors (2007) examined the medical history of 184 people at a memory clinic. All of them had a medical diagnosis of dementia. However, the bilinguals had received this diagnosis at the average age of 75.5, in contrast to an average age of 71.4 for the monolinguals. This difference is especially important because the monolingual individuals actually had an average of 1.6 *more* years of formal education than did the bilingual individuals.

The disadvantages of being bilingual are relatively minor. People who use two languages extensively may subtly alter how they pronounce some speech sounds in both languages (Gollan et al., 2005). Bilingual individuals may also process language slightly more slowly, in comparison to monolinguals. Furthermore, bilingual children may have somewhat smaller vocabularies for words that are used in a home setting (Bialystok, 2009; Bialystok et al., 2010). However, these disadvantages are far outweighed by the advantages of being able to communicate effectively in two languages (Michael & Gollan, 2005).

Second-Language Proficiency as a Function of Age of Acquisition

The term **age of acquisition** refers to the age at which you learned a second language. Does your ability to learn a new language decrease as you grow older? Some theorists have proposed a critical period hypothesis (e.g., Johnson & Newport, 1989). According to the **critical period hypothesis**, your ability to acquire a second language is strictly limited to a specific period of your life. Specifically, the critical period hypothesis proposes that individuals who have already reached a specified age—perhaps early puberty—will no longer be able to acquire a new language with native-like fluency. Fortunately, however, the current research evidence does not support a clear-cut, biologically based "deadline" for learning a second language (Bialystok 2001; Birdsong, 2006; De Groot, 2011; Wiley et al., 2005).

Even if we reject the critical period hypothesis, we still need to explore a more general issue: Do older people have more difficulty than younger people in mastering a new language? Like so many psychological controversies, the answer varies as a function of the dependent variable. As you'll see, researchers draw different conclusions, depending on whether the dependent variable is vocabulary, phonology, or grammar.

Vocabulary. When the measure of language proficiency is vocabulary, age of acquisition is *not* related to language skills (Bialystok, 2001). Several studies report that adults and children are equally skilled in learning words in their new language (Bialystok & Hakuta, 1994).

This finding makes sense, because people continue to learn new terms in their own language throughout their lifetime. For example, you have already learned several hundred new terms in cognitive psychology since you began this course!

Phonology. The research suggests that age of acquisition *does* influence the mastery of **phonology,** or the sounds of a person's speech. Specifically, people who acquire a second language during childhood are more likely to pronounce words like a native speaker of that language. In contrast, those who acquire a second language during adulthood are more likely to have a foreign accent when they speak their new language (Bialystok, 2001; Flege et al., 1999; MacKay et al., 2006).

For example, Flege and his coauthors (1999) tested people who had immigrated to the United States from Korea when they were between the ages of 1 and 23 years. At the time of the study, all participants had lived in the United States for at least eight years.

To test phonology, Flege and his colleagues asked their participants to listen to an English sentence, and then repeat it. The phonology of each sentence was later judged by speakers whose native language was English.

As you can see, Figure 10.3 shows that Korean immigrants who had arrived in the United States during childhood typically had minimal accents when speaking English; you can see that most have scores of 7 or 8. Those who had arrived as adolescents or adults usually had stronger accents, with scores of 2 to 4. However, notice the fairly smooth decline with age of acquisition, rather than the abrupt drop predicted by the critical period hypothesis (Bialystok, 2001). In later research, MacKay and his coauthors (2006) found similar results in phonology, with people who had emigrated from Italy.

FIGURE 10.3

The Average Rating for Foreign Accent, as a Function of the Individual's Age of Arrival in the United States (9 = no accent; 1 = strong accent).

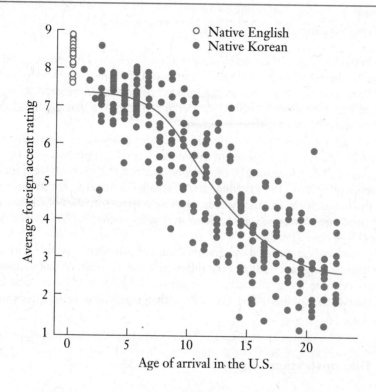

Note: For comparison, the study by Flege and his coauthors (1999) also provided an average rating of foreign accent, for 10 speakers whose native language was English. In the upper left corner of the graph, you can see that the judges rated them as having virtually no foreign accent.

Source: Flege, J. E., Yeni-Komshiam, G. H., & Lui, S. (1999). Age constraints on second-language acquisition. *Journal of Memory and Language, 41*, 78–104.

Grammar. Let's review the conclusions—so far—about age of acquisition and mastering a second language. As far as vocabulary, age doesn't matter. As far as phonology, age *does* matter; if people learn a new language when they are young, they will have a less noticeable accent.

The controversy about age of acquisition is strongest when we consider mastery of grammar (e.g., Bialystok, 2001; Johnson & Newport, 1989). Let's focus on another component of the study by Flege and his coauthors (1999); we just discussed this study in connection with phonology. These researchers also examined how the native speakers of Korean had mastered English grammar. Specifically, the researchers asked the participants to judge whether a variety of English sentences were grammatical. Here are three representative examples of ungrammatical sentences:

1. Should have Timothy gone to the party?
2. Susan is making some cookies for we.
3. Todd has many coat in his closet.

The initial analysis of the data showed that those who had learned English during childhood had better mastery of English grammar. However, Flege and his colleagues (1999) then discovered that the "early arrivers" had much more experience in U.S. schools and therefore more formal education in the English language. In other words, the "early arrivers" had an unfair advantage.

The researchers therefore conducted a second analysis, by carefully matching some of the early arrivers with some of the late arrivers. Each subgroup had an average of 10.5 years of U.S. education. In this second analysis, the early arrivers received an average score of 84% on the grammar test, virtually identical to the average score of 83% for the late arrivers. In other words, once we control for years of education in the United States, age of acquisition is not related to an individual's mastery of English grammar (Flege et al., 1999).

So far, we have emphasized the grammatical performance of people with an Asian first language, a language that is very different from English. What happens when researchers examine the grammatical competence of bilinguals whose first language is more similar to English? The research with Spanish and Dutch does not show

---

⑨ Demonstration 10.6

Exploring Bilingualism

If you are fortunate enough to be bilingual or multilingual, you can answer these questions yourself. If you are not, locate someone you know well enough to ask the following questions:

1. How old were you when you were first exposed to your second language?
2. Under what circumstances did you acquire this second language? For example, did you have formal lessons in this language?
3. When you began to learn this second language, did you find yourself becoming any less fluent in your native language? If so, can you provide any examples?
4. Do you think you have any special insights about the nature of language that a monolingual may not have?
5. Does the North American culture (including peer groups) discourage bilinguals from using their first language?

any consistent relationship between age of arrival and mastery of English grammar (Bahrick et al., 1994; Birdsong & Molis, 2001; Jia et al., 2002).

In short, the studies show that English-speaking people can begin to learn a new language during adulthood. Specifically, the research shows the following:

1. Age of acquisition is not related to vocabulary in the new language.

2. Age of acquisition is related to phonology.

3. Age of acquisition is sometimes related to grammar for people whose first language is different from English; but there may be no relationship when the first language is similar to English.

As an exercise in helping you understand bilingualism, try Demonstration 10.6 at your next opportunity. Quite clearly, bilinguals and multilinguals provide the best illustration of how Theme 2 applies to language. These fortunate people often manage to achieve accurate and rapid communication in two or more languages.

Next, this chapter's Individual Differences feature will focus on the superstars of bilingualism. These are the people who listen to speech in one language and simultaneously produce the translation in a different language.

Individual Differences: Simultaneous Interpreters and Working Memory

If you have studied another language, you've probably had the experience of looking at a written passage in that language and writing down the English equivalent of that passage. The technical term **translation** refers to this process of translating from a text written in one language into a second *written* language. In contrast, the technical term **interpreting** usually refers to the process of changing from a spoken message in one language into a second *spoken* language. (One exception is sign language, which refers to the process of changing between a spoken message in one language into a second language that is signed, or else from a signed message into a spoken form.)

Simultaneous interpreting is one of the most challenging linguistic tasks that humans can perform (Christoffels & De Groot, 2005). Imagine that you are a simultaneous interpreter, listening to a person speaking in Spanish and producing the English version of that message for a group of listeners who are fluent in English but are not familiar with Spanish. You would need to manage three working-memory tasks at exactly the same time:

1. Comprehend one Spanish segment (perhaps a sentence or two).

2. Mentally transform the previous Spanish segment into English.

3. Actually speak out loud—in English—an even earlier segment.

Furthermore, you must manage to perform these cognitive gymnastics at the rate of between 100 to 200 words per minute!

It's hard to think of any other occupation that would create such an ongoing challenge for a person's working memory. Let's look at research that compares simultaneous interpreters with other bilingual individuals, on two kinds of working-memory tasks.

Ingrid Christoffels, Annette De Groot, and Judith Kroll (2006) studied three groups of bilingual people whose native language was Dutch. In addition, all of these individuals were also fluent in English. These groups included 39 Dutch undergraduate students at the University of Amsterdam, 15 Dutch teachers of English who had an average of 19 years of professional experience, and 13 Dutch simultaneous interpreters who had an average of 16 years of professional experience. Christoffels and her colleagues hypothesized that the professional interpreters would have higher scores than the other two groups on tests of working memory. Let's consider two of these working-memory tasks, which the researchers called the reading-span test and the speaking-span test.

For the *reading-span test*, the researchers created 42 sentences in both English and Dutch. The final word of each sentence was matched for the two languages, in terms of both word length and the frequency of the word in the appropriate language. The researchers showed several series of sentences, which were two, three, four, or five sentences in length. Each sentence was shown on a screen, for half a second. At the end of each series, the participants tried to recall the last word of each of the sentences in that specific series. Furthermore, the participants completed this reading-span test in both English and Dutch.

For the *speaking-span test*, the researchers selected 42 words in both English and Dutch, matching for both word length and the frequency of the word in the appropriate language. The researchers presented several series of words, which were two, three, four, or five words in length. Each word was shown on a screen, for only half a second. At the end of each series, the participants tried to produce—out loud—a grammatically correct sentence for each word in the series that they could recall. Again, the participants tried this speaking-span test in both English and Dutch.

Figure 10.4 shows that all three groups of bilinguals recalled more words in their native language of Dutch, compared to their second language of English. The more interesting comparison focuses on the three groups of people. As you can see, the simultaneous interpreters remembered significantly more Dutch and English words than the other two groups, in terms of both their reading span and their speaking span.

As you know, psychologists emphasize that it's sometimes difficult to explain significant differences between groups. In this case, we know that simultaneous interpreters perform better than either bilingual students or teachers. One possible explanation is that the experience of managing simultaneous tasks increased the working-memory skills for the simultaneous interpreters. However, another possibility is that only people with superb working-memory skills can manage to survive in a profession that requires an extremely high level of proficiency in working memory. In reality, both of these explanations may be correct.

FIGURE 10.4

Average Score on the Reading-Span Test and the Speaking-Span Test, as a Function of the Language (Dutch and English) and Profession.

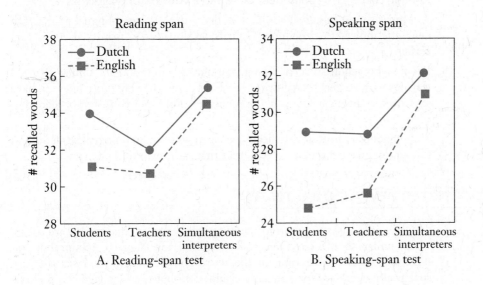

A. Reading-span test

B. Speaking-span test

Source: Christoffels, I. K., De Groot, A. M. B., & Kroll, J. F. (2006). Memory and language skills in simultaneous interpreters: The role of expertise and language proficiency. *Journal of Memory and Language, 54,* 324–345.

Section Summary: *Bilingualism and Second-Language Acquisition*

1. More than half of the world's population are at least somewhat bilingual. Many residents of Canada and the United States speak a first language other than English; children's schools may not value fluency in another language.

2. Research shows that motivation and attitudes are important determinants of bilingual skills.

3. If people are fluent in a second language, they tend to be more positive toward people who speak that language.

4. Bilingual people tend to have more positive impressions of people whose language is currently being spoken (e.g., attitudes toward Jews when the message is spoken in Hebrew).

5. Bilinguals have an advantage over monolinguals in their ability to communicate in two languages, their understanding of first-language structure, their

awareness of the arbitrary nature of concept names, and their ability to pay attention to subtle aspects of language.

6. Bilinguals also show superior ability in following complex instructions and forming concepts; they also tend to be more sensitive to pragmatics.

7. A comparison of bilingual adults with dementia and monolingual adults with dementia showed that the monolinguals developed this disorder about 4 years earlier.

8. People who acquire a second language during adulthood are similar to child learners with respect to acquiring vocabulary, but they are more likely to have an accent in this new language; age of acquisition is not consistently related to competency in grammar.

9. Simultaneous interpreters typically perform better than bilingual students and foreign-language teachers on two tasks that assess working memory.

CHAPTER REVIEW QUESTIONS

1. The cognitive tasks required for language production (Chapter 10) are somewhat similar to the cognitive tasks required for language comprehension (Chapter 9). Describe some of the more complex cognitive tasks that are specifically necessary for language production, but not language comprehension.

2. Think of a slip-of-the-tongue that you recently made or heard in a conversation. What kind of error is this, according to Dell's classification, and how would Dell's theory explain this particular error? What slips-of-the-tongue would you be *least* likely to make?

3. Recall several conversations you've had in the last day or two. Describe how these conversations reflected the pragmatic components of speech production, such as common ground, and directives.

4. What is "embodied cognition"? How is it relevant in language production in Chapter 10? How is it similar to the findings about mirror neurons in Chapter 9?

5. What is the linearization problem? In what way is it more relevant in language production (either speaking or writing) than it would be when you create a mental image (Chapter 7)?

6. "Language is more than simply a sequence of words." Discuss this statement with respect to the social aspects of language production, including topics such as gestures, prosody, and bilingualism.

7. Based on the material in the section on writing, what hints could you adopt to produce a better paper, when you next begin to work on a formal writing assignment?

8. Think of another language that you would like to speak with some fluency. What factors could facilitate your mastery of that language? Describe several

tasks in which bilinguals are likely to perform better than monolinguals. Which tasks would monolinguals probably perform better than bilinguals?

9. The section on bilingualism mentioned metalinguistics, or the knowledge of the form and structure of language. Review this chapter, noting several topics related to metalinguistics that would be interesting to explore. Suggest several specific research projects. (For example, how could you test people's knowledge about how they write a paper?)

10. Language is perhaps the most social of our cognitive activities. Describe how social factors are relevant in our speaking and writing, as well as in bilingual interactions.

KEYWORDS

slips-of-the-tongue	direct request	sequential bilingualism
morphemes	indirect request	first language
gestures	frame	second language
embodied cognition	working memory	Implicit Association Test (IAT)
gist	phonological loop	metalinguistics
linearization problem	visuospatial sketchpad	dementia
prosody	central executive	age of acquisition
discourse	prewriting	critical period hypothesis
narrative	bilingual speaker	phonology
pragmatics	multilingual speaker	translation
common ground	simultaneous bilingualism	interpreting
directive		

RECOMMENDED READINGS

Bazerman, C. (Ed.). (2008). *Handbook of research on writing: History, society, school, individual, text*. Mahwah, NJ: Erlbaum. Many of the chapters in this book explore topics unrelated to psychology. However, the last 13 chapters focus on psychological aspects of writing.

De Groot, A. M. B. (2011). *Language and cognition in bilinguals and multilinguals: An introduction*. New York: Psychology Press. I strongly recommend Annette De Groot's book for anyone who would like an in-depth examination of the topic. It is current, well organized, and comprehensive.

Gaskell, M. G. (Ed.). (2009a). *The Oxford handbook of psycholinguistics*. New York: Oxford University Press. Most books on psycholinguistics ignore the topic of language production; Gaskell's handbook includes nine chapters on this topic.

Segalowitz, N. (2010). *Cognitive bases of second language fluency*. New York: Routledge. Norman Segalowitz's book is briefer than De Groot's book, and it is written more from the perspective of cognitive psychology. It examines topics such as the pragmatics of second-language usage, as well as the important topic of fluency in a second language.

CHAPTER 11
Problem Solving and Creativity

Chapter Introduction

Understanding the Problem

Problem-Solving Strategies

Factors That Influence Problem Solving

Creativity

PREVIEW

You use problem solving when you want to reach a particular goal, but you cannot immediately figure out the best pathway toward that goal. This chapter considers four aspects of problem solving: (1) understanding the problem, (2) problem-solving strategies, (3) factors that influence problem solving, and (4) creativity.

In order to understand a problem, you must pay attention to the relevant information. Then you can represent the problem, for instance by using symbols or diagrams. In some cases, people may solve a complex problem in their daily life, even though they cannot solve a similar problem on a classroom exam. According to current research, problem representation is often influenced by environmental cues and by cues related to your own body.

After you understand a problem, you must figure out how to solve it. Many problem-solving approaches are based on heuristics. A heuristic is a general rule that typically produces a correct solution. One heuristic is the analogy approach, in which you solve the current problem based on a your experience with similar previous problems. A second approach is the means-ends heuristic, in which you break a problem into subproblems and then solve these individual subproblems. A third heuristic is the hill-climbing heuristic; at every choice point, you simply choose the alternative that seems to lead most directly toward your goal.

The third section of this chapter examines factors that influence problem solving. It emphasizes that top-down processing and bottom-up processing are both important in effective problem solving. Experts benefit by using their well-developed top-down skills. In contrast, overactive top-down processing can interfere with effective problem solving, as we'll see in the discussions of mental set and functional fixedness. An additional problem occurs when overactive top-down processing encourages stereotype threat, a problem that can decrease women's math performance. Furthermore, if you try to solve a standard, noninsight problem, top-down processing is typically helpful. In contrast, to solve an insight problem, you need to overcome incorrect top-down assumptions.

Creativity can be defined as finding solutions that are novel and useful. We'll discuss a classic theory about creativity, as well as some general characteristics about creativity. The research shows that people are generally more creative when they are working on a project because it is enjoyable, rather than because they might win a competition.

CHAPTER INTRODUCTION

Every day, you solve dozens of problems. For example, think about the problems you worked on today. Perhaps you wanted to reach a student in your social psychology class, but you didn't know his last name or his e-mail address. Also, you may have tried to solve the problem of choosing a topic for your cognitive psychology paper. Then maybe you took a break by working on a Sudoku puzzle, which is yet another example of problem solving.

You use **problem solving** when you want to reach a specified goal; however, the solution is not immediately obvious because you are missing important information and/or it is not clear how to reach the goal (Bassok & Novick, 2012; D'Zurilla & Maydeu-Olivares, 2004; Reif, 2008). These problems vary widely. For example, a toddler could try to solve the problem of conveying pasta to her mouth, without spilling (Keen, 2011). An English-speaking student—studying in France—might try to solve the problem of asking for directions, with only a limited vocabulary (Segalowitz, 2010). A counseling psychologist may try to help a high school student solve a personal problem about his interactions with his peers (Heppner, 2008).

The nature of these problems may differ. However, every problem includes three components: (1) the initial state, (2) the goal state, and (3) the obstacles. For example, suppose that you need to reach Jim in your social psychology class. The **initial state** describes the situation at the beginning of the problem. In this case, your initial state might be, "I need to reach Jim tonight so that we can begin to work on our social psychology project . . . but I don't know his last name, his e-mail address, or his phone number." You reach the **goal state** when you solve the problem (Levy, 2010). Here, it could be, "I have Jim's last name and his e-mail address." The **obstacles** describe the restrictions that make it difficult to proceed from the initial state to the goal state (Thagard, 2005). The obstacles in this hypothetical problem might include the following: "Jim wasn't in class yesterday," "The professor said she was going to be away this afternoon," and "We need to turn in a draft of our project on Friday."

Take a moment to recall a problem you solved recently. Determine the initial state, the goal state, and the obstacles, so that you are familiar with these three concepts. Then try Demonstration 11.1.

In Chapter 1, we defined the term *cognition* as the acquisition, storage, transformation, and use of knowledge. So far in this textbook, we've paid the least attention to the component called "transformation of knowledge." However, in this chapter and in the next chapter on reasoning and decision making, we focus on how people must

---

⊚ Demonstration 11.1

Attention and Problem Solving

Suppose you are a bus driver. On the first stop, you pick up 4 men and 4 women. At the second stop, 3 men, 2 woman, and 1 child board the bus. Then at the third stop, 2 men leave and 2 women get on. At the fourth stop, 3 women get off. At the fifth stop, 2 men get off, 3 men get on, 1 woman gets off, and 2 women get on. What is the bus driver's name?

Source: Based on Halpern, 2003, p. 389.

gather the information that they acquired. Then they must *transform* this information to reach an appropriate answer.

Chapters 11 and 12 are both included within the general category called "thinking." **Thinking** requires you to go beyond the information you were given, so that you can reach a goal; the goal may be a solution, a belief, or a decision.

Throughout this chapter, we will emphasize the active nature of cognitive processes in problem solving, as emphasized in Theme 1. When some people try to solve a problem, they may take a trial-and-error approach, randomly trying different options until they find a solution (Reif, 2008). However, effective problem solvers typically plan their attack. They often break a problem into its component parts and devise a strategy for solving each part. In addition, people use certain strategies that are likely to produce a solution relatively quickly.

People also use metacognition to monitor whether their problem-solving strategies seem to be working effectively (Hinsz, 2004; Mayer, 2004; Reif, 2008). As this textbook emphasizes, humans do not passively absorb information from the environment. Instead, we plan our approach to problems, and we choose strategies that are likely to provide useful solutions.

The initial step in problem solving is understanding the problem, so we will consider this topic in the first section of this chapter. Once you understand a problem, the next step is to select a strategy for solving it; we will examine several problem-solving approaches in the second section. Next we will examine some factors that influence effective problem solving; for example, expertise is clearly helpful, but a mental set is counterproductive. Our final topic in this chapter is creativity—an area that requires finding novel solutions to challenging problems.

UNDERSTANDING THE PROBLEM

Some years ago, several companies located in a New York City skyscraper faced a major problem. The people in the building were continually complaining that they had to wait too long for the slow-moving elevators. Numerous consultants were brought in, but the complaints only increased. When several companies threatened to move out, the architects made plans to incorporate an extremely expensive new set of elevators.

Before reconstruction began, however, someone decided to add mirrors in the lobbies next to the elevators. The complaints stopped. Apparently, the original problem solvers had not properly understood the problem. In fact, the real problem wasn't the speed of the elevators, but the boredom of waiting for them to arrive (Thomas, 1989).

In problem-solving research, the term **understanding** means that you have constructed a well-organized mental representation of the problem, based on both the information provided in the problem and your own previous experience (Benjamin & Ross, 2011; Fiore & Schooler, 2004). Think about an occasion when you realized that your mental representation was inaccurate. I recall my mother giving her friend a recipe for homemade yogurt. The instructions included the sentence, "Then you put the yogurt in a warm blanket." The friend looked alarmed, and she asked, "But

---

⑨ Demonstration 11.2

Using Symbols in Problem Solving

Solve the following problem: Mary is 10 years younger than twice Susan's age. Five years from now, Mary will be 8 years older than Susan's age at that time. How old are Mary and Susan? (You can find the answer in the discussion of "Symbols" a little later in the text.)

---

isn't it awfully messy to wash the blanket out?" Unfortunately, the friend's internal representation had omitted the fact that the yogurt was in a container.

In this first section of the chapter, we'll consider several topics related to understanding a problem: (1) paying attention to the relevant information; (2) methods of representing the problem; and (3) *situated cognition*, which emphasizes how context helps you understand a problem, as well as *embodied cognition*, which emphasizes how your own body helps you understand a problem.

Paying Attention to Important Information

To understand a problem, you need to decide which information is most relevant to the problem's solution and then attend to that information. Notice, then, that one cognitive task—problem solving—relies on other cognitive activities such as attention, memory, and decision making. Once again, our cognitive processes are interrelated (Theme 4).

Attention is important in understanding problems, because competing thoughts can produce divided attention. For instance, Bransford and Stein (1984) presented algebra "story problems" to a group of college students. You'll remember these problems—a typical one might ask about a train traveling north, while a car is traveling south. In this particular study, the students were asked to record their thoughts and emotions as they inspected the problem.

Many students had an immediate negative reaction to the algebra problem. A typical comment was, "Oh no, this is a math word problem—I hate those things." These negative thoughts occurred frequently throughout the 5 minutes allotted to the task. The thoughts clearly distracted the students' attention away from the central task of problem solving.

A second major challenge in understanding a problem is focusing on the appropriate part. Researchers have found that effective problem solvers read the description of a problem very carefully. They pay particular attention to inconsistencies (Mayer & Hegarty, 1996). Effective problem solvers also scan strategically, deciding which information is most important (Nievelstein et al., 2011).

Incidentally, if you paid attention to the question about the bus driver on page 371, you could solve it without needing to read it a second time. However, if you didn't pay attention, you can locate the answer in the first sentence of Demonstration 11.1. In summary, then, attention is a necessary initial component of understanding a problem.

Methods of Representing the Problem

As soon as the problem solver has decided which information is essential and which can be ignored, the next step is to find a good method to represent the problem. **Problem representation** refers to the way you translate the elements of the problem into a different format. If you choose an appropriate representation, you are more likely to reach an effective solution to the problem.

Chapter 1 introduced the gestalt psychologists, who emphasized that we actively organize our cognitive experiences. When they studied problem solving, they emphasized the importance of finding an effective method of representing the problem (Bassok & Novick, 2012; Schnotz et al., 2010).

The research shows that working-memory capacity is correlated with a person's ability to solve algebra word problems (Lee et al., 2009) and with the ability to categorize geometric patterns (Lewandowsky, 2011). If you have a good working memory, you can keep the relevant parts of the problem in your mind simultaneously. As a result, you are more likely to create a helpful representation of the problem (Leighton & Sternberg, 2003; Ward & Morris, 2005).

Your representation of the problem must show the essential information that you need in order to solve it. Some of the most effective methods of representing problems include symbols, matrices, diagrams, and visual images.

Symbols. Sometimes the most effective way to represent an abstract problem is by using symbols, as you learned to do in high school algebra (Mayer, 2004; Nickerson, 2010). Consider Demonstration 11.2. The usual way of solving this problem is to let a symbol such as m represent Mary's age and a symbol such as s represent Susan's age. We can then "translate" each sentence into a formula. The first sentence becomes $m = 2s - 10$ and the second sentence becomes $m + 5 = s + 5 + 8$. We can then substitute for m in the second sentence and perform the necessary arithmetic. We then learn that Susan must be 18 and Mary must be 26.

A major challenge is that problem solvers often make mistakes when they try to translate words into symbols (Mayer, 2004). One common error is that they reverse the roles of the two variables (Fisher et al., 2011). For example, suppose that college students read the sentence, "There are 8 times as many cats as dogs." Many students make a mistake by translating this sentence into the equation: $8 \times C = D$. Instead, the equation should be: $8 \times D = C$.

An additional error may occur when problem solvers try to translate sentences into symbols: They may oversimplify the sentence, so that they misrepresent the information (Mayer, 2004). For example, Mayer and Hegarty (1996) asked college students to read a series of algebra word problems and then to recall them later. The students often misremembered the problems that contained relational statements. Consider a sentence in an algebra problem about a boat travelling in water: "The engine's rate in still water is 12 miles per hour more than the rate of the current." Many students transformed this statement into a simpler, incorrect form, for example, "The engine's rate in still water is 12 miles per hour." Now try Demonstration 11.3.

ⓢ Demonstration 11.3

Representing a Problem

Read the following information, and fill in the information in the matrix. Then answer the following question, "What disease does Ms. Anderson have, and what is her room number?" (The answer is at the end of the chapter.)

Five people are in a hospital. Each person has only one disease, and each has a different disease. Each person occupies a separate room; the room numbers are 101 through 105.

1. The person with asthma is in Room 101.
2. Ms. Lopez has heart disease.
3. Ms. Green is in Room 105.
4. Ms. Smith has influenza.
5. The woman with a liver problem is in Room 104.
6. Ms. Thomas is in Room 101.
7. Ms. Smith is in Room 102.
8. One of the patients, other than Ms. Anderson, has gallbladder disease.

	Room Number				
	101	102	103	104	105
Anderson					
Lopez					
Green					
Smith					
Thomas					

Source: Based on Schwartz, 1971.

Matrices. You can solve some problems effectively by using a **matrix**, which is a grid consisting of rows and columns; it that shows all possible combinations of items (Hurley & Novick, 2010). A matrix is an excellent way to keep track of items, particularly if the problem is complex and if the relevant information is categorical (Halpern, 2003). For example, you can solve Demonstration 11.3 most effectively by using a matrix like the one at the bottom of this demonstration.

---

⑨ Demonstration 11.4

The Buddhist Monk Problem

At sunrise one morning, a Buddhist monk began to climb a tall mountain. The path was narrow, and it wound around the mountain to a beautiful, gleeming temple at the very top of the mountain.

The monk sometimes climbed the path quickly, and he sometimes went more slowly. From time to time, he also stopped along the way to rest or to eat the fruit he had brought with him. Finally, he reached the temple, just a few minutes before sunset. At the temple, he meditated for several days. Then he began his descent back along the same path. He left the temple at sunrise. As before, he walked slowly at times, but more quickly when the pathway was smooth. Again, he made many stops along the way. Of course, he walked down the hill more quickly than when he was walking up the hill.

Demonstrate that there must be a spot along the path that the monk will pass on both trips at exactly the same time of day. (The answer is found in Figure 11.1.)

Demonstration 11.3 is based on research by Steven Schwartz and his colleagues (Schwartz, 1971; Schwartz & Fattaleh, 1972; Schwartz & Polish, 1974). Schwartz and his coworkers found that students who represented the problem by a matrix were likely to solve the problem correctly. In contrast, students who used alternative problem representations were less successful. Furthermore, you need to use the appropriate labels for a matrix, such as the one in Demonstration 11.3. Otherwise, you are less likely to solve the problem correctly (Hurley & Novick, 2010).

The matrix method is especially suitable when the information is stable, as in Demonstration 11.3, rather than changing over time (Novick, 2006). Now try Demonstration 11.4 before you read further.

Diagrams. If you've ever assembled a new piece of equipment, you probably know that diagrams can be helpful. For example, Novick and Morse (2000) asked students to construct origami objects—such as a miniature piano—using folded paper. People who received both a verbal description and a step-by-step diagram were much more accurate than people who received only a verbal description. Diagrams allow you to represent abstract information in a concrete fashion. They also let you discard unnecessary details (Bassok & Novick, 2012; Reed, 2010; Reif, 2008; Schneider et al., 2010).

Diagrams can also be useful when you want to represent a large amount of information. For example, a **hierarchical tree diagram** is a figure that uses a tree-like structure to show various possible options in a problem. This kind of diagram is especially helpful in showing the relationship between categorized items (Hurley & Novick, 2010; Reed, 2010). Figure 6.3 on page 181 shows a hierarchical tree diagram in a different context.

Furthermore, diagrams can represent complicated information in a clear, concrete form. As a result, you have more "mental space" in your working memory for solving other parts of the problem (Halpern, 2003; Hurley & Novick, 2006). Students can master some kinds of diagrams with relatively little effort (Reed, 2010). For example, Novick and her colleagues (1999) provided students with a brief training session on matrices and hierarchical diagrams. After this training session, students were more skilled in choosing the most appropriate method for representing a variety of problems.

Diagrams can also help people understand a problem. For instance, Grant and Spivey (2003) found that the participants' eye movements were drawn to the most relevant areas of a diagram that accompanied the verbal part of the problem. As a result, they solved problems more successfully.

A graph is sometimes the most effective kind of diagram for representing visual information during problem solving. Consider, for example, the Buddhist monk problem you tried to solve in Demonstration 11.4. As Figure 11.1 illustrates, you could use one line to show the monk going up the mountain on the first day. You could then use a second line to show the monk coming down the mountain several days later. Notice where the lines cross in this figure. This crossing point tells us the spot where the monk will pass at the same time on each of the two days. I have arbitrarily drawn the lines so that they cross at a point 900 feet up the mountain at 12 noon. However, the two paths must always cross at some point, even if you vary the monk's rate of ascent and descent.

FIGURE 11.1

A Graphic Representation of the Buddhist Monk Problem in Demonstration 11.4.

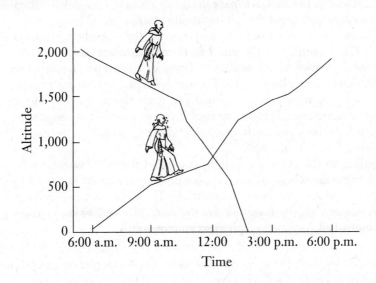

Visual Images. Other people prefer to solve problems like the one about the Buddhist monk by using visual imagery. One young woman reported that she suddenly saw a visual image of one monk walking up the hill. He was then joined by a second monk walking down. As she said, "I realized in a flash that the two figures must meet at some point, some time—regardless at what speed they walk and how often each of them stops" (Koestler, 1964, p. 184).

Notice that a visual image allows us to escape from the boundaries of traditional, concrete representations. Good visual-imagery skills also provide an advantage when a problem requires you to construct a figure (Gorman, 2006; Pylyshyn, 2006).

So far, our discussion of problem solving began by emphasizing that attention is an important component of understanding problems. We've also seen that problems can be represented according to several different formats, including symbols, matrices, diagrams, and visual images. Our final topic in this section moves into a new dimension because it emphasizes the rich external and internal context in which we understand the problems that we must solve.

Situated Cognition, Embodied Cognition, and Problem Solving

When you think about your problem-solving skills, it's tempting to focus only on the information inside your head, which you acquired by reading or listening. However, in recent years, psychologists and cognitive scientists have begun to emphasize additional factors that help us think more quickly and more accurately.

For instance, Chapter 7 introduced the situated cognition approach, in connection with mental maps (pp. 242–243). According to the **situated cognition approach**, we often use helpful information in our immediate environment to create spatial representations. For instance, we make decisions about the up–down dimension more quickly than decisions about the left–right dimension (e.g., Tversky, 2009).

In Chapter 10, we discussed a related concept, the embodied cognition approach (pp. 340–342). According to the **embodied cognition approach**, we often use our own body and our own motor actions, in order to express our abstract thoughts and knowledge (Kirsh, 2009; Reed, 2010; Thomas & Lleras, 2009a). For example, suppose that you are trying to remember a word that is on the tip of your tongue, such as *metronome.* You are more likely to succeed if you are allowed to use gestures, such as waving your hand back and forth, using the same motion as a metronome (Hostetter, 2011; Hostetter & Alibali, 2008).

According to the current research, you often use both situated cognition and embodied cognition when you try to solve problems. You do not need to rely only on the most obvious sources of information. These two terms may sound similar. However, situated cognition emphasizes the external *situation* that surrounds you. In contrast, embodied cognition emphasizes your own *body.*

Situated Cognition. One of the first examples of *situated cognition* comes from studies conducted in Brazil. On the streets of several large Brazilian cities, 10-year-old boys frequently sold candy to people passing by.

Researchers studied these children, who had no formal education. Nevertheless, they demonstrated a sophisticated understanding of mathematics. During that era, Brazil was using an inflated monetary system in which an entire box of candy bars could sell for 20,000 Brazilian cruzeiros. However, the children managed to figure out how to compare two ratios, involving large numbers. For instance, a young boy might offer two candy bars for 500 cruzeiros, but five candy bars for 1,000 cruzeiros. In other words, this 10-year-old needed to understand that a buyer might be tempted to pay less for each candy bar, by purchasing a greater number of candy bars (Carraher et al., 1985; Robertson, 2001; Woll, 2002).

How can children understand ratio comparisons, with such large numbers? This is a concept that 10-year-olds seldom learn in North American schools. The situated cognition approach argues that our ability to solve a problem is tied into the specific physical and social context in which we learned to solve that problem (Chiu et al., 2010; Lave, 1997; Proctor & Vu, 2010; Robertson, 2001). These theorists also argue that an abstract intelligence test often fails to reveal how competent a person would be in solving problems in real-life settings (Kyllonen & Lee, 2005).

The traditional cognitive approach to thinking emphasizes the processes that take place inside an individual person's head. The situated cognition approach argues that the traditional cognitive approach is too simplistic. After all, in real life, our cognitive processes take advantage of an information-rich environment (Chrisley, 2004; Olson & Olson, 2003; Wilson, 2002). In real life, we also interact with other people, who provide information and help us clarify our cognitive processes. All these factors help us become more competent in understanding and solving problems (Glaser, 2001; Kirsh, 2009; Seifert, 1999).

As you can imagine, the situated cognition perspective has important implications for education. It suggests that children should have experience in solving authentic math problems that they are likely to encounter outside a school setting. The situated cognition perspective also suggests that college students can learn especially effectively during internships and other practical settings (Hakel, 2001; Jitendra et al., 2007). We will return to this issue later in the chapter, when we examine how people often fail to appreciate an analogy between previous abstract problem-solving tasks and the problem they are currently trying to solve.

This situated cognition perspective is consistent with the idea that psychologists should emphasize ecological validity if they want to accurately understand cognitive processes. As we discussed earlier in this book, a study has **ecological validity** if the conditions in which the research is conducted are similar to the natural setting in which the results will be applied. For example, a study of children's mathematical skills in selling candy would have greater ecological validity than a study of children's mathematical skills on a paper-and-pencil, standardized examination.

Embodied Cognition. **Many** studies have shown that we solve certain kinds of problems more quickly or more accurately if we are allowed to move parts of our body. For example, Chapter 7 discussed mental rotation tasks, in which people must mentally rotate a geometric figure, to see if it matches another similar figure. (See pp. 213–217.) This research also shows that people perform more accurately on these mental-rotation tasks if they are allowed to move their hands (Chu & Kita, 2011).

Another study about embodied cognition focused on a classic problem-solving task, which required the participants to tie together two ropes that were suspended from the ceiling. This problem could be solved if the participant managed to swing one of the ropes toward the other rope. The research on embodied cognition shows that people are more likely to solve this problem correctly if they had been instructed—during an "exercise break"—to move their arms in a swinging motion (Thomas & Lleras, 2009b). Similarly, participants are more likely to choose a hand-movement strategy to solve a mechanical problem about the movement of gears, if they had previous experience with hand gestures (Alibali et al., 2011).

Section Summary: *Understanding the Problem*

1. During problem solving, you begin with the initial state and try to overcome the obstacles in order to reach the goal state.

2. To understand a problem, you need to create an accurate mental representation of the problem.

3. Attention is relevant in problem solving because attention is limited, because competing thoughts can produce divided attention, and because problem solvers must focus their attention on the appropriate part of the problem.

4. You can represent a problem by using approaches such as symbols, matrices, diagrams, and visual images.

5. Environmental cues (situated cognition) and cues related to your own body (embodied cognition) can influence the way you represent a problem; as a result, you can solve the problem more accurately.

PROBLEM-SOLVING STRATEGIES

Once you have represented the problem, you try to solve it by using a strategy. Some strategies are very time consuming. For instance, an **algorithm** is a method that will always produce a solution to the problem, although the process can sometimes be inefficient (Sternberg & Ben-Zeev, 2001; Thagard, 2005). One example of an algorithm is a method called an **exhaustive search**, in which you try out all possible answers using a specified system.

Algorithms are often inefficient and unsophisticated. Other, more sophisticated methods reduce the possibilities that must be explored to find a solution. For example, suppose that you have been working on some anagrams, rearranging a random string of letters to create an English word. The next anagram is LSSTNEUIAMYOUL. You might begin to solve that lengthy anagram by trying to identify the first two letters of your target word. Specifically, you decide to pick out only pronounceable two-letter combinations that frequently appear at the beginning of an English word. Perhaps you would reject combinations such as LS, LT, and LY, but you consider LE, LU, and—ideally—SI. This strategy would probably lead you to a solution much faster than an exhaustive search of all the more than 87 billion possible arrangements of the fourteen letters in SIMULTANEOUSLY.

The strategy of looking only for pronounceable letter combinations is an example of a heuristic. As you know from other chapters, a **heuristic** is a general rule that is usually correct (Nickerson, 2010). If you use a heuristic strategy to solve a problem, you would ignore some alternatives and explore only those alternatives that seem especially likely to produce a solution.

We noted that algorithms such as an exhaustive search will always produce a solution, although you may grow a few years older in the process. Heuristics, in contrast, do not guarantee a correct solution. For instance, suppose you were given the anagram IPMHYLOD. Suppose also that you use the heuristic of rejecting a combination of letters if it seldom appears at the beginning of a word. If you reject words beginning with LY, then you would fail to find the correct solution, LYMPHOID. When solving a problem, you'll need to weigh the benefits of a heuristic's speed against the costs of possibly missing the correct solution.

Psychologists have conducted more research on problem solvers' heuristics than on their algorithms. One reason is that we are more likely to successfully solve everyday problems with heuristics than algorithms. Three of the most widely used heuristics are the analogy, the means-ends heuristic, and the hill-climbing heuristic. Let's examine these three heuristics.

The Analogy Approach

Every day, you use analogies to solve problems. When confronted with a problem in a statistics course, for example, you refer to previous examples in your textbook. When you write a paper for your cognitive psychology course, you use many of the same strategies that were helpful when you wrote a previous paper for social psychology. When you use the **analogy approach** in problem solving, you employ a solution to a similar, earlier problem to help you solve a new problem (Benjamin & Ross, 2011; Leighton & Sternberg, 2003; Schelhorn et al., 2007).

Analogies are widely used in problem solving (Bassok & Novick, 2012). For example, one study reported that engineers created an average of 102 analogies during 9 hours spent on problem solving (Christensen & Schunn, 2007). In a cross-cultural study, students in Brazil, India, and the United States typically chose the analogy approach as their preferred strategy in solving problems (Güss & Wiley, 2007). Take a moment to think about several times when you used the analogy approach.

Analogies are also prominent when people make creative breakthroughs in areas such as art, politics, science, and engineering (Kyllonen & Lee, 2005; Schwering et al., 2009; Young, 2007). For example, Wilbur and Orville Wright designed some of the features of their airplanes by creating an analogy between the wings of a bird and the wings of an airplane. Specifically, they noticed that birds could control their flight patterns by making small adjustments in the orientation of their wing tips. They therefore designed airplane wing tips so that pilots could make subtle adjustments by using metal rods and gears (Weisberg, 2006).

Let's first consider the general structure of the analogy approach. Then we'll look at some of the factors that can encourage problem solvers to use the analogy approach most effectively. First, however, try Demonstration 11.5.

The Structure of the Analogy Approach. The major challenge for people who use the analogy strategy is to determine the real problem—that is, the abstract puzzle underneath all the details. In the section on understanding the problem, we emphasized that problem solvers must peel away the irrelevant, superficial details in

---

⦿ Demonstration 11.5

The Elves-and-Goblins Problem

Try solving this problem. (The answer is at the end of the chapter.)

As you may know, Elves and Goblins are mythical creatures. Imagine that three Elves and three Goblins all arrive at the right side of a riverbank, and they all want to cross to the left side. Fortunately, there is a boat. However, the boat is small, and it can hold only two creatures at one time. There is another problem. The three hostile-looking creatures at the bottom of this sketch are Goblins, and Goblins are vicious creatures. The three gentle-looking creatures are Elves. Here is the problem: Whenever there are more Goblins than Elves on one side of the river, the Goblins will immediately attack the Elves and gobble them up. Therefore, you must be absolutely certain that you never leave more Goblins than Elves on any riverbank. How would you solve this dilemma? (Please note that the Goblins, though vicious, can be trusted to bring the boat back!)

order to reach the core of the problem (Whitten & Graesser, 2003). Researchers use the term **problem isomorphs** to refer to a set of problems that have the same underlying structures and solutions, but different specific details.

Unfortunately, people tend to focus more on the superficial content of the problem than on its abstract, underlying meaning (Bassok, 2003; Whitten & Graesser, 2003). In other words, they pay attention to the obvious **surface features** such as the specific objects and terms used in the question. As a result, they fail to emphasize the **structural features**, the underlying core that they must understand in order to solve the problem correctly. (Try Demonstration 11.5 before you read further.)

For example, Rutgers University wanted to design a system that would allow prospective students to keep track of the status of their college applications. At first, Rutgers staff members looked only at the systems used by other universities, which were similar to their own existing system in terms of surface features. This analogy was not effective. Fortunately, however, the Rutgers staff then shifted their attention to structural features, rather than superficial features. At this point, the staff realized that the *real* problem involved tracking the applicants. So then they decided to examine Federal Express, to see how this company solved the problem of tracking the location of its packages. Their system provided a highly effective solution to Rutgers' college-application problem (Ruben, 2001).

The research clearly shows that people often fail to see the analogy between a problem they have solved and a new problem isomorph that has similar structural features (e.g., Barnett & Ceci, 2002; Bassok & Novick, 2012; Leighton & Sternberg, 2003; Lovett, 2002). As we saw in the discussion of the situated cognition perspective (pp. 242–243), people often have trouble solving the same problem in a new setting; they fail to transfer their knowledge. Similarly, they have trouble solving the same problem when it is "dressed up" with a superficially different cover story (Bassok, 2003). People who have limited problem-solving skills and limited metacognitive ability are especially likely to have difficulty using analogies (Chen et al., 2004; Davidson & Sternberg, 1998).

Factors that Encourage Appropriate Use of Analogies. Fortunately, people often overcome the influence of context, and they can use the analogy method appropriately (Lovett, 2002). They are more likely to use the analogy strategy correctly when they try several structurally similar problems before they tackle the target problem (Bassok, 2003). Furthermore, students solve statistics problems more accurately if they have been trained to sort problems into categories on the basis of structural similarities (Quilici & Mayer, 2002).

The Means-Ends Heuristic

The means-ends heuristic has two important components: (1) First, you divide the problem into a number of **subproblems**, or smaller problems, and (2) then you try to reduce the difference between the initial state and the goal state for each of the subproblems (Bassok & Novick, 2012; Davies, 2005; Ormerod, 2005). The name **means-ends heuristic** is appropriate because it requires you to identify the "ends" (or final result) that you want and then figure out the "means" or methods that you will use to reach those ends (Feltovich et al., 2006; Ward & Morris, 2005). When problem solvers use the means-ends heuristic, they must focus their attention on the difference between the initial problem state and the goal state. Researchers emphasize that this heuristic is one of the most effective and flexible problem-solving strategies (Dunbar, 1998; Lovett, 2002).

On a daily basis, we solve problems by using means-ends analysis. For example, several years ago, a student I knew well came running into my office saying, "Can I use your stapler, Dr. Matlin?" When I handed her the stapler, she immediately inserted the bottom edge of her skirt and deftly tacked up the hem. As she explained in a more leisurely fashion later that day, she had been faced with a problem: At 11:50, she realized that the hem of her skirt had come loose, and she was scheduled to deliver a class presentation in 10 minutes. Using the means-ends heuristic, she divided the problem into two subproblems: (1) identifying an object that could fix the hem—even though this object was not a traditional "hem-fixer"—and (2) locating this object.

Research on the Means-Ends Heuristic. Research demonstrates that people do organize problems in terms of subproblems. For example, Greeno (1974) examined how people solve the Elves-and-Goblins problem in Demonstration 11.5. His study showed that people pause at points in the problem when they begin to tackle a subproblem and need to organize a sequence of moves. Working memory is especially active when people are planning one of these movement sequences (Simon, 2001; Ward & Allport, 1997).

Sometimes the correct solution to a problem requires you to move backward, temporarily *increasing* the difference between the initial state and the goal state. For example, how did you solve the Elves-and-Goblins problem in Demonstration 11.5? Maybe you concentrated on *decreasing* the difference between the initial state (all creatures on the right side) and the goal state (all creatures on the left side). You therefore moved them only from right to left. If you did, you would have ignored some steps that were crucial for solving the problem. For example, in Step 6 you needed to move two creatures backward across the river to the riverbank on the right. (See the steps in the answer on page 405.)

The research confirms that people are reluctant to move away from the goal state—even if the correct solution requires you to make this temporary detour (Bassok & Novick, 2012; R. Morris et al., 2005). In real life, as in the Elves-and-Goblins problem, the most effective way to move forward is sometimes to move backward temporarily.

Computer Simulation. One of the best-known examples of computer simulation was devised to account for the way humans use means-ends analysis to solve well-defined problems. Specifically, Allen Newell and Herbert Simon developed a theory that featured subgoals and reducing the difference between the initial state and the goal state (Newell & Simon, 1972; Simon, 1995, 1999). Let's first consider some general characteristics of computer simulation, when applied to problem solving. Then we'll briefly discuss Newell and Simon's approach, as well as more recent developments in computer simulation.

When researchers use **computer simulation**, they write a computer program that will perform a task in the same way that a human would. For example, a researcher might try to write a computer program for the Elves-and-Goblins problem, which you tried in Demonstration 11.5. The program should make some false starts, just as a human would. The program should be no better at solving the problem than a human would be, and it also should be no worse. The researchers test the program by having it solve a problem and noting whether the steps it takes would match the steps that humans would take in solving the problem.

In 1972, Newell and Simon developed a now-classic computer simulation called General Problem Solver. **General Problem Solver (GPS)** is a program whose basic strategy is means-ends analysis. The goal of the GPS is to mimic the processes that normal humans use when they tackle these problems (Lovett, 2002; Simon, 1996). GPS has several different methods of operating, including the difference-reduction strategy.

Newell and Simon (1972) began by asking participants to talk out loud while working on a relevant problem. They used the narrative from the participants to create specific computer simulations, to solve problems such as the Elves-and-Goblins transport problem.

The General Problem Solver was the first program to simulate a variety of human symbolic behaviors (Sobel, 2001; Sternberg & Ben-Zeev, 2001). As a result, GPS has had an important impact on the history of cognitive psychology (Bassok & Novick, 2012). However, Newell and Simon eventually discarded the GPS because its generality was not as great as they had wished, especially because real-life problems are not so clear cut (Gardner, 1985; Sobel, 2001).

More recently, John Anderson and his colleagues have designed and tested many computer simulations for solving problems similar to the Elves-and-Goblins one, as well as problems in algebra, geometry, and computer science (e.g., Anderson et al., 1995; Anderson et al., 2008; Anderson & Gluck, 2001). These projects are related to Anderson's ACT-R theory, which was summarized in Chapter 8. These programs were originally developed to learn more about how people acquire skills in problem solving. However, these researchers have also developed "cognitive tutors" that can be used in high school mathematics classes (Anderson et al., 1995; Anderson et al., 2005). Notice, then, that a project initially designed to examine theoretical questions can be applied to real-life situations.

The Hill-Climbing Heuristic

One of the most straightforward problem-solving strategies is called the hill-climbing heuristic. To understand this heuristic, imagine that you are hiking along a path in an unfamiliar area. Your goal is to reach the top of a hill. Just ahead, you see a fork in this path. Unfortunately, you cannot see far into the distance on either of the two paths. Because your goal is to climb upward, you select the path that has the steepest incline. Similarly, if you are using the **hill-climbing heuristic**—and you reach a choice point—you consistently choose the alternative that seems to lead most directly toward your goal (Lovett, 2002; Ward & Morris, 2005).

The hill-climbing heuristic can be useful when you do not have enough information about your alternatives, because you can see only the immediate next step. However, like many heuristics, the hill-climbing heuristic can lead you astray. The biggest drawback to this heuristic is that problem solvers must consistently choose the alternative that appears to lead most directly toward the goal. In doing so, they may fail to choose an *indirect* alternative, which may have greater long-term benefits. For example, a hillside path that seems to lead upward may quickly come to an abrupt end. The hill-climbing heuristic does not guarantee that you'll end up on the top of the hill (Robertson, 2001).

Similarly, a student whose career goal is to earn a high salary may decide to take a job immediately after graduating from college, although a graduate degree would probably yield greater long-term benefits. Sometimes the best solution to a problem requires us to move temporarily backward—away from the goal (Lovett, 2002). The major point to remember about the hill-climbing heuristic is that it encourages short-term goals, rather than long-term solutions.

◉ Section Summary: *Problem-Solving Strategies*

1. With algorithms, such as exhaustive search, the problem solver eventually reaches a solution. However, this method is often very time consuming. In contrast, heuristics are faster because they examine only a few of the alternatives; unfortunately, they do not guarantee an appropriate solution.

2. One important heuristic is the analogy approach, in which people solve a new problem by referring to an earlier problem. They may be distracted by superficial similarity, but several precautions can encourage people to emphasize structural similarity.

3. The means-ends heuristic requires dividing a problem into subproblems and then trying to reduce the difference between the initial state and the goal state for each of the subproblems. The General Problem Solver (GPS) is a computer simulation that was designed to use means-ends analysis.

4. One of the simplest problem-solving strategies is the hill-climbing heuristic; at every choice point, you select the alternative that seems to lead most directly to the goal. However, this strategy may not produce the best long-term solution.

FACTORS THAT INFLUENCE PROBLEM SOLVING

According to Theme 5 of this book, our cognitive processes rely on both bottom-up processing and top-down processing. **Bottom-up processing** emphasizes the information about the stimulus, as registered on our sensory receptors. In contrast, **top-down processing** emphasizes our concepts, expectations, and memory, which we have acquired from past experience.

As you'll see in this section, these two types of processing help us understand how several important factors can influence our ability to solve a problem. For example, people with expertise use top-down processing effectively when they solve problems; they take advantage of factors such as their knowledge, memory, and strategies. In contrast, both mental set and functional fixedness can interfere when we try to solve a problem; both of these factors rely too heavily on top-down processing. This chapter's In-Depth section also shows how gender stereotypes may encourage people to rely on overactive top-down processing, which leads to poor problem-solving performance. Finally, if the problem requires insight, we must also overcome overactive top-down processing in order to approach the problem from an unfamiliar perspective. In short, effective problem solving requires an ideal blend of both top-down and bottom-up processing (Theme 5).

Expertise

An individual with **expertise** demonstrates consistently exceptional skill and performance on representative tasks for a particular area (Ericsson, 2006; Ericsson & Towne, 2010; Ericsson et al., 2009). For many years, researchers also specified that an expert needed at least 10 years of experience in a particular area of expertise. However, many researchers have dropped that criterion. The problem was that the number of years of experience was not strongly correlated with excellent performance in a variety of fields, such as being skilled as a psychotherapist.

Earlier in this book, we noted that experts in a particular discipline are likely to have superior long-term memory related to that discipline (Chapter 5), as well as the detailed structure of their concepts (Chapter 8). Now we'll explore how expertise facilitates performance in problem solving. Specifically, experts have developed top-down processes that allow them to perform well on many different components of problem solving in their particular area. However, people with expertise in one area typically do not excel in another areas (Feltovich et al., 2006; Robertson, 2001). Let's trace how experts differ from novices on a variety of dimensions that are crucial to problem solving.

Knowledge Base. Experts and novices differ substantially in their knowledge base and schemas (Bransford et al., 2000; Ericsson & Towne, 2010; Feltovich et al., 2006; Robertson, 2001). As Michelene Chi (1981) found in her classic study of physics problem solving, the novices simply lacked important knowledge about the principles of physics.

As we discussed in previous chapters, you need the appropriate schemas in order to understand a topic properly. Experts may solve problems especially well if they have had training in a variety of relevant settings, and if the training includes immediate detailed feedback (Barnett & Koslowski, 2002; Ericsson & Towne, 2010).

Memory. Experts differ from novices with respect to their memory for information related to their area of expertise (Bransford et al., 2000; Chi, 2006; Robertson, 2001). The memory skills of experts tend to be very specific. For example, expert chess players have much better memory than novices for various chess positions.

According to one estimate, chess experts can remember about 50,000 "chunks," or familiar arrangements of chess pieces (Chi, 2006; Gobet & Simon, 1996a). Expert chess players can also rapidly retrieve information from long-term memory (Ericsson & Towne, 2010).

Surprisingly, though, chess experts are only slightly better than novices at remembering random arrangements of the chess pieces (Gobet et al., 2004). In other words, experts' memory is substantially better only if the chess arrangement fits into a particular schema (Feltovich et al., 2006; Lovett, 2002).

Problem-Solving Strategies. When experts encounter a novel problem in their area of expertise, they are more likely than novices to use the means-ends heuristic effectively (Sternberg & Ben-Zeev, 2001). That is, they divide a problem into several

---

⑨ Demonstration 11.6

Mental Set

Try these two examples to see the effects of mental set.

A. Luchins's Water-Jar Problem. Suppose that you have three jars, A, B, and C. Each of six problems (listed below) shows the capacity of the three jars. You must use these jars in order to obtain the amount of liquid specified in the Goal column. You may obtain the goal amount by adding or subtracting the quantities listed in A, B, and C. (The answers can be found later in the text, in the discussion of mental set.)

Problem	A	B	C	Goal
1	24	130	3	100
2	9	44	7	21
3	21	58	4	29
4	12	160	25	98
5	19	75	5	46
6	23	49	3	20

B. A Number Puzzle. You are no doubt familiar with the kind of number puzzles in which you try to figure out the pattern for the order of numbers. Why are these numbers arranged in this order?

8, 5, 4, 9, 1, 7, 6, 3, 2, 0

The answer appears at the end of the chapter.

Source: Part A of this demonstration is based on Luchins, 1942.

subproblems, which they solve in a specified order. They are also more likely to approach a problem systematically, whereas novices are more likely to have a haphazard approach (Reif, 2008).

In addition, experts and novices differ in the way they use the analogy approach. When solving physics problems, experts are more likely to emphasize the structural similarity between problems. In contrast, novices are more likely to be distracted by surface similarities (Chi, 2006; Leighton & Sternberg, 2003). Now try Demonstration 11.6 before you read further.

Speed and Accuracy. As you might expect, experts are much faster than novices, and they solve problems very accurately (Chi, 2006; Ericsson, 2003b; Ericsson & Towne, 2010). Their operations become more automatic, and a particular stimulus situation also quickly triggers a response (Bransford et al., 2000; Glaser & Chi, 1988; Robertson, 2001).

On some tasks, experts may solve problems faster because they use parallel processing, rather than serial processing. As we noted earlier in the book, **parallel processing** handles two or more items at the same time. In contrast, **serial processing** handles only one item at a time. Novick and Coté (1992) discovered that experts frequently solved anagrams in less than 2 seconds. In fact, they typically solved the anagrams so quickly that they must have been considering several possible solutions at the same time. In contrast, the novices solved the anagrams so slowly that they were probably using serial processing.

Metacognitive Skills. Experts are better than novices at monitoring their problem solving. You may recall from Chapter 6 that self-monitoring is a component of metacognition. For example, experts seem to be better at judging the difficulty of a problem, and they are more skilled at allocating their time appropriately when solving problems (Bransford et al., 2000). According to a study of people who are inventors, the expert inventors skillfully monitor ideas, to see that they are useful, as well as creative (Mieg, 2011). Experts can also recover relatively quickly when they realize that they have made an error (Feltovich et al., 2006).

Experts are definitely more skilled at numerous phases of problem solving, and they are also more skilled at monitoring their progress while working on a problem. However, experts perform poorly on one task related to metacognition. Specifically, experts underestimate the amount of time that novices will require to solve a problem in the experts' area of specialization (Hinds, 1999). In contrast, the novices are more accurate in realizing that they will have trouble solving the problem!

Mental Set

Before you read further, be sure to try Demonstration 11.6, which illustrates two examples of a mental set. In a situation when you have a **mental set**, you keep trying the same solution you used in previous problems, even though you could solve the problem by using a different, easier method. If you have a mental set, you close your mind prematurely, and you stop thinking about how to solve a problem effectively (Kruglanski, 2004; Zhao et al., 2011). Interestingly, recent research shows that people have a greater change in their event-related brain potentials (ERPs) on trials when they break a mental set, compared to trials when they keep trying their customary problem-solving strategy (Zhao et al., 2011).

We noted earlier that problem solving requires both top-down and bottom-up processing (Theme 5). Experts make appropriate use of top-down processing, because they can use their previous knowledge to solve problems both quickly and accurately. In contrast, both mental set and functional fixedness—which we'll discuss in a moment—represent overactive top-down processing. In both of these cases, problem solvers are so strongly guided by their previous experience that they fail to consider more effective solutions to their problems.

The classic experiment on mental set is Abraham Luchins's (1942) water-jar problem, illustrated in Part A of Demonstration 11.6. The best way to solve Problem 1 in Part A is to fill up jar B and remove one jarful with jar A and two jarfuls with jar C. You can solve Problems 1 through 5 by using this strategy, so you develop a mental set. Most people will keep using this complex method when they reach Problem 6. Unfortunately, however, the previous learning will actually hinder your performance, because you can solve these last two problems by using easier, more direct methods. For example, you can solve Problem 6 by subtracting C from A, and you can solve Problem 7 by adding C to A.

Luchins also tested a group who began right away with problems such as Problem 6 in Demonstration 11.6. These people almost always solved these problems in the easier fashion.

Mental sets are related to a concept that Carol Dweck (2006) calls a "fixed mindset." If you have a **fixed mindset,** you believe that you possess a certain amount of intelligence and other skills, and no amount of effort can help you perform better. You give up on trying to discover new ways to improve your abilities. In contrast, if you have a **growth mindset,** you believe that you can cultivate your intelligence and other skills. You challenge yourself to perform better, whether you are trying to learn how to play tennis, how to adjust to a new roommate, or how to perform better on your next examination in your course in cognitive psychology.

Functional Fixedness

Like a mental set, functional fixedness occurs when our top-down processing is overactive. We therefore rely too heavily on our previous concepts, expectations, and memory. However, mental set refers to our problem-solving *strategies,* whereas functional fixedness refers to the way we think about *physical objects.* Specifically, **functional fixedness** means that we tend to assign stable (or "fixed") functions to an object. As a result, we fail to think about the features of this object that might be useful in helping us solve a problem (German & Barrett, 2005).

The classic study in functional fixedness is called *Duncker's candle problem* (Duncker, 1945). Imagine that a researcher has led you into a room that contains a table. On the table are three objects: a candle, a matchbox holding some matches, and a box of thumbtacks. Your task is to find a way to attach a candle to the wall of the room so that it burns properly, using only the objects on the table. The solution requires overcoming functional fixedness by thinking flexibly about other ways to use an object (Bassok & Novick, 2012). In this situation, you need to realize that the matchbox can also be used for a different purpose—holding a candle—rather than just holding some matches. In fact, you can use the tack to fasten the empty matchbox to the wall, so that it can serve as a candle-holder.

In our everyday life, most of us have access to a variety of tools and objects, so functional fixedness does not create a significant handicap. In contrast, consider the quandary of Dr. Angus Wallace and Dr. Tom Wong, who provided a heroic example of overcoming functional fixedness. These physicians had just left on a plane for Hong Kong when they learned that another passenger was experiencing a collapsed lung. The only surgical items they had brought onboard were a segment of rubber tubing and a scalpel. Still, they operated on the woman and saved her life, using only this modest equipment and objects in the airplane that normally have fixed functions—a coat hanger, a knife, a fork, and a bottle of Evian water (Adler & Hall, 1995).

Interestingly, functional fixedness can also be demonstrated in cultures with little experience using manufactured objects. For example, German and Barrett (2005) showed some simple kitchen objects to adolescents living near the Amazon River in Ecuador. If the adolescents saw a spoon being used to stir rice, they later had difficulty imagining that the spoon could also serve as a bridge between two other objects.

Mental set and functional fixedness are two examples of part of Theme 2: Mistakes in cognitive processing can often be traced to a strategy that is basically very rational. It is generally a wise strategy to use the knowledge you learned in solving earlier problems to solve a current dilemma. If an old idea happens to work well, keep using it! However, in the case of a mental set, we are too rigid in applying a strategy that we learned from previous experience. We therefore fail to think about more efficient solutions.

Similarly, objects in our world normally have fixed functions. For example, we use a screwdriver to tighten a screw, and we use a coin to purchase something. In general, the strategy of using one object for one task and a second object for a different task is appropriate. Functional fixedness occurs, however, when we apply that strategy too rigidly. For example, we fail to realize that—if we don't have a screwdriver—a coin may provide a handy substitute.

IN DEPTH

Gender Stereotypes and Math Problem Solving

So far, we have examined mental set and functional fixedness, two situations in which top-down processes are overactive. Let's now focus on a third situation: Our top-down processes may be overactive because stereotypes can influence our beliefs about our own abilities (Walton & Dweck, 2009). Psychologists have conducted studies on stereotypes based on ethnic group, social class, and age. However, the most widely researched topic is gender stereotypes that focus on problem solving in mathematics.

As we noted in Chapter 8, **gender stereotypes** are the beliefs and opinions that we associate with females and males (Jackson, 2011; Matlin, 2012; Whitley & Kite, 2010). A typical gender stereotype is that men are more skilled than women in solving mathematics problems. Gender stereotypes about cognitive skills may sometimes be partially accurate, but they do not apply to everybody. Let's examine the research, as it relates to problem solving.

For example, Janet Hyde and her colleagues (2008) analyzed scores on standardized mathematics tests for 7,200,000 U.S. students. They found consistent gender similarities for students of all ages, from second grade through eleventh grade. One gender comparison is especially relevant for this chapter: The researchers found gender similarities, even when the test required students to solve complex math problems. The same pattern of gender similarities is found in studies conducted with international samples (Else-Quest et al., 2010; Halpern, 2012). Furthermore, females earn *higher* grades in math courses, beginning with elementary school and continuing up through college (Halpern, 2012; Kimball, 1989).

To provide a context for our discussion here, glance back at the research about inferences based on gender stereotypes. Pages 288 to 289 of Chapter 8 reported, for example, that many women do not associate themselves with mathematics, and this tendency holds true even for women who are math majors.

The Nature of Stereotype Threat. Imagine two high school seniors, Jennifer and Matthew, who are about to begin the math portion of the Scholastic Assessment Test (SAT). Both are excellent students, with A averages in their math courses. They know that this may be the most important test they will ever take, because the results could determine which college they will attend.

Both students are anxious, but Jennifer has an additional source of anxiety: She must struggle with the wide-spread stereotype that, because she is a female, she should score lower than male students (Quinn & Spencer, 2001). This additional anxiety may in fact lead her to solve math problems less effectively and to earn a relatively low score on the math portion of the SAT. In this example, Jennifer is experiencing **stereotype threat**: If you belong to a group that is hampered by a negative stereotype—and you think about your membership in that group—your performance may suffer (Smith et al., 2007; Steele, 1997; Whitley & Kite, 2010).

Research with Asian American Females. Let's examine a study conducted by Margaret Shih and her coauthors (1999), in which all of the participants were Asian American female college students. In North America, one stereotype is that Asian Americans are "good at math," compared to those from other ethnic groups. In contrast, as we just discussed, another stereotype is that women are "bad at math," compared to men.

Shih and her coworkers (1999) divided these Asian American women into three different conditions. Let's examine how these conditions influenced their scores on a challenging math test.

1. *Ethnicity-emphasis condition*: One group of participants were asked to indicate their ethnicity and then answer several questions about their ethnic identity. Then they took a challenging math test. These women answered 54% of the questions correctly.

2. *Control-group condition*: A second group of participants did not answer any questions beforehand. They simply took the challenging math test. These women answered 49% of the questions correctly.

3. *Gender-emphasis condition*: A third group of participants were asked to indicate their gender and then answer several questions about their gender identity. Then they took the challenging math test. These women answered only 43% of the questions correctly.

Apparently, when Asian American women are reminded of their ethnicity, they perform relatively well. However, when Asian American women are reminded of their gender, they may experience stereotype threat, and their problem-solving ability can decline. Nalini Ambady and her coauthors (2001) demonstrated this same pattern among Asian American girls enrolled in elementary and middle school.

Research with European American Females. The effects of stereotype threat have also been replicated in samples where most of the women are European American (O'Brien & Crandall, 2003; Quinn & Spencer, 2001). For instance, O'Brien and Crandall (2003) studied a group of college women who were taking a difficult math test. Some women had been told that they would take a math test that was known to show higher scores for men than for women. These women performed significantly worse than women in a second group, who had been told that the math test had not shown gender differences.

In a similar study, Dustin Thoman and his colleagues (2008) told one group of female students that males tend to perform better than females on math tests because males have greater *ability*. A second group of female students heard the same instructions, except that the males' better performance occurred because males *try harder*. A third group served as the control group; they received no information about gender differences. Interestingly, the women in the "try harder" condition answered a significantly greater percentage of questions correctly, compared to the women in the other two conditions.

Potential Explanations. Why should stereotype threat often lead to poorer performance? Two factors probably contribute to the problem. One factor is that stereotype threat can produce high arousal (Blascovich et al., 2001; O'Brien & Crandall, 2003). High arousal is likely to interfere with working memory, especially on difficult tasks. Research shows that people may "choke under pressure" on a challenging math test. This anxiety apparently reduces the capacity of working memory (Beilock & Carr, 2005).

A second factor is that females who are taking a difficult math test may work hard to suppress the thought that they are supposed to perform poorly (Quinn &

Spencer, 2001). As Chapter 3 pointed out, thought suppression requires great effort, which reduces the capacity of working memory even further.

In what way do the increased arousal and reduced working memory actually decrease women's ability to solve math problems? Quinn and Spencer (2001) proposed that these factors decrease women's abilities to construct problem-solving strategies. They studied female and male undergraduates. Half of each group completed a test with word problems; these items required strategies in order to convert the words into algebraic equations. The other half of each group completed a test with algebra problems that were presented as numerical equations. These items did not require any conversion strategies. Figure 11.2 shows that the men performed signifiantly better than the women on the word-problem test, but there were no gender differences on the numerical test.

FIGURE 11.2

Average Performance by Men and Women on Word-Problem Test and Numerical Test.

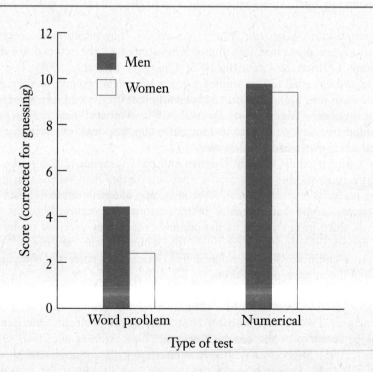

Source: Quinn, D. M., & Spencer, S. J. (2001). The interference of stereotype threat with women's generation of mathematical problem-solving strategies. *Journal of Social Issues, 57*, 55–71.

As this in-depth section has shown, researchers have examined numerous gender comparisons in mathematical problem solving. In general, these studies show gender similarities in problem-solving skills. The studies also show that female students may earn lower scores if they receive messages that females are less competent than males in mathematics. Now, before you read further, try Demonstration 11.7.

---

⑨ Demonstration 11.7

Two Insight Problems

A. **The Sahara Problem** (based on Perkins, 2001). Suppose that you are driving through the Sahara Desert in Africa. Suddenly, you see someone lying facedown in the sand. When you explore further, you see that it's a dead man. You cannot see any tracks anywhere nearby, and there have been no recent winds to erase the tracks. You look in a pack on the man's back. What do you find?

B. **The Triangle Problem**. With six matches, construct four equilateral triangles. One intact match (not broken or bent) must make up one side of each triangle. The answers to these two problems are at the end of the chapter.

Insight Versus Noninsight Problems

When you solve an **insight problem**, the problem initially seems impossible to solve, but then an alternative approach suddenly bursts into your consciousness. You immediately realize that your new solution is correct (Gibson et al., 2011; Johnson-Laird, 2005b; Reed, 2010). In general, people who have a large working-memory capacity solve insight problems relatively quickly (Chein et al., 2010).

In contrast, when you work on a **noninsight problem**, you solve the problem gradually, by using your memory, reasoning skills, and a routine set of strategies (Davidson, 1995; Schooler et al., 1995). For example, Demonstration 11.1 was a noninsight problem, because you gradually pursued the answer in a logical, step-by-step fashion.

When cartoonists represent insight, they show a gleaming light bulb above a person's head. You can probably think of a time when you or someone you know suddenly experienced an "aha!" moment. For example, I recall a vivid "aha!" moment that our daughter Sally demonstrated in connection with the Tooth Fairy. As you may know, many North American families have an eccentric custom. When a child has lost a tooth, he or she places it in a sealed envelope, underneath a pillow at nighttime. Then, when the child is asleep, an adult quietly replaces that envelope with a different envelope that contains a modest amount of money, presumably brought by the small, surreptitious Tooth Fairy.

After several visits from the Tooth Fairy, we noticed that our daughter wore a perplexed expression. She then described her puzzlement: "What I don't understand is how the Tooth Fairy can take out the tooth and put the money in the envelope without tearing the envelope... *unless* there are two different envelopes!!!" If you solved the problems successfully in Demonstration 11.7, you experienced a similar feeling of sudden success.

Let's examine several components of insight. Then we'll consider people's metacognitions when working on insight and noninsight problems.

The Nature of Insight. The concept of insight was very important to gestalt psychologists (Fioratou & Cowley, 2011; Johnson-Laird, 2005b; Lovett, 2002). As Chapters 1 and 2 noted, gestalt psychologists emphasized organizational tendencies, especially in perception and in problem solving. They argued that the parts of a problem may initially seem unrelated to one another, but a sudden flash of insight could make the parts instantly fit together into a solution. In contrast to the gestalt psychologists, the behaviorists rejected the concept of insight.

According to the psychologists who favor this concept of insight, people who are working on an insight problem usually hold some incorrect assumptions when they begin to solve the problem (Chi, 2006; Ormerod et al., 2006; Reed, 2010). For example, when you began to solve Part B of Demonstration 11.7, at first you probably assumed that the six matches needed to be arranged on a flat surface. In other words, top-down processing inappropriately dominated your thinking, and you were considering the wrong set of alternatives (Ormerod et al., 2006).

We've noted that top-down processing may prevent you from solving an insight problem. In contrast, noninsight problems—such as straightforward algebra problems—typically do benefit from top-down processing (McCormick, 2003). The strategies you learned in high school math classes offer guidance as you work, step-by-step, toward the proper conclusion of the problem.

Metacognition During Problem Solving. When you are working on a problem, how confident are you that you are on the right track? Janet Metcalfe (1986) emphasizes that the pattern of your metacognitions differs for noninsight and insight problems. Specifically, people's confidence builds gradually for problems that do not require insight, such as standard high-school algebra problems. In contrast, when people work on insight problems, they experience a sudden leap in confidence when they are close to a correct solution. In fact, this sudden rise in confidence can be used to distinguish insight from noninsight problems (Hélie & Sun, 2010; Herzog & Robinson, 2005; Metcalfe & Wiebe, 1987).

Let us examine Metcalfe's (1986) classic research on metacognitions about insight problems. Metcalfe presented students with problems like this one:

A stranger approached a museum curator and offered him an ancient bronze coin. The coin had an authentic appearance and was marked with the date 544 B.C. The curator had happily made acquisitions from suspicious sources before, but this time he promptly called the police and had the stranger arrested. Why? (p. 624).

As students worked on this kind of insight problem, they supplied ratings every 10 seconds on a "feeling-of-warmth" scale. A rating of 0 indicated that they were completely "cold" about the problem, with no glimmer of a solution. A score of 10 meant that they were certain they had a solution.

As you can see from the left-hand side of Figure 11.3, the participants' warmth ratings initially showed only gradual increases for the insight problems. However, their warmth ratings soared dramatically when they discovered the correct solution. If you figured out the answer to the coin question, did you experience this same sudden burst of certainty? (Incidentally, the answer to this problem is that someone who had actually lived in 544 B.C. could not possibly have used the designation "B.C." to indicate the birth of Christ half a millennium later.) Metcalfe's results have been replicated (Davidson, 1995), confirming that problem solvers typically report a dramatic increase in their confidence when they believe they have located the correct solution to an insight problem.

FIGURE 11.3

"Warmth Ratings" for Answers That Were Correct, as a Function of Time of Rating Prior to Answering.

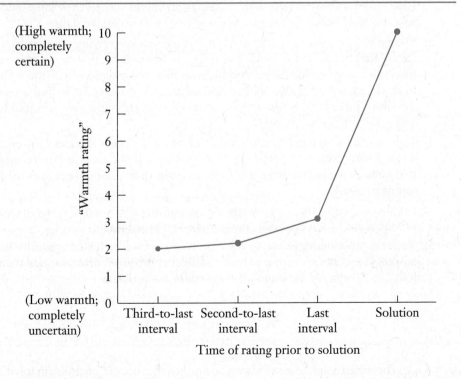

Advice About Problem Solving. The potential difference between noninsight problems and insight problems suggests some strategies. You might begin to solve a problem by contemplating whether you have had previous experience with similar problems. Top-down processing will be especially useful when you approach a noninsight problem.

From time to time, however, you should also consider whether the problem might require insight. You'll need a different approach to solve an insight problem, because there are no clear rules for these problems (Chi, 2006). You might try to represent the problem in a different way or think about a different meaning for an ambiguous word (Lovett, 2002; Perkins, 2001). In some cases, it's helpful to draw sketches, work with physical objects, or use gestures when you are trying to solve an insight problem (Fioratou & Cowley, 2011; Shapiro, 2011). An insight problem forces you to search for the answer "outside the box" by abandoning your customary top-down assumptions and looking for novel solutions.

Section Summary: *Factors That Influence Problem Solving*

1. Experts differ from novices with respect to attributes such as their knowledge base, problem-solving strategies, accuracy, and metacognitive skills.

2. Mental set can influence your problem solving; you keep trying the same ineffective strategy, although another strategy would be more effective. Functional fixedness can also infuence your problem solving; you assign a specific function to an object, although this object could be used for other tasks. In both cases, top-down processing is overactive. However, both strategies can be traced to a basically intelligent strategy.

3. Males and females typically earn similar scores on mathematics tasks. However, females may experience stereotype threat if they think about the stereotype that females are less skilled in math. As a result, their performance on a math test may suffer.

4. Insight problems are solved when the answer appears suddenly; noninsight problems are solved gradually, using top-down processing.

5. Research on metacognition shows that your confidence builds gradually for *noninsight* problems; in contrast, your confidence on *insight* problems is initially low, but it suddenly increases when you solve the problem.

CREATIVITY

Perhaps you breathed a sigh of relief when you finished the sections on problem solving and prepared to read a section on creativity. Problem solving sounds so routine. People who solve problems trudge along while they work out their means-ends analyses. In contrast, creativity sounds inspired! People who think creatively often experience moments of genius, and light bulbs flash continuously above their heads. Truthfully, however, creativity is an area of problem solving. Like the problem-solving tasks we have already considered, creativity requires moving from an initial state to a goal state.

Creativity is definitely a popular topic, both within and beyond psychology. In fact, more than 10,000 papers about creativity were published between 1999 and 2009 (Kaufman & Sternberg, 2010b).

It would be easy to write an entire chapter on the variety of definitions for creativity. However, most theorists emphasize that **creativity** requires solutions that are both novel and useful (Hennessey & Amabile, 2010; Kaufman & Sternberg, 2010b; Runco, 2007). Incidentally, take a few minutes to complete Demonstration 11.8.

---

⑨ Demonstration 11.8

Divergent Production Tests

Try the following items, which are similar to Guilford's divergent production tests.

1. Many words begin with an L and end with an N. In 1 minute, list as many words as possible that have the form L _____ N. (The words can have any number of letters between the L and the N.)

2. Suppose that people reached their final height at the age of 2, and so normal adult height would be less than 3 feet. In 1 minute, list as many consequences as possible that would result from this change.

3. Below is a list of names. They can be classified in many ways. For example, one classification would be in terms of the number of syllables: JACOB, MAYA, and HAROLD have two syllables, whereas BETH, GAIL, and JUAN have one syllable. Classify them in as many other ways as possible in 1 minute.

   BETH HAROLD GAIL JACOB JUAN MAYA

4. Below are four shapes. In 1 minute, combine them to make each of the following objects: a face, a lamp, a piece of playground equipment, and a tree. Each shape may be used once, many times, or not at all in forming each object, and it may be expanded or shrunk to any size. Each shape may also be rotated.

Although many theorists agree on the basic definition of creativity, their views differ on other characteristics. For instance, some psychologists argue that creativity is based on ordinary thinking, a process similar to our everyday problem solving (e.g., De Dreu et al., 2008; Halpern, 2003; Kozbelt et al., 2010). In contrast, other psychologists argue that ordinary people seldom produce creative products. Instead, certain exceptional people are extraordinarily creative in their specific area of expertise, such as music, literature, or science (e.g., Feldman et al., 1994; Kozbelt et al., 2010; Simonton, 2010).

Guilford's Classic Approach to Creativity

For more than a century, researchers have devised a variety of theories about creativity. However, the initial scientific research is typically traced to J. P. Guilford (Runco, 2010). Guilford (1967) proposed that psychologists should measure creativity in terms of **divergent production**, or the number of different responses made to a test item. Many researchers agree that creativity requires divergent thinking, rather than one single best answer (Runco, 2007; Russ, 2001; Smith & Ward, 2012). Demonstration 11.8 shows several ways in which Guilford measured divergent production. To earn a high score, the problem solver must explore in many different directions from the initial problem state. As you can see, some items require test takers to overcome functional fixedness.

Research on tests of divergent production has found moderate correlations between people's test scores and other judgments of their creativity (Guilford, 1967; Runco, 2010). However, the number of different ideas may not be the best measure of creativity. After all, this measure does not assess whether the solutions meet the two criteria for creativity: The solution must be both novel and useful.

The Nature of Creativity

As mentioned earlier, more than 10,000 papers on creativity have been published between 1999 and 2009. Therefore, no list of characteristics can capture the rich variety of the research. However, here are three general observations, which psychologists have discovered about the nature of creativity. As you will see, these observations do not match the reports that you find in the popular media.

1. *Creativity includes convergent thinking, as well as divergent thinking* (Dietrich & Kanso, 2010; Ward & Kolomyts, 2010). On page 399, you saw that divergent production is measured by the number of different responses that the test-taker makes. In contrast, **convergent production** asks the test-taker to supply a single, best response, and the researchers measure the quality of that response. Many situations require one especially creative solution, rather than several less useful solutions.

2. *Creativity is associated with many regions within the left hemisphere, as well as many regions within the right brain.* We saw in Chapter 9 that language is not limited to the left brain (see pp. 310–311). Similarly, creativity is associated with many locations in both of the brain's hemispheres, as well as other regions and structures in the brain (Dietrich, 2007; Dietrich & Kanso, 2010; Feist, 2010).

3. *Creativity can occur when we use focused attention (conscious attention) as well as defocused attention (altered states of consciousness).* People can be creative when they are consciously focusing on a task. If ideas occur to people when they are daydreaming, these ideas are not especially creative (Dietrich & Kanso, 2010).

The Relationship Between Extrinsic Motivation and Creativity

Think about a recent time when you worked especially hard on a course assignment, or else some project at your job. Researchers propose two general types of motivation. One type is called **extrinsic motivation**, or the motivation to work on a task—not because you find it enjoyable—but in order to earn a promised reward or to win a competition. However, people are often less creative if their extrinsic motivation is high.

The research about extrinsic motivation shows that people often produce less creative projects if they are working on these projects for external reasons (Amabile, 1996; Hennessey, 2000; Prabhu et al., 2008). When people believe that a particular task is just a means of earning a reward, a good grade, or a positive evaluation, their extrinsic motivation is high. Consequently, their creativity is also likely to decrease (Hennessey, 2000; Prabhu et al., 2008; Runco, 2007).

For many years, researchers had adopted a simple perspective that extrinsic motivation is consistently harmful. You've probably studied psychology long enough to know that no conclusions in our discipline could be that straightforward. In fact, the research suggests that creativity can actually be enhanced if the extrinsic factors provide *useful feedback* (Collins & Amabile, 1999; Eisenberger & Rhoades, 2001).

Individual Differences: The Relationship Between Intrinsic Motivation and Creativity

So far, we have only considered *extrinsic* motivation. The other type of creativity is called **intrinsic motivation**, or the motivation to work on tasks for their own sake, because you find them interesting, exciting, or personally challenging (Collins & Amabile, 1999; Eliott & Mapes, 2002; Runco, 2005). Let's now examine *intrinsic* motivation. The research confirms that people are more likely to be creative when they are working on a task that they truly enjoy (e.g., Amabile, 1997; Hennessey, 2000; Runco, 2005).

For example, Ruscio and his coauthors (1998) gave college students a standardized test of intrinsic motivation. The test asked them to rate their level of interest in three representative kinds of creative activities: writing, art, and problem solving. Several

---

⑨ Demonstration 11.9

Writing a Creative Poem

For this demonstration, you will write an American haiku. These instructions are similar to those that Ruscio and his colleagues (1998) supplied to the participants in their study, as follows:

> An American haiku is a five-line poem. As you can see from the sample poem below, the first line simply contains a noun, in this case the noun *ocean*. The second line has two adjectives describing the noun. The third line features three verbs related to the noun. The fourth line is a phrase of any length, which is related to the noun. Notice that the last line simply repeats the first line.
>
>> Ocean
>> Wavy, foamy
>> Roll, tumble, crash
>> All captured in this shell at my ear.
>> Ocean
>
> Your task is to write a similar American haiku, featuring the noun *summer*. Take 5 minutes to write this poem.

Source: Based on Ruscio et al., 1998, p. 249.

---

weeks later, the students were asked to perform tasks in these three areas. Demonstration 11.9 is similar to the writing task, for example. Take a few minutes to try this demonstration. A group of trained judges then rated the students' creative projects. The results showed that the students who had earned high intrinsic-motivation scores on the standardized test were also more likely to produce more creative projects.

Now we'll consider a study about intrinsic motivation in more detail. Veena Prabhu, Charlotte Sutton, and William Sauser (2008) proposed that certain personality traits might be related to creativity, but only if the person has high intrinsic motivation. Prabhu and her colleagues therefore gave several self-rating questionnaires to 124 undergraduate students who were enrolled in an introductory management course at Auburn University. These questionnaires assessed a variety of characteristics, such as intrinsic motivation and extrinsic motivation. They also assessed personality traits, such as **self-efficacy**, which is the belief that you have the ability to organize and carry out a specific task, and **perseverance**, which is the ability to keep working on a task, even when you encounter obstacles. Let's look at the results of this study:

1. Consistent with the previous research, the students with high scores on intrinsic motivation tended to earn high scores on creativity. If you are working on a project because you find it interesting, your work is likely to be *more* creative.

2. Also consistent with the previous research, the students with high scores on extrinsic motivation tended to earn low scores on creativity. As we discussed

earlier, if you are working on a project because you want some kind of reward, your work is likely to be *less* creative.

3. Prabhu and her coauthors (2008) also found that self-efficacy was closely correlated with creativity. Furthermore, a more detailed statistical analysis showed that this correlation could be explained by the students' intrinsic motivation. That is, when students are high in self-efficacy, they tend to have high intrinsic motivation, and this high intrinsic motivation encourages their creativity.

4. Surprisingly, Prabhu and her colleagues discovered that perseverance was *not* consistently correlated with creativity.

Prabhu and her coauthors (2008) point out a potential problem that might have occurred to you: Can self-reports be trusted? The students' responses on the questionnaires were completely anonymous, so they would not be especially likely to answer the questions in a socially desirable fashion. Still, Prabhu and her coauthors (2008) suggest that future research should evaluate the participants' *actual* creative performance, rather than the participants' own evaluation of their creativity.

Section Summary: *Creativity*

1. Many definitions have been proposed for creativity; one common definition is that creativity requires finding a solution that is both novel and useful.

2. Guilford's measure of divergent production is the classic approach to creativity.

3. The research demonstrates that extrinsic motivation can reduce creativity.

4. The research also demonstrates that intrinsic motivation promotes high levels of creativity. However, self-reported perseverance does not seem to be correlated with creativity.

CHAPTER REVIEW QUESTIONS

1. This chapter examined several different methods of representing a problem. Return to pages 374 to 378 and point out how each method could be used to solve a problem that you have recently faced, either in college classes or in your personal life. In addition, identify how the situated cognition and the embodied cognition perspectives can be applied to your understanding of this problem.

2. What barriers prevent people from successfully using the analogy approach to problem solving? Think of an area in which you are an expert, such as an academic subject, a hobby, or knowledge related to your work. When are you most likely to recognize the structural similarities shared by problem isomorphs?

3. In problem solving, how do algorithms differ from heuristics? When you solve problems, what situations encourage each of these two approaches? Describe a situation in where the means-ends heuristic was more useful than an algorithm. Identify a time when you used the hill-climbing heuristic, and note whether it helped you solve the problem.

4. Think of someone you know well, who is an expert in a particular area. Explain the cognitive areas in which he or she may have an advantage over a novice. When discussing this area of expertise, does this person fail to realize that other people might not understand this discussion?

5. How are mental set and functional fixedness related to each other, and how do they limit problem solving? How could insight help you to overcome these two barriers to effective problem solving?

6. On two occasions, this chapter discussed metacognition. Discuss these two topics, and point out how metacognitive measures can help us determine which problems require insight and which do not.

7. Imagine that you are teaching seventh grade, and your students are about to take a series of standardized tests in mathematics. Assume that your students hold the stereotype that boys are better at math than girls are. Just before the test, you hear the students discussing whether the boys or the girls will earn a higher score. How might stereotype threat influence their performance? Describe two specific ways in which stereotype threat could influence the students' cognitive processes.

8. Think of an example of an insight problem and a noninsight problem that you have solved recently. Based on the discussion of this topic, how would these two problems differ with respect to the way you made progress in solving the problem and the nature of your metacognitions about your progress in problem solving?

9. We discussed how the external environment can influence problem solving, in connection with (a) situated cognition, (b) the analogy approach, and (c) factors influencing creativity. Using this information, point out why environmental factors are important in problem solving.

10. Imagine that you are supervising ten employees in a small company. Describe how you might use the material in this chapter to encourage more effective problem solving and greater creativity. Then describe the activities you would want to *avoid* because they might hinder problem solving and creativity.

KEYWORDS

problem solving	situated cognition approach	structural features
initial state	embodied cognition approach	subproblems
goal state	ecological validity	means-ends heuristic
obstacles	algorithm	computer simulation
thinking	exhaustive search	General Problem Solver
understanding	heuristic	(GPS)
problem representation	analogy approach	hill-climbing heuristic
matrix	problem isomorphs	bottom-up processing
hierarchical tree diagram	surface features	top-down processing

expertise
parallel processing
serial processing
mental set
fixed mindset
growth mindset

functional fixedness
gender stereotypes
stereotype threat
insight problem
noninsight problem
creativity

divergent production
convergent production
extrinsic motivation
intrinsic motivation
self-efficacy
perseverance

RECOMMENDED READINGS

Ericsson, K. A., Charness, N., Feltovich, P. J., & Hoffman, R. R. (Eds.). (2006). *The Cambridge handbook of expertise and expert performance*. New York: Cambridge University Press. K. Anders Ericsson is the acknowledged "expert on expertise"; this handbook includes 42 chapters on theoretical, empirical, and applied aspects of expertise.

Hennessey, B. A., & Amabile, T. M. (2010). Creativity. *Annual Review of Psychology, 61*, 569–598. Beth Hennessey and Teresa Amabile are well-known researchers in the area of creativity, and this chapter provides an excellent summary of the research.

Kaufman, J. C., & Sternberg, R. J. (Eds.). (2010a). *The Cambridge handbook of creativity*. New York: Cambridge University Press. This handbook examines topics such as theories of creativity, everyday creativity, and the relationship between creativity and mental illness.

Nickerson, R. S. (2010). *Mathematical reasoning: Patterns, problems, conjectures, and proofs*. New York: Psychology Press. Most books about mathematics are written by mathematicians, but Raymond Nickerson is a psychology professor. This book examines topics such as young children's understanding of numbers, representation in mathematics, and the concept of infinity.

ANSWERS TO DEMONSTRATION 11.3

In the hospital room problem, Ms. Anderson has a liver problem, and she is in Room 104.

ANSWERS TO DEMONSTRATION 11.5

In the Elves-and-Goblins problem (with R representing the right bank and L representing the left bank), here are the steps in the solution:

1. Move 2 Goblins, R to L.
2. Move 1 Goblin, L to R.
3. Move 2 Goblins, R to L.
4. Move 1 Goblin, L to R.
5. Move 2 Elves, R to L.
6. Move 1 Goblin, 1 Elf, L to R.
7. Move 2 Elves, R to L.
8. Move 1 Goblin, L to R.
9. Move 2 Goblins, R to L.
10. Move 1 Goblin, L to R.
11. Move 2 Goblins, R to L.

ANSWER TO DEMONSTRATION 11.6B

The numbers are in alphabetical order; your mental set probably suggested that the numbers were in some mathematical sequence, not a language-based sequence.

ANSWER TO DEMONSTRATION 11.7A

The pack on the man's back contained an unopened parachute. (Other solutions would also be possible.)

ANSWER TO DEMONSTRATION 11.7B

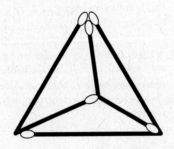

CHAPTER 12
Deductive Reasoning and Decision Making

PREVIEW

This chapter considers how we perform two complex cognitive tasks: deductive reasoning and decision making. The topic of thinking includes problem solving (Chapter 11), as well as deductive reasoning and decision making.

In deductive reasoning tasks, you need to draw some logical conclusions, based on the information supplied to you. This chapter focuses on conditional reasoning, using statements such as, "If today is Saturday, then Abyssinia Restaurant is open for dinner." People make several systematic errors on conditional reasoning tasks. For example, our prior beliefs may influence our conclusions; we may also fail to test whether our hypotheses could be incorrect.

In decision making, we evaluate and choose among several alternatives; we often use three heuristics, or general strategies, to make decisions. Heuristics usually lead to the correct decision, but we sometimes apply them inappropriately.

1. When we use the *representativeness heuristic*, we judge a sample to be likely because it looks similar to the population from which it was selected. For example, if you toss a coin six times, an outcome of six heads in a row looks very unlikely. However, sometimes we pay so much attention to representativeness that we ignore other important information such as the size of the sample.

2. When we use the *availability heuristic*, we estimate frequency in terms of how easily we think of examples of something. For instance, you estimate that the number of unethical corporations is large if you can easily think of many relevant examples from the news. Unfortunately, availability is often influenced by two irrelevant factors—recency and familiarity—and so this heuristic sometimes leads to decision errors.

3. When we use the *anchoring and adjustment heuristic*, we begin by guessing a first approximation (an anchor) and then make an adjustment, based on other information. This strategy is frequently useful, except that our adjustments are typically too small.

We'll also discuss how context and wording can influence decisions, why we are often overconfident, and why our hindsight is often inaccurate. We'll also explore current theoretical perspectives on human decision making. Then we'll see that people may actually be less happy if they have a wide variety of choices. Our final topic raises a moral qustion: How should wealth be distributed?

CHAPTER INTRODUCTION

You use deductive reasoning every day, although you might not use this label. For example, suppose that a student named Jenna wants to enroll next semester in a course called "Biopsychology." The course description says, "To enroll in this course, students must have completed a course in research methods." However, Jenna has not completed this course; she plans to enroll in it next semester. Therefore, we draw the logical conclusion, "Jenna cannot enroll in Biopsychology next semester." You use decision making more frequently. Many decisions are trivial: Do you want mustard on your sandwich? Other decisions are momentous: Should you apply to graduate programs for next year, or should you try to find a job?

The topics of problem solving (Chapter 11), deductive reasoning, and decision making are all interrelated, and we will note several similarities among these tasks throughout this chapter. All three topics are included in the general category called "thinking." **Thinking** requires you to go beyond the information you were given; thinking also has a goal such as a solution, a belief, or a decision. In other words, you begin with several pieces of information, and you must mentally transform that information so that you can solve a problem, draw a conclusion about a deductive reasoning task, or make a decision.

Furthermore, all three thinking tasks illustrate Theme 2. This theme argues that we often use a heuristic that is typically helpful, but we sometimes overgeneralize this heuristic to inappropriate situations. As a result, when we are engaged in a thinking task, we often make a "smart mistake" (Levy, 2010; Stanovich, 2011).

Our two topics for this chapter—deductive reasoning and decision making—are clearly related to each other. In **deductive reasoning**, you begin with some specific premises that are true, and you need to judge whether those premises allow you to draw a particular conclusion, based on the principles of logic (Halpern, 2003; Johnson-Laird, 2005a; Levy, 2010). A deductive-reasoning task provides you with all the information you need to draw a conclusion. Furthermore, the premises are either true or false, and you must use the rules of formal logic in order to draw conclusions (Levy, 2010; Roberts & Newton, 2005; Wilhelm, 2005).

In **decision making**, you must assess the information and choose among two or more alternatives. Compared to deductive reasoning, the area of decision making is much more ambiguous. Some information may be missing or contradictory. In addition, we do not have clear-cut rules that tell us how to proceed from the information to the conclusions. Also, you may never know whether your decision was correct, the consequences of that decision won't be immediately apparent, and you may need to take additional factors into account (Johnson-Laird et al., 2004; Simon et al., 2001). In fact, you may never know whether you should have applied to grad school or looked for a job.

In real life, the uncertainty of decision making is more common than the certainty of deductive reasoning. However, people have difficulty with both kinds of tasks, and they do not always reach the appropriate conclusions (Goodwin & Johnson-Laird, 2005; Stanovich, 2009, 2011).

When contemporary psychologists study reasoning and decision making, they may adopt a **dual-process theory**, which distinguishes between two types of cognitive processing (De Neys & Goel, 2011; Evans, 2006, 2012; Kahneman, 2011; Stanovich, 2009, 2011). In general, **Type 1 processing** is fast and automatic; it requires little conscious attention. For example, we use Type 1 processing during depth perception, recognition of facial expression, and automatic stereotyping.

In contrast, **Type 2 processing** is relatively slow and controlled; it requires focused attention, and it is typically more accurate. For example, we use Type 2 processing when we think of exceptions to a general rule, when we realize that we made a stereotyped response, and when we acknowledge that our Type 1 response may have been incorrect.

DEDUCTIVE REASONING

One of the most common kinds of deductive reasoning tasks is called conditional reasoning. A **conditional reasoning task** (also called a **propositional reasoning task**) describes the relationship between conditions. Here's a typical conditional reasoning task:

> If a child is allergic to peanuts, then eating peanuts produces a breathing problem.
> A child has a breathing problem.
> Therefore, this child has eaten peanuts.

Notice that this task tells us about the relationship between two conditions, such as the relationship between eating peanuts and a breathing problem. The kind of conditional reasoning we consider in this chapter explores reasoning tasks that have an "if…then…" kind of structure. When researchers study conditional reasoning, people judge whether the conclusion is valid or invalid. In the example above, the conclusion, "Therefore, this child has eaten peanuts" is *not* valid, because some other substance or medical condition could have caused the problem.

Another common kind of deductive reasoning task is called a syllogism. A **syllogism** consists of two statements that we must assume to be true, plus a conclusion. Syllogisms refer to quantities, so they use the words *all*, *none*, *some*, and other similar terms. Here's a typical syllogism:

> Some psychology majors are friendly people.
> Some friendly people are concerned about poverty.
> Therefore, some psychology majors are concerned about poverty.

In a syllogism, you must judge whether the conclusion is valid, invalid, or indeterminate. In this example, the answer is indeterminate. In fact, those psychology majors who are friendly people and those friendly people who are concerned about poverty could really be two separate populations, with no overlap whatsoever.

Notice that your everyday experience tempts you to conclude, "Yes, the conclusion is valid." After all, you know many psychology majors who are concerned about poverty. To use the terminology from page 409, Type 1 processing is likely to operate; many people would automatically respond, "valid conclusion." In contrast, if you use Type 2 processing, you'll re-examine that syllogism and realize that the strict rules of deductive reasoning require you to respond, "The conclusion is indeterminate" (Stanovich, 2009, 2011; Tsujii & Watanabe, 2009).

In a college course in logic, you could spend an entire semester learning about the structure and solution of deductive reasoning tasks like these. However, we will emphasize the *cognitive* factors that influence deductive reasoning. Furthermore, we will limit ourselves to conditional reasoning, a kind of deductive reasoning that students typically find more approachable than syllogisms (Schmidt & Thompson, 2008).

As it happens, researchers have found that conditional reasoning tasks and syllogisms are influenced by similar cognitive factors (Mercier & Sperber, 2011; Schmidt & Thompson, 2008; Stanovich, 2011). In addition, people's performance on conditional reasoning tasks is correlated with their performance on syllogism tasks (Stanovich & West, 2000).

Let's first explore the four basic kinds of conditional reasoning tasks. Next, we'll see how reasoning is influenced by two factors: (1) whether the statements include negative terms and (2) whether the statements are concrete or abstract. Then we'll discuss two cognitive errors that people often make when they solve these reasoning tasks.

An Overview of Conditional Reasoning

Conditional reasoning situations occur frequently in our daily life. However, these reasoning tasks are surprisingly difficult to solve correctly (Evans, 2004; Johnson-Laird, 2011). People are likely to use Type 1 processing, without pausing to engage in Type 2 processing (page 411). Let's examine the formal principles that have been devised for solving these tasks correctly.

Table 12.1 illustrates **propositional calculus**, which is a system for categorizing the four kinds of reasoning used in analyzing **propositions** or statements. Let's first introduce some basic terminology. The word **antecedent** refers to the first proposition

TABLE 12.1

Propositional Calculus: The Four Kinds of Reasoning Tasks

Action taken	Portion of the Statement	
	Antecedent	Consequent
Affirm	Affirming the antecedent (valid)	Affirming the consequent (invalid)
	This is an apple; therefore this a fruit.	*This is a fruit; therefore this is an apple.*
Deny	Denying the antecedent (invalid)	Denying the consequent (valid)
	This is not an apple; therefore it is not a fruit.	*This is not a fruit; therefore this is not an apple.*

Note: Each of these examples is based on the statement, "If this is an apple, then this is a fruit."

or statement; the antecedent is contained in the "if..." part of the sentence. The word **consequent** refers to the proposition that comes second; it is the consequence. The consequent is contained in the "then..." part of the sentence.

Furthermore, when we work on a conditional reasoning task, we can perform two possible actions: (1) We can *affirm* part of the sentence, saying that it is true; or (2) we can *deny* part of the sentence, saying that it is false. By combining the two parts of the sentence with these two actions, we have four conditional reasoning situations. As you can see, two of them are valid, and two of them are invalid.

---

⑨ Demonstration 12.1

Propositional Calculus

Decide which of the following conclusions are valid and which are invalid. The answers are at the end of the chapter.

1. *Affirming the antecedent.*

   If today is Tuesday, then I have my bowling class.
   Today is Tuesday.
   Therefore, I have my bowling class.

2. *Affirming the consequent.*

   If Sarita is a psychology major, then she is a student.
   Sarita is a student.
   Therefore, Sarita is a psychology major.

3. *Denying the antecedent.*

   If I am a first-year student, then I must register for next semester's classes today.
   I am not a first-year student.
   Therefore, I must not register for next semester's classes today.

4. *Denying the consequent.*

   If the judge is fair, then Susan is the winner.
   Susan is not the winner.
   Therefore, the judge is not fair.

1. **Affirming the antecedent** means that you say that the "if..." part of the sentence is true. As shown in the upper-left corner of Table 12.1, this kind of reasoning leads to a valid, or correct, conclusion.

2. The fallacy (or error) of **affirming the consequent** means that you say that the "then..." part of the sentence is true. This kind of reasoning leads to an invalid conclusion. Notice the upper-right corner of Table 12.1; the conclusion "This is an apple" is incorrect. After all, the item could be a pear, or a mango, or numerous other kinds of non-apple fruit. (We will discuss this second reasoning situation in more detail in a moment.)

3. The fallacy of **denying the antecedent** means that you say that the "if..." part of the sentence is false. Denying the antecedent also leads to an invalid conclusion, as you can see from the lower-left corner of Table 12.1. Again, the item could be some fruit other than an apple.

4. **Denying the consequent** means that you say that the "then..." part of the sentence is false. In the lower-right corner of Table 12.1, notice that this kind of reasoning leads to a correct conclusion.*

Now test yourself on the four kinds of conditional reasoning tasks by trying Demonstration 12.1. Then be sure to engage your Type 2 processing, by consulting Table 12.1 to see if your reasoning was correct.

Let's now reconsider the "affirming the consequent" task in more detail, because this task causes the largest number of errors (Byrne & Johnson-Laird, 2009). It's easy to see why people are tempted to affirm the consequent. In real life, we are likely to be correct when we make this kind of conclusion (Evans, 2000). For example, consider the two propositions, "If a person is a talented singer, then he or she has musical abilities" and "Paula has musical abilities." In reality, it's often a good bet that Paula *is* a talented singer. However, in logical reasoning, we cannot rely on statements such as, "It's a good bet that...." For example, I remember a student whose musical skills as a violinist were exceptional, yet she sang off-key.

As Theme 2 emphasizes, many cognitive errors can be traced to a **heuristic**, a general strategy that usually works well. In this example of logical reasoning, however, "it's a good bet" is not the same as "always" (Leighton & Sternberg, 2003). In the second part of this chapter, you'll see that decision-making tasks actually do allow us to use the concept, "it's a good bet." However, propositional reasoning tasks require us to use the word "always" before we conclude that the conclusion is valid.

Still, many people do manage to solve these reasoning tasks correctly. How do they succeed? Remember dual-process theory (see pp. 409–410). People may initially use Type 1 processing, which is quick and generally correct. However, they sometimes pause and then shift to Type 2 processing, which requires a more effortful analytic

---

*If you have taken courses in research methods or statistics, you will recognize that scientific reasoning is based on the strategy of denying the consequent—that is, ruling out the null hypothesis.

approach. This approach requires focused attention and working memory, so that people can realize that their initial conclusion would not necessarily be correct (De Neys & Goel, 2011; Evans, 2004, 2006; Kahneman, 2011; Stanovich, 2009, 2011).

Our performance on reasoning tasks is a good example of Theme 4, which emphasizes that our cognitive processes are interrelated. For example, conditional reasoning relies upon working memory, especially the central-executive component of working memory that we discussed in Chapter 4 (Evans, 2006; Gilhooly, 2005; Reverberi et al., 2009). Reasoning also requires general knowledge and language skills (Rips, 2002; Schaeken et al., 2000; Wilhelm, 2005). In addition, it often uses mental imagery (Evans, 2002; Goodwin & Johnson-Laird, 2005).

We would expect the cognitive burden to be especially heavy when some of the propositions contain negative terms (rather than just positive terms) and when people try to solve abstract reasoning tasks (rather than concrete terms). Let's examine these two topics, and then we will consider two cognitive tendencies that people demonstrate on these conditional reasoning tasks.

Difficulties with Linguistically Negative Information

Theme 3 of this book states that people can handle positive information better than negative information. As you may recall from Chapter 9, people have trouble processing sentences that contain words such as *no* or *not*. This same issue is also true for conditional reasoning tasks. For example, try the following reasoning task:

> If today is not Friday, then we will not have a quiz today.
>
> We will not have a quiz today.
>
> Therefore, today is not Friday.

This item has four instances of the word *not*, and it is definitely more challenging than a similar but linguistically positive item that begins, "If today is Friday...."

Research shows that people take longer to evaluate problems that contain linguistically negative information, and they are also more likely to make errors on these problems (Garnham & Oakhill, 1994; Halpern, 2003). A reasoning problem is especially likely to strain our working memory if the problem involves denying the antecedent or denying the consequent. Most of us squirm when we see a reasoning task that includes a statement like, "It is not true that today is not Friday." Furthermore, we often make errors when we translate either the initial statement or the conclusion into more accessible, linguistically positive forms.

Difficulties with Abstract Reasoning Problems

In general, people are more accurate when they solve reasoning problems that use concrete examples about everyday categories, rather than abstract, theoretical examples. For instance, you probably worked through the items in Demonstration 12.1 somewhat easily. In contrast, even short reasoning problems are difficult if they refer to abstract items with abstract characteristics (Evans, 2004, 2005; Manktelow, 1999). For example, try this problem about geometric objects, and decide whether the conclusion is valid or invalid:

> If an object is red, then it is rectangular.
>
> This object is not rectangular.
>
> Therefore, it is not red.

Now check the answer to this item, located at the bottom of Demonstration 12.2 (p. 416). Incidentally, the research shows that people's accuracy typically increases when they use diagrams to make the problem more concrete (Halpern, 2003). However, we often make errors on concrete reasoning tasks if our everyday knowledge overrides the principles of logic (Evans, 2011; Mercier & Sperber, 2011). The belief-bias effect illustrates how this principle operates.

The Belief-Bias Effect

In our lives outside the psychology laboratory, our background (or top-down) knowledge helps us function well. Inside the psychology laboratory—or in a course on logic—this background information sometimes encourages us to make mistakes. For example, try the following reasoning task (Markovits et al., 2009, p. 112):

> If a feather is thrown at a window, the window will break.
>
> A feather is thrown at a window.
>
> Therefore, the window will break.

In everyday life, it's a good bet that this conclusion is *incorrect*; how could a feather possibly break a window? However, in the world of logic, this feather-window task actually affirms the antecedent, so it must be correct. Similarly, your common sense may have encouraged you to decide that the conclusion was valid for the syllogism on page 410, about the psychology majors who are concerned about poverty.

The **belief-bias effect** occurs in reasoning when people make judgments based on prior beliefs and general knowledge, rather than on the rules of logic. In general, people make errors when the logic of a reasoning problem conflicts with their background knowledge (Dube et al., 2010, 2011; Levy, 2010; Markovits et al., 2009; Stanovich, 2011).

The belief-bias effect is one more example of top-down processing (Theme 5). Our prior expectations help us to organize our experiences and understand the world. For example, when we see a conclusion in a reasoning task that looks correct in the "real world," we may not pay attention to the reasoning process that generated this conclusion (Stanovich, 2003; Thompson et al., 2011). As a result, we may question a valid conclusion.

People vary widely in their susceptibility to the belief-bias effect. For example, people with low scores on an intelligence test are especially likely to demonstrate the belief-bias effect (Macpherson & Stanovich, 2007). People are also likely to demonstrate the belief-bias effect if they have low scores on a test of flexible thinking (Stanovich, 1999; Stanovich & West, 1997, 1998). An inflexible person is likely to agree with statements such as, "No one can talk me out of something I know is right."

In contrast, people who are flexible thinkers agree with statements such as, "People should always take into consideration any evidence that goes against their beliefs." These people are more likely to solve the reasoning problems correctly, without being distracted by the belief-bias effect. In fact, these people actively *block* their everyday knowledge, such as their knowledge that a feather could not break a window (Markovitz et al., 2009). In general, they also tend to carefully inspect a reasoning problem, trying to determine whether the logic is faulty (Macpherson & Stanovich, 2007; Markovitz et al., 2009). Fortunately, when students have been taught about the belief-bias effect, they make fewer errors (Kruglanski & Gigerenzer, 2011).

The Confirmation Bias

Be sure to try Demonstration 12.2 (below) before you read any further. Peter Wason's (1968) selection task has inspired more psychological research than any other

---

⑥ Demonstration 12.2

The Confirmation Bias

Imagine that each square below represents a card. Suppose that you are participating in a study in which the experimenter tells you that every card has a letter on one side and a number on the other side.

You are then given this rule about these four cards: "IF A CARD HAS A VOWEL ON ONE SIDE, THEN IT HAS AN EVEN NUMBER ON THE OTHER SIDE."

Your task is to decide which card (or cards) you would need to turn over, so that you can find out whether this rule is valid or invalid. What is your answer? The correct answer is discussed later in the chapter.

| E | J | 6 | 7 |

(Incidentally, the answer to the problem about the objects on p. 415 is "valid.")

Source: The confirmation-bias task in this demonstration is based on Wason, 1968.

deductive reasoning problem. It has also raised many questions about whether humans are basically rational (Mercier & Sperber, 2011; Lilienfeld et al., 2009; Oswald & Grosjean, 2004). Let's first examine the original version of the selection task. Then we'll see how people typically perform better on a more concrete variation of this task.

The Standard Wason Selection Task. **Demonstration 12.2** shows the original version of the selection task. Peter Wason (1968) found that people show a **confirmation bias**; they would rather try to confirm or support a hypothesis than try to disprove it (Kida, 2006; Krizan & Windschitl, 2007; Levy, 2010).

When people try this classical selection task, they typically choose to turn over the E card (Mercier & Sperber, 2011; Oaksford & Chater, 1994). This strategy allows the participants to confirm the hypothesis by the valid method of affirming the antecedent, because this card has a vowel on it. If this E card has an even number on the other side, then the rule is correct. If the number is odd, then the rule is incorrect.

As we discussed on pages 412–413, the other valid method in deductive reasoning is to deny the consequent. To accomplish this goal, you must choose to turn over the 7 card. The information about the other side of the 7 card is very valuable. In fact, it is just as valuable as the information about the other side of the E card. Remember that the rule is: "If a card has a vowel on its letter side, then it has an even number on its number side."

To deny the consequent in this Wason Task, we need to check out a card that does *not* have an even number on its number side. In this case, then, we must check out the 7 card. We noted that many people are eager to affirm the antecedent. In contrast, they are reluctant to deny the consequent by searching for counterexamples. This approach would be a smart strategy for rejecting a hypothesis, but people seldom choose this appropriate strategy (Lilienfeld et al., 2009; Oaksford & Chater, 1994). Keep in mind that most participants in these selection-task studies are college students, so they should be able to master an abstract task (Evans, 2005).

You may wonder why we did not need to check on the J and the 6. Take a moment to read the rule again. Actually, the rule did not say anything about consonants, such as J. The other side of the J could show an odd number, an even number, or even a Vermeer painting, and we wouldn't care. A review of the literature showed that most people appropriately avoid the J card (Oaksford & Chater, 1994).

The rule also does not specify what must appear on the other side of the even numbers, such as 6. However, most people select the 6 card to turn over (Oaksford & Chater, 1994). People often assume that the two parts of the rule can be switched, so that it reads, "If a card has an even number on its number side, then it has a vowel on its letter side." Thus, they make an error by choosing the 6.

This preference for confirming a hypothesis—rather than disproving it—corresponds to Theme 3 of this book. On the Wason selection task, we see that people who are given a choice would rather know what something *is* than what it *is not*.

Concrete Versions of the Wason Selection Task. **In most of the recent research on the Wason Task, psychologists focus on versions in which the numbers and letters on the cards are replaced by concrete situations that we encounter in our everyday lives.**

As you might guess, people perform much better when the task is concrete, familiar, and realistic (Evans, 2011; Mercier & Sperber, 2011).

For example, Griggs and Cox (1982) tested college students in Florida using a variation of the selection task. This task focused on the drinking age, which was then 19 in the state of Florida. Specifically, the students were asked to test this rule: "If a person is drinking beer, then the person must be over 19 years of age" (p. 415). Each participant was instructed to choose two cards to turn over—out of four—in order to test whether people were lying about their age.

Griggs and Cox (1982) found that 73% of the students who tried the drinking age problem made the correct selections, in contrast to 0% of the students who tried the standard, abstract form of the selection task. According to later research, people are especially likely to choose the correct answer when the wording of the selection task implies some kind of social contract designed to prevent people from cheating (Barrett & Kurzban, 2006; Cosmides & Tooby, 2006).

Applications in Medicine. Several studies point out that the confirmation bias can be applied in medical situations. For example, researchers have studied people who seek medical advice for insomnia (Harvey & Tang, 2012). As it happens, when people believe that they have insomnia, they overestimate how long it takes them to fall asleep. They also underestimate the amount of time they spend sleeping at night. One explanation for these data is that people seek confirming evidence that they are indeed "bad sleepers," and they provide estimates that are consistent with this diagnosis.

Another study focused on the diagnosis of psychological disorders (Mendel et al., 2011). Medical students and psychiatrists first read a case vignette about a 65-year-old man, and then they were instructed to provide a preliminary diagnosis of either Alzheimer's disease or severe depression. Each person then decided what kind of additional information they would like; six items were consistent with each of the two diagnoses. The results showed that 25% of the medical students and 13% of the psychiatrists selected only the information that was consistent with their original diagnosis. In other words, they did not investigate information that might be consistent with the other diagnosis.

Further Perspectives. How can we translate the confirmation bias into real-life experiences? Try noticing your own behavior when you are searching for evidence. Do you consistently look for information that will *confirm* that you are right, or do you valiantly pursue ways in which your conclusion can be wrong?

The confirmation bias might sound relatively harmless. However, thousands of people die each year because our political leaders fall victim to this confirmation bias (Kida, 2006). For example, suppose that Country A wants to start a war in Country B. The leaders in Country A will keep seeking support for their position. These leaders will also *avoid* seeking information that their position may not be correct. Here's a remedy for the confirmation bias: Try to explain why another person might hold the opposite view (Lilienfeld et al., 2009; Myers, 2002). In an ideal world, for example, the leaders of Country A should sincerely try to construct arguments *against* attacking Country B.

This overview of conditional reasoning does not provide much evidence for Theme 2 of this book. At least in the psychology laboratory, people are not especially accurate when they try to solve "if...then..." kinds of problems. However, the circumstances are usually more favorable in our daily lives, where problems are more concrete and situations are more consistent with our belief biases (Mercier & Sperber, 2011). Deductive reasoning is such a challenging task that we are not as efficient and accurate as we are in perception and memory—two areas in which humans are generally very competent.

Section Summary: *Deductive Reasoning*

1. Conditional reasoning focuses on "if...then..." relationships.

2. People's accuracy is higher for linguistically positive sentences, rather than linguistically negative statements. Accuracy is also higher for concrete problems, rather than abstract problems.

3. The belief-bias effect encourages people to trust their prior knowledge, rather than the rules of logic; overactive top-down processing therefore leads to errors.

4. Furthermore, people often fall victim to the confirmation bias; they keep trying to confirm a hypothesis, rather than rejecting it.

5. The Wason selection task provides strong evidence for the confirmation bias; however, people are more accurate when the task describes a concrete situation that is governed by societal rules.

6. Other examples of the confirmation bias can be found in medical diagnoses and in political situations.

DECISION MAKING

When you engage in reasoning, you use the established rules of propositional calculus to draw clear-cut conclusions. In contrast, when you make a decision, there is no comparable list of rules. Furthermore, you may never even know whether your decision is correct. Some critical information may be missing, and you may suspect that other information is not accurate. Should you apply to graduate school or get a job after college? Should you take social psychology in the morning or in the afternoon? In addition, emotional factors frequently influence our everyday decision making (Kahneman, 2011; Lehrer, 2009; Stanovich, 2009, 2011).

Decision making is an interdisciplinary field that includes research in all the social sciences, including psychology, economics, political science, and sociology (LeBoeuf & Shafir, 2012; Mosier & Fischer, 2011). It also includes other areas such as statistics, philosophy, medicine, education, and law (Reif, 2008; Mosier & Fischer, 2011; Schoenfeld, 2011).

Within the discipline of psychology, decision making inspires numerous books and articles each year. For example, many books provide a general overview of decision making (e.g., Bazerman & Tenbrunsel, 2011; Bennett & Gibson, 2006; Hallinan, 2009; Herbert, 2010; Holyoak & Morrison, 2012; Kahneman, 2011; Kida, 2006; Lehrer, 2009; Schoenfeld, 2011; Stanovich, 2009, 2011). Other recent books consider decision-making approaches, such as critical thinking (Levy, 2010).

Many other books consider decision making in specific areas, such as business (Bazerman & Tenbrunsel, 2011; Henderson & Hooper, 2006; Mosier & Fischer, 2011; Useem, 2006); politics (Thaler & Sunstein, 2008; Weinberg, 2012); the neurological correlates of decision making (Delgado et al., 2011; Vartanian & Mandel, 2011); healthcare (Groopman, 2007; Mosier & Fischer, 2011); and education (Reif, 2008; Schoenfeld, 2011). In general, the research on decision making examines concrete, realistic scenarios, rather than the kind of abstract situations used in research on deductive reasoning.

As you'll see, this section emphasizes several kinds of decision-making heuristics. We've noted that heuristics are general strategies that typically produce a correct solution. When we need to make a decision, we often use a heuristic that is simple, fast, and easy to access (Bazerman & Tenbrunsel, 2011; Kahneman, 2011; Kahneman & Frederick, 2005; Stanovich, 2009, 2011). These heuristics reduce the difficulty of making a decision (Shah & Oppenheimer, 2008). In many cases, however, humans fail to appreciate the limitations of these heuristics. When we use this fast, Type 1 processing, we can make inappropriate decisions (see p. 409). However, if we pause and shift to slow, Type 2 processing, we can correct that original error and end up with a good decision.

Throughout this section, you will often see the names of two researchers, Daniel Kahneman and Amos Tversky. Kahneman won the Nobel Prize in economics in 2002 for his research in decision making. (Unfortunately, Tversky had died in 1996.) Their research emphasized decision-making heuristics, an approach that connected decision making with the heuristics that we have discussed in other parts of this book.

Kahneman and Tversky proposed that a small number of heuristics guide human decision making. As they emphasized, the same strategies that normally guide us toward the correct decision may sometimes lead us astray (Kahneman, 2011; Kahneman & Frederick, 2002, 2005; Kahneman & Tversky, 1996). Notice that this heuristics approach is consistent with Theme 2 of this book: Our cognitive processes are usually efficient and accurate, and our mistakes can often be traced to a rational strategy.

In this part of the chapter, we will discuss many studies that illustrate errors in decision making. These errors should not lead us to conclude that humans are foolish creatures. Instead, people's decision-making heuristics are well adapted to handle a wide range of problems (Kahneman, 2011; Kahneman & Frederick, 2005; Kahneman & Tversky, 1996). However, these same heuristics become a liability when they are applied too broadly, for example, when we emphasize heuristics rather than other important information.

We will now explore three classic decision-making heuristics: representativeness, availability, and anchoring and adjustment. Then, in a discussion of framing, we'll examine how background information and wording can influence decisions. The In-Depth feature of this chapter discusses people's overconfidence about their decisions. Similarly, the hindsight bias shows that we are also overconfident that we would have made wise decisions in the past. We'll then summarize the current status of heuristics and decision making. Then the Individual Differences feature examines how people are often less happy if they agonize about relatively trivial decisions. Finally, we will consider how people in the United States view the actual and the ideal distribution of personal wealth.

The Representativeness Heuristic

Here's a remarkable coincidence: Three early U.S. presidents—Adams, Jefferson, and Monroe—all died on the Fourth of July, although in different years (Myers, 2002). This information doesn't seem correct, because the dates should be randomly scattered throughout the 365 days a year.

You've probably discovered some personal coincidences in your own life. For example, one afternoon, I was searching for some resources on political decision making, and I found two relevant books. While recording the citations, I noticed an amazing coincidence: One was published by Stanford University Press, and the other by the University of Michigan Press. As it happened, I had earned my bachelor's degree from Stanford and my Ph.D. from the University of Michigan.

Now consider this example. Suppose that you have a regular penny with one head (H) and one tail (T), and you toss it six times. Which outcome seems most likely, T H H T H T or H H H T T T? Most people choose T H H T H T (Teigen, 2004). After all, you know that coin tossing should produce heads and tails in random order, and the order T H H T H T looks much more random.

A sample looks **representative** if it is similar in important characteristics to the population from which it was selected. For instance, if a sample was selected by a random process, then that sample must look random in order for people to say it looks representative. Thus, T H H T H T is a sample that looks representative because it has an equal number of heads and tails (which would be the case in random coin tosses). Furthermore, T H H T H T looks more representative because the order of the Ts and Hs looks random rather than orderly.

The research shows that we often use the **representativeness heuristic**; we judge that a sample is likely if it is similar to the population from which this sample was selected (Kahneman, 2011; Kahneman & Tversky, 1972; Levy, 2010). According to the representativeness heuristic, we believe that random-looking outcomes are more likely than orderly outcomes. Suppose, for example, that a cashier adds up your grocery bill, and the total is $21.97. This very random-looking outcome is a representative kind of answer, and so it looks "normal."

However, suppose that the total bill is $22.22. This total does not look random, and you might even decide to check the arithmetic. After all, addition is a process that should yield a random-looking outcome. In reality, though, a random process occasionally produces an outcome that look nonrandom. In fact, chance alone can produce an orderly sum like $22.22, just as chance alone can produce an orderly pattern like the three presidents dying on the Fourth of July.

---

⑨ Demonstration 12.3

Base Rates and Representativeness

Imagine that a psychologist wrote the following description of Tom W, when Tom was a senior in high school. This description was based on some psychological tests that had uncertain validity.

Tom W is highly intelligent, but he is not genuinely creative. Tom needs everything to be orderly and clear, and he likes every detail to be in its appropriate place. His writing is quite dull and mechanical, although he loves corny puns. He sometimes makes up plots about science fiction. Tom has a strong drive for competence. He seems to have little feeling for other people, and he has little sympathy for their problems. He does not actually like interacting with others. Although he is self-centered, he does have a deep moral sense. [Based on a description by Kahneman, 2011, p. 147]

Now suppose that Tom W is a graduate student at a large university. Rank the following nine fields of specialization, in terms of the likelihood that Tom W is now a student in that program. Write 1 for "most likely," and 7 for "least likely."

_____ business administration

_____ computer science

_____ engineering

_____ humanities and education

_____ law

_____ medicine

_____ library science

_____ physical and life sciences

_____ social sciences and social work

The representativeness heuristic raises a major problem: This heuristic is so persuasive that people often ignore important statistical information that they should consider (Kahneman, 2011; Newell et al., 2007; Thaler & Sunstein, 2008). We'll see that two especially useful statistics are the sample size and the base rate. In addition, people have trouble thinking about the probability of two combined characteristics. Be sure to try Demonstration 12.3 (above) before you read further.

Sample Size and Representativeness. When we make a decision, representativeness is such a compelling heuristic that we often fail to pay attention to sample size. For example, Kahneman and Tversky (1972) asked college students to consider a hypothetical small hospital, where about 15 babies are born each day, and a hypothetical large hospital, where about 45 babies are born each day. Which hospital would be more likely to report that more than 60% of the babies on a given day would be boys, or would they both be equally likely to report more than 60% boys?

The results showed that 56% of the students responded, "About the same." In other words, the majority of students thought that a large hospital and a small hospital were equally likely to report having at least 60% baby boys born on a given day. Thus, they ignored sample size.

In reality, however, sample size is an important characteristic that you *should* consider whenever you make decisions. A large sample is statistically more likely to reflect the true proportions in a population. In contrast, a small sample will often reveal an extreme proportion (for example, at least 60% baby boys). However, people are often unaware that deviations from a population proportion are more likely in these small samples (Newell et al., 2007; Teigen, 2004).

In one of their first publications, Tversky and Kahneman (1971) pointed out that people often commit the **small-sample fallacy** because they assume that a small sample will be representative of the population from which it is selected (Poulton, 1994). Unfortunately, the small-sample fallacy leads us to incorrect decisions.

We often commit the small-sample fallacy in social situations, as well as in relatively abstract statistics problems. For example, we may draw unwarranted stereotypes about a group of people on the basis of a small number of group members (Hamilton & Sherman, 1994). One effective way of combating inappropriate stereotypes is to become acquainted with a large number of people from the target group—for example, through exchange programs with groups of people from other countries.

Base Rate and Representativeness. Representativeness is such a compelling heuristic that people often ignore the **base rate**, or how often the item occurs in the population. Be sure you have tried Demonstration 12.3 on page 422 before reading further.

Using problems like the one in this demonstration, Kahneman and Tversky (1973) showed that people rely on representativeness when they are asked to judge category membership. In other words, we focus on whether a description is representative of members of each category. When we emphasize representativeness, we commit the **base-rate fallacy**, paying too little attention to important information about base rate (Kahneman, 2011; Levy, 2010; Swinkels, 2003).

If people pay appropriate attention to the base rate in this demonstration, they should select graduate programs that have a relatively high enrollment (base rate). These would include the two options "humanities and education" and "social science and social work." However, most students in this study used the representativeness heuristic, and they most frequently guessed that Tom W was a graduate student in either computer science or engineering (Kahneman, 2011; Kahneman & Tversky, 1973). The description of Tom W was highly similar to (that is, representative of) the stereotype of a computer scientist or an engineer.

You might argue, however, that the Tom W study was unfair. After all, the base rates of the various graduate programs were not even mentioned in the problem. Maybe the students failed to consider that there are more graduate students in the "social sciences and social work" category than in the "computer science" category. However, when Kahneman and Tversky's (1973) study included this base-rate information, most people ignored it. Instead, they judged mostly on the basis of representativeness. In fact, this description for Tom W is highly representative of our stereotype for students

---

⑨ Demonstration 12.4

The Conjunction Fallacy

Read the following paragraph:

> Linda is 31 years old, single, outspoken, and very bright. She majored in philosophy. As a student, she was deeply concerned with issues of discrimination and social justice, and she also participated in antinuclear demonstrations.

Now rank the following options in terms of the probability of their describing Linda. Give a ranking of 1 to the most likely option and a ranking of 8 to the least likely option:

_____ Linda is a teacher at an elementary school.
_____ Linda works in a bookstore and takes yoga classes.
_____ Linda is active in the feminist movement.
_____ Linda is a psychiatric social worker.
_____ Linda is a member of the League of Women Voters.
_____ Linda is a bank teller.
_____ Linda is an insurance salesperson.
_____ Linda is a bank teller and is active in the feminist movement.

Source: Tversky, A., & Kahneman, D. (1983). Extensional versus intuitive reasoning: The conjunction fallacy in probability judgment. *Psychological Review, 90,* 293–315.

---

in computer science. As a result, people tend to select this particular answer. Now complete Demonstration 12.4 before you read further.

We should emphasize, however, that the representativeness heuristic—like all heuristics—frequently helps us make a correct decision (Levy, 2010; Newell et al., 2007; Shepperd & Koch, 2005). Heuristics are also relatively simple to use (Hogarth & Karelaia, 2007). In addition, some problems—and some alternative wording of problems—produce more accurate decisions (Gigerenzer, 1998; Shafir & LeBoeuf, 2002).

Incidentally, research on this kind of "base-rate" task provides support for the dual-process approach. Specifically, different parts of the brain are activated when people use automatic, Type 1 processing, rather than slow, Type 2 processing (De Neys & Goel, 2011).

Furthermore, training sessions can encourage students to use base-rate information appropriately (Krynski & Tenenbaum, 2007; Shepperd & Koch, 2005). Training would make people more aware that they should pause and use Type 2 processing to examine the question more carefully.

You should also be alert for other everyday examples of the base-rate fallacy. For instance, one study of pedestrians killed at intersections showed that 10% were killed when crossing at a signal that said "walk." In contrast, only 6% were killed when crossing at a signal that said "stop" (Poulton, 1994). So—for your own safety—should you cross the street only when the signal says "stop"? Now compare the two base rates: Many more people cross the street when the signal says "walk."

The Conjunction Fallacy and Representativeness. Be sure to try Demonstration 12.4 on page 424 before you read further. Now inspect your answers. Now compare which of these two choices you ranked more likely: (1) Linda is a bank teller, or (2) Linda is a bank teller and is active in the feminist movement.

Tversky and Kahneman (1983) presented the "Linda" problem and another similar problem to three groups of people. One was a "statistically naïve" group of undergraduates. The "intermediate-knowledge" group consisted of first-year graduate students who had taken one or more courses in statistics. The "statistically sophisticated" group consisted of doctoral students in a decision science program who had taken several advanced courses in statistics. In each case, the participants were asked to rank all eight statements according to their probability, with the rank of 1 assigned to the most likely statement.

Figure 12.1 shows the average rank for each of the three groups for the two critical statements: (1) "Linda is a bank teller" and (2) "Linda is a bank teller and

FIGURE 12.1

The Influence of Type of Statement and Level of Statistical Sophistication on Likelihood Rankings. Low numbers on the ranking indicate that people think the event is very likely.

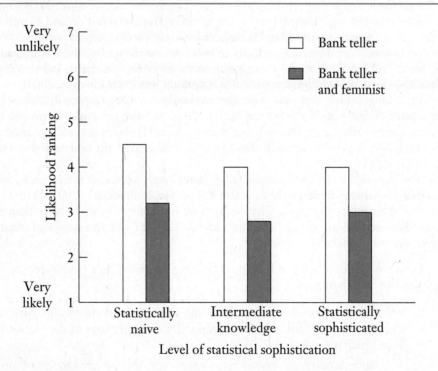

Source: Tversky, A., & Kahneman, D. (1983). Extensional versus intuitive reasoning: The conjunction fallacy in probability judgment. *Psychological Review, 90,* 293–315.

is active in the feminist movement." Notice that the people in all three groups believed—incorrectly—that the second statement would be more likely than the first.

Think for a moment why this conclusion is mathematically impossible. According to the **conjunction rule**, the probability of the conjunction of two events cannot be larger than the probability of either of its constituent events (Newell et al., 2007). In the Linda problem, the conjunction of the two events—bank teller and feminist—cannot occur more often than either event by itself, for instance, being a bank teller. Consider another situation where the conjunction rule operates: The number of murders last year in Detroit cannot be greater than the number of murders last year in Michigan (Kahneman & Frederick, 2005).

As we saw earlier in this section, representativeness is such a powerful heuristic that people may ignore useful statistical information, such as sample size and base rate. Apparently, they also ignore the mathematical implications of the conjunction rule (Kahneman, 2011; Kahneman & Frederick, 2005). Specifically, when most people try the "Linda problem," they commit the conjunction fallacy. When people commit the **conjunction fallacy**, they judge the probability of the conjunction of two events to be greater than the probability of either constituent event.

Tversky and Kahneman (1983) traced the conjunction fallacy to the representativeness heuristic. They argued that people judge the conjunction of "bank teller" and "feminist" to be more likely than the simple event "bank teller." After all, "feminist" is a characteristic that is very representative of (that is, similar to) someone who is single, outspoken, bright, a philosophy major, concerned about social justice, and an antinuclear activist. A person with these characteristics doesn't seem likely to become a bank teller. However, she seems highly likely to be a feminist. By adding the extra detail of "feminist" to "bank teller," the description seems more representative and also more plausible—even though this description is *statistically* less likely (Swoyer, 2002).

Psychologists are intrigued with the conjunction fallacy, especially because it demonstrates that people can ignore one of the most basic principles of probability theory. Furthermore, research by Keith Stanovich (2011) shows that college students with high SAT scores are actually *more* likely than other students to demonstrate this conjunction fallacy.

The results for the conjunction fallacy have been replicated many times, with generally consistent findings (Fisk, 2004; Kahneman & Frederick, 2005; Stanovich, 2009). For example, the probability of "spilling hot coffee" seems greater than the probability of "spilling coffee" (Moldoveanu & Langer, 2002)…until you identify the conjunction fallacy.

Before we discuss a second decision-making heuristic, let's briefly review the representativeness heuristic.

1. We use the representativeness heuristic when we make decisions based on whether a sample looks similar in important characteristics to the population from which it is selected.

2. The representativeness heuristic is so appealing that we tend to ignore other important characteristics that we should consider, such as sample size and base rate.

3. We also fail to realize that the probability of two events occurring together (for example, bank teller and feminist) needs to be smaller than the probability of just one of those events (for example, bank teller).

In summary, the representativeness heuristic is basically helpful in our daily lives. However, we sometimes use it inappropriately (Ben-Zeev, 2002; Kahneman, 2011).

The Availability Heuristic

A second important heuristic that people use in making decisions is availability. You use the **availability heuristic** when you estimate frequency or probability in terms of how easy it is to think of relevant examples of something (Hertwig et al., 2005; Kahneman, 2011; Tversky & Kahneman, 1973). In other words, people judge frequency by assessing whether they can easily retrieve relevant examples from memory or whether this memory retrieval is difficult.

The availability heuristic is generally helpful in everyday life. For example, suppose that someone asked you whether your college had more students from Illinois or more from Idaho. You haven't memorized these geography statistics, so you would be likely to answer the question in terms of the relative availability of examples of Illinois students and Idaho students. Let's also say that your memory has stored the names of dozens of Illinois students, and so you can easily retrieve their names ("Jessica, Akiko, Bob . . ."). Let's also say that your memory has stored only one name of an Idaho student, so you cannot think of many examples of this category. Because examples of Illinois students were relatively easy to retrieve, you conclude that your college has more Illinois students. In general, then, this availability heuristic is a relatively accurate method for making decisions about frequency (Kahneman, 2011).

As you know, a heuristic is a general strategy that is typically accurate. The availability heuristic is accurate as long as availability is correlated with true, objective frequency—and it usually is. However, the availability heuristic can lead to errors (Levy, 2010; Thaler & Sunstein, 2008). As we will see in a moment, several factors can influence memory retrieval, even though they are not correlated with true, objective frequency. These factors can bias availability, and so they may decrease the accuracy of our decisions. We will see that recency and familiarity—both factors that influence memory—can potentially distort availability. Figure 12.2 illustrates how these two factors can contaminate the relationship between true frequency and availability.

Before exploring the research about availability, let's briefly review how representativeness—the first decision-making heuristic—differs from availability. When we use the representativeness heuristic, we are given a specific example (such as T H H T H T or Linda the bank teller). We then make judgments about whether the specific example is *similar* to the general category that it is supposed to represent (such as coin tosses or philosophy majors concerned about social justice). In contrast, when we use the availability heuristic, we are given a general category, and we must recall the specific examples (such as examples of Illinois students). Then we make

FIGURE 12.2

The Relationship Between True Frequency and Estimated Frequency, with Recency and Familiarity as "Contaminating" Factors.

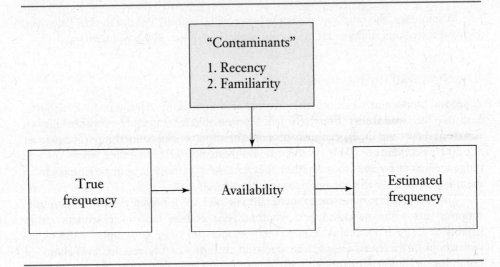

decisions based on whether the specific examples come easily to mind. So here is a way to remember the two heuristics:

1. If the problem is based on a judgment about *similarity*, you are dealing with the representativeness heuristic.
2. If the problem requires you to *remember examples*, you are dealing with the availability heuristic.

We'll begin our exploration of availability by considering two factors that can bias availability: recency and familiarity. Next, we'll consider the recognition heuristic, an application of the availability heuristic that typically leads to accurate decisions. Finally, we will examine a consequence of availability, called illusory correlations.

Recency and Availability. As you know from Chapters 4, 5, and 6, your memory is better for items that you've recently seen, compared to items you saw long ago. In other words, those more recent items are more *available*. As a result, we judge recent items to be more likely than they really are. For example, take yourself back to the fall of 2011. Several university coaches and administrators had been fired following the discovery that young boys had been sexually abused (e.g., Bartlett, 2011; Bazerman & Tenbrunsel, 2011). If you had been asked to estimate the frequency of these crimes—and the cover-ups—you probably would have provided a high estimate.

Research on the availability heuristic has important implications for clinical psychology. Consider a study by MacLeod and Campbell (1992), who encouraged one group of people to recall pleasant events from their past. These individuals later judged pleasant events to be more likely in their future. The researchers also encouraged another group to recall unpleasant events. These individuals later judged unpleasant events to be more likely in their future. Psychotherapists might encourage depressed clients to envision a more hopeful future by having them recall and focus on previous pleasant events.

Familiarity and Availability. The familiarity of the examples—as well as their recency—can also produce a distortion in frequency estimation (Kahneman, 2011). Norman Brown and his colleagues conducted research on this topic in Canada, the United States, and China (Brown, Cui, & Gordon, 2002; Brown & Siegler, 1992). They discovered that the media can distort people's estimates of a country's population.

For example, Brown and Siegler (1992) conducted a study during an era when El Salvador was frequently mentioned in the news because of U.S. intervention in Latin America. In contrast, Indonesia was seldom mentioned. Brown and Siegler found that the students' estimates for the population of these two countries were similar, even though the population of Indonesia was about 35 times as large as the population of El Salvador.

Try asking a friend to estimate the population of Israel (population = 7,400,000) and Cambodia (population = 14,800,000). How about Afghanistan (population = 29,100,000) and Algeria (population = 34,600,000)? Are your friend's estimates for these two pairs of countries distorted by the frequency of the media coverage about Israel and Afghanistan?

The media can also influence viewers' ideas about the prevalence of different points of view. For instance, the media often give equal coverage to several thousand protesters and to several dozen counterprotesters. Notice whether you can spot the same tendency in current news broadcasts. Does the media coverage create our cognitive realities?

How can we counteract Type 1 processing, which happens when we first encounter some information? Kahneman (2011) suggests that we can overcome that initial reaction by using critical thinking and shifting to Type 2 processing. For example, someone might analyze a friend's use of the availability heuristic and argue, "He underestimates the risks of indoor pollution because there are few media stories on them. That's an availability effect. He should look at the statistics" (p. 136).

The Recognition Heuristic. We have emphasized that the decision-making heuristics are generally helpful and accurate. However, most of the examples have emphasized that judgment accuracy is hindered by factors such as recency and familiarity. Let's discuss a special case of the availability heuristic, which often leads to an *accurate* decision (Goldstein & Gigerenzer, 2002; Kahneman, 2011; Volz et al., 2006).

Suppose that someone asks you which of two Italian cities has the larger population, Milan or Modena. Most U.S. students have heard of Milan, but they may not recognize the name of a nearby city called Modena. The **recognition heuristic** typically operates when you must compare the relative frequency of two categories; if you recognize one category, but not the other, you conclude that the recognized category has the higher frequency. In this case, you would correctly respond that Milan has the greater population (Volz et al., 2006). Keep this example of correct decision making in mind as you read the remainder of this chapter.

Illusory Correlation and Availability. So far, we have seen that availability—or the ease with which examples come to mind—is typically a useful heuristic. However, this heuristic can become "contaminated" by factors such as recency and familiarity, leading to inappropriate decisions about the true frequency of an event. Now we turn to a third topic, to see how the availability heuristic can contribute to a cognitive error called an *illusory correlation*.

The word *illusory* means deceptive or unreal, and a correlation is a statistical relationship between two variables. Therefore, an **illusory correlation** occurs when people believe that two variables are statistically related, even though there is no actual evidence for this relationship. According to the research, we often believe that a certain group of people tends to have certain kinds of characteristics, even though an accurate tabulation would show that the relationship is not statistically significant (Fiedler & Walther, 2004; Hamilton et al., 1993; Risen et al., 2007).

Think of some stereotypes that arise from illusory correlations. These illusory correlations may either have no basis in fact or much less basis than is commonly believed. For example, consider the following illusory correlations: (1) Females have poor math skills, (2) people on welfare are cheaters, (3) gay males and lesbians have psychological problems, and so forth.

According to the **social cognition approach**, stereotypes can be traced to our normal cognitive processes. In the case of illusory correlations, an important cognitive factor is the availability heuristic (Reber, 2004; Risen et al., 2007). You may recall that Chapter 8 discussed how gender stereotypes are related to schemas, another important cognitive factor.

Chapman and Chapman (1969) performed a classic investigation of the illusory correlation. Their data showed that students formed an illusory correlation between people's reported sexual orientation and their responses on an inkblot test. Let's see how the availability heuristic might help to explain illusory correlations.

When we try to figure out whether two variables are related to each other, we should consider the data about four categories in a 2 × 2 matrix. For example, suppose that we want to determine whether people who are lesbians or gay males are more likely than heterosexuals to have psychological problems.* Imagine, for example, that researchers gathered the data in Table 12.2. These data show that 6 out of 60 gay people (or 10%) have psychological problems, and 8 out of 80 straight people (also 10%) have psychological problems. We should therefore conclude that sexual orientation is not related to psychological problems.

Unfortunately, however, people typically pay the most attention to only one cell in the matrix, especially if the two descriptive characteristics are statistically less frequent

---

*Although some people believe in this illusory correlation, the research does not show a consistent relationship between sexual orientation and psychological problems (e.g., Garnets, 2008; Herek & Garnets, 2007; Rothblum & Factor, 2001).

TABLE 12.2

A Matrix Showing Hypothetical Information About Sexual Orientation and Psychological Problems

	Number in Each Category		
	Gay people	Straight people	Totals
People with psychological problems	6	8	14
People without psychological problems	54	72	126
Totals	60	80	140

(Risen et al., 2007). In this example, some people notice only the six gay people who have psychological problems, ignoring the important information in the other three cells.

People with an established bias against gay people might be especially likely to pay attention to this cell. Furthermore, they may continue to look for information that confirms their hypothesis that gay people have problems. You'll recall from the earlier discussion of conditional reasoning that people would rather try to confirm a hypothesis than try to disprove it, consistent with Theme 3.

Try applying the information about illusory correlations to some stereotype that you hold. Notice whether you tend to focus on only one cell in the matrix, ignoring the other three. Have you specifically tried to *disconfirm* the stereotypes? Also, notice how politicians and the media often base their arguments on illusory correlations (Myers, 2002). For example, they may focus on the number of welfare recipients with fraudulent claims. This number is meaningless unless we know additional information, such as the number of welfare recipients *without* fraudulent claims.

Before we move on to a third heuristic in decision making, let us summarize information about the availability heuristic:

1. We use the availability heuristic when we estimate frequency or probability in terms of how easily we can think of examples of something. This heuristic is generally accurate in our daily lives, and people can estimate relative frequency with impressive accuracy.

2. However, availability may be contaminated by two factors that are not related to objective frequency: recency and familiarity. Therefore, when you make frequency judgments, ask yourself whether you are giving a special advantage to items that occurred more recently or that are somehow more familiar.

3. In contrast, the recognition heuristic is usually helpful when we judge relative frequency, for example, in guessing which of two cities has the larger population.

4. The availability heuristic can also create illusory correlations, when two variables appear to be correlated, although there is no statistical relationship.

The Anchoring and Adjustment Heuristic

You've probably had a number of incidents like this one. A friend asks you, "Can you meet me at the library in 15 minutes?" You know that it takes longer than 15 minutes to get there, so you make a modest adjustment and agree to meet in 20 minutes. However, you didn't count on needing to find your coat, or your cell phone ringing, or stopping to tie a shoelace, or several other trivial events. Basically, you could have arrived in 20 minutes (well, maybe 25), if everything had gone smoothly. In retrospect, you failed to make large enough adjustments to account for the inevitable delays. (Try Demonstration 12.5 when it's convenient, but complete Demonstration 12.6 before you read further.)

According to the **anchoring and adjustment heuristic**—also known as the **anchoring effect**—we begin with a first approximation, which serves as an **anchor**; then we make adjustments to that number, based on additional information (Mussweiler et al., 2004; Thaler & Sunstein, 2008; Tversky & Kahneman, 1982). This heuristic often leads to a reasonable answer, just as the representativeness and availability heuristics often lead to reasonable answers. However, people typically rely too heavily on the anchor, and their adjustments are too small (Kahneman, 2011).

The anchoring and adjustment heuristic illustrates once more that people tend to endorse their current hypotheses or beliefs, rather than trying to question them (Baron, 2000; Kida, 2006). They emphasize top-down processing, consistent

---

◎ Demonstration 12.5

The Anchoring and Adjustment Heuristic

Copy the two multiplication problems listed below on separate pieces of paper. Show Problem A to at least five friends, and show Problem B to at least five other friends. In each case, ask the participants to estimate the answer within 5 seconds.

A. $8 \times 7 \times 6 \times 5 \times 4 \times 3 \times 2 \times 1$

B. $1 \times 2 \times 3 \times 4 \times 5 \times 6 \times 7 \times 8$

Now tally the answers separately for the two problems, listing the answers from smallest to largest. Calculate the median for each problem. (If you have an uneven number of participants, the median is the answer in the middle of the distribution—with half larger and half smaller. If you have an even number of participants, take the average between the two answers in the middle of the distribution.)

⑨ Demonstration 12.6

Estimating Confidence Intervals

For each of the following questions, answer in terms of a range, rather than a single number. Specifically, you should supply a 98% confidence interval. A confidence interval is the range within which you expect the correct answer to fall. For example, suppose you answer a question by supplying a 98% confidence interval that is 2,000 to 7,000. This means that you think there is only a 2% chance that the real answer is either less than 2,000 or more than 7,000. The correct answers can be found at the end of the chapter on page 452.

1. How many full-time students were enrolled in U.S. colleges and universities in 2011?
2. According to the official count, how many people died in the 2011 earthquake and tsunami in Japan?
3. In what year did Martin Van Buren begin his term as the president of the United States?
4. In 2009, what was the average life expectancy in Canada?
5. How many dollars did the United States spend for military expenditures in 2010?
6. In what year did New Zealand give women the right to vote?
7. What was the median salary of a U.S. male college graduate in 2009?
8. What is the total area of Canada (in either square kilometers or square miles)?
9. What was the estimated population of France in 2010?
10. Of the residents of Canada, what percentage report that they are Roman Catholics?

Source: All questions are based on information from "Countries of the World," 2012; "Student Demographics," 2011; and Statistics Canada, 2012b.

with Theme 5. We've seen several other examples of this tendency in the present chapter:

1. The *belief-bias effect*: We rely too heavily on our established beliefs.
2. The *confirmation bias*: We prefer to confirm a current hypothesis, rather than to reject it.
3. The *illusory correlation*: We rely too strongly on one well-known cell in a 2 × 2 data matrix, and we fail to seek information about the other three cells.

Let's begin by considering some research on the anchoring and adjustment heuristic. Then we will see how this heuristic can be applied to estimating confidence intervals.

Research on the Anchoring and Adjustment Heuristic. Demonstration 12.5 illustrates the anchoring and adjustment heuristic. In a classic study, high school students were asked to estimate the answers to these two multiplication problems (Tversky & Kahneman, 1982). The students were allowed only 5 seconds to respond. The results showed that the two problems generated widely different answers. If the first number in this sequence was 8, a relatively large number, the median of their estimates was 2,250. (That is, half the students estimated higher than 2,250, and half estimated lower.) In contrast, if the first number was 1, a small number, their median estimate was only 512.

Furthermore, both groups anchored too heavily on the initial impression that every number in the problem was only a single digit, because both estimates were far too low. The correct answer for both problems is 40,320. Did the anchoring and adjustment heuristic influence the people you tested?

The anchoring and adjustment heuristic is so powerful that it operates even when the anchor is obviously arbitrary or impossibly extreme, such as a person living to the age of 140. It also operates for both novices and experts (Herbert, 2010; Kahneman, 2011; Mussweiler et al., 2004; Tversky & Kahneman, 1974).

Researchers have not developed precise explanations for the anchoring and adjustment heuristic. However, one likely mechanism is that the anchor restricts the search for relevant information in memory. Specifically, people concentrate their search on information relatively close to the anchor, even if this anchor is not a realistic number (Kahneman, 2011; Pohl et al., 2003).

The anchoring and adjustment heuristic has many applications in everyday life (Janiszewski, 2011; Mussweiler et al., 2004; Newell et al., 2007). For example, Englich and Mussweiler (2001) studied anchoring effects in courtroom sentencing. Trial judges with an average of 15 years of experience listened to a typical legal case. The role of the prosecutor was played by a person who was introduced as a computer science student. This student was obviously a novice in terms of legal experience, so the judges should not take him seriously. However, when the "prosecutor" demanded a sentence of 12 months, these experienced judges recommended 28 months. In contrast, when the "prosecutor" demanded a sentence of 34 months, these judges recommended a sentence of 36 months. (Incidentally, be sure to try Demonstration 12.6 on page 433 before you read further.)

Estimating Confidence Intervals. We use anchoring and adjustment when we estimate a single number. We also use this heuristic when we estimate a confidence interval. A **confidence interval is the range** within which we expect a number to fall a certain percentage of the time. For example, you might guess that the 98% confidence interval for the number of students at a particular college is 3,000 to 5,000. This guess would mean that you think there is a 98% chance that the number is between 3,000 and 5,000, and only a 2% chance that the number is outside of this range.

Demonstration 12.6 tested the accuracy of your estimates for various kinds of numerical information. Check page 452 to see how many of your confidence-interval estimates included the correct answer. Suppose that a large number of people were instructed to provide a confidence interval for each of these 10 questions. Then we would expect their confidence intervals to include the correct answer about 98% of the time, assuming that their estimation techniques had been correct.

However, studies have shown that people provide 98% confidence intervals that actually include the correct answer only about 60% of the time (Block & Harper, 1991; Hoffrage, 2004). In other words, our estimates for these confidence intervals are definitely too narrow.

The research by Tversky and Kahneman (1974) pointed out how the anchoring and adjustment heuristic is relevant when we make confidence-interval estimates. We first provide a best estimate, and we use this figure as an anchor. Next we make adjustments upward and downward from this anchor to construct the confidence-interval estimate. However, our adjustments are typically too small.

For example, let's consider Question 1 in Demonstration 12.6. Perhaps you initially guessed that the United States currently has 8 million full-time students in college. You might then say that your 98% confidence interval was between 6 million and 10 million. This interval would be too narrow, because you had made a large error in your original estimate. Check the correct answers on page 452. Again, we establish our anchor, and we do not wander far from it in the adjustment process (Kahneman, 2011; Kruglanski, 2004). When we shut our minds to new possibilities, we rely too heavily on top-down processing.

An additional problem is that most people don't really understand confidence intervals. For instance, when you estimated the confidence intervals in Demonstration 12.6, did you emphasize to yourself that each confidence interval should be so wide that there was only a 2% chance of the actual number being either larger or smaller than this interval? Teigen and Jørgensen (2005) found that college students tend to misinterpret these confidence intervals. In their study, the students' 90% confidence intervals were associated with an actual certainty of only about 50%.

Let's summarize the last of the three major decision-making heuristics:

1. When we use the anchoring and adjustment heuristic, we begin by guessing a first approximation or anchor. Then we make adjustments to that anchor.

2. This heuristic is generally useful, but we typically fail to make large enough adjustments.

3. The anchoring and adjustment heuristic also explains our errors when we estimate confidence intervals; we usually supply a range that is too narrow, given our uncertainty about the anchor.

You can overcome potential biases from the anchoring and adjustment heuristic. First, think carefully about your initial estimate. Then ask yourself whether you are paying enough attention to the features of this specific situation that might require you to change your anchor, or else to make large adjustments away from your initial anchor.

The Framing Effect

When I was writing this chapter on decision making, I took a break to read the mail that had just arrived. I opened an envelope from an organization I support, called "The Feminist Majority." The letter pointed out that in a previous year, right-wing organizations had introduced legislation in 17 state governments that would eliminate affirmative action programs for women and people of color. This figure surprised and saddened me; apparently the anti–affirmative action supporters had more influence than I had imagined! And then I realized that the framing effect might be operating. Perhaps, at that very moment, other people throughout the United States were opening their mail from organizations that endorsed the other perspective. Perhaps their letter pointed out that their organization—and others with a similar viewpoint—had failed to introduce legislation in 33 state governments. Yes, a fairly subtle change in the wording of a sentence can produce a very different emotional reaction! Are political organizations perhaps hiring cognitive psychologists?

The **framing effect** demonstrates that the outcome of your decision can be influenced by two factors: (1) the background context of the choice and (2) the way in which a question is worded (or framed). However, before we discuss these two factors, be sure you have tried Demonstration 12.7, which appears below.

Chapter 2 examined framing, in connection with illusory contours. On page 39, for example, notice how the three outer shapes create the illusion of a large white inverted triangle. Hide the frame—the three blue shapes—and you no longer see this triangle (Keren, 2011a).

⦿ Demonstration 12.7

The Framing Effect and Background Information

Try the following two problems:

Problem 1

Imagine that you decided to see a concert, and you paid $20 for the admission price of one ticket. You are about to enter the theater, when you discover that you cannot find your ticket. The theater doesn't keep a record of ticket purchases, so you cannot simply get another ticket. You have $60 in your wallet. Would you pay $20 for another ticket for the concert?

Problem 2

Imagine that you decided to buy a ticket for a concert; the ticket will cost $20. You go to the theater box office. Then you open your wallet and discover that a $20 bill is missing. (Fortunately, you still have $40 left in your wallet.) Would you pay $20 for a ticket for the concert?

Source: Based on Tversky & Kahneman, 1981.

Chapter 10 discussed framing, with respect to how language can frame our thinking. For example, some people use the word "responsibility" to mean individual responsibility, defined in terms of their own wealth and power. Other people use the word "responsibility" to mean social responsibility, defined in terms of helping people who have less wealth and power than they do (Lakoff, 2009, 2011). Now we'll examine how decision making can be influenced by (a) the background information and (b) the specific wording of a question (LeBoeuf & Shafir, 2012; McGraw et al., 2010).

Background Information and the Framing Effect. Take a moment to read Demonstration 12.7 once more. Notice that the amount of money is $20 in both cases. If decision makers were perfectly "rational," they would respond identically to both problems (Kahneman, 2011; LeBoef & Shafir, 2012; Moran & Ritov, 2011). However, the decision frame differs for these two situations, so they seem psychologically different from each other.

⊚ Demonstration 12.8

The Framing Effect and the Wording of a Question

Try the following two problems:

Problem 1

Imagine that a country in Europe is preparing for the outbreak of an unusual disease, which is expected to kill 600 people. The public health officials have proposed two alternative programs to combat the disease. Assume that these officials have scientifically estimated the consequences of the programs, as follows:

> If they adopt Program A, 200 people will be saved.
> If they adopt Program B, there is a one-third probability that 600 people will be saved, and a two-thirds probability that zero people will be saved.
> Which of these two programs would you choose?

Problem 2

Now imagine the same situation, but with these two alternatives:

> If Program C is adopted, 400 people will die.
> If Program D is adopted, there is a one-third probability that no one will die, and a two-thirds probability that 600 people will die.
> Which of these two programs would you choose?

Source: Based on Tversky & Kahneman, 1981.

We frequently organize our mental expense accounts according to topics. Specifically, we view going to a concert as a transaction in which the cost of the ticket is exchanged for the experience of seeing a concert. If you buy another ticket, the cost of seeing that concert has increased to a level that many people find unacceptable. When Kahneman and Tversky (1984) asked people what they would do in the case of Problem 1, only 46% said that they would pay for another ticket.

In contrast, in Problem 2, people did not tally the lost $20 bill in the same account as the cost of a ticket. In this second case, people viewed the lost $20 as being generally irrelevant to the ticket. In Kahneman and Tversky's (1984) study, 88% of the participants said that they would purchase the ticket in Problem 2. In other words, the background information provides different frames for the two problems, and the specific frame strongly influences the decision. Now, before you read the next section, be sure that you have tried Demonstration 12.8, which appeared on page 437.

The Wording of a Question and the Framing Effect. In Chapter 11, we saw that people often fail to realize that two problems may share the same deep structure, for instance in algebra problems. In other words, people are distracted by the differences in the surface structure of the problems. When people make decisions, they are also distracted by differences in surface structure. For example, people who conduct surveys have found that the exact wording of a question can have a major effect on the answers that respondents provide (Bruine de Bruin, 2011).

Tversky and Kahneman (1981) tested college students in both Canada and the United States, using Problem 1 in Demonstration 12.8. Notice that both choices emphasize the number of lives that would be *saved*. They found that 72% of their participants chose Program A, and only 28% chose Program B. Notice that the participants in this group were "risk averse." That is, they preferred the certainty of saving 200 lives, rather than the risky prospect of a one-in-three possibility of saving 600 lives. Notice, however, that the benefits of Programs A and B in Problem 1 are statistically identical.

Now inspect your answer to Problem 2, in which both choices emphasize the number of lives that would be *lost* (that is, the number of deaths). Tversky and Kahneman (1981) presented this problem to a different group of students from the same colleges that they had tested with Problem 1. Only 22% favored Program C, but 78% favored Program D. Here the participants were "risk taking"; they preferred the two-in-three chance that 600 would die, rather than the guaranteed death of 400 people. Again, however, the benefits of the two programs are statistically equal. Furthermore, notice that Problem 1 and Problem 2 have identical deep structures. The only difference is that the outcomes are described in Problem 1 in terms of the lives saved, but in Problem 2 in terms of the lives lost.

The way that a question is framed—lives saved or lives lost—has an important effect on people's decisions (Hardman, 2009; Moran & Ritov, 2011; Stanovich, 2009). This framing changes people from focusing on the possible gains (lives saved) to focusing on the possible losses (lives lost). In the case of Problem 1, we tend to prefer the certainty of having 200 lives saved, so we avoid the option where it's possible that no lives will be saved. In the case of Problem 2, however, we tend to prefer the risk that nobody will die (even though there is a good chance that 600 will die); we avoid the option where 400 face certain death. Tversky and Kahneman (1981) chose the name **prospect theory** to refer to people's tendencies to think that possible gains are different from possible losses. Specifically:

1. When dealing with possible *gains* (for example, lives saved), people tend to avoid risks.
2. When dealing with possible *losses* (for example, lives lost), people tend to seek risks.

Numerous studies have replicated the general framing effect, and the effect is typically strong (Kahneman, 2011; LeBoeuf & Shafir, 2012; Stanovich, 1999). Furthermore, the framing effect is common among statistically sophisticated people as well as statistically naive people, and the magnitude of the effect is relatively large. In addition, Mayhorn and his colleagues (2002) found framing effects with both students in their 20s and with older adults.

Let's review the framing effect. Background context (e.g., lost ticket vs. lost $20 bill) can influence decisions; we do not make choices in a vacuum. In addition, the wording of the question can influence decisions. Specifically, people avoid risks when the wording implies gains, and they seek risks when the wording implies losses.

The research on framing suggests some practical advice: When you are making an important decision, try rewording the description of this decision. For example, suppose that you need to decide whether to accept a particular job offer. Ask yourself how you would feel about having this job, and then ask yourself how you would feel about *not* having this job. This kind of Type 2 processing can help you make wiser decisions (Kahneman, 2011).

IN DEPTH

Overconfidence About Decisions

So far, we have seen that decisions can be influenced by three decision-making heuristics: the representativeness heuristic, the availability heuristic, and the anchoring and adjustment heuristic. Furthermore, the framing effect demonstrates that both the background information and the wording of a statement can encourage us to make unwise decisions.

Given these sources of error, people should realize that their decision-making skills are nothing to boast about. Unfortunately, however, the research shows that people are frequently overconfident (Johnson, 2004; Kahneman, 2011; Krizan & Windschitl, 2007; Moore & Healy, 2008). **Overconfidence** means that your confidence judgments are higher than they should be, based on your actual performance on the task.

We have already discussed two examples of overconfidence in decision making in this chapter. In an illusory correlation, people are confident that two variables are related, when in fact the relationship is either weak or nonexistent. In anchoring and adjustment, people are so confident in their estimation abilities that they supply very narrow confidence intervals for these estimates.

Overconfidence is a characteristic of other cognitive tasks, in addition to decision making. For example, Chapter 5 noted that people are often overconfident about the accuracy of their eyewitness testimony. Furthermore, Chapter 6 pointed out that people are typically overconfident about how well they understood material they had read and how accurately they remember information. Let's now consider research on several aspects of overconfidence; then we'll discuss several factors that help to create overconfidence.

General Studies on Overconfidence. A variety of studies show that humans are overconfident in many decision-making situations. For example, people are overconfident about how long a person with a fatal disease will live, which firms will go bankrupt, and whether the defendant is guilty in a court trial (Kahneman & Tversky, 1995). People typically have more confidence in their own decisions than in predictions that are based on statistically objective measurements. In addition, people tend to overestimate their own social skills, creativity, leadership abilities, and a wide range of academic skills (Kahneman & Renshon, 2007; Matlin, 2004; Matlin & Stang, 1978; Moore & Healy, 2008). In addition, physicists, economists, and other researchers are overconfident that their theories are correct (Trout, 2002).

We need to emphasize, however, that individuals differ widely with respect to overconfidence (Oreg & Bayazit, 2009; Steel, 2007). For example, a large-scale study showed that 77% of the student participants were overconfident about their accuracy in answering general-knowledge questions like those in Demonstration 12.6. Still, these results tell us that 23% were either on target or underconfident (Stanovich, 1999).

Furthermore, people from different countries may differ with respect to their confidence (Weber & Morris, 2010). For example, a cross-cultural study in three countries reported that Chinese residents showed the greater overconfidence, and the U.S. residents were intermediate. However, the least confident group was Japanese residents, who also took the longest to make their decisions (Yates, 2010).

Let's consider two research areas in which overconfidence has been extensively documented. As you'll see, politicians are often overconfident about the decisions they make. Furthermore, if we explore an area that is personally more familiar, students are usually overconfident that they will complete their academic projects on time.

Overconfidence in Political Decision Making. Even powerful politicians can make unwise personal decisions, as we have recently seen with elected officials in the United States. I live in western New York, where both our governor Elliot Spitzer and our congressman Christopher Lee resigned because of sexual scandals. Within recent years, we've seen many similar resignations. How could so many politicians be so confident that their secret lives would not be discovered?

Let's shift to the decisions that politicians make about international policy—decisions that can affect thousands of people. Unfortunately, political leaders seldom think systematically about the risks involved in important decisions. For instance, they often fail to consider the risks involved when they (a) invade another country, (b) continue a war that they cannot win, and (c) leave the other country in a worse situation following the war. In an international conflict, each side tends to overestimate its own chances of success (Johnson, 2004; Kahneman & Renshon, 2007; Kahneman & Tversky, 1995).

When politicians need to make a decision, they are also overconfident that their data are accurate (Moore & Healy, 2008). For example, the United States went to war with Iraq because our political leaders were overconfident that Iraq had owned weapons of mass destruction.

For instance, Vice President Dick Cheney had stated on August 26, 2002, "There is no doubt that Saddam Hussein now has weapons of mass destruction." President George W. Bush had declared on March 17, 2003, "Intelligence gathered by this and other governments leaves no doubt that the Iraq regime continues to possess and conceal some of the most lethal weapons ever devised." However, it then became clear that crucial information had been a forgery, and these weapons did not exist (Tavris & Aronson, 2007).

Researchers have created methods for reducing overconfidence about decisions. For example, the **crystal-ball technique** asks decision makers to imagine that a completely accurate crystal ball has determined that their favored hypothesis is actually incorrect; the decision makers must therefore search for alternative explanations for the outcome (Cannon-Bowers & Salas, 1998; Paris et al., 2000). They must also find reasonable evidence to support these alternative explanations. If the Bush administration had used the crystal-ball technique, for example, they would have been instructed to describe several reasons why Saddam Hussein could *not* have weapons of mass destruction.

Unfortunately, political leaders apparently do not use de-biasing techniques to make important political decisions. As Griffin and Tversky (2002) point out,

It can be argued that people's willingness to engage in military, legal, and other costly battles would be reduced if they had a more realistic assessment of their chances of success. We doubt that the benefits of overconfidence outweigh its costs. (p. 249)

Overconfidence About Completing Projects on Time. Are you surprised to learn that students are frequently overly optimistic about how quickly they can complete a project? In reality, this overconfidence applies to most people. Even Daniel Kahneman (2011) describes examples of his own failure in completing projects on time.

According to the **planning fallacy**, people typically underestimate the amount of time (or money) required to complete a project; they also estimate that the task will be relatively easy to complete (Buehler et al., 2002; Buehler et al., 2012; Kahneman, 2011; Peetz et al., 2010; Sanna et al., 2009). Notice why this fallacy is related to overconfidence. Suppose that you are overconfident when you make decisions. You will then estimate that your paper for cognitive psychology will take only 10 hours to complete, and you can easily finish it on time if you start next Tuesday.

Researchers certainly have not discovered a method for eliminating the planning fallacy. However, the research suggests several strategies that can help you make more realistic estimates about the amount of time a large project will require.

1. Divide your project into several parts, and estimate how long each part will take. This process will provide a more realistic estimate of the time you will need to complete the project (Forsyth & Burt, 2008).

2. Envision each step in the process of completing your project, such as gathering the materials, organizing the project's basic structure, and so forth. Each day, rehearse these components (Taylor et al., 1998).

3. Try thinking about some person other than yourself, and visualize how long this person took to complete the project; be sure to visualize the potential obstacles in your imagery (Buehler et al., 2012).

The planning fallacy has been replicated in several studies in the United States, Canada, and Japan. How can we explain people's overconfidence that they will complete a task on time? One factor is that people create an optimistic scenario that represents the ideal way in which they will make progress on a project. This scenario fails to consider the large number of problems that can arise (Buehler et al., 2002).

People also recall that they completed similar tasks relatively quickly in the past (Roy & Christenfeld, 2007; Roy et al., 2005). In addition, they estimate that they will have more free time in the future, compared to the free time they have right now (Zauberman & Lynch, 2005). In other words, people use the anchoring and adjustment heuristic, and they do not make large enough adjustments to their original scenario, based on other useful information.

Reasons for Overconfidence. We have seen many examples demonstrating that people tend to be overconfident about the correctness of their decisions. This overconfidence arises from errors during many different stages in the decision-making process:

1. People are often unaware that their knowledge is based on very tenuous, uncertain assumptions and on information from unreliable or inappropriate sources (Bishop & Trout, 2002; Johnson, 2004).

2. Examples that *confirm* our hypotheses are readily available, but we resist searching for counterexamples (Hardman, 2009; Lilienfeld et al., 2009;

Mercier & Sperber, 2011). You'll recall from the discussion of deductive reasoning that people also persist in confirming their current hypothesis, rather than looking for negative evidence.

3. People have difficulty recalling the other possible hypotheses, and decision making depends on memory (Theme 4). If you cannot recall the competing hypotheses, you will be overly confident about the hypothesis you have endorsed (Trout, 2002).

4. Even if people manage to recall the other possible hypotheses, they do not treat them seriously. The choice once seemed ambiguous, but the alternatives now seem trivial (Kida, 2006; Simon et al., 2001).

5. Researchers do not educate the public about the overconfidence problem (Lilienfeld et al., 2009). As a result, we typically do not pause—on the brink of making a decision—and ask ourselves, "Am I relying only on Type 1 thinking? I need to switch over to Type 2 thinking!"

When people are overconfident in a risky situation, the outcome can often produce disasters, deaths, and widespread destruction. The term **my-side bias** describes the overconfidence that your own view is correct in a confrontational situation (Stanovich, 2009; Toplak & Stanovich, 2002). Conflict often arises when individuals (or groups or national leaders) each fall victim to my-side bias. People are so confident that their position is correct that they cannot even consider the possibility that their opponent's position may be at least partially correct. If you find yourself in conflict with someone, try to overcome my-side bias. Could some part of the other people's position be worth considering?

More generally, try to reduce the overconfidence bias when you face an important decision. Emphasize Type 2 processing, and review the five points listed above. Are you perhaps overconfident that this decision will have a good outcome?

The Hindsight Bias

In the preceding In-Depth feature, we discussed how people are overconfident about predicting events that will happen in the future. In contrast, **hindsight** refers to our judgments about events that already happened in the past. The **hindsight bias** occurs when an event has happened, and we say that the event had been inevitable; we had actually "known it all along" (Hastie & Dawes, 2010).

In other words, the hindsight bias reflects our overconfidence that we could have accurately predicted a particular outcome at some point in the past (Hardt et al., 2010; Pezzo & Beckstead, 2008; Pohl, 2004; Sanna & Schwarz, 2006). The hindsight bias demonstrates that we often reconstruct the past so that it matches our present knowledge (Schacter, 2001).

Research About the Hindsight Bias. The hindsight bias can operate for the judgments we make about people. In a thought-provoking study, Linda Carli (1999) asked students to read a two-page story about a young woman named Barbara and her relationship with Jack, a man she had met in graduate school. The story, told from Barbara's viewpoint, provided background information about Barbara and her growing relationship with Jack. Half of the students read a version that had a tragic ending, in which Jack rapes Barbara. The other half read a version that was identical except that it had a happy ending, in which Jack proposes marriage to Barbara.

After reading the story, each student then completed a true/false memory test. This test examined recall for the facts of the story, but it also included questions about information that had not been mentioned in the story. Some of these questions were consistent with a stereotyped version of a rape scenario, such as, "Barbara met many men at parties." Other questions were consistent with a marriage-proposal scenario, such as, "Barbara wanted a family very much."

The results of Carli's (1999) study demonstrated the hindsight bias. People who read the version about the rape responded that they could have predicted Barbara would be raped. Furthermore, people who read the marriage-proposal version responded that they could have predicted Jack would propose to Barbara. (Remember that the two versions were actually identical, except for the final ending.) Furthermore, each group committed systematic errors on the memory test. Each group recalled items that were consistent with the ending they had read, even though this information had not appeared in the story.

Carli's (1999) study is especially important because it helps us understand why many people "blame the victim" following a tragic event such as a rape. In reality, this person's earlier actions may have been perfectly appropriate. However, people often search the past for reasons why a victim deserved that outcome. As we've seen in Carli's research, people may even "reconstruct" some reasons that did not actually occur.

The hindsight bias has been demonstrated in a number of different studies, though the effect is not always strong (e.g., Hardt et al., 2010; Harley et al., 2004; Kahneman, 2011; Koriat et al., 2006; Pohl, 2004). The bias has also been documented in North America, Europe, Asia, and Australia (Pohl et al., 2002). Furthermore, doctors show the hindsight bias when guessing a medical diagnosis (Kahneman, 2011). People also demonstrate the hindsight bias for political events and for business decisions (Hardt et al., 2010; Kahneman, 2011).

Explanations for the Hindsight Bias. Despite all the research, the explanations for the hindsight bias are not clear (Hardt et al., 2010; Pohl, 2004). However, one likely cognitive explanation is that people might use anchoring and adjustment. After all, they have been told that a particular outcome actually did happen—that it was 100% certain. Therefore, they use this 100% value as the anchor in estimating the likelihood that they would have predicted the answer, and then they do not adjust their certainty downward as much as they should.

We also noted in discussing Carli's (1999) study that people may misremember past events, so that those events are consistent with current information. These events help to justify the outcome. Did the results of Carli's study about the tragic ending versus the upbeat story ending surprise anyone? Of course not . . . we knew it all along.

Demonstration 12.9

Decision-Making Style

1	2	3	4	5	6	7

Completely disagree   Completely agree

Using the scale above, answer each of the following questions:

1. Whenever I'm faced with a choice, I try to imagine what all the other possibilities are, even ones that aren't present at the moment.
2. Whenever I make a choice, I try to get information about how the other alternatives turned out.
3. When I am in the car listening to the radio, I often check other stations to see if something better is playing, even if I am relatively satisfied with what I'm listening to.
4. When I watch TV, I channel surf, often scanning through the available options even while attempting to watch one program.
5. I treat relationships like clothing: I expect to try a lot on before finding the perfect fit.
6. I often find it difficult to shop for a gift for a friend.
7. Renting videos or DVDs is really difficult. I'm always struggling to pick the best one.
8. When shopping, I have a hard time finding clothing that I really love.
9. I'm a big fan of lists that attempt to rank things (the best movies, the best singers, the best athletes, the best novels, etc.).
10. I find that writing is very difficult, even if it's just writing a letter to a friend, because it's so hard to word things just right. I often do several drafts of even simple things.
11. No matter what I do, I have the highest standards for myself.
12. I never settle for second best.
13. I often fantasize about living in ways that are quite different from my actual life.

Source: Schwartz, B., et al., (2002). Maximizing versus satisfaction: Happiness is a matter of choice. *Journal of Personality and Social Psychology, 83,* 1178–1197.

Current Status of Heuristics and Decision Making

Some researchers have argued that the heuristic approach—developed by Kahneman and Tversky—may underestimate people's decision-making skills. For example, research by Adam Harris and his colleagues found that people make fairly realistic judgments about future events (Harris et al., 2009; Harris & Hahn, 2011).

Furthermore, Gerd Gigerenzer and his colleagues agree that people are not perfectly rational decision makers, especially under time pressure. However, they emphasize that people can do relatively well when they are given a fair chance on decision-making tasks. For instance, we saw on pages 429 to 430 that the recognition heuristic is reasonably accurate. Other research shows that people answer questions more accurately in naturalistic settings, especially if the questions focus on frequencies, rather than probabilities (e.g., Gigerenzer, 2006a, 2006b, 2008; Todd & Gigerenzer, 2007).

Peter Todd and Gerd Gigerenzer (2007) devised a term called **ecological rationality** to describe how people create a wide variety of heuristics to help themselves make useful, adaptive decisions in the real world. This point resembles the observation in Chapter 11 that Brazilian children can accurately solve complex math problems when selling candy in the streets, but not in a classroom (Carraher et al., 1985; Woll, 2002). Similarly, adults typically make wise decisions, if we examine the specific characteristics of the environment in which we live.

For example, only 28% of U.S. residents become potential organ donors, in contrast to 99.9% of French residents. Gigerenzer (2008) suggests that both groups are using a simple **default heuristic**; specifically, if there is a standard option—which happens if people do nothing—then people will choose it. In the United States, you typically need to sign up to become an organ donor. Therefore, the majority of U.S. residents—using the default heuristic—remain in the non-donor category. In France, you are an organ donor unless you specifically opt out of the donor program. Therefore, the majority of French residents—using the default heuristic—remain in the donor category.

Furthermore, people bring their world knowledge into the research laboratory, where researchers often design the tasks to specifically contradict their schemas. For example, do you really believe that Linda *wouldn't* be a feminist (p. 424) given her long-time commitment to social justice?

The two approaches—one proposed by Kahneman and one by Gigerenzer—may seem fairly different. However, both approaches suggest that decision-making heuristics generally serve us well in the real world. Furthermore, we can become more effective decision makers by realizing the limitations of these important strategies (Kahneman & Tversky, 2000).

Now, before reading the next section, try Demonstration 12.9 (p. 445).

Individual Differences: Decision-Making Style and Psychological Well-Being

Think back to the last time you needed to buy something in a fairly large store. Let's say that you needed to buy a shirt. Did you carefully inspect every shirt that seemed to be the right size, and then reconsider the top contenders before buying the shirt? **Maximizers** are people who have a **maximizing decision-making style**; they tend to examine as many options as possible. The task becomes even more challenging as the number of options increases, leading to "choice overload" (Schwartz, 2009).

In contrast, did you look through an assortment of shirts until you found one that was good enough to meet your standards, even if it wasn't the best possible shirt? **Satisficers** are people who have a **satisficing decision-making style**; they tend to settle for something that is satisfactory (Simon, 1955). Satisficers are not concerned about a potential shirt in another location that might be even better (Campitelli & Gobet, 2010; Schwartz, 2004, 2009).

Now look at your answers to Demonstration 12.9, and add up the total number of points. If your total is 65 or higher, you would tend toward the "maximizer" region of the scale. If your total is 40 or lower, you would tend toward the "satisficer" region of the scale. (Scores between 41 and 64 would be in the intermediate region.)

Barry Schwartz and his coauthors (2002) administered the questionnaire in Demonstration 12.9 to a total of 1,747 individuals, including college students in the United States and Canada, as well as groups such as healthcare professionals and people waiting at a train station. The researchers also administered several other measures. One of these assessed regret about past choices. It included such items as "When I think about how I'm doing in life, I often assess opportunities I have passed up" (p. 1182).

Schwartz and his colleagues found a significant correlation ($r = +.52$) between people's scores on the maximizing–satisficing scale and their score on the regret scale. Those who were maximizers tended to experience more regret. They blame themselves for picking a less-than-ideal item (Schwartz, 2009).

The researchers also found a significant correlation ($r = +.34$) between people's scores on the maximizing–satisficing scale and their score on a standard scale of depressive symptoms, the Beck Depression Inventory. The maximizers tended to experience more depression (Schwartz, 2004, 2009).

Keep in mind that these data are correlational, so they do not necessarily demonstrate that a maximizing decision-making style actually *causes* depression. However, people seem to pay a price for their extremely careful decision-making style. They keep thinking about how their choice might not have been ideal, and so they experience regret. The research by Schwartz and his coauthors (2002) suggests that this regret contributes to a person's more generalized depression.

An important conclusion from Schwartz's (2004) research is that having an abundance of choices certainly doesn't make the maximizers any happier. In fact, if they are relatively wealthy, they will need to make even more choices about their purchases, leading to even greater regret about the items that they did not buy. Schwartz (2009) chose a thought-provoking title for a recent chapter: "Be careful what you wish for: The dark side of freedom."

In a recent article, Schwartz (2012) makes an interesting suggestion. If the economic downturn in the United States continues, many "middle class" people may have lower incomes. They may decide that shopping—and finding that perfect shirt—isn't all that important. Instead, they may choose to re-examine their values and decide to enjoy other less materialist activities.

Demonstration 12.10

The Distribution of Wealth in an Ideal Nation

For this demonstration, you will need to think about how wealth is *actually* distributed in the United States, and how it *should* be distributed. In each case, divide the U.S. population into five groups (or quintiles). For example, consider the top 20% of the population for "actual wealth"—those who are the wealthiest 20%. Because they are the wealthiest, they have more than 20% of all the wealth. However, what percentage of all the U.S. wealth do you think that they *actually* own? Continue with these estimates for all five quintiles. The five numbers for "actual distribution" must add up to 100%.

1. Actual distribution of wealth

___ Top 20%   ___2nd 20%   ___3rd 20%   ___4th 20%   ___Bottom 20%

Now think about an ideal nation. How do you believe that the money should be divided? For example, consider the top 20% of the population. What percentage of all the wealth do you think that they *should* actually own? Continue with these estimates for all five quintiles. Again, the five numbers for "ideal nation" must add up to 100%.

2. Ideal distribution of wealth

___ Top 20%   ___2nd 20%   ___3rd 20%   ___4th 20%   ___Bottom 20%

Now turn to page 452, and check your answers against the percentages that Norton and Ariely (2011) found in their nationwide survey.

Hypothetical Decision Making: How Should Wealth Be Distributed?

Most studies in decision making focus on decisions that affect a limited number of people. However, a thought-provoking study by Norton and Ariely (2011) examined an important moral question: How should wealth be distributed? These authors surveyed a randomly drawn sample of 5,522 people living in the United States. Their survey focused on the distribution of wealth, which they defined as the total value of everything someone owns (e.g., property, stocks, etc.), minus the value of debts (e.g., loans and mortgages).

Before you read further, try Demonstration 12.10, which is based on their study. When you have finished your two sets of estimates, check page 452 to see the estimates that were provided by Norton and Ariely's sample, for both the actual and the ideal distribution of wealth. Compare the actual and the ideal distributions of wealth, as shown in Norton and Ariely's study. Were you surprised by either of these two responses to the survey? Then compare your actual distribution with your ideal distributions. Describe whether this comparison matched the results in Norton and Ariely's research. Page 452 also shows a third set of scores, people's estimates about how wealth is actually distributed in the U.S.

⑨ Section Summary: *Decision Making*

1. Decision-making heuristics are typically helpful in our daily lives; however, we can make errors in decision making when we overemphasize heuristics and underemphasize other important information.

2. According to the representativeness heuristic, we judge that a sample is likely if it resembles the population from which it was. For example, the sample should look random if it was gathered by random selection.

3. We are so persuaded by the representativeness heuristic that we tend to ignore important statistical information such as the size of the sample and the base rates in the population; furthermore, the representativeness heuristic helps to create the conjunction fallacy.

4. According to the availability heuristic, we estimate frequency or probability in terms of how easily we think of relevant examples of something. The availability heuristic produces errors when availability is influenced by biasing factors such as recency and familiarity. However, a related phenomenon—called the recognition heuristic—helps us make accurate decisions about relative frequency.

5. The availability heuristic helps to explain the phenomenon of illusory correlation, which is related to stereotypes.

6. According to the anchoring and adjustment heuristic, we establish an anchor, and then we make adjustments, based on other information; the problem is that these adjustments are usually too small.

7. We also use the anchoring and adjustment heuristic when we estimate confidence intervals. We begin with a single best estimate, and then we make very small adjustments on either side of that estimate; however, this confidence interval is usually too narrow.

8. The way in which a question is framed can influence our decisions; background information can influence our decisions inappropriately. The framing effect also depends on wording. When the wording implies gains, we tend to avoid risks; when the wording implies losses, we tend to seek out risks.

9. People are frequently overconfident about their decisions. For instance, political decision makers may risk lives when they are overconfident. In addition, college students tend to be overconfident when they estimate the completion time for various projects.

10. In the hindsight bias, people already know the outcome of an event, and they are overly optimistic that they could have predicted that specific outcome before it actually happened.

11. Gigerenzer and his colleagues emphasize that humans are reasonably skilled at making decisions in natural settings, using a wide variety of heuristics. This approach and the heuristics approach of Kahneman and his colleagues both emphasize that heuristics usually lead to appropriate decisions.

12. Satisficers make decisions quickly; in contrast, maximizers agonize over their decisions, which may lead to regret and depressive symptoms.

13. Norton and Ariely's survey shows that people make significant errors in estimating the actual distribution of wealth in the United States. Their choices for the ideal distribution of wealth show much more equality.

CHAPTER REVIEW QUESTIONS

1. Describe the basic differences between deductive reasoning and decision making. Provide an example from your daily life that illustrates each of these cognitive processes. Why can both of them be categorized as "thinking"?

2. To make certain that you understand conditional reasoning, begin with this sentence: "If today is Monday, the art museum is closed." Apply the four conditional reasoning situations (propositional calculus) to this sentence, and point out which are valid and which are invalid.

3. Many of the errors that people make in reasoning can be traced to overreliance on previous knowledge or overactive top-down processes. Discuss this point, and then relate it to the anchoring and adjustment heuristic.

4. Throughout this chapter, you have seen many examples of a general cognitive tendency: We tend to accept the status quo (or the currently favored hypothesis), without sufficiently exploring other options. Describe how this statement applies to deductive reasoning and to several kinds of decision-making tasks.

5. Describe which heuristic is illustrated in each of the following everyday errors: (a) Someone asks you whether cardinals or robins are more common, and you make this decision based on the number of birds of each kind that you have seen this winter. (b) You are looking at a deck of cards that are in random order, and you see that there are three cards in a row that are Kings, which doesn't seem likely by chance alone. (c) You estimate the number of bottles of soda you will need for a picnic in July, based on the Christmas party consumption, taking into account the fact that the weather will be warmer in July.

6. In the case of the representativeness heuristic, people fail to take into account two important factors that should be emphasized. In the case of the availability heuristic, people take into account two important factors that should be ignored. Discuss these two statements, with reference to the information in this chapter. Give examples of each of these four kinds of errors.

7. Describe the variety of ways in which people tend to be overconfident in their decision making. Think of relevant examples from your own experience. Then point out methods for avoiding the planning fallacy when you face a deadline for a class assignment.

8. Think of a recent example from the news in which a politician made a decision for which he or she was criticized by news commentators. How could overconfidence have led to this unwise decision? Why might the hindsight bias be relevant here? Also, how could a politician use the results from the study by Norton and Ariely on wealth distribution on pages 448–449?

9. Suppose that you are planning to enroll in a course in social psychology next semester. Summarize at least five topics from this material on decision making that would have implications for that particular course.

10. Imagine that you have been hired by your local high school district to create a course in critical thinking. Review the chapter and make 15 to 20 suggestions (each only one sentence long) about precautions that should be included in such a program.

KEYWORDS

thinking
deductive reasoning
decision making
dual-process theory
Type 1 processing
Type 2 processing
conditional reasoning task
propositional reasoning task
syllogism
propositional calculus
propositions
antecedent
consequent
affirming the antecedent
affirming the consequent
denying the antecedent
denying the consequent

heuristic
belief-bias effect
confirmation bias
representative
representativeness heuristic
small-sample fallacy
base rate
base-rate fallacy
conjunction rule
conjunction fallacy
availability heuristic
recognition heuristic
illusory correlation
social cognition approach
anchoring and adjustment
  heuristic
anchoring effect

anchor
confidence intervals
framing effect
prospect theory
overconfidence
crystal-ball technique
planning fallacy
my-side bias
hindsight
hindsight bias
ecological rationality
default heuristic
maximizers
maximizing decision-making
  style
satisficers
satisficing decision-making style

RECOMMENDED READINGS

Holyoak, K. J., & Morrison, R. G. (Eds.). (2012). *The Oxford handbook of thinking and reasoning*. New York: Oxford University Press. This handbook has 40 chapters on a variety of topics that are related to reasoning and decision making. It also includes some chapters in specialty areas, such as legal reasoning, musical thought, and cross-cultural components of thinking.

Kahneman, D. (2011). *Thinking, fast and slow*. New York: Farrar, Straus and Giroux. Daniel Kahneman's book is superb, because he clearly describes how he and Amos Tversky collaborated in developing their approach to decision making. He also provides examples of numerous heuristics. Each chapter ends with critical-thinking examples that readers can model if they want to improve their Type 2 processing. For example, page 422 of your textbook shows an example for the representativeness heuristic.

Keren, G. (Ed.). (2011b). *Perspectives on framing*. New York: Psychology Press. Here is an excellent book that discusses both the framing effect and the anchor and adjustment heuristic. It also discusses both theoretical and practical issues in decision making.

Manktelow, K. D., Over, D., & Elqayam, S. (Eds.). (2011). *The science of reason: A festschrift for Jonathan St B. T. Evans* (pp. 119–143). New York: Psychology Press. This book was created to honor Dr. Evans, a British psychologist whose research has focused on logical reasoning. This book would be useful for students who are searching for an advanced-level examination of the discipline.

Schwartz, B. (2004). *The paradox of choice: Why more is less: How the culture of abundance robs us of satisfaction*. New York: HarperCollins. Schwartz's book explores the topic of maximizers and satisficers, discussed in this chapter's Individual Differences feature. The book goes beyond decision making to examine our cultural values. Although this book was published during the previous decade, it certainly has current relevance.

ANSWERS TO DEMONSTRATION 12.1

1. valid   2. invalid   3. invalid   4. valid

ANSWERS TO DEMONSTRATION 12.6

1. 12,198,540 students were enrolled full-time in the United States.
2. 15,839 people died.
3. Martin Van Buren began his term in 1837.
4. The average life expectancy in Canada in 2009 was 81.3 years.
5. The United States paid $698,000,000,000 for military expenditures in 2010.
6. New Zealand gave women the right to vote in 1893. (They were the first country to do so.)
7. The median salary of a U.S. male college graduate in 2009 was $51,000.
8. The total area of Canada is 9,984,670 square kilometers or 3,855,102 square miles.
9. The population of France is 64,057.792.
10. Of the residents of Canada, 43% report that their religion is Roman Catholic.

Did most of your confidence intervals include the correct answers, or were your confidence intervals too narrow?

ANSWERS TO DEMONSTRATION 12.10

Below are the average percentages supplied by participants in Norton and Ariely's study, for each of the two distributions. How do your own answers compare with these percentages?

1. The actual distribution of wealth in the U.S. How accurate were your predictions?
    84% Top 20%   11% 2nd 20%   4% 3rd 20%   0.2% 4th 20%   0.1% Bottom 20%

2. The *ideal* distribution of wealth in the U.S., as judged by people in this study. Do they match your own?
    32% Top 20%   22% 2nd 20%   22% 3rd 20%   13% 4th 20%   11% Bottom 20%

3. Here are the participants' estimates of the actual distribution of wealth in the U.S. Were you more accurate than they were?
    59% Top 20%   19% 2nd 20%   13% 3rd 20%   6% 4th 20%   3% Bottom 20%

CHAPTER 13

Cognitive Development Throughout the Lifespan

This chapter examines how cognitive processes develop in several areas that we've discussed in earlier chapters. Rather than discussing many topics briefly, we will explore three important topics in detail: memory, metamemory, and language. One purpose of this chapter is to describe how humans develop in these three important areas. You'll see that some skills improve as children mature to adulthood, and some decline as adults reach old age. However, many skills show less change than you might expect. A second purpose of this chapter is to encourage you to review some important concepts that were introduced earlier in the book. As you know from Chapter 6, you'll learn more effectively if you spread your learning over time. You can now refresh your memory about concepts that you initially learned several weeks ago.

According to the current research, even young infants can remember people, objects, and events. For example, young infants can remember how to activate a mobile by using a kicking motion that they learned several weeks earlier. Children's long-term recognition memory is surprisingly accurate, but their working memory and various kinds of long-term recall are considerably less accurate than in adults. Young children also fail to use memory strategies spontaneously when they want to remember something. When conditions are ideal, children can provide accurate eyewitness testimony. Errors are more likely if the children are young, if they heard some misleading information, or if they have intellectual disabilities.

Elderly adults are somewhat similar to young adults when the tasks require straightforward working memory, implicit memory, or recognition memory. However, they have more difficulty on tasks that require complex working memory, prospective memory, or explicit recall.

Children's metamemory skills improve as they grow older. For example, young children are much too confident about their memory accuracy, whereas older children and adults provide more accurate assessments. Elderly adults and young adults have similar beliefs about how memory operates. However, elderly adults tend to be more overconfident about the accuracy of their memory.

With respect to language development, young infants are remarkably competent in perceiving speech sounds and other important components of language. When interacting with infants, people typically produce language that encourages infants' linguistic skills. As children mature, their language skills increase dramatically in areas such as word meaning, grammatical relationships, and the pragmatic aspects of language.

CHAPTER INTRODUCTION

A friend described an interesting example of her granddaughter's cognitive sophistication. Five-year-old Isabelle had been on a family outing to go ice skating, a new experience for her. As they left the skating rink, Isabelle said, "That wasn't as much fun as I thought it was going to be." This chapter examines cognitive development in three areas, and Isabelle's remark reveals her expertise in all of these areas.

1. Memory: Isabelle remembers her original expectation that ice skating would be fun.

2. Metacognition: Isabelle had predicted that the skating experience would be fun.

3. Language: Isabelle's description successfully navigates among the three time periods, beginning with her anticipation of an enjoyable skating experience, and then the actual (not-so-enjoyable) skating experience, and finally her current acknowledgment of the discrepancy between the first and second time periods.

This interaction captures the considerable cognitive potential of young children. It also illustrates Theme 1 of this textbook, because children actively pursue information, and they try to make sense of their experiences (Gelman & Frazier, 2012).

A 4-year-old boy remarked to his mother one morning, "You know, I thought I'd be a grown-up by now . . . It sure is taking a long time!" (Rogoff, 1990, p. 3). As we will see in this chapter, the boy is certainly correct. Young children have mastered some important components of memory, metacognition, and language. However, they still need to develop their skills in areas such as memory performance, memory strategies, metacognition, syntax, and pragmatics.

Why should we study the cognitive processes of infants and children? One reason is theoretical: This research helps us understand the origins of cognitive skills, as well as the evolution of more complex skills (Gelman & Frazier, 2012; Rovee-Collier & Cuevas, 2009a). Another reason is practical: Many of you will have careers that require background knowledge about infancy and childhood.

Furthermore, why should we study the cognitive processes of older adults? Most cognitive psychology textbooks limit their discussion of cognitive development to infancy and childhood. However, this textbook emphasizes the **lifespan approach to development**, which emphasizes that developmental changes continue beyond young adulthood; we continue to change and adapt throughout our entire lives (Smith & Baltes, 1999; Whitbourne & Whitbourne, 2011). One reason for studying older adults is theoretical: The research shows that some cognitive skills decline during the aging process, but many other capabilities remain stable.

A second reason for studying older adults is practical: Many students will choose careers that require background knowledge about elderly people. At present, 14% of Canadian residents and 13% of U.S. residents are 65 years of age or older (Statistics Canada, 2012a; U.S. Census Bureau, 2012a). A third reason is personal: You probably have relatives who are older . . . and most young people in North America will become older adults. You need to know that most older adults are cognitively competent, with age differences in only a few areas.

When we study the cognitive abilities of infants, children, and elderly adults, the research problems are more complex than when we study young adults. For example, how can young infants convey their cognitive abilities, given their limited language and motor skills? With creative research techniques, however, researchers can partially overcome these limitations and discover that even young infants can understand information about the people and objects in their world (e.g., Gelman & Frazier, 2012; Mandler, 2004a; Rovee-Collier & Cuevas, 2009a, 2009b).

Research with elderly individuals presents a different set of methodological problems (Boker & Bisconti, 2006; Whitbourne & Whitbourne, 2011). Hundreds of studies have compared the cognitive performance of young, healthy college students with the performance of elderly people whose health, self-confidence, formal education, and familiarity with technology are relatively poor. Furthermore, college students are much more likely than elderly adults to have recent experiences with memorizing material and taking tests.

These differences present a methodology problem: Suppose that a poorly controlled memory study determines that young adults recall 25% more items than elderly adults. Perhaps the superior performance of the young adults can be traced to confounding variables—such as health or education—rather than to the aging process itself. In general, researchers believe that confounding variables can explain a major portion of the differences in cognitive performance. However, researchers have identified some age-related differences that persist, even when they eliminate confounding variables (Rabbitt, 2002; Salthouse, 2012; Whitbourne & Whitbourne, 2011).

This chapter focuses on cognitive development in three areas: memory, metamemory, and language. I organized this textbook so that the final chapter would encourage you to review many of the major concepts from these three important areas within cognitive psychology. As you'll also learn, infants and young children possess cognitive skills that you might not expect. In addition, you'll see that elderly people are much more cognitively competent than the popular stereotype suggests (Whitley & Kite, 2010).

THE LIFESPAN DEVELOPMENT OF MEMORY

We have examined memory in many parts of this textbook. Chapters 4, 5, and 6 focused specifically on memory, and the remaining chapters frequently discussed how memory contributes to other cognitive processes. Now we will examine how memory develops during infancy (the first two years of life), childhood, and old age.

Memory in Infants

Try to picture an infant who is about 4 months old—not yet old enough to sit upright without support. Would you expect that this baby would recognize his or her mother or remember how to make a mobile move? Several decades ago, psychologists believed that infants as young as 4 months of age could not remember anything for more than a brief period (Gelman, 2002). Of course, we cannot expect young infants to demonstrate sophisticated memory feats, because regions of the cortex most relevant to working memory and long-term memory are not yet fully developed (Bauer, 2004; Kagan & Herschkowitz, 2005).

Furthermore, early researchers underestimated infants' memory capacities because of methodological problems. Fortunately, current developmental psychologists have devised several research methods to test infants' ability to remember people and objects (Gelman & Frazier, 2012; Reznick, 2009). This research shows that infants have greater memory capabilities than you might expect. For example, we now know that 6-month-old infants can create an association between two objects, even if they have never previously seen the objects together at the same time and even if they were never reinforced for creating these associations (Cuevas et al., 2006; Giles & Rovee-Collier, 2011). Clearly Theme 2—which emphasizes cognitive competence—applies to infants, as well as children and adults.

One way to assess infants' memory is to see whether they look longer at one stimulus than another (e.g., Kibbe & Leslie, 2011; Sangrigoli & de Schonen, 2004). Let's consider two other research techniques that demonstrate infants' memory skills: (1) recognizing mother and (2) conjugate reinforcement with a mobile. As you'll see, babies can demonstrate substantial memory ability, even during their first month of life.

Recognizing Mother. Research on visual recognition shows that 3-day-old infants can distinguish their mother from a stranger (Rovee-Collier et al., 2001; Slater & Butterworth, 1997).

Infants' ability to recognize their mother's voice is especially remarkable (Markowitsch & Welzer, 2010; Siegler et al., 2003). For example, Kisilevsky and her coauthors (2003) tested infants about one or two weeks *before* they were born. Specifically, these researchers approached pregnant women who were receiving prenatal care at a hospital in China. The researchers asked each woman about testing her infant's voice-recognition ability, while she was still pregnant. If the mother agreed, the researchers presented either the mother's voice reading a Chinese poem or a female stranger's voice reading the same poem. Impressively, the infants' heart rate changed more when they listened to their mother's voice, rather than the stranger's voice.

Conjugate Reinforcement. Obviously, young infants cannot verbally tell us that they remember something they saw earlier. Carolyn Rovee-Collier and her colleagues designed a nonverbal measure to assess infant memory. Many studies now use this conjugate reinforcement technique to examine infant memory (Markowitsch & Welzer, 2010; Ornstein & Haden, 2009; Rovee-Collier & Cuevas, 2009a, 2009b). In the **conjugate reinforcement technique**, a mobile hangs above a young infant's crib; a ribbon connects the infant's ankle and the mobile, so that the infant's kicks will make the mobile move (see Figure 13.1).

This game is especially appealing to 2- to 6-month-old infants. After several minutes, they begin to kick rapidly and pump up the mobile. Then the infants lie quietly and watch parts of the mobile move. As the movement dies down, they typically shriek and then kick vigorously, thereby pumping it up again. In operant conditioning terms, the response is a foot kick, and the reinforcement is the movement of the mobile (Barr et al., 2005; Rovee-Collier & Cuevas, 2009a, 2009b).

FIGURE 13.1

The Conjugate Reinforcement Setup in Rovee-Collier's Research.

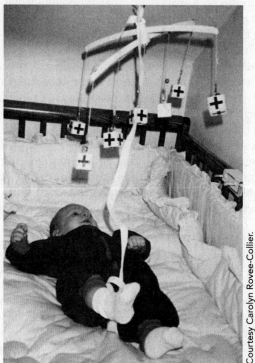

Courtesy Carolyn Rovee-Collier.

Let's see how the conjugate reinforcement technique can be used to assess infant memory. All the training and testing take place in the infant's crib at home, so that measurements are not distorted by the infant's reactions to the new surroundings. For a 3-minute period at the beginning of the first session, the experimenter takes a baseline measure. During this time, the ribbon is connected from the infant's ankle to an "empty" mobile stand, rather than to the mobile. Thus, the experimenters can measure the amount of spontaneous kicking that occurs in the presence of the mobile, before the infant learns how to make the mobile move (Rovee-Collier & Barr, 2002; Rovee-Collier & Cuevas, 2009a).

Next, the experimenter moves the ribbon so that it runs from the baby's ankle to the stand from which the mobile is hung. The babies are allowed 9 minutes to discover that their kicks can activate the mobile; this is the acquisition phase. The infants typically receive two training sessions like this, spaced 24 hours apart. At the end of the second training session, the ribbon is unhooked and returned to the empty stand for 3 minutes in order to measure what the infants remember. The number of kicks that the infant produces is a test of immediate retention.

Researchers then measure long-term memory after 1 to 42 days have elapsed. The mobile is once again hung above the infant's crib, with the ribbon hooked to the empty stand. Suppose that 3-month-old Jason recognizes the mobile and recalls how his kicking had produced movement. Then Jason will soon produce the foot-kick response.

Notice, then, that Rovee-Collier devised a clever way to "ask" infants if they remember how to activate the mobile. She also devised an objective method for assessing long-term memory, because she can compare two measures: (1) the number of kicks produced in the immediate retention test and (2) the number of kicks produced following the delay.

Rovee-Collier later devised a second operant conditioning task that is more appealing to infants between the ages of 6 and 18 months. In this second task, older infants learn to press a lever in order to make a miniature train move along a circular track. By combining information from the two tasks, researchers can trace infant memory from 2 months through 18 months of age (Barr et al., 2011; Hsu & Rovee-Collier, 2006; Rovee-Collier & Barr, 2002).

Figure 13.2 shows how much time can pass before infants no longer show significant recall for the relevant task. For example, 6-month-olds can recall how to move the mobile and also how to move the train, even after a two-week delay. This research demonstrates that long-term retention shows a steady, linear improvement during the first 18 months of life (Hsu & Rovee-Collier, 2006).

Several decades ago, researchers thought that infant memory was extremely limited. However, Rovee-Collier and her coworkers have demonstrated that infants can remember actions, even after a substantial delay. Furthermore, infant memory and adult memory are influenced by many of the same factors (Barr et al., 2011; Rovee-Collier & Barr, 2002; Rovee-Collier & Cuevas, 2009a, 2009b; Rovee-Collier et al., 2001).

For example, you saw in Chapter 5 that context sometimes influences adult memory. Context effects are even stronger for infants. Rovee-Collier and her colleagues (1985) used the conjugate reinforcement technique to test 3-month-old infants whose cribs were lined with a fabric that had a distinctive, colorful pattern. The infants' delayed recall was significantly stronger when they were tested 7 days later with the same, familiar crib liner, rather than an unfamiliar crib liner. Without the proper environmental context, infants' memories decline sharply (Markowitsch & Welzer, 2010; Rovee-Collier & Cuervas, 2009a; Rovee-Collier & Hayne, 2000).

In additional research, Rovee-Collier and her associates have discovered numerous other similarities between infant and adult memory. For example, Chapter 6 (pages 176–177) discussed the spacing effect: College students learn most effectively if their practice is distributed over time (**spaced learning**), rather than if they learn the material all at once (**massed learning**). A number of studies have also demonstrated that infants can also remember better with distributed practice (Barr et al., 2005; Bearce & Rovee-Collier, 2006).

FIGURE 13.2

The Maximum Duration for Which Different Groups of Infants Demonstrated Significant Retention. In this study, 2- to 6-month-old infants kicked to activate a mobile, and 6- to 18-month-old infants pressed a lever to activate a train.

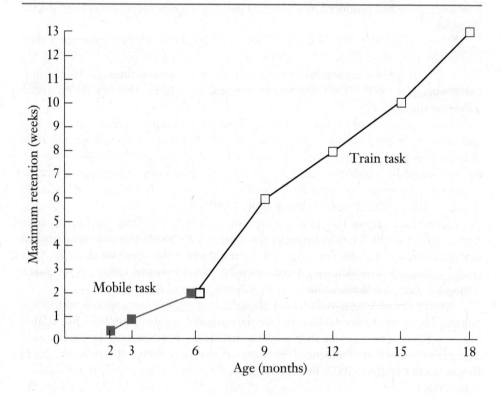

Source: Rovee-Collier, C. K. (1999). The development of infant memory. *Current Directions in Psychological Science, 8,* 80–85.

Furthermore, infants show a levels-of-processing effect, with better recall for items that were processed at a deep level (Rovee-Collier et al., 2001). As you can see, researchers have designed several creative techniques. These techniques allow them to discover that many principles of adult memory are also relevant for infants who have not yet reached their first birthday.

In summary, a number of tasks allow infants to demonstrate their memory skills. For example, babies can recognize their mother's voice, even prior to birth. Furthermore, 6-month-olds can remember how to activate a mobile after a 2-week delay, and some of the same factors that influence an adult's memory also influence an infant's memory.

Memory in Children

We have seen that researchers need to be extremely inventive when they study infant memory. By using the conjugate reinforcement technique and other creative methods, they have concluded that infants' memory is reasonably impressive.

Children can respond verbally, so it's much easier to assess their memory than infants' memory. However, the task is still challenging. Young children may have trouble understanding the task instructions, and they might not recognize letters of the alphabet or printed words. With these problems in mind, let's consider five topics: (1) children's working memory, (2) their long-term memory, (3) their memory strategies, (4) their eyewitness testimony, and (5) the relationship between children's intelligence and the accuracy of their eyewitness testimony.

Children's Working Memory. Working memory is often measured in terms of memory span, or the number of items that can be correctly recalled in order, immediately after presentation. Memory spans improve dramatically during childhood (Cowan & Alloway, 2009; Gathercole et al., 2006; Hitch, 2006). According to one estimate, for example, a 2-year-old can recall an average of two numbers in a row, whereas a 9-year-old can recall six (Kail, 1992). By the age of 11 or 12, children's working memory is even more impressive. In fact, under ideal conditions, typically developing children almost match the performance of college students (Cowan et al., 2009).

As you saw in Chapter 4, Alan Baddeley (2006) and other theorists propose that adult working memory has three especially important components: the central executive, the phonological loop, and the visuospatial sketchpad. Susan Gathercole and her colleagues (2004) found that this same structural model also applies to the working memory of children as young as 4, with older children, and with adolescents.

As you might expect, children's working-memory skills are correlated with their performance in school. For instance, children with high scores on *phonological* working memory are likely to excel in reading, writing, and listening (Alloway et al., 2005). Furthermore, children with high scores on *visuospatial* working memory are likely to excel in mathematics (Gathercole & Pickering, 2000; Hitch, 2006).

Unfortunately, children with reading disabilities or ADHD (see pages 192–193) are likely to have problems with working memory (Holmes et al., 2010; Swanson et al., 2010). For example, they may have trouble remembering their teacher's instructions, a situation that could create challenges in all subject areas (Cowan & Alloway, 2009; Moulin & Gathercole, 2008).

Now let's turn our attention to long-term memory in children. Later, we'll see how older children's use of memory strategies helps to explain the improvement in their memory performance.

Children's Long-Term Memory. With respect to long-term memory, young children typically have excellent recognition memory but relatively poor recall memory (e.g., Flavell et al., 2002; Howe, 2000; Schwenk et al., 2009). In a classic study, Myers and Perlmutter (1978) administered research tasks similar to those in Demonstration 13.1, using 2- and 4-year-old children. To test *recognition*, the researchers began by showing children 18 objects. Then they presented 36 items, including the 18 previous

---

⑨ **Demonstration 13.1**

Age Differences in Recall and Recognition

In this study, you will need to test a college-age person and a preschool child. You should reassure the child's parents that you are simply testing memory as part of a class project.

    You will be examining both recall and recognition in this demonstration. First, assemble 20 common objects, such as a pen, pencil, piece of paper, leaf, stick, rock, book, key, apple, and so forth. Place the objects in a box or cover them with a cloth.

    You will use the same testing procedure for both people, although the preschool child will require a more extensive explanation. Remove 10 objects in all, one at a time. Show each object for about 5 seconds and then conceal it again. After you have shown all 10 objects, ask each person to recall as many of the objects as possible. Do not provide feedback about the correctness of the responses. After recall is complete, test for recognition. Show one object at a time, randomly presenting the old objects mixed in sequence with several new objects. For each item, ask whether the object is old or new.

    Count the number of correct recalls and the number of correct recognitions for each person. You should find that both the child and the adult are quite accurate on the *recognition* measures, but the adult *recalls* more items than the child.

---

objects as well as 18 new objects. The 2-year-olds recognized an impressive 80% of the items, and the 4-year-olds recognized about 90% of the items.

    To examine *recall*, Myers and Perlmutter (1978) tested two additional groups of children. These researchers began by showing the children nine items. The 2-year-olds recalled only about 20% of the items, and the 4-year-olds recalled about 40% of the items. Recall memory seems to require the active use of memory strategies. As you'll see later in this section, children do not develop these strategies until middle childhood (Schneider & Bjorklund, 1998). Let's now consider two additional topics related to long-term memory: (1) autobiographic memory for events from childhood and (2) children's source monitoring.

    1. *Autobiographical memory and early childhood.* As we discussed in Chapter 5, **autobiographical memory** refers to your memory for experiences and information that are related to yourself (Brewin, 2011). When researchers study autobiographical memory in children, they emphasize how children link their previous experiences together. Children therefore create a personal history or "life narrative" (Fivush, 2011). Most children's language skills grow rapidly as they approach the age of 2. These skills help them remember their personal experiences more accurately. Notice that this connection between language and memory is a good example of Theme 4 of your textbook.

Children who are 3 years old can typically produce simple scripts to describe a recent experience (Howe et al., 2009; Hudson & Mayhew, 2009; Pipe & Salmon, 2009). As Chapter 8 pointed out, a **script** is a simple, well-structured sequence of events—in a specified order—that are associated with a highly familiar activity (Baddeley et al., 2009). After the age of 2, children are increasingly likely to reminisce about their previous experiences, especially with their parents (Fivush, 2011; Laible & Panfile, 2009; Ornstein et al., 2011). According to the research, when mothers encourage their children to provide detailed descriptions of events, these children are more likely to develop a narrative style that is detailed and coherent (Fivush, 2009, 2011).

Now take a moment to answer this question: Can you clearly recall any events that happened when you were 2 or 3 years old? Are you sure that you're not actually recalling another person's description of this event? David Rubin (2000) located previous studies that had asked adolescents and adults to recall autobiographical memories from the first 10 years of their lives. As you can see in Figure 13.3, people seldom recalled events that happened when they were younger than 3. Recent studies confirm Rubin's results (e.g., Fitzgerald, 2010; Janssen et al., 2011; Markowitsch & Welzer, 2010; Peterson et al., 2011).

FIGURE 13.3

The Proportion of Memories Supplied by Adolescents and Adults That Occurred for Each Year, 1 to 10 Years of Age.

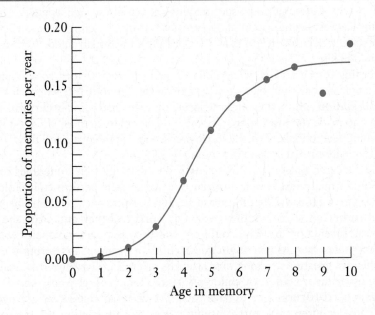

Source: Rubin, D. C. (2000). The distribution of early childhood memories. *Memory, 8,* 265–269.

The reason for this phenomenon is not clear, especially because 2-year-old children frequently describe an event that occurred several weeks or months ago. This observation suggests that they must be able to store verbal memories for several months (Gauvain, 2001; Ornstein & Haden, 2001).

One possibility is that children younger than 2 do not have a well-organized sense of who they are (Fivush & Nelson, 2004; Goodman & Melinder, 2007; Markowitsch & Welzer, 2010). As a result, they may have difficulty encoding and retrieving a series of events connected with themselves, when the interval is longer than several months (Newcombe et al., 2000). This explanation could be especially relevant, because the study by Rubin (2000) examined adolescents and adults. Apparently, they have trouble accessing their memories about early childhood.

2. *Children's source monitoring.* Chapter 5 discussed **source monitoring**, which is the process of trying to identify the origin of a particular memory. In general, children younger than about 7 years of age typically have more difficulty than adults in distinguishing between reality and pure fantasy (Foley, 2012; Ratner et al., 2001; Sluzenski et al., 2004). For example, I know an extremely bright child who had participated in an imaginary trip to the moon one day at school. Later that day, she insisted to her parents that she really *had* visited the moon. Children who are younger than 7 years of age also have difficulty distinguishing between something they saw in real life, as opposed to something from a storybook or a video (Thierry et al., 2010).

Research by Mary Ann Foley, Hilary Horn Ratner, and their colleagues has systematically clarified the conditions in which young children are most likely to make these source-monitoring errors. For example, Foley and Ratner (1998) asked one group of 6-year-olds to perform specific physical activities, such as making a motion like an airplane. A second group of 6-year-olds was instructed, "Try to imagine what it would actually feel like to do that." A third group was instructed, "Try to picture what you look like . . . ."

According to the results, when children had actually performed an action, they seldom reported that they had simply imagined it. In contrast, when children had simply *imagined* an action, they often reported that they had actually performed it. The children who made the most source-monitoring errors were those who had imagined how it would feel to make airplane movements; they often convinced themselves that they had actually circled around the room.

Other research on source monitoring shows that children sometimes recall that they had performed a task, when someone else had actually performed it (Foley, 2012; Foley, Ratner, & House, 2002; Ratner et al., 2002). Apparently, children between the ages of 4 and 6 can watch another person at work, and they anticipate the steps in the project. Later, they become confused, and they remember actually completing the project themselves. As you might guess, children's source monitoring is especially poor if they are questioned a long time after the original event (Sluzenski et al., 2004).

In another investigation of children's source monitoring, Mary Ann Foley and her colleagues (2010) arranged to have pairs of 4-year-old children work together on a task. These children took turns placing pieces of construction paper on a poster board to make a collage. Consistent with earlier research, children often claimed "I did it," when the other child had actually made the placement. Incidentally, you might wonder if the children's responses simply reflect an egocentric bias. However, the "I did it" bias seldom occurs when an adult and a child take turns (Foley, 2012).

In one of these studies, the researcher asked the child to think what the adult would feel like, raising her arms and moving them like an airplane (Foley et al., 2010). This procedure provided a framework for imagining the adult make other motor movements. Then the researcher told the child to watch the adult placing each piece on the collage, and think what it would feel like to actually go through the motions of placing the piece. The results showed that these "feel like" instructions actually increased the likelihood that the child would claim, "I did it." Notice, then, that preschool children seem to have a significant problem with source monitoring.

Children's Memory Strategies. So far, our exploration of children's memory has demonstrated that young children are fairly similar to adults in recognizing items. However, children are much less accurate than adults in terms of recall and source monitoring. Adults have another advantage: When they want to remember something that must be recalled at a later time, they often use memory strategies. Here is one important reason that young children have relatively poor recall: They cannot use memory strategies effectively (Cowan & Alloway, 2009; Kail, 2010; Torbeyns et al., 2010). During elementary school, children become increasingly skilled in using these strategies (Bjorklund et al., 2009; Grammer et al., 2011).

Memory strategies are intentional, goal-oriented activities that we use to improve our memories. Young children may not realize that strategies can be helpful. Their working memory may not be developed enough to choose a strategy and actually use it on a memory task (Torbeyns et al., 2010). Furthermore, some young children may not actually *use* the strategies effectively; this problem is called **utilization deficiency** (Pressley & Hilden, 2006; Schneider et al., 2004). As a result, the strategies may not improve their recall (Ornstein et al., 2006; Schneider, 2002).

In contrast, older children are more likely than younger children to realize that strategies are helpful. In addition, they choose their strategies more carefully and use them more consistently. Also, older children often use a variety of strategies when they need to learn several items, and they may monitor how they use these strategies (Bjorkland et al., 2009; Schneider, 1998). As a result, older children can recall items with reasonable accuracy. Let's survey three major kinds of memory strategies: rehearsal, organization, and imagery.

1. *Rehearsal*, or merely repeating items over and over, is not a particularly effective strategy, but it may be useful for maintaining items in working memory. Research suggests that 4- and 5-year-olds do not spontaneously rehearse material they want to remember. However, 7-year-olds do use rehearsal strategies, often silently rehearsing several words together (Bjorklund et al., 2009; Gathercole, 1998; Schneider & Bjorklund, 1998).

Another important point is that younger children can benefit from learning to use rehearsal strategies, even though they may not use these strategies spontaneously (e.g., Flavell et al., 2002; Gathercole, 1998). Children with reading disorders also tend to recall more items when they have been taught about rehearsal (Swanson et al., 2010).

As we will see in the section on metamemory, young children often fail to realize that they could improve their memory performance by using strategies.

2. *Organizational strategies*, such as categorizing and grouping, are helpful for adults, as we saw in Chapter 6. However, young children are typically less likely than older children to spontaneously group similar items together to aid memorization (Flavell et al., 2002; Ornstein et al., 2006; Pressley & Hilden, 2006; Schwenck et al., 2009). Try Demonstration 13.2 on page 467; are the children in your sample reluctant to adopt an organizational strategy?

Demonstration 13.2 is based on a classic study by Moely and her colleagues (1969), in which children studied pictures from four categories: animals, clothing, furniture, and vehicles. During the 2-minute study period, they were told that they could rearrange the pictures in any order they wished. Younger children rarely moved the pictures next to other similar pictures, but older children frequently organized the pictures into categories. The researchers specifically urged other groups of children to organize the pictures. Even the younger children saw that the organizational strategy was useful, and this strategy increased their recall.

3. *Imagery*, a topic discussed in Chapters 6 and 7, is an extremely useful device for improving memory in adults. Research shows that even 6-year-olds can be trained to use visual imagery effectively (Foley et al., 1993; Howe, 2006). However, young children usually do not use imagery spontaneously. In fact, the spontaneous use of imagery does not develop until adolescence. Even most college students do not use this helpful strategy often enough (Pressley & Hilden, 2006; Schneider & Bjorklund, 1998).

In short, preschool children are unlikely to use memory strategies in a careful, consistent fashion. In fact, as we have suggested here—and will further discuss in connection with metamemory—young children seldom appreciate that they need to use memory strategies (Ornstein et al., 2006; Schneider, 1999). However, as children develop, they learn how to use memory strategies such as rehearsal, organization, and (eventually) imagery.

It's also worth mentioning that teachers can help children by showing them how to use age-appropriate memory strategies. Furthermore, teachers can use spaced rather than massed presentation (see pages 176–177) in the classroom to improve their students' recall (Seabrook et al., 2005).

Children's Eyewitness Testimony. So far, we have examined children's working memory, long-term memory, and memory strategies. We've seen that young children's performance in those three areas is definitely inferior when compared with adults' performance. This information has implications for an applied area of cognition, the accuracy of their eyewitness testimony. As you might guess, older children typically provide much more accurate eyewitness testimony than younger children (Melnyk et al., 2007; Pipe & Salmon, 2009; Schwartz, 2011).

A real-life court case inspired Michelle Leichtman and Stephen Ceci (1995) to conduct an experiment. In the original court case, a 9-year-old girl had provided eyewitness testimony, and it seemed likely that both stereotypes and suggestions could

⊚ Demonstration 13.2

Organizational Strategies in Children

Make a photocopy of the pictures on this page and use scissors to cut them apart. In this study you will test a child between the ages of 4 and 8; ideally, it would be interesting to test children of several different ages. Arrange these pictures in random order in a circle facing the child. Instruct him or her to study the pictures so that they can be remembered later. Mention that the pictures can be rearranged in any order they want. After a 4-minute study period, remove the pictures and ask the child to list as many items as possible. Notice two things in this demonstration: (1) Does the child spontaneously rearrange the items at all during the study period? (2) Does the child show clustering during recall, with similar items appearing together?

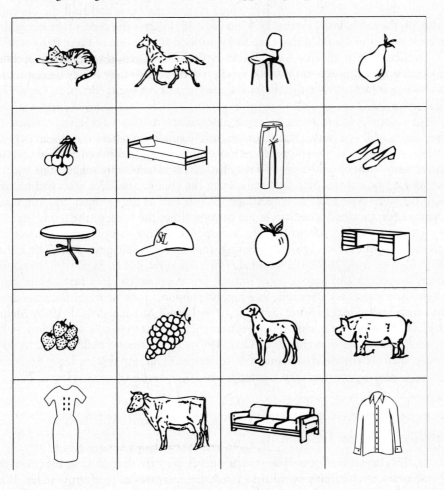

have influenced her report. Leichtman and Ceci's classic study explored the impact of these two factors.

Leichtman and Ceci tested 176 preschoolers, assigning each child to one of four conditions. In the *control condition*, a stranger named Sam Stone visited the classroom, strolling around and making several bland comments for a period of about 2 minutes. In the *stereotype condition*, a research assistant presented one story each week to the children, for 3 weeks prior to Sam Stone's visit. Each story emphasized that Sam Stone was nice but very clumsy. In the *suggestion condition*, the research assistant told the children two incorrect suggestions after Sam Stone's visit—that Sam Stone had ripped a book and that he had spilled a chocolate drink on a white teddy bear. Finally, in the *stereotype-plus-suggestion condition*, children were exposed to both the stereotype before Sam Stone's visit and the incorrect suggestions afterwards.

Ten weeks after Sam Stone's classroom visit, a new interviewer asked the children what Sam Stone had done during his visit. The children were specifically asked whether they had actually seen Sam Stone tear up the book and spill the chocolate drink on the teddy bear. Figure 13.4 (on page 469) shows the percentage of children in each condition who said that they had witnessed at least one of these two events.

Notice, first of all, that the children in the control group were highly accurate. In other words, children can provide valid eyewitness testimony if they do not receive misleading information, either before or after the target event (Bruck & Ceci, 1999; Schneider, 2002).

As Figure 13.4 also shows, however, a worrisome number of children claimed that they had actually witnessed these actions, in the condition where the researchers had established a previous stereotype. Even more of the younger children claimed that they had actually witnessed the actions if they had received inaccurate suggestions after the event. The most worrisome data came from the younger children who had received both the stereotype and the suggestions. Almost half of the younger children falsely reported that they had seen Sam Stone damage either the book or the teddy bear.

Other research confirms that the accuracy of children's eyewitness testimony is influenced by the child's age, stereotyping, and misleading suggestions (Melnyk et al., 2007; Memon et al., 2006; Roebers et al., 2005; Schwartz, 2011). As you might imagine, social factors can also have a major impact. For example, children make more errors when interviewers ask questions in a highly emotional tone or when the interviewer uses complex language (Bruck & Ceci, 1999; Imhoff & Baker-Ward, 1999; Melnyk et al., 2007). In addition, children are extremely reluctant to say, "I don't know" when an adult asks a question (Bruck & Ceci, 1999). Furthermore, children are likely to change their statements if someone cross-examines them, and this tendency is stronger among 5- and 6-year-olds than among 9- and 10-year-olds (Zajac & Hayne, 2006).

Individual Differences: Children's Intellectual Abilities and Eyewitness Testimony

So far, this chapter has focused on typically developing children, and we have seen that the accuracy of children's eyewitness testimony increases as they grow older. What happens for children with intellectual disabilities? Lucy Henry and Gisli Gudjonsson

FIGURE 13.4

The Effects of Stereotypes and Suggestions on Young Children's Eyewitness Testimony. Graph shows the percentage who reported actually seeing events that had not occurred.

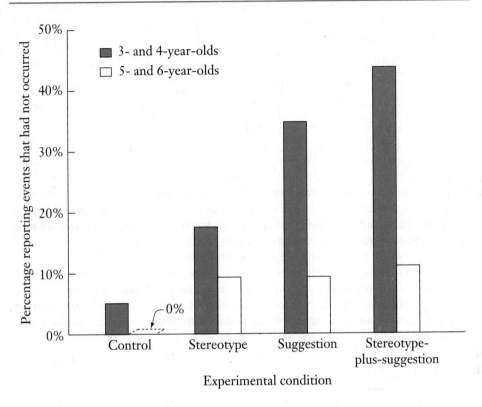

Source: Leichtman, M. D., & Ceci, S. J. (1995). The effects of stereotypes and suggestions of preschoolers' reports. *Developmental Psychology, 31,* 568–578.

(2007) studied children in England, who were either enrolled in special schools for children with intellectual disabilities or enrolled in mainstream schools. In each of these two groups, they tested children who were an average of either 9 years 2 months old or 12 years 8 months old.

All the children saw a 3-minute video clip that featured four people pulling up to a gas station in a car, filling up the car with gas, and driving off without paying for the gas. Each child then performed a short irrelevant task, and then the researcher asked the child to describe as much as possible about the video. The researchers scored the recall narrative in terms of the total number of correct items supplied by the child. As Table 13.1 shows, older children recalled more items than the younger children. Furthermore, this age difference was especially strong for the typically developing children.

TABLE 13.1

The Number of Correct Items Supplied by Children in Free Recall

Category of Children	Average Age of Child	
	9 Years 2 Months	12 Years 8 Months
Children with intellectual disability	7.2 items	13.6 items
Typically developing children	18.9 items	34.5 items

Source: Henry, L. A., & Gudjonsson, G. H. (2007). Individual and developmental differences in eyewitness recall and suggestibility in children with intellectual disabilities. *Applied Cognitive Psychology, 21,* 361–381.

In addition, Henry and Gudjonsson (2007) asked some specific misleading questions, for example, about the color of the police car, even though there was no police car. In this misleading-question situation, the older children made the same number of errors as the younger children. However, within each age group, the typically developing children provided a greater number of correct answers and a smaller number of errors in response to misleading questions. These results are consistent with the outcomes of other research (e.g., Pipe & Salmon, 2009).

However, Henry and Gudjonsson (2007) point out that there was only a short delay period between seeing the event and providing eyewitness testimony. Further research would need to include a longer delay, consistent with the real-life situations in which children are asked to supply eyewitness testimony.

> **IN DEPTH**

Memory in Elderly People

The popular stereotype for elderly people is that they may be pleasant, but they are typically forgetful and cognitively incompetent (Cuddy & Fiske, 2002; Hess et al., 2003; Levy & Banaji, 2002). Here's an example of this stereotype (Hulicka, 1982). A 78-year-old woman served a meal to her guests, and the meal was excellent, except that she had used bleach instead of vinegar in the salad dressing. Her concerned relatives attributed the error to impaired memory and general intellectual decline, and they discussed placing her in a nursing home. As it turned out, someone else had placed the bottle of bleach in the cupboard where the vinegar was kept. Understandably, the woman had reached for the wrong bottle, which was similar in size, shape, and color to the vinegar bottle.

Some time later, the same people were guests in another home. A young woman in search of hair spray reached into a bathroom cabinet and found a can of the correct size and shape. She proceeded to drench her hair with Lysol. In this case, however, no one suggested that the younger woman should be institutionalized; they merely teased her about her absentmindedness.

In mainstream North American culture, people often believe that elderly people have substantial cognitive deficits. Unfortunately, this stereotype can lead elderly people to think that they actually *are* less competent. As a result, elderly people may remember less information (Moulin & Gathercole, 2008; Whitbourne & Whitbourne, 2011; Zacks & Hasher, 2006).

The research on age-related changes in memory has increased dramatically during the last 10 years, and we now have a wide variety of review articles and books (e.g., Bialystok & Craik, 2006; Erber, 2005; Park & Reuter-Lorenz, 2009; Whitbourne & Whitbourne, 2011). However, the research shows large individual differences and complex developmental trends in various components of memory. Let's first consider the research on working memory and long-term memory in elderly people. Then we will examine some potential explanations for the memory changes during aging.

Working Memory in Elderly People. How well do elderly adults perform on tasks requiring working memory, when they need to retain information in memory for less than a minute? You've probably noticed that your psychology professors frequently use the phrase, "It all depends on...." In the case of working memory, factors such as the nature of the task determine whether we find age similarities or age differences (Craik, 2006; Whitbourne & Whitbourne, 2011).

In general, we find age similarities in working memory when the task is relatively straightforward and requires simple storage. In contrast, we typically find age differences when the task is complicated and requires manipulation of information (Craik, 2006; Park & Payer, 2006; Schwartz, 2011; Whitbourne & Whitbourne, 2011; Zacks & Hasher, 2006).

For example, younger and older adults perform similarly on a standard digit-span test of working memory. On these tasks, people are instructed to recall a list of numbers in order (Bäckman et al., 2001; Dixon & Cohen, 2003; Fabiani & Wee, 2001).

In contrast, age differences are substantial on a working-memory task in which people must either ignore irrelevant information, manipulate information, or perform two simultaneous tasks (Cansino et al., 2011; Carstensen, 2007; Kramer & Kray, 2006; Schwartz, 2011). For instance, in one study, people were given short lists of unrelated words, with the instructions to remember them, and report these words in correct alphabetical order (Craik, 1990). On this complex task, the average young participant reported 3.2 correct items on the alphabetical-order task, whereas the average elderly participant reported 1.7 correct items. Incidentally, an occupation that requires superb working memory is air traffic controller. U.S. regulations require controllers to retire at age 56, a policy that is clearly appropriate (Salthouse, 2012).

Long-Term Memory in Elderly People. Do elderly people differ from younger adults in their long-term memory? Once again, the answer depends on the characteristics of the task. In general, elderly people perform quite well on tests of semantic memory (Park & Reuter-Lorenz, 2009; Schwartz, 2011; Whitbourne & Whitbourne, 2011; Zacks & Hasher, 2006). In fact, a study by Salthouse (2012) showed that 50- to 80-year-olds actually perform *better* than 30- to 40-year-olds on crossword puzzles.

Elderly individuals also tend to perform well on tasks that they can do relatively automatically (Economou et al., 2006; Little et al., 2004). However, age differences emerge on more challenging tasks, such as source monitoring (Mitchell & Johnson, 2009; Whitbourne & Whitbourne, 2011).

In this discussion of long-term memory, we will consider four topics: (1) prospective memory, (2) implicit memory; (3) explicit recognition memory, and (4) explicit recall memory.

1. *Prospective memory.* Chapter 6 discussed **prospective memory**, or remembering to do something in the future. In general, older adults have difficulty on many prospective-memory tasks (Craik, 2006; Scullin et al., 2011; Zimmermann & Meier, 2010). For example, one prospective-memory task—high in ecological validity—simulates a shopping task. Participants saw a list of items they were supposed to purchase. For example, when they saw an image of a fast-food restaurant, they were supposed to "buy" a hamburger. On these tasks, younger adults successfully completed a greater number of tasks than the older adults (Farrimond et al., 2006; McDermott & Knight, 2004).

Why would older adults tend to make more errors on prospective-memory tasks? One important reason is that prospective memory relies heavily on working memory. People need to keep reminding themselves to do the relevant task, and—as we saw on pages 471–472—older adults often show a decline in working memory.

In contrast, older adults perform relatively accurately when they have an environmental cue, such as a book placed near the door, reminding them to take it to the library (Craik, 2006; Einstein & McDaniel, 2004; Scullin et al., 2011). Occasionally, older adults even perform more accurately than younger adults, for example, when instructed to take a certain medicine on a daily basis (Park & Hedden, 2001; Park et al., 1999).

2. *Implicit Memory.* Chapter 5 pointed out that an **explicit memory task** requires people to remember information that they have previously learned. In contrast, an **implicit memory task** requires people to perform a perceptual or cognitive task (for example, to complete a series of word fragments); previous experience with the material facilitates their performance on the task.

In a representative study, Light and her colleagues (1995) measured implicit memory in terms of the amount of time that the participants needed to read a letter sequence that was either familiar or unfamiliar. People demonstrated implicit memory if they read a familiar sequence faster than an unfamiliar sequence. On this implicit memory task, adults between the ages of 64 and 78 performed just as well as the younger adults, who were between the ages of 18 and 24.

Other research on implicit memory shows either similar performance by younger adults, or else just a slight deficit for older adults (e.g., Craik, 2006; Economou et al., 2006; Park & Reuter-Lorenz, 2009; Whitbourne & Whitbourne, 2011; Zacks & Hasher, 2006). Thus, age differences are minimal when the memory task does not require effortful remembering.

3. *Recognition Memory*. The research shows that long-term recognition memory declines either slowly or not at all, as people grow older (Burke, 2006; Erber, 2005; Moulin et al., 2007; Schwartz, 2011). For example, a classic study on recognition memory found that 20-year-olds correctly recognized 67% of words that had been presented earlier. On this same task, the 70-year-olds recalled a nearly identical 66% of the words (Intons-Peterson et al., 1999).

4. *Explicit Recall Memory*. So far, our discussion of long-term memory has shown that elderly people often have difficulty with prospective memory, but they perform reasonably well on two kinds of long-term memory tasks: (1) implicit memory and (2) recognition memory. Let us now turn to performance on explicit recall tasks. Here, the differences between a young adult and an older adult are frequently more substantial (Brown, 2012; Schwartz, 2011; Zacks & Hasher, 2006).

Consider a study by Alaitz Aizpurua and her colleagues (2009). These researchers compared college students (age range = 19 to 25 years) with people who were enrolled in a college course designed for older adults (age range = 56 to 72 years). Notice that the researchers chose appropriate comparison groups for this study. In fact, the two groups were similar in the number of years of formal education and also similar in their self-rated health.

The participants in this study watched a short video of a robbery. After a short delay, they were given 10 minutes to recall the events from the video. The results showed that the older adults recalled less information than the younger adults. However, the two age groups were similar in (1) the number of events they described that did not occur in the video and (2) the nature of these errors.

Elderly individuals differ widely in their performance on long-term recall tasks. For example, people with low verbal ability and little education are more likely to show a decline in recall as they grow older. In contrast, age differences are minimal for people who have high verbal ability and are well educated (Manly et al., 2003; Rabbitt, 2002). Suppose that the two groups in the previous study had differed greatly in both education and health. The memory differences would have been substantially larger.

Lynn Hasher and her coauthors have explored another variable that can influence researchers' conclusions about age differences in memory. This variable is the time of day when people's memory is tested (Hasher et al., 2002; Zacks & Hasher, 2006). Specifically, older adults tend to function relatively well when they are tested in the morning. In contrast, older adults make substantially more memory errors than younger adults when both groups are tested in the afternoon. Interestingly, most research on memory is scheduled for afternoons, so the data underestimate the memory of older adults.

So, are older people more likely than younger people to have trouble with their long-term memory? As you can see, it's impossible to provide a simple answer. Instead, the research results are consistent with the "It all depends on . . . ." principle. Elderly people are fairly similar to younger people on implicit memory tasks and on recognition tasks.

What happens when we examine an area in which age differences are more prominent, for example, on an explicit recall task? Here we cannot draw a simple conclusion. For instance, highly verbal, well-educated elderly people perform relatively well. Elderly people also perform relatively well when tested in the morning.

In other words, memory deficits are far from universal among elderly people. In fact, Zacks and Hasher (2006) end their chapter on aging and long-term memory with the following statement: "Taken together, these recent findings suggest that we may have seriously underestimated the memory abilities of older adults" (p. 174).

Explanations for Age Differences in Memory. We have examined a complex pattern of age-related memory effects. On some tasks, young people remember better than older people; in other cases, the age differences are minimal. As you might expect, this complex pattern of effects requires a complex explanation, rather than just one straightforward cause.

1. *Neurocognitive changes.* Research in cognitive neuroscience demonstrates that some changes in brain structures occur during normal aging. Remember that explicit recall memory is especially likely to show a deficit. From a neuroscience perspective, this makes sense, because explicit recall relies on a complex network of different brain structures. Because parts of the brain must work together, explicit recall memory can be disrupted if one component of the network is not functioning appropriately. Furthermore, many of these brain structures are known to decrease in volume during normal aging (Moulin et al., 2007; Park & Reuter-Lorenz, 2009).

Surprisingly, however, the research with elderly individuals shows *increased* activation in the frontal lobe, even though its actual size may decrease. This frontal-lobe activation helps to compensate for some of the age-related decreases in other parts of the brain (Park & Reuter-Lorenz, 2009).

Let's now consider several psychological processes that help to explain the pattern of changes in memory performance during normal aging. To account for these changes, we would need to identify several mechanisms, because no single explanation would be sufficient (Moulin et al., 2007).

2. *Difficulty paying attention.* In general, the research suggests that elderly adults are more likely than younger adults to have difficulty paying attention (Guerreiro & Van Gerven, 2011; Mueller-Johnson & Ceci, 2007; Whitbourne & Whitbourne, 2011). In fact, when elderly adults work on a standard memory task, they often perform about the same as when young adults work on a memory task that requires

divided attention (Craik, 2006; Naveh-Benjamin et al., 2005; Naveh-Benjamin et al., 2007).

3. *Less effective use of memory strategies.* Elderly people could have impaired memory because they use memory strategies and metamemory less effectively. Some research suggests that elderly adults construct fewer chunks in working memory, compared to younger adults (Naveh-Benjamin et al., 2007). As you may recall from Chapter 4, a **chunk** is a memory unit that consists of several components that are strongly associated with one another (Schwartz, 2011). If elderly people have trouble using working-memory strategies, they are likely to make errors on tasks such as prospective memory and explicit recall.

In contrast, many studies conclude that elderly adults and young adults use similar memory strategies in *long-term memory* (Dunlosky & Hertzog, 1998; Light, 2000). Therefore, the strategy-deficit hypothesis cannot explain age differences in long-term memory.

4. *The contextual-cues hypothesis.* As we saw earlier, elderly people perform relatively well on recognition tasks. Contextual cues are present on recognition tasks, because researchers display an item, and the participants report whether they had seen it previously. In other words, these contextual cues can encourage recognition for elderly individuals.

In contrast, contextual cues are absent on explicit recall tasks; instead, these recall tasks require people to use effortful, deliberate processing. The research shows that young adults are relatively skilled in remembering contextual cues, such as where they were and what date it was when they heard a particular news item (Grady & Craik, 2000; Light, 2000). These contextual cues may therefore boost the accuracy of young adults' explicit recall. In contrast, we noted that elderly adults typically recall fewer contextual cues. Therefore, elderly adults must rely on effortful, deliberate processing in order to retrieve the information, and the explicit recall task is more challenging.

5. *Cognitive slowing.* A final explanation is one that has been acknowledged for decades: Elderly people often experience **cognitive slowing**, or a slower rate of responding on cognitive tasks (e.g., Bunce & Macready, 2005; Einstein & McDaniel, 2004; Schwartz, 2011). The cognitive-slowing explanation can account for some of the age-related differences in memory, but it cannot fully explain why elderly people function relatively well on some other memory tasks.

In summary, several hypotheses can each explain some portion of the memory differences between older and younger adults. Perhaps researchers will develop a more refined version of several of these hypotheses, or they may propose additional hypotheses. At this point, we currently have a complex set of findings about memory in elderly individuals, but no comprehensive explanation for these results.

◎ Section Summary: *The Lifespan Development of Memory*

1. The lifespan approach to development emphasizes that changes and adaptations continue throughout the lifespan, from infancy through old age.

2. Psychologists interested in the development of cognition encounter methodological problems in their research, particularly when they study infants and elderly people.

3. Research demonstrates that 3-day-olds can recognize their mothers' face and voice. Older infants can recall how to move a mobile—following a delay of several days—when they are tested with the conjugate reinforcement technique.

4. Infant memory is influenced by many factors—such as context effects and the spacing effect—that are also important in adulthood.

5. Compared to adults, children have reduced working memory, reasonably strong recognition memory, and poor memory on long-term recall tasks.

6. Studies of autobiographical memory show that most people cannot recall events that occurred prior to the age of 2 or 3. In general, children have poor source monitoring.

7. In general, children have difficulty with source monitoring. For example, they sometimes recall that they had performed a task that someone else had actually performed.

8. As children grow older, they increasingly use memory strategies such as rehearsal and organization. By adolescence, they can also use imagery appropriately.

9. Under ideal circumstances, children's eyewitness reports can be trustworthy, but young children's reports may be unreliable when they have been supplied with stereotypes and suggestive questions.

10. Compared to others in their age group, children with intellectual disabilities tend to recall fewer items on an eyewitness-testimony task; they also make more errors following misleading information.

11. As adults grow older, their working memory remains intact for some tasks, but it is limited if the task is complicated or if it requires manipulation of information.

12. With respect to long-term memory in adulthood, age differences are relatively large for prospective memory tasks; in contrast, age differences are relatively small for implicit memory tasks and for recognition tasks.

13. Age differences on explicit recall tasks are typically more substantial, but the deficits depend on a variety of factors. For instance, elderly individuals perform relatively well if they have high verbal ability, if they are well educated, or if they are tested early in the day.

14. Cognitive neuroscience research shows changes in the brain structure during normal aging. Potential psychological explanations for age-related memory

changes during adulthood include (a) neurocognitive changes, (b) difficulty paying attention, (c) less effective use of memory strategies, (d) the contextual-cues hypothesis, and (e) cognitive slowing.

THE LIFESPAN DEVELOPMENT OF METAMEMORY

As we discussed in Chapter 6, **metacognition** is a term that refers to your thoughts about thinking; it is your knowledge about your cognitive processes, as well as your control of these cognitive processes. One important kind of metacognition is **metamemory**, a term that refers to your knowledge, monitoring, and control of your memory.

Another kind of metacognition is called **theory of mind**, a term that refers to your ideas about how your mind works, as well as how other people's minds work. For example, you know that other people hold certain beliefs that are different from your own. However, young children have trouble with this concept (Dunlosky & Metcalfe, 2009; Schneider & Lockl, 2008; Schwartz, 2011).

A third kind of metacognition is **metacomprehension**, a term that refers to your thoughts about your comprehension, such as your understanding of written material or spoken language. Although there are a small number of exceptions (e.g., Baker et al., 2010; Hacker et al., 2009), researchers have not explored metacomprehension in children or elderly individuals. In this chapter of your textbook, we will therefore focus specifically on *metamemory* in children and elderly people.

Metamemory in Children

In this discussion of children's metamemory, we will examine children's beliefs about how their memory works, their awareness that learning requires an effort, and their judgments about their own memory performance. Then we'll discuss how metamemory is related to memory performance.

Children's Understanding of How Memory Works. An important component of metamemory is a person's knowledge about how memory works. Demonstration 13.3 includes some questions about this aspect of children's metamemory. Try this demonstration when you have an opportunity. You may need to simplify the questions for young children, because their responses might be influenced by their limited language skills (Fritz et al., 2010).

Children often have unsophisticated ideas about some aspects of their memory (Fritz et al., 2010; Larkin, 2010). For example, 7-year-olds are not yet aware that words are easier to remember when they are related to one another, rather than randomly selected (Schneider & Pressley, 1997). Furthermore, when young children are taught to use a memory strategy, they often fail to realize that the strategy actually improved their memory performance (Bjorklund, 2005). If children don't know how their memory works, they won't know how to plan effective study strategies (Bjorklund, 2005; Schneider, 2002).

---

⑨ Demonstration 13.3

Metamemory in Children

Locate a child who is at least 5 years old, and ask the following questions about his or her memory. Compare the accuracy and the completeness of the answers with your own responses. If the child is young, you may need to modify the wording.

1. Suppose that a child named Katie is supposed to bring her favorite book to school tomorrow. She is afraid that she might forget to bring it. What kind of things can she do, to make sure that she brings the book to school?

2. Suppose that I decide to read you a list of 10 words. How many words do you think that you could remember, in the correct order? (Then read the following list fairly slowly, and count how many words the child recalls correctly. If the child is young, substitute the number "5" for "10" and read only the first five words.)

     dog   chair   flower   sky   ball   bicycle   apple   pencil   house   car

3. Suppose that you memorize a friend's address. Will you remember the address better after *2 minutes* have passed or after *2 days* have passed?

4. Two children want to remember a list of words. One child has a list of 10 words, and the other has a list of five words. Which child will be more likely to remember all the words on the list correctly?

5. Suppose that a boy named Bob is telling you a story about a birthday party he went to. Later on, you tell this story to a friend. Would it be easier for you to tell the whole story word for word? Or would it be easier for you to tell the main idea about the story?

Children's Awareness That Effort Is Necessary. **Another important component of metamemory is the awareness that memory is not an automatic process. Instead, you need to make an effort, if you really want to remember something (Bjorklund, 2005; Schwartz, 2011). Unfortunately, young children do not appreciate this principle. Furthermore, they are not accurate in judging whether they have successfully committed some information to memory. They typically report to the experimenter that they have satisfactorily memorized a list, yet they recall little on a test (Pressley & Hilden, 2006).

In addition, children often fail to realize that they need to make an effort to use a memory strategy. However, they are more likely to successfully use a memory strategy if they have received instructions about why the strategy should help their memory (Pressley & Hilden, 2006).

Older children also have naive ideas about the effort required in memorization. I recall a visit from an 11-year-old in our neighborhood who had been memorizing some information about the U.S. Constitution. My husband asked her how she was doing and whether she would like him to quiz her on the material. She replied that she knew the material well, but he could quiz her if he wanted. Her recall turned out to be minimal for both factual and conceptual information. She had assumed that by allowing her eyes to wander over the text several times, the material had magically worked its way into her memory.

Children's Judgments About Their Memory Performance. In general, young children are extremely overconfident when they assess their memory performance. In contrast, older children are somewhat more accurate (Dunlosky & Metcalfe, 2009; Keast et al., 2007; Larkin, 2010; Schneider & Lockl, 2008).

FIGURE 13.5

Average Level of Confidence for Questions Answered Correctly and Questions Answered Incorrectly. (1 = Very Unsure; 5 = Very Sure)

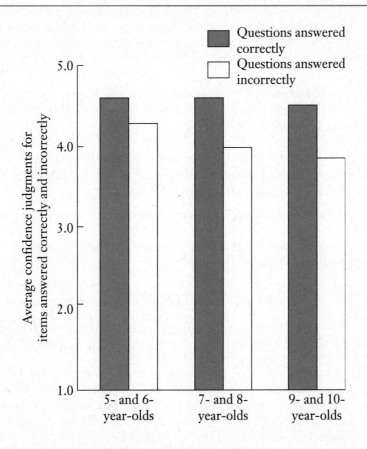

Source: Roebers, C. M., Gelhar, T., & Schneider, W. (2004). "It's magic!" The effects of presentation modality on children's event memory, suggestibility, and confidence judgments. *Journal of Experimental Child Psychology, 87,* 320–355.

For example, Claudia Roebers and her colleagues (2004) gathered measures of metamemory as part of their larger study on children's eyewitness testimony. Children between the ages of 5 and 10 years of age watched a live magic show, which lasted 8 minutes.

One week later, an interviewer met with each child individually and asked a series of 56 questions about the show. In this study by Roebers and her colleagues, a typical question was, "Where did the magician get the bag from?" (p. 326). After answering each question, children rated how confident they were that their answer had been correct. Specifically, they used a rating scale consisting of five cartoon faces. The facial expressions varied from a very frowning face ("very unsure," corresponding to a rating of 1) to a very smiling face ("very sure," corresponding to a rating of 5).

Figure 13.5 shows the results. As you can see, when children answered a question correctly, all three age groups were very sure that their answer had been correct. In contrast, when they answered a question *incorrectly*, they should have circled either the very frowning face or the somewhat frowning face. Notice that even the older children were overconfident that their incorrect answer had been correct. However, this overly optimistic assessment may be adaptive: If children knew that their performance had been so dismal, they would not persist on a difficult task (Dunlosky & Metcalfe, 2009).

Children's Metamemory: The Relationship Between Metamemory and Memory Performance. Let us summarize several observations from this chapter that are related to memory in young children:

1. Their metamemory is faulty; they do not realize that they need to make an effort to memorize, and they also do not realize how little they can remember.

2. They do not spontaneously use helpful memory strategies.

3. Relative to older children, their performance on a memory test is poor.

Does a causal relationship link these three observations? Perhaps the three are related in this fashion:

Metamemory → Strategy use → Memory performance

According to this argument, when children have poor metamemory, they will not be aware that they must use strategies to commit material to memory. If they do not use strategies, then their memory performance will be poor.

We have some evidence that metamemory is related to strategy use. For example, children with sophisticated metamemory skills are more likely to report using memory strategies. They are also somewhat more likely to use these strategies effectively (e.g., Dunlosky & Metcalfe, 2009; L. M. Taylor, 2005). In addition, we have extensive evidence to support the second link in the chain. As we've just seen, children's strategy use is related to memory performance.

So, metamemory is linked to strategy use, and strategy use is linked to memory performance. Is there a relationship between the two ends in that chain—that is, a relationship between metamemory and memory performance? Analysis of the research shows that the correlation between metamemory and memory performance is moderate (Ornstein et al., 2006; Schneider, 2002).

It makes sense that the correlations are not stronger. One reason is that it's difficult to test children's metamemory, because they haven't yet developed the sophisticated vocabulary necessary to describe their mental states (Joyner & Kurtz-Costes, 1997; Sodian, 2005). Furthermore, children may already know that memory strategies would be helpful, but they do not actually use them. After all, bright college students may have finely tuned metamemory skills; however, they may lack either the time or the motivation to actually use some potentially useful memory strategies.

To some extent, elementary-school teachers can take advantage of "teachable moments" in the classroom, and they can help children understand how to think about improving their memory (Duffy et al., 2009; Grammer et al., 2011; Ornstein et al., 2011). Parents can also provide guidance. Furthermore, when parents reminisce with their young children, they provide a model that helps children understand how to think about future events (Laible & Panfile, 2009).

In summary, we can conclude that metamemory is moderately related to memory performance (Dunlosky & Metcalfe, 2009; Schneider, 2002). Consequently, the proposed causal sequence (Metamemory → Strategy use → Memory performance) could account for a substantial portion of the improvement in memory performance as children grow older.

Metamemory in Elderly People

What do elderly adults believe about their memory? Let's begin by examining comparisons between older and younger adults in two areas: (1) their beliefs about how memory operates, and (2) their skill in monitoring their memory. Then we will consider another topic: (3) whether elderly people are aware of their memory problems.

Beliefs About Memory. Older and younger adults share similar beliefs about the properties of memory tasks (Dunlosky & Metcalfe, 2009; Light, 1996). Both groups have the same fundamental knowledge about how memory works. They also have similar ideas about which strategies are most effective, and what kinds of material can be remembered most readily (Hertzog et al., 1999).

Memory Monitoring. On some tasks, older and younger adults are equally skilled in monitoring their memory performance (Bieman-Copland & Charness, 1994; Hertzog & Dixon, 1994). For example, the two groups are similar in their ability to predict—on an item-by-item basis—which items they can recall at a later time (Connor et al., 1997).

Older and younger adults are also similar with respect to selecting the most difficult items for further study, rather than studying the items that they have already mastered (Dunlosky & Hertzog, 1997). The two groups also perform equally well in judging their accuracy when answering general-knowledge questions and when deciding whether a particular item is old or new (Dodson et al., 2007).

However, older adults are more likely than younger adults to be overconfident on some memory tasks (e.g., Dunlosky & Metcalfe, 2009). For example, Chad Dodson and his colleagues (2007) studied adults whose average age was 67 and college students whose average age was 21. The older adults were more likely than the young adults to overestimate their overall performance on a test of memory for specific details about a recent event.

Furthermore, older adults are especially likely to overestimate their performance on a task where their working memory is "overworked" (Shake et al., 2009). In addition, older adults may be skilled in monitoring their memory, but then they may not use this information to decide how to remember some information (Krätzig & Arbuthnot, 2009).

Finally, some older adults have **dementia**, a medical disorder that includes memory problems and other cognitive impairments (American Psychiatric Association, 2000). These individuals typically have difficulty in estimating their memory abilities (Youn et al., 2009).

Awareness of Memory Problems.   The research about memory-problem awareness does not compare older and younger adults. Instead, it focuses on surveys of elderly individuals. Elderly people are likely to report problems with their everyday memory, especially on explicit recall tasks such as remembering names and phone numbers (Dunlosky & Metcalfe, 2009; Kester et al., 2002; Rendell et al., 2005). They are also likely to say that their memory failures have increased over the years. Based on the research we reviewed on explicit recall in elderly individuals, these reports may be accurate.

The problem is that the popular stereotype about elderly people's poor memory may encourage elderly individuals to think that memory decline is inevitable. As a result, many elderly people will not try to develop helpful memory strategies (Dunlosky & Metcalfe, 2009; Hess, 2005). In contrast, some elderly people are high in **memory self-efficacy**, which is a person's belief in his or her own potential to perform well on memory tasks. They think that it's important to keep developing their memory. As a result, they typically use effective memory strategies, and they perform relatively well (Dunlosky & Metcalfe, 2009; Zacks & Hasher, 2006).

In summary, our examination of metamemory has revealed that elderly adults and young adults are similar in some respects (Dodson et al., 2007; Light, 2000). We saw earlier in this section that young children's metamemory is less accurate than young adults' metamemory. In contrast, most elderly adults do not experience overwhelming metamemory impairments, and they remain quite competent on some metamemory tasks.

⊙ Section Summary: *The Lifespan Development of Metamemory*

1. Young children have some knowledge of the factors that influence memory, and their knowledge increases as they mature.

2. Young children are not aware that they need to make an effort to learn a list of items, and they also cannot accurately judge when they have mastered the material.

3. Older children and adults are much more accurate than younger children in judging their accuracy on a memory task that they had performed; younger children tend to be extremely overconfident.

4. To some extent, children's deficits in metamemory partly explain their poor performance on memory tasks.

5. As children grow older, their metamemory improves, leading to increased strategy use, which helps to produce better memory performance.

6. Elementary-school teachers and parents can help children think about how to think about improving their memory.

7. Elderly adults and young adults have similar beliefs about memory tasks. They also have a similar ability to monitor their memory on an item-by-item basis. However, on some tasks, elderly adults are more likely to overestimate their overall performance.

8. Elderly adults report an increase in the frequency of some memory problems; this assessment this probably correct.

9. When elderly adults believe that a memory decline is inevitable, they may not try to develop useful memory strategies.

THE DEVELOPMENT OF LANGUAGE

"Mama!" (8 months old)
"Wash hair." (1 year, 4 months old)
"Don't tickle my tummy, Mommy!" (1 year, 11 months old)
"My grandma gave me this dolly, Cara. My grandma is my mommy's mommy. I have another grandma, too. She's my daddy's mommy. And Aunt Elli is my daddy's sister." (2 years, 9 months old)

These selections from the early language of my daughter Sally are typical of children's remarkable achievements during language acquisition. Individual children differ in the rate at which they master language (e.g., Fernald & Marchman, 2006; Hayne & Simcock, 2009; Tomasello, 2006). Still, within a period of 2 to 3 years, all normal children progress from one-word utterances to complex discourse. In fact, by the age of 5, most children produce sentences that resemble adult speech (Kuhl, 2000).

Many linguists say that language acquisition is the most spectacular of human accomplishments (Thompson & Madigan, 2005; Tomasello, 2006). Therefore, as you might expect, children's linguistic skills clearly exemplify Theme 2. For instance, the average 6-year-old can speak between about 10,000 and 14,000 words (MacWhinney, 2011).

To acquire a vocabulary of this size, children must learn approximately seven new words each day, from the time they start speaking until their sixth birthday (Carroll, 2008; Wellman, 2000). If you are not impressed by a 14,000-word vocabulary, consider how much effort high school students must exert to learn 1,000 words in another language—and those 6-year-old language learners are only waist-high!

However, language acquisition includes much more than the simple acquisition of new words. For example, children combine these words into phrases that they have never heard before, such as, "My dolly dreamed about toys" (2 years, 2 months).

Researchers have typically ignored developmental changes in language during late adulthood, although some research is emerging (e.g., de Bot & Makoni, 2005; Kemper, 2006; Stine-Morrow et al., 2006; Whitbourne & Whitbourne, 2011). Our discussion of language development will therefore be limited to infancy and childhood.

Language in Infants

During the first 18 months of life—and even shortly before birth—human infants are preparing to use language (Curtin & Werker, 2009). Let's begin by considering how young infants perceive the basic sounds of speech. Then we will look at several early skills in language comprehension and language production. We will also see that adults provide infants with a very helpful kind of language, which clearly helps them acquire language. Our last topic in this part of the chapter focuses on a question from applied psychology: Can infants learn language by watching a popular DVD?

Speech Perception During Infancy. To acquire language, infants must be able to distinguish between **phonemes**, which are the smallest sound units in a language. However, the ability to make distinctions is only half of the struggle. Infants must also be able to group together the sounds that are phonetically equivalent. For example, infants must be able to recognize that the sounds *b* and *p* are different from each other. In addition, they must recognize that the sound *b*, spoken by the deepest bass voice, is the same as the sound *b*, spoken by the highest soprano voice (Harley, 2008; Jusczyk & Luce, 2002; Saffran et al., 2006).

If you have recently observed a baby who is younger than 6 months old, you might have concluded that the baby's mastery of language was roughly equivalent to the linguistic skills of your elbow. Until the early 1970s, psychologists were not much more optimistic. However, more than 40 years of research have demonstrated that infants' speech perception is surprisingly advanced (Fennell, 2012). Infants can perceive almost all the speech-sound contrasts used in language, either at birth or within the first few weeks of life (Houston, 2005; Todd et al., 2006; Traxler, 2012). They can also recognize similarities, an important early stage in language comprehension. Young infants' abilities clearly encourage them to learn languages (Curtin & Werker, 2009; Saffran et al., 2006; Traxler, 2012).

In some cases, young infants are even more skilled than older infants and adults in making phonemic distinctions (Curtin & Werker, 2009). For example, Hindi is a language spoken in India. In Hindi, the *t* sound is sometimes made by placing the tongue against the back of the teeth. However, the *t* sound can also be made by placing the tongue farther back along the roof of the mouth. Hindi speakers can easily distinguish between these two sounds in their language.

As it happens, English-speaking adults *cannot* distinguish between these two *t* sounds. Do the children of English speakers tend to be more skilled? Werker and Tees (1984) tested infants who were being raised in an English-speaking environment. Impressively, infants could distinguish between these two Hindi phonemes with about 95% accuracy when they are 6 to 8 months old. Their accuracy drops to about 70% at 8 to 10 months of age, and to about 20% at 10 to 12 months of age. In contrast, consider 10- to 12-month-old infants who have been raised in a Hindi-speaking environment. These infants distinguish between these two phonemes with close to 100% accuracy (Werker & Tees, 1984).

Apparently, young infants can appreciate numerous phonetic distinctions in every language. Later, however, they reorganize their perceptual categories so that they focus on the important distinctions from their own language environment (Curtin & Werker, 2009; Lany & Saffran, 2010; MacWhinney, 2011; Todd et al., 2006).

According to other research on speech perception, newborns can discriminate between two languages that have different rhythms, such as English and Italian (Saffran et al., 2006). Furthermore, research by Bosch and Sebastián-Gallés (2001) focused on children being raised in bilingual homes where the parents spoke two rhythmically similar languages, Spanish and Catalan. (Catalan is a language spoken in Barcelona, Spain, and the surrounding region.) Impressively, 4-month-olds could discriminate between these two languages! These discrimination skills help infants to keep these two languages from being confused with each other (Curtin & Werker, 2009; Saffran et al., 2006).

Language Comprehension During Infancy. The research about speech perception in infancy has been active for several decades. In contrast, researchers have been slower to explore how infants master the more complex aspects of language *comprehension*, beyond the level of the phoneme. However, we now have information about young infants' comprehension skills in several areas: (1) recognizing important words, (2) understanding the correspondence between a speaker's facial expression and the emotional tone of the speaker's voice, and (3) appreciating semantic concepts.

1. *Recognizing important words.* Interestingly, infants between the ages of 4 and 5 months can already recognize the sound patterns in their own name. Specifically, Mandel and her colleagues (1995) found that infants are likely to turn their heads to look at a location from which their own name is spoken. In contrast, they seldom turn their heads when a different name is spoken that is similar in length and accented syllable (e.g., *Megan* for an infant named *Rachel*).

Young infants can also understand a few selected words (Curtin & Werker, 2009; Piotroski & Naigles, 2012; Saffran et al., 2006). For example, Tincoff and Jusczyk (1999) showed each 6-month-old two videos placed next to each other. One video showed the infant's mother, and the other showed the infant's father. Meanwhile, the infants heard either the word *mommy* or the word *daddy*. When *mommy* was presented, the infants preferred to look at the video of their mother. When *daddy* was presented, they preferred to look at the video of their father.

2. *Understanding the correspondence between sound and sight.* Infants also appreciate another component of language comprehension: the emotional tone of spoken language (Flavell et al., 2002). For example, Walker-Andrews (1986) played recordings of either a happy voice or an angry voice to 7-month-old infants. Meanwhile, the infants saw a pair of films—one of a happy speaker and one of an angry speaker—projected side-by-side. The mouth region of each face was covered so that the infants could not rely on lip movements to match the voice with the film. Therefore, the infants had to look for emotional cues only in the speaker's cheeks and eyes, rather than in the most obvious location, the speaker's mouth.

The results of Walker-Andrews's (1986) study showed that infants who heard a happy voice watched the happy face more often. In contrast, the infants who heard an angry voice watched the angry face more often. In other words, even young infants appreciate that facial expression must correspond with vocal intonation.

3. *Appreciating semantic concepts.* So far, we've seen that infants respond when they hear their own names. They also link the words "mommy" and "daddy" with the visual image of the appropriate parent. In addition, they know that sight and sound must be linked together.

According to research by Jean Mandler and her colleagues, infants also show remarkable skills when we consider their concepts about objects. For example, by about 9 months of age, infants can distinguish between animate objects, which move by themselves, and inanimate objects, which cannot move independently (Mandler, 2003, 2004a, 2007).

In another study, McDonough and Mandler (1998) showed 9-month-old infants a dog drinking from a cup and a car giving a doll a ride. The researchers then handed the infants some new objects from two categories—such as a cat and an anteater for the animal category and a truck and a forklift for the vehicle category. The infants showed the appropriate imitation patterns for the new objects, even for the relatively unfamiliar ones. For example, they showed the anteater drinking, whereas they showed the forklift giving the doll a ride. Infants therefore have the ability to generalize across a category such as "animal" or "vehicle" (Mandler, 2003, 2004a). In other words, children can understand concepts before they are 1 year old (Mandler, 2007).

As children mature, their categories become more refined. For example, 14-month-old children watched a researcher give a toy dog a drink from a cup. Then the researcher handed the cup to a child, together with a different dog, a cat, an unfamiliar mammal, and a bird. Children typically gave the cup to all three mammals, but not to the bird (Mandler, 2004a, 2004b). By their actions, young children reveal their sophisticated knowledge about categories: "Land animals can drink from a cup, but birds cannot" (Mandler, 2007).

Chapter 8 emphasized that your conceptual ability allows you to categorize similar objects together and to make inferences based on these categories. As we've just seen, this skill begins to develop before a child's first birthday.

The word "infant" originally meant "not capable of speech" (Pan, 2012). In a moment, you will see that the language *production* of young infants is definitely limited. However, their speech perception and language comprehension are impressively sophisticated, even when they are only a few months old.

Language Production During Infancy. The early vocalizations of infants pass through a series of stages. By about 2 months of age, infants begin to make **cooing** noises, sounds that involve vowels such as *oo*. By about 6 months they have developed **babbling**, a vocalization that uses both consonants and vowels, often repeating sounds in a series such as *dadada* (Harley, 2010; Kail, 2010). By about 10 months of age, these vocalizations begin to sound like the infant's native language (DeHart et al., 2004; Thompson & Madigan, 2005). This observation coincides with infants' decreased ability to discriminate between phonemes that are irrelevant in their native language (MacWhinney, 2011; Werker & Tees, 1999). We discussed this research on page 485.

At about 8 to 10 months of age, babies begin to produce actions that are designed to capture the attention of other people. They may hand an object to an adult or point to an object. They may also repeat an action—such as clapping—that has attracted attention in the past (Herriot, 2004; Taylor, 2005). Let's now consider the nature of the language that adults provide to infants.

Adults' Language to Infants. Infants learn language relatively quickly because of their impressive auditory skills, their memory capacity, and their receptivity to language. In addition, most infants receive superb assistance from their parents and other adults. Adults tend to make language acquisition somewhat simpler by adjusting their language when speaking with the children. The term **child-directed speech** refers to the language spoken to children. Child-directed speech uses repetition, short sentences, simple vocabulary, basic syntax, a slow pace, a high pitch, exaggerated changes in pitch, and exaggerated facial expressions (Harley, 2008; Kuhl, 2006). Demonstration 13.4 illustrates child-directed speech.

Incidentally, **motherese** is a term that linguists previously used for child-directed speech. However, this gender-biased term neglects the fact that many fathers, other adults, and older children speak "motherese" to infants and young children (DeHart et al., 2004; Harley, 2008; Kail, 2010).

Research in a variety of language communities throughout the world shows that adults typically use a different language style when speaking to infants and young children than when speaking to older people. In general, the features of child-directed language help young language learners understand the meaning and structure of language (Kail, 2010).

⊚ Demonstration 13.4

Producing Child-Directed Speech

Locate a doll that resembles an infant as closely as possible in features and size. Select a friend who has had experience with infants, and ask him or her to imagine that the doll is a niece or nephew who just arrived with parents for a first visit. Encourage your friend to interact with the "baby" in a normal fashion. Observe your friend's language for qualities such as pitch, variation in pitch, vocabulary, sentence length, repetition, and intonation. Also observe any nonverbal communication. What qualities are different from the language used with adults?

Can Infants Learn Language from a DVD? Have you seen advertisements for DVDs that claim to increase an infant's vocabulary? Since the release of the first baby media—called "Baby Einstein"—people have spent hundreds of millions of dollars on these items (DeLoache et al., 2010). The ads claim that parents can boost their infants' vocabulary by playing a video that shows objects with their spoken names. For example, one ad featured a parent who reported that her 18-month-old child had shown a sudden increase in vocabulary after watching one of these videos.

However, you have probably completed many psychology courses that emphasize research methods. As a result, you should ask, "Are there any factors—other than the DVD—that could explain these results?" or "Where's the control group?" As Judy DeLoache and her coauthors (2010) point out, young children normally show a rapid increase in their vocabulary at about 18 months of age. Without a control group, we cannot trust the advertisements' claims.

DeLoache and her colleagues therefore decided to conduct a well-controlled study to determine whether a best-selling language DVD actually does lead to an increase in infants' language. The researchers located 72 infants between the ages of 12 and 18 months. (None of these infants had any previous experience with any "baby media.") The infants were randomly assigned to one of four groups:

1. *The parent-teaching condition* did not use any DVD; instead, the parents were given a list of the 25 words from the DVD, and they were instructed to try to teach their infant as many words as possible for a 4-week period.

2. In the *DVD-with-interaction condition*, the child and the parent watched the DVD together at least five times each week for a 4-week period.

3. In the *DVD-with-no-interaction condition*, the children watched the DVD by themselves, at least five times each week for a 4-week period.

4. In the *control condition*, there was no DVD and the parents did not try to teach specific words to their children.

After 4 weeks, each child was shown a pair of objects: one object represented in the DVD (perhaps a clock) and one control object (perhaps a plate), which had not

FIGURE 13.6

Infants' Average Performance on the Word-Recognition Test, as a Function of Group.

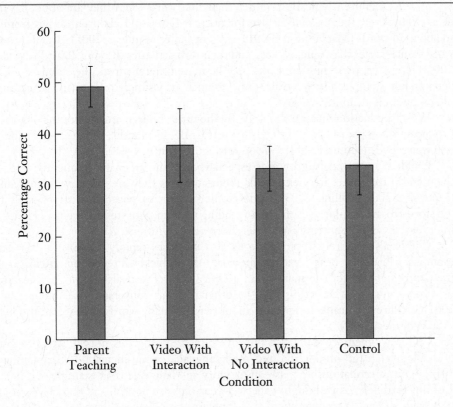

Note: The vertical bars are a measure of variability.

Source: DeLoache, J. S., et al. (2010). Do babies learn from baby media? *Psychological Science, 21,* 1570–1574.

been shown in the DVD. The child was asked, for example, "Can you show me the clock?" Figure 13.6 shows the results of this experiment. A statistical analysis showed that the children in the parent-teaching condition were more likely to point to the correct answer, compared to the children in all the other three groups. The bottom line? If you've considered buying a language DVD for an infant you know, you will want to consider a more useful gift.

Language in Children

Sometime around their first birthday, most infants throughout the world speak their first word (Harley, 2010; MacWhinney, 2011). Let's look at the characteristics of these initial words, as well as the words spoken by older children. Then we will consider two components of children's grammar, morphology and syntax. Finally, we will examine how children master pragmatics, or the social rules of language.

Words. Children typically produce their first word when they are about 1 year of age. However, the vocabulary size for normal 1-year-old children ranges from 0 to about 50 words (MacWhinney, 2011; Thompson & Madigan, 2005). A child's first words usually refer to people, objects, and their own activities (Bloom, 2001; Waxman, 2002). However, these first concepts may be quite different from the standard adult version. For example, a baby's concept of "animal" may simply refer to any object that moves by itself (Mandler, 2006).

Word production increases rapidly. By the time children are 20 months old, they produce an average of about 150 to 180 words. By 28 months, the average is about 380 words (MacWhinney, 2011; Woodward & Markman, 1998).

Children's vocabulary growth is especially rapid if caregivers frequently read to them and if caregivers frequently talk about activities they are doing with the child (Patterson, 2002; Rollins, 2003). In developing countries, parents are more likely to tell stories to their children, rather than reading to them. Storytelling is equally helpful in developing children's language skills (Bornstein & Putnick, 2012).

Children's comprehension of words also increases rapidly (Rollins, 2003). For example, when they hear a particular word, they quickly direct their attention to the appropriate object (Fernald et al., 1998). Children can also learn the meaning of some words by overhearing them in other people's conversations (Akhtar et al., 2001). Children typically understand about twice as many words as they can produce (MacWhinney, 2011).

Children's memory skills also improve rapidly during this period, which boosts both their language production and their language comprehension (MacWhinney, 2011). This interrelationship between memory and language is an example of Theme 4 of this textbook. As you might expect, 5-year-olds are more likely than 3-year-olds to provide a detailed account about their previous experiences (Hayne et al., 2011).

Another factor that helps children learn new words is called **fast mapping**, or using context to make a reasonable guess about a word's meaning after just one or two exposures (Harley, 2008; Mandler, 2004b). Chapter 9 emphasized that adults are guided by the context in which a word appears. Fast mapping demonstrates that context is also critically important for young children.

Young children may apply a newly learned label to a category that is either too broad or too narrow. An **overextension** is the use of a word to refer to other objects in addition to objects that adults would consider appropriate (Donaldson, 2004; Harley, 2010). For example, when my daughter Beth was 1 year old, she used the word *baish* to refer initially to her blanket. Then she later applied the term to a diaper, a diaper pin, and a vitamin pill. Often an object's shape or function is important in determining overextensions. However, sometimes—as in the case of the vitamin pill—word usage can wander away from the original meaning.

Around the age of 2, children often produce overextensions for words such as *dog* and *ball*. For example, one child produced the name *dog* for nine species of dog and one toy dog—all correct answers. However, he also used the word *dog* for two bears, a wolf, a fox, a doe, a rhinoceros, a hippopotamus, and a fish—all overextensions. Some overextensions occur when a child does not yet know the correct word for an unfamiliar item (Harley, 2010; Taylor, 2005). Few 2-year-olds have ever seen a rhinoceros or a hippopotamus. However, in many cases, a child may be confused about the exact differences between two similar concepts, such as a tulip versus a daffodil.

Morphology. Children initially use the simple form of a word in every context—for example, "girl run," rather than "girl runs." However, they soon begin to master how to add on morphemes. **Morphemes** are the basic units of meaning, which include endings such as *-s* and *-ed*, as well as simple words such as *run*. **Morphology** is the study of these basic units of meaning.

After children have learned many words with regular plurals and past tenses—like *girls* and *kicked*—they progress to a more advanced understanding of morphology. At this point, they sometimes create their own regular forms, such as *mouses* and *runned*, although children are typically accurate (Bates et al., 2001; Harley, 2008). These errors show that language acquisition is not simply a matter of imitating the words produced by parents, because parents seldom produce mistakes such as *mouses* and *runned* (Stromswold, 1999).

This tendency to add the most customary grammatical morphemes to create new forms of irregular words is called **overregularization**. Keep in mind, then, that *overextension* refers to the tendency to extend a word's meaning inappropriately. In contrast, *overregularization* refers to the tendency to add regular morphemes inappropriately. Later still, children learn that many words have regular plurals and past tenses, but some words have irregular forms, such as *mice* and *ran* (Kail, 2010).

Theorists have developed several different explanations of children's overregularizations. For example, Gary Marcus (1996) has proposed an explanation for overregularization. According to Marcus's **rule-and-memory theory**, children learn a general rule for past-tense verbs, which specifies that they must add *-ed*; however, they also store in memory the past tenses for many irregular verbs. English has about 200 verbs with irregular past tenses, so young children would store only the most common of these irregular verbs (Kagan & Herschkowitz, 2005; Marcus, 1996).

Marcus's theory also proposes that children who remember an irregular form will consistently use it, rather than applying the default "add *-ed*" rule. As children gather more expertise about language, they gradually replace the overregularized words with the appropriate past-tense verbs. Marcus (1996) applied his theory to a sample of more than 11,000 past-tense verbs that children had generated. He found that specific components of the theory predicted the patterns of overregularization. He also observed a linear decrease in the number of overregularizations, from 4% among preschoolers to 1% among fourth graders.

Syntax. At about 18 to 24 months of age, the average child begins to combine two words—usually after acquiring between 50 and 100 words (de Boysson-Bardies, 1999; Flavell et al., 2002; Tomasello, 2006). An important issue that arises at this point is syntax. **Syntax** refers to the grammatical rules that govern how words can be combined into sentences. An important factor that contributes to this rapid increase in word combinations is the growing capacity of children's working memory.

Children's two-word utterances express many different kinds of relationships, such as possessor–possession ("Mama dress"), action–object ("Eat cookie"), and agent–action ("Teddy fall"). Furthermore, a two-word phrase can have different meanings in different contexts. "Daddy sock" may signify that the father is putting the child's sock on her or his foot, or that a particular sock belongs to the father (de Villiers & de Villiers, 1999). Many of these utterances, such as "me going" may not be grammatically correct, but they obviously convey the message (Tomasello, 2006).

After children have reached the two-word stage, they begin to fill in the missing words and word endings, and they also improve their word order. "Baby cry" becomes "The baby is crying," for example. By 3½ years of age, most children are reasonably accurate with respect to both morphology and syntax (Kail, 2010).

Language learning is definitely an active process, consistent with Theme 1 of this book. Children learn language by actively constructing their own speech. They produce phrases that adults would never say, such as "Allgone sticky," "Bye-bye hot," and "More page" (Rogers, 1985). These phrases show us that children's speech is far richer than a simple imitation of adult language.

As children grow increasingly skilled in producing sophisticated language, they also grow increasingly skilled in understanding it. Consider, for example, how a child manages to understand the sentence, "Pat hit Chris." How does the child know who is the actor in that sentence and who is the recipient of the action? In English, the word order of the sentence is the most important cue, and children use this information appropriately (Hirsh-Pasek & Golinkoff, 1996). We might be tempted to assume that word order is similarly helpful in all languages. However, young children learning Turkish or Polish use the endings of words—rather than word-order information—to decode the meaning of sentences (Weist, 1985).

Children seem to be clever strategists who can use whatever syntax cues are available in their language. Furthermore, children usually realize that the purpose of language is to communicate with others. Therefore, it's no surprise that they try to produce language that adults can comprehend (Baldwin & Meyer, 2007).

Pragmatics. As we discussed in Chapter 10, **pragmatics** focuses on the social rules and world knowledge that allow speakers to successfully communicate messages to other people (De Groot, 2011). Research on pragmatics focuses on how speakers successfully communicate messages to their listeners.

Children need to learn what should be said (and what should *not* be said) in certain circumstances. They must also understand that they should use different language styles when speaking to their parents, their teachers, their peers, and younger children (Bjorklund, 2005; MacWhinney, 2011). In addition, they have to learn that two speakers need to coordinate a conversation by taking turns and by being a responsive listener.

Every family has stories about children's wildly inappropriate remarks to elderly relatives, friendly neighbors, and complete strangers. A student in my child development class described an example of a pragmatic violation. Her family was attending a church service, and her 4-year-old brother noticed that their father was starting to fall asleep during the sermon. So the little boy stood up on the church pew and announced in a loud voice, "Be quiet everyone! My daddy is trying to sleep!" As you can imagine, everyone reacted more strongly to the fact that the child had broken a pragmatic rule than to the fact that he had tried to help his dozing daddy.

Another pragmatic skill that children learn is to adapt their language to the listener. For instance, they must determine whether their listener has the appropriate background information about a topic (MacWhinney, 2011; Pan & Snow, 1999). Until the early 1970s, psychologists believed that children's language ignored the listener's level of understanding.

However, an influential study by Shatz and Gelman (1973) showed that children often make appropriate adjustments. In this study, 4-year-olds modified their speech substantially when the listener was a 2-year-old, rather than a peer or an adult. For example, the 4-year-olds described a toy to their 2-year-old listeners using short, simple utterances. However, when describing the toy to another 4-year-old or an adult, their descriptions were much longer and more complex.

Even 2-year-olds tend to simplify their language when speaking to their infant siblings (Dunn & Kendrick, 1982). If you know any young preschoolers, you may wish to repeat Demonstration 13.3 with them. Children clearly understand some of the social aspects of language before they enter kindergarten.

Children also learn to take turns in a conversation. Sophisticated turn taking requires each speaker to anticipate when the conversational partner will complete his or her remark. This requirement demands an impressive knowledge of language structure (Siegal, 1996; Snow, 1999).

The next time you observe two adults conversing, notice how the listener responds to the speaker by smiling, gazing, and other gestures of interest. In one study, researchers recorded these kinds of listener responses in young children who were talking with an adult about topics such as toys, a popular film, and siblings (Miller et al., 1985). All these listener responses were more abundant in the older children. For example, 8% of 3-year-olds said "uh-hum" at some point while the adult was speaking, in contrast to 50% of 5-year-olds. Furthermore, only 67% of 3-year-old listeners nodded their heads, in contrast to an impressive 100% of 5-year-olds. Thus, children learn how to be pragmatically skilled listeners, as well as speakers (MacWhinney, 2011; Snow, 1999).

Infants and children seem to be specially prepared to notice and interact socially (Wellman & Gelman, 1992). Children are eager to master language and to become active participants in ongoing conversations. This enthusiasm about learning language encourages children to master the words, morphemes, syntax, and pragmatics of speech.

Throughout this chapter, we have seen examples of the early competence of infants and children. For instance, young infants are remarkably skilled at remembering faces and distinguishing speech sounds. These early skills foreshadow the impressive cognitive skills that adults exhibit (Theme 2). Furthermore, children's active, inquiring interactions with the people, objects, and concepts in their world (Theme 1) help them develop memory, metamemory, and language. Finally, the research on the cognitive skills of elderly people reveals some specific deficits. However, many cognitive abilities remain both accurate and active throughout the life span.

Section Summary: *The Development of Language*

1. Research with infants reveals their impressive speech perception abilities. For example, infants can perceive the difference between two similar phonemes and discriminate between two similar languages,

2. Infants can also recognize their name, understand that a happy voice should be accompanied by a smiling face, and appreciate some important semantic concepts.

3. During late infancy, babbling begins to resemble the language that is spoken to the infant, and the infant attempts intentional communication.

4. The child-friendly language that parents use with infants helps to encourage their language development.

5. Infants cannot learn vocabulary by merely watching a DVD in which spoken words are linked with appropriate objects.

6. Young children rapidly acquire new words from context (fast mapping), but their word usage frequently includes overextensions.

7. During language acquisition, children show overregularization, adding regular morphemes to words that have irregular plurals and past tenses.

8. Between the ages of 18 and 24 months, children begin active efforts to master syntax by combining words into simple phrases.

9. Young children sometimes violate pragmatic rules. As children mature, however, they adapt their language to the listener, and they develop turn-taking strategies. They also learn how they are supposed to respond to someone who is speaking with them.

CHAPTER REVIEW QUESTIONS

1. Prior to the 1970s, most psychologists were pessimistic about the cognitive skills of infants and young children. However, psychologists have become more optimistic. If you wanted to impress someone with infants' and children's cognitive skills, what information would you provide about their memory and their language abilities?

2. Part of the challenge in studying infants is designing experiments that reveal an infant's true abilities. Describe several procedures that researchers have developed so that they can discover infants' skills in memory and language.

3. Compare children, young adults, and elderly adults with respect to their skills in the following areas: working memory, recognition memory, and recall memory. Be sure to list factors that might influence your conclusions.

4. Suppose that the outcome of an important court case in your community depends on the eyewitness testimony of a young child. What factors would

encourage you to trust the child's report? What factors would make you think that the child's memory might not be accurate?

5. Describe the proposed explanation for children's memory performance, which focuses on memory strategies and metamemory. Discuss the evidence for this explanation, including information about the correlation between metamemory and memory performance.

6. In general, what kinds of memory tasks are especially difficult for elderly people? What explanations can best account for memory deficits in elderly individuals? How might overconfidence and stereotypes about older adults help to explain these difficulties?

7. This chapter describes children's metamemory and strategy use. What could a third-grade teacher do to encourage students' memory skills? What should this teacher know about children's metacognitive ability?

8. In 1985, Branthwaite and Rogers commented that being a child is like being a spy who is trying to break a code to discover how the world works. Apply this idea to a child's understanding of word meaning, morphology, word order, and pragmatic rules.

9. Describe some of the pragmatic rules of language that are important in our culture. How does the mastery of these rules change as children develop?

10. Consider the information about cognitive processes in this chapter. Are infants as different from children as you had originally thought? Do any of the findings on elderly people surprise you, or do they match your original impressions?

ONE LAST TASK

This final task will help you review this book as comprehensively as possible. On separate sheets of paper, list each of the five themes of this book. Then skim through each chapter. Write a brief description of every example of a theme, using the appropriate sheet each time a theme is mentioned. You can check the completeness of your lists by consulting the entries for Theme 1, 2, 3, 4, and 5 in the subject index. After completing your lists, try to synthesize the material within each of the five themes.

KEYWORDS

lifespan approach to
   development
conjugate reinforcement
   technique
spaced learning
massed learning

autobiographical memory
script
source monitoring
memory strategies
utilization deficiency
prospective memory

explicit memory task
implicit memory task
chunk
cognitive slowing
metacognition
metamemory

KEYWORDS   (continued)

theory of mind
metacomprehension
dementia
memory self-efficacy
phonemes
cooing

babbling
child-directed speech
motherese
fast mapping
overextension
morphemes

morphology
overregularization
rule-and-memory theory
syntax
pragmatics

RECOMMENDED READINGS

Courage, M. L., & Cowan, N. (Eds.). (2009). *The development of memory in infancy and childhood*. New York: Psychology Press. This excellent book includes chapters about memory development in both infants and toddlers, as well as the development of processes such as working memory, memory strategies, and autobiographical memory.

Dunlosky, J., & Metcalfe, J. (2009). *Metacognition*. Los Angeles: Sage. The two final chapters in this book focus on metacognition during childhood development and older adulthood. These authors provide an excellent summary of the research in these two areas, and their writing style is superb.

Hacker, D. J., Dunlosky, J., & Graesser, A. C. (Eds.). (2009). *Handbook of metacognition in education*. New York: Routledge. Here's a perfect book for someone interested in cognitive development and education. In addition to the topics discussed in your textbook, this handbook examines how metacognition is relevant in reading, mathematics, and judgment.

Whitbourne, S. K., & Whitbourne, S. B. (2011). *Adult development and aging: Biopsychosocial perspectives* (4th ed.). Hoboken, NJ: Wiley. Susan K. Whitbourne and her daughter Stacey B. Whitbourne are both experts in development during adulthood and old age. Their book provides a clear overview of the research about memory and related areas in older adults; they also explore related topics such as perception, health, and social interactions.

Glossary

abstraction A memory process that stores the meaning of a message, rather than the exact words.

acoustic confusions In memory research, the observation that people are likely to confuse similar-sounding stimuli.

ACT-R An acronym for "Adaptive Control of Thought-Rational"; this approach uses a series of network models in an attempt to account for a wide variety of tasks including memory, learning, spatial cognition, language, reasoning, problem solving, and decision making.

ADHD See Attention-Deficit/Hyperactivity Disorder (ADHD).

affirming the antecedent In conditional reasoning tasks, claiming that the "if..." part of the statement is true. This kind of reasoning leads to a correct, conclusion.

affirming the consequent In conditional reasoning tasks, the fallacy (or error) of claiming that the "then..." part of the sentence is true. This kind of reasoning leads to an invalid conclusion.

age of acquisition In psycholinguistics, the age at which a person begins to learn a second language.

AI See artificial intelligence.

algorithm A method that will always produce a solution to the problem, although the process can sometimes be inefficient.

alignment heuristic In cognitive maps, the finding that people tend to remember a series of separate geographic structures as being more lined up than they really are.

ambiguous figure-ground relationship A perceptual phenomenon studied by gestalt psychologists, in which the figure and the ground of a visual stimulus reverse from time to time, so that the figure becomes the ground and then becomes the figure again.

ambiguous sentences Two sentences that have identical surface structures but very different deep structures.

amnesia Severe deficits in episodic memory.

analog code In the imagery debate, a mental representation that closely resembles the physical object.

analogy approach In problem solving, the use of a solution to a similar, earlier problem to help solve a new problem.

anchor In decision making, the first approximation, used in the anchoring and adjustment heuristic.

anchoring and adjustment heuristic In decision making, beginning with a first approximation, which serves as an anchor, and then making adjustments to that anchor, based on additional information. Typically people rely too heavily on the anchor and their adjustments are too small. This heuristic is also known as the *anchoring effect*.

anchoring effect See anchoring and adjustment heuristic.

antecedent In conditional reasoning tasks, the first proposition or statement; the antecedent is contained in the "if..." part of the sentence.

anterograde amnesia The inability to form memories for events that occur after brain damage.

anxiety disorders A broad category of psychological disorders that includes problems such as generalized anxiety disorder, post-traumatic stress disorder, and social phobia.

aphasia Difficulty communicating, caused by damage to the speech areas of the brain. This damage is typically caused by a stroke or a tumor.

artificial intelligence (AI) A branch of computer science that explores human cognitive processes by creating computer models. These models demonstrate "intelligent behavior" and also accomplish the same tasks that humans do.

Atkinson-Shiffrin model The proposal that memory involves a sequence of separate steps; in each step, information is transferred from one storage area to another.

attention A concentration of mental activity, so that you can take in limited information.

Attention-Deficit/Hyperactivity Disorder (ADHD) A psychological disorder characterized by difficulty paying attention at school, at work, and in other activities, as well as hyperactivity and impulsivity. People with ADHD often have more difficulty than others on central-executive tasks, especially when they must perform another task at the same time.

auditory imagery The mental representation of auditory stimuli (sounds) when the sounds are not physically present.

autobiographical memory   Memory for experiences and information related to oneself. Autobiographical memory usually includes a verbal narrative. Research in this area typically examines recall for events that happen outside the laboratory.

availability heuristic   Estimating frequency or probability in terms of how easy it is to think of relevant examples of something.

babbling   A vocalization that uses both consonants and vowels, often repeating sounds in a series such as *dadada*. Infants develop these vocalizations by about 6 months of age.

base rate   In decision making, how often an item occurs in the population. People often ignore this useful information.

base-rate fallacy   In decision making, paying too little attention to important information about how often an item occurs in the population (its base rate).

basic-level categories   In the prototype approach to semantic memory, categories that are moderately specific; "chair," "dog," and "screwdriver" are examples of basic-level categories.

behaviorism   An approach to psychology that focuses on objective, observable reactions to stimuli in the environment.

belief-bias effect   When people make reasoning judgments based on prior beliefs and general knowledge, rather than on the rules of logic. In general, people make errors when the logic of a reasoning problem conflicts with their background knowledge.

betrayal trauma   An explanation of recovered memory that emphasizes the adaptive nature of memory; actively inhibiting memories of abuse may be necessary in order to maintain an attachment to a parent or caretaker.

bilingual speaker   Someone who is fluent in two different languages.

binding problem   A characteristic of the visual system, in which characteristics such as color and shape can be registered separately; as a result, the visual system may not represent these important features of an object as a unified whole.

blindsight   A visual condition in which an individual with a damaged visual cortex claims not to see an object; however, he or she can accurately report some characteristics of this object, such as its location.

border bias   In cognitive maps, the finding that people tend to estimate that the distance between two locations—on different sides of a geographic border—are larger than two locations that are the same distance apart, but on the same side of a geographic border.

bottleneck theories   In early theories about attention, the proposal that a narrow passageway in human information processing limits the quantity of information to which one can pay attention.

bottom-up processing   The kind of cognitive processing that emphasizes stimulus characteristics in object recognition and other cognitive tasks. For example, the physical stimuli from the environment are registered on the sensory receptors. This information is then passed on to higher, more sophisticated levels in the cognitive system.

boundary extension   The tendency to remember having viewed a greater portion of a scene than was actually shown at an earlier time.

brain lesion   Specific brain damage caused by strokes, tumors, blows to the head, accidents, or other traumas.

Broca's aphasia   An expressive-language deficit—trouble producing speech—characterized by hesitant speech using isolated words and short phrases. This deficit is caused by damage to Broca's area.

Broca's area   A region toward the front of the brain that is important in speech production.

Brown/Peterson & Peterson technique   A technique designed by John Brown, Lloyd Peterson, and Margaret Peterson. Researchers present several items to a participant, who is instructed to remember these items. Next the participant performs a distracting task and then attempts to recall the original items. This classic technique was created in order to assess short-term memory.

calibration   People's accuracy in estimating their own actual performance.

categorical perception   A phenomenon in which people report hearing a clear-cut phoneme (e.g., a clear-cut *b* or a clear-cut *p*) even though they actually heard an ambiguous sound, between the two phonemes (e.g., a sound partway between a *b* and a *p*).

category   A set of objects that belong together and are considered by the cognitive system to be at least partly equivalent. Categories provide useful information about their members.

central executive   The component of working memory that integrates information from the phonological loop, the visuospatial sketchpad, the episodic buffer, and long-term memory. The central executive also plays a role in attention, planning, and coordinating other cognitive activities.

cerebral cortex The outer layer of the brain that is essential for cognitive processes.

change blindness The failure to detect a change in an object or a scene due to the overuse of top-down processing.

child-directed speech The kind of language spoken to children. Child-directed speech typically includes characteristics such as repetition, short sentences, simple vocabulary, basic syntax, a slow pace, a high pitch, exaggerated changes in pitch, and exaggerated facial expressions.

chunk A memory unit that consists of several components, which are strongly associated with one another.

chunking A memory strategy in which the learner combines several small units to create larger units.

coarticulation One of the causes of phoneme variation, in this case created by surrounding phonemes. Specifically, when pronouncing a particular phoneme, the mouth remains in somewhat the same shape as when it pronounced the previous phoneme in a word; in addition, the mouth is preparing to pronounce the next phoneme.

cocktail party effect The phenomenon of noticing one's own name, when it is mentioned in a nearby conversation, even when paying close attention to another conversation.

cognition Mental activity, including the acquisition, storage, transformation, and use of knowledge.

cognitive approach A theoretical orientation that emphasizes people's thought processes and their knowledge.

cognitive map The mental representation of geographic information, including a person's surrounding environment.

cognitive neuroscience An approach to studying mental activity that uses the research techniques of cognitive psychology, along with various neuroscience techniques for assessing the structure and function of the brain.

cognitive psychology (1) A synonym for cognition. (2) The theoretical approach to psychology that focuses on studying people's thought processes and knowledge.

cognitive science An interdisciplinary field that tries to answer questions about the mind. Cognitive science includes cognitive psychology, neuroscience, artificial intelligence, philosophy, linguistics, anthropology, sociology, and economics.

cognitive slowing A reduced rate of responding on cognitive tasks; often observed in elderly individuals.

cognitive-behavioral approach The theory that psychological problems arise from inappropriate thinking (cognitive factors) and inappropriate learning (behavioral factors).

cognitive-functional approach The idea that the function of human language in everyday life is to communicate meaning to other individuals.

common ground A situation where the people in a conversation share similar background knowledge, schemas, and perspectives. These elements of common ground are necessary for mutual understanding.

computer metaphor A way of describing cognition as a complex, multipurpose machine that processes information quickly and accurately.

computer modeling *See* computer simulation.

computer simulation Programming a computer to perform a specific cognitive task in the same way that humans actually perform this task. Also called *computer modeling*.

concept The mental representation of a category.

conditional reasoning task A deductive reasoning task that describes the relationship between conditions. Conditional reasoning tasks are often presented in an "if . . . then . . . " format. Also called a *propositional reasoning task*.

confidence interval In decision making, the range within which a number is expected to fall a certain percentage of the time.

confirmation bias The tendency to try to confirm or support a hypothesis rather than trying to disprove it.

conjugate reinforcement technique A method for investigating cognition in infants, using a mobile hanging above a young infant's crib. A ribbon connects the infant's ankle and the mobile, so that the infant's kicks will make the mobile move. Researchers can test an infant's memory by determining the amount of time that can elapse between the original learning and the infant's recall of the kicking response.

conjunction fallacy A decision-making error that occurs when people judge the probability of the conjunction of two events to be greater than the probability of either constituent event.

conjunction rule A rule stating that the probability of the conjunction of two events cannot be larger than the probability of either of its constituent events.

connection weights In parallel distributed processing, a characteristic of neural networks that determines how much activation one unit can pass on to another unit.

connectionism   *See* parallel distributed processing approach (PDP).

connectionist approach   *See* parallel distributed processing approach (PDP).

consciousness   A person's awareness of the external world and of her or his own perceptions, images, thoughts, memories, and feelings.

consequent   In conditional reasoning tasks, the proposition that comes second; it is the consequence. The consequent is contained in the "then..." part of the sentence.

consistency bias   In autobiographical memory, the tendency to exaggerate the consistency between past feelings or beliefs and one's current viewpoint.

constructionist view of inferences   In long-term memory, the observation that readers usually draw inferences about the causes of events and about the relationships between events.

constructive model of memory   In long-term memory, the proposal that people integrate information from individual sentences in order to construct larger ideas.

constructivist approach   In long-term memory, the proposal that people construct knowledge by integrating the information they know. As a result, their understanding of an event or a topic is coherent, and it makes sense.

control processes   Intentional strategies—such as rehearsal—that people may use to improve their memory.

convergent production   A measure of creativity requiring the test-taker to supply a single, best response; the researchers assess the quality of that response.

cooing   Sounds involving vowels such as *oo* that infants begin to make by about 2 months of age.

creativity   In problem solving, finding solutions that are both novel and useful.

critical period hypothesis   In linguistics, the proposal that the ability to acquire a new language is strictly limited to a specific period of life. The critical period hypothesis proposes that individuals who have already reached a specified age—perhaps early puberty—will no longer be able to acquire a new language with native-like fluency. In general, the research does not support this hypothesis.

cross-ethnicity effect   *See* own-ethnicity bias.

crystal-ball technique   In decision making, imagining that a completely accurate crystal ball has determined that a favored hypothesis is actually incorrect. Therefore, the decision makers must search for alternative explanations for the outcome.

decision making   Assessing information and choosing among two or more alternatives. Compared to deductive reasoning, decision making is much more ambiguous.

declarative knowledge   In semantic memory, knowledge about facts and things.

deductive reasoning   The type of reasoning that begins with some specific premises, which are assumed to be true. Next, you judge whether those premises allow a particular conclusion to be drawn, based on the principles of logic.

deep structure   In psycholinguistics, the underlying, more abstract meaning of a sentence, in contrast to *surface structure*.

default assignment   In parallel distributed processing, a method used to fill in missing information about a particular person or object based on information from other similar people or objects.

default heuristic   In decision making, the tendency to choose a default option (i.e., the standard option), when one is presented.

demand characteristics   Cues that might convey the experimenter's hypothesis to a participant in a research study.

dementia   A disorder that includes memory problems and other cognitive deficits. Individuals with dementia typically have difficulty estimating their memory abilities.

denying the antecedent   In conditional reasoning tasks, the fallacy (or error) of claiming that the "if..." part of the sentence is false. This kind of reasoning leads to an invalid conclusion.

denying the consequent   In conditional reasoning tasks, claiming that the "then..." part of the sentence is false. This kind of reasoning leads to a correct conclusion.

depth-of-processing approach   *See* levels-of-processing approach.

desirable difficulties   A learning situation that is somewhat challenging, but not too difficult; this situation is helpful for increasing long-term recall.

dichotic listening A laboratory technique in which one message is presented to the left ear and a different message is presented to the right ear.

direct request In language, resolving an interpersonal situation or problem by using a very obvious statement or question.

direct-access route During reading, when a word is recognized directly through vision, without "sounding out" the word.

directive In language, a sentence that asks someone to do something.

discourse Interrelated units of language that are longer than a sentence.

dissociation In research areas such as cognitive neuroscience, an outcome that occurs (1) when a variable has large effects on Test A, but little or no effects on Test B; or (2) when a variable has one kind of effect if measured by Test A, and the opposite effect if measured by Test B. A dissociation is similar to the concept of a statistical interaction.

distal stimulus In perception, the actual object that is "out there" in the environment, for example, a pen on a desk.

distinctive feature In visual perception, an important characteristic of the visual stimulus.

distinctiveness In the levels-of-processing approach to memory, the situation in which one memory trace is different from all other memory traces. People tend to forget information if it is not distinctly different from the other memory traces in their long-term memory.

distributed attention In feature-integration theory, a relatively fast, low-level kind of processing, in which the viewer registers the features of the stimulus automatically and simultaneously, using parallel processing.

distributed-practice effect The observation that memory is better when the learning trials are spread over time (spaced learning), as compared with trying to learn the material all at once (massed learning). The studies generally support this effect for both recall tasks and recognition tasks.

divergent production A measure of creativity that emphasizes the number of different responses made to a test item.

divided-attention task A situation in which people try to pay attention to two or more simultaneous messages, responding appropriately to each message. Both speed and accuracy frequently suffer during a divided-attention task.

dual-process theory In reasoning and decision making, the approach that distinguishes between two types of cognitive processing: *Type 1 processing* is fast and automatic, requiring little conscious attention. In contrast, *Type 2 processing* is relatively slow and controlled, requiring focused attention, and it is typically more accurate.

dual-route approach to reading The proposal that skilled readers use both (1) a direct-access route and (2) an indirect-access route to recognize words during reading.

ecological rationality In decision making, a description of how people create a wide variety of heuristics to help make useful, adaptive choices in the real world.

ecological validity A principle of research design in which the research uses conditions that are similar to the natural setting where the results will be applied.

elaboration In the levels-of-processing approach to memory, rich processing that emphasizes the meaning of a particular concept; it also relates the concept to prior knowledge and interconnected concepts already mastered.

embodied cognition approach The proposal that people often use their own bodies and motor actions in order to express their abstract thoughts and knowledge.

emotion A brief psychological reaction to a specific stimulus, in contrast to a mood, which is a more general, long-lasting experience.

emotional Stroop task When people are instructed to name the ink color of words that could have strong emotional significance to them, they often require more time to name the color of the stimuli, presumably because they have trouble ignoring their emotional reactions to those specific words.

empirical evidence Scientific evidence obtained by careful observation and experimentation.

encoding The initial acquisition of information. During encoding, we process and represent this information in memory.

encoding-specificity principle The observation that recall is often better if the context at the time of encoding matches the context at the time of retrieval.

episodic buffer In working memory, a temporary storehouse that can hold and combine information from the phonological loop, visuospatial sketchpad, and long-term memory.

episodic memory   People's memories for events that happened to them personally, in contrast with semantic memory.

ERP   *See* event-related potential (ERP) technique.

event-related potential (ERP) technique   A procedure for recording the very brief, small fluctuations in the brain's electrical activity in response to a stimulus such as an auditory tone.

executive attention network   A cognitive system that is responsible for the kind of attention one uses when a task focuses on conflicting information, for example on the Stroop task.

exemplar   In concept representation, the examples of a concept stored in memory. A new stimulus is classified by comparing it with these exemplars.

exemplar approach   In concept representation, the proposal that people first learn information about some specific examples of a concept; then they classify each new stimulus by deciding how closely it resembles all of those specific examples.

exhaustive search   In problem solving, a kind of algorithm in which a person tests all of the possible answers, using a specified system.

experimenter expectancy   In research, when researchers' biases and expectations influence the outcomes of an experiment.

expertise   A person's impressive cognitive abilities or this person's consistently exceptional performance on representative tasks in a particular area.

explicit memory task   A memory task in which participants are instructed to remember some information. Later, a recall or recognition test requires them to intentionally retrieve that previously learned information.

external memory aid   Any device, external to one's self, which facilitates memory in some way; this memory aid is especially helpful on prospective-memory tasks.

extrinsic motivation   The motivation to work on a task—not because it is enjoyable—but in order to earn a promised reward or to win a competition.

face-inversion effect   The observation that people are much more accurate in identifying upright faces, compared to upside-down faces.

false alarm   In memory research, when people "remember" an item that was not originally presented.

false-memory perspective   The proposal that most recovered memories are actually incorrect memories; in other words, these recovered memories are constructed stories about events that never occurred. This perspective is contrasted with the recovered-memory perspective.

family resemblance   In the prototype approach to semantic memory, the observation that—for some concepts—no single attribute is shared by all examples of the concept. However, each example has at least one attribute in common with some other example of the concept.

fast mapping   In language learning, using context to make a reasonable guess about a word's meaning after just one or two exposures.

feature-analysis theories   In perception, the proposal that we recognize visual objects, based on a small number of characteristics or components known as distinctive features.

feature-integration theory   This theory of attention, developed by Anne Treisman, proposes two elements: (1) distributed attention, processing all parts of the scene at the same time, and (2) focused attention, processing each item in the scene, one at a time.

feature-present/feature-absent effect   In visual search studies, the finding that people can typically locate a feature that is *present* more quickly than a feature that is *absent*.

feeling-of-knowing effect   In memory, the subjective experience of knowing some information, but not being able to recall it right now.

figure   In gestalt psychology, when two areas share a common boundary, the figure is the area that has a distinct shape with clearly defined edges. This area seems closer and more dominant. In contrast, the ground is the area that forms the background.

first language   In linguistics, the initial language that a person learned; this term is typically applied to someone who later learned a different language. *See* sequential bilingualism.

first-letter technique   A memory strategy in which a person is learning a list of items; he or she composes a word or a sentence from the first letters of each word on the list to be remembered.

fixations   Brief pauses occurring between saccadic eye movements, in which the visual system acquires information that is useful for reading and other visual tasks.

fixed mindset The belief that a person possesses a certain amount of intelligence and other skills, and no amount of effort can improve performance, in contrast to the *growth mindset.*

flashbulb memory Memory for the circumstances in which one first learned about a very surprising and emotionally arousing event.

fMRI *See* functional magnetic resonance imaging (fMRI).

focused attention In feature-integration theory, slower serial processing, in which a person identifies objects, one at a time. This kind of processing is necessary when objects are more complex.

foresight bias The tendency, when studying for a future exam, to be overconfident about performance on that exam.

fovea A very small region in the center of the retina, which has better acuity than other retinal regions.

frame In linguistics, mental structures that simplify reality. Frames tend to structure what "counts" as facts. George Lakoff uses this term in discussing how language can structure people's thinking.

framing effect In decision making, when decisions are influenced by (1) the background context of the choice or (2) the way in which a question is worded (or framed).

functional fixedness The tendency to assign stable (or "fixed") functions to an object. As a result, people do not think about the features of this object that might be useful in helping solve a problem.

functional magnetic resonance imaging (fMRI) A method of measuring brain activity, based on the principle that oxygen-rich blood is an index of brain activity. A magnetic field produces changes in the oxygen atoms in the brain while a person performs a cognitive task. A scanning device takes a "photo" of the changes.

gender stereotypes The beliefs and opinions that people associate with females and males.

general mechanism approach The idea that speech perception can be explained without proposing any specialized phonetic module. In other words, humans use the same neural mechanisms to process both speech sounds and nonspeech sounds.

General Problem Solver (GPS) In problem solving, a computer program whose basic strategy is means-ends analysis. The goal of the GPS is to mimic the processes that normal humans use when they tackle these problems.

generalized anxiety disorder A psychological disorder characterized by at least 6 months of intense, long-lasting anxiety and worry.

geons In recognition-by-components theory, the simple 3-D shapes that people use in order to recognize visual objects.

gestalt (pronounced "geh-*shtahlt*") In perception and problem solving, an overall quality that transcends the individual elements in the stimulus.

gestalt psychology (pronounced "geh-*shtahlt*") The theoretical approach emphasizing that: (1) humans actively organize what they see; (2) they see patterns; and (3) the whole is greater than the sum of its parts.

gestures Communication using visible movements of any part of the body.

gist In psycholinguistics, the overall meaning of a message.

goal state In problem solving, the situation when the problem is solved.

GPS *See* General Problem Solver (GPS).

graceful degradation In parallel distributed processing, the brain's ability to provide partial memory. Graceful degradation explains why the brain continues to work somewhat accurately, even when an accident, stroke, or dementia has destroyed portions of the cortex.

graded structure In the prototype approach to category representation, a description of the variation between the category's most representative or prototypical members, less prototypical members, and nonprototypical members.

grammar In psycholinguistics, a term encompassing both morphology and syntax. The psycholinguistic study of grammar examines both word structure and sentence structure.

ground In gestalt psychology, when two areas share a common boundary, the area that is seen as being behind the figure, forming the background.

growth mindset The belief that people can cultivate intelligence and other skills by challenging themselves to perform better.

heuristic (pronounced "hyoo-*riss*-tick") A general rule or problem-solving strategy that usually produces a correct solution; however, it can sometimes lead to cognitive errors.

hierarchical tree diagram A figure that uses a tree-like structure to show various possible options in a problem. This kind of diagram is especially helpful in showing the relationship between categorized items.

hierarchy   A memory strategy in which the learner arranges items in a series of classes, from the most general classes to the most specific.

hill-climbing heuristic   In problem solving, consistently choosing—at each choice point—the alternative that seems to lead most directly toward the goal.

hindsight   In decision making, people's judgments about events that already happened in the past.

hindsight bias   In decision making, the belief, after an event has already happened, that the event had been inevitable and was predicted all along.

hippocampus   A structure located underneath the cortex that is important in many learning and memory tasks.

holistic   A term describing the recognition of faces and other selected stimuli, based on their overall shape and structure, or gestalt.

IAT   *See* Implicit Association Test (IAT).

iconic memory   Sensory memory for visual information. Iconic memory preserves an image of a visual stimulus for a brief period after the stimulus has disappeared.

illusory conjunction   An inappropriate combination of features (e.g., combining one object's shape with a nearby object's color). An illusory conjunction is formed when the visual system is overwhelmed by too many simultaneous tasks.

illusory contours   The perception of edges in a visual stimulus, even though edges are not physically present. Also known as *subjective contours*.

illusory correlation   In decision making, a person's belief that two variables are statistically related, even though there is no actual evidence for this relationship.

imagery   *See* mental imagery.

imagery debate   An important controversy: Do mental images resemble perception (using an analog code), or do they resemble language (using a propositional code)?

Implicit Association Test (IAT)   A research tool based on the principle that people can mentally pair two related words together much more easily than they can pair two unrelated words. The IAT is useful in assessing stereotypes, such as stereotypes about gender.

implicit memory task   An indirect measure of memory. Participants see the material (usually a series of words

or pictures). Later, during the test phase, they are instructed to complete a cognitive task that does not directly ask for either recall or recognition. Previous experience with the material facilitates performance on the later task.

inattentional blindness   The failure to notice an unexpected but completely visible object that suddenly appears while attention is focused on some other events in a scene. Inattentional blindness results from the overuse of top-down processing.

indirect request   In language, using subtle suggestions to resolve an interpersonal problem, rather than stating the request in a straightforward manner.

indirect-access route   During reading, when—as soon as a word is seen—the letters on the page are translated into some form of sound, before the word and its meaning can be accessed.

individual differences   Systematic variation in the way that groups of people perform on the same cognitive task.

inference   In connection with schemas (Chapter 8), an *inference* refers to the logical interpretations or conclusions that go beyond the original material. In connection with reading (Chapter 9), an *inference* refers to the use of world knowledge in order to create information that is not explicitly stated in a written passage.

information-processing approach   A theory of cognition proposing that (1) mental processes are similar to the operations of a computer and (2) information progresses through the cognitive system in a series of stages, one step at a time.

initial state   In problem solving, the situation at the beginning of a problem.

insight problem   The problem-solving situation in which a problem initially seems impossible to solve, but then an alternative approach suddenly bursts into consciousness. The problem solver immediately realizes that the new solution is correct.

interpreting   The process of converting a spoken message in one language into a second spoken (or signed) language. In contrast, *translation* refers to the process of converting a text written in one language into a second written language.

intrinsic motivation   The motivation to work on a task for its own sake, because it is interesting, exciting, or personally challenging.

introspection   An early approach to studying mental activity, in which carefully trained observers systematically analyzed their own sensations and reported them as objectively as possible, under standardized conditions.

ironic effects of mental control The observation that people's efforts often backfire when they attempt to control the contents of consciousness; as a result, people are even more likely to think about the topic that they are trying to avoid.

isolated-feature/combined-feature effect In visual-search studies, the finding that people can typically locate an isolated feature (e.g., an X) more quickly than a combined feature (e.g., a blue X).

keyword method A memory technique for learning vocabulary words or people's names. The learner identifies an actual word (the keyword) that sounds similar to the new word. Then she or he creates an image that links the keyword with the meaning of this new word.

landmark effect In cognitive maps, people tend to provide shorter distance estimates when traveling to a landmark—an important geographical location—rather than a nonlandmark.

language-localizer task A relatively new neuroscience technique that compensates for the problem of individual differences in the anatomical structure of the language-related regions of the brain. Researchers gather fMRI data while a person performs several relatively complex language tasks, and then use this information to create a "linguistic map" that applies only to this specific person.

latent semantic analysis (LSA) A computer program that can perform many fairly sophisticated language tasks, such as evaluating creative writing or analyzing a person's self-descriptions.

lateralization The proposal that each hemisphere of the brain has somewhat different functions.

levels of processing The observation that recall is generally more accurate when people process information at a deep, meaningful level, rather than a shallow, sensory kind of processing.

levels-of-processing approach A theory of memory proposing that deep, meaningful processing of information leads to more accurate recall than shallow, sensory kinds of processing.

life script A list of events that a person believes would be most important throughout his or her lifetime.

lifespan approach to development The view that developmental changes continue beyond young adulthood; people continue to change and adapt throughout their entire lives.

linearization problem In language production, the difficulty of arranging words in an ordered, linear sequence.

long-term memory The large-capacity memory for experiences and information accumulated throughout one's lifetime. Atkinson and Shiffrin proposed that information stored in long-term memory is relatively permanent and not likely to be lost.

LSA *See* latent semantic analysis (LSA).

major depression A psychological disorder characterized by feeling sad, discouraged, and hopeless; fatigue and lack of interest in leisure activities are also common. This disorder can interfere with the ability to perform daily cognitive and physical tasks.

massed learning When learning new material, the situation in which the learner practices the material all at the same time, by "cramming"; this learning strategy is less effective than *spaced learning*.

matrix In problem solving, a grid consisting of rows and columns that shows all possible combinations of the items in the problem.

maximizers In decision making, people who tend to examine as many options as possible, rather than settling for something that is satisfactory.

maximizing decision-making style The tendency to examine as many options as possible—when making a decision—to make the best possible choice, instead of settling for something that is merely satisfactory.

McGurk effect The observation that visual information influences speech perception; listeners integrate both visual and auditory information when perceiving speech.

means-ends heuristic An approach to problem solving that consists of two important components: (1) dividing the problem into a number of subproblems, and (2) reducing the difference between the initial state and the goal state for each of the subproblems. The name *means-ends heuristic* is appropriate because it requires identifying the "ends" desired and then figuring out the "means" or methods to reach those ends.

memory The process of maintaining information over time.

memory integration Using background knowledge to incorporate new information into memory in a schema-consistent manner.

memory self-efficacy A person's belief in his or her own potential to perform well on memory tasks.

memory strategy Intentional, goal-oriented mental activities that a person performs, in order to improve encoding and retrieval of information in memory.

mental imagery The mental representation of stimuli when those stimuli are not physically present. Sensory receptors do not receive any input when a mental image is created.

mental set In problem solving, applying the same solution used in previous problems, even though there is a different, easier way to solve the problem.

meta-analysis A statistical method for combining numerous studies on a single topic. A meta-analysis computes a statistical index (known as effect size, or *d*) that tells us whether a particular variable has a statistically significant effect, when combining all the studies.

metacognition Knowledge and control of cognitive processes; metacognition helps to supervise the way one selects and uses memory strategies. The general term, *metacognition*, includes metamemory, metacomprehension, and metalinguistics. It is also related to both the tip-of-the-tongue phenomenon and the feeling of knowing.

metacomprehension A kind of metacognition, referring to a person's thoughts, which specifically focus on language comprehension. Most research about metacomprehension focuses on reading comprehension, rather than on the comprehension of spoken language or on other kinds of knowledge about language.

metalinguistics Knowledge about the form and structure of language, as opposed to knowledge about language comprehension. On many measures of metalinguistic skill—but not all of them—bilinguals outperform monolinguals.

metamemory A kind of metacognition that refers to one's knowledge, monitoring, and control of memory.

mind wandering A situation that occurs when a person's thoughts shift away from the external environment, and the person begins thinking about another topic.

mindless reading A situation that occurs when your eyes may move forward, but you do not process the meaning of the material being read.

mirror system A network of neurons in the brain's motor cortex. These neurons can be activated when a person watches someone else perform an action.

mnemonics Mental strategies designed to improve memory.

modular In theories of language, the proposal that people have a set of specific language skills that are separate from other cognitive processes, such as memory and decision making.

mood A general, long-lasting experience, in contrast to an emotion, which is a reaction to a specific stimulus.

mood congruence The observation that material is recalled more accurately if it is congruent with a person's current mood.

morpheme (pronounced "*more*-feem") The basic unit of meaning in language. For example, the word *reactivated* actually contains four morphemes: *re-*, *active*, *-ate*, and *-ed*. Each of those segments conveys meaning.

morphology The study of morphemes; morphology examines how words are created by combining morphemes.

motherese A term that linguists previously used for *child-directed speech*.

multilingual speaker Someone who uses more than two languages; psycholinguists often use the term *bilingual* to include multilinguals as well.

multitask An attempt to accomplish two or more tasks at the same time. However, the research shows that people frequently work more slowly or make more mistakes when they try to multitask.

my-side bias In decision making, people are overconfident that their own view is correct in a confrontational situation.

narrative In language, a category of discourse in which someone describes a series of actual or fictional events.

narrative technique In memory, making up stories that link a series of words together, in order to enhance memory.

nested structure In language, when one phrase is embedded within another phrase. People often experience a memory overload when they try to read a sentence that has a nested structure.

network models Proposals that semantic memory consists of a netlike organization of concepts in memory, with numerous interconnections.

neural-network approach A theory describing cognitive processing in terms of networks that link together neuron-like units. These networks perform operations simultaneously and in parallel, rather than one step at a time. Also known as the *parallel distributed processing approach* (abbreviated *PDP*) and the *connectionist approach*.

neurolinguistics The discipline that examines how the brain processes language.

90-degree-angle heuristic In cognitive maps, when angles in a mental map are represented as being closer to 90 degrees than they really are.

node In network models, the representation of each concept, or one unit located within the network. When people see or hear the name of a concept, the node representing that concept is activated. The activation expands or spreads from that node to other connected nodes, a process called *spreading activation*.

noninsight problem A problem that a person solves gradually, by using memory, reasoning skills, and a routine set of strategies.

object recognition The process of identifying a complex arrangement of sensory stimuli and perceiving that this pattern is separate from its background.

obstacles In problem solving, the restrictions that make it difficult to proceed from the initial state to the goal state.

operational definition In psychology research, a precise definition that specifies exactly how researchers will measure a concept.

organization A mnemonic strategy in which a person applies a systematic order to the material that must be learned.

orienting attention network A system responsible for the kind of attention required for visual search, in which a person must shift her or his attention around to various spatial locations.

other-ethnicity effect *See* own-ethnicity bias.

overconfidence When a person's confidence judgments are higher than they should be, based on actual performance on the task.

overextension In children's language, the use of a word to refer to other objects, in addition to objects that adults would consider appropriate.

overregularization In language learning, the tendency to add the most customary grammatical morphemes to create new forms of irregular words.

own-ethnicity bias The observation that people are generally more accurate in identifying members of their own ethnic group than members of another ethnic group; also known as *own-race bias*, the *other-ethnicity effect*, or the *cross-ethnicity effect*.

parallel distributed processing approach (PDP) A theory describing cognitive processing in terms of networks that link together neuron-like units. These networks perform operations simultaneously and in parallel, rather than one step at a time. Also known as the *connectionist approach* and the *neural-network approach*.

parallel processing A type of cognitive processing in which a person performs many operations simultaneously, in contrast to *serial processing*.

pattern recognition The process of identifying a complex arrangement of sensory stimuli and perceiving that this pattern is separate from its background.

PDP *See* parallel distributed processing approach (PDP).

perception The use of previous knowledge to gather and interpret stimuli registered by the senses. Perception requires both bottom-up and top-down processing.

perceptual span In reading, the number of letters and spaces perceived during a fixation.

perseverance The ability to keep working on a task, even when obstacles are encountered.

PET scan *See* positron emission tomography (PET scan).

phobic disorder An anxiety disorder characterized by excessive fear of a specific object.

phoneme (pronounced "*foe*-neem") The basic unit of spoken language, such as the sounds *a*, *k*, and *th*. The English language has about 40 phonemes.

phonemic restoration In speech perception, filling in a missing phoneme based on contextual meaning.

phonetic module A theoretical, special-purpose neural mechanism that specifically handles all aspects of speech perception, but not other kinds of auditory perception. Also known as the *speech module*.

phonics approach The proposal that readers recognize words by trying to pronounce ("sounding out") the individual letters in the word.

phonological loop The part of working memory that processes a limited number of sounds for a short period of time. The phonological loop processes language and other sounds that a person hears, as well as the sounds that they make. It is also active when he or she silently sounds out a word during reading.

phonology The sounds of a person's speech. People who acquire a second language during childhood are more likely to pronounce words like a native speaker of that language, compared to people who attempt to learn that language later in life.

pitch   A characteristic of a sound stimulus that can be arranged on a scale from low to high.

planning fallacy   The tendency (1) to underestimate the amount of time (or money) required to complete a project and (2) to estimate that the task will be relatively easy to complete.

Pollyanna Principle   In memory and other cognitive processes, the principle that people usually process pleasant items more efficiently and more accurately than less pleasant items.

positivity effect   A phenomenon showing that people tend to rate previous negative events more positively with the passage of time.

positron emission tomography (PET scan)   A procedure for measuring blood flow in the brain by injecting the participant with a radioactive chemical, just before this person performs a cognitive task. A special camera makes an image of this accumulated radioactive chemical in the regions of the brain active during the task.

post-event misinformation effect   In eyewitness testimony, when people first view an event and then are given misleading information about the event. Later on, they mistakenly recall the misleading information, rather than the event they actually saw.

post-traumatic stress disorder   An anxiety disorder characterized by repeated re-experiencing of an extremely traumatic event.

pragmatic view of memory   The proposal (developed by Murphy and Shapiro) that people pay attention to the aspect of a message that is most relevant to their current goals. For example, knowing when only the gist of a sentence is important and when to pay attention to the specific wording.

pragmatics   In language, the social rules and world knowledge that allow speakers to successfully communicate messages to other people.

prewriting   Beginning a formal writing project by generating a list of ideas. Prewriting is difficult and strategic—much different from many relatively automatic language tasks.

primacy effect   A tendency for items at the beginning of a list to be recalled better than items in the middle of a list, at least partly because people rehearse these early items more frequently.

primary visual cortex   The portion of the cerebral cortex located in the occipital lobe of the brain that is concerned with basic processing of visual stimuli. It is also the first place where information from the two eyes is combined.

proactive interference   Difficulty learning or recalling new material because some previously learned material continues to interfere with the formation of new memories.

problem isomorphs   In problem solving, a set of problems that have the same underlying structures and solutions but different specific details.

problem representation   In problem solving, the process of translating the elements of a problem into a different format. Choosing an appropriate representation will increase the likelihood of solving the problem effectively.

problem solving   The processes that a person uses to reach a specified goal for which the solution is not immediately obvious. Either important information is missing and/or it is unclear how to reach the goal.

procedural memory   A person's knowledge about how to do something.

proposition   In John Anderson's ACT-R model, a *proposition* is the smallest unit of knowledge that people can judge to be either true or false.

proposition   In deductive reasoning, propositions are the statements that are made up of antecedents and consequents.

propositional calculus   In deductive reasoning, a system for categorizing the four kinds of reasoning used in analyzing statements that are made up of antecedents and consequents. When working on a conditional reasoning task, a person can perform two possible actions: (1) affirm part of the sentence, saying that it is true; or (2) deny part of the sentence, saying that it is false.

propositional code   In the imagery debate (Chapter 7), an abstract, language-like representation. This form of storage is neither visual nor spatial, and it does not physically resemble the original stimulus.

propositional network   According to Anderson's ACT-R model, the pattern of interconnected propositions representing a sentence.

propositional reasoning task   *See* conditional reasoning task.

propositions   In deductive reasoning, propositions are the statements that are made up of antecedents and consequents.

prosody   In language, the "melody" of an utterance; its intonation, rhythm, and emphasis.

prosopagnosia (pronounced "pros-o-pag-*no*-zhe-ah") The inability to recognize human faces visually, though other objects may be perceived relatively normally. People with prosopagnosia also have comparable problems in creating visual imagery for faces.

prospect theory In decision making, people's tendencies to think that possible gains are different from possible losses. When dealing with possible gains (for example, *lives saved*), people tend to avoid risks. When dealing with possible losses (for example, *lives lost*), people tend to seek risks.

prospective memory Remembering that one needs to do something in the future, such as buying an item on the way home from classes. In contrast, retrospective memory refers to remembering things that happened in the past.

prototype The item that is the best, most typical example of a category; the ideal representative of a category.

prototype approach In semantic memory, the proposal that people decide whether a particular item belongs to a category, based on a comparison between this item and a prototype. If the item is similar to the prototype, then it will be included within this category.

prototypicality According to the prototype theory of semantic memory, the degree to which a member of a category is representative of its category.

proximal stimulus In perception, the information registered on the sensory receptors—for example, the image on the retina created by a pen on a desk.

psycholinguistics An interdisciplinary field that examines how people use language to communicate ideas.

pure AI *See* pure artificial intelligence.

pure artificial intelligence (pure AI) An approach that designs a computer program to accomplish a cognitive task as efficiently as possible, even if the computer's processes are completely different from the processes used by humans.

reality monitoring The attempt to identify whether an event really occurred, or whether the event was imagined.

recall task In memory research, a task requiring the participants to reproduce items learned earlier.

recency effect A tendency for items at the end of a list to be recalled better than items in the middle of a list.

recognition heuristic A situation in decision making that occurs when someone is trying to decide which of two categories occurs more frequently. If this person recognizes one category, but not the other, then she or he concludes that the recognized category has the higher frequency.

recognition task An explicit memory task that requires participants to identify which items on a list had been presented at an earlier time.

recognition-by-components theory In visual perception, a theory proposing that people can recognize three-dimensional shapes, in terms of an arrangement of simple 3-D shapes called geons. Geons can be combined to form meaningful objects.

recovered-memory perspective The proposal that some individuals who experienced sexual abuse during childhood managed to forget that memory for many years. At a later time, this presumably forgotten memory may come flooding back into consciousness. This perspective is contrasted with the false-memory perspective.

regressions In reading, moving one's eyes backward to words that appear earlier in a sentence.

rehearsal Silently repeating the information to be learned. Rehearsal is not considered to be an effective memory strategy.

release from proactive interference A memory phenomenon in which proactive interference is reduced when a person switches from one category of stimuli, to a new category. (For example, a person may initially see the names of occupations, but then he or she sees the names of fruits.) This release from proactive interference leads to increased recall for the new category.

repetition priming task A memory task in which recent exposure to a word increases the likelihood that a person will think of that particular word, when given a cue that could evoke many different words.

representative In decision making, when a sample looks similar in important characteristics to the population from which it was selected.

representativeness heuristic A general rule in decision making that people use when trying to decide which outcome would be more likely. People who use this heuristic make judgments in terms of the similarity between the sample and the population from which the sample was selected. For instance, people believe that a coin toss of HTTHTH is more likely than a coin toss of HHHTTT.

retina The part of the visual system covering the inside back portion of the eye. The retina contains millions of neurons that register and transmit visual information from the outside world.

retrieval Locating information in memory storage and accessing that information.

retrieval practice Preparing for an exam by trying to recall important concepts from memory. If retrieval is difficult, but successful, learning is enhanced and test performance is improved.

retroactive interference In memory, people often experience difficulty in learning or recalling old material, because some recently learned material interferes with these older memories.

retrograde amnesia Loss of memory for events that occurred prior to brain damage. This deficit is especially severe for events that occurred during the years just before the damage.

retrospective memory Remembering information that was acquired in the past. In contrast, prospective memory applies to remembering a task that needs to be done in the future.

rotation heuristic In cognitive maps, people tend to remember a figure that is slightly tilted as being either more vertical or more horizontal than it really is.

rule-and-memory theory In children's language learning, the proposal that children learn a general rule for past-tense verbs, which specifies that they must add -*ed*; however, they also store in memory the past tenses for many irregular verbs.

ruminative style Worrying continuously about the problems that are wrong in one's life.

saccadic eye movement Small changes in eye position during reading, in order to bring the center of the retina into position over the words currently being read.

satisficers In decision making, people who tend to settle for something that is satisfactory rather than examining numerous options.

satisficing decision-making style The tendency to settle for something that is satisfactory, rather than examining numerous options.

schema Generalized, well-integrated knowledge about a situation, an event, or a person. Schemas allow people to predict what will happen in a new situation. These predictions are generally correct.

schema therapy When a clinician and client work together in order to explore the client's core beliefs, and they also create appropriate new, more helpful strategies.

schizophrenia A serious psychological disorder characterized by lack of emotional expression, as well as hallucinations, disordered thinking, and poor performance on many cognitive tasks.

script A simple, well-structured sequence of events in a specified order. Scripts are usually associated with a highly familiar activity.

second language In linguistics, the second language that a person learned; this term is typically applied to someone who first learned a different language. *See* sequential bilingualism.

selective-attention task A situation in which people are instructed to pay attention to certain kinds of information, while ignoring other ongoing information.

self-efficacy The belief that one has the ability to organize and carry out a specific task.

self-instruction Subvocal reminders about something that needs to be done. This process involves the phonological loop.

self-knowledge The information that people believe about themselves, including factual information, as well as knowledge of one's own social behavior, personality, and attitudes.

self-reference effect The enhancement of long-term memory by relating the material to oneself.

semantic memory A person's organized knowledge about the world, including knowledge about words and other factual information.

semantic priming effect The observation that people respond faster to an item if it was preceded by an item with similar meaning.

semantics The area of psycholinguistics that examines the meanings of words and sentences.

sensory memory The large-capacity storage system that records information from each of the senses with reasonable accuracy.

sequential bilingualism In linguistics, a term referring to people who speak two or more languages, but did not learn them at the same time. Their native language is referred to as their *first language*, and the non-native language that they acquire is their *second language*.

serial processing A type of cognitive processing in which a person performs operations one item at a time, rather than simultaneously, in contrast to *parallel processing*.

serial-position effect The U-shaped relationship between a word's position in a list and its probability of recall. Recall is especially accurate for the initial words and the final words in a list, and recall is least accurate for the words in the middle of the list.

shadow In attention research, a task in which participants can hear two messages; however, they are instructed to listen to only one message and then repeat it after the speaker.

short-term memory The part of memory that holds only the small amount of information that a person is actively using. The more current term for this type of memory is *working memory*.

short-term visual memory *See* visuospatial sketchpad.

simultaneous bilingualism In linguistics, a term referring to people who learned two languages at the same time during childhood.

situated cognition approach The proposal that a person makes use of information in the immediate environment or situation; thus, knowledge typically depends on the context surrounding the person.

slips-of-the-tongue Errors during speaking, in which sounds or entire words are rearranged between two or more different words. Slips-of-the-tongue are informative because they reveal people's extensive knowledge about the sounds, structure, and meaning of the language that they are speaking.

small-sample fallacy In decision making, the assumption that a small sample will be representative of the population from which it is selected. This assumption often leads to incorrect decisions.

social cognition approach The view that stereotypes and many other components of social psychology can be traced to normal cognitive processes.

social cognitive neuroscience A new discipline that uses neuroscience techniques to explore the kind of cognitive processes used in interactions with other people.

social phobia An anxiety disorder characterized by extreme anxiety in social situations.

source monitoring The process of trying to identify the origin of a particular memory.

spaced learning When learning new material, the situation in which the learner distributes her or his practice over time; this learning strategy is more effective than *massed learning*.

spatial cognition The mental processes involved in (1) thoughts about cognitive maps, (2) memory for the world that we navigate, and (3) keeping track of objects in a spatial array.

spatial framework model The proposal that the above–below spatial dimension is especially important in spatial imagery, the front–back dimension is moderately important, and the right–left dimension is least important.

special mechanism approach In psycholinguistics, the theory that humans are born with a specialized device that allows them to decode speech stimuli. As a result, speech sounds are processed more quickly and more accurately than other auditory stimuli, such as instrumental music.

speech module A hypothetical, special-purpose neural mechanism that specifically handles all aspects of speech perception, but not other kinds of auditory perception. Also known as the *phonetic module*.

speech perception The process by which the auditory system records sound vibrations that are generated by someone talking. The auditory system then translates these vibrations into a sequence of sounds that are perceived as speech.

speech-is-special approach *See* special mechanism approach.

spontaneous generalization In the parallel distributed processing approach, when information is missing, people use individual cases to draw inferences about general information.

spreading activation In network models of semantic memory, the process by which nodes excite nearby or related nodes.

STEM disciplines The fields of Science, Technology, Engineering, and Mathematics; spatial ability is especially important in these disciplines.

stereotype threat In social cognitive theory, people may be hampered by a negative stereotype about belonging to a group that is perceived as being less competent in a specific area. This theory proposes that, when these individuals are reminded of their membership in this group, their performance may suffer.

Stroop effect The observation that people take a long time to name an ink color that has been used in printing an incongruent word (for example, if blue ink is used in printing the word *red*), even though they can quickly name that same ink color when it appears as a solid patch.

structural features In problem solving, the underlying core of a problem that must be understood in order to solve the problem correctly. Often contrasted with the *surface features* of a problem.

subjective contours The perception of edges in a visual stimulus, even though edges are not physically present. Also known as *illusory contours*.

subordinate-level categories In the prototype approach to semantic memory, lower-level or more specific categories; "desk chair," "collie," and "Phillips screwdriver" are examples of subordinate-level categories.

subproblems In problem solving, a complex problem may be difficult to solve. One strategy is to divide that problem into two or more smaller problems and solve each of these subproblems separately.

subvocalization Silently pronouncing words during reading.

superordinate-level categories In the prototype approach to semantic memory, higher-level or more general categories; "furniture," "animal," and "tool" are all examples of superordinate-level categories.

surface features In problem solving, the specific objects and terms used in the question. These elements are often not relevant to the underlying core of the problem, known as the *structural features*.

surface structure In psycholinguistics, the representation of a sentence based on the words that are actually spoken or written, in contrast to *deep structure*.

syllogism A common deductive reasoning task consisting of two statements that one must assume to be true, plus a conclusion. Syllogisms refer to quantities, so they use the words *all, none, some,* and other similar terms.

symmetry heuristic In cognitive maps, people tend to remember figures as being more symmetrical and regular than they truly are.

syntax The grammatical rules that govern how words can be combined into sentences.

templates According to an early theory of visual object recognition, the specific perceptual patterns stored in memory.

testing effect The observation that the act of taking a test is actually an excellent way to boost long-term recall for academic material.

the good-enough approach In language comprehension, the observation that people frequently process only part of a sentence.

Theme 1: *The cognitive processes are active, rather than passive.*

Theme 2: *The cognitive processes are remarkably efficient and accurate.*

Theme 3: *The cognitive processes handle positive information better than negative information.*

Theme 4: *The cognitive processes are interrelated with one another; they do not operate in isolation.*

Theme 5: *Many cognitive processes rely on both bottom-up and top-down processing.*

theory of mind A specific kind of metacognition, which refers to your ideas about how your own mind works, as well as how other people's minds work.

thinking In problem solving and decision making, going beyond the information given to reach a goal such as a solution, a decision, or a belief.

thought suppression The attempt, usually unsuccessful, to push an undesirable idea out of consciousness.

timbre (pronounced "*tam*-ber") The sound quality of a tone. Different musical instruments playing the same note differ in their timbre.

tip-of-the-finger effect In the Deaf Community, the subjective experience of knowing a target sign, but not being able to produce that sign because it is temporarily inaccessible.

tip-of-the-tongue effect The subjective experience of knowing which word is being sought, but not being able to retrieve the actual word. A person may know the word's first letter and the general sound of the word—even though the word itself refuses to leap into memory. Also known as the *tip-of-the-tongue phenomenon*.

tip-of-the-tongue phenomenon *See* tip-of-the-tongue effect.

TMS *See* Transcranial Magnetic Stimulation.

top-down processing The kind of cognitive processing that emphasizes the importance of concepts, expectations, and memory in object recognition and other cognitive tasks.

total-time hypothesis The concept that the amount of information you learn depends on the total time devoted to learning. This hypothesis is generally true, although the quality of study strategies used during the time is also important.

Transcranial Magnetic Stimulation (TMS) A non-surgical neuroscience technique that uses a magnetic field to briefly stimulate a specific location on the cortex. This stimulation interferes—very briefly—with information processing, but it does not harm the brain.

transformational rules According to Noam Chomsky, the processes used to convert deep structure (the basic idea in a sentence) into a surface structure (a spoken or written sentence).

translation The process of converting a text written in one language into a second written language. In contrast, *interpreting* refers to the process of converting a spoken message in one language into a second spoken (or signed) language.

Type 1 processing According to dual-process theory in reasoning and decision making, Type 1 processing is relatively fast and automatic. It also requires little conscious attention, and performance is typically less accurate than Type 2 processing on the same task.

Type 2 processing According to dual-process theory in reasoning and decision making, Type 2 processing is relatively slow and controlled. It also requires focused attention, and performance is typically more accurate than Type 1 processing on that same task.

typicality effect In the prototype theory of semantic memory, the observation that people judge typical items (prototypes) faster than items that are not typical (nonprototypes).

understanding In problem solving, having a well-organized mental representation of the problem, based on both the information provided in the problem and one's own previous experience.

unilateral spatial neglect A perceptual condition, resulting from brain damage to the parietal region, in which a person ignores part of his or her visual field.

utilization deficiency The problem of not using memory strategies effectively; common in young children.

validity A test's ability to predict a person's performance in another situation.

verbatim memory Word-for-word recall of material presented at an earlier time; the research shows that people usually have poor verbatim memory.

viewer-centered approach A modification of the recognition-by-components theory of object recognition. The viewer-centered approach proposes that people store a small number of views of a three-dimensional object, rather than just one view.

visual imagery The mental representation of visual stimuli.

visual search A task requiring the observer to find a target in a visual display that has numerous distractors.

visual sensory memory *See* iconic memory.

visuospatial sketchpad The component of working memory that processes both visual and spatial information. The visuospatial sketchpad has also been known as visuospatial working memory and short-term visual memory.

visuospatial working memory *See* visuospatial sketchpad.

Wernicke's aphasia (pronounced either "*Ver*-nih-kees" or "*Wer*-nih-kees") Severe problems with language comprehension (e.g., understanding instructions), caused by damage to Wernicke's area. Many people with Wernicke's aphasia also have problems with language production.

Wernicke's area (pronounced either "*Ver*-nih-kees" or "*Wer*-nih-kees") An area toward the back of the brain that is especially important in language comprehension.

whole-language approach The idea that, in order to increase children's enthusiasm about learning to read, reading instruction should emphasize meaning, and it should also be enjoyable.

whole-word approach The proposal that readers can directly connect the written word—as an entire unit—with the meaning that this word represents.

word superiority effect In visual perception, the observation that a single letter is more accurately and rapidly recognized when it appears in a meaningful word, rather than when it appears alone or in a meaningless string of unrelated letters.

working memory The brief, immediate memory for the limited amount of material that a person is currently processing. Part of working memory also actively coordinates ongoing mental activities. In the current research, the term *working memory* is more popular than a similar but older term, *short-term memory*.

working-memory approach Baddeley's model of immediate memory, which proposed a system with several components that temporarily hold and manipulate information while cognitive tasks are performed.

References

Abelson, R. P. (1981). Psychological status of the script concept. *American Psychologist, 36,* 715–729.

Acheson, D. J., & M. C. MacDonald (2009). Verbal working memory and language production: Common approaches to the serial ordering of verbal information. *Psychological Bulletin, 135,* 50–68.

Adler, J., & Hall, C. (1995, June 5). Surgery at 33,000 feet. *Newsweek,* p. 36.

Adler, T. (1991, July). Memory researcher wins Troland award. *APA Monitor,* pp. 12–13.

Ainsworth, W., & Greenberg, S. (2006). Auditory processing of speech. In S. Greenberg & W. A. Ainsworth (Eds.), *Listening to speech: An auditory perspective* (pp. 3–17). Mahwah, NJ: Erlbaum.

Aizpurua, A., Garcia-Bajos, E., & Migueles, M. (2009). False memories for a robbery in young and older adults. *Applied Cognitive Psychology, 23,* 341–363.

Akhtar, N., Jipson, J., & Callanan, M. A. (2001). Learning words through overhearing. *Child Development, 72,* 416–430.

Alibali, M. W., Spencer, R. C., Knox, L., & Kita, S. (2011). Spontaneous gestures influence strategy choices in problem solving. *Psychological Science, 22,* 1138–1144.

Allen, G. L. (2004). Preface: Routes of human spatial memory research. In G. L. Allen (Ed.), *Human spatial memory: Remembering where* (pp. xiii–xx). Mahwah, NJ: Erlbaum.

Alloway, T. P. (2011). *Improving working memory: Supporting students' learning.* Los Angeles: Sage.

Alloway, T. P., et al. (2005). Working memory and phonological awareness as predictors of progress towards early learning goals at school entry. *British Journal of Developmental Psychology, 23,* 417–426.

Almeida, J., Mahon, B. Z., & Caramazza, A. (2010). The role of the dorsal visual processing stream in tool identification. *Psychological Science, 21,* 772–778.

Alter, J. (2000, July 3). A reckoning on death row. *Newsweek,* p. 31.

Alvarez, G. A., & Cavanaugh, P. (2004). The capacity of visual short-term memory is set both by visual information load and by number of objects. *Psychological Science, 15,* 106–111.

Amabile, T. M. (1996). *Creativity in context: Update to the social psychology of creativity.* Boulder, CO: Westview.

Amabile, T. M. (1997). Motivating creativity in organizations: On doing what you love and loving what you do. *California Management Review, 40,* 39–58.

Ambady, N., Shih, M., Kim, A., & Pittinsky, T. L. (2001). Stereotype susceptibility in children: Effects of identity activation on quantitative performance. *Psychological Science, 12,* 385–390.

Ambady, N., & Weisbuch, M. (2010). Nonverbal behavior. In S. T. Fiske, D. T. Gilbert, & G. Lindzey (Eds.), *Handbook of social psychology* (5th ed., Vol. 1, pp. 464–497). Hoboken, NJ: Wiley.

American Psychiatric Association. (2000). *Diagnostic and statistical manual of mental disorders* (4th ed., text revision). Washington, DC: Author.

American Psychological Association. (2010). *Publication manual of the American Psychological Association* (6th ed.). Washington, DC: Author.

Amir, N., & Selvig, A. (2005). Implicit memory tasks in clinical research. In A. Wenzel & D. C. Rubin (Eds.), *Cognitive methods and their application to clinical research* (pp. 153–171). Washington, DC: American Psychological Association.

Anastasi, J. S., & Rhodes, M. G. (2003). Evidence for an own-age bias in face recognition. *North American Journal of Psychology, 8,* 237–252.

Anderson, J. R. (1990). *The adaptive character of thought.* Hillsdale, NJ: Erlbaum

Anderson, J. R. (2000). *Learning and memory: An integrated approach* (2nd ed.). New York: Wiley.

Anderson, J. R. (2009). *Cognitive psychology and its implications* (7th ed.). New York: Worth.

Anderson, J. R., Corbett, A. T., Koedinger, K. R., & Pelletier, R. (1995). Cognitive tutors: Lessons learned. *The Journal of Learning Science, 4,* 167–207.

Anderson, J. R., Douglass, S., & Qin, Y. (2005). How should a theory of learning and cognition inform instruction? In A. F. Healy (Ed.), *Experimental cognitive psychology and its applications* (pp. 47–59). Washington, DC: American Psychological Association.

Anderson, J. R., Fincham, J. M., Qin, Y., & Stocco, A. (2008). A central circuit of the mind. *Trends in Cognitive Science, 12,* 136–143.

Anderson, J. R., & Gluck, K. A. (2001). What role do cognitive architectures play in intelligent tutoring systems? In S. M. Carver & D. Klahr (Eds.),

Cognition and instruction: Twenty-five years of progress (pp. 227–261). Mahwah, NJ: Erlbaum.

Anderson, J. R., & Schooler, L. J. (2000). The adaptive nature of memory. In E. Tulving & F. I. M. Craik (Eds.), *The Oxford handbook of memory* (pp. 557–581). New York: Oxford University Press.

Anderson, J. R., & Schunn, C. D. (2000). Implications of the ACT-R learning theory: No magic bullets. In R. Glaser (Ed.), *Advances in instructional psychology* (Vol. 5, pp. 1–33). Mahwah, NJ: Erlbaum.

Anderson, J. R., et al. (2004). An integrated theory of mind. *Psychological Review, 111*, 1036–1060.

Anderson, R. E. (1998). Imagery and spatial representation. In W. Bechtel & G. Graham (Eds.), *A companion to cognitive science* (pp. 204–211). Malden, MA: Blackwell.

Ariel, R., & Dunlosky, J. (2011). The sensitivity of judgment-of-learning resolution to past test performance, new learning, and forgetting. *Memory & Cognition, 39*, 171–184.

Arvidsson, D., Sikström S., & Werbart, A. (2011). Changes in self and object representations following psychotherapy measured by a theory-free, computational, semantic space method. *Psychotherapy Research, 21*, 430–446.

Ashby, F. G., Prinzmetal, W., Ivry, R., & Maddox, W. T. (1996). A formal theory of feature binding in object perception. *Psychological Review, 103*, 165–192.

Atkinson, D., & Connor, U. (2008). Multilingual writing development. In C. Bazerman (Ed.), *Handbook of research on writing: History, society, school, individual, text* (pp. 515–532). Mahwah, NJ: Erlbaum.

Atkinson, R. C., & Shiffrin, R. M. (1968). Human memory: A proposed system and its control processes. In K. W. Spence & J. T. Spence (Eds.), *The psychology of learning and motivation: Advances in research and theory* (Vol. 2, pp. 89–105). New York: Academic Press.

Awh, E., et al. (1999). Rehearsal in spatial working memory: Evidence from neuroimaging. *Psychological Science, 10*, 433–437.

Bäckman, L., Small, B. J., & Wahlin, A. (2001). Aging and memory: Cognitive and biological perspectives. In J. E. Birren & K. W. Schaie (Eds.), *Handbook of the psychology of aging* (5th ed., pp. 349–377). San Diego: Academic Press.

Bacon, E. (2010). Further insight into cognitive and metacognitive processes of the tip-of-the-tongue state with an amnesic drug as cognitive tool. In A. Efklides

& Misailidi (Eds.), *Trends and prospects in metacognition research* (pp. 81–104). New York: Springer.

Baddeley, A. D. (1986). *Working memory*. Oxford, UK: Clarendon.

Baddeley, A. D. (1994). The magical number seven: Still magic after all these years? *Psychological Review, 101*, 353–356.

Baddeley, A. D. (1997). *Human memory: Theory and practice* (Rev. ed.). East Sussex, UK: Psychology Press.

Baddeley, A. D. (1999). *Essentials of human memory*. East Sussex, UK: Psychology Press.

Baddeley, A. D. (2000a). Short-term and working memory. In E. Tulving & F. I. M. Craik (Eds.), *The Oxford handbook of memory* (pp. 77–92). New York: Oxford University Press.

Baddeley, A. D. (2000b). The episodic buffer: A new component of working memory? *Trends in Cognitive Sciences, 4*, 417–423.

Baddeley, A. D. (2001). Is working memory still working? *American Psychologist, 56*, 849–864.

Baddeley, A. D. (2003). Working memory and language: An overview. *Journal of Communication Disorders, 36*, 189–208.

Baddeley, A. D. (2004). Memory and context. In R. L. Gregory (Ed.), *The Oxford companion to the mind* (2nd ed., pp. 571–572). New York: Oxford University Press.

Baddeley, A. D. (2006). Working memory: An overview. In S. J. Pickering (Ed.), *Working memory and education* (pp. 3–31). Burlington, MA: Elsevier.

Baddeley, A. D. (2007). *Working memory, thought, and action*. Oxford, UK: Oxford University Press.

Baddeley, A. D. (2012). Working memory: Theories, models, and controversies. *Annual Review of Psychology, 63*, 1–29.

Baddeley, A. D., Allen, R., & Hitch, G. J. (2011). Binding in visual working memory: The role of the episodic buffer. *Neuropsychologia, 49*, 1393–1400.

Baddeley, A. D., Allen, R., & Vargha-Khadem, F. (2010). Is the hippocampus necessary for visual and verbal binding in working memory? *Neuropsychologia, 48*, 1089–1095.

Baddeley, A. D., & Andrade, J. (1998). Working memory and consciousness: An empirical approach. In M. A. Conway, S. E. Gathercole, & C. Cornoldi (Eds.), *Theories of memory II* (pp. 1–24). Hove, UK: Psychology Press.

Baddeley, A., Eysenck, M. W., & Anderson, M. C. (2009). *Memory*. New York: Psychology Press.

Baddeley, A. D., Grant, S., Wight, E., & Thomson, N. (1973). Imagery and visual working memory. In P. M. A. Rabbitt & S. Dornic (Eds.), *Attention and performance V* (pp. 205–217). London: Academic Press.

Baddeley, A. D., & Hitch, G. J. (1974). Working memory. In G. Bower (Ed.), *Recent advances in learning and memory* (Vol. 8, pp. 47–90). New York: Academic Press.

Bahrick, H. P. (2005). The long-term neglect of long-term memory: Reasons and remedies. In A. F. Healy (Ed.), *Experimental cognitive psychology and its applications* (pp. 89–100). Washington, DC: American Psychological Association.

Bahrick, H. P., & Hall, L. K. (2005). The importance of retrieval failures to long-term retention: A metacognitive explanation of the spacing effect. *Journal of Memory and Language, 52,* 566–577.

Bahrick, H. P., et al. (1994). Fifty years of language maintenance and language dominance in bilingual Hispanic immigrants. *Journal of Experimental Psychology: General, 123,* 264–283.

Baker, J. M. C., & Dunlosky, J. (2006). Does momentary accessibility influence metacomprehension judgments? The influence of study-judgment lags on accessibility effects. *Psychonomic Bulletin & Review, 13,* 60–65.

Baker, J. M. C., Dunlosky, J., & Hertzog, C. (2010). How accurately can older adults evaluate the quality of their text recall? The effect of providing standards on judgment accuracy. *Applied Cognitive Psychology, 24,* 134–147.

Baker, K. D. (1999). Personal communication.

Baker, L. (2005). Developmental differences in metacognition: Implications for metacognitively oriented reading instruction. In S. E. Israel, C. C. Block, K. L. Bauserman, & K. Kinnucan-Welsch (Eds.), *Metacognition in literacy learning: Theory, assessment, instruction, and professional development* (pp. 61–79). Mahwah, NJ: Erlbaum.

Balch, W. R. (2006). Introducing psychology students to research methodology: A word-pleasantness experiment. *Teaching of Psychology, 33,* 132–134.

Baldwin, D., & Meyer, M. (2007). How inherently social is language? In E. Hoff & M. Shatz (Eds.), *Blackwell handbook of language development* (pp. 87–106). Malden, MA: Blackwell.

Baldwin, M. W., & Dandeneau, S. D. (2005). Understanding and modifying the relational schemas underlying insecurity. In M. W. Baldwin (Ed.), *Interpersonal cognition* (pp. 33–61). New York: Guilford.

Barash, D. P. (2006, July 14). I am, therefore I think. *Chronicle of Higher Education,* pp. B9–B10.

Bardovi-Harlig, K. (2010). Pragmatics and second language acquisition. In R. B. Kaplan (Ed.), *The Oxford handbook of applied linguistics* (2nd ed., pp. 233–243). New York: Oxford University Press.

Bargh, J., & Ferguson, M. J. (2000). Beyond behaviorism: On the automaticity of higher mental processes. *Psychological Bulletin, 126,* 925–945.

Barkley, R. A. (2006). *Attention deficit hyperactivity disorder: A handbook for diagnosis and treatment* (3rd ed.). New York: Guilford.

Barkley, R. A. (2010). *Taking charge of adult ADHD.* New York: Guilford.

Barnes, J. B. (2004). Aristotle. In R. L. Gregory (Ed.), *The Oxford companion to the mind* (2nd ed., pp. 45–46). New York: Oxford University Press.

Barnett, S. M., & Ceci, S. J. (2002). When and where do we apply what we learn? A taxonomy for far transfer. *Psychological Bulletin, 128,* 612–637.

Barnett, S. M., & Koslowski, B. (2002). Adaptive expertise: Effects of type of experience and the level of theoretical understanding it generates. *Thinking and Reasoning, 8,* 237–267.

Barnhart, A. S., & Goldinger, S. D. (2010). Interpreting chicken-scratch: Lexical access for handwritten words. *Journal of Experimental Psychology: Human Perception and Performance, 36,* 906–923.

Baron, J. (2000). *Thinking and deciding* (3rd ed.). New York: Cambridge University Press.

Barr, D. J., & Keysar, B. (2006). Perspective taking and the coordination of meaning in language use. In M. J. Traxler & M. A. Gernsbacher (Eds.), *Handbook of psycholinguistics* (2nd ed., pp. 901–938). Amsterdam: Elsevier.

Barr, R., Rovee-Collier, C., & Campanella, J. (2005). Retrieval protracts deferred imitation by 6-month-olds. *Infancy, 7,* 263–283.

Barr, R., Rovee-Collier, C., & Learmonth, A. (2011). Potentiation in young infants: The origin of the prior knowledge effect? *Memory & Cognition, 39,* 625–636.

Barrett, H. C., & Kurzban, R. (2006). Modularity in cognition: Framing the debate. *Psychological Review, 113,* 628–647.

Barrett, L. F. (2009). The future of psychology: Connecting mind to brain. *Perspectives on Psychological Science, 4,* 326–339.

Barron, E., Roby, L. M., Greer, J., & Smallwood, J. (2011). Absorbed in thought: The effect of mind wandering on the processing of relevant and irrelevant events. *Psychological Science, 22*, 596–601.

Barsalou, L. W. (1990). On the indistinguishability of exemplar memory and abstraction in category representation. In T. K. Srull & R. S. Wyer (Eds.), *Advances in social cognition* (Vol. 3, pp. 61–88). Hillsdale, NJ: Erlbaum.

Barsalou, L. W. (1992). Frames, concepts, and conceptual fields. In A. Lehrer & E. F. Kittay (Eds.), *Frames, fields, and contrasts* (pp. 21–74). Hillsdale, NJ: Erlbaum.

Barsalou, L. W. (2003). Situated simulation in the human conceptual system. *Language and Cognitive Processes, 18*, 513–562.

Barsalou, L. W. (2009). Situating concepts. In P. Robbins & M. Aydede (Eds.), *The Cambridge handbook of situated cognition* (pp. 236–263). New York: Cambridge University Press.

Barshi, I., & Healy, A. F. (2011). The effects of spatial representation on memory for verbal navigation instructions. *Memory & Cognition, 39*, 47–62.

Bartlett, F. C. (1932). *Remembering: An experimental and social study*. Cambridge, UK: Cambridge University Press.

Bartlett, T. (2011, November 25). "Motivated blindness": One take on what went wrong at Penn State. *Chronicle of Higher Education*, p. A9.

Baruss, I. (2003). *Alterations of consciousness: An empirical analysis for social scientists*. Washington, DC: American Psychological Association.

Bassetti, B., & Cook, V. (2011). Relating language and cognition: The second language user. In V. Cook & B. Bassetti (Eds.), *Language and bilingual cognition* (pp. 143–190). New York: Psychology Press.

Bassok, M. (2003). Analogical transfer in problem solving. In J. E. Davidson & R. J. Sternberg (Eds.), *The psychology of problem solving* (pp. 343–369). New York: Cambridge University Press.

Bassok, M., & Novick, L. R. (2012). Problem solving. In K. J. Holyoak & R. G. Morrison (Eds.), *Oxford handbook of thinking and reasoning* (pp. 413–432). Oxford University Press.

Bates, E., Devescovi, A., & Wulfeck, B. (2001). Psycholinguistics: A cross-language perspective. *Annual Review of Psychology, 52*, 369–396.

Bauer, B., & Jolicoeur, P. (1996). Stimulus dimensionality effects in mental rotation. *Journal of Experimental Psychology: Human Perception and Performance, 22*, 82–94.

Bauer, P. J. (2004). Getting explicit memory off the ground: Steps toward construction of a neuro-developmental account of changes in the first two years of life. *Developmental Review, 24*, 347–373.

Baumeister, R. F., Masicampo, E. J., & Vohs, K. D. (2011). Do conscious thoughts cause behavior? *Annual Review of Psychology, 62*, 331–361.

Bayliss, D. M., Jarrold, C., Baddeley, A. D., & Leigh, E. (2005). Differential constraints on the working memory and reading abilities of individuals with learning difficulties and typically developing children. *Journal of Experimental Child Psychology, 92*, 76–99.

Bazerman, C. (Ed.). (2008). *Handbook of research on writing: History, society, school, individual, text*. Mahwah, NJ: Erlbaum.

Bazerman, M. H., &Tenbrunsel, A. E. (2011). *Blind spots: Why we fail to do what's right and what to do about it*. Princeton: Princeton University Press.

Bearce, K. H., & Rovee-Collier, C. (2006). Repeated priming increases memory accessibility in infants. *Journal of Experimental Child Psychology, 93*, 357–376.

Beauchamp, M. S., Nath, A. R., & Passler, S. (2010). FMRI-guided transcranial magnetic stimulation reveals that the superior temporal sulcus is a cortical locus of the McGurk effect. *Journal of Neuroscience, 30*, 2414–2417.

Beauvais, C., Olive, T., & Passerault, J.-M. (2011). Why are some texts good and others not? Relationship between text quality and management of the writing process. *Journal of Educational Psychology, 103*, 415–428.

Bechtel, W., Abrahamsen, A., & Graham, G. (1998). The life of cognitive science. In W. Bechtel & G. Graham (Eds.), *A companion to cognitive science* (pp. 2–104). Malden, MA: Blackwell.

Beck, J. S. (2011). *Cognitive behavior therapy: Basics and beyond* (2nd ed.). New York: Guilford.

Bediou, B., et al. (2005). Effects of emotion and identity on facial affect processing in schizophrenia. *Psychiatric Research, 133*, 149–157.

Beeman, M., Bowden, E. M., & Gernsbacher, M. A. (2000). Right and left hemisphere cooperation for drawing predictive and coherence inferences during normal story comprehension. *Brain and Language, 71*, 310–336.

Beilock, S. I., & Carr, T. H. (2005). When high-powered people fail: Working memory and "choking under pressure" in math. *Psychological Science, 16*, 101–105.

Bellezza, F. S. (1984). The self as a mnemonic device: The role of internal cues. *Journal of Personality and Social Psychology, 47,* 506–516.

Bellezza, F. S., & Hoyt, S. K. (1992). The self-reference effect and mental cueing. *Social Cognition, 10,* 51–78.

Beni, R. D., Pazzaglia, F., & Gardini, S. (2006). The role of mental rotation and age in spatial perspective-taking tasks: When age does not impair perspective-taking performance. *Applied Cognitive Psychology, 20,* 807–821.

Benjamin, A. S. (Ed.). (2011). *Successful remembering and successful forgetting: A festschrift in honor of Robert A. Bjork.* New York: Psychology Press.

Benjamin, A. S., & Ross, B. H. (2011). The causes and consequences of reminding. In A. S. Benjamin (Ed.), *Successful remembering and successful forgetting: A festschrift in honor of Robert A. Bjork* (pp. 71–87). New York: Psychology Press.

Benjamin, L. T., Jr. (2009). *A history of psychology* (3rd ed.). Malden, MA: Blackwell.

Bennett, M. D., & Gibson, J. M. (2006). *A field guide to good decisions.* Westport, CT: Praeger.

Ben-Zeev, T. (2002). If "ignorance makes us smart," then does reading books make us less smart? [Review of simple heuristics that make us smart.] *Contemporary Psychology, 47,* 653–656.

Berg, T. (2002). Slips of the typewriter key. *Applied Psycholinguistics, 23,* 185–207.

Berger, C. R. (1997). Producing messages under uncertainty. In J. O. Greene (Ed.), *Message production* (pp. 221–224). Mahwah, NJ: Erlbaum.

Bermúdez, J. L. (2010). *Cognitive science: An introduction to the science of the mind.* New York: Cambridge University Press.

Bernstein, D. M., Laney, C., Morris, E. K., & Loftus, E. F. (2005). False memories about food can lead to food avoidance. *Social Cognition, 23,* 11–34.

Bernstein, D. M., & Loftus, E. F. (2009). The consequences of false memories for food preferences and choices. *Perspectives on Psychological Science, 4,* 135–139.

Bernstein, S. E., & Carr, T. H. (1996). Dual-route theories of pronouncing printed words: What can be learned from concurrent task performance? *Journal of Experimental Psychology: Learning, Memory, and Cognition, 22,* 86–116.

Bialystok, E. (1988). Levels of bilingualism and levels of linguistic awareness. *Developmental Psychology, 24,* 560–567.

Bialystok, E. (1992). Selective attention in cognitive processing: The bilingual edge. In R. J. Harris (Ed.), *Language processing in bilingual children* (pp. 501–513). Amsterdam: Elsevier.

Bialystok, E. (2001). *Bilingualism in development: Language, literacy, & cognition.* New York: Cambridge University Press.

Bialystok, E. (2005). Consequences of bilingualism for cognitive development. In J. F. Kroll, & A. M. de Groot (Eds.), *Handbook of bilingualism: Psycholinguistic approaches* (pp. 417–432). New York: Oxford University Press.

Bialystok, E. (2009). Bilingualism: The good, the bad, and the indifferent. *Bilingualism: Language and Cognition, 12,* 3–11.

Bialystok, E. (2010). Bilingualism. *Wiley Interdisciplinary Reviews: Cognitive Science, 1,* 559–572.

Bialystok, E., & Codd, J. (1997). Cardinal limits: Evidence from language awareness and bilingualism for developing concepts of number. *Cognitive Development, 12,* 85–106.

Bialystok, E., & Craik, F. I. M. (Eds.). (2006). *Lifespan cognition: Mechanisms of change.* New York: Oxford University Press.

Bialystok, E., Craik, F. I. M., & Freedman, M. (2007). Bilingualism as a protection against the onset of symptoms of dementia. *Neuropsychologia, 45,* 459–464.

Bialystok, E., & Feng, X. (2009). Language proficiency and executive control in proactive interference: Evidence from monolingual and bilingual children and adults. *Brain & Language, 109,* 93–100.

Bialystok, E., & Hakuta, K. (1994). *In other words: The science and psychology of second-language acquisition.* New York: Basic Books.

Bialystok, E., Luk, G., Peets, K. F., & Yang, S. (2010). Receptive vocabulary differences in monolingual and bilingual children. *Bilingualism: Language and Cognition, 13,* 525–531.

Bialystok, E., & Majumder, S. (1998). The relationship between bilingualism and the development of cognitive processes in problem solving. *Applied Psycholinguistics, 19,* 69–85.

Bialystok, E., & Martin, M. (2004). Attention and inhibition in bilingual children: Evidence from the dimensional change card sort task. *Developmental Science, 7,* 325–339.

Bialystok, E., & Viswanathan, M. (2009). Components of executive control with advantages for bilingual children in two cultures. *Cognition, 112,* 494–500.

Biber, D., & Vásquez, C. (2008). Writing and speaking. In C. Bazerman (Ed.), *Handbook of research on writing: History, society, school, individual, text* (pp. 535–548). Mahwah, NJ: Erlbaum.

Biederman, I. (1990). Higher-level vision. In E. N. Osherson, S. M. Kosslyn, & J. M. Hollerbach (Eds.), *An invitation to cognitive science* (Vol. 2, pp. 41–72). Cambridge, MA: MIT Press.

Biederman, I. (1995). Visual object recognition. In S. F. Kosslyn & D. N. Osherson (Eds.), *An invitation to cognitive science* (2nd ed., pp. 121–165). Cambridge, MA: MIT Press.

Bieman-Copland, S., & Charness, N. (1994). Memory knowledge and memory monitoring in adulthood. *Psychology and Aging, 9,* 287–302.

Bingham, A. (2011). "The Makioka sisters." *Cineaste, 36* (4), 65–66.

Biorge, A. K. (2007). Power distance in English lingua franca email communication. *International Journal of Applied Linguistics, 17,* 60–80.

Birdsong, D. (2006). Age and second language acquisition and processing: A selective overview. *Language Learning, 56,* 9–48.

Birdsong, D., & Molis, M. (2001). On the evidence for maturational constraints in second-language acquisition. *Journal of Memory and Language, 44,* 235–249.

Bisby, J. A., et al. (2010). Acute effects of alcohol on intrusive memory development and viewpoint dependence in spatial memory support a dual representation model. *Biological Psychiatry, 68,* 280–286.

Bishop, M. A., & Trout, J. D. (2002). 50 years of successful predictive modeling should be enough. *Lessons for Philosophy of Science, 69,* S197–S208.

Bjork, E. L., & Bjork, R. A. (1988). On the adaptive aspects of retrieval failure in autobiographical memory. In M. M. Gruneberg, P. E. Morris, & R. N. Sykes (Eds.), *Practical aspects of memory* (Vol. 2). London: Academic Press.

Bjork, E. L., Bjork, R. A., & MacLeod, M. D. (2005). Types and consequences of forgetting: Intended and unintended. In L.-G. Nilsson & Nobuo Ohta (Eds.), *Memory and society: Psychological perspectives* (pp. 134–158). New York: Psychology Press.

Bjork, E. L., Storm, B. C., & deWinstanley, P. A. (2011). Learning from the consequences of retrieval: Another test effect. In A. S. Benjamin (Ed.), *Successful remembering and successful forgetting: A festschrift in honor of Robert A. Bjork* (pp. 347–364). New York: Psychology Press.

Bjork, R. A. (2011). On the symbiosis of remembering, forgetting, and learning. In A. S. Benjamin (Ed.), *Successful remembering and successful forgetting: A festschrift in honor of Robert A. Bjork* (pp. 1–22). New York: Psychology Press.

Bjorklund, D. F. (2005). *Children's thinking: Cognitive development and individual differences* (4th ed.). Belmont, CA: Thomson Wadsworth.

Bjorklund, D. F., Dukes, C., & Brown, R. D. (2009). The development of memory strategies. In M. Courage & N. Cowan (Eds.), *The development of memory in childhood* (pp. 145–175). Hove, UK: Psychology Press.

Bjorklund, D. F., Miller, P. H., Coyle, T. R., & Slawinski, J. L. (1997). Instructing children to use memory strategies: Evidence of utilization deficiencies in memory training studies. *Developmental Review, 17,* 411–441.

Blascovich, J., Spencer, S. J., Quinn, D., & Steele, C. (2001). African Americans and high blood pressure: The role of stereotype threat. *Psychological Science, 12,* 225–229.

Block, R. A., & Harper, D. R. (1991). Overconfidence in estimation: Testing the anchoring-and-adjustment hypothesis. *Organizational Behavior and Human Decision Processes, 49,* 188–207.

Bloom, F. E., & Lazerson, A. (1988). *Brain, mind, and behavior* (2nd ed.). New York: Freeman.

Bloom, L. C., & Mudd, S. A. (1991). Depth of processing approach to face recognition: A test of two theories. *Journal of Experimental Psychology: Learning, Memory, and Cognition, 17,* 556–565.

Bloom, P. (2001). Précis of how children learn the meaning of words. *Behavioral and Brain Sciences, 24,* 1095–1103.

Blumenthal, A. L. (2009). A reappraisal of Wilhelm Wundt. In L. T. Benjamin, Jr. (Ed.), (2009), *A history of psychology* (3rd ed., pp. 64–72). Malden, MA: Blackwell.

Bock, K., & Garnsey, S. M. (1998). Language processing. In W. Bechtel & G. Graham (Eds.), *A companion to cognitive science* (pp. 226–234). Malden, MA: Blackwell.

Bock, K., & Griffin, Z. M. (2000). Producing words: How mind meets mouth. In L. Wheeldon (Ed.), *Aspects of language production* (pp. 7–47). Philadelphia: Psychology Press.

Bock, K., Loebell, H., & Morey, R. (1992). From conceptual roles to structural relations: Bridging the syntactic cleft. *Psychological Review, 99,* 150–171.

Boden, M. (2004). Artificial intelligence (AI). In R. L. Gregory (Ed.), *The Oxford companion to the mind* (2nd ed., pp. 59–61). New York: Oxford University Press.

Bodenhausen, G. V., Macrae, C. N., & Hugenberg, K. (2003). Social cognition. In I. B. Weiner (Ed.),

Handbook of psychology (Vol. 5, pp. 257–282). Hoboken, NJ: Wiley.

Bohanek, J. G., Fivush, R., & Walker, E. (2005). Memories of positive and negative emotional events. *Applied Cognitive Psychology, 19,* 51–66.

Bohn, A. (2010). Generational differences in cultural life scripts and life story memories of younger and older adults. *Applied Cognitive Psychology, 24,* 1324–1345.

Bohn-Gettler, C. M., et al. (2011). Adults' and children's monitoring of story events in the service of comprehension. *Memory & Cognition, 39,* 992–1011.

Boker, S. M., & Bisconti, T. L. (2006). Dynamical systems modeling for aging research. In C. S. Bergeman & S. M. Boker (Eds.), *Methodological issues in aging research* (pp. 185–229). Mahwah, NJ: Erlbaum.

Boot, W. E., Brockmole, J. R., & Simons, D. J. (2005). Attention capture is modulated in dual-task situations. *Psychonomic Bulletin & Review, 12,* 662–668.

Bornkessel, I., & Schlesewsky, M. (2006). The extended argument dependency model: A neurocognitive approach to sentence comprehension across languages. *Psychological Review, 113,* 787–821.

Bornstein, M. H., & Putnick, D. L. (2012). Cognitive and socioemotional caregiving in developing countries. *Child Development, 83,* 46–61.

Borst, G., & Kosslyn, S. M. (2008). Visual mental imagery and visual perception: Structural equivalence revealed by scanning processes. *Memory & Cognition,* 849–862.

Borst, G., & Kosslyn, S. M. (2010). Individual differences in spatial mental imagery. *Quarterly Journal of Experimental Psychology, 63,* 2031–2050.

Borst, G., Thompson, W. L., & Kosslyn, S. M. (2011). Understanding the dorsal and ventral systems of the human cerebral cortex. *American Psychologist, 66,* 624–632.

Bosch, L., & Sebastián-Gallés, N. (2001). Early language differentiation in bilingual infants. In J. Cenoz & F. Genesee (Eds.), *Trends in bilingual acquisition* (pp. 71–93). Amsterdam: Benjamins.

Botella, J., Privado, J., Gil-Gómez de Liaño, B., & Suero, M. (2011). Illusory conjunctions reflect the time course of the attentional blink. *Attention, Perception, & Psychophysics, 73,* 1361–1373.

Bouvier, S., & Treisman, A. (2010). Visual feature binding requires reentry. *Psychological Science, 21,* 202–204.

Bower, G. H. (2000). A brief history of memory research. In E. Tulving & F. I. M. Craik (Eds.), *The Oxford handbook of memory* (pp. 3–32). New York: Oxford University Press.

Bower, G. H. (2008). The evolution of a cognitive psychologist: A journey from simple behavior to complex mental acts. *Annual Review of Psychology, 59,* 1–27.

Bower, G. H., & Clark, M. C. (1969). Narrative stories as mediators for serial learning. *Psychonomic Science, 14,* 181–182.

Bower, G. H., Clark, M. C., Lesgold, A. M., & Winzenz, D. (1969). Hierarchical retrieval schemes in recall of categorized word lists. *Journal of Verbal Learning and Verbal Behavior, 8,* 323–343.

Bower, G. H., & Forgas, J. P. (2000). Affect, memory, and social cognition. In E. Eich, et al. (Eds.), *Cognition and emotion* (pp. 87–168). New York: Oxford University Press.

Bower, G. H., & Springston, F. (1970). Pauses as recoding points in letter series. *Journal of Experimental Psychology, 83,* 421–430.

Bower, G. H., & Winzenz, D. (1970). Comparison of associative learning strategies. *Psychonomic Science, 20,* 119–120.

Bowman, L. L., Levine, L. E., Waite, B. M., & Gendron, M. (2010). Can students really multitask? An experimental study of instant messaging while reading. *Computers & Education, 54,* 927–931.

Bradshaw, J. L., & Nettleton, N. C. (1974). Articulatory inference and the MOWN-DOWN heterophone effect. *Journal of Experimental Psychology, 102,* 88–94.

Brainerd, C. J., & Reyna, V. F. (2005). *The science of false memory.* New York: Oxford University Press.

Brandimonte, M. A., & Gerbino, W. (1996). When imagery fails: Effects of verbal recoding on accessibility of visual memories. In C. Cornoldi, et al. (Eds.), *Stretching the imagination: Representation and transformation in mental imagery* (pp. 31–76). New York: Oxford University Press.

Brandimonte, M. A., Hitch, G. J., & Bishop, D. V. M. (1992). Influence of short-term memory codes on visual image processing: Evidence from image transformation tasks. *Journal of Experimental Psychology: Learning, Memory, and Cognition, 18,* 157–165.

Brandt, K. R., Cooper, L. M., & Dewhurst, S. A. (2005). Expertise and recollective experience: Recognition memory for familiar and unfamiliar academic subjects. *Applied Cognitive Psychology, 19,* 1113–1125.

Bransford, J. D., Brown, A. L., & Cocking, R. R. (2000). *How people learn: Brain, mind, experience, and school* (expanded edition). Washington, DC: National Academy Press.

Bransford, J. D., & Franks, J. J. (1971). Abstraction of linguistic ideas. *Cognitive Psychology, 2,* 331–350.

Bransford, J. D., Franks, J. J., Morris, C. D., & Stein, B. S. (1979). Some general constraints on learning and memory research. In L. S. Cermak & F. I. M. Craik (Eds.), *Levels of processing in human memory* (pp. 331–354). Hillsdale, NJ: Erlbaum.

Bransford, J. D., & Stein, B. S. (1984). *The IDEAL problem solver.* New York: Freeman.

Branthwaite, A., & Rogers, D. (1985). Introduction. In A. Branthwaite & D. Rogers (Eds.), *Children growing up* (pp. 1–2). Milton Keynes, UK: Open University Press.

Brewer, N., Weber, N., & Semmler, C. (2005). Eyewitness identification. In N. Brewer & K. D. Williams (Eds.), *Psychology and law: An empirical perspective* (pp. 177–221). New York: Guilford.

Brewer, W. F. (2000). Bartlett's concept of the schema and its impact on theories of knowledge representation in contemporary cognitive psychology. In A. Saito (Ed.), *Bartlett, culture and cognition* (pp. 69–89). East Sussex, UK: Psychology Press.

Brewer, W. F., & Treyens, J. C. (1981). Role of schemata in memory for places. *Cognitive Psychology, 13,* 207–230.

Brewin, C. R. (2011). The nature and significance of memory disturbance in posttraumatic stress disorder. *Annual Review of Clinical Psychology, 7,* 203–227.

Brewin, C. R., Gregory, J. D., Lipton, M., & Burgess, N. (2010). Intrusive images in psychological disorders: Characteristics, neural mechanisms, and treatment implications. *Psychological Review, 117,* 210–232.

Briggs, F., & Usrey, W. M. (2010). Visual system structure. In E. B. Goldstein (Ed.), *Encyclopedia of perception* (Vol. 2, pp. 1130–1134). Thousand Oaks, CA: Sage.

Brigham, J. C., Bennett, L. B., Meissner, C. A., & Mitchell, T. L. (2007). The influence of race on eyewitness memory. In R. C. L. Lindsay, D. F. Ross, J. D. Read, & M. P. Toglia (Eds.), *Handbook of eyewitness psychology* (Vol. 2, pp. 257–281). Mahwah, NJ: Erlbaum.

Britton, B. K. (1996). Rewriting: The arts and sciences of improving expository instructional text. In C. Michael Levy & S. Ransdell (Eds.), *The science of writing: Theories, methods, individual differences, and applications* (pp. 323–345). Mahwah, NJ: Erlbaum.

Broadbent, D. E. (1958). *Perception and communication.* New York: Pergamon.

Brockmole, J. R. (Ed.). (2009). *The visual world in memory.* New York: Psychology Press.

Bromme, R., Jucks, R., & Wagner, T. (2005). How to refer to 'diabetes'? Language in online health advice. *Applied Cognitive Psychology, 19,* 569–586.

Brown, A. S. (2012). *The tip of the tongue state.* New York: Psychology Press.

Brown, C. H., & Sinnott, J. M. (2006). Cross-species comparisons of vocal perception. In S. Greenberg & W. A. Ainsworth (Eds.), *Listening to speech: An auditory perspective* (pp. 183–201). Mahwah, NJ: Erlbaum.

Brown, J. (1958). Some tests of the decay theory of immediate memory. *Quarterly Journal of Experimental Psychology, 10,* 12–21.

Brown, J. (2004). Memory: Biological basis. In R. L. Gregory (Ed.), *The Oxford companion to the mind* (2nd ed., pp. 564–568). New York: Oxford University Press.

Brown, N. R., Cui, X., & Gordon, R. D. (2002). Estimating national populations: Cross-cultural differences and availability effects. *Applied Cognitive Psychology, 16,* 811–827.

Brown, N. R., & Siegler, R. S. (1992). The role of availability in the estimation of national populations. *Memory & Cognition, 20,* 406–412.

Brown, R., & Kulik, J. (1977). Flashbulb memories. *Cognition, 5,* 73–99.

Brown, R., & McNeill, D. (1966). The "tip of the tongue" phenomenon. *Journal of Verbal Learning and Verbal Behavior, 5,* 325–377.

Brown, T. L., Gore, C. L., & Carr, T. H. (2002). Visual attention and word recognition in Stroop color naming: Is word recognition "automatic"? *Journal of Experimental Psychology: General, 131,* 220–240.

Bruce, V., Green, P. R., & Georgeson, M. A. (2003). *Visual perception* (4th ed.). Hove, UK: Psychology Press.

Bruce, V., Henderson, A., Newman, C., & Burton, A. M. (2001). Matching identities of familiar and unfamiliar faces caught on CCTV images. *Journal of Experimental Psychology: Applied, 7,* 207–218.

Bruck, M., & Ceci, S. J. (1999). The suggestibility of children's memory. *Annual Review of Psychology, 50,* 419–439.

Bruine de Bruin, W. (2011). Framing effects in surveys: How respondents make sense of the questions we ask. In G. Keren (Ed.), *Perspectives on framing* (pp. 303–324). New York: Psychology Press.

Bruner, J. (1997). Will cognitive revolutions ever stop? In D. M. Johnson & C. E. Erneling (Eds.), *The future of the cognitive revolution* (pp. 279–292). New York: Oxford University Press.

Bruning, R. H., Schraw, G. J., & Ronning, R. R. (1999). *Cognitive psychology and instruction* (3rd ed.). Upper Saddle River, NJ: Prentice Hall.

Bruno, L., Zarrinpar, A., & Kosslyn, S. M., (2003). Do separate processes identify objects as exemplars versus members of basic-level categories? Evidence from hemispheric specialization. *Brain and Cognition, 53,* 15–27.

Bryant, D. J., & Tversky, B. (1999). Mental representations of perspective and spatial relations from diagrams and models. *Journal of Experimental Psychology: Learning, Memory, and Cognition, 25,* 137–156.

Buckner, R. L. (2010). The role of the hippocampus in prediction and imagination. *Annual Review of Psychology, 61,* 27–48.

Buckner, R. L., & Logan, J. M. (2001). Functional neuroimaging methods: PET and fMRI. In R. Cabeza & A. Kingstone (Eds.), *Handbook of functional neuroimaging of cognition* (pp. 27–48). Cambridge, MA: MIT Press.

Buehler, R., Griffin, D., Lama, C. H., & Deslaurier, J. (2012). Perspectives on prediction: Does third-person imagery improve task completion estimates? *Organizational Behavior and Human Decision Processes, 117,* 138–149.

Buehler, R., Griffin, D., & Ross, M. (2002). Inside the planning fallacy: The causes and consequences of optimistic time predictions. In T. Gilovich, D. Griffin, & D. Kahneman (Eds.), *Heuristics and biases: The psychology of intuitive judgment* (pp. 250–270). New York: Cambridge University Press.

Bull, R., & Espy, K. A. (2006). Working memory, executive functioning, and children's mathematics. In S. J. Pickering (Ed.), *Working memory and education* (pp. 93–123). Burlington, MA: Elsevier.

Bunce, D., & Macready, A. (2005). Processing speed, executive function, and age differences in remembering and knowing. *Quarterly Journal of Experimental Psychology, 58A,* 155–168.

Bundesen, C., & Habekost, T. (2005). Attention. In K. Lamberts & R. L. Goldstone (Eds.), *Handbook of cognition.* Thousand Oaks, CA: Sage.

Burke, D. M. (2006). Representation and aging. In E. Bialystok & F. I. M. Craik (Eds.), *Lifespan cognition: Mechanisms of change* (pp. 193–206). New York: Oxford University Press.

Burns, D. J. (2006). Assessing distinctiveness: Measures of item-specific and relational processing. In R. R. Hunt & J. B. Worthen (Eds.), *Distinctiveness and memory* (pp. 109–130). New York: Oxford University Press.

Burstein, J., & Chodorow, M. (2010). Progress and new directions in technology for automated essay evaluation. In R. B. Kaplan (Ed.), *The Oxford handbook of applied linguistics* (2nd ed., pp. 529–547). New York: Oxford University Press.

Burton, A. M., Wilson, S., Cowan, M., & Bruce, V. (1999). Face recognition in poor-quality video: Evidence from security surveillance. *Psychological Science, 10,* 243–248.

Bus, A. G., & van IJzendoorn, M. H. (1999). Phonological awareness and early reading: A meta-analysis of experimental training studies. *Journal of Educational Psychology, 91,* 403–414.

Bushman, B. J. (1998). Effects of television violence on memory for commercial messages. *Journal of Experimental Psychology: Applied, 4,* 291–307.

Bushman, B. J. (2005). Violence and sex in television programs do not sell products in advertisements. *Psychological Science, 16,* 702–708.

Bushman, B. J., & Gibson, B. (2011). Violent video games cause an increase in aggression long after the game has been turned off. *Social Psychological and Personality Science, 2,* 29–32.

Bushman, B. J., & Huesmann, L. R. (2010). Aggression. In S. K. Fiske, D. T. Gilbert, & G. Lindzey (Eds.), *Handbook of social psychology* (5th ed., pp. 833–863). Hoboken, NJ: Wiley.

Butcher, K. R., & Kintsch, W. (2003). Text comprehension and discourse processing. In A. F. Healy & R. W. Proctor (Eds.), *Handbook of psychology* (Vol. 4, pp. 575–595). Hoboken, NJ: Wiley.

Byrne, R. M. J. & Johnson-Laird, P. N. (2009). "If" and the problems of conditional reasoning. *Trends in Cognitive Sciences, 13,* 282–287.

Cacioppo, J. T. (2007, December). The structure of psychology. *Association for Psychological Science,* pp. 3, 50–51.

Cacioppo, J. T., & Berntson, G. G. (Eds.). (2005a). *Social neuroscience: Key readings.* New York: Psychology Press.

Cacioppo, J. T., & Berntson, G. G. (2005b). Volume overview: Analyses of the social brain through the lens of human brain imaging. In J. T. Cacioppo & G. G. Berntson (Eds.), *Social neuroscience: Key readings* (pp. 1–17). New York: Psychology Press.

Cain, K. (2006). Children's reading comprehension: The role of working memory in normal and impaired development. In S. J. Pickering (Ed.), *Working memory and education* (pp. 61–91). Burlington, MA: Elsevier.

Calbris, G. (2011). *Elements of meaning in gesture.* Philadelphia: John Benjamins.

Calkins, M. W. (1910). The teaching of elementary psychology in colleges supposed to have no laboratory. *Psychological Monographs, 124* (Whole No. 51), 41–53.

Calvo-Merino, B., et al., (2005). Action observation and acquired motor skills: An fMRI study with expert dancers. *Cerebral Cortex, 15,* 1243–1249.

Campbell, J., & Mayer, R. E. (2009). Questioning as an instructional method: Does it affect learning from lectures? *Applied Cognitive Psychology, 23,* 747–759.

Campbell, R., & Sais, E. (1995). Accelerated metalinguistic (phonological) awareness in bilingual children. *British Journal of Developmental Psychology, 13,* 61–68.

Campitelli, G., & Gobet, F. (2010). Herbert Simon's decision-making approach: Investigations of cognitive processes in experts. *Review of General Psychology, 14,* 354–364.

Cannon-Bowers, J. A., & Salas, E. (Eds.). (1998). *Making decisions under stress: Implications for individuals and team training.* Washington, DC: American Psychological Association.

Cansino, S., et al. (2011). Effects of aging on interference control in selective attention and working memory. *Memory & Cognition, 39,* 1409–1422.

Caplan, P. J., & Caplan, J. B. (2009). *Thinking critically about research on sex and gender* (3rd ed.). Boston, MA: Pearson.

Caramazza, A., & Miozzo, M. (1997). The relation between syntactic and phonological knowledge in lexical access: Evidence from the "tip-of-the-tongue" phenomenon. *Cognition, 69,* 309–343.

Carli, L. L. (1999). Cognitive reconstruction, hindsight, and reactions to victims and perpetrators. *Personality and Social Psychology Bulletin, 25,* 966–979.

Carlson, L. A. (2010) Top-down and bottom-up processing. In E. B. Goldstein (Ed.), *Encyclopedia of perception* (Vol. 2, pp. 1011–1013). Thousand Oaks, CA: Sage.

Carney, R. N., & Levin, J. R. (2001). Remembering the names of unfamiliar animals: Keywords as keys to their kingdom. *Applied Cognitive Psychology, 15,* 133–143.

Carney, R. N., & Levin, J. R. (2011). Delayed mnemonic benefits for a combined pegword-keyword strategy, time after time, rhyme after rhyme. *Applied Cognitive Psychology, 25,* 204–2011.

Carpenter, P. A., & Just, M. A. (1999). Computational modeling of high-level cognition versus hypothesis testing. In R. J. Sternberg (Ed.), *The nature of cognition* (pp. 245–293). Cambridge, MA: MIT Press.

Carpenter, P. A., Miyake, A., & Just, M. A. (1995). Language comprehension: Sentence and discourse processing. *Annual Review of Psychology, 46,* 91–120.

Carpenter, S. K., & DeLosh, E. L. (2005). Application of the testing and spacing effects to name learning. *Applied Cognitive Psychology, 19,* 619–636.

Carr, W., & Roskos-Ewoldsen, B. (1999). Spatial orientation by mental transformation. *Psychological Research/ Psychologische Forschung, 62,* 36–47.

Carraher, T. N., Carraher, D. W., & Schliemann, A. D. (1985). Mathematics in the streets and in schools. *British Journal of Developmental Psychology, 3,* 21–29.

Carroll, D. W. (2004). *Psychology of language* (4th ed.). Belmont, CA: Thomson Wadsworth.

Carroll, D. W. (2008). *Psychology of language* (5th ed.). Belmont, CA: Thomson Wadsworth.

Carstensen, L. L. (2007, *Winter*). Growing old or living long: Take your pick. *Issues in Science and Technology,* pp. 41–50.

Cassady, J. (2004). The impact of cognitive test anxiety on text comprehension and recall in the absence of external evaluative pressure. *Applied Cognitive Psychology, 18,* 311–325.

Castelhano, M. S., & Rayner, K. (2008). Eye movements during reading, visual search and scene perception: An overview. In K. Rayner, D. Shen, X. Bai, & G. Yan (Eds.), *Cognitive and cultural influences on eye movements* (pp. 3–33). Tianjin, China: Tianjin People's Publishing House.

Castelli, P., et al. (2006). Evaluating eyewitness testimony in adults and children. In I. B. Weiner & A. K. Hess (Eds.), *The handbook of forensic psychology* (3rd ed., pp. 243–304). Hoboken, NJ: Wiley.

Ceballo, R. (1999). Negotiating the life narrative: A dialogue with an African American social worker. *Psychology of Women Quarterly, 23,* 309–321.

Ceci, S. J., & Liker, J. K. (1986). A day at the races: A study of IQ, expertise, and cognitive complexity. *Journal of Experimental Psychology: General, 115*, 255–266.

Cepeda, N. J., et al. (2006). Distributed practice in verbal recall tasks: A review and quantitative synthesis. *Psychological Bulletin, 132*, 354–380.

Cha, C. B., et al. (2010). Attentional bias toward suicide-related stimuli predicts suicidal behavior. *Journal of Abnormal Psychology, 119*, 616–622.

Chabris, C. F., & Simons, D. J. (2010). *The invisible gorilla and other ways our intuitions deceive us.* New York: Crown.

Chafe, W., & Danielewicz, J. (1987). Properties of spoken and written language. In R. Horowitz & S. J. Samuels (Eds.), *Comprehending oral and written language* (pp. 83–113). San Diego: Academic Press.

Chalmers, D. (2007). The hard problem of consciousness. In M. Velmans & S. Schneider (Eds.), *The Blackwell companion to consciousness* (pp. 225–235). Malden, MA: Blackwell.

Chambers, D., & Reisberg, D. (1985). Can mental images be ambiguous? *Journal of Experimental Psychology: Human Perception and Performance, 11*, 317–328.

Chan, J. C. K., & McDermott, K. B. (2006). Remembering pragmatic inferences. *Applied Cognitive Psychology, 20*, 633–639.

Chapman, L. J., & Chapman, J. P. (1969). Illusory correlations as an obstacle to the use of valid psychodiagnostic signs. *Journal of Abnormal Psychology, 74*, 271–280.

Chapman, P., & Underwood, G. (2000). Forgetting near-accidents: The roles of severity, culpability and experience in the poor recall of dangerous driving situations. *Applied Cognitive Psychology, 14*, 31–44.

Chein, J. M., Weisberg, R. W., Streeter, N. L., & Kwok, S. (2010). Working memory and insight in the nine-dot problem. *Memory & Cognition, 38*, 883–892.

Chen, Z., Mo, L., & Honomichl, R. (2004). Having the memory of an elephant: Long-term retrieval and the use of analogues in problem solving. *Journal of Experimental Psychology: General, 133*, 415–433.

Chenoweth, N. A., & Hayes, J. R. (2001). Fluency in writing. *Written Communication, 18*, 80–98.

Cherry, C. (1953). Some experiments on the recognition of speech with one and with two ears. *Journal of the Acoustical Society of America, 25*, 975–979.

Chi, M. T. H. (1981). Knowledge development and memory performance. In M. Friedman, J. P. Das, & N. O'Connor (Eds.), *Intelligence and learning* (pp. 221–230). New York: Plenum.

Chi, M. T. H. (2006). Two approaches to the study of experts' characteristics. In K. A. Ericsson, N. Charness, P. J. Feltovich, & R. R. Hoffman (Eds.), *The Cambridge handbook of expertise and expert performance* (pp. 21–30). New York: Cambridge University Press.

Chi, M. T. H., & Ohlsson, S. (2005). Complex declarative learning. In K. J. Holyoak & R. G. Morrison (Eds.), *The Cambridge handbook of thinking and reasoning* (pp. 371–399). New York: Cambridge University Press.

Chiang, E. S., Therriault, D. J., & Franks, B. A. (2010). Individual differences in relative metacomprehension accuracy: Variation within and across task manipulations. *Metacognition and Learning, 5*, 121–135.

Chin-Parker, S., & Ross, B. H. (2004). Diagnosticity and prototypicality in category learning: A comparison of inference learning and classification learning. *Journal of Experimental Psyhcology: Learning, Memory, and Cognition, 30*, 216–236.

Chipman, S. F. (2004). Research on the women and mathematics issue: A personal case history. In A. M. Gallagher & J. C. Kaufman (Eds.), *Gender differences in mathematics: An integrative psychological approach* (pp. 1–24). New York: Cambridge University Press.

Chiroro, P. M., Tredoux, C. G., Radaelli, S., & Meissner, C. A. (2008). Recognizing faces across continents: The effect of within-race variations on the own-race bias in face recognition. *Psychonomic Bulletin & Review, 15*, 1089–1092.

Chiu, C,-Y., et al. (2010). Intersubjective culture: The role of intersubjective perceptions in cross-cultural research. *Perspectives on Psychological Sciences, 5*, 482–493.

Chomsky, N. (1957). *Syntactic structures.* The Hague: Mouton.

Chomsky, N. (1965). *Aspects of the theory of syntax.* Cambridge, MA: MIT Press.

Chomsky, N. (1975). *Reflections on language.* New York: Pantheon

Chomsky, N. (1981). *Lectures on government and binding.* Dordrecht, Netherlands: Foris.

Chomsky, N. (2000). *New horizons in the study of language and mind.* Cambridge, UK: Cambridge University Press.

Chomsky, N. (2002). *On nature and language.* Cambridge, UK: Cambridge University Press.

Chomsky, N. (2004). Language: Chomsky's theory. In R. L. Gregory (Ed.), *The Oxford companion to the mind* (2nd ed., pp. 511–513). New York: Oxford University Press.

Chomsky, N. (2006). *Language and mind* (3rd ed.). New York: Cambridge University Press.

Chong, S. C., Joo, S. J., Emmanouil, T.-A., & Treisman, A. (2008). Statistical processing: Not so implausible after all. *Perception & Psychophysics, 70*, 1327–1334.

Chrisley, R. (2004). Artificial intelligence (AI). In R. L. Gregory (Ed.), *The Oxford companion to the mind* (2nd ed., pp. 61–63). New York: Oxford University Press.

Christensen, B. T., & Schunn, C. D. (2007). The relationship of analogical distance to analogical function and pre-inventive structure: The case of engineering design. *Memory & Cognition, 35*, 29–38.

Christianson, K., Luke, S. G., & Ferreira, F. (2010). Effects of plausibility on structural priming. *Journal of Experimental Psychology: Learning, Memory, and Cognition, 36*, 538–544.

Christoffels, I. K., & De Groot, A. M. B. (2005). Simultaneous interpreting: A cognitive perspective. In J. F. Kroll & A. M. B. De Groot (Eds.), *Handbook of bilingualism: Psycholinguistic approaches* (pp. 454–479). New York: Oxford University Press.

Christoffels, I. K., De Groot, A. M. B., & Kroll, J. F. (2006). Memory and language skills in simultaneous interpreters: The role of expertise and language proficiency. *Journal of Memory and Language, 54*, 324–345.

Christopher, G., & MacDonald, J. (2005). The impact of clinical depression on working memory. *Cognitive Neuropsychiatry, 10*, 379–399.

Chu, M., & Kita, S. (2011). The nature of gestures' beneficial role in spatial problem solving. *Journal of Experimental Psychology: General, 140*, 102–116.

Chun, M. M., Golumb, J. D., & Turk-Browne, N. B. (2011). A taxonomy of external and internal attention. *Annual Review of Psychology, 62*, 73–101.

Chun, M. M., & Wolfe, J. M. (2001). Visual attention. In E. B. Goldstein (Ed.), *Blackwell handbook of perception* (pp. 272–310). Malden, MA: Blackwell.

Clark, D. A. (2005). *Intrusive thoughts in clinical disorders: Theory, research, and treatment.* New York: Guilford Press.

Clark, H. H. (1985). Language use and language users. In G. Lindzey & E. Aronson (Eds.), *Handbook of social psychology* (2nd ed., Vol. 2, pp. 179–231). New York: Random House.

Clark, H. H. (1994). Discourse in production. In M. A. Gernsbacher (Ed.), *Handbook of psycholinguistics* (pp. 985–1021). San Diego: Academic Press.

Clark, H. H., & Chase, W. G. (1972). On the process of comparing sentences against pictures. *Cognitive Psychology, 3*, 472–517.

Clark, H. H., & Van Der Wege, M. M. (2002). Psycholinguistics. In D. Medin (Ed.), *Stevens' handbook of experimental psychology* (3rd ed., Vol. 2, pp. 209–259). New York: Wiley.

Clark, H. H., & Wilkes-Gibbs, D. (1986). Referring as a collaborative process. *Cognition, 22*, 1–39.

Cleary, M., & Pisoni, D. B. (2001). Speech perception and spoken word recognition: Research and theory. In E. B. Goldstein (Ed.), *Blackwell handbook of perception* (pp. 499–534). Malden, MA: Blackwell.

Close, J., Hahn, U., Hodgetts, C. J., & Pothos, E. M. (2010). Rules and similarity in adult concept learning. In D. Mareschal, P. C. Quinn, & S. E. G. Lea (Eds.), *The making of human concepts* (pp. 29–51). New York: Oxford University Press.

Clump, M. A. (2006). An active learning classroom activity for the "Cocktail Party Phenomenon." *Teaching of Psychology, 33*, 51–53.

Cohen, D. J., White, S., & Cohen, S. B. (2011). A time use diary: Study of adult everyday writing behavior. *Written Communication, 28*, 3–33.

Cohen, J. D., Usher, M., & McClelland, J. C. (1998). A PDP approach to set size effects within the Stroop task: Reply to Kanne, Balota, Spieler, and Faust (1998). *Psychological Review, 105*, 188–194.

Collet, C., et al. (2009). Physiological and behavioural changes associated to the management of secondary tasks while driving. *Applied Ergonomics, 40*, 1041–1046.

Collins, A. M., & Loftus, E. F. (1975). A spreading-activation theory of semantic memory. *Psychological Review, 82*, 407–428.

Collins, D. (2008). Personal communication.

Collins, J. L. (1998). *Strategies for struggling writers.* New York: Guilford.

Collins, M. A., & Amabile, T. M. (1999). Motivation and creativity. In R. J. Sternberg (Ed.), *Handbook of creativity* (pp. 297–312). New York: Cambridge University Press.

Coltheart, M. (2005). Modeling reading: The dual-route approach. In J. Snowling & C. Hulme (Eds.), *The science of reading: A handbook* (pp. 6–23). Malden, MA: Blackwell.

Coluccia, E. (2008). Learning from maps: The role of visuo-spatial working memory. *Applied Cognitive Psychology, 22,* 217–233.

Coluccia, E., Bianco, C., & Brandimonte, M. A. (2010). Autobiographical and event memories for surprising and unsurprising events. *Applied Cognitive Psychology, 24,* 177–199.

Comeau, L., & Genesee, F. (2001). Bilingual children's repair strategies during dyadic communication. In J. Cenoz & F. Genesee (Eds.), *Trends in bilingual acquisition* (pp. 231–256). New York: John Benjamins.

Connor, L. T., Dunlosky, J., & Hertzog, C. (1997). Age-related differences in absolute but not relative metamemory accuracy. *Psychology and Aging, 12,* 50–71.

Connor-Greene, P. A. (2000). Making connections: Evaluating the effectiveness of journal writing in enhancing student learning. *Teaching of Psychology, 27,* 44–46.

Conrad, R., & Hull, A. J. (1964). Information, acoustic confusion, and, memory span. *British Journal of Psychology, 55,* 432–439.

Conway, A. R. A., Cowan, N., & Bunting, M. F. (2001). The cocktail party phenomenon revisited: The importance of working memory capacity. *Psychonomic Bulletin & Review, 8,* 331–335.

Conway, A. R. A., Skitka, L. J., Hemmerich, J. A., & Kershaw, T. C. (2009). Flashbulb for 11 September 2001. *Applied Cognitive Psychology, 23,* 605–623.

Conway, A. R. A., et al. (Eds.). (2007). *Variation in working memory.* New York: Oxford University Press.

Conway, C. M., Loebach, J. L., & Pisoni, D. B. (2010). Speech perception. In E. B. Goldstein (Ed.), *Encyclopedia of perception* (Vol. 2, pp. 918–923). Thousand Oaks, CA: Sage.

Conway, M. A., & Fthenaki, A. (2000). Disruption and loss of autobiographical memory. In F. Boller & J. Grafman (Eds.), *Handbook of neuropsychology* (2nd ed., Vol. 2, pp. 281–312). Amsterdam: Elsevier.

Cook, G. I., Marsh, R. L., & Hicks, J. L. (2005). Associating a time-based prospective memory task with an expected context can improve or impair intention completion. *Applied Cognitive Psychology, 19,* 345–360.

Cook, V., & Bassetti, B. (Eds.). (2011). *Language and bilingual cognition.* New York: Psychology Press.

Cooper, L. A., & Lang, J. M. (1996). Imagery and visual-spatial representations. In E. L. Bjork & R. A. Bjork (Eds.), *Memory* (pp. 129–164). San Diego: Academic Press.

Corballis, M. C. (2006). Language. In K. Pawlik & G. d'Ydewalle (Eds.), *Psychological concepts: An international historical perspective* (pp. 197–221). New York: Psychology Press.

Corballis, M. C., & Suddendorf, T. (2010). The evolution of concepts: A timely look. In D. Mareschal, P. C. Quinn, & S. E. G. Lea (Eds.), *The making of human concepts* (pp. 365–384). New York: Oxford University Press.

Coren, S., Ward, L. M., & Enns, J. T. (2004). *Sensation and perception* (6th ed.). Hoboken, NJ: Wiley.

Cosmides, L., & Tooby, J. (2006). Evolutionary psychology, moral heuristics, and the law. In G. Gigerenzer & C. Engel (Eds.), *Heuristics and the law* (pp. 175–205). Cambridge, MA: MIT Press.

Costa, A., Alario, F.-X., & Sebastián-Gallés, N. (2009). Cross-linguistic research on language production. In M. G. Gaskell (Ed.), *The Oxford handbook of psycholinguistics* (pp. 531–546). New York: Oxford University Press.

Countries of the World. (2012). Information about France, Canada, and Japan. Retrieved March 14, 2012, from www.infoplease.com/countries.html

Courage, M. L., & Cowan, N. (Eds.). (2009). *The development of memory in infancy and childhood.* New York: Psychology Press.

Cowan, N. (2005). *Working memory capacity.* New York: Psychology Press.

Cowan, N. (2010). The magical mystery four: How is working memory capacity limited, and why? *Current Directions in Psychological Science, 19,* 51–57.

Cowan, N., & Alloway, T. (2009). Development of working memory in childhood. In M. Courage & N. Cowan (Eds.), *The development of memory in childhood* (pp. 303–342). Hove, UK: Psychology Press.

Cowan, N., Johnson, T. D., & Saults, J. S. (2005). Capacity limits in list item recognition: Evidence from proactive interference. *Memory, 13,* 293–299.

Cowan, N., Morey, C. C., Chen, Z., & Bunting, M. F. (2007). What do estimates of working memory capacity tell us? In N. Osaka & R. Logie (Eds.), *Working memory: Behavioural & neural correlates.* New York: Oxford University Press.

Cowan, N., et al. (2009). Seven-year-olds allocate attention like adults unless working memory is overloaded. *Developmental Science, 13,* 120–133.

Coward, L. A., & Sun, R. (2004). Criteria for an effective theory of consciousness and some preliminary attempts. *Consciousness and Cognition, 13,* 268–301.

Cowley, S. J. (2011). Distributed language. In S. J. Cowley (Ed.), *Distributed language* (pp. 1–14). Philadelphia: John Benjamins.

Cox, W. M., Fadardi, J. S., & Pothos, E. M. (2006). The addiction-Stroop test: Theoretical considerations and procedural recommendations. *Psychological Bulletin, 132,* 443–476.

Craik, F. I. M. (1990). Changes in memory with normal aging: A functional view. In R. J. Wurtman (Ed.), *Advances in neurology*: Vol. 51. *Alzheimer's disease* (pp. 201–205). New York: Raven.

Craik, F. I. M. (1999). Levels of encoding and retrieval. In B. H. Challis & B. M. Velichkovsky (Eds.), *Stratification in cognition and consciousness* (pp. 97–104). Philadelphia: John Benjamins.

Craik, F. I. M. (2006). Age-related changes in human memory: Practical consequences. In L.-G. Nilsson & N. Ohta (Eds.), *Memory and society: Psychological perspectives* (pp. 175–191). New York: Psychology Press.

Craik, F. I. M., & Lockhart, R. S. (1972). Levels of processing: A framework for memory research. *Journal of Verbal Learning and Verbal Behavior, 11,* 671–684.

Craik, F. I. M., & Tulving, E. (1975). Depth of processing and the retention of words in episodic memory. *Journal of Experimental Psychology: General, 104,* 268–294.

Craske, M. G. (2010). *Cognitive-behavioral therapy.* Washington, DC: American Psychological Association.

Craver-Lemley, C., & Reeves, A. (1992). How visual imagery interferes with vision. *Psychological Review, 99,* 633–649.

Credé, M., & Kuncel, N. R. (2008). Study habits, skills, and attitudes: The third pillar supporting collegiate academic performance. *Perspectives on Psychological Science, 3,* 425–453.

Cromdal, J. (1999). Childhood bilingualism and metalinguistic skills: Analysis and control in young Swedish-English bilinguals. *Applied Psycholinguistics, 20,* 1–20.

Cromer, L. D., & Freyd, J. J. (2007). What influences believing child sexual abuse disclosures? The roles of depicted memory persistence, participant gender, trauma history, and sexism. *Psychology of Women, 31,* 13–22.

Cuddy, A. J. C., & Fiske, S. T. (2002). Doddering but dear: Process, content, and function in stereotyping of older persons. In T. D. Nelson (Ed.), *Ageism: Stereotyping and prejudice against older persons* (pp. 3–26). Cambridge, MA: MIT Press.

Cuevas, K., Rovee-Collier, C., & Learmonth, A. E. (2006). Infants form associations between memory representations of stimuli that are absent. *Psychological Science, 17,* 543–549.

Curci, A., & Luminet, O. (2009). Flashbulb memories for expected events: A test of the emotional-integrative model. *Applied Cognitive Psychology, 23,* 98–114.

Curtin, S., & Werker, J. E. (2009). The perceptual foundations of phonological development. In M. G. Gaskell (Ed.), *The Oxford handbook of psycholinguistics* (pp. 579–599). New York: Oxford University Press.

Dahan, D. (2010). Word recognition. In E. B. Goldstein (Ed.), *Encyclopedia of perception* (Vol. 2, pp. 1141–1145). Thousand Oaks, CA: Sage.

Dahan, D., & Magnuson, J. S. (2006). Spoken word recognition. In M. J. Traxler & M. A. Gernsbacher (Eds.), *Handbook of psycholinguistics* (2nd ed., pp. 249–283). Amsterdam: Elsevier.

Dahlstrom-Hakki, I., et al. (2008). Eye movements and individual differences in mental rotation. In K. Rayner, D. Shen, X. Bai, & G. Yan (Eds.), *Cognitive and cultural influences on eye movements* (pp. 210–232). Tianjin, China: Tianjin People's Publishing House.

Damian, M. F., & Martin, R. C. (1999). Semantic and phonological codes interact in a single word production. *Journal of Experimental Psychology: Learning, Memory, and Cognition, 25,* 345–361.

Daneman, M. F., & Stainton, M. (1993). The generation effect in reading and proofreading. *Reading and Writing: An Interdisciplinary Journal, 5,* 297–313.

Danziger, S., & Ward, R. (2010). Language changes implicit associations between ethnic groups and evaluation in bilinguals. *Psychological Science, 21,* 799–800.

Darwin, C. J., Turvey, M. T., & Crowder, R. G. (1972). An auditory analogue of the Sperling partial report procedure: Evidence for brief auditory storage. *Cognitive Psychology, 3,* 255–267.

Davelaar, E. J., Haarmann, H. J., Goshen-Gottstein, Y., & Usher, M. (2006). Semantic similarity dissociates short- from long-term effects: Testing a neurocomputational model of list memory. *Memory & Cognition, 34,* 323–334.

Davelaar, E. J., et al. (2005). The demise of short-term memory revisited: Empirical and computational investigations of recency effects. *Psychological Review, 112,* 3–42.

Davenport, T., & Coulson, S. (2011). Predictability and novelty in literal language comprehension: An ERP study. *Brain Research, 1418,* 70–82.

Davidson, D. (1994). Recognition and recall of irrelevant and interruptive atypical actions in script-based stories. *Journal of Memory and Language, 33,* 757–775.

Davidson, D. (2006). Memory for bizarre and other unusual events: Evidence from script research. In R. R. Hunt & J. B. Worthen (Eds.), *Distinctiveness and memory* (pp. 157–179). New York: Oxford University Press.

Davidson, J. E. (1995). The suddenness of insight. In R. J. Sternberg & J. E. Davidson (Eds.), *The nature of insight* (pp. 125–155). Cambridge, MA: MIT Press.

Davidson, J. E., & Sternberg, R. J. (1998). Smart problem solving: How metacognition helps. In D. J. Hacker, J. Dunlosky, & A. C. Graesser (Eds.), *Metacognition in educational theory and practice* (pp. 47–65). Mahwah, NJ: Erlbaum.

Davies, G. M., & Wright, D. B. (Eds.). (2010a). *Current issues in applied memory research* (pp. 1–7). New York: Psychology Press.

Davies, G. M., & Wright, D. B. (2010b). Introduction. In G. M. Davies & D. B. Wright (Eds.), *Current issues in applied memory research* (pp. 1–7). New York: Psychology Press.

Davies, S. P. (2005). Planning and problem solving in well-defined domains. In R. Morris & G. Ward (Eds.), *The cognitive psychology of planning* (pp. 35–51). Hove, UK: Psychology Press.

Davis, D., & Friedman, R. D. (2007). Memory for conversation: The orphan child of witness memory researchers. In M. P. Toglia, J. D. Read, D. F. Ross, & R. C. L. Lindsay (Eds.), *Handbook of eyewitness psychology* (Vol. 1, pp. 3–52). Mahwah, NJ: Erlbaum.

Davis, D., & Loftus, E. F. (2007). Internal and external sources of misinformation in adult witness memory. In M. P. Toglia, J. D. Read, D. F. Ross, & R. C. L. Lindsay (Eds.), *Handbook of eyewitness psychology* (Vol. 1, pp. 195–237). Mahwah, NJ: Erlbaum.

Davis, D., & Loftus, E. F. (2008). Expectancies, emotion, and memory reports for visual events. In J. R. Brockmole (Ed.), *The visual world in memory* (pp. 178–214). New York: Psychology Press.

Davis, M. H., Marslen-Wilson, W. D., & Gaskell, M. G. (2002). Leading up the lexical garden path: Segmentation and ambiguity in spoken word recognition. *Journal of Experimental Psychology: Human Perception and Performance, 28,* 218–244.

Davis, T., & Love, B. C. (2010). Memory for category information is idealized through contrast with competing options. *Psychological Science, 21,* 234–242.

de Bot, K., & Makoni, S. (2005). *Language and aging in multilingual contexts.* Clevedon, UK: Multilingual Matters.

de Boysson-Bardies, B. (1999). *How language comes to children: From birth to two years.* Cambridge, MA: MIT Press.

De Dreu, C., Baas, M., & Nijstad, B. A. (2008). Hedonic tone and activation level in the mood-creativity link: Toward a dual pathway to creativity model. *Journal of Personality and Social Psychology, 94,* 739–756.

Defeldre, A.-C. (2005). Inadvertent plagiarism in everyday life. *Applied Cognitive Psychology, 19,* 1033–1040.

De Groot, A. M. B. (2011). *Language and cognition in bilinguals and multilinguals: An introduction.* New York: Psychology Press.

Dehaene, S., & Naccache, L. (2001). Towards a cognitive neuroscience of consciousness: Basic evidence and a workspace framework. In S. Dehaene (Ed.), *The cognitive neuroscience of consciousness* (pp. 1–37). Cambridge, MA: MIT Press.

Dehaene, S., et al. (2006). Conscious, preconscious, and subliminal processing: A testable taxonomy. *Trends in Cognitive Sciences, 10,* 204–211.

DeHart, G. B., Sroufe, L. A., & Cooper, R. G. (2004). *Child development: Its nature and course* (5th ed.). New York: McGraw Hill.

De Houwer, J., Teige-Mocigemba, S., Spruyt, A., & Moors, A. (2009). Implicit measures: A normative analysis and review. *Psychological Bulletin, 135,* 347–368.

de Jong, P. F. (2006). Understanding normal and impaired reading development: A working memory perspective. In S. J. Pickering (Ed.), *Working memory and education* (pp. 33–60). Burlington, MA: Elsevier.

De Koning, B. B., Tabbers, H. K., Rikers, R. M. J. P., & Paas, F. (2011). Improved effectiveness of cueing by self-explanations when learning from a complex animation. *Applied Cognitive Psychology, 25,* 183–194.

Delgado, M. R., Phelps, E. A., & Robbins, T. W. (Eds.). (2011). *Decision making, affect, and learning.* New York: Oxford University Press.

De Lissnyder, E., Koster, E. H. W., Derakshan, N., & De Raedt, R. (2010). The association between depressive symptoms and executive control impairments in response to emotional and non-emotional information. In N. Derakshan & M Eysenck (Eds.), *Emotional states, attention, and working memory* (pp. 264–280). New York: Psychology Press.

Dell, G. S. (1986). A spreading-activation theory of retrieval in sentence production. *Psychological Review, 93*, 283–321.

Dell, G. S. (1995). Speaking and misspeaking. In L. R. Gleitman & M. Liberman (Eds.), *Language* (pp. 183–208). Cambridge, MA: MIT Press.

Dell, G. S. (2005). Language production, lexical access, and aphasia. In G. Houghton (Ed.), *Connectionist models in cognitive psychology* (pp. 373–401). New York: Psychology Press.

Dell, G. S., Burger, L. K., & Svec, W. R. (1997). Language production and serial order: A functional analysis and a model. *Psychological Review, 104*, 123–147.

Dell, G. S., Reed, K. D., Adams, D. R., & Meyer, A. S. (2000). Speech errors, phonotactic constraints, and implicit learning: A study of the role of experience in language production. *Journal of Experimental Psychology: Learning, Memory, and Cognition, 26*, 1355–1367.

Dell, G. S., Warker, J. A., & Whalen, C. A. (2008). Speech errors and the implicit learning of phonological sequences. In E. Morsella, J. A. Bargh, & P. M. Gollwitzer (Eds.), *The psychology of action*. New York: Oxford University Press.

Dell, G. S., et al. (1997). Lexical access in aphasic and nonaphasic speakers. *Psychological Review, 104*, 801–838.

DeLoache, J. S., et al. (2010). Do babies learn from baby media? *Psychological Science, 21*, 1570–1574.

De Neys, W., & Goel, V. (2011). Heuristics and biases in the brain: Dual neural pathways for decision making. In O. Vartanian & D. R. Mandel (Eds.), *Neuroscience of decision making* (pp. 125–141). New York: Psychology Press.

Denis, M., & Kosslyn, S. M. (1999a). Does the window really need to be washed? More on the mental scanning paradigm. *Cahiers de Psychologie Cognitive, 18*, 593–616.

Denis, M., & Kosslyn, S. M. (1999b). Scanning visual mental images: A window on the mind. *Cahiers de Psychologie Cognitive, 18*, 409–465.

Denis, M., Mellet, E., & Kosslyn, S. M. (2004). Neuroimaging of mental imagery: An introduction. *European Journal of Cognitive Psychology, 16*, 625–630.

Department of Veterans Affairs. (2010). Mild traumatic brain injury-concussion. Retrieved April 28, 2012, from http://www.publichealth.va.gov/docs/exposures/TBI-pocketcard.pdf

DePrince, A. P., & Freyd, J. J. (2004). Forgetting trauma stimuli. *Psychological Science, 15*, 488–492.

Derakshan, N., & Eysenck, M. (Eds.). (2010a). *Emotional states, attention, and working memory.* New York: Psychology Press.

Derakshan, N., & Eysenck, M. (2010b). Introduction to the special issue: Emotional states, attention, and working memory. In N. Derakshan & M. Eysenck (Eds.), *Emotional states, attention, and working memory* (pp. 189–199). New York: Psychology Press.

D'Esposito, M., Zarahn, E., & Aguirre, G. K. (1999). Event-related functional MRI: Implications for cognitive psychology. *Psychological Bulletin, 125*, 155–164.

de Villiers, J. G., & de Villiers, P. A. (1999). Language development. In M. H. Bornstein & M. E. Lamb (Eds.), *Developmental psychology: An advanced textbook* (4th ed., pp. 313–373). Mahwah, NJ: Erlbaum.

Devlin, A. S. (2001). *Mind and maze: Spatial cognition and environmental behavior.* Westport, CT: Praeger.

deWinstanley, P. A., & Bjork, R. A. (2002). Successful lecturing: Presenting information in ways that engage effective processing. In D. F. Halpern & M. D. Hakel (Eds.), *Applying the science of learning to university teaching and beyond* (pp. 19–31). San Francisco: Jossey-Bass.

Diana, R. A., & Reder, L. M. (2004). Visual and verbal metacognition: Are they really different? In D. T. Levin (Ed.), *Thinking and seeing: Visual metacognition in adults and children* (pp. 187–201). Cambridge, MA: MIT Press.

Diaz, M., & Benjamin, A. S. (2011). The effects of proactive interference (PI) and release from PI on judgments of learning. *Memory & Cognition, 39*, 196–203.

Diaz, R. M. (1985). Bilingual cognitive development: Addressing three gaps in current research. *Child Development, 56*, 1376–1388.

Dick, F., et al. (2001). Language deficits, localization, and grammar: Evidence for a distributive model of language breakdown in aphasic patients and neurologically intact individuals. *Psychological Review, 108*, 759–788.

Diehl, R. L., Lotto, A. J., & Holt, L. L. (2004). Speech perception. *Annual Review of Psychology, 55*, 149–179.

Dietrich, A. (2007). Who's afraid of a cognitive neuroscience of creativity? *Methods, 42*, 22–27.

Dietrich, A., & Kanso, R. (2010). A review of EEG, ERP, and neuroimaging studies of creativity and insight. *Psychological Bulletin, 136*, 822–848.

Dijkerman, C. H., Ietswaart, M., & Johnston, M. (2010). Motor imagery and the rehabilitation of movement disorders: An overview. In A. Guillot & C. Collet (Eds.), *The neurophysiological foundations of mental and motor imagery* (pp. 127–142). New York: Oxford University Press.

Dijksterhuis, A., & Aarts, H. (2010). Goals, attention and (un)consciousness. *Annual Review of Psychology*, *61*, 467–490.

Dismukes, R. K., & Nowinski, J. L. (2007). Prospective memory, concurrent task management, and pilot error. In A. Kramer, D. Wiegmann, & A. Kirlik (Eds.), *Attention: From theory to practice*. New York: Oxford University Press.

Diwadkar, V. A., Carpenter, P. A., & Just, M. A. (2000). Collaborative activity between parietal and dorsolateral prefrontal cortex in dynamic spatial working memory revealed by fMRI. *NeuroImage*, *12*, 85–99.

Dixon, R. A., & Cohen, A. L. (2003). Cognitive development in adulthood. In R. M. Lerner, M. A. Easterbrooks, & J. Mistry (Eds.), *Handbook of psychology* (Vol. 6, pp. 443–461). Hoboken, NJ: Wiley.

Dodson, C. S., Bawa, S., & Krueger, L. F. (2007). Aging, metamemory, and high-confidence errors: A misrecollection account. *Psychology and Aging*, *22*, 122–133.

Dominowski, R. L. (2002). *Teaching undergraduates*. Mahwah, NJ: Erlbaum.

Donaldson, M. (2004). Language: Learning word meanings. In R. L. Gregory (Ed.), *The Oxford companion to the mind* (2nd ed., pp. 513–515). New York: Oxford University Press.

Donderi, D. C. (2006). Visual complexity: A review. *Psychological Bulletin*, *132*, 73–97.

Douglass, A. B., & Steblay, N. (2006). Memory distortion in eyewitnesses: A meta-analysis of the post-identification feedback effect. *Applied Cognitive Psychology*, *20*, 859–869.

Doumas, L. A. A., & Hummel, J. E. (2010). A computational account of the development of the generalization of shape information. *Cognitive Science*, *34*, 698–712.

Doumas, L. A. A., & Hummel, J. E. (2012). Computation models of higher cognition. In K. J. Holyoak & R. G. Morrison (Eds.), *The Oxford handbook of thinking and reasoning* (pp. 52–66). New York: Oxford University Press.

Drieghe, D., Brysbaert, M., Desmet, T., & DeBaecke, C. (2004). Word skipping in reading: On the interplay of linguistic and visual factors. In R. Radach, A. Kennedy, & K. Rayner (Eds.), *Eye movements and information processing during reading* (pp. 79–103). Hove, UK: Psychology Press.

Dror, I. E., & Kosslyn, S. M. (1994). Mental imagery and aging. *Psychology and Aging*, *9*, 90–102.

Dube, C., Rotello, C. M., & Heit, E. (2010). Assessing the belief bias effect with ROCs: It's a response bias effect. *Psychological Review*, *117*, 831–863.

Dube, C., Rotello, C. M., & Heit, E. (2011). The belief bias effect is aptly named: A reply to Klauer and Kellen (2011). *Psychological Review*, *118*, 155–163.

Duchaine, B. C., & Nakayama, K. (2006). Developmental prosopagnosia: A window to content-specific face processing. *Current Opinion in Neurobiology*, *16*, 166–173.

Duckworth, A. L., et al. (2011). Deliberate practice spells success: Why grittier competitors triumph at the National Spelling Bee. *Social Psychological and Personality Science*, *2*, 174–181.

Dudukovic, N. M., Marsh, E. J., & Tversky, B. (2004). Telling a story or telling it straight: The effects of entertaining versus accurate retellings on memory. *Applied Cognitive Psychology*, *18*, 125–143.

Duffy, G. G., Miller, S., Parsons, S., & Meloth, M. (2009). Teachers as metacognitive professionals. In D. J. Hacker, J. Dunlosky, & A. C. Graesser (Eds.), *Handbook of metacognition in education* (pp. 240–256). New York: Routledge.

Dunbar, K. (1998). Problem solving. In W. Bechtel & G. Graham (Eds.), *A companion to cognitive science* (pp. 289–298). Malden, MA: Blackwell.

Duncan, J. (1999). Attention. In R. A. Wilson & F. C. Keil (Eds.), *The MIT encyclopedia of the cognitive sciences* (pp. 39–41). Cambridge, MA: MIT Press.

Duncan, J., et al. (2000). A neural basis for general intelligence. *Science*, *289*, 457–460.

Duncker, K. (1945). On problem solving. *Psychological Monographs*, *58* (Whole No. 270).

Dunlosky, J., & Bjork, R. A. (2008a). *Handbook of metamemory and memory*. New York: Psychology Press.

Dunlosky, J., & Bjork, R. A. (2008b). The integrated nature of metamemory and memory. In J. Dunlosky & R. A. Bjork (Eds.), *Handbook of metamemory and memory* (pp. 11–28). New York: Psychology Press.

Dunlosky, J., & Hertzog, C. (1997). Older and younger adults use a functionally identical algorithm to select items for restudy during multitrial learning. *Journal of Gerontology: Psychological Sciences*, *52B*, P178–P186.

Dunlosky, J., & Hertzog, C. (1998). Aging and deficits in associative memory: What is the role of strategy production? *Psychology and Aging*, *13*, 597–607.

Dunlosky, J., & Lipko, A. R. (2007). Metacomprehension: A brief history and how to improve its accuracy. *Current Directions in Psychological Science*, *16*, 228–232.

Dunlosky, J., & Metcalfe, J. (2009). *Metacognition.* Thousand Oaks, CA: Sage.

Dunlosky, J., Rawson, K. A., & Middleton, E. L. (2005). What constrains the accuracy of metacomprehension judgments? Testing the transfer-appropriate-monitoring and accessibility hypotheses. *Journal of Memory and Language, 52,* 551–565.

Dunn, J., & Kendrick, C. (1982). The speech of two- and three-year-olds to infant siblings: "Baby talk" and the context of communication. *Journal of Child Language, 9,* 579–595.

Dunning, D., Johnson, K., Ehrlinger, J., & Kruger, J. (2003). Why people fail to recognize their own incompetence. *Current Directions in Psychological Science, 12,* 83–87.

Dunning, D., & Sherman, D. A. (1997). Stereotypes and tacit inference. *Journal of Personality and Social Psychology, 73,* 459–471.

Dweck, C. S. (2006). *Mindset: The new psychology of success.* New York: Random House.

Dysart, J. E., & Lindsay, R. C. L. (2007). The effects of delay on eyewitness identification accuracy: Should we be concerned? In R. C. L. Lindsay, D. F. Ross, J. D. Read, & M. P. Toglia (Eds.), *Handbook of eyewitness psychology* (Vol. 2, pp. 361–376). Mahwah, NJ: Erlbaum.

D'Zurilla, T. J, & Maydeu-Olivares, A. (2004). Social problem solving: Theory and assessment. In E. C. Chang, T. J. D'Zurilla, & L. J. Sanna (Eds.), *Social problem solving: Theory, research, and training* (pp. 11–27). Washington, DC: American Psychological Association.

Eagly, A. H., & Carli, L. L. (2007). *Through the labyrinth: The truth about how women become leaders.* Boston: Harvard Business School Press.

Easton, A., & Emery, N. J. (Eds.). (2005). *The cognitive neuroscience of social behaviour* (pp. 1–16). New York: Psychology Press.

Economou, A., Simos, P. G., & Papanicolaou, A. C. (2006). Age-related memory decline. In A. C. Papanicolaou (Ed.), *The amnesias: A clinical textbook of memory disorders* (pp. 57–74). New York: Oxford University Press.

Edelman, G. M. (2005). *Wider than the sky: The phenomenal gift of consciousness.* New Haven: Yale University Press.

Edwards, D. (1997). *Discourse and cognition.* London: Sage.

Ehrlich, M. (1998). Metacognitive monitoring in the processing of anaphoric devices in skilled and less skilled comprehenders. In C. Cornoldi & J. Oakhill (Eds.), *Reading comprehension difficulties: Processes and interventions* (pp. 221–249). Mahwah, NJ: Erlbaum.

Eich, E. (1995). Mood as a mediator of place dependent memory. *Journal of Experimental Psychology: General, 124,* 293–308.

Einstein, G. O., & McDaniel, M. A. (2004). *Memory fitness: A guide for successful aging.* New Haven, CT: Yale University Press.

Eisen, M. L., Quas, J. A., & Goodman, G. S. (Eds.). (2002). *Memory and suggestibility in the forensic interview.* Mahwah, NJ: Erlbaum.

Eisenberger, R., & Rhoades, L. (2001). Incremental effects of rewards on creativity. *Journal of Personality and Social Psychology, 81,* 728–741.

Eliott, A. J., & Mapes, R. R. (2002). Enhancing the yield. [Review of the book *Intrinsic and extrinsic motivation: The search for optimal motivation and performance*]. *Contemporary Psychology, 47,* 200–202.

Else-Quest, N., Hyde, J. S., & Linn, M. C. (2010). Cross-national patterns of gender differences in mathematics: A meta-analysis. *Psychological Bulletin, 136,* 103–127.

Emberson, L. J., Lupyan, G., Goldstein, M. H., & Spivey, M. J. (2010). Overheard cell-phone conversations: When less speech is more distracting. *Psychological Science, 21,* 1383–1388.

Emery, N. J., & Easton, A. (2005). Introduction: What is social cognitive neuroscience (SCN)? In A. Easton & N. J. Emery (Eds.), *The cognitive neuroscience of social behaviour* (pp. 1–16). New York: Psychology Press.

Emmanouil, T.-A., & Treisman, A. (2008). Divided attention across feature dimensions in statistical processing of perceptual groups. *Perception & Psychophysics, 70,* 946–954.

Emmorey, K., Klima, E., & Hickok, G. (1998). Mental rotation within linguistic and non-linguistic domains in users of American Sign Language. *Cognition, 68,* 221–246.

Endsley, M. R. (2006). Expertise and situation awareness. In K. A. Ericsson, N. Charness, P. J. Feltovich, & R. R. Hoffman (Eds.), *The Cambridge handbook of expertise and expert performance* (pp. 633–651). New York: Cambridge University Press.

Engbert, R., & Krügel, A. (2010). Readers use Bayesian estimation for eye movement control. *Psychological Science, 21,* 366–371.

Engbert, R., Nuthman, A., Richter, E. M., & Kliegl, R. (2005). SWIFT: A dynamic model of saccade generation during reading. *Psychological Review, 112,* 777–813.

Engelkamp, J. (1998). *Memory for actions.* Hove, UK: Psychology Press.

Engle, R. W. (2011, May). *Perspectives on scientific writing.* Presented at the annual meeting of the Association for Psychological Science, Washington, DC.

Englich, B., & Mussweiler, T. (2001). Sentencing under uncertainty: Anchoring effects in the courtroom. *Journal of Applied Social Psychology, 31,* 1535–1551.

Epstein, R. (2004). Watson, John Broadus. In R. L. Gregory (Ed.), *The Oxford companion to the mind* (2nd ed., pp. 942–943). New York: Oxford University Press.

Erber, J. T. (2005). *Aging and older adulthood.* Belmont, CA: Thomson Wadsworth.

Erdoğan, A., et al. (2008). On the persistence of positive events in life scripts. *Applied Cognitive Psychology, 22,* 95–111.

Erickson, M. A., & Kruschke, J. K. (1998). Rules and exemplars in category learning. *Journal of Experimental Psychology: General, 127,* 107–140.

Erickson, M. A., & Kruschke, J. K. (2002). Rule-based extrapolation in perceptual categorization. *Psychonomic Bulletin & Review, 9,* 160–168.

Ericsson, K. A. (2003a). Exceptional memorizers: Made, not born. *TRENDS in Cognitive Psychology, 7,* 233–235.

Ericsson, K. A. (2003b). The search for general abilities and basic capacities: Theoretical implications from the modifiability and complexity of mechanisms mediating expert performance. In R. J. Sternberg & E. L. Grigorenko (Eds.), *The psychology of abilities, competencies, and expertise* (pp. 93–125). New York: Cambridge University Press.

Ericsson, K. A. (2006). An introduction to Cambridge handbook of expertise and expert performance: Its development, organization and content. In K. A. Ericsson, N. Charness, P. J. Feltovich, & R. R. Hoffman (Eds.), *The Cambridge handbook of expertise and performance* (pp. 3–19). New York: Cambridge University Press.

Ericsson, K. A., Charness, N., Feltovich, P. J., & Hoffman, R. R. (Eds.). (2006). *The Cambridge handbook of expertise and expert performance.* New York: Cambridge University Press.

Ericsson, K. A., Delaney, P. F., Weaver, G., & Mahadevan, R. (2004). Uncovering the structure of a memorist's "basic" memory capacity. *Cognitive Psychology, 49,* 191–237.

Ericsson, K. A., & Fox, M. C. (2011). Thinking aloud is not a form of introspection but a qualitatively different methodology: Reply to Schooler (2011). *Psychological Bulletin, 137,* 351–354.

Ericsson, K. A., & Kintsch, W. (1995). Long-term working memory. *Psychological Review, 102,* 211–245.

Ericsson, K. A., & Lehmann, A. C. (1996). Expert and exceptional performance: Evidence of maximal adaptation to task constraints. *Annual Review of Psychology, 47,* 273–305.

Ericsson, K. A., Nandagopal, K., & Roring, R. W. (2009). Toward a science of exceptional achievement: Attaining superior performance through deliberate practice. *Longevity, Regeneration, and Optimal Health: Annals of the New York Academy of Sciences,* 199–217.

Ericsson, K. A, & Towne, T. J. (2010). Expertise. *Wiley Interdisciplinary Reviews: Cognitive Science, 1,* 404–416.

Ericsson, K. A., et al. (2009). The measurement and development of professional performance: An introduction to the topic and a background on the design and origin of this book. In K. Anders Ericsson (Ed.), *Development of professional expertise; Toward measurement of expert performance and design of optimal learning environments* (pp. 1–24). New York: Cambridge.

Erskine, J. A. K., Georgiou, G. J., & Kvavilashvili, L. (2010). I suppress, therefore I smoke: Effects of thought suppression on smoking behavior. *Psychological Science, 21,* 1225–1230.

Erwin-Tripp, S. (2011). Advances in the study of bilingualism: A personal view. In V. Cook & B. Bassetti (Eds.), *Language and bilingual cognition* (pp. 219–228). New York: Psychology Press.

Esgate, A., & Groome, D. (2005). *An introduction to applied cognitive psychology.* Hove, UK: Psychology Press.

Ethnologue Languages of the World. (2011). Statistical summaries. Retrieved June 23, 2011, from http://www.ethnologue.com/ethno_docs/distribution.asp?by=size

Evans, J. St. B. T. (2000). What could and could not be a strategy in reasoning. In W. Schaeken, G. DeVooght, A. Vandierendonck, & G. d'Ydewalle (Eds.), *Deductive reasoning and strategies* (pp. 1–22). Mahwah, NJ: Erlbaum.

Evans, J. St. B. T. (2002). Logic and human reasoning: An assessment of the deduction paradigm. *Psychological Bulletin, 128,* 978–996.

Evans, J. St. B. T. (2004). Biases in deductive reasoning. In R. F. Pohl (Eds.), *Cognitive illusions: A handbook on fallacies and biases in thinking, judgement, and memory* (pp. 127–144). Hove, UK: Psychology Press.

Evans, J. St. B. T. (2005). Insight and self-insight in reasoning and decision making. In V. Girotto &

P. N. Johnson-Laird (Eds.), *The shape of reason: Essays in honour of Paolo Legrenzi* (pp. 27–47). Hove, UK: Psychology Press.

Evans, J. St. B. T. (2006). The heuristic-analytic theory of reasoning: Extension and evaluation. *Psychonomic Bulletin & Review, 13*, 378–395

Evans, J. St. B. T. (2011). Reasoning is for thinking, not just for arguing. *Behavioral and Brain Sciences, 34*, 57–111.

Evans, J. St. B. T. (2012). Dual-process theories of deductive reasoning: Facts and fallacies. In K. J. Holyoak & R. G. Morrison (Eds.), *The Oxford handbook of thinking and reasoning* (pp. 115–133). New York: Oxford University Press.

Evans, V., & Green, M. (2006). *Cognitive linguistics: An introduction.* Mahwah, NJ: Erlbaum.

Everett, D. L. (2005). Cultural constraints on grammar and cognition in Pirahã: Another look at the design features of human language. *Current Anthropology, 76*, 621–646.

Everett, D. L. (2007). Challenging Chomskyan Linguistics: The case of Pirahã. *Human Development, 50*, 297–299.

Eysenck, M. W., & Keane, M. T. (2010). *Cognitive psychology: A student's handbook* (6th ed.). Hove, UK: Psychology Press.

Fabiani, M., & Wee, E. (2001). Age-related changes in working memory and frontal lobe function: A review. In C. A. Nelson & M. Luciana (Eds.), *Handbook of developmental cognitive neuroscience* (pp. 473–488). Cambridge, MA: MIT Press.

Falsetti, S. A., Monnier, J., & Resnick, H. S. (2005). Intrusive thoughts in postraumatic stress disorder. In D. A. Clark (Ed.), *Intrusive thoughts in clinical disorders: Theory, research, and treatment* (pp. 30–53). New York: Guilford Press.

Fan, J., et al. (2002). Testing the efficiency and independence of attentional networks. *Journal of Cognitive Neuroscience, 14*, 340–347.

Farah, M. J. (2000). *The cognitive neuroscience of vision.* Malden, MA: Blackwell.

Farah, M. J. (2001). Consciousness. In B. Rapp (Ed.), *The handbook of cognitive neuropsychology* (pp. 159–182). Philadelphia: Psychology Press.

Farah, M. J. (2002). Emerging ethical issues in neuroscience. *Nature Neuroscience, 5*, 1123.

Farah, M. J. (2004). *Visual agnosia* (2nd ed.). Cambridge, MA: MIT Press.

Farrimond, S., Knight, R. G., & Titov, N. (2006). The effects of aging on remembering intentions:

Performance on a simulated shopping task. *Applied Cognitive Psychology, 20*, 533–555.

Fay, N., et al. (2008). Speaker overestimation of communication effectiveness and fear of negative evaluation: Being realistic is unrealistic. *Psychonomic Bulletin & Review, 15*, 1160–1165.

Fedorenko, E., Behr, M. K., & Kanwisher, N. (2011). Functional specificity for high-level linguistic processing in the human brain. *PNAS Early Edition*, pp. 1–6. doi: 10.1073/pnas.1112937108.

Fedorenko, E., Nieto Castañón, A., & Kanwisher, N. (2011). Syntactic processing in the human brain: What we know, what we don't know, and a suggestion for how to proceed. *Brain & Language*, doi: 10.1016/j.bandl.2011.01.001.

Fehr, B. (2005). The role of prototypes in interpersonal cognition. In M. W. Baldwin (Ed.), *Interpersonal cognition* (pp. 180–205). New York: Guilford.

Fehr, B., & Sprecher, S. (2009). Prototype analysis of the concept of compassionate love. *Personal Relationships, 16*, 343–364.

Feist, G. J. (2006). Why the studies of science need a psychology of science. *Review of General Psychology, 10*, 183–187.

Feist, G. J. (2010). The function of personality in creativity: The nature and nurture of the creative personality. In J. C. Kaufman & R. J. Sternberg (Eds.), *The Cambridge handbook of creativity* (pp. 113–130). New York: Cambridge University Press.

Feldman, D. H., Csikszentmihalyi, M., & Gardner, H. (1994). *Changing the world: A framework for the study of creativity.* Westport, CT: Praeger.

Feltovich, P. J., Prietula, M. J., & Ericsson, K. A. (2006). Studies of expertise from psychological perspectives. In K. A. Ericsson, N. Charness, P. J. Feltovich, & R. R. Hoffman (Eds.), *The Cambridge handbook of expertise and expert performance* (pp. 41–67). New York: Cambridge University Press.

Fennell, C. T. (2012). *Habituation procedures. Research methods in child language: A practical guide* (pp. 3–16). Malden, MA: Blackwell.

Fernald, A., & Marchman, V. A. (2006). Language learning in infancy. In M. J. Traxler & M. A. Gernsbacher (Eds.), *Handbook of psycholinguistics* (2nd ed., pp. 1027–1071). Amsterdam: Elsevier.

Fernald, A., et al. (1998). Rapid gains in speed of verbal processing by infants in the 2nd year. *Psychological Science, 9*, 228–231.

Ferreira, F., Bailey, K. G. D., & Ferraro, V. (2002). Good-enough representations in language comprehension. *Current Directions in Psychological Science, 11,* 11–15.

Ferreira, F., & Patson, N. D. (2007). The "good enough" approach to language comprehension. *Language and Linguistics Compass, 1,* 71–83.

Ferreira, V. S., & Slevc, L. R. (2009). Grammatical encoding. In M. G. Gaskell (Ed.), *The Oxford handbook of psycholinguistics* (pp. 453–487). New York: Oxford University Press.

Fetzer, A., & Oishi, E. (Eds.). (2011). *Context and contexts.* Amsterdam: John Benjamins Publishing Company.

Fiedler, K., Friese, M., & Wänke, M. (2011). Psycholinguistic methods in social psychology. In K. C. Klauer, A. Voss, & C. Stahl (Eds.), *Cognitive methods in social psychology* (206–235). New York: Guilford.

Fiedler, K., Nickel, S., Asbeck, J., & Pagel, U. (2003). Mood and the generation effect. *Cognition and Emotion, 17,* 585–608.

Fiedler, K., & Walther, E. (2004). *Stereotyping as inductive hypothesis testing.* Hove, UK: Psychology Press.

Field, J. (2004). *Psycholinguistics: The key concepts.* New York: Routledge.

Fields, A. W., & Shelton, A. L. (2006). Individual skill differences and large-scale environmental learning. *Journal of Experimental Psychology: Learning, Memory, and Cognition, 32,* 506–515.

Findlay, J. M., & Gilchrist, I. D. (2001). Visual attention: The active vision perspective. In M. Jenkin & L. Harris (Eds.), *Vision and attention* (pp. 83–103). New York: Springer-Verlag.

Finke, R. A., Pinker, S., & Farah, M. J. (1989). Reinterpreting visual patterns in mental imagery. *Cognitive Science, 13,* 51–78.

Finstad, K., Bink, M., McDaniel, M., & Einstein, G. O. (2006). Breaks and task switches in prospective memory. *Applied Cognitive Psychology, 20,* 705–712.

Fioratou, E., & Cowley, S. J. (2011). Insightful thinking: Cognitive dynamics and material artifacts. In S. J. Cowley (Ed.), *Distributed language* (pp. 57–80). Amsterdam: John Benjamins.

Fiore, S., & Schooler, J. W. (2004). Process mapping and shared cognition: Teamwork and the development of shared problem models. In E. Salas & S. M. Fiore (Eds.), *Team cognition: Understanding the factors that drive process and performance* (pp. 133–152). Washington, DC: American Psychological Association.

Fisher, D. L., & Pollatsek, A. (2007). Novice driver crashes: Failure to divide attention or failure to recognize risks. In A. F. Kramer, D. A. Wiegmann, & A. Kirlik (Eds.), *Attention: From theory to practice* (pp. 134–153). New York: Oxford University Press.

Fisher, K. J., Borchert, K., & Bassok, M. (2011). Following the standard form: Effects of equation format on algebraic modeling. *Memory & Cognition, 39,* 502–515.

Fishman, J. A. (2006). The new linguistic order. In H. Luria, D. M. Seymour, & T. Smoke (Eds.), *Language and linguistics in context: Readings and applications for teachers* (pp. 175–189). Mahwah, NJ: Erlbaum.

Fisk, J. E. (2004). Conjunction fallacy. In R. Pohl (Ed.), *Cognitive illusions: Handbook on fallacies and biases in thinking, judgment, and memory* (pp. 23–42) Hove, UK: Psychology Press.

Fitzgerald, J. M. (2010). Culture, gender, and the first memories of black and white American students. *Memory & Cognition, 38,* 785–796.

Fivush, R. (2009). Co-constructing memories and meaning over time. In J. A. Quas & R. Fivush (Eds.), *Emotion and memory in development: Biological, cognitive, and social considerations* (pp. 343–354). New York: Oxford University Press.

Fivush, R. (2011). The development of autobiographical memory. *Annual Review of Psychology, 62,* 559–582.

Fivush, R., & Nelson, K. (2004). Culture and language in the emergence of autobiographical memory. *Psychological Science, 15,* 573–577.

Flavell, J. H., Miller, P. H., & Miller, S. A. (2002). *Cognitive development* (4th ed.). Upper Saddle River, NJ: Prentice-Hall.

Flege, J. E., Yeni-Komshiam, G. H., & Liu, S. (1999). Age constraints on second-language acquisition. *Journal of Memory and Language, 41,* 78–104.

Flores Salgado, E. F. (2011). *The pragmatics of requests and apologies.* Philadelphia: John Benjamins.

Flower, L. S., & Hayes, J. R. (1980). The dynamics of composing: Making plans and juggling constraints. In L. W. Gregg & E. R. Steinberg (Eds.), *Cognitive processes in writing* (pp. 31–50). Hillsdale, NJ: Erlbaum.

Foley, H. J., & Matlin, M. W. (2010). *Sensation and perception* (5th ed.). Boston, MA: Allyn & Bacon.

Foley, M. A. (2012). Remember *imagining that?* Children's source monitoring of memories for imagination. In M. Taylor (Ed.), *Development of imagination.* New York: Oxford University Press.

Foley, M. A., & Foley, H. J. (1998). A study of face identification: Are people looking beyond disguises?

In M. J. Intons-Peterson & D. L. Best (Eds.), *Memory distortions and their prevention* (pp. 29–47). Mahwah, NJ: Erlbaum.

Foley, M. A., Belch, C., Mann, R., & McLean, M. (1999). Self-referencing: How incessant the stream? *American Journal of Psychology, 112,* 73–96.

Foley, M. A., Foley, H. J., & Korenman, L. M. (2002). Adapting a memory framework (source monitoring) to the study of closure processes. *Memory & Cognition, 30,* 412–422.

Foley, M. A., & Ratner, H. H. (1998). Distinguishing between memories for thoughts and deeds: The role of prospective processing in children's source monitoring. *British Journal of Developmental Psychology, 16,* 465–484.

Foley, M. A., Ratner, H. H., & Gentes, E. (2010). Helping children enter into another's experiences: The look and feel of it. *Journal of Cognition and Development, 11,* 217–239.

Foley, M. A., Ratner, H. H., & House, A. T. (2002). Anticipation and source-monitoring errors: Children's memory for collaborative activities. *Journal of Cognition and Development, 3,* 385–414.

Foley, M. A., Wilder, A., McCall, R., & Van Vorst, R. (1993). The consequences for recall of children's ability to generate interactive imagery in the absence of external supports. *Journal of Experimental Child Psychology, 56,* 173–200.

Folk, C. L. (2010). Attention: Divided. In E. B. Goldstein (Ed.), *Encyclopedia of perception* (Vol. 1, pp. 84–87). Thousand Oaks, CA: Sage.

Foltz, P. W. (2003). Quantitative cognitive models of text and discourse processing. In A. C. Graesser, M. A. Gernsbacher, & S. R. Goldman (Eds.), *Handbook of discourse processes* (pp. 487–523). Mahwah, NJ: Erlbaum.

Forgas, J. P. (2001). The Affect Infusion Model (AIM): An integrative theory of mood effects on cognition and judgment. In L. L. Martin & G. L. Clore (Eds.), *Theories of mood and cognition* (pp. 99–134). Mahwah, NJ: Erlbaum.

Forster, K. I. (1981). Priming and the effects of sentence and lexical contexts on naming time: Evidence for autonomous lexical processing. *Quarterly Journal of Experimental Psychology, 33A,* 465–495.

Forsyth, D. K., & Burt, C. D. B. (2008). Allocating time to future tasks: The effect of task segmentation on planning fallacy bias. *Memory & Cognition, 36,* 791–798.

Fowler, C. A. (2003). Speech production and perception. In A. F. Healy & R. W. Proctor (Eds.), *Handbook of psychology* (Vol. 4, pp. 237–266). Hoboken, NJ: Wiley.

Fowler, C. A., & Galantucci, B. (2005). The relation of speech perception and speech production. In D. B. Pisoni & R. E. Remez (Eds.), *The handbook of speech perception* (pp. 633–652). Malden, MA: Blackwell.

Fox, E. (Ed.). (2005). *Visual social cognition.* Hove, UK: Psychology Press.

Fox, M. C., Ericsson, K. A., & Best, R. (2011). Do procedures for verbal reporting of thinking have to be reactive? A meta-analysis and recommendations for best reporting methods. *Psychological Bulletin, 137,* 316–344.

Fox Tree, J. E. (2000). Coordinating spontaneous talk. In L. Wheeldon (Ed.), *Aspects of language production* (pp. 375–406). Hove, UK: Psychology Press.

Franconeri, S. I., Hollingworth, A., & Simons, D. J. (2005). Do new objects capture attention? *Psychological Science, 16,* 275–281.

Franklin, N., & Tversky, B. (1990). Searching imagined environments. *Journal of Experimental Psychology: General, 119,* 63–76.

Franklin, S. (1995). *Artificial minds.* Cambridge, MA: MIT Press.

Freyd, J. J., & DePrince, A. A. (Eds.). (2001). *Trauma and cognitive science.* New York: Haworth.

Freyd, J. J., Klest, B., & DePrince, A. P. (2010). Avoiding awareness of betrayal: Comment on Lindblom and Gray (2009). *Applied Cognitive Psychology, 24,* 20–26.

Freyd, J. J., & Quina, K. (2000). Feminist ethics in the practice of science: The contested memory controversy as an example. In M. M. Brabeck (Ed.), *Practicing feminist ethics in psychology* (pp. 101–123). Washington, DC: American Psychological Association.

Freyd, J. J., et al. (2005). The science of child sexual abuse. *Science, 308,* 501–503.

Frick-Horbury, D., & Guttentag, R. E. (1998). The effects of restricting hand gesture production on lexical retrieval and free recall. *American Journal of Psychology, 111,* 43–62.

Friedman, A., Brown, N. R., & McGaffey, A. P. (2002). A basis for bias in geographical judgments. *Psychonomic Bulletin & Review, 9,* 151–159.

Friedman, A., & Montello, D. R. (2006). Global-scale location and distance estimates: Common representations and strategies in absolute and relative judgments. *Journal of Experimental Psychology: Learning, Memory, and Cognition, 32,* 333–346.

Friedman, A., Spetch, M. L., & Ferrey, A. (2005). Recognition by humans and pigeons of novel views of 3-D objects and their photographs. *Journal of Experimental Psychology: General, 134,* 149–162.

Frishman, L. J. (2001). Basic visual processes. In E. B. Goldstein (Ed.), *Blackwell handbook of perception* (pp. 53–91). Malden, MA: Blackwell.

Frith, C., & Rees, G. (2004). Brain imaging: The methods. In R. L. Gregory (Ed.), *The Oxford companion to the mind* (2nd ed., pp. 131–133). New York: Oxford University Press.

Fritz, K., Howie, P., & Kleitman, S. (2010). "How do I remember when I got my dog?" The structure and development of children's metamemory. *Metacognition, 5,* 207–228.

Fuchs, A. H., & Milar, K. J. (2003). Psychology as a science. In D. F. Freedheim (Ed.), *Handbook of psychology* (Vol. 1: *The history of psychology,* pp. 1–26). Hoboken, NJ: Wiley.

Fuster, J. M. (2003). *Cortex and mind: Unifying cognition.* New York: Oxford University Press.

Galambos, S. J., & Goldin-Meadow, S. (1990). The effects of learning two languages on levels of metalinguistic awareness. *Cognition, 34,* 1–56.

Gallese, V., et al. (2011). Mirror neuron forum. *Perspectives on Psychological Science, 6,* 369–407.

Gallistel, C. R., & King, A. P. (2009). *Memory and the computational brain: Why cognitive science will transform neuroscience.* Hoboken, NJ: Wiley-Blackwell.

Gallo, D. A. (2006). *Associative illusions of memory.* New York: Psychology Press.

Gallo, D. A. (2010). False memories and fantastic beliefs: 15 years of the DRM illusion. *Memory & Cognition, 38,* 833–848.

Ganellen, R. J., & Carver, C. S. (1985). Why does self-reference promote incidental encoding? *Journal of Experimental Social Psychology, 21,* 284–300.

Ganis, G., Thompson, W. L., & Kosslyn, S. M. (2009). Visual mental imagery: More than "seeing with the mind's eye." In J. R. Brockmole (Ed.), *The visual world in memory* (pp. 211–249). New York: Routledge.

Gardner, H. (1985). *The mind's new science: A history of the cognitive revolution.* New York: Basic Books.

Gardner, R. C. (2010). Second language acquisition: A social psychological perspective. In R. B. Kaplan (Ed.), *The Oxford handbook of applied linguistics* (2nd ed., pp. 204–216). New York: Oxford University Press.

Gardner, R. C., & Lambert, W. E. (1959). Motivational variables in second-language acquisition. *Canadian Journal of Psychology, 13,* 266–272.

Garnets, L. D. (2008). Life as a lesbian: What does gender have to do with it? In J. C. Chrisler, C. Golden, & P. D. Rozee (Eds.), *Lectures on the psychology of women* (4th ed., pp. 232–267). New York: Boston.

Garnham, A. (2005). Language comprehension. In K. Lamberts & R. L. Goldstone (Eds.), *Handbook of cognition* (pp. 241–254). Thousand Oaks, CA: Sage.

Garnham, A., & Oakhill, J. (1994). *Thinking and reasoning.* Oxford, UK: Blackwell.

Garrett, M. (2009). Thinking across boundaries: Psycholinguistics perspectives. In M. G. Gaskell (Ed.), *The Oxford handbook of psycholinguistics* (pp. 805–820). New York: Oxford University Press.

Gaskell, M. G. (Ed.). (2009a). *The Oxford handbook of psycholinguistics.* New York: Oxford University Press.

Gaskell, M. G. (2009b). Statistical and connectionist models of speech perception and word recognition. In M. G. Gaskell (Ed.), *The Oxford handbook of psycholinguistics* (pp. 55–69). New York: Oxford University Press.

Gathercole, S. E. (1998). The development of memory. *Journal of Child Psychology and Psychiatry, 39,* 3–27.

Gathercole, S. E., & Baddeley, A. D. (1993). *Working memory and language.* Hove, UK: Erlbaum.

Gathercole, S. E., Lamont, E., & Alloway, T. P. (2006). Working memory in the classroom. In S. J. Pickering (Ed.), *Working memory and education* (pp. 219–240). Burlington, MA: Elsevier.

Gathercole, S. E., & Pickering, S. J. (2000). Working memory deficits in children with low achievement in the national curriculum at 7 years of age. *British Journal of Educational Psychology, 70,* 177–194.

Gathercole, S. E., Pickering, S. J., Ambridge, B., & Wearing, H. (2004). The structure of working memory from 4 to 15 years of age. *Developmental Psychology, 40,* 177–190.

Gauvain, M. (2001). *The social context of cognitive development.* New York: Guilford.

Gazzaniga, M. S., Ivry, R. B., & Mangun, G. R. (2009). *Cognitive neuroscience: The biology of the mind.* New York: Norton.

Geisler, W. S. (2008). Visual perception and statistical properties of natural scenes. *Annual Review of Psychology, 59,* 167–192.

Geisler, W. S., & Super, B. J. (2000). Perceptual organization of two-dimensional patterns. *Psychological Review, 107,* 677–708.

Gelman, R. (2002). Cognitive development. In H. Pashler (Ed.), *Stevens' handbook of experimental psychology* (Vol. 2, pp. 533–550). New York: Wiley.

Gelman, S. A., & Frazier, B. N. (2012). Development of thinking in children. In K. J. Holyoak & R. G. Morrison (Eds.), *The Cambridge handbook of thinking and reasoning* (pp. 513–528). New York: Cambridge University Press.

Genesee, F., & Gándara, P. (1999). Bilingual education programs: A cross-national perspective. *Journal of Social Issues, 55,* 665–685.

Genesee, F., Tucker, R., & Lambert, W. E. (1975). Communication skills of bilingual children. *Child Development, 46,* 1010–1014.

Geraerts, E., Raymaekers, & Merkelbach, H. (2010). Mechanisms underlying recovered memories. In G. M. Davies & D. B. Wright (Eds.), *Current issues in applied memory research* (pp. 101–118). New York: Psychology Press.

German, T. P., & Barrett, H. C. (2005). Functional fixedness in a technologically sparse culture. *Psychological Science, 16,* 1–5.

Gernsbacher, M. A., & Kaschak, M. P. (2003). Neuroimaging studies of language production and comprehension. *Annual Review of Psychology, 54,* 91–114.

Gernsbacher, M. A., & Robertson, D. A. (2005). Watching the brain comprehend discourse. In A. F. Healy (Ed.), *Experimental cognitive psychology and its applications* (pp. 157–167). Washington, DC: American Psychological Association.

Gerrie, M. P., Garry, M., & Loftus, E. F. (2005). False memories. In N. Brewer & K. D. Williams (Eds.), *Psychology and law: An empirical perspective* (pp. 222–253). New York: Guilford.

Gerrig, R. J. (1998). *Experiencing narrative words.* Boulder, CO: Westview Press.

Gerrig, R. J., & McKoon, G. (2001). Memory processes and experiential continuity. *Psychological Science, 12,* 81–85.

Gibbs, R. W., Jr. (1998). The varieties of intentions in interpersonal communication. In S. R. Fussell & R. J. Kreuz (Eds.), *Social and cognitive approaches to interpersonal communications* (pp. 19–37). Mahwah, NJ: Erlbaum.

Gibson, E. J. (1969). *Principles of perceptual learning and development.* New York: Prentice Hall.

Gibson, J. M., Dhuse, S., Hrachovec, L., & Grimm, L. R. (2011). Priming insight in groups: Facilitating and inhibiting solving an ambiguously worded insight problem. *Memory & Cognition, 39,* 128–146.

Gigerenzer, G. (1998). Ecological intelligence: An adaptation for frequencies. In D. D. Cummins & C. Allen (Eds.), *The evolution of mind* (pp. 9–29). New York: Oxford University Press.

Gigerenzer, G. (2006a). Bounded and rational. In R. J. Stainton (Ed.), *Contemporary debates in cognitive science* (pp. 115–133). Oxford, UK: Blackwell.

Gigerenzer, G. (2006b). Heuristics. In G. Gigerenzer & C. Engel (Eds.), *Heuristics and the law* (pp. 17–44). Cambridge, MA: MIT Press.

Gigerenzer, G. (2008). Why heuristics work. *Perspectives in Psychological Science, 3,* 20–29.

Giles, A., & Rovee-Collier, C. (2011). Infant long-term memory for associations formed during mere exposure. *Infant Behavior and Development, 34,* 327–338.

Gilhooly, K. J. (2005). Working memory and strategies in reasoning. In M. J. Roberts & E. J. Newton (Eds.), *Methods of thought: Individual differences in reasoning strategies* (pp. 57–80). Hove, UK: Psychology Press.

Gillam, B., Sedgwick, H. A., & Peterson, M. A. (2007). Introduction. In M. A. Peterson, B. Gillam, & H. A Sedgwick (Eds.), *In the mind's eye: Julian Hochberg on the perception of pictures, films, and the world.* New York: Oxford University Press.

Gillihan, S. J., & Farah, M. J. (2005). Is self special? A critical review of evidence from experimental psychology and cognitive neuroscience. *Psychological Bulletin, 131,* 76–97.

Glaser, R. (2001). Progress then and now. In S. M. Carver & D. Klahr (Eds.), *Cognition and instruction: Twenty-five years of progress* (pp. 493–507). Mahwah, NJ: Erlbaum.

Glaser, R., & Chi, M. T. H. (1988). Overview. In M. T. H. Chi, R. Glaser, & M. J. Farr (Eds.), *The nature of expertise* (pp. xv–xxxvi). Hillsdale, NJ: Erlbaum.

Glenberg, A. M. (2011a). Introduction to the mirror neuron forum. *Perspectives on Psychological Science, 6,* 363–368.

Glenberg, A. M. (2011b). Positions in the mirror are closer than they appear. *Perspectives on Psychological Science, 6,* 408–410.

Glenberg, A. M., Goldberg, A., Zhu, X. (2011). Improving early reading comprehension using embodied CAI. *Instructional Science, 39,* 27–39. DOI 10.1007/s11251-009-9096-7.

Glicksohn, J. (1994). Rotation, orientation, and cognitive mapping. *American Journal of Psychology, 107,* 39–51.

Gluck, M. A., & Myers, C. E. (2001). *Gateway to memory: An introduction to neural network modeling of the hippocampus and learning.* Cambridge, MA: MIT Press.

Gobet, F., de Voogt, A., & Retschitzki, J. (2004). *Moves in mind: The psychology of board games.* Hove, UK: Psychology Press.

Gobet, F., & Simon, H. A. (1996a). Recall of random and distorted chess positions: Implications for the theory of expertise. *Memory & Cognition, 24,* 493–503.

Gobet, F., & Simon, H. A. (1996b). Recall of rapidly presented random chess positions is a function of skill. *Psychonomic Bulletin & Review, 3,* 159–163.

Goldenberg, C., & Coleman, R. (2010). *Promoting academic achievement among English learners: A guide to the research.* Thousand Oaks, CA: Corwin.

Goldin-Meadow, S., & Beilock, S. L. (2010). Action's influence on thought: The case of gesture. *Perspectives on Psychological Science, 5,* 664–674.

Goldsmith, M., Koriat, A., & Pansky, A. (2005). Strategic regulation of grain size in memory reporting over time. *Journal of Memory and Language, 52,* 505–525.

Goldstein, D. G., & Gigerenzer, G. (2002). Models of ecological rationality: The recognition heuristic. *Psychological Review, 109,* 75–90.

Goldstein, E. B. (Ed.). (2010a). *Encyclopedia of perception.* Thousand Oaks, CA: Sage.

Goldstein, E. B. (2010b). *Sensation and perception* (8th ed.). Belmont, CA: Wadsworth.

Goldstone, R. L., & Kersten, A. (2003). Concepts and categorization. In I. B. Weiner (Ed.), *Handbook of psychology* (Vol. 4). Hoboken, NJ: Wiley.

Gollan, T. H., & Acenas, L.-A. R. (2004). What is a TOT? Cognate and translation effects on tip-of-the-tongue states in Spanish-English and Tagalog-English bilinguals. *Journal of Experimental Psychology: Learning, Memory, and Cognition, 29,* 1095–1105.

Gollan, T. H., Bonanni, M. P., & Montoya, R. I. (2005). Proper names get stuck on bilingual and monolingual speakers' tip of the tongue equally often. *Neuropsychology, 19,* 278–287.

Goodwin, G. P., & Johnson-Laird, P. N. (2005). Reasoning about relations. *Psychological Review, 112,* 468–493.

Goodman, G. S., & Melinder, A. (2007). The development of autobiographical memory: A new model. In S. Magnussen & T. Helstrup (Eds.), *Everyday memory* (pp. 111–135). New York: Psychology Press.

Goodman, G. S., & Paz-Alonso, P. M. (2006). Trauma and memory: Normal versus special memory mechanisms. In B. Uttl, N. Ohta, & A. L. Siegenthaler (Eds.), *Memory and emotion: Interdisciplinary perspectives* (pp. 234–257). Malden, MA: Blackwell.

Goodman, G. S., et al. (2003). A prospective study of memory for child sexual abuse: New findings relevant to the repressed-memory controversy. *Psychological Science, 14,* 113–118.

Goodman, G. S., et al. (2007). Memory illusions and false memories in the real world. In S. Magnussen & T. Helstrup (Eds.), *Everyday memory* (pp. 157–182). New York: Psychology Press.

Goodwin, G. P. & Johnson-Laird, P. N., (2005). Reasoning about relations. *Psychological Review, 112,* 468–493.

Gordon, I. E. (2004). *Theories of visual perception* (3rd ed.). Hove, UK: Psychology Press.

Gordon, R., Franklin, N., & Beck, J. (2005). Wishful thinking and source monitoring. *Memory & Cognition, 33,* 418–438.

Gorman, M. E. (2006). Scientific and technological thinking. *Review of General Psychology, 10,* 113–129.

Gorrell, P. (1999). Sentence processing. In R. A. Wilson & F. C. Keil (Eds.), *The MIT encyclopedia of the cognitive sciences* (pp. 748–751). Cambridge, MA: MIT Press.

Grady, C. L., & Craik, F. I. M. (2000). Changes in memory processing with age. *Current Opinion in Neurobiology, 10,* 224–231.

Graesser, A. C., Gernsbacher, M. A., & Goldman, S. R. (2003). Introduction to the handbook of discourse processes. In A. C. Graesser, M. A. Gernsbacher, & S. R. Goldman (Eds.), *Handbook of discourse processes* (pp. 1–23). Mahwah, NJ: Erlbaum.

Graesser, A. C., et al. (2007). Using LSA in AutoTutor: Learning through mixed-initiative dialogue in natural language. In T. K. Landauer, D. S. McNamara, S. Dennis, & W. Kintsch (Eds.), *Handbook of latent semantic analysis* (pp. 243–262). Mahwah, NJ: Erlbaum.

Graf, M., Kaping, D., & Bülthoff, H. H. (2005). Orientation congruency effects for familiar objects: Coordinate transformations in object recognition. *Psychological Science, 16,* 214–221.

Grainger, J., & Jacobs, A. M. (2005). Pseudoword context effects on letter perception: The role of word misperception. *European Journal of Cognitive Psychology, 17,* 289–318.

Grammer, J. K., Purtell, K. M., Coffman, J. L., & Ornstein, P. A. (2011). Relations between children's metamemory and strategic performance: Time-varying covariates in early elementary school. *Journal of Experimental Child Psychology, 108*, 139–155.

Grant, E. R., & Spivey, M. J. (2003). Eye movements and problem solving: Guiding attention guides thought. *Psychological Science, 14*, 462–466.

Greeno, J. G. (1974). Hobbits and orcs: Acquisition of a sequential concept. *Cognitive Psychology, 6*, 270–292.

Greenwald, A. G., McGee, D. E., & Schwartz, J. L. K. (1998). Measuring individual differences in implicit cognition: The Implicit Association Test. *Journal of Personality and Social Psychology, 74*, 1464–1480.

Greenwald, A. G., & Nosek, B. A. (2001). Health of the Implicit Association Test at age 3. *Zeitschrift für Experimentelle Psychologie, 48*, 85–93.

Gregory, R. L. (2004a). Perception. In R. L. Gregory (Ed.), *The Oxford companion to the mind* (2nd ed., pp. 707–710). New York: Oxford University Press.

Gregory, R. L. (2004b). Piaget and education. In R. L. Gregory (Ed.), *The Oxford companion to the mind* (2nd ed., pp. 732–733). New York: Oxford University Press.

Grice, H. P. (1989). *Studies in the way of words.* Cambridge, MA: Harvard University Press.

Griffin, D., Gonzales, R., Koehler, D., & Gilovich, T. (2012). Judgmental heuristics: A historical overview. In K. J. Holyoak & R. G. Morrison (Eds.), *The Oxford handbook of thinking and reasoning* (pp. 322–345). New York: Oxford University Press.

Griffin, D., & Tversky, A. (2002). The weighing of evidence and the determinants of confidence. In T. Gilovich, D. Griffin, & D. Kahneman (Eds.), *Heuristics and biases: The psychology of intuitive judgment* (pp. 230–249). New York: Cambridge University Press.

Griffin, T. D., Wiley, J., & Thiede, K. W. (2008). Individual differences, rereading, and self-explanation: Concurrent processing and cue validity as constraints on metacomprehension accuracy. *Memory & Cognition, 36*, 93–103.

Griffin, Z. M. (2004). Why look? Reasons for eye movements related to language production. In J. M. Henderson & F. Ferreira (Eds.), *The interface of language, vision, and action: Eye movements and the visual world* (pp. 213–247). New York: Psychology Press.

Griffin, Z. M., & Bock, K. (2000). What the eyes say about speaking. *Psychological Science, 11*, 274–279.

Griffin, Z. M., & Ferreira, V. S. (2006). Properties of spoken language production. In M. J. Traxler & M. A. Gernsbacher (Eds.), *Handbook of psycholinguistics* (2nd ed., pp. 505–527). Amsterdam: Elsevier.

Griffith, P. L., & Ruan, J. (2005). What is metacognition and what should be its role in literacy instruction? In S. E. Israel, C. C. Block, K. L. Bauserman, & K. Kinnucan-Welsch (Eds.), *Metacognition in literacy learning: Theory, assessment, instruction, and professional development* (pp. 3–18). Mahwah, NJ: Erlbaum.

Griggs, R. A., & Cox, J. R. (1982). The elusive thematic-materials effect in Wason's selection task. *British Journal of Psychology, 73*, 407–420.

Grill-Spector, K., & Kanwisher, N. (2005). Visual recognition: As soon as you know it is there, you know what it is. *Psychological Science, 16*, 152–160.

Grodzinsky, Y. (2006). A blueprint for a brain map of syntax. In Y. Grodzinsky & K. Amunts (Eds.), *Broca's region* (pp. 83–107). New York: Oxford University Press.

Groninger, L. D. (1971). Mnemonic imagery and forgetting. *Psychonomic Science, 23*, 161–163.

Groome, D. (1999). *An introduction to cognitive psychology: Processes and disorders.* Hove, UK: Psychology Press.

Groopman, J. (2007). *How doctors think.* Boston: Houghton Mifflin.

Gross, T. F. (2009). Own-race/ethnicity bias in the recognition of Hispanic-Mestiso, African, Asian, and Caucasian children and adult faces. *Basic and Applied Social Psychology, 31*, 128–135.

Grossberg, S. (2000). The complementary brain: Unifying brain dynamics and modularity. *Trends in Cognitive Sciences, 4*, 233–245.

Grossberg, S., Govindarajan, K. K., Wyse, L. L., & Cohen, M. A. (2004). ARTSTREAM: A neural network model of auditory scene analysis and source segregation. *Neural Networks, 17*, 511–536.

Guerin, B. (2003). Language use as social strategy: A review and an analytic framework for the social sciences. *Review of General Psychology, 7*, 251–298.

Guerreiro, M. J. S., & Van Gerven, P. W. M. (2011). Now you see it, now you don't: Evidence for age-dependent and age-independent cross-modal distraction. *Psychology and Aging, 26*, 415–426.

Guilford, J. P. (1967). *The nature of human intelligence.* New York: McGraw-Hill.

Gunter, B., Furman, A., & Pappa, E. (2005). Effects of television violence on memory for violent and nonviolent advertising. *Journal of Applied Social Psychology, 35*, 1680–1697.

Gurung, R. A. R. (2003). Pedagogical aids and student performance. *Teaching of Psychology, 30*, 92–95.

Gurung, R. A. R. (2004). Pedagogical aids: Learning enhancers or dangerous detours? *Teaching of Psychology*, *31*, 164–166.

Gurung, R. A. R., & McCann, L. I. (2011, April). How should students study? Tips, advice, and pitfalls. *Association for Psychological Sciences Observer*, pp. 33–35.

Güss, C. D., & Wiley, B. (2007). Metacognition of problem-solving strategies in Brazil, India, and the United States. *Journal of Cognition and Culture*, 7, 1–25.

Guynn, M. J., McDaniel, M. A., & Einstein, G. O. (1998). Prospective memory: When reminders fail. *Memory & Cognition*, *26*, 287–298.

Gyselinck, V., & Meneghetti, C. (2011). The role of spatial working memory in understanding descriptions. In A. Vandierendonck & A. Szmalec (Eds.), *Spatial working memory* (pp. 159–180). New York: Psychology Press.

Haberlandt, K. (1999). *Human memory: Exploration and application*. Boston: Allyn and Bacon.

Hacker, D. J., Bol, L., & Keener, M. C. (2008). Metacognition in education: A focus on calibration. In J. Dunlosky & R. A. Bjork (Eds.), *Handbook of metamemory and memory* (pp. 429–455). New York: Psychology Press.

Hacker, D. J., Dunlosky, J., & Graesser, A. C. (Eds.). (2009). *Handbook of metacognition in education*. New York: Routledge.

Hakel, M. D. (2001). Learning that lasts. *Psychological Science*, *12*, 433–434.

Hakuta, K. (1986). *Mirror of language: The debate on bilingualism*. New York: Basic Books.

Hall, J., et al. (2004). Social cognition and face processing and schizophrenia. *British Journal of Psychiatry*, *185*, 169–170.

Hallinan, J. T. (2009). *Why we make mistakes*. New York: Broadway Books.

Halpern, A. R., Zatorre, R. J., Bouffard, M., & Johnson, J. A. (2004). Behavioral and neural correlates of perceived and imagined musical timbre. *Neuropsychologia*, *42*, 1281–1292.

Halpern, D. F. (2003). *Thought and knowledge: An introduction to critical thinking* (4th ed.). Mahwah, NJ: Erlbaum.

Halpern, D. F. (2012). *Sex differences in cognitive abilities* (4th ed.). New York: Psychology Press.

Hamilton, D. L. (2005). Social cognition: An introductory overview. In D. L. Hamilton (Ed.), *Social cognition: Key readings* (pp. 1–36). New York: Psychology Press.

Hamilton, D. L., & Sherman, J. W. (1994). Stereotypes. In R. S. Wyer, Jr., & T. K. Srull (Eds.), *Handbook of social cognition* (2nd ed., Vol. 2, pp. 1–68). Hillsdale, NJ: Erlbaum.

Hamilton, D. L., Stroessner, S. J., & Mackie, D. M. (1993). The influence of affect on stereotyping: The case of illusory correlations. In D. M. Mackie & D. L. Hamilton (Eds.), *Affect, cognition, and stereotyping: Interactive processes in group perception* (pp. 39–61). San Diego: Academic Press.

Hampton, J. A. (1997a). Conceptual combination. In K. Lamberts & D. Shanks (Eds.), *Knowledge, concepts, and categories* (pp. 133–159). Cambridge, MA: MIT Press.

Hampton, J. A. (1997b). Psychological representation of concepts. In M. A. Conway (Ed.), *Cognitive models of memory* (pp. 81–110). Cambridge, MA: MIT Press.

Handbook of eyewitness psychology. Memory for people (Vol. 1, Toglia, M. P., et al., Eds.) & *Memory for events* (Vol. 2, Lindsay, R. C. L., et al., Eds.). (2007). Mahwah, NJ: Erlbaum.

Hannon, B., et al. (2010). Differential-associative processing: A new strategy for learning highly-similar concepts. *Applied Cognitive Psychology*, *24*, 1222–1244.

Hardman, D. (2009). *Judgment and decision making: Psychology perspectives*. Chichester, Sussex, UK: Blackwell.

Hardt, O., Einarsson, E. Ö., & Nader, K. (2010). A bridge over troubled water: Reconsolidation as a link between cognitive and neuroscientific memory research traditions. *Annual Review of Psychology*, *61*, 141–167.

Harley, E. M., Carlsen, K. A., & Loftus, G. R. (2004). The "saw-it-all-along" effect: Demonstrations of visual hindsight bias. *Journal of Experimental Psychology: Learning, Memory, and Cognition*, *30*, 960–968.

Harley, T. A. (2001). *The psychology of language: From data to theory* (2nd ed.). East Sussex, UK: Psychology Press.

Harley, T. A. (2008). *The psychology of language: From data to theory* (3rd ed.). New York: Psychology Press.

Harley, T. A. (2010). *Talking the talk: Language, psychology and science*. New York: Psychology Press.

Harris, A. J. L., Corner, A., & Hahn, U. (2009). Estimating the probability of negative events. *Cognition*, *110*, 51–64.

Harris, A. J. L., & Hahn, U. (2011). Unrealistic optimism about future life events: A cautionary note. *Psychological Review*, *118*, 135–154.

Harris, C. R., & Pashler, H. (2004). Attention and the processing of emotional words and names: Not so special after all. *Psychological Science, 15*, 171–178.

Harris, R. J., Sardarpoor-Bascom, F., & Meyer, T. (1989). The role of cultural knowledge in distorting recall for stories. *Bulletin of the Psychonomic Society, 27*, 9–10.

Hartwig, M. K., & Dunlosky, J. (2012). Study strategies of college students: Are self-testing and scheduling related to achievement? *Psychonomic Bulletin & Review, 19*, 126–134.

Harvey, A. G. (2005). Unwanted intrusive thoughts in insomnia. In D. A. Clark (Ed.), *Intrusive thoughts in clinical disorders: Theory, research, and treatment* (pp. 86–118). New York: Guilford Press.

Harvey, A. G., & Tang, N. K. Y. (2012). (Mis)perception of sleep in insomnia: A puzzle and a resolution. *Psychological Bulletin, 138*, 77–101.

Hasher, L., Chung, C., May, C. P., & Foong, N. (2002). Age, time of testing, and proactive interference. *Canadian Journal of Experimental Psychology, 56*, 200–207.

Hasher, L., Lustig, C., & Zacks, R. (2007). Inhibitory mechanisms and the control of attention. In A. R. A. Conway, et al. (Eds.), *Variations in working memory* (pp. 227–249). New York: Oxford University Press.

Hassin, R. R. (2005). Nonconscious control and implicit working memory. In R. R. Hassin, J. E. Uleman, & J. A. Bargh (Eds.), *The new unconscious* (pp. 196–222). New York: Oxford University Press.

Hassin, R. R., Uleman, J. S., & Bargh, J. A. (2005). *The new unconscious*. New York: Oxford University Press.

Hastie, R., & Dawes, R. M. (2010). *Rational choice in an uncertain world: The psychology of judgment and decision making* (2nd ed.). Los Angeles: Sage.

Hayes, J. R. (1989). Writing research: The analysis of a very complex task. In D. Klahr & K. Kotovsky (Eds.), *Complex information processing: The impact of Herbert A. Simon* (pp. 209–234). Hillsdale, NJ: Erlbaum.

Hayes, J. R. (1996). A new framework for understanding cognition and affect in writing. In C. M. Levy & S. Randsell (Eds.), *The science of writing: Theories, methods, individual differences, and applications* (pp. 1–27). Mahwah, NJ: Erlbaum.

Hayes, J. R., et al. (1987). Cognitive processes in revision. In S. Rosenberg (Ed.), *Advances in psycholinguistics: Vol. 2. Reading, writing, and languages processing*. Cambridge, UK: Cambridge University Press.

Hayne, H., & Simcock, G. (2009). Memory development in toddlers. In M. Courage & N. Cowan (Eds.), *The development of memory in childhood* (pp. 43–68). Hove, UK: Psychology Press.

Hayne, H., et al. (2011). Episodic memory and episodic foresight in 3- and 5-year-old children. *Cognitive Development, 26*, 343–355.

Haywood, S. J., Pickering, M. J., & Branigan, H. P. (2005). Do speakers avoid ambiguities during dialogue? *Psychological Science, 16*, 362–366.

Hayworth, K. J., & Biederman, I. (2006). Neural evidence for intermediate representations in object recognition. *Vision Research, 46*, 4024–4031.

Hazeltine, R. E., Prinzmetal, W., & Elliott, K. (1997). If it's not there, where is it? Locating illusory conjunctions. *Journal of Experimental Psychology: Human Perception and Performance, 23*, 263–277.

Healy, A. F., et al. (2011). Data entry: A window to principles of training. In A. S. Benjamin (Ed.), *Successful remembering and successful forgetting: A festschrift in honor of Robert A. Bjork* (pp. 277–296). New York: Psychology Press.

Hearst, E. (1991). Psychology and nothing. *American Scientist, 79*, 432–443.

Hein, G., & Knight, R. T. (2008). Superior temporal sulcus—it's my area: Or is it? *Journal of Cognitive Neuroscience, 20*, 2125–2136.

Heine, S. J. (2010). Cultural psychology. In S. T. Fiske, D. T. Gilbert, & G. Lindzey (Eds.), *Handbook of social psychology* (6th ed., pp. 1423–1464). Hoboken, NJ: Wiley.

Heit, E., & Barsalou, L. W. (1996). The instantiation principle in natural categories. *Memory, 4*, 413–451.

Hélie, S., & Sun, R. (2010). Incubation, insight, and creative problem solving: A united theory and a connectionist model. *Psychological Review, 117*, 994–1024.

Henderson, D. R., & Hooper, C. L. (2006). *Making great decisions in business and life*. Chicago Park, CA: Chicago Park Press.

Henderson, J. M. (Ed.). (2005). *Real-world scene perception*. Hove, UK: Psychology Press.

Henderson, J. M., & Ferreira, F. (Eds.). (2004a). *The interface of language, vision, and action: Eye movements and the visual world*. New York: Psychology Press.

Henderson, J. M., & Ferreira, F. (2004b). Scene perception for psycholinguists. In J. M. Henderson & F. Ferreira (Eds.), *The interface of language, vision, and action: Eye movements and the visual world* (pp. 1–58). New York: Psychology Press.

Henderson, Z., Bruce, V., & Burton, A. M. (2001). Matching the faces of robbers captured on video. *Applied Cognitive Psychology, 15*, 445–464.

Henkel, L. A. (2011). Photograph-induced memory errors: When photographs make people claim they have done things they have not. *Applied Cognitive Psychology, 25*, 78–86.

Hennessey, B. A. (2000). Rewards and creativity. In C. Sansone & J. M. Harackiewicz (Eds.), *Intrinsic and extrinsic motivation: The search for optimal motivation and perormance* (pp. 55–78). San Diego, CA: Academic Press.

Hennessey, B. A., & Amabile, T. M. (2010). Creativity. *Annual Review of Psychology, 61*, 569–598.

Henry, L. A., & Gudjonsson, G. H. (2007). Individual and developmental differences in eyewitness recall and suggestibility in children with intellectual disabilities. *Applied Cognitive Psychology, 21*, 361–381.

Heppner, P. P. (2008). Expanding the conceptualization and measurement of applied problem solving and coping: From stages to dimensions to the almost forgotten cultural context. *American Psychologist, 63*, 805–816.

Herbert, W. (2010). *On second thought.* New York: Crown.

Herek, G. M., & Garnets, L. D. (2007). Sexual orientation and mental health. *Annual Review of Clinical Psychology, 3*, 353–375.

Hernandez-García, L., Wager, T., & Jonides, J. (2002). Functional brain imaging. In H. Pashler & J. Wixted (Eds.), *Stevens' handbook of experimental psychology* (3rd ed., Vol. 4, pp. 175–221). New York: Wiley.

Herriot, P. (2004). Language development in children. In R. L. Gregory (Ed.), *The Oxford companion to the mind* (2nd ed., pp. 519–521). New York: Oxford University Press.

Herrmann, D. J., Gruneberg, M., et al. (2006). Memory failures and their causes in everyday life. In L.-G. Nilsson & Nobuo Ohta (Eds.), *Memory and society: Psychological perspectives* (pp. 251–268). New York: Psychology Press.

Herrmann, D. J, Raybeck, D., & Gruneberg, M. (2002). *Improving memory and study skills.* Kirkland, WA: Hogrefe & Huber.

Herrmann, D. J., Yoder, C. Y., Gruneberg, M., & Payne, D. G. (2006). *Applied cognitive psychology: A textbook.* Mahwah, NJ: Erlbaum.

Hertel, P. T., & Matthews, A. (2011). Cognitive bias modification: Past perspectives, current findings, and future applications. *Perspectives on Psychological Science, 6*, 521–536.

Hertwig, R., Pachur, T., & Kurzenhäuser, S. (2005). Judgments of risk frequencies: Tests of possible cognitive mechanisms. *Journal of Experimental Psychology: Learning, Memory, and Cognition, 31*, 621–642.

Hertzog, C., & Dixon, R. A. (1994). Metacognitive development in adulthood and old age. In J. Metcalfe & A. P. Shimamura (Eds.), *Metacognition: Knowing about knowing* (pp. 227–251). Cambridge, MA: MIT Press.

Hertzog, C., Dunlosky, J., & Sinclair, S. M. (2010). Episodic feeling-of-knowing resolution derives from the quality of original encoding. *Memory & Cognition, 38*, 771–784.

Hertzog, C., Lineweaver, T. T., & McGuire, C. L. (1999). Beliefs about memory and aging. In F. Blanchard-Fields & T. M. Hess (Eds.), *Social cognition and aging* (pp. 43–68). New York: Academic Press.

Herzog, C., & Robinson, A. E. (2005). Metacognition and intelligence. In O. Wilhelm & R. W. Engle (Eds.), *Handbook of understanding and measuring intelligence* (pp. 101–123). Thousand Oaks: Sage.

Hess, T. M. (2005). Memory and aging in context. *Psychological Bulletin, 131*, 383–406.

Hess, T. M., Auman, C., Colcombe, S. J., & Rahhal, T. A. (2003). The impact of stereotype threat on age differences in memory performance. *Journal of Gerontology Psychological Sciences, 58B*, P3–P11.

Heth, C. D., Cornell, E. H., & Flood, T. L. (2002). Self-ratings of sense of direction and route reversal performance. *Applied Cognitive Psychology, 16*, 309–324.

Higham, P., Luna, K., & Bloomfield, J. (2011). Trace strength and source-monitoring accounts of accuracy and metacognitive resolution in the misinformation paradigm. *Applied Cognitive Psychology, 25*, 324–335.

Hinds, P. J. (1999). The curse of expertise: The effects of expertise and debiasing methods on predictions of novice performance. *Journal of Experimental Psychology: Applied, 5*, 205–211.

Hinsz, V. B. (2004). Metacognition and mental models in groups: An illustration with metamemory of group recognition memory. In E. Salas & S. M. Fiore (Eds.), *Team cognition: Understanding the factors that drive process and performance* (pp. 33–58). Washington, DC: American Psychological Association.

Hintzman, D. L. (2011). Research strategies in the study of memory: Fads, falacies, and the search for the "coordinates of truth." *Perspectives on Psychological Science, 6,* 253–271.

Hirsh-Pasek, K., & Golinkoff, R. M. (1996). *The origins of grammar: Evidence from early language comprehension.* Cambridge, MA: MIT Press.

Hirt, E. R., McDonald, H. E., & Markman, K. D. (1998). Expectancy effects in reconstructive memory: When the past is just what we expected. In S. J. Lynn & K. M. McConkey (Eds.), *Truth in memory* (pp. 62–89). New York: Guilford.

Hirtle, S. C., & Mascolo, M. F. (1986). Effect of semantic clustering on the memory of spatial locations. *Journal of Experimental Psychology: Learning, Memory, and Cognition, 12,* 182–189.

Hitch, G. J. (2006). Working memory in children: A cognitive approach. In E. Bialystok & F. I. M. Craik (Eds.), *Lifespan cognition: Mechanisms of change* (pp. 112–127). New York: Oxford University Press.

Hoffman, D. D. (2010). Consciousness. In E. B. Goldstein (Ed.), *Encyclopedia of perception* (Vol. 1, pp. 300–304). Thousand Oaks, CA: Sage.

Hoffrage, U. (2004). Overconfidence. In R. Pohl (Ed.), *Cognitive illusions: Handbook on fallacies and biases in thinking, judgment, and memory.* Hove, UK: Psychology Press.

Hogarth, R. M., & Karelaia, N. (2007). Heuristic and linear models of judgment: Matching rules and environments. *Psychological Review, 114,* 733–758.

Holcombe, A. O. (2010). Binding problem. In E. B. Goldstein (Ed.), *Encyclopedia of perception* (Vol. 1, pp. 205–208). Thousand Oaks, CA: Sage.

Hollingworth, A. (2004). Constructing visual representations of natural scenes. The roles of short- and long-term visual memory. *Journal of Experimental Psychology: Human Perception and Performance, 30,* 519–537.

Hollingworth, A. (2006a). Scene and position specificity in visual memory for objects. *Journal of Experimental Psychology: Learning, Memory, and Cognition, 32,* 58–69.

Hollingworth, A. (2006b). Visual memory for natural scenes: Evidence from change detection and visual search. *Visual Cognition, 14,* 781–807.

Hollingworth, A., & Henderson, J. M. (2004). Sustained change blindness to incremental scene rotation: A dissociation between explicit change detection and visual memory. *Perception and Psychophysics, 66,* 800–807.

Hollingworth, H. (1910). The oblivescence of the disagreeable. *Journal of Philosophy, Psychology and Scientific Methods, 7,* 709–714.

Holmes, J. B., Waters, H. S., & Rajaram, S. (1998). The phenomenology of false memories: Episodic content and confidence. *Journal of Experimental Psychology: Learning, Memory, and Cognition, 24,* 1026–1040.

Holmes, J., et al. (2010). Working memory deficits can be overcome: Impacts of training and medication on working memory in children with ADHD. *Applied Cognitive Psychology, 24,* 827–836.

Holtgraves, T. (2010). Social psychology and language: Words, utterances, and conversations. In S. T. Fiske, D. T. Gilbert, & G. Lindzey (Eds.), *Handbook of social psychology* (5th ed., Vol. 2, pp. 13–86). Hoboken, NJ: Wiley.

Holyoak, K. J., & Morrison, R. G. (Eds.). (2012). *The Oxford handbook of thinking and reasoning.* New York: Oxford University Press.

Hong, Y., Morris, M. W., Chiu, C., & Benet-Martínez, V. (2000). Multicultural minds: A dynamic constructivist approach to culture and cognition. *American Psychologist, 55,* 709–720.

Honig, E. (1997). Striking lives: Oral history and the politics of memory. *Journal of Women's History, 9,* 139–157.

Hopkins, J. R. (2011, December). The enduring influence of Jean Piaget. *APS Observer,* pp. 35–36.

Horowitz, L. M., & Turan, B. (2008). Prototypes and personal templates: Collective wisdom and individual differences. *Psychological Review, 115,* 1054–1068.

Horowitz, T. S. (2010). Visual search. In E. B. Goldstein (Ed.), *Encyclopedia of perception* (Vol. 2, pp. 1119–1122). Thousand Oaks, CA: Sage.

Hostetter, A. B. (2011). When do gestures communicate? A meta-analysis. *Psychological Bulletin, 137,* 297–315.

Hostetter, A. B., & Alibali, M. W. (2008). Visible embodiment: Gestures as simulated action. *Psychonomic Bulletin & Review, 15,* 495–514.

Hostetter, A. B., & Alibali, M. W. (2010). Language, gesture, action! A test of the gesture as simulated action framework. *Journal of Memory and Language, 63,* 245–257.

Houston, D. M. (2005). Speech perception in infants. In D. B. Pisoni & R. E. Remez (Eds.), *The handbook of speech perception* (pp. 417–448). Malden, MA: Blackwell.

Howard, D. J., & Kerin, R. A. (2011). The effects of name similarity on message processing and persuasion. *Journal of Experimental Social Psychology, 47,* 63–71.

Howe, M. L. (2000). *The fate of early memories.* Washington, DC: American Psychological Association.

Howe, M. L. (2006). Distinctiveness effects in children's memory. In R. R. Hunt & J. B. Worthen (Eds.), *Distinctiveness and memory.* New York: Oxford University Press.

Howe, M. L., Courage. M. L., & Rooksby, M. (2009). The genesis and development of autobiographical memory. In M. Courage & N. Cowan (Eds.), *The development of memory in childhood* (pp. 177–196). Hove, UK: Psychology Press.

Howes, M. B. (2007). *Human memory: Structures and images.* Thousand Oaks, CA: Sage.

Hsu, V. C., & Rovee-Collier, C. (2006). Memory reactivation in the second year of life. *Infant Behavior & Development, 29,* 91–107.

Hu, Y., Ericsson, K. A., Yang, D., & Lu, C. (2009). Superior self-paced memorization of digits in spite of a normal digit span: The structure of a memorist's skill. *Journal of Experimental Psychology: Learning, Memory, and Cognition, 35,* 1426–1442.

Hubbard, T. L. (2010). Auditory imagery: Empirical findings. *Psychological Bulletin, 136,* 302–329.

Hubel, D. H. (1982). Explorations of the primary visual cortex, 1955–1978. *Nature, 299,* 515–524.

Hubel, D. H., & Wiesel, T. N. (1965). Receptive fields of single neurons in two nonstriate visual areas (18 and 19) of the cat. *Journal of Neurophysiology, 28,* 229–289.

Hubel, D. H., & Wiesel, T. N. (1979). Brain mechanisms and vision. *Scientific American, 241* (3), 150–162.

Hubel, D. H., & Wiesel, T. N. (2005). *Brain and visual perception: The story of a 25-year collaboration.* New York: Oxford University Press.

Hudson, J. A., & Mayhew, E. M. Y. (2009). The development of memory for recurring events. In M. Courage & N. Cowan (Eds.), *The development of memory in childhood* (pp. 69–91). Hove, UK: Psychology Press.

Huettel, S. A., Song, A. W., & McCarthy, G. (2004). *Functional magnetic resonance imaging.* Sunderland, MA: Sinauer.

Hugenberg, K., Young, S. G., Bernstein, M. J., & Sacco, D. F. (2010). The categorization-individuation model: An integrative account of the other-race recognition deficit. *Psychological Review, 117,* 1168–1187.

Huitema, J. S., Dopkins, S., Klin, C. M., & Myers, J. L. (1993). Connecting goals and actions during reading. *Journal of Experimental Psychology: Learning, Memory, and Cognition, 19,* 1053–1060.

Hulicka, I. M. (1982). Memory functioning in late adulthood. In F. I. M. Craik & S. Trehub (Eds.), *Advances in the study of communication and affect* (Vol. 8, pp. 331–351). New York: Plenum.

Hulme, C., & Snowling, M. J. (2011). Children's reading comprehension difficulties: Nature, causes, and treatments. *Current Directions in Psychological Science, 20,* 139–142.

Humphreys, G. W., & Riddoch, M. J. (2001). The neuropsychology of visual object and space perception. In E. B. Goldstein (Ed.), *Blackwell handbook of perception* (pp. 204–236). Malden, MA: Blackwell.

Hunter, I. M. L. (2004a). James, William. In R. L. Gregory (Ed.), *The Oxford companion to the mind* (2nd ed., pp. 492–494). New York: Oxford University Press.

Hunter, I. M. L. (2004b). Mnemonics. In R. L. Gregory (Ed.), *The Oxford companion to the mind* (2nd ed., 610–612). New York: Oxford University Press.

Hurley, M. M. (2011). *Inside jokes: Using humor to reverse-engineer the mind.* Cambridge, MA: MIT Press.

Hurley, S. M., & Novick, L. R. (2006). Context and structure: The nature of students' knowledge about three spatial diagram representations. *Thinking & Reasoning, 12,* 281–308.

Hurley, S. M., & Novick, L. R. (2010). Solving problems using matrix, network, and hierarchy diagrams: The consequences of violating construction conventions. *The Quarterly Journal of Experimental Psychology, 63,* 275–290.

Hyde, J. S. (2005). The gender similarities hypothesis. *American Psychologist, 60,* 581–592.

Hyde, J. S., et al. (2008). Gender similarities characterize math performance. *Science, 321,* 494–495.

Hyman, I. E., Jr. (2010). Did you see the unicycling clown? Inattentional blindness while walking and talking on a cell phone. *Applied Cognitive Psychology, 24,* 597–607.

Hyman, I. E., Jr., Husband, T. H., & Billings, F. J. (1995). False memories of childhood experiences. *Applied Cognitive Psychology, 9,* 181–197.

Hyman, I. E., Jr., & Kleinknecht, E. E. (1999). False childhood memories: Research, theory, and applications. In L. M. Williams & V. L. Banyard (Eds.), *Trauma & memory* (pp. 175–188). Thousand Oaks, CA: Sage.

Hyman, I. E., Jr., & Loftus, E. F. (2002). False childhood memories and eyewitness memory errors. In M. L. Eisen, J. A. Quas, & G. S. Goodman (Eds.), *Memory and suggestibility in the forensic interview* (pp. 63–84). Mahwah, NJ: Erlbaum.

Imhoff, M. C., & Baker-Ward, L. (1999). Preschoolers' suggestibility: Effects of developmentally appropriate language and interviewer supportiveness. *Journal of Applied Developmental Psychology, 20,* 407–429.

Intons-Peterson, M. J. (1983). Imagery paradigms: How vulnerable are they to experimenters' expectations? *Journal of Experimental Psychology: Learning, Memory, and Cognition, 10,* 699–715.

Intons-Peterson, M. J., Russell, W., & Dressel, S. (1992). The role of pitch in auditory imagery. *Journal of Experimental Psychology: Learning, Memory, and Cognition, 13,* 490–500.

Intons-Peterson, M. J., et al. (1999). Age, testing at preferred or nonpreferred times (testing optimality) and false memory. *Journal of Experimental Psychology: Learning, Memory, and Cognition, 25,* 23–40.

Intraub, H. (1997). The representation of visual scenes. *TRENDS in Cognitive Sciences, 1,* 217–222.

Intraub, H., & Berkowits, D. (1996). Beyond the edges of a picture. *American Journal of Psychology, 109,* 581–598.

Intraub, H., & Richardson, M. (1989). Wide-angle memories of close-up scenes. *Journal of Experimental Psychology: Learning, Memory, and Cognition, 15,* 179–187.

Intraub, H., Gottesman, C. V., & Bills, A. J. (1998). Effects of perceiving and imagining scenes on memory for pictures. *Journal of Experimental Psychology: Learning, Memory, and Cognition, 24,* 186–201.

Irwin, D. E. (2003). Eye movements and visual cognitive suppression. *The Psychology of Learning and Motivation, 42,* 265–293.

Irwin, D. E. (2004). Fixation location and fixation duration as indices of cognitive processing. In J. M. Henderson & F. Ferreira (Eds.), *The interface of language, vision, and action: Eye movements and the visual world* (pp. 105–133). New York: Psychology Press

Irwin, D. E., & Zelinsky, G. J. (2002). Eye movements and scene perception: Memory for things observed. *Perception & Psychophysics, 64,* 882–895.

Ishai, A., & Sagi, D. (1995). Common mechanisms of visual imagery and perception. *Science, 268,* 1772–1774.

Isikoff, M., & Lipper, T. (2003, July 21). A spy takes the bullet. *Newsweek,* pp. 24–25.

Israel, S. E., & Massey, D. (2005). Metacognitive think-aloud: Using a gradual release model with middle school students. In S. E. Israel, C. C. Block, K. L. Bauserman, & K. Kinnucan-Welsch (Eds.), *Metacognition in literacy learning: Theory, assessment, instruction, and professional development* (pp. 183–198). Mahwah, NJ: Erlbaum.

Ito, T. A., Urland, G. R., Willadsen-Jensen, E., & Correll, J. (2006). The social neuroscience of stereotyping and prejudice: Using event-related brain potentials to study social perception. In J. T. Cacioppo, P. S. Visser, & C. L. Pickett (Eds.), *Social neuroscience: People thinking about thinking people* (pp. 189–208). Cambridge, MA: MIT Press.

Jackendoff, R. (1994). *Patterns in the mind.* New York: Basic Books.

Jackendoff, R. (1997). *The architecture of the language faculty.* Cambridge, MA: MIT Press.

Jackson, L. M. (2011). *The psychology of prejudice: From attitudes to social action.* Washington, DC: American Psychological Association.

Jacobs, N., & Garnham, A. (2007). The role of conversational hand gestures in a narrative task. *Journal of Memory and Language, 56,* 291–303.

Jahn, G. (2004). Three turtles in danger: Spontaneous construction of causally relevant spatial situation models. *Journal of Experimental Psychology: Learning, Memory, and Cognition, 30,* 969–987.

Jain, A. K., & Duin, R. P. W. (2004). Pattern recognition. In R. L. Gregory (Ed.), *The Oxford companion to the mind* (2nd ed., p. 698–703). New York: Oxford University Press.

Jäkel, F., Schölkopf, B., & Wickmann, F. A. (2008). Generalization and similarity in exemplar models of categorization: Insights from machine learning. *Psychonomic Bulletin & Review, 15,* 256–271.

Jalbert, A., Neath, I., Bireta, T. J., & Suprenant, A. M. (2011). When does length cause the word length effect? *Journal of Experimental Psychology: Learning, Memory, and Cognition, 37,* 338–357.

James, L. E., & MacKay, D. G. (2001). H.M., word knowledge, and aging: Support for a new theory of long-term retrograde amnesia. *Psychological Science, 12,* 485–492.

James, W. (1890). *The principles of psychology.* New York: Henry Holt.

Janiszewski, C. (2011). Too many views to capture: Reference sets in human judgment. In G. Keren

(Ed.), *Perspectives on framing* (pp. 93–115). New York: Psychology Press.

Janssen, S. M. J., & Rubin, D. C. (2011). Age effects in cultural life scripts. *Applied Cognitive Psychology, 25*, 291–298.

Janssen, S. M. J., Rubin, D. C., & St. Jacques, P. L. (2011). The temporal distribution of autobiographical memory: Changes in reliving and vividness over the life span do not explain the reminiscence bump. *Memory & Cognition, 39*, 1–11.

Jared, D., Levy, B. A., & Rayner, K. (1999). The role of phonology in the activation of word meanings during reading: Evidence from proofreading and eye movements. *Journal of Experimental Psychology: General, 128*, 219–264.

Jarrold, C., & Bayliss, D. M. (2007). Variation in working memory due to typical and atypical development. In A. R. A. Conway, et al. (Eds.), *Variations in working memory* (pp. 134–161). New York: Oxford University Press.

Jenkins, J. J. (1974). Remember that old theory of memory? Well, forget it. *American Psychologist, 29*, 785–795.

Jia, G., Aaronson, D., & Wu, Y. (2002). Long-term language attainment of bilingual immigrants: Predictive variables and language group differences. *Applied Psycholinguistics, 23*, 599–621.

Jitendra, A. K., et al. (2007). A comparison of single and multiple strategy instruction on third-grade students' mathematical problem solving. *Journal of Educational Psychology, 99*, 115–127.

Jobard, G., Crivello, E., & Tzourio-Mazoyer, N. (2003). Evaluation of the dual route theory of reading: A meta-analysis of 35 neuroimaging studies. *Neuroimage, 20*, 693–712.

Johansson, P., et al. (2006). How something can be said about telling more than we can know: On choice blindness and introspection. *Consciousness and Cognition, 15*, 673–692.

Johnson, D. D. P. (2004). *Overconfidence and war: The havoc and glory of positive illusions.* Cambridge, MA: Harvard University Press.

Johnson, J. S., & Newport, E. L. (1989). Critical effects in second language learning: The influence of maturational state on the acquisition of English as a second language. *Cognitive Psychology, 21*, 60–99.

Johnson, M. H., & Bolhuis, J. J. (2000). Predispositions in perceptual and cognitive development. In J. J. Bolhuis (Ed.), *Brain, perception, memory* (pp. 68–84). New York: Oxford University Press.

Johnson, M. K. (1996). Fact, fantasy, and public policy. In D. J. Herrmann, et al. (Eds.), *Basic and applied memory research theory in context* (Vol. 1, pp. 83–103). Mahwah, NJ: Erlbaum.

Johnson, M. K. (1997). Identifying the origin of mental experience. In M. S. Myslobodsky (Ed.), *The mythomanias: The nature of deception and self-deception* (pp. 133–180). Mahwah, NJ: Erlbaum.

Johnson, M. K. (1998). Individual and cultural reality monitoring. *Annals of the American Academy of Political and Social Science, 560*, 179–193.

Johnson, M. K. (2002, October). Reality monitoring: Varying levels of analysis. *APS Observer*, pp. 8, 28–29.

Johnson-Laird, P. N. (2005a). Mental models and thought. In K. J. Holyoak & R. G. Morrison (Eds.), *The Cambridge handbook of thinking and reasoning* (pp. 185–208). New York: Cambridge University Press.

Johnson-Laird, P. N. (2005b). The shape of problems. In V. Girotto & P. N. Johnson-Laird (Eds.), *The shape of reason: Essays in honour of Paolo Legrenzi* (pp. 3–26). Hove, UK: Psychology Press.

Johnson-Laird, P. N. (2011). The truth about conditionals. In K. Manktelow, D. Over, & S. Elqayam (Eds.), *The science of reason: A festschrift for Jonathan St B. T. Evans* (pp. 119–143). New York: Psychology Press.

Johnson-Laird, P. N., Girotto, V., & Legrenzi, P. (2004). Reasoning from inconsistency to consistency. *Psychological Review, 111*, 640–661

Jolicoeur, P., & Kosslyn, S. M. (1985a). Demand characteristics in image scanning experiments. *Journal of Mental Imagery, 9*, 41–50.

Jolicoeur, P., & Kosslyn, S. M. (1985b). Is time to scan visual images due to demand characteristics? *Memory & Cognition, 13*, 320–332.

Jones, D. M., Macken, W. J., & Nicholls, A. P. (2004). The phonological store of working memory: Is it phonological and is it a store? *Journal of Experimental Psychology, Learning, Memory, and Cognition, 30*, 656–674.

Jones, E. L., & Ross, B. H. (2011). Classification versus inference learning contrasted with real-world categories. *Memory and Cognition, 39*, 764–777.

Jones, J. (1999). *The psychotherapist's guide to human memory*. New York: Basic Books.

Jonides, J., et al. (2008). The mind and brain of short-term memory. *Annual Review of Psychology, 59,* 193–224.

Joorman, J., & Siemer, M. (2004). Memory accessibility, mood regulation, and dysphoria: Difficulties in repairing sad mood with happy memories? *Journal of Abnormal Psychology, 113,* 179–188.

Joyner, M. H., & Kurtz-Costes, B. (1997). Metamemory development. In N. Cowan & C. Hulme (Eds.), *The development of memory in childhood* (pp. 275–300). East Sussex, UK: Psychology Press.

Juffs, A. (2010). Perspectives from formal linguistics on second language acquisition. In R. B. Kaplan (Ed.), *The Oxford handbook of applied linguistics* (2nd ed., pp. 143–162). New York: Oxford University Press.

Jusczyk, P. W., & Luce, P. A. (2002). Speech perception. In H. Pashler (Ed.), *Stevens' handbook of experimental psychology* (3rd ed., Vol. 1, pp. 493–536). New York: Wiley.

Just, M. A., et al. (2004). Imagery in sentence comprehension: An fMRI study. *NeuroImage, 21,* 112–124.

Kagan, J., & Herschkowitz, N. (2005). *A young mind in a growing brain*. Mahwah, NJ: Erlbaum.

Kahneman, D. (2011). *Thinking, fast and slow*. New York: Farrar, Straus and Giroux.

Kahneman, D., & Frederick, S. (2002). Representativeness revisited: Attribute substitution in intuitive judgment. In T. Gilovich, D. Griffin, & D. Kahneman (Eds.), *Heuristics and biases: The psychology of intuitive judgment* (pp. 49–81). New York: Cambridge University Press.

Kahneman, D., & Frederick, S. (2005). A model of heuristic judgment. In K. J. Holyoak & R. G. Morrison (Eds.), *The Cambridge handbook of thinking and reasoning* (pp. 267–293). New York: Cambridge University Press.

Kahneman, D., & Renshon, J. (2007, January/February). Why hawks win. *Foreign Policy*, pp. 34–38.

Kahneman, D., & Tversky, A. (1972). Subjective probability: A judgment of representativeness. *Cognitive Psychology, 3,* 430–454.

Kahneman, D., & Tversky, A. (1973). On the psychology of prediction. *Psychological Review, 80,* 237–251.

Kahneman, D., & Tversky, A. (1984). Choices, values, and frames. *American Psychologist, 39,* 341–350.

Kahneman, D., & Tversky, A. (1995). Conflict resolution: A cognitive perspective. In K. Arrow, et al.

(Eds.), *Barriers to conflict resolution* (pp. 44–60). New York: Norton.

Kahneman, D., & Tversky, A. (1996). On the reality of cognitive illusions. *Psychological Review, 103,* 582–591.

Kahneman, D., & Tversky, A. (2000). *Choice, values, and frames*. New York: Cambridge University Press.

Kail, R. V. (1992). Development of memory in children. In L. R. Squire (Ed.), *Encyclopedia of learning and memory* (pp. 99–102). New York: Macmillan.

Kail, R. V. (2010). *Children and their development* (5th ed.). Upper Saddle River, NJ: Prentice Hall.

Kalat, J. W. (2009). *Biological psychology* (10th ed.). Belmont, CA: Wadsworth.

Kanwisher, N. (2010). Functional specificity in the human brain: A window into the functional architecture of the mind. *PNAS Proceedings of the National Academy of Sciences of the United States of America, 107,* 11163–11170.

Kanwisher, N., Downing, P., Epstein, R., & Kourtzi, Z. (2001). Functional neuroimaging of visual recognition. In R. Cabeza & A. Kingstone (Eds.), *Handbook of functional neuroimaging of cognition* (pp. 110–151). Cambridge, MA: MIT Press.

Kaplan, R. B. (Ed.). (2010a). *The Oxford handbook of applied linguistics* (2nd ed.). New York: Oxford University Press.

Kaplan, R. B. (2010b). Whence applied linguistics: The twentieth century. In R. B. Kaplan (Ed.), *The Oxford handbook of applied linguistics* (2nd ed., pp. 3–33). New York: Oxford University Press.

Kaschak, M. P., Kutta, T. & Schachneider, C. (2011). Long-term cumulative structural priming persists for (at least) one week. *Memory & Cognition, 39,* 381–388.

Kaufman, J. C., & Sternberg, R. J. (Eds.). (2010a). *The Cambridge handbook of creativity*. New York: Cambridge University Press.

Kaufman, J. C., & Sternberg, R. J. (2010b). Preface. In J. C. Kaufman & R. J. Sternberg (Eds.), *The Cambridge handbook of creativity* (pp. xiii–xv). New York: Cambridge University Press.

Kaufman, N. J., Randlett, A. L., & Price, J. (1985). Awareness of the use of comprehension strategies in good and poor college readers. *Reading Psychology, 6,* 1–11.

Kayaert, G., Biederman, I., & Vogels, R. (2003). Shape tuning in macaque inferior temporal cortex. *Journal of Neuroscience, 23,* 3016–3027.

Keast, A., Brewer, N., & Wells, G. L. (2007). Children's metacognitive judgments in an eyewitness identification task. *Journal of Experimental Child Psychology, 97*, 286–314.

Keating, P. A. (2006). Phonetic encoding of prosodic structure. In J. Harrington & M. Tabain (Eds.), *Speech production: Models, phonetic processes, and techniques* (pp. 167–186). New York: Psychology Press.

Keehner, M., et al. (2006). Learning a spatial skill for surgery: How the contributions of abilities change with practice. *Applied Cognitive Psychology, 20*, 487–503.

Keen, R. (2011). The development of problem solving in young children: A critical cognitive skill. *Annual Review of Psychology, 62*, 1–21.

Keller, T. A., Carpenter, P. A., & Just, M. A. (2003). Brain imaging of tongue-twister sentence comprehension: Twisting the tongue and the brain. *Brain and Language, 84*, 189–203.

Kellogg, R. T. (1994). *The psychology of writing*. New York: Oxford University Press.

Kellogg, R. T. (1996). A model of working memory in writing. In C. M. Levy & S. Ransdell (Eds.), *The science of writing: Theories, methods, individual differences, and applications* (pp. 57–71). Mahwah, NJ: Erlbaum.

Kellogg, R. T. (1998). Components of working memory in text production. In M. Torrance & G. C. Jeffery (Eds.), *The cognitive demands of writing: Processing capacity and working memory effects in text production*. Amsterdam: Amsterdam University Press.

Kellogg, R. T. (2001a). Competition for working memory among writing processes. *American Journal of Psychology, 114*, 175–191.

Kellogg, R. T. (2001b). Long-term working memory in text production. *Memory & Cognition, 29*, 43–52.

Kellogg, R. T., Olive, T., & Piolat, A. (2007). Verbal, visual, and spatial working memory in written language production. *Acta Psychologica, 124*, 382–397.

Kellogg, R. T., & Whiteford, A. P. (2009). Training advanced writing skills: The case for deliberate practice. *Educational Psychologist, 44*, 250–266.

Kelly, F., & Grossberg, S. (2000). Neural dynamics of 3-D surface perception: Figure-ground separation and lightness perception. *Perception & Psychophysics, 62*, 1596–1618.

Kemp, R., Towell, N., & Pike, G. (1997). When seeing should not be believing: Photographs, credit cards, and fraud. *Journal of Applied Psychology, 11*, 211–222.

Kemper, S. (2006). Language and adulthood. Aging and attention. In E. Bialystok & F. I. M. Craik (Eds.), *Lifespan cognition: Mechanisms of change* (pp. 223–238). New York: Oxford University Press.

Keren, G. (2011a). On the definition and possible underpinnings of framing effects: A brief review and a critical evaluation. In G. Keren (Ed.), *Perspectives on framing* (pp. 3–33). New York: Psychology Press.

Keren, G. (Ed.). (2011b). *Perspectives on framing*. New York: Psychology Press.

Kersten, D., Mamassian, P., & Yuille, A. (2004). Object perception as Bayesian inference. *Annual Review of Psychology, 55*, 271–304.

Kesibir, S., & Oishi, S. (2010). Spontaneous self-reference effect in memory: Why some birthdays are harder to remember than others. *Psychological Science, 21*, 1525–1531.

Kester, J. D., Benjamin, A. S., Castel, A. D., & Craik, F. I. M. (2002). Memory in elderly people. In A. D. Baddeley, M. D. Kopelman, & B. A. Wilson (Eds.), *The handbook of memory disorders* (2nd ed., pp. 543–567). New York: Wiley.

Ketelsen, K., & Welsh, M. (2010). Working memory and mental arithmetic: A case for dual central executive resources. *Brain and Cognition, 74*, 203–209.

Kibbe, M. M., & Leslie, A. M. (2011). What do infants remember when they forget? Location and identity in 6-month-olds' memory for objects. *Psychological Science, 22*, 1500–1505.

Kida, T. (2006). *Don't believe everything you think: The 6 basic mistakes we make in thinking*. Amherst, NY: Prometheus Books.

Kiesel, A., et al. (2010). Control and interference in task switching—a review. *Psychological Bulletin*, 849–874.

Kifner, J. (1994, May 20). Pollster finds error on Holocaust doubts. *New York Times* (Late New York Edition), p. A12.

Kihlstrom, J. F. (2009). 'So that we might have roses in December': The function of autobiographical memory. *Applied Cognitive Psychology*, 1179–1192.

Kihlstrom, J. F., Dorfman, J., & Park, L. (2007). Implicit and explicit memory and learning. In M. Velmans & S. Schneider (Eds.), *The Blackwell companion to consciousness* (pp. 526–539). Malden, MA: Blackwell.

Kimball, D. R., & Holyoak, K. K. (2000). Transfer and expertise. In E. Tulving & F. I. M. Craik (Eds.), *The Oxford handbook of memory* (pp. 109–122). New York: Oxford University Press.

Kimball, M. M. (1989). A new perspective on women's math achievement. *Psychological Bulletin, 105,* 198–214.

Kinsbourne, M. (1998). The right hemisphere and recovery from aphasia. In B. Stemmer & H. A. Whitaker (Eds.), *Handbook of neurolinguistics* (pp. 385–392). San Diego: Academic Press.

Kintsch, W. (1998). *Comprehension: A paradigm for cognition.* New York: Cambridge University Press.

Kintsch, W., & Buschke, H. (1969). Homophones and synonyms in short-term memory. *Journal of Experimental Psychology, 80,* 403–407.

Kintsch, W., et al. (1999). Models of working memory. In A. Miyake & P. Shah (Eds.), *Models of working memory: Mechanisms of active maintenance and executive control* (pp. 412–441). New York: Cambridge University Press.

Kirsh, D. (2009). Problem solving and situated cognition. In P. Robbins & M. Aydede (Eds.), *The Cambridge handbook of situated cognition* (pp. 264–306). New York: Cambridge University Press.

Kirsh, S. J. (2011). *Children, adolescents, and media violence: A critical look at the research* (2nd ed.). Los Angeles: Sage.

Kisilevsky, B. S., et al. (2003). Effects of experience on fetal voice recognition. *Psychological Science, 14,* 220–224.

Kitchin, R., & Blades, M. (2002). *The cognition of geographic space.* London: Tauris.

Klein, S. B., & Kihlstrom, J. F. (1986). Elaboration, organization, and the self-reference effect in memory. *Journal of Experimental Psychology: General, 115,* 26–38.

Kliegl, R., Grabner, E., Rolfe, M., & Engbert, R. (2004). Length, frequency, and predictability effects of words on eye movements in reading. In R. Radach, A. Kennedy, & K. Rayner (Eds.), *Eye movements and information processing during reading* (pp. 262–284). Hove, UK: Psychology Press.

Klin, C. M., Guzmán, A. E., & Levine, W. H. (1999). Prevalence and persistence of predictive inferences. *Journal of Memory and Learning, 40,* 593–604.

Knott, R., & Marslen-Wilson, W. (2001). Does the medial temporal lobe bind phonological memories? *Journal of Cognitive Neuroscience, 13,* 593–609.

Knouse, L. E., Paradise, M. J., & Dunlosky, J. (2006). Does ADHD in adults affect the relative accuracy of metamemory judgments? *Journal of Attention Disorders, 10,* 160–170.

Knowlton, B. (1997). Declarative and nondeclarative knowledge: Insights from cognitive neuroscience. In K. Lamberts & D. Shanks (Eds.), *Knowledge, concepts and categories* (pp. 215–246). Cambridge, MA: MIT Press.

Koestler, A. (1964). *The act of creation.* London: Hutchin.

Kolb, B., & Whishaw, I. Q. (2009). *Fundamentals of human neuropsychology* (6th ed.). New York: Worth.

Kolb, B., & Whishaw, I. Q. (2011). *An introduction to brain and behavior* (3rd ed.). New York: Worth.

Koriat, A. (2000). Control processes in remembering. In E. Tulving & F. I. M. Craik (Eds.), *The Oxford handbook of memory* (pp. 333–346). New York: Oxford University Press.

Koriat, A. (2007). Metacognition and consciousness. In P. D. Zelazo, M. Moscovitch, & E. Thompson (Eds.), *The Cambridge handbook of consciousness* (pp. 289–325). Cambridge, UK: Cambridge University Press.

Koriat, A., & Bjork, R. A. (2005). Illusions of competence in monitoring one's knowledge during study. *Journal of Experimental Psychology: Learning, Memory, and Cognition, 31,* 187–194.

Koriat, A., & Bjork, R. A. (2006a). Illusions of competence during study can be remedied by manipulations that enhance learners' sensitivity to retrieval conditions at test. *Memory & Cognition, 34,* 959–972.

Koriat, A., & Bjork, R. A. (2006b). Mending metacognitive illusions: A comparison of mnemonic-based and theory-based procedures. *Journal of Experimental Psychology: Learning, Memory, and Cognition, 32,* 1133–1145.

Koriat, A., Fiedler, K., & Bjork, R. A. (2006). Inflation of conditional predictions. *Journal of Experimental Psychology: General, 135,* 429–447.

Koriat, A., Goldsmith, M., & Pansky, A. (2000). Toward a psychology of memory accuracy. *Annual Review of Psychology, 51,* 481–537.

Koriat, A., & Helstrup, T. (2007). Metacognitive aspects of memory. In S. Magnussen & T. Helstrup (Eds.), *Everyday memories* (pp. 251–274). New York: Psychology Press.

Koriat, A., Nussinson, R., Bless, H., & Shaked, N. (2008). Information-based and experience-based metacognitive judgments: Evidence from subjective confidence. In J. Dunlosky & R. A. Bjork (Eds.), *Handbook of metamemory and memory* (pp. 117–135). New York: Psychology Press.

Kornell, N. (2009). Optimising learning using flash-cards: Spacing is more effective than cramming. *Applied Cognitive Psychology, 23,* 1297–1317.

Kornell, N., & Metcalfe, J. (2006). Study efficacy and the region of proximal learning framework. *Journal of Experimental Psychology: Learning, Memory, and Cognition, 37,* 609–622.

Kornell, N., Rhodes, M. G., Castel, A. D., & Tauber, S. K. (2011). The ease-of-processing heuristic and the stability bias: Dissociating memory, memory beliefs, and memory judgments. *Psychological Science, 22,* 787–794.

Kosslyn, S. M. (1983). *Ghosts in the mind's machine: Creating and using images in the brain.* New York: Norton.

Kosslyn, S. M. (2001). Visual consciousness. *Advances in Consciousness Research, 8,* 79–103.

Kosslyn, S. M. (2007). *Clear and to the point: 8 psychological principles for compelling PowerPoint® presentations.* New York: Oxford University Press.

Kosslyn, S. M., Alpert, N. M., & Thompson, W. L. (1995). Identifying objects at different levels of hierarchy: A positron emission tomography study. *Human Brain Mapping, 3,* 107–132.

Kosslyn, S. M., Ball, T. M., & Reiser, B. J. (1978). Visual images preserve metric spatial information: Evidence from studies of image scanning. *Journal of Experimental Psychology: Human Perception & Performance, 4,* 47–60.

Kosslyn, S. M., Ganis, G., & Thompson, W. L. (2001). Neural foundations of imagery. *Nature Reviews/Neuroscience, 2,* 635–642.

Kosslyn, S. M., Ganis, G., & Thompson, W. L. (2003). Mental imagery: Against the nihilistic hypothesis. *TRENDS in Cognitive Sciences, 7,* 109–111.

Kosslyn, S. M., Ganis, G., & Thompson, W. L. (2010). Multimodal images in the brain. In A. Guillot & C. Collet (Eds.), *The neurophysiological foundations of mental and motor imagery* (pp. 3–16). New York: Oxford University Press.

Kosslyn, S. M., Seger, C., Pani, J. R., & Hillger, L. A. (1990). When is imagery used in everyday life? A diary study. *Journal of Mental Imagery, 14,* 131–152.

Kosslyn, S. M., & Thompson, W. L. (2000). Shared mechanisms in visual imagery and visual perception: Insights from cognitive neurosciences. In M. S. Gazzaniga (Ed.), *The new cognitive neurosciences* (2nd ed., pp. 975–985). Cambridge, MA: MIT Press.

Kosslyn, S. M., Thompson, W. L., & Ganis, G. (2006). *The case for mental imagery.* New York: Oxford University Press.

Kosslyn, S. M., Thompson, W. L., Wraga, M., & Alpert, N. M. (2001). Imagining rotation by endogenous versus exogenous forces: Distinct neural mechanisms. *Cognitive Neuroscience and Neuropsychology, 12,* 2519–2525.

Kovera, K. B., & Borgida, E. (2010). Social psychology and law. In S. T. Fiske, D. T. Gilbert, & G. Lindzey (Eds.), *The handbook of social psychology* (5th ed., Vol. 2, pp. 1343–1385). Hoboken, NJ: Wiley.

Kozbelt, A., Beghetto, R. A., & Runco, M. A. (2010). Theories of creativity. In J. C. Kaufman & R. J. Sternberg (Eds.), *The Cambridge handbook of creativity* (pp. 20–47). New York: Cambridge University Press.

Kramer, A. F., & Kray, J. (2006). Aging and attention. In E. Bialystok & F. I. M. Craik (Eds.), *Lifespan cognition: Mechanisms of change* (pp. 57–69). New York: Oxford University Press.

Krätzig, G. P., & Arbuthnot, K. D. (2009). Metacognitive learning: The effect of item-specific experience and age on metamemory calibration and planning. *Metacognition and Learning, 4,* 125–144.

Krizan, Z., & Windschitl, P. D. (2007). The influence of outcome desirability on optimism. *Psychological Bulletin, 133,* 95–121.

Kroll, J. F., & De Groot, A. M. (Eds.). (2005). *Handbook of bilingualism: Psycholinguistic approaches.* New York: Oxford University Press.

Krueger, L. E. (1992). The word-superiority effect and phonological recoding. *Memory & Cognition, 20,* 685–694.

Kruglanski, A. W. (2004). *The psychology of closed mindedness.* New York: Psychology Press.

Kruglanski, A. W., & Gigerenzer, G. (2011). Intuitive and deliberate judgments are based on common principles. *Psychological Review, 118,* 97–109.

Krynski, R. R., & Tenenbaum, J. B. (2007). The role of causality in judgments under uncertainty. *Journal of Experimental Psychology: General, 136,* 430–450.

Ku, R. J.-S. (2006). Confessions of an English professor: Globalization and the anxiety of the (standard) English practice. In H. Luria, D. M. Seymour, & T. Smoke (Eds.), *Language and linguistics in context: Readings and applications for teachers* (pp. 377–384). Mahwah, NJ: Erlbaum

Kubose, T. T., et al. (2006). The effects of speech production and speech comprehension on simulated driving performance. *Applied Cognitive Psychology, 20,* 43–64.

Kuhl, P. K. (1994). Learning and representation in speech and language. *Current Opinion in Neurobiology, 4,* 812–822.

Kuhl, P. K. (2000). Language, mind, and brain: Experience alters perception. In M. Gazzaniga (Ed.), *The new cognitive neurosciences* (pp. 99–115). Cambridge, MA: MIT Press.

Kuhl, P. K. (2006). A new view of language acquisition. In H. Luria, D. M. Seymour, & T. Smoke (Eds.), *Language and linguistics in context: Readings and applications for teachers* (pp. 29–41). Mahwah, NJ: Erlbaum.

Kutas, M., & Federmeier, K. D. (2011). Thirty years and counting: Finding meaning in the N400 component of the event-related brain potential (ERP). *Annual Review of Psychology, 62,* 621–647.

Kvavilashvili, L., Mirani, J., Schlagman, S., & Kornbrot, D. E. (2003). Comparing flashbulb memories of September 11 and the death of Princess Diana: Effects of time delays and nationalities. *Applied Cognitive Psychology, 17,* 1017–1031.

Kyllonen, P. C., & Lee, S. (2005). Assessing problem solving in context. In O. Wilhelm & R. W. Engle (Eds.), *Handbook of understanding and measuring intelligence* (pp. 11–25). Thousand Oaks, CA: Sage.

LaBerge, D. (1995). *Attentional processing: The brain's art of mindfulness.* Cambridge, MA: Harvard University Press.

Laeng, B., Zarrinpar, A., & Kosslyn, S. M. (2003). Do separate processes identify objects as exemplars versus members of basic-level categories? Evidence from hemispheric specialization. *Brain and Cognition, 53,* 15–27.

Laible, D., & Panfile, T. (2009). Mother-child reminiscing in the context of secure attachment relationships: Lessons in understanding and coping with negative emotions. In J. A. Quas & R. Fivus (Eds.), *Emotion and memory in development: Biological, cognitive, and social considerations* (pp. 166–195). New York: Oxford University Press.

Lakoff, G. (1987). *Women, fire and dangerous things: What categories reveal about the mind.* Chicago: University of Chicago Press.

Lakoff, G. (2007). *Whose freedom? The battle over America's most important idea.* New York: Picador.

Lakoff, G. (2009). *The political mind: A cognitive scientist's guide to your brain and its politics.* New York: Penguin.

Lakoff, G. (2011, October 19). *Framing Occupy Wall Street.* Retrieved January 23, 2012, from www.truth-out.org/how-frame-yourself-framing/131 >9031142

Lambert, W. E. (1987). The effects of bilingual and bicultural experiences on children's attitudes and social perspectives. In P. Homel, M. Palij, & D. Aaronson (Eds.), *Childhood bilingualism: Aspects of linguistic, cognitive, and social development* (pp. 197–228). Hillsdale, NJ: Erlbaum.

Lambert, W. E. (1990). Persistent issues in bilingualism. In B. Harley, P. Allen, J. Cummins, & M. Swain (Eds.), *The development of second language proficiency* (pp. 201–218). Cambridge, UK: Cambridge University Press.

Lambert, W. E. (1992). Challenging established views on social issues. *American Psychologist, 47,* 533–542.

Lambert, W. E., Genesee, F., Holobow, N., & Chartrand, L. (1991). *Bilingual education for majority English-speaking children.* Montreal: McGill University, Psychology Department.

Lampinen, J. M., Beike, D. R., & Behrend, D. A. (2004). The self and memory: It's about time. In D. R. Beike, J. M., & Behrend (Eds.), *The self and memory* (pp. 255–262). New York: Psychology Press.

Lampinen, J. M., Copeland, S. M., & Neuschatz, J. S. (2001). Recollection of things schematic: Room schemas revisited. *Journal of Experimental Psychology: Learning, Memory, & Cognition, 27,* 1211–1222.

Lampinen, J. M., Faries, J. M., Neuschatz, J. S., & Toglia, M. P. (2000). Recollections of things schematic: The influence of scripts on recollective experience. *Applied Cognitive Psychology, 14,* 543–554.

Landau, M. J., Meier, B. P., & Keefer, L. A. (2010). A metaphor-enriched social cognition. *Psychological Bulletin, 136,* 1045–1067.

Landauer, T. K. (2011). Distributed learning and the size of memory: A 50-year spacing odyssey. In A. S. Benjamin (Ed.), *Successful remembering and successful forgetting: A festschrift in honor of Robert A. Bjork* (pp. 49–69). New York: Psychology Press.

Landauer, T. K., & Dumais, S. T. (1997). A solution to Plato's problem: The latent semantic analysis theory of acquisition, induction, and representation of knowledge. *Psychological Review, 104,* 211–240.

Landauer, T. K., McNamara, D. S., Dennis, S., & Kintsch, W. (Eds.). (2007). *Handbook of latent semantic analysis.* Mahwah, NJ: Erlbaum.

Lane, K. A., Banaji, M. R., & Greenwald, A. G. (2007). Understanding and using the Implicit Association Test: IV. What we know (so far) about the method. In B. Wittenbrink & N. Schwarz (Eds.), *Implicit measures of attitudes*. New York: Guilford.

Lane, K. A., Kang, J., & Banaji, M. R. (2007). Implicit social cognition and law. *Annual Review of Law and Social Psychology, 3*, 427–451.

Lany, J., & Saffran, J. B. (2010). From statistics to meaning: Infants' acquisition of lexical categories. *Psychological Science, 21*, 284–291.

Lappin, J. S., & Craft, W. D. (2000). Foundations of spatial vision: From retinal images to perceived shapes. *Psychological Review, 107*, 6–38.

Larkin, S. (2010). *Metacognition in young children*. London: Routledge.

Larsen, A., & Bundesen, C. (1996). A template-matching pandemonium recognizes unconstrained handwritten characters with high accuracy. *Memory & Cognition, 24*, 136–143.

Lave, J. (1997). What's special about experiments as contexts for thinking. In M. Cole, Y. Engeström, & O. Vasquez (Eds.), *Mind, culture, and activity* (pp. 56–69). New York: Cambridge University Press.

Lavie, N. (2007). Attention and consciousness. In M. Velmans & S. Schneider (Eds.), *The Blackwell companion to consciousness* (pp. 489–503). Malden, MA: Blackwell.

Lea, R. B., Mulligan, E. J., & Walton, J. L. (2005). Accessing distant premise information: How memory feeds reasoning. *Journal of Experimental Psychology: Learning, Memory, and Cognition, 31*, 387–395.

Leahey, T. H. (2003). Cognition and learning. In D. F. Freedheim (Ed.), *Handbook of psychology* (Vol. 1: *The history of psychology*, pp. 109–133). Hoboken, NJ: Wiley.

Leary, D. E. (2009). William James and the art of human understanding. In L. T. Benjamin, Jr. (Ed.), *A history of psychology* (3rd ed., pp. 88–100). Malden, MA: Blackwell.

Leavitt, J. D., & Christenfeld, N. J. S. (2011). Story spoilers don't spoil stories. *Psychological Science, 22*, 1152–1154.

LeBoeuf, R. A., & Shafir, E. B. (2012). Decision making. In K. J. Holyoak & R. G. Morrison (Eds.), *The Cambridge handbook of thinking and reasoning* (pp. 301–321). New York: Cambridge University Press.

Lee, J. J., & Pinker, S. (2010). Rationales for indirect speech: The theory of the strategic speaker. *Psychological Review, 117*, 785–807.

Lee, K., Ng, E. L., & Ng, S. F. (2009). The contributions of working memory and executive functioning to problem representation and solution generation in algebraic word problems. *Journal of Educational Psychology, 101*, 373–387.

Lehrer, J. (2009). *How we decide*. Boston: Houghton Mifflin Harcourt.

Leichtman, M. D., & Ceci, S. J. (1995). The effects of stereotypes and suggestions on preschoolers' reports. *Developmental Psychology, 31*, 568–578.

Leighton, J. P., & Sternberg, R. J. (2003). Reasoning and problem solving. In A. F. Healy & R. W. Proctor (Eds.), *Handbook of psychology* (Vol. 4, pp. 623–648). Hoboken, NJ: Wiley.

Leippe, M., & Eisenstadt, D. (2007). Eyewitness confidence and the confidence-accuracy relationship in memory for people. In R. C. L. Lindsay, D. F. Ross, J. D. Read, & M. P. Toglia (Eds.), *Handbook of eyewitness psychology* (Vol. 2, pp. 377–425). Mahwah, NJ: Erlbaum.

LeMoult, J., Hertel, P. T., & Joormann, J. (2010). Training the forgetting of negative words: The role of direct suppression and the relation to stress reactivity. *Applied Cognitive Psychology, 24*, 365–375.

Lenzner, T., Kaczmirek, L., & Lenzner, A. (2010). Cognitive burden of survey questions and response times: A psycholinguistic experiment. *Applied Cognitive Psychology, 24*, 1003–1020.

Levelt, W. J. M. (1998). The genetic perspective in psycholinguistics or where do spoken words come from? *Journal of Psycholinguistic Research, 27*, 167–180.

Levin, D. S., Thurman, S. K., & Kiepert, M. H. (2010). More than just a memory: The nature and validity of working memory in educational settings. In G. M. Davies & D. B. Wright (Eds.), *Current issues in applied memory research* (pp. 72–95). New York: Psychology Press.

Levin, D. T. (2004). Introduction. In D. T. Levin (Ed.), *Thinking and seeing: Visual metacognition in adults and children* (pp. 1–11). Cambridge, MA: MIT Press.

Levine, D. S. (2002). Neural network modeling. In H. Pashler (Ed.), *Stevens' handbook of experimental psychology* (3rd ed., Vol. 4, pp. 223–269). New York: Wiley

Levy, B. A. (1999). Whole words, segments, and meaning: Approaches to reading education. In R. M. Klein

& P. McMullen (Eds.), *Converging methods for understanding reading and dyslexia* (pp. 77–110). Cambridge, MA: MIT Press.

Levy, B., & Banaji, M. R. (2002). Implicit ageism. In T. D. Nelson (Ed.), *Ageism: Stereotyping and prejudice against older persons* (pp. 49–75). Cambridge, MA: MIT Press.

Levy, C. M., & Ransdell, S. (1995). Is writing as difficult as it seems? *Memory & Cognition, 23*, 767–779.

Levy, D. A. (2010). *Tools of critical thinking: Metathoughts for psychology* (2nd ed.). Long Grove, IL: Waveland Press.

Lewandowsky, S. (2011). Working memory capacity and categorization: Individual differences and modeling. *Journal of Experimental Psychology: Learning, Memory, and Cognition, 37*, 720–738.

Liberman, A. M. (1996). *Speech: A special code.* Cambridge, MA: MIT Press.

Liberman, A. M., & Mattingly, I. G. (1989). A specialization for speech perception. *Science, 243*, 489–494.

Lieberman, M. D. (2007). Social cognitive neuroscience: A review of core processes. *Annual Review of Psychology, 58*, 259–259.

Liederman, J., et al. (2011). Are women more influenced than men by top-down semantic information when listening to disrupted speech? *Language and Speech, 54*, 33–48.

Light, L. L. (1996). Memory and aging. In E. L. Bjork & R. A. Bjork (Eds.), *Memory* (2nd ed., pp. 443–490). San Diego: Academic Press.

Light, L. L. (2000). Memory changes in adulthood. In S. H. Qualls & N. Abeles (Eds.), *Psychology and the aging revolution* (pp. 73–97). Washington, DC: American Psychological Association.

Light, L. L., La Voie, D., & Kennison, R. (1995). Repetition priming of nonwords in young and older adults. *Journal of Experimental Psychology: Learning, Memory, and Cognition, 21*, 327–346.

Lilienfeld, S. O., Ammirati, R., & Landfield, K. (2009). Giving debiasing away: Can psychological research on correcting cognitive errors promote human welfare? *Perspectives on Psychological Science, 4*, 390–398.

Little, D. M., Prentice, K. J., & Wingfield, A. (2004). Adult age differences in judgments of semantic fit. *Applied Psycholinguistics, 25*, 135–142.

Lockhart, R. S. (2001). Commentary: Levels of processing and memory theory. In M. Naveh-Benjamin, M. Moscovitch, & H. L. Roediger, III (Eds.), *Perspectives on human memory and cognitive aging: Essays in honour of Fergus Craik* (pp. 99–102). New York: Psychology Press.

Loftus, E. F., Miller, D. G., & Burns, H. J. (1978). Semantic integration of verbal information into visual memory. *Journal of Experimental Psychology: Human Learning and Memory, 4*, 19–31.

Logie, R. H. (1995). *Visuo-spatial working memory.* Hove, UK: Erlbaum.

Logie, R. H. (2003). Spatial and visual working memory: A mental workspace. *The Psychology of Learning and Motivation, 42*, 37–78.

Logie, R. H. (2011). The visual and the spatial of a multicomponent working memory. In A. Vandierendonck & A. Szmalec (Eds.), *Spatial working memory* (pp. 19–45). New York: Psychology Press.

Logie, R. H., & Della Sala, S. (2005). Disorders of visuospatial working memory. In P. Shah & A. Miyaki (Eds.), *The Cambridge handbook of visuospatial thinking* (pp. 81–120). New York: Cambridge University Press.

Logie, R. H., Trawley, S., & Law, A. (2011). Multitasking: Multiple, domain-specific cognitive functions in a virtual environment. *Memory & Cognition, 39*, 1561–1574.

Logie, R. H., & van der Meulen, M. (2009). Fragmenting and integrating visuospatial working memory. In J. R. Brockmole (Ed.), *The visual world in memory* (pp. 1–32). New York: Psychology Press.

Long, D. L., Johns, C. L., & Morris, P. E. (2006). Comprehension ability in mature readers. In M. J. Traxler & M. A. Gernsbacher (Eds.), *Handbook of psycholinguistics* (2nd ed., pp. 801–833). Amsterdam: Elsevier.

Long, G. M., & Toppino, T. C. (2004). Enduring interest in perceptual ambiguity: Alternating views of reversible figures. *Psychological Bulletin, 130*, 748–768.

Lovatt, P., Avons, S. E., & Masterson, J. (2002). Output decay in immediate serial recall: Speech time revisited. *Journal of Memory and Language, 46*, 227–243.

Love, B. C., & Tomlinson, M. (2010). Mechanistic models of associative and rule-based category learning. In D. Mareschal, P. C. Quinn, & S. E. G. Lea (Eds.), *The making of human concepts* (pp. 53–74). New York: Oxford University Press.

Lovelace, E. A. (1984). Metamemory: Monitoring future recallability during study. *Journal of Experimental Psychology: Learning, Memory, and Cognition, 10*, 756–766.

Lovett, M. C. (2002). Problem solving. In D. Medin (Ed.), *Stevens' handbook of experimental psychology* (pp. 317–362). New York: Wiley.

Luchins, A. S. (1942). Mechanization in problem solving. *Psychological Monographs, 54* (Whole No. 248).

Luck, S. J., & Vecera, S. P. (2002). Attention. In H. Pashler (Ed.), *Stevens' handbook of experimental psychology* (3rd ed., Vol. 1, pp. 235–286). New York: Wiley.

Luna, D. (2011). Advertising to the buy-lingual consumer. In V. Cook & B. Bassetti (Eds.), *Language and bilingual cognition* (pp. 543–558). New York: Psychology Press.

Luo, C. R., Johnson, R. A., & Gallo, D. A. (1998). Automatic activation of phonological information in reading: Evidence from the semantic relatedness decision task. *Memory & Cognition, 26*, 833–843.

Lupyan, G., & Dale, R. (2010). Language structure is partly determined by social structure. *PloS ONE, 5* (1), e8559.

Luria, H. (2006). Introduction to Unit III: Literacy and education in a globalized world. In H. Luria, D. M. Seymour, & T. Smoke (Eds.), *Language and linguistics in context: Readings and applications for teachers* (pp. 233–242). Mahwah, NJ: Erlbaum.

Lynch, T. (2010). Listening: Sources, skills, and strategies. In R. B. Kaplan (Ed.), *The Oxford handbook of applied linguistics* (2nd ed., pp. 74–87). New York: Oxford University Press.

MacDonald, M. C. (1999). Distributional information in language comprehension, production, and acquisition: Three puzzles and a moral. In B. MacWhinney (Ed.), *The emergence of language* (pp. 177–196). Mahwah, NJ: Erlbaum.

MacKay, D. (2004). Information theory. In R. L. Gregory (Ed.), *The Oxford companion to the mind* (2nd ed., pp. 456–467). New York: Oxford University Press.

MacKay, I. R. A., Flege, J. E., & Imai, S. (2006). Evaluating the effects of chronological age and sentence duration on degree of perceived foreign accent. *Applied Psycholinguistics, 27*, 153–183.

MacLeod, C. (2005). The Stroop task in clinical research. In A. Wenzel & D. C. Rubin (Eds.), *Cognitive methods and their application to clinical research* (pp. 41–62). Washington, DC: American Psychological Association.

MacLeod, C., & Campbell, L. (1992). Memory accessibility and probability judgments: An experimental evaluation of the availability heuristic. *Journal of Personality and Social Psychology, 63*, 890–902.

MacLeod, C. M. (2005). The Stroop task in cognitive research. In A. Wenzel & D. C. Rubin (Eds.), *Cognitive methods and their application to clinical research* (pp. 17–40). Washington, DC: American Psychological Association.

MacLin, O. H., & Malpass, R. S. (2001). Racial categorization of faces: The ambiguous race face effect. *Psychology, Public Policy, and Law, 7*, 98–118.

Macpherson, R., & Stanovich, K. E. (2007). Cognitive ability, thinking dispositions, and instructional set as predictors of critical thinking. *Learning and Individual Differences, 17*, 115–127.

Macrae, C. N., & Quadflieg, S. (2010). Perceiving people. In S. T. Fiske, D. T. Gilbert, & G. Lindzey (Eds.), *Handbook on social psychology* (5th ed., Vol. 2, pp. 428–463). Hoboken, NJ: Wiley.

MacWhinney, B. (2011). Language development. In M. H. Bornstein & M. E. Lamb (Eds.), *Developmental science: An advanced textbook* (pp. 389–423). Mahwah, NJ: Erlbaum.

Magnussen, S., et al. (2006). What people believe about memory. *Memory, 14*, 595–613.

Mahon, B. Z., Schwarzbach, J., & Caramazza, A. (2010). The representation of tools in the left parietal cortex is independent of visual experience. *Psychological Science, 21*, 764–771.

Maki, R. H., Jonas, D., & Kallod, M. (1994). The relationship between comprehension and metacomprehension ability. *Psychonomic Bulletin & Review, 1*, 126–129.

Maki, R. H., & McGuire, M. J. (2002). Metacognition for text: Findings and implications for education. In T. J. Perfect & B. L. Schwartz (Eds.), *Applied metacognition* (pp. 39–67). Cambridge, UK: Cambridge University Press.

Maki, R. H., & Serra, M. (1992). The basis of test prediction for text material. *Journal of Experimental Psychology: Learning, Memory, and Cognition, 18*, 116–126.

Maki, R. H., Shields, M., Wheeler, A. E., & Zacchilli, T. L. (2005). Individual differences in absolute and relative metacomprehension accuracy. *Journal of Educational Psychology, 97*, 723–731.

Maki, R. H., Willmon, C., & Pietan, A. (2009). Basis of metamemory judgments for text with multiple-choice, essay and recall tests. *Applied Cognitive Psychology, 23*, 204–222.

Maki, W. S., & Maki, R. H. (2000). Evaluation of a web-based introductory psychology course: II. Contingency management to increase use of on-line study aids. *Behavior Research Methods, Instruments & Computers, 32*, 240–245.

Mandel, D. R., Jusczyk, P. W., & Pisoni, D. B. (1995). Infants' recognition of the sound patterns of their own names. *Psychological Science, 6*, 314–317.

Mandler, G. (2002). Origins of the cognitive (R)evolution. *Journal of the Behavioral Sciences, 38*, 339–353.

Mandler, J. M. (2003). Conceptual categorization. In D. Rakison & L. M. Oakes (Eds.), *Early category and concept development*. New York: Oxford University Press.

Mandler, J. M. (2004a). *The foundations of mind: Origins of conceptual thought*. New York: Oxford University Press.

Mandler, J. M. (2004b). Thought before language. *TRENDS in Cognitive Science, 8*, 508–524.

Mandler, J. M. (2006). Actions organize the infant's world. In K. Hirsh-Pasek & R. M. Golinkoff (Eds.), *Action meets word: How children learn verbs* (pp. 111–133). New York: Oxford University Press.

Mandler, J. M. (2007). On the origins of the conceptual system. *American Psychologist, 62*, 741–751.

Manktelow, K. D. (1999). *Reasoning and thinking*. East Sussex, UK: Psychology Press.

Manktelow, K. D., Over, D., & Elqayam, S. (Eds.). (2011). *The science of reason: A festschrift for Jonathan St B. T. Evans* (pp. 119–143). New York: Psychology Press.

Manly, J. J., Touradji, P., Tang, M., & Stern, Y. (2003). Literacy and memory decline among ethnically diverse elders. *Journal of Clinical and Experimental Neuropsychology, 25*, 680–690.

Mäntylä, T. (1997). Recollections of faces: Remembering differences and knowing similarities. *Journal of Experimental Psychology: Learning, Memory, and Cognition, 23*, 1203–1216.

Mar, R. A. (2011). The neural bases of social cognition and story comprehension. *Annual Review of Psychology, 62*, 103–134.

Mar, R. A., Tackett, J. L., & Moore, C. (2010). Exposure to media and theory-of-mind development in preschoolers. *Cognitive Development, 25*, 69–78.

Marcus, G. F. (1996). Why do children say "breaked"? *Current Directions in Psychological Science, 5*, 81–85.

Mareschal, D., Quinn, P. C., & Lea, S. E. G. (Eds.). (2010). *The making of human concepts*. New York: Oxford University Press.

Marian, V., & Fausey, C. M. (2006). Language-dependent memory in bilingual learning. *Applied Cognitive Psychology, 20*, 1025–1047.

Maril, A., Simons, J. S., Weaver, J. J., & Schacter, D. L. (2005). Graded recall success: An event-related fMRI comparison of tip of the tongue and feeling of knowing. *NeuroImage, 24*, 1130–1138.

Markman, A. B. (1999). *Knowledge representation*. Mahwah, NJ: Erlbaum.

Markman, A. B. (2002). Knowledge representation. In D. Medin (Ed.), *Stevens' handbook of experimental psychology* (3rd ed., Vol. 2, pp. 165–208). New York: Wiley.

Markman, A. B., & Ross, B. H. (2003). Category use and category learning. *Psychological Bulletin, 129*, 592–613.

Markovits, H., Saelen, C., & Forgues, H. L. (2009). An inverse belief-bias effect: More evidence for the role of inhibitory processes in logical reasoning. *Experimental Psychology, 56*, 112–120.

Markowitsch, H. J., & Welzer, H. (2010). *The development of autobiographical memory*. New York: Psychology Press.

Marsh, E. J., & Sink, H. E. (2010). Access to handouts of presentation slides during lecture: Consequences for learning. *Applied Cognitive Psychology, 24*, 691–706.

Marsh, E. J., & Tversky, B. (2004). Spinning the stories of our lives. *Applied Cognitive Psychology, 18*, 491–503.

Marsh, R. L., Hicks, J. L., & Hancock, T. W. (2000). On the interaction of ongoing cognitive activity and the nature of an event-based intention. *Applied Cognitive Psychology, 14*, S29–S41.

Marsh, R. L., Landau, J. D., & Hicks, J. L. (1997). Contributions of inadequate source monitoring to unconscious plagiarism during idea generation. *Journal of Experimental Psychology: Learning, Memory, and Cognition, 23*, 886–897.

Marsh, R. L., et al. (2007). Memory for intention-related material presented in a to-be-ignored channel. *Memory & Cognition, 35*, 1197–1204.

Marshall, P. J. (2009). Relating psychology and neuroscience: Taking up the challenges. *Perspectives on Psychological Science, 4*, 113–125.

Marslen-Wilson, W. D., Tyler, L. K., & Koster, C. (1993). Integrative processes in utterance resolution. *Journal of Memory and Language, 32*, 647–666.

Martin, E. (1967). Personal communication.

Martin, F., Baudouin, J., Tiberghien, G., & Franck, N. (2005). Processing emotional expression and facial identity in schizophrenia. *Psychiatry Research, 134,* 43–53.

Martin, R. C., & Wu, D. H. (2005). The cognitive neuropsychology of language. In K. Lamberts & R. L. Goldstone (Eds.), *Handbook of cognition* (pp. 382–404). Thousand Oaks, CA: Sage.

Martins, M., Silva, C., & Pereira, M. (2010). The impact of the articulatory properties of phonemes on the evolution of preschool children's writing. *Applied Psycholinguistics, 31,* 693–709.

Martinussen, R., Hayden, J., Hogg-Johnson, S., & Tannock, R. (2005). A meta-analysis of working memory impairments in children with attention-deficit/hyperactivity disorder. *Journal of the American Academy of Child and Adolescent Psychology, 44,* 377–384.

Mason, R. A., & Just, M. A. (2006). Neuroimaging contributions to the understanding of discourse processes. In M. J. Traxler & M. A. Gernsbacher (Eds.), *Handbook of psycholinguistics* (2nd ed., pp. 765–799). New York: Academic Press.

Masoura, E., & Gathercole, S. E. (2005). Contrasting contributions of phonological short-term memory and long-term knowledge to vocabulary learning in a foreign language. *Memory, 13,* 422–429.

Massaro, D. W. (1998). *Perceiving talking faces.* Cambridge, MA: MIT Press.

Massaro, D. W. (1999). Speechreading: Illusion or window into pattern recognition. *Trends in Cognitive Sciences, 3,* 310–317.

Massaro, D. W., Cohen, M. M., & Smeele, P. M. T. (1995). Cross-linguistic comparisons in the integration of visual and auditory speech. *Memory & Cognition, 23,* 113–131.

Massaro, D. W., & Cole, R. (2000, August). From "speech is special" to talking heads in language learning. *Proceedings of Integrating Speech Technology in the (Language) Learning and Assistive Interface,* pp. 153–161. New York: Association for Computer Machinery.

Massaro, D. W., & Stork, D. G. (1998). Speech recognition and sensory integration. *American Scientist, 86,* 236–244.

Mast, F., Kosslyn, S. M., & Berthoz, A. (1999). Visual mental imagery interferes with allocentric orientation judgements. *NeuroReport, 10,* 3549–3553.

Mather, G. (2006). *Foundations of perception.* Hove, UK: Psychology Press.

Mather, M. (2006). Why memories may become more positive as people age. In B. Uttl, N. Ohta, & A. L. Siegenthaler (Eds.), *Memory and emotion: Interdisciplinary perspectives* (pp. 135–158). Malden, MA: Blackwell.

Matlin, M. W. (2004). Pollyanna Principle. In R. Pohl (Ed.), *Cognitive illusions: Handbook on fallacies and biases in thinking, judgment, and memory* (pp. 255–272). Hove, UK: Psychology Press.

Matlin, M. W. (2012). *The psychology of women* (7th ed.). Belmont, CA: Wadsworth Cengage.

Matlin, M. W., & Stang, D. J. (1978). *The Pollyanna Principle: Selectivity in language, memory, and thought.* Cambridge, MA: Schenkman.

Matsumoto, E. (2010). Bias in attending to emotional facial expressions: Anxiety and visual search efficiency. *Applied Cognitive Psychology, 24,* 414–424.

Mattys, S. L., & Liss, J. M. (2008). On building models of spoken-word recognition: When there is as much to learn from natural "oddities" as artificial normality. *Perception & Psychophysics, 70,* 1235–1242.

Mayer, R. E. (2003). Memory and information processing. In W. M. Reynolds & G. E. Miller (Eds.), *Handbook of psychology* (Vol. 7, pp. 47–57). Hoboken, NJ: Wiley.

Mayer, R. E. (2004). Teaching of subject matter. *Annual Review of Psychology, 55,* 715–744.

Mayer, R. E., & Hegarty, M. (1996). The process of understanding mathematical problems. In R. J. Sternberg & T. Ben-Zeev (Eds.), *The nature of mathematical thinking* (pp. 29–53). Mahwah, NJ: Erlbaum.

Mayhorn, C. B., Fisk, A. B., & Whittle, J. D. (2002). Decisions, decisions: Analysis of age, cohort, and time of testing on framing of risky decision options. *Human Factors, 44,* 515–521.

Maynard, A. M. (2006). Personal communication.

Maynard, A. M., Maynard, D. C., & Rowe, K. A. (2004). Exposure to the fields of psychology: Evaluation of an introductory psychology project. *Teaching of Psychology, 31,* 37–40.

Mazzoni, G. A. L., & Memon, A. (2003). Imagination can create false autobiographical memories. *Psychological Science, 14,* 186–188.

McAdams, D. P. (2004). The redemptive self: Narrative identity in America today. In D. R. Beike, J. M., & Behrend (Eds.), *The self and memory* (pp. 95–115). New York: Psychology Press.

McAdams, S., & Drake, C. (2002). Auditory perception and cognition. In S. Yantis (Ed.), *Stevens' handbook of experimental psychology* (3rd ed., Vol. 1, pp. 397–452). New York: Wiley.

McCabe, J. (2011). Metacognitive awareness of learning strategies in undergraduates. *Memory & Cognition, 39,* 462–476.

McClelland, J. L. (1981). Retrieving general and specific knowledge from stored knowledge of specifics. *Proceedings of the Third Annual Conference of the Cognitive Science Society,* 170–172.

McClelland, J. L. (1995). Constructive memory and memory distortions: A parallel-distributed processing approach. In D. L. Schacter (Ed.), *Memory distortion: How minds, brains, and societies reconstruct the past* (pp. 71–89). Cambridge, MA: Harvard University Press.

McClelland, J. L. (1999). Cognitive modeling, connectionist. In R. A. Wilson & F. C. Keil (Eds.), *The MIT encyclopedia of the cognitive sciences* (pp. 137–139). Cambridge, MA: MIT Press.

McClelland, J. L. (2000). Connectionist models of memory. In E. Tulving & F. I. M. Craik (Eds.), *The Oxford handbook of memory* (pp. 583–597). New York: Oxford University Press.

McClelland, J. L., & Rumelhart, D. E. (Eds.). (1986). *Parallel distributed processing: Explorations in the microstructure of cognition* (Vol. 2). Cambridge, MA: MIT Press.

McClelland, J. L., Rumelhart, D. E., & Hinton, G. E. (1986). The appeal of parallel distributed processing. In D. E. Rumelhart, J. L. McClelland, & the PDP Research Group (Eds.), *Parallel distributed processing* (Vol. 1, pp. 3–44). Cambridge, MA: MIT Press.

McCormick, C. B. (2003). Metacognition and learning. In W. M. Reynolds & G. E. Miller (Eds.), *Handbook of psychology* (Vol. 7, pp. 79–102). Hoboken, NJ: Wiley.

McCutchen, D., Teske, P., & Bangston, C. (2008). In C. Bazerman (Ed.), *Handbook of research on writing: History, society, school, individual, text* (pp. 451–470). Mahwah, NJ: Erlbaum.

McDaniel, M. A., & Butler, A. C. (2011). A contextual framework for understanding when difficulties are desirable. In A. S. Benjamin (Ed.), *Successful remembering and successful forgetting: A festschrift in honor of Robert A. Bjork* (pp. 175–198). New York: Psychology Press.

McDaniel, M. A., & Einstein, G. O. (2005). Material appropriate difficulty: A framework for determining when difficulty is desirable for improving learning.

In A. F. Healy (Ed.), *Experimental cognitive psychology and its applications* (pp. 73–85). Washington, DC: American Psychological Association.

McDaniel, M. A., & Einstein, G. O. (2007). *Prospective memory: An overview and synthesis of an emerging field.* Thousand Oaks, CA: Sage.

McDaniel, M. A., Einstein, G. O., Graham, T., & Rall, E. (2004). Delaying execution of intentions: Overcoming the costs of interruptions. *Applied Cognitive Psychology, 18,* 533–547.

McDaniel, M. A., Waddill, P. J., & Shakesby, P. S. (1996). Study strategies, interest, and learning from text: The application of material appropriate processing. In D. J. Herrmann, et al. (Eds.), *Basic and applied memory research: Practical applications* (Vol. 1, pp. 385–397). Mahwah, NJ: Erlbaum.

McDermott, K., & Knight, R. G. (2004). The effects of aging on a measure of prospective remembering using naturalistic stimuli. *Applied Cognitive Psychology, 18,* 349–362.

McDonald, S. A., & Shillcock, R. C. (2003). Eye movements reveal the on-line computation of lexical probabilities during reading. *Psychological Science, 14,* 648–652.

McDonough, L., & Mandler, J. M. (1998). Inductive generalization in 9- and 11-month-olds. *Developmental Science, 1,* 227–232.

McDougall, S., & Gruneberg, M. (2002). What memory strategy is best for examinations in psychology? *Applied Cognitive Psychology, 16,* 451–458.

McGovern, T. V., & Brewer, C. L. (2003). Undergraduate education. In D. F. Freedheim (Ed.), *Handbook of psychology* (Vol. 1: *The history of psychology,* pp. 465–481). Hoboken, NJ: Wiley.

McGraw, A. P., Larsen, J. T., Kahneman, D., & Schkade. D. (2010). Comparing gains and losses. *Psychological Science, 21,* 1438–1435.

McGuinness, D. (2004). *Early reading instruction: What science really tells us about how to teach reading.* Cambridge, MA: Bradford.

McGurk, H., & MacDonald, J. (1976). Hearing lips and seeing voices. *Nature, 264,* 746–748.

McKelvie, S. J., Sano, E. K., & Stout, D. (1994). Effects of colored separate and interactive pictures on cued recall. *Journal of General Psychology, 12,* 241–251.

McKone, E. (2004). Isolating the special component of face recognition: Peripheral identification and a Mooney face. *Journal of Experimental Psychology: Learning, Memory, and Cognition, 30,* 181–197.

McKoon, G., & Ratcliff, R. (1998). Memory-based language processing: Psycholinguistic research in the 1990s. *Annual Review of Psychology, 49,* 25–42.

McNamara, D. S. (2011). Measuring deep, reflective comprehension and learning strategies: Challenges and successes. *Metacognition and Learning, 6,* 195–203.

McNamara, T. P. (2005). *Semantic priming: Perspectives from memory and word recognition.* New York: Psychology Press.

McNamara, T. P., & Diwadkar, V. A. (1997). Symmetry and asymmetry of human spatial memory. *Cognitive Psychology, 34,* 160–190.

McNamara, T. P., & Holbrook, J. B. (2003). The native mind: Biological categorization and reasoning in development across cultures. *Psychological Review, 111,* 960–983.

McNeill, D. (2005). *Gesture and thought.* Chicago: University of Chicago Press.

McQueen, J. M. (2005). Speech perception. In K. Lamberts & R. L. Goldstone (Eds.), *Handbook of cognition* (pp. 255–275). London, UK: Sage.

McVay, J. C., & Kane, M. C. (2010). Does mind wandering reflect executive function or executive failure? Comment on Smallwood and Schooler (2006) and Watkins (2008). *Psychological Bulletin, 136,* 188–197.

Medin, D. L., Lynch, E. B., & Solomon, K. O. (2000). Are there kinds of concepts? *Annual Review of Psychology, 51,* 121–147.

Medin, D. L., & Rips, L. J. (2005). Concepts and categories: Memory, meaning and metaphysics. In K. J. Holyoak & R. G. Morrison (Eds.), *The Cambridge handbook of thinking and reasoning* (pp. 37–72). New York: Cambridge University Press.

Meeter, M., Eijsackers, E. V., & Mulder, J. L. (2006). Retrograde amnesia for autobiographical memories and public events in mild and moderate Alzheimer's disease. *Journal of Clinical and Experimental Neuropsychology, 28,* 914–927.

Meeter, M., & Murre, J. M. J. (2004). Consolidation of long-term memory: Evidence and alternatives. *Psychological Bulletin, 130,* 843–857.

Meissner, C. A., & Brigham, J. C. (2001). Thirty years of investigating the own-race bias in memory for faces: A meta-analytic review. *Psychology, Public Policy, & Law, 7,* 3–35.

Meissner, C. A., Brigham, J. C., & Butz, D. A. (2005). Memory for own- and other-race faces: A dual-process approach. *Applied Cognitive Psychology, 19,* 545–567.

Melnyk, L., Crossman, A. M., & Scullin, M. H. (2007). The suggestibility of children's memory. In M. Toglia, J. D. Read, D. F. Ross, & R. C. L. Lindsay (Eds.), *Handbook of eyewitness psychology* (Vol. 1, pp. 401–451). Mahwah, NJ: Erlbaum.

Memon, A., Holliday, R., & Hill, C. (2006). Pre-event stereotypes and misinformation effects in young children. *Memory, 14,* 104–114.

Mendel, R., et al. (2011). Confirmation bias: Why psychiatrists stick to wrong preliminary diagnoses. *Psychological Medicine, 41,* 2651–2659.

Mendola, J. (2003). Contextual shape processing in human visual cortex: Beginning to fill-in the blanks. In L. Pessoa & P. De Weerd (Eds.), *Filling-in: From perceptual completion to cortical reorganization* (pp. 38–58). New York: Oxford University Press.

Mercier, H., & Sperber, D. (2011). Why do humans reason? Arguments for an argumentative theory. *Behavioral and Brain Sciences, 34,* 57–111.

Mervis, C. B., Catlin, J., & Rosch, E. (1976). Relationships among goodness-of-example, category norms, and word frequency. *Bulletin of the Psychonomic Society, 7,* 283–284.

Metcalfe, J. (1986). Premonitions of insight predict impending error. *Journal of Experimental Psychology: Learning, Memory, and Cognition, 12,* 623–634.

Metcalfe, J. (1998). Insight and metacognition. In G. Mazzoni & T. O. Nelson (Eds.), *Metacognition and cognitive neuropsychology* (pp. 181–197). Mahwah, NJ: Erlbaum.

Metcalfe, J. (2000). Metamemory. In E. Tulving & F. I. M. Craik (Eds.), *The Oxford handbook of memory* (pp. 197–211). New York: Oxford University Press.

Metcalfe, J. (2002). Is study time allocated selectively to a region of proximal learning? *Journal of Experimental Psychology: General, 131,* 349–363.

Metcalfe, J. (2011). Desirable difficulties and studying in the region of proximal learning. In A. S. Benjamin (Ed.), *Successful remembering and successful forgetting: A festschrift in honor of Robert A. Bjork* (pp. 259–276). New York: Psychology Press.

Metcalfe, J., & Wiebe, D. (1987). Intuition in insight and noninsight problem solving. *Memory & Cognition, 15,* 238–246.

Meyer, A. S. (2004). The use of eye tracking in studies of sentence generation. In J. M. Henderson & F. Ferreira (Eds.), *The interface of language, vision, and action: Eye movements and the visual world* (p. 191–211). New York: Psychology Press.

Meyer, A. S., & Belke, E. (2009). Word form retrieval in language production. In M. G. Gaskell (Ed.), *The Oxford handbook of psycholinguistics* (pp. 471–487). New York: Oxford University Press.

Michael, E. B., & Gollan, T. H. (2005). Being and becoming bilingual: Individual differences and consequences for language production. In J. F. Kroll & A. M. B. de Groot (Eds.), *Handbook of bilingualism: Psycholinguistic approaches* (pp. 389–407). New York: Oxford University Press.

Michie, D. (2004). Computer chess. In R. L. Gregory (Ed.), *The Oxford companion to the mind* (2nd ed., pp. 196–199). New York: Oxford University Press.

Mieg, H. A. (2011). Focused cognition: Information integration and complex problem solving by top inventors. In K. L. Mosier & U. M. Fisher (Eds.), *Informed by knowledge: Expert performance in complex situations* (pp. 41–54). New York: Psychology Press.

Miller, G. A. (1956). The magical number seven, plus or minus two: Some limits on our capacity for processing information. *Psychological Review, 63,* 81–97.

Miller, G. A. (1967). The psycholinguists. In G. A. Miller (Ed.), *The psychology of communication* (pp. 70–92). London, UK: Penguin.

Miller, L. C., Lechner, R. E., & Rugs, D. (1985). Development of conversational responsiveness: Preschoolers' use of responsive listener cues and relevant comments. *Developmental Psychology, 21,* 473–480.

Millis, K. K., & Graesser, A. C. (1994). The time-course of constructing knowledge-based inferences for scientific texts. *Journal of Memory and Language, 33,* 583–599.

Milner, B. (1966). Amnesia. In C. W. M. Whitty & O. L. Zangwill (Eds.), *Amnesia following operation on the temporal lobes* (pp. 109–133). London, UK: Butterworth.

Milton, F., & Wills, A. J. (2004). The influence of stimulus properties on category construction. *Journal of Experimental Psychology: Learning, Memory, and Cognition, 30,* 407–415.

Minda, J. P., & Smith, J. D. (2011). Prototype models of categorization: Basic formulation, predictions, and limitations. In D. M. Pothos & A. J. Wills (Eds.), *Formal approaches in categorization* (pp. 40–64). New York: Cambridge University Press.

Miozzo, M., & Caramazza, A. (1997). Retrieval of lexical-syntactic features in tip-of-the-tongue states. *Journal of Experimental Psychology: Learning, Memory, and Cognition, 23,* 1410–1423.

Mishra, A., & Mishra, H. (2010). Border bias: The belief that state borders can protect against disasters. *Psychological Science, 21,* 1582–1586.

Mitchell, K. J., & Johnson, M. K. (2009). Source monitoring 15 years later: What have we learned from fMRI about the neural mechanisms of source memory? *Psychological Bulletin, 135,* 638–677.

Mitte, K. (2008). Memory bias for threatening information in anxiety and anxiety disorders: A meta-analytic review. *Psychological Bulletin, 134,* 886–911.

Miyake, A., & Shah, P. (1999). Toward unified theories of working memory. In A. Miyake & P. Shah (Eds.), *Models of working memory: Mechanisms of active maintenance and executive control* (pp. 442–481). New York: Cambridge University Press.

Moar, I., & Bower, G. H. (1983). Inconsistency in spatial knowledge. *Memory & Cognition, 11,* 107–113.

Moely, B. E., Olson, F. A., Halwes, T. G., & Flavell, J. H. (1969). Production deficiency in young children's clustered recall. *Developmental Psychology, 1,* 26–34.

Mol, S. E., & Bus, A. G. (2011). To read or not to read: A meta-analysis of print exposure from infancy to early adulthood. *Psychology Bulletin, 137,* 267–296.

Moldoveanu, M., & Langer, E. (2002). When "stupid" is smarter than we are. In R. J. Sternberg (Ed.), *Why smart people can be so stupid* (pp. 212–231). New Haven, CT: Yale University Press.

Montello, D. R. (2005). Navigation. In P. Shah & A. Miyake (Eds.), *The Cambridge handbook of visuospatial thinking* (pp. 257–294). New York: Cambridge University Press.

Montello, D. R., Waller, D., Hegarty, M., & Richardson, A. E. (2004). Spatial memory of real environments, virtual environments, and maps. In G. L. Allen (Ed.), *Human spatial memory: Remembering where* (pp. 251–285). Mahwah, NJ: Erlbaum.

Moore, C. M. (2010). Attention and consciousness. In E. B. Goldstein (Ed.), *Encyclopedia of perception* (Vol. 1, pp. 112–116). Thousand Oaks, CA: Sage.

Moore, D. A., & Healy, P. J. (2008). The trouble with overconfidence. *Psychological Review, 115,* 502–517.

Moore, J. D., & Wiemer-Hastings, P. (2003). Discourse in computational linguistics and artificial intelligence. In A. C. Graesser, M. A. Gernsbacher, & S. R. Goldman (Eds.), *Handbook of discourse processes* (pp. 439–485). Mahwah, NJ: Erlbaum.

Moran, S. & Ritov, I., (2011). Valence framings in negotiations. In G. Keren (Ed.), *Perspectives on framing* (pp. 239–254). New York: Psychology Press.

Morey, C. C., & Cowan, N. (2004). When visual and verbal memories compete: Evidence of cross-domain limits in working memory. *Psychonomic Bulletin & Review, 11*, 296–301.

Morey, C. C., & Cowan, N. (2005). When do visual and verbal memories conflict? The importance of working-memory load and retrieval. *Journal of Experimental Psychology: Learning, Memory, and Cognition, 31*, 703–713.

Morris, P. E., et al. (2005). Strategies for learning proper names: Expanding retrieval practice, meaning and imagery. *Applied Cognitive Psychology, 19*, 779–798.

Morris, R. K., & Binder, K. S. (2001). What happens to the unselected meaning of an ambiguous word in skilled reading? In D. S. Gorfein (Ed.), *On the consequences of meaning selection: Perspectives on resolving lexical ambiguity* (pp. 139–153). Washington, DC: American Psychological Association.

Morris, R., Kotitsa, M., & Bramham, J. (2005). Planning in patients with focal brain damage: From simple to complex task performance. In R. Morris & G. Ward (Eds.), *The cognitive psychology of planning* (pp. 153–198). Hove, UK: Psychology Press.

Morrison, A. P. (2005). Psychosis and the phenomenon of unwanted intrusive thoughts. In D. A. Clark (Ed.), *Intrusive thoughts in clinical disorders: Theory, research, and treatment* (pp. 175–198). New York: Guilford.

Morrison, R. G. (2005). Thinking in working memory. In K. J. Holyoak & R. G. Morrison (Eds.), *The Cambridge handbook of thinking and reasoning* (pp. 457–473). New York: Cambridge University Press.

Morrison, R. G., & Knowlton, B. J. (2012). Neurocognitive methods in higher cognition. In K. J. Holyoak & R. G. Morrison (Eds.), *The Oxford handbook of thinking and reasoning* (pp. 67–89). New York: Oxford University Press.

Moscovitch, M., & Craik, F. I. M. (1976). Depth of processing, retrieval cues, and uniqueness of encoding as factors in recall. *Journal of Verbal Learning and Verbal Behavior, 15*, 447–458.

Mosier, K. L., & Fischer, U. M. (Eds.). (2011). *Informed by knowledge: Expert performance in complex situations*. New York: Psychology Press.

Most, S. B. (2010). Attention and emotion. In E. B. Goldstein (Ed.), *Encyclopedia of perception* (Vol. 1, pp. 116–119). Thousand Oaks, CA: Sage.

Most, S. B., Scholl, B. J., Clifford, E. R., & Simons, D. J. (2005). What you see is what you set: Sustained inattentional blindness and the capture of awareness. *Psychological Review, 112*, 217–242.

Most, S. B., et al. (2001). How not to be seen: The contribution of similarity and selective ignoring to sustained inattentional blindness. *Psychological Science, 12*, 9–17.

Moulin, C. J. A., & Gathercole, S. E. (2008). Memory changes across the lifespan. In G. Cohen & M. A. Conway (Eds.), *Memory in the real world* (pp. 305–326). New York: Psychology Press.

Moulin, C. J. A., Thompson, R. G., Wright, D. B., & Conway, M. A. (2007). Eyewitness memory in older adults. In M. P. Toglia, J. D. Read, D. F. Ross, & R. C. L. Lindsay (Eds.), *Handbook of eyewitness psychology* (Vol. 1, pp. 627–646). Mahwah, NJ: Erlbaum.

Mueller, T. (2005, December 12). Your move: How computer chess programs are changing the game. *New Yorker*, pp. 62–69.

Mueller-Johnson, K., & Ceci, S. J. (2007). The elderly eyewitness: A review and prospectus. In M. P. Toglia, J. D. Read, D. F. Ross, & R. C. L. Lindsay (Eds.), *Handbook of eyewitness psychology* (Vol. 1, pp. 577–605). Mahwah, NJ: Erlbaum.

Müller, H. J., & Krummenacher, J. (2006). Visual search and selective attention. *Visual Cognition, 14*, 389–410.

Munger, M. P., Owens, T. R., & Conway, J. E. (2005). Are boundary extension and representational momentum related? *Visual Cognition, 12*, 1041–1056.

Murphy, G. L. (2002). *The big book of concepts*. Cambridge, MA: MIT Press.

Murphy, G. L. (2010). What are categories and concepts? In D. Mareschal, P. C. Quinn, & S. E. G. Lea (Eds.), *The making of human concepts* (pp. 11–28). New York: Oxford University Press.

Murphy, G. L., & Shapiro, A. M. (1994). Forgetting of verbatim information in discourse. *Memory & Cognition, 22*, 85–94.

Murray, L. A., Whitehouse, W. G., & Alloy, L. B. (1999). Mood congruence and depressive deficits in memory: A forced-recall analysis. *Memory, 7*, 175–196.

Muscatell. K. A., et al. (2012). Social status modulates neural activity in the mentalizing network. *NeuroImage, 60*, 1771–1777.

Mussweiler, T., Englich, B., & Strack, F. (2004). Anchoring effects. In R. Pohl (Ed.), *Cognitive illusions: Handbook on fallacies and biases in thinking, judgment, and memory* (pp. 183–200). Hove, UK: Psychology Press.

Myers, D. G. (2002). *Intuition: Its powers and perils*. New Haven, CT: Yale University Press.

Myers, N. A., & Perlmutter, M. (1978). Memory in the years from two to five. In P. A. Ornstein (Ed.), *Memory development in children* (pp. 191–218). Hillsdale, NJ: Erlbaum.

Nairne, J. S. (2005). The functionalist agenda in memory. In A. F. Healy (Ed.), *Experimental cognitive psychology and its applications* (pp. 115–126). Washington, DC: American Psychological Association.

Narens, L., Nelson, T. O., & Scheck, P. (2008). Memory monitoring and the delayed JOL effect. In J. Dunlosky & R. A. Bjork (Eds.), *Handbook of metamemory and memory* (pp. 137–153). New York: Psychology Press.

National Center for Education Statistics. (2004). *Highlights from the Trends in International Mathematics and Science Study (TIMSS) 2003*. Washington, DC: U.S. Department of Education.

Naveh-Benjamin, M., Cowan, N., Kilb, A., & Chen, Z. (2007). Age-related differences in immediate serial recall: Dissociating chunk formation and capacity. *Memory & Cognition, 35*, 724–737.

Naveh-Benjamin, M., Craik, F. I. M., Guez, J., & Kreuger, S. (2005). Divided attention in younger and older adults: Effects of strategy and relatedness on memory performance and secondary task costs. *Journal of Experimental Psychology: Learning, Memory, and Cognition, 31*, 520–537.

Neisser, U. (1967). *Cognitive psychology*. New York: Appleton.

Neisser, U. (2003). New directions for flashbulb memories: Comments on the ACP special issue. *Applied Cognitive Psychology, 17*, 1149–1155.

Neisser, U., & Libby, L. K. (2000). Remembering life experiences. In E. Tulving & F. I. M. Craik (Eds.), *The Oxford handbook of memory* (pp. 315–332). New York: Oxford University Press.

Nelson, J. R., Balass, M., & Perfetti, C. A. (2005). Differences between written and spoken input in learning new words. *Written Language and Literacy, 8*, 101–120.

Nelson, T. O., Dunlosky, J., Graf, A., & Narens, L. (1994). Utilization of metacognitive judgments in the allocation of study during multitrial learning. *Psychological Science, 5*, 207–213.

Nelson, T. O., & Leonesio, R. J. (1988). Allocation of self-paced study time and the "labor-in-vain effect." *Journal of Experimental Psychology: Learning, Memory, and Cognition, 14*, 676–686.

Neuschatz, J. S., et al. (2002). The effect of memory schemata on memory and the phenomenological experience of naturalistic situations. *Applied Cognitive Psychology, 16*, 687–708.

Neuschatz, J. S., et al. (2007). False memory research: History, theory, and applied implications. In M. P. Toglia, J. D. Read, D. F. Ross, & R. C. L. Lindsay (Eds.), *Handbook of eyewitness psychology* (Vol. 1, pp. 239–260). Mahwah, NJ: Erlbaum.

Newcombe, N. S. (2002). Spatial cognition. In D. Medin (Ed.), *Stevens' handbook of experimental psychology* (3rd ed., Vol. 2, pp. 113–163). New York: Wiley.

Newcombe, N. S. (2006, March 3). A plea for spatial literacy. *Chronicle of Higher Education*, p. B20.

Newcombe, N. S. (2010, Summer). Picture this: Increasing math and science learning by improving spatial thinking. *American Educator*, pp. 29–34, 43.

Newcombe, N. S., & Huttenlocher, J. (2000). *Making space: The development of spatial representation and reasoning*. Cambridge, MA: MIT Press.

Newcombe, N. S., et al. (2000). Remembering early childhood: How much, how, and why (or why not). *Current Directions in Psychological Science, 9*, 55–58.

Newell, A., & Simon, H. A. (1972). *Human problem solving*. Englewood Cliffs, NJ: Prentice-Hall.

Newell, B. R., Lagnado, D. A., & Shanks, D. R. (2007). *Straight choices: The psychology of decision making*. New York: Psychology Press.

Newmeyer, F. J. (1998). *Language form and language function*. Cambridge, MA: MIT Press.

Ng, W.-K., & Lindsay, R. C. L. (1994). Cross-race facial recognition: Failure of the contact hypothesis. *Journal of Cross-Cultural Psychology, 25*, 217–232.

Nicholls, M. E. R., Searle, D. A., & Bradshaw, J. L. (2004). Read my lips. *Psychological Science, 15*, 138–141.

Nickerson, R. S. (2010). *Mathematical reasoning: Patterns, problems, conjectures, and proofs*. New York: Psychology Press.

Nickerson, R. S., Perkins, D. N., & Smith, E. E. (1985). *The teaching of thinking*. Hillsdale, NJ: Erlbaum.

Nievelstein, F., Van Gog, T., Van Dijck, G., & Boshuizen, H. P. (2011). Instructional support for novice law students: Reducing search processes and explaining concepts in cases. *Applied Cognitive Psychology, 25*, 408–413.

Nisbett, R. E., & Wilson, T. D. (1977). Telling more than we can know: Verbal reports on mental processes. *Psychological Review, 84*, 231–259.

Noice, T., & Noice, H. (1997). *The nature of expertise in professional acting: A cognitive view*. Mahwah, NJ: Erlbaum.

Noice, T., & Noice, H. (2002). Very long-term recall and recognition of well-learned material. *Applied Cognitive Psychology, 16*, 259–272.

Nolen-Hoeksema, S. (2006). The etiology of gender differences in depression. In C. M. Mazure & G. P. Keita (Eds.), *Understanding depression* (pp. 9–43). Washington, DC: American Psychological Association.

Norman, E., Price, M. C., & Duff, S. C. (2010). Fringe consciousness: A useful framework for clarifying the nature of experience-based metacognitive feelings. In A. Efklides & Misailidi (Eds.), *Trends and prospects in metacognition research* (pp. 63–80). New York: Springer.

Norton, M. I., & Ariely, D. (2011). Building a better America—one wealth quintile at a time. *Perspectives on Psychological Science, 6*, 9–12.

Nosek, B. A., Banaji, M. R., & Greenwald, A. G. (2002). Math = male, me = female, therefore math ≠ me. *Journal of Personality and Social Psychology, 83*, 44–59.

Nosek, B. A., Greenwald, A. G., & Banaji, M. R. (2007). The Implicit Association Test at age 7: A methodological and conceptual review. In J. A. Bargh (Ed.), *Social psychology and the unconscious: The automaticity of higher mental processes* (pp. 265–292). New York: Psychology Press.

Nosek, B. A., et al. (2009). National differences in gender-science stereotypes predict national sex differences in science and math achievement. *Proceedings of the National Academy of Sciences, 106*, 10593–10597.

Nosofsky, R. M., & Palmeri, T. J. (1998). A rule-plus-exception model for classifying objects in continuous-dimension spaces. *Psychonomic Bulletin & Review, 5*, 345–369.

Novick, L. R. (2003). At the forefront of thought: The effect of media exposure on airplane typicality. *Psychonomic Bulletin & Review, 10*, 971–974.

Novick, L. R. (2006). Understanding spatial diagram structure: An analysis of hierarchies, matrices, and networks. *The Quarterly Journal of Experimental Psychology, 59*, 1826–1856.

Novick, L. R., & Coté, N. (1992). The nature of expertise in anagram solution. *Proceedings of the Fourteenth Annual Conference of the Cognitive Science Society* (pp. 450–455). Hillsdale, NJ: Erlbaum.

Novick, L. R., Hurley, S. M., & Francis, M. (1999). Evidence for abstract, schematic knowledge of three spatial diagram representations. *Memory & Cognition, 27*, 288–308.

Novick, L. R., & Morse, D. L. (2000). Folding a fish, making a mushroom: The role of diagrams in executing assembly procedures. *Memory & Cognition, 28*, 1242–1256.

Nusbaum, H. C., & Small, S. L. (2006). In J. T. Caciaoppi, P. S. Visser, & C. L. Pickett (Eds.), *Social neuroscience: People thinking about thinking people* (pp. 131–165). Cambridge, MA: MIT Press.

Oakes, S., & North, A. C. (2006). The impact of background musical tempo and timbre congruity upon ad content recall and affective response. *Applied Cognitive Psychology, 20*, 505–520.

Oakhill, J., Garnham, A., & Reynolds, D. (2005). Immediate activation of stereotypical gender information. *Memory & Cognition, 33*, 972–983.

Oakie, S. (2005). Traumatic brain injury in the war zone. *New England Journal of Medicine, 352*, 2043–2047.

Oaksford, M., & Chater, N. (1994). A rational analysis of the selection task as optimal data selection. *Psychological Review, 101*, 608–631.

Oberauer, K., Süss, H.-M., Wilhelm, O., & Sander, N. (2007). Individual differences in working memory capacity and reasoning ability. In A. R. A. Conway, et al. (Eds.), *Variations in working memory* (pp. 49–75). New York: Oxford University Press.

Oberlander, J. & Gill, A. J. (2006). Language with character: A stratified corpus comparison of individual differences in e-mail communication. *Discourse Processes, 42*, 239–270.

O'Boyle, C. G. (2006). *History of psychology: A cultural perspective*. Mahwah, NJ: Erlbaum.

O'Brien, L. T., & Crandall, C. S. (2003). Stereotype threat and arousal: Effects on women's math performance. *Personality and Social Psychology Bulletin, 29*, 782–789.

Olesen, P. J., Westerberg, H., & Klingberg, T. (2004). Increased prefrontal and parietal activity after training of working memory. *Nature Neuroscience, 7*, 75–79.

Olson, G. M., & Olson, J. S. (2003). Human-computer interaction: Psychological aspects of the human use of computing. *Annual Review of Psychology, 54*, 491–516.

Oppenheimer, D. M. (2006). Consequences of erudite vernacular utilized irrespective of necessity: Problems with using long words needlessly. *Applied Cognitive Psychology, 20*, 139–156.

Oreg, S., & Bayazit, M. (2009). Prone to bias: Development of a bias taxonomy from an individual differences perspective. *Review of General Psychology, 13,* 175–193.

Ormerod, T. C. (2005). Planning and ill-defined problems. In R. Morris & G. Ward (Eds.), *The cognitive psychology of planning* (pp. 53–70). Hove, UK: Psychology Press.

Ormerod, T. C., Chronicle, E. P., & MacGregor, J. V. (2006). *The remnants of insight.* Proceedings of the Annual Cognitive Science Society Conference, Vancouver, CA.

Ornstein, P. A., & Haden, C. A. (2001). Memory development or the development of memory? *Current Directions in Psychological Science, 10,* 202–205.

Ornstein, P. A., & Haden, C. A. (2009). Developments in the study of the development of memory. In M. Courage & N. Cowan (Eds.), *The development of memory in childhood* (pp. 367–385). Hove, UK: Psychology Press.

Ornstein, P. A., Haden, C. A., & Coffman, J. L. (2011). Learning to remember: Mothers and teachers talking with children. In N. L. Stein & Rauadenbush, S. W. (Eds.), *Developmental cognitive science goes to school* (pp. 69–83). New York: Routledge.

Ornstein, P. A., Haden, C. A., & Elischberger, H. B. (2006). Children's memory development: Remembering the past and preparing for the future. In E. Bialystok & F. I. M. Craik (Eds.), *Lifespan cognition: Mechanisms of change* (pp. 143–161). New York: Oxford University Press.

Osterhout, L., Bersick, M., & McLaughlin, J. (1997). Brain potentials reflect violations of gender stereotypes. *Memory & Cognition, 25,* 273–285.

Oswald, M. E., & Grosjean, S. (2004). Confirmation bias. In R. Pohl (Ed.), *Cognitive illusions: Handbook on fallacies and biases in thinking, judgment, and memory* (pp. 77–96). Hove, UK: Psychology Press.

Owens, R. E., Jr. (2001). *Language development: An introduction.* Boston: Allyn and Bacon.

Öztekin, I., Davachi, L., & McElree, B. (2010). Are representations in working memory distinct from representations in long-term memory? Neural evidence in support of a single store. *Psychological Science, 21,* 1123–1133.

Paas, F., & Kester, L. (2006). Learner and information characteristics in the design of powerful learning environments. *Applied Cognitive Psychology, 20,* 281–285.

Paivio, A. (1978). Comparison of mental clocks. *Journal of Experimental Psychology: Human Perception and Performance, 4,* 61–71.

Paivio, A. (1995). Imagery and memory. In M. S. Gazzaniga (Ed.), *The cognitive neurosciences* (pp. 977–986). Cambridge, MA: MIT Press.

Paller, K. A., Voss, J. L., & Westerberg, C. E. (2009). Investigating the awareness of remembering. *Perspectives on Psychological Science, 4,* 185–199.

Palmer, S. E. (1999). *Vision science: Photons to phenomenology.* Cambridge, MA: MIT Press.

Palmer, S. E. (2002). Perceptual organization in vision. In S. Yantis (Ed.), *Stevens' handbook of experimental psychology* (3rd ed., Vol. 1, pp. 177–234). New York: Wiley.

Palmer, S. E. (2003). Visual perception of objects. In A. F. Healy & R. W. Proctor (Eds.), *Handbook of psychology* (Vol. 4, pp. 179–211). Hoboken, NJ: Wiley.

Pan, B. A. (2012). Assessing vocabulary skills. In E. Hoff (Ed.), *Research methods in child language: A practical guide* (pp. 100–112). Malden, MA: Wiley Blackwell.

Pan, B. A., & Snow, C. E. (1999). The development of conversational and discourse skills. In M. Barrett (Ed.), *The development of language* (pp. 229–249). Hove, UK: Psychology Press.

Pansky, A. & Koriat, A. (2004). The basic-level convergence effect on memory distortions. *Psychological Science, 15,* 52–59.

Pansky, A., Koriat, A., & Goldsmith, M. (2005). Eyewitness recall and testimony. In N. Brewer & K. D. Williams (Eds.), *Psychology and law: An empirical perspective* (pp. 93–150). New York: Guilford.

Papadopoulos, C., Hayes, B. K., & Newell, B. R. (2011). Noncategorical approaches to feature prediction with uncertain categories. *Memory & Cognition, 39,* 304–318.

Parasuraman, R., & Greenwood, P. (2007). Individual differences in attention and working memory: A molecular genetic approach. In A. F. Kramer, D. A. Wiegmann, & A. Kirlik (Eds.), *Attention: From theory to practice* (pp. 59–72). New York: Oxford University Press.

Paris, C. R., Salas, E., & Cannon-Bowers, J. A. (2000). Teamwork in multi-person systems: A review and analysis. *Ergonomics, 43,* 1052–1075.

Park, D. C., & Hedden, T. (2001). Working memory and aging. In M. Naveh-Benjamin, M. Moscovitch, & H. L. Roediger, III (Eds.), *Perspectives on human memory and cognitive aging: Essays in honour of Fergus Craik* (pp. 148–169). New York: Psychology Press.

Park, D. C., & Payer, D. (2006). Working memory across the adult lifespan. In E. Bialystok & F. I. M. Craik (Eds.), *Lifespan cognition: Mechanisms of change* (pp. 128–142). New York: Oxford University Press.

Park, D. C., & Reuter-Lorenz, P. (2009). The adaptive brain: Aging and neurocognitive scaffolding. *Annual Review of Psychology, 60,* 173–196.

Park, D. C., et al. (1999). Medication adherence in rheumatoid arthritis patients: Older is wiser. *Journal of the American Geriatric Society, 47,* 172–183.

Parks, T. (2004). Iconic image. In R. L. Gregory (Ed.), *The Oxford companion to the mind* (2nd ed., p. 425). New York: Oxford University Press.

Parry, K. (2006). People and language. In H. Luria, D. M. Seymour, & T. Smoke (Eds.), *Language and linguistics in context: Readings and applications for teachers* (pp. 153–168). Mahwah, NJ: Erlbaum.

Pashler, H., Rohrer, D., Cepeda, N. J., & Carpenter, S. K. (2007). Enhancing learning and retarding forgetting: Choice and consequences. *Psychonomic Bulletin and Review, 14,* 187–193.

Pasternak, T., Bisley, J. W., & Calkins, D. (2003). Visual processing in the primate brain. In M. Gallagher & R. J. Nelson (Eds.), *Handbook of psychology* (Vol. 3, pp. 139–185). Hoboken, NJ: Wiley.

Patel, A. D., et al. (1998). Processing syntactic relations in language and music: An event-related potential study. *Journal of Cognitive Neuroscience, 10,* 717–733.

Patterson, J. L. (2002). Relationships of expressive vocabulary to frequency of reading and television experience among bilingual toddlers. *Applied Psycholinguistics, 23,* 493–508.

Pauker, K., Rule, N. O., & Ambady, N. (2010). Ambiguity and social perception. In E. Balcetis & G. D. Lassiter (Eds.), *Social psychology of visual perception* (pp. 7–26). New York: Psychology Press.

Peal, E., & Lambert, W. E. (1962). The relation of bilingualism to intelligence. *Psychological Monographs,* 546.

Peetz, J., Buehler, R., & Wilson, A. (2010). Planning for the near and distant future: How does temporal distance affect task completion predictions? *Journal of Experimental Social Psychology, 46,* 709–720.

Perfetti, C. (2003). The universal grammar of reading. *Scientific Studies of Reading, 7,* 3–24.

Perfetti, C. (2011). Phonology is critical in reading but a phonological deficit is not the only source of low reading skill. In S. A. Brady, D. Braze, & C. A. Fowler (Eds.), *Explaining individual differences in reading: Theory and evidence* (pp. 153–171). New York: Psychology Press.

Perfetti, C. A., Landi, N., & Oakhill, J. (2005). The acquisition of reading comprehension skill. In M. J. Snowling & C. Hulme (Eds.), *The science of reading: A handbook* (pp. 227–250). Oxford, UK: Blackwell.

Perkins, D. (2001). *The Eureka Effect: The art and logic of breakthrough thinking.* New York: Norton.

Peterson, C., Warren, K. L., & Short, M. M. (2011). Infantile amnesia across the years: A 2-year follow-up of children's earliest memories. *Child Development, 82,* 1092–1105.

Peterson, L. R., & Peterson, M. (1959). Short-term retention of individual verbal items. *Journal of Experimental Psychology, 58,* 193–198.

Pexman, P. M., Hino, Y., & Lunker, S. J. (2004). Semantic ambiguity and the process of generating meaning from print. *Journal of Experimental Psychology: Learning, Memory, and Cognition, 30,* 1252–1270.

Pezdek, K. (Ed.). (2003). Memory and cognition for the events of September 11, 2001 [Special issue]. *Applied Cognitive Psychology, 17* (9).

Pezdek, K., Finger, K., & Hodge, D. (1997). Planting false childhood memories: The role of event plausibility. *Psychological Science, 8,* 437–441

Pezdek, K., & Freyd, J. J. (2009). The fallacy of generalizing from egg salad in false-belief research. *Analysis of Social Issues and Public Policy, 9,* 177–183.

Pezdek, K., & Taylor, J. (2002). Memory for traumatic events in children and adults. In M. L. Eisen, J. A. Quas, & G. S. Goodman (Eds.), *Memory and suggestibility in the forensic interview* (pp. 165–183). Mahwah, NJ: Erlbaum.

Pezzo, M. V., & Beckstead, J. W. (2008). The effects of disappointment on hindsight bias for real-world outcomes. *Applied Cognitive Psychology, 22,* 491–506.

Phillips, W. D. (1995). Personal communication.

Phillipson, R. (Ed.). (2000). *Rights to language: Equity, power, and education.* Mahwah, NJ: Erlbaum.

Pickering, M. J., & Ferreira, V. S. (2008). Structural priming: A critical review. *Psychological Bulletin, 134,* 427–459.

Pickering, S. J. (2006a). Assessment of working memory in children, In S. J. Pickering (Ed.), *Working memory and education* (pp. 241–271). Burlington, MA: Elsevier.

Pickering, S. J. (2006b). Introduction. In S. J. Pickering (Ed.), *Working memory and education* (pp. xv–xxii). Burlington, MA: Elsevier.

Pickford, R. W., & Gregory, R. L. (2004). Bartlett, Sir Frederic Charles. In R. L. Gregory (Ed.), *The Oxford companion to the mind* (2nd ed., pp. 86–87). New York: Oxford University Press.

Pickrell, J. E., Bernstein, D. M., & Loftus, E. E. (2004). Misinformation effect. In R. Pohl (Ed.), *Cognitive illusions: Handbook on fallacies and biases in thinking, judgment, and memory* (pp. 345–361) Hove, UK: Psychology Press.

Pickren, W. E., & Rutherford, A. (2010). *A history of modern psychology in context.* Hoboken, NJ: Wiley.

Pinker, S. (1993). The central problem for the psycholinguist. In G. Harman (Ed.), *Conceptions of the human mind* (pp. 59–84). Hillsdale, NJ: Erlbaum.

Pinker, S. (2002). *The blank slate: The modern denial of human nature.* New York: Viking.

Pinker, S., Nowak, M. A., & Lee, J. J. (2008). The logic of indirect speech. *PNAS, 105,* 833–838.

Piotroski, J., & Naigles, L. R. (2012). Intermodal preferential looking. In E. Hoff (Ed.), *Research methods in child language: A practical guide* (pp. 17–28). Malden, MA: Blackwell.

Pipe, M.-E., & Salmon, K. (2009). Memory development and forensic context. In M. Courage & N. Cowan (Eds.), *The development of memory in childhood* (pp. 241–282). Hove, UK: Psychology Press.

Pita, M. D., & Utakis, S. (2006). Educational polity for the transnational Dominican community. In H. Luria, D. M. Seymour, & T. Smoke (Eds.), *Language and linguistics in context: Readings and applications for teachers* (pp. 333–341). Mahwah, NJ: Erlbaum.

Pitt, M. A. (2009). The strength and time course of lexical activation of pronunciation variants. *Journal of Experimental Psychology: Human Perception and Performance, 35,* 896–910.

Plack, C. J. (2005). *The sense of hearing.* Mahwah, NJ: Erlbaum.

Plack, C. J., & Oxenham, A. J. (2005). Overview: The present and future of pitch. In C. J. Plack, A. J. Oxenham, R. R. Fay, & A. N. Popper (Eds.), *Pitch: Neural coding and perception* (pp. 1–6). New York: Springer.

Plant, E. A., Ericsson, K. A., Hill, L., & Asberg, K. (2005). Why study time does not predict grade point average across college students: Implications of deliberate practice for academic performance. *Contemporary Educational Psychology, 30,* 96–116.

Plucker, J. A., & Renzulli, J. S. (1999). Psychometric approaches to the study of human creativity. In R. J. Sternberg (Ed.), *Handbook of creativity* (pp. 35–61). New York: Cambridge University Press.

Pohl, R. F. (2004). Hindsight bias. In R. Pohl (Ed.), *Cognitive illusions: Handbook on fallacies and biases in thinking, judgment, and memory* (pp. 363–378). Hove, UK: Psychology Press.

Pohl, R. F., Bender, M., & Lachmann, G. (2002). Hindsight bias around the world. *Experimental Psychology, 49,* 270–282.

Pohl, R. F., Schwarz, S., Sczesny, S., & Stahlberg, D. (2003). Hindsight bias in gustatory judgments. *Experimental Psychology, 50,* 107–115.

Poirel, N., Zago, L., Petit, L., & Mellet, E. (2010). Neural bases of topographical representation in humans: Contribution of neuroimaging studies. In A. Guillot & C. Collet (Eds.), *The neurophysiological foundations of mental and motor imagery* (pp. 17–30). New York: Oxford University Press.

Polk, T. A., et al. (2002). Neural specialization for letter recognition. *Journal of Cognitive Neuroscience, 14,* 145–159.

Pomarol-Clotet, E., et al. (2010). Facial emotion processing in schizophrenia: A non-specific neuropsychological deficit? *Psychological Medicine, 40,* 911–919.

Poole, D., & Samraj, B. (2010). Discourse analysis and applied linguistics. In R. B. Kaplan (Ed.), *The Oxford handbook of applied linguistics* (2nd ed., pp. 128–140). New York: Oxford University Press.

Posner, M. I. (2004). Progress in attention research. In M. I. Posner (Ed.), *Cognitive neuroscience of attention* (pp. 3–9). New York: Guilford.

Posner, M. I., & Rothbart, M. K. (2007a). *Educating the human brain.* Washington, DC: American Psychological Association.

Posner, M. I., & Rothbart, M. K. (2007b). Research on attention networks as a model for the integration of psychological science. *Annual Review of Psychology, 58,* 1–23.

Potter, M. C. (1999). Understanding sentences and scenes: The role of conceptual short-term memory. In V. Coltheart (Ed.), *Fleeting memories: Cognition of brief visual stimuli* (pp. 13–46). Cambridge, MA: MIT Press.

Poulton, E. C. (1994). *Behavioral decision theory: A new approach.* Cambridge, UK: Cambridge University Press.

Powell, M. B., Thomson, D. M., & Ceci, S. J. (2003). Children's memory of recurring events: Is the first event always the best remembered? *Applied Cognitive Psychology, 17,* 127–146.

Prabhu, V., Sutton, C., & Sauser, W. (2008). Creativity and certain personality traits: Understanding the mediating effects of intrinsic motivation. *Creativity Research Journal, 20,* 53–66.

Pressley, M. (1996). Personal reflections on the study of practical memory in the mid-1990s: The complete cognitive researcher. In D. J. Herrmann, et al. (Eds.), *Basic and applied memory research: Practical applications* (Vol. 2, pp. 19–33). Mahwah, NJ: Erlbaum.

Pressley, M., & Ghatala, E. S. (1988). Delusions about performance on multiple-choice comprehension tests. *Reading Research Quarterly, 23,* 454–464.

Pressley, M., & Hilden, K. (2006). Cognitive strategies. In D. Kuhn & R. Siegler (Eds.), *Handbook of child psychology* (6th ed., Vol. 2, pp. 511–556). Hoboken, NJ: Wiley.

Pressley, M., Levin, J. R., & Ghatala, E. S. (1984). Memory strategy monitoring in adults and children. *Journal of Verbal Learning and Verbal Behavior, 23,* 270–288.

Pressley, M., Levin, J. R., & Ghatala, E. S. (1988). Strategy-comparison opportunities promote long-term strategy use. *Contemporary Educational Psychology, 13,* 157–168.

Pringle, A., Harmer, C. J., & Cooper, M. J. (2010). Investigating vulnerability to eating disorders: Biases in emotional processing. *Psychological Medicine, 40,* 645–655.

Proctor, R. W., & Vu, K.-P. L. (2010). Cumulative knowledge and progress in human factors. *Annual Review of Psychology, 2010,* 623–651.

Puce, A., & Perrett, D. (2005). Electrophysiology and brain imaging of biological motion. In J. T. Cacioppo & G. G. Berntson (Eds.), *Social neuroscience: Key readings* (pp. 115–129). New York: Psychology Press.

Purdon, C., Rowa, K., & Antony, M. M. (2005). Thought suppression and its effects on thought frequency, appraisal and mood state in individuals with obsessive-compulsive disorder. *Behavior Research and Therapy, 43,* 93–108.

Purves, D., & Lotto, R. B. (2003). *Why we see what we do.* Sunderland, MA: Sinauer.

Pylyshyn, Z. W. (2003). Return of the mental image: Are there pictures in the brain? *TRENDS in Cognitive Sciences, 7,* 113–118.

Pylyshyn, Z. W. (2004). Mental imagery. In R. L. Gregory (Ed.), *The Oxford companion to the mind* (pp. 582–585). New York: Oxford University Press.

Pylyshyn, Z. W. (2006). *Seeing and visualizing: It's not what you think.* Cambridge, MA: MIT Press.

Pynte, J., Kennedy, A., & Ducrot, S. (2004). The influence of parafoveal typographical errors on eye movements in reading. In R. Radach, A. Kennedy, & K. Rayner (Eds.), *Eye movements and information processing during reading* (pp. 178–202). Hove, UK: Psychology Press.

Qu, Q., Damian, M. F., Zhang, Q., & Zhu, X. (2011). Phonology contributes to writing: Evidence from written word production in a nonalphabetic script. *Psychological Science, 22,* 1107–1112.

Quilici, J. L., & Mayer, R. E. (2002). Teaching students to recognize structural similarities between statistics word problems. *Applied Cognitive Psychology, 16,* 325–342.

Quinlan, P. (2010). Feature integration theory. In E. B. Goldstein (Ed.), *Encyclopedia of perception* (Vol. 1, pp. 452–456). Thousand Oaks, CA: Sage.

Quinn, D. M., & Spencer, S. J. (2001). The interference of stereotype threat with women's generation of mathematical problem-solving strategies. *Journal of Social Issues, 57,* 55–71.

Quinn, P. C., et al. (2002). Development of form similarity as a Gestalt grouping principle in infancy. *Psychological Science, 13,* 320–328.

Raaijmakers, J. G. W., & Shiffrin, R. M. (2002). Models of memory. In D. Medin (Ed.), *Stevens' handbook of experimental psychology* (3rd ed., pp. 43–76). New York: Wiley.

Rabbitt, P. (2002). Aging and cognition. In H. Pashler (Ed.), *Stevens' handbook of experimental psychology* (3rd ed., Vol. 4, pp. 793–860). New York: Wiley.

Rachlinski, J. J. (2004). Misunderstanding ability, mislocating responsibility. In D. T. Levin (Ed.), *Thinking and seeing: Visual metacognition in adults and children* (pp. 251–276). Cambridge, MA: MIT Press.

Radach, R., & Kennedy, A. (2004). Theoretical perspectives on eye movements in reading: Past controversies, current issues, and an agenda for future research. In R. Radach, A. Kennedy, & K. Rayner (Eds.), *Eye movements and information processing during reading* (pp. 3–26). Hove, UK: Psychology Press.

Radach, R., Kennedy, A., & Rayner, K. (Eds.). (2004a). Eye movements and information processing during reading (pp. 3–26). Hove, UK: Psychology Press.

Radach, R., Kennedy, A., & Rayner, K. (2004b). Preface. In R. Radach, A. Kennedy, & K. Rayner (Eds.), *Eye movements and information processing during reading* (pp. 1–2). Hove, UK: Psychology Press.

Radvansky, G. A. (2008). Situation models in memory: Texts and stories. In G. Cohen & M. Conway (Eds.), *Memory in the real world* (3rd ed., pp. 230–247). New York: Psychology Press.

Rahman, R. A., & Sommer, W. (2008). Seeing what we know and understand: How knowledge shapes perception. *Psychonomic Bulletin & Review, 15,* 1055–1063.

Randi, J., Grigorenko, E. L., & Sternberg, R. J. (2005). Revisiting definitions of reading comprehension: Just what is reading comprehension anyway? In S. E. Israel, C. C. Block, K. L. Bauserman, & K. Kinnucan-Welsch (Eds.), *Metacognition in literacy learning: Theory, assessment, instruction, and professional development* (pp. 19–39). Mahwah, NJ: Erlbaum.

Ransdell, S., & Levy, C. M. (1999). Writing, reading, and speaking memory spans and the importance of resource flexibility. In M. Torrance & G. C. Jeffery (Eds.), *The cognitive demands of writing: Processing capacity and working memory in text production* (pp. 99–113). Amsterdam: Amsterdam University Press.

Rapp, B., & Goldrick, M. (2000). Discreteness and interactivity in spoken word production. *Psychological Review, 107,* 460–499.

Rapp, D. N., & Gerrig, R. J. (2006). Predilections for narrative outcomes: The impact of story contexts and reader preferences. *Journal of Memory and Language, 54,* 54–67.

Rasmussen, E. B. (2006). Expanding your coverage of neuroscience: An interview with Michael Gazzaniga. *Teaching of Psychology, 33,* 212–215.

Rathbone, C. K., & Moulin, C. J. A. (2010). When's your birthday? The self-reference effect in retrieval of dates. *Applied Cognitive Psychology, 24,* 737–743.

Ratner, H. H., Foley, M. A., & Gimpert, N. (2002). The role of collaborative planning in children's source-monitoring errors and learning. *Journal of Experimental Child Psychology, 81,* 44–73.

Ratner, H. H., Foley, M. A., & McCaskill, P. (2001). Understanding children's activity memory: The role of outcomes. *Journal of Experimental Child Psychology, 79,* 162–191.

Ratner, N. B., & Gleason, J. B. (1993). An introduction to psycholinguistics: What do language users know? In J. B. Gleason & N. B. Ratner (Eds.), *Psycholinguistics.* Fort Worth: Harcourt Brace Jovanovich.

Raulerson, B. A., III, Donovan, M. J., Whitford, A. B., & Kellogg, R. T. (2010). Differential verbal, visual, and spatial working memory in written language production. *Perceptual and Motor Skills, 110,* 229–244.

Rayner, K. (1998). Eye movements in reading and information processing: 20 years of research. *Psychological Bulletin, 124,* 372–422.

Rayner, K. (2009). The 35th Sir Frederick Bartlett Lecture: Eye movements and attention in reading, scene perception, and visual search. *Quarterly Journal of Experimental Psychology, 62,* 1457–1506.

Rayner, K., & Clifton, C., Jr. (2002). Language processing. In D. Medin (Ed.), *Stevens' handbook of experimental psychology* (3rd ed., Vol. 2, pp. 261–316). New York: Wiley.

Rayner, K., Juhasz, B. J., & Pollatsek, A. (2005). Eye movements during reading. In J. Snowling & C. Hulme (Eds.), *The science of reading: A handbook* (pp. 61–78). Malden, MA: Blackwell.

Rayner, K., & Liversedge, S. P. (2004). Visual and linguistic processing during eye fixations in reading. In J. M. Henderson & F. Ferreira (Eds.), *The interface of language, vision, and action: Eye movements and the visual world* (pp. 59–104). New York: Psychology Press.

Rayner, K., Liversedge, S. P., & White, S. J. (2006). Eye movements when reading disappearing text: The importance of the word to the right of fixation. *Vision Research, 46,* 310–323.

Rayner, K., Pollatsek, A., & Starr, M. S. (2003). Reading. In I. B. Weiner (Ed.), *Handbook of psychology* (Vol. 4, pp. 549–574). Hoboken, NJ: Wiley.

Rayner, K., Shen, D., Bai, X., & Yan, G. (Eds.). (2008). *Cognitive and cultural influences on eye movements.* Tianjin, China: Tianjin People's Publishing House.

Rayner, K., Warren, T., Juhasz, B. J., & Liversedge, S. P. (2004). The effect of plausibility on eye movements in reading. *Journal of Experimental Psychology: Learning, Memory, and Cognition, 30,* 1290–1301.

Rayner, K., et al. (2001). How psychological science informs the teaching of reading. *Psychological Science in the Public Interest, 2,* 31–74

Read, J. D., & Connolly, D. A. (2007). The effects of delay on long-term memory for witnessed events. In M. P. Toglia, J. D. Read, D. F. Ross, & R. C. L. Lindsay (Eds.), *Handbook of eyewitness psychology* (Vol. 1, pp. 117–155). Mahwah, NJ: Erlbaum.

Reber, R. (2004). Availability. In R. Pohl (Ed.), *Cognitive illusions: Handbook on fallacies and biases in thinking, judgment, and memory.* Hove, UK: Psychology Press.

Reddy, L., Tsuchiya, N., & Serre, T. (2010). Reading the mind's eye: Decoding category information during mental imagery. *NeuroImage, 50,* 818–835.

Reder, L. M., Park, H., &Keiffaber, P. D. (2009). Memory systems do not divide on consciousness: Reinterpreting memory in terms of activation and binding. *Psychological Bulletin, 135,* 23–49.

Reed, S. K. (1974). Structural descriptions and the limitations of visual images. *Memory & Cognition, 2,* 329–336.

Reed, S. K. (2010).*Thinking visually.* New York: Psychology Press.

Rehder, B., & Hoffman, A. B. (2005). Thirty-something categorization results explained: Selective attention, eyetracking, and models of category learning. *Journal of Experimental Psychology: Learning Memory, and Cognition, 31,* 811–929.

Reichenberg, A., & Harvey, P. D. (2007). Neuropsychological impairments in schizophrenia: Integration of performance-based and brain imaging findings. *Psychological Bulletin, 133,* 833–858.

Reicher, G. M. (1969). Perceptual recognition as a function of meaningfulness of stimuli material. *Journal of Experimental Psychology, 81,* 275–280.

Reichle, E. D., & Laurent, P. A. (2006). Using reinforcement learning to understand the emergence of "intelligent" eye-movement behavior during reading. *Psychological Review, 113,* 390–408.

Reichle, E. D., Pollatsek, A., Fisher, D. L., & Rayner, K. (1998). Toward a model of eye movement control in reading. *Psychological Review, 105,* 125–157.

Reichle, E. D., Reineberg, A. E., & Schooler, J. W. (2010). Eye movements during mindless reading. *Psychological Science, 21,* 1300–1310.

Reif, F. (2008). *Applying cognitive science to education: Thinking and learning in scientific and other complex domains.* Cambridge, MA: MIT Press.

Reisberg, D., & Heuer, F. (2005). Visuospatial images. In P. Shah & A. Miyake (Eds.), *The Cambridge handbook of visuospatial thinking* (pp. 35–80). New York: Cambridge University Press.

Reisberg, D., Pearson, D. G., & Kosslyn, S. M. (2003). Intuitions and introspections about imagery: The role of imagery experience in shaping an investigator's theoretical views. *Applied Cognitive Psychology, 17,* 147–160.

Rendell, P. G., Castel, A. D., & Craik, F. I. M. (2005). Memory for proper names in old age: A disproportionate impairment? *Quarterly Journal of Experimental Psychology, 58A,* 54–71.

Rensink, R. A. (2010). Change detection. In E. B. Goldstein (Ed.), *Encyclopedia of perception* (Vol. 1, pp. 241–244). Thousand Oaks, CA: Sage.

Rensink, R. A., O'Regan, J. K., & Clark, J. J. (1997). To see or not to see: The need for attention to perceive changes in scenes. *Psychological Science, 8,* 368–373.

Reuter-Lorenz, P. A., & Jonides, J. (2007). The executive is central to working memory: Insights from age, performance, and task variations. In A. R. A. Conway, et al. (Eds.), *Variations in working memory* (pp. 250–271). New York: Oxford University Press.

Reverberi, C., et al. (2009). Cortical bases of elementary deductive reasoning: Inference, memory, and metadeduction. *Neuropsychologia, 47,* 1107–1116.

Revonsuo, A. (2010). *Consciousness: The science of subjectivity.* New York: Psychology Press.

Reyna, V. F., Mills, B., Estreada, S., & Brainerd, C. J. (2007). False memory in children: Data, theory, and legal implications. In M. P. Toglia, J. D. Read, D. F. Ross, & R. C. L. Lindsay (Eds.), *Handbook of eyewitness psychology* (Vol. 1, pp. 479–507). Mahwah, NJ: Erlbaum.

Reynolds, D. J., Garnham, A., & Oakhill, J. (2006). Evidence of immediate activation of gender information from a social role name. *Quarterly Journal of Experimental Psychology, 59,* 886–903.

Reznick, J. S. (2009). Working memory in infants and toddlers. In M. Courage & N. Cowan (Eds.), *The development of memory in childhood* (pp. 343–365). Hove, UK: Psychology Press.

Rhodes, M. G. (2009). Age estimation of faces: A review. *Applied Cognitive Psychology, 23,* 1–12.

Rhodes, M. G., & Castel, A. D. (2009). Metacognitive illusions for auditory information: Effects on monitoring and control. *Psychonomic Bulletin & Review, 16,* 550–554.

Rhodes, M. G., & Tauber, S. K. (2011). The influence of delaying Judgments of Learning (JOLs) on metacognitive accuracy: A meta-analytic review. *Psychological Bulletin, 137,* 131–148.

Rhodes, R. L., Ochoa, S. H., & Ortiz, S. O. (2005). *Assessing culturally and linguistically diverse students: A practical guide.* New York: Guilford.

Riccio, D. C., Millin, P. M., & Gisquet-Verrier, P. (2003). Retrograde amnesia: Forgetting back. *Current Directions in Psychological Science, 12*, 41–44.

Richardson, J. T. E. (1999). *Imagery.* East Sussex, UK: Psychology Press.

Richardson-Klavehn, A., & Gardiner, J. M. (1998). Depth-of-processing effects on priming in stem completion: Tests of the voluntary-contamination, conceptual-processing, and lexical-processing hypotheses. *Journal of Experimental Psychology: Learning, Memory, and Cognition, 24*, 593–609.

Richler, J. J., Cheung, O. S., & Gauthier, I. (2011). Holistic processing predicts face recognition. *Psychological Science, 22*, 464–471.

Riddoch, M. J., & Humphreys, G. W. (2001). Object recognition. In B. Rapp (Ed.), *The handbook of cognitive neuropsychology* (pp. 45–74). Philadelphia: Psychology Press.

Rips, L. J. (2002). Reasoning. In D. Medin (Ed.), *Stevens' handbook of experimental psychology* (3rd ed., Vol. 2, pp. 363–411). New York: Wiley.

Rips, L. J., Smith, E. E., & Medin, D. L. (2012). Concepts and categories: Memory, meaning, and metaphysics. In K. J. Holyoak & R. G. Morrison (Eds.), *The Oxford handbook of thinking and reasoning* (pp. 177–209). New York: Oxford University Press.

Risen, J. L., Gilovich, T., & Dunning, D. (2007). One-shot illusory correlations and stereotype formation. *Personality and Social Psychology Bulletin, 33*, 1492–1502.

Rizzolatti, G., & Craighero, L. (2009). Language and mirror neurons. In M. G. Gaskell (Ed.), *The Oxford handbook of psycholinguistics* (pp. 771–785). New York: Oxford University Press.

Rizzolatti, G., Fadiga, L., Fogassi, L., & Gallese, V. (1996). Premotor cortex and the recognition of motor actions. *Cognitive Brain Research, 3*, 131–141.

Robbins, P., & Aydede, M. (2009). A short primer on situated cognition. In P. Robbins & M. Aydede (Eds.), *The Cambridge handbook of situated cognition* (pp. 3–10). New York: Cambridge University Press.

Roberts, M. J., & Newton, E. J. (2005). Introduction: Individual differences in reasoning strategies. In M. J. Roberts & E. J. Newton (Eds.), *Methods of thought: Individual differences in reasoning strategies* (pp. 1–9). Hove, UK: Psychology Press.

Robertson, L. C., & Treisman, A. (2010). Consciousness: Disorders. In E. B. Goldstein (Ed.), *Encyclopedia of perception* (Vol. 1, pp. 304–309). Thousand Oaks, CA: Sage.

Robertson, S. I. (2001). *Problem solving.* East Sussex, UK: Psychology Press.

Robins, R. W., Gosling, S. D., & Craik, K. H. (1999). An empirical analysis of trends in psychology. *American Psychologist, 54*, 117–128.

Robins, S., & Treiman, R. (2009). Talking about writing: What we can learn from conversations between parents and their young children. *Applied Psycholinguistics, 30*, 463–484.

Rodd, J., Gaskell, G., & Marslen-Wilson, W. (2002). Making sense of semantic ambiguity: Semantic competition in lexical access. *Journal of Memory and Language, 46*, 245–266.

Roebers, C. M., Gelhar, T., & Schneider, W. (2004). "It's magic!" The effects of presentation modality on children's event memory, suggestibility, and confidence judgments. *Journal of Experimental Child Psychology, 87*, 320–335.

Roebers, C. M., & Schneider, W. (2000). The impact of misleading questions on eyewitness memory in children and adults. *Applied Cognitive Psychology, 14*, 509–526.

Roebers, C. M., Schwarz, S., & Neumann, R. (2005). Social influence and children's event recall and suggestibility. *European Journal of Developmental Psychology, 2*, 47–69.

Roediger, H. L., III. (2000). Why retrieval is the key process in understanding human memory. In E. Tulving (Ed.), *Memory, consciousness, and the brain* (pp. 52–75). Philadelphia: Psychology Press.

Roediger, H. L., III. (2008). Relativity of remembering: Why the laws of memory vanished. *Annual Review of Psychology, 59*, 225–254.

Roediger, H. L. III, Agarwal, P. K., Kang. S. H. K., & Marsh, E. J. (2010). Benefits of testing memory: Best practices and boundary conditions. In G. M. Davies & D. B. Wright (Eds.), *Current issues in applied memory research* (pp. 13–49). New York: Psychology Press.

Roediger, H. L., III, & Amir, N. (2005). Implicit memory tasks: Retention without conscious recollection. In A. Wenzel & D. C. Rubin (Eds.), *Cognitive methods and their application to clinical research* (pp. 121–127). Washington, DC: American Psychological Association.

Roediger, H. L., III, & Gallo, D. A. (2001). Levels of processing: Some unanswered questions. In M. Naveh-Benjamin, M. Moscovitch, & H. L. Roediger,

III (Eds.), *Perspectives on human memory and cognitive aging: Essays in honour of Fergus Craik* (pp. 28–47). New York: Psychology Press.

Roediger, H. L., III, Gallo, D. A., & Geraci, L. (2002). Processing approaches to cognition: The impetus from the levels-of-processing framework. *Memory, 10*, 319–332.

Roediger, H. L., III, & Guynn, M. J. (1996). Retrieval processes. In E. L. Bjork & R. A. Bjork (Eds.), *Memory* (pp. 197–236). San Diego: Academic Press.

Roediger, H. L., III, & Karpicke, J. D. (2006a). The power of testing memory: Basic research and implications for educational practice. *Perspectives on Psychological Science, 1*, 181–210.

Roediger, H. L., III, & Karpicke, J. D. (2006b). Test-enhanced learning: Taking memory tests improves long-term retention. *Psychological Science, 17*, 249–255.

Roediger, H. L., III, Marsh, E. J., & Lee, S. C. (2002). Kinds of memory. In D. Medin (Ed.), *Stevens' handbook of experimental psychology* (3rd ed., pp. 1–41). New York: Wiley.

Roediger, H. L., III, & McDermott, K. B. (1995). Creating false memories: Remembering words not presented in lists. *Journal of Experimental Psychology: Learning, Memory, and Cognition, 21*, 803–814.

Roediger, H. L., III, & McDermott, K. B. (2000). Distortions of memory. In E. Tulving & F. I. M. Craik (Eds.), *The Oxford handbook of memory* (pp. 149–162). New York: Oxford University Press.

Roelofs, A., & Baayen, H. (2002). Morphology by itself in planning the production of spoken words. *Psychonomic Bulletin & Review, 9*, 132–138.

Rogers, D. (1985). Language development. In A. Branthwaite & D. Rogers (Eds.), *Children growing up* (pp. 82–93). Milton Keynes, UK: Open University Press.

Rogers, T. B., Kuiper, N. A., & Kirker, W. S. (1977). Self-reference and the encoding of personal information. *Journal of Personality and Social Psychology, 35*, 677–688.

Rogers, T. T. & McClelland, J. L. (2004). *Semantic cognition: A parallel distributed processing approach.* Cambridge, MA: MIT Press.

Rogers, T. T., & McClelland, J. L. (2011). Semantics without categorization. In E. M. Pothos & A. J. Wills (Eds.), *Formal approaches in categorization* (pp. 88–119). New York: Cambridge University Press.

Rogoff, B. (1990). *Apprenticeship in thinking: Cognitive development in social context.* New York: Oxford University Press.

Rohrer, D., & Taylor, K. (2006). The effects of overlearning and distributed practice on the retention of mathematics knowledge. *Applied Cognitive Psychology, 20*, 1209–1224.

Rollins, P. R. (2003). Caregivers' contingent comments to 9-month-old infants: Relationships with later language. *Applied Psycholinguistics, 24*, 221–234.

Rolls, E. T. (2004). Neural networks in the brain. In R. L. Gregory (Ed.), *The Oxford companion to the mind* (2nd ed., pp. 639–641). New York: Oxford University Press.

Rolls, E. T., & Tovee, M. J. (1995). Sparseness of the neuronal representation of stimuli in the primate temporal visual cortex. *Journal of Neurophysiology, 73*, 713–726.

Romero Lauro, L. J., et al. (2010). A case for the involvement of phonological loop in sentence comprehension. *Neuropsychologia, 48*, 4003–4011.

Rosch, E. H. (1973). Natural categories. *Cognitive Psychology, 4*, 328–350.

Rosch, E. H. (1975). The nature of mental codes for color categories. *Journal of Experimental Psychology: Human Perception and Performance, 1*, 303–322.

Rosch, E. H., & Mervis, C. B. (1975). Family resemblances: Studies in the internal structure of categories. *Cognitive Psychology, 7*, 573–605.

Rosch, E. H., et al. (1976). Basic objects in natural categories. *Cognitive Psychology, 8*, 382–439.

Rose, S. P. R. (2004). Memory: Biological basis. In R. L. Gregory (Ed.), *The Oxford companion to the mind* (2nd ed., pp. 564–568). New York: Oxford University Press.

Rosenblum, L. D. (2005). Primacy of multimodal speech perception. In D. B. Pisoni & R. E. Remez (Eds.), *The handbook of speech perception* (pp. 51–78). Malden, MA: Blackwell.

Roskos-Ewoldsen, B., McNamara, T. P., Shelton, A. L., & Carr, W. (1998). Mental representations of large and small spatial layouts are orientation dependent. *Journal of Experimental Psychology: Learning, Memory, and Cognition, 24*, 215–226.

Ross, M., & Wang, Q. (2010). Why we remember and what we remember: Culture and autobiographical memory. *Perspectives on Psychological Science, 5*, 401–409.

Ross, N., & Tidwell, M. (2010). Concepts and culture. In D. Mareschal, P. C. Quinn, & S. E. G. Lea (Eds.), *The making of human concepts* (pp. 131–148). New York: Oxford University Press.

Rothbart, M. K., Sheese, B. F., Rueda, M. R., & Posner, M. J. (2011). Developing mechanisms of self-regulation in early life. *Emotion Review, 3,* 207–213.

Rothblum, E. D., & Factor, R. (2001). Lesbians and their sisters as a control group. *Psychological Science, 12,* 63–69.

Rouw, R., Kosslyn, S. M., & Hamel, R. (1997). Detecting high-level and low-level properties in visual images and visual precepts. *Cognition, 63,* 209–226.

Rovee-Collier, C. K., & Barr, R. (2002). Infant cognition. In H. Pashler (Ed.), *Stevens' handbook of experimental psychology* (Vol. 4, pp. 693–791). New York: Wiley.

Rovee-Collier, C. K., & Cuevas, K. (2009a). The development of infant memory. In M. Courage & N. Cowan (Eds.), *The development of memory in childhood* (pp. 11–41). Hove, UK: Psychology Press.

Rovee-Collier, C., & Cuevas, K. (2009b). Multiple memory systems are unnecessary to account for infant memory development: An ecological model. *Developmental Psychology, 43,* 160–174.

Rovee-Collier, C. K., Griesler, P. C., & Earley, L. A. (1985). Contextual determinants of retrieval in three-month-old infants. *Learning and Motivation, 16,* 139–157.

Rovee-Collier, C., & Hayne, H. (2000). Memory in infancy and early childhood. In E. Tulving & F. I. M. Craik (Eds.), *The Oxford handbook of memory* (pp. 267–282). New York: Oxford University Press.

Rovee-Collier, C., Hayne, H., & Colombo, M. (2001). *The development of implicit and explicit memory.* Philadelphia: John Benjamins Publishing Company.

Roy, M. M., & Christenfeld, N. J. S. (2007). Bias in memory predicts bias in estimation of future task duration. *Memory & Cognition, 35,* 557–564.

Roy, M. M., Christenfeld, N. J. S., & McKenzie, C. R. M. (2005). Underestimating the duration of future events: Memory incorrectly used or memory bias? *Psychological Review, 131,* 738–756.

Royden, C. S., Wolfe, J. M., & Klempen, N. (2001). Visual search asymmetries in motion and optic flow fields. *Perception & Psychophysics, 63,* 436–444.

Ruben, B. D. (2001, July 13). We need excellence beyond the classroom. *Chronicle of Higher Education,* pp. B15–B16.

Rubin, D. C. (2000). The distribution of early childhood memories. *Memory, 8,* 265–269.

Rubin, D. C., & Berentsen, D. (2009). The frequency of voluntary and involuntary autobiographical memories across the life span. *Memory & Cogniton, 37,* 679–688.

Rubin, D. C., Berntsen, D., & Bohni, M. K. (2008). A memory-based model of posttraumatic stress disorder: Evaluating basic assumptions underlying the PTSD Diagnosis. *Psychological Review, 115,* 985–1011.

Rubin, E. (1915/1958). Synoplevede Figurer [Figure and ground]. In D. C. Beardslee & M. Wertheimer (Eds.), *Readings in perception* (pp. 194–203). Princeton, NJ: Van Nostrand.

Rucker, D. D., Briñol, P., & Petty, R. E. (2011). Metacognition: Methods to assess primary versus secondary cognition. In K. C. Klauer, A. Voss, & C. Stahl (Eds.), *Cognitive methods in social psychology* (pp. 236–264). New York: Guilford.

Ruddle, R. A., Volkova, E., Mohler, B., & Bülthoff, H. H., et al. (2011). The effect of landmark and body-based sensory information on route knowledge. *Memory & Cognition, 39,* 686–699.

Rudman, L. A. (2005). Rejection of women? Beyond prejudice as antipathy. In J. F. Dovidio, P. Glick, & L. A. Rudman (Eds.), *On the nature of prejudice: Fifty years after Allport* (pp. 106–120). Malden, MA: Blackwell.

Rueckl, J. G. (1995). Ambiguity and connectionist networks: Still settling into a solution—comment on Joordens and Besner (1994). *Journal of Experimental Psychology: Learning, Memory, and Cognition, 21,* 501–508

Rueckl, J. G., & Oden, G. C. (1986). The integration of contextual and featural information during word identification. *Journal of Memory and Language, 25,* 445–460.

Rumelhart, D. E., McClelland, J. L., & the PDP Research Group (Eds.). (1986). *Parallel distributed processing* (Vol. 1). Cambridge, MA: MIT Press.

Runco, M. A. (2005). Motivation, competence, and creativity. In A. J. Elliot & C. S. Dweck (Eds.), *Handbook of competence and motivation* (pp. 609–623). New York: Guilford.

Runco, M. A. (2007). *Creativity: Theories and themes: Research, development, and practice.* London: Elsevier Academic Press.

Runco, M. A. (2010). Divergent thinking, creativity, and ideation. In J. C. Kaufman & R. J. Sternberg (Eds.), *The Cambridge handbook of creativity* (pp. 413–446). New York: Cambridge University Press.

Rundus, D. (1971). Analysis of rehearsal processes in free recall. *Journal of Experimental Psychology, 89*, 63–77.

Ruscio, J., Whitney, D. M., & Amabile, T. M. (1998). Looking inside the fishbowl of creativity: Verbal and behavioral predictors of creative performance. *Creativity Research Journal, 11*, 243–263.

Russ, S. W. (2001). Writing creatively: How to do it. [Review of the book *Writing in flow: Keys to enhanced creativity.*] *Contemporary Psychology, 46*, 181–182.

Rutherford, A. (2009). *Beyond the box: B.F. Skinner's technology of behavior from laboratory to life, 1950s–1970s.* Toronto: University of Toronto Press.

Sachs, J. (1967). Recognition memory for syntactic and semantic aspects of a connected discourse. *Perception & Psychophysics, 2*, 437–442.

Saffran, E. M., & Schwartz, M. F. (2003). Language. In I. B. Weiner (Ed.), *Handbook of psychology* (Vol. 4, pp. 595–636). Hoboken, NJ: Wiley.

Saffran, J. B., Werker, J. F., & Werner, L. A. (2006). The infant's auditory world: Hearing, speech, and the beginnings of language. In D. Kuhn & R. Siegler (Eds.), *Handbook of child psychology* (6th ed., Vol. 2, pp. 58–108). Hoboken, NJ: Wiley.

Salthouse, T. (2012). Consequences of age-related cognitive declines. *Annual Review of Psychology, 63*, 201–226.

Salvucci, D. D., & Taatgen, N. A. (2008). Threaded cognition: An integrated theory of concurrent multitasking. *Psychological Review, 115*, 101–130.

Samelson, F. (2009). Struggle for scientific authority. In L. T. Benjamin, Jr. (Ed.), *A brief history of psychology: Original sources and contemporary research* (pp. 265–280). Malden, MA: Blackwell.

Samuel, A. G. (2011). Speech perception. *Annual Review of Psychology, 62*, 49–72.

Sangrigoli, S., & de Schonen, S. (2004). Recognition of own-face and other-race faces by three-month-old infants. *Journal of Child Psychology and Psychiatry, 45*, 1219–1227.

Sanna, L. J., & Schwarz, N. (2006). Metacognitive experiences and human judgment: The case of hindsight bias and its debiasing. *Current Directions in Psychological Science, 15*, 172–176.

Sanna, L. J., Schwarz, N., & Kennedy, L. A. (2009). It's hard to imagine: Mental simulation, metacognitive experiences, and the success of debiasing. In K. D. Markman, W. M. P. Klein, & Suhr, J. A. (Eds.), *Handbook of imagination and mental simulation* (pp. 197–210). New York: Psychology Press.

Saylor, M. M., & Baldwin, D. A. (2004). Action analysis and change blindness: Possible links. In D. T. Levin (Ed.), *Thinking and seeing: Visual metacognition in adults and children* (pp. 37–56). Cambridge, MA: MIT Press.

Schacter, D. L. (1999). The seven sins of memory: Insights from psychology and cognitive neuroscience. *American Psychologist, 54*, 182–203.

Schacter, D. L. (2001). *The seven sins of memory.* Boston: Houghton Mifflin.

Schacter, D. L., Church, B., & Treadwell, J. (1994). Implicit memory in amnesic patients: Evidence for spared auditory priming. *Psychological Science, 5*, 20–25.

Schacter, D. L., Norman, K. A., & Koustaal, W. (1998). The cognitive neuroscience of constructive memory. *Annual Review of Psychology, 49*, 289–318.

Schacter, D. L., & Wiseman, A. L. (2006). Reducing memory errors: The distinctiveness heuristic. In R. R. Hunt & J. B. Worthen (Eds.), *Distinctiveness and memory* (pp. 89–107). New York: Oxford University Press.

Schaeken, W., DeVooght, G., Vandierendonck, A., & d'Ydewalle, G. (2000). Strategies and tactics in deductive reasoning. In W. Schaeken, G. DeVooght, A. Vandierendonck, & G. d'Ydewalle (Eds.), *Deductive reasoning and strategies* (pp. 301–309). Mahwah, NJ: Erlbaum.

Schank, R. C., & Abelson, R. P. (1977). *Scripts, plans, goals, and understanding.* Hillsdale, NJ: Erlbaum.

Schank, R. C., & Abelson, R. P. (1995). Knowledge and memory: The real story. In R. S. Wyer, Jr. (Ed.), *Knowledge and memory: The real story* (pp. 1–85). Hillsdale, NJ: Erlbaum.

Schawlow, A. (1982, *Fall*). Going for the gaps. *Stanford Magazine*, 42.

Schelhorn, S.-E., Griego, J., & Schmid, U. (2007). Transformational and derivational strategies in analogical problem solving. *Cognitive Processes, 8*, 45–55.

Schirillo, J. A. (2010). Gestalt approach. In E. B. Goldstein (Ed.), *Encyclopedia of perception* (Vol. 1, pp. 469–472). Thousand Oaks, CA: Sage.

Schmeichel, B. J., & Hoffman, W. (2011). Working memory capacity in social psychology. In K. C. Klauer, A. Voss, & C. Stahl, *Cognitive methods in social psychology* (pp. 184–205). New York: Guilford.

Schmidt, J. R., & Thompson, V. A. (2008). "At least one" problem with "some" formal reasoning paradigms. *Memory & Cognition, 36*, 217–229.

Schmidt, S. R. (2006). Emotion, significance, distinctiveness, and memory. In R. R. Hunt & J. B. Worthen (Eds.), *Distinctiveness and memory* (pp. 47–64). New York: Oxford University Press.

Schneider, M., Rode, C., & Stern, E. (2010). Secondary school students' availability and activation of diagrammatic strategies for learning from texts. In L. Verschaffel, E. De Corte, T. de Jong, & J. Elen (Eds.), *Use of representations in reasoning and problem solving: Analysis and improvement* (pp. 112–130). London: Routledge.

Schneider, V. I., Healy, A. F., Barshi, I., & Kole, J. A. (2011). Following navigation instructions presented verbally or spatially: Effects on training, retention and transfer. *Applied Cognitive Psychology, 25,* 53–67.

Schneider, W. (1998). The development of procedural metamemory in childhood and adolescence. In G. Mazzoni & T. O. Nelson (Eds.), *Metacognition and cognitive neuropsychology* (pp. 1–21). Mahwah, NJ: Erlbaum.

Schneider, W. (1999). The development of metamemory in children. In D. Gopher & A. Koriat (Eds.), *Attention and performance XVII* (pp. 487–514). Cambridge, MA: MIT Press.

Schneider, W. (2002). Memory development in childhood. In U. Goswami (Ed.), *Blackwell handbook of childhood cognitive development* (pp. 236–256). Malden, MA: Blackwell.

Schneider, W., & Bjorklund, D. F. (1998). Memory. In D. Kuhn & R. S. Siegler (Eds.), *Handbook of child psychology* (5th ed., Vol. 2, pp. 467–521). New York: Wiley.

Schneider, W., & Lockl, K. (2008). Procedural metacognition in children: Evidence for developmental trends. In J. Dunlosky & R. A. Bjork (Eds.), *Handbook of metamemory and memory* (pp. 391–409). New York: Psychology Press.

Schneider, W., Kron, V., Hünnerkopf, M., & Krajewsi, K. (2004). The development of young children's memory strategies: First findings from the Würzburg Longitudinal Memory Study. *Journal of Experimental Child Psychology, 88,* 191–209.

Schneider, W., & Pressley, M. (1997). *Memory development: Between two and twenty* (2nd ed.). Mahwah, NJ: Erlbaum.

Schnotz, W., Baadtem C., Müller, A., & Rasch, R. (2010). Creative thinking and problem solving with depictive and descriptive representations. In L. Verschaffel, E. De Corte, T. de Jong, & J. Elen (Eds.), *Use of representations in reasoning and problem solving: Analysis and improvement* (pp. 11–35). London: Routledge.

Schober, M. F., & Brennan, S. E. (2003). Processes of interactive spoken discourse: The role of the partner. In A. C. Graesser, M. A. Gernsbacher, & S. R. Goldman (Eds.), *Handbook of discourse processes* (pp. 123–164). Mahwah, NJ: Erlbaum.

Schoenfeld, A. H. (2011). *How we think: A theory of goal-oriented decision making and its educational applications.* New York: Routledge.

Scholl, B. J., Simons, D. J., & Levin, D. T. (2004). "Change blindness" blindness: An implicit measure of a metacognitive error. In D. T. Levin (Ed.), *Thinking and seeing: Visual metacognition in adults and children* (pp. 145–165). Cambridge, MA: MIT Press.

Schönpflug, U. (2008). The influence of instruction on verbatim and content text recall. *Educational Psychology, 28,* 97–108.

Schooler, J. W., & Eich, E. (2000). Memory for emotional events. In E. Tulving & F. I. M. Craik (Eds.), *The Oxford handbook of memory* (pp. 379–392). New York: Oxford University Press.

Schooler, J. W., Fallshore, M., & Fiore, S. M. (1995). Epilogue: Putting insight into perspective. In R. J. Sternberg & J. E. Davidson (Eds.), *The nature of insight* (pp. 559–587). Cambridge, MA: MIT Press.

Schooler, J. W., Reichle, E. D., & Halpern, D. V. (2004). Zoning out while reading: Evidence for dissociations between experience and metaconsciousness. In D. T. Levin (Ed.), *Thinking and seeing: Visual metacognition in adults and children* (pp. 204–226). Cambridge, MA: MIT Press.

Schraw, G. (2005). An interview with K. Anders Ericsson. *Educational Psychology Review, 17,* 389–412.

Schreiber, F. J. (2005). Metacognition and self-regulation in literacy. In S. E. Israel, C. C. Block, K. L. Bauserman, & K. Kinnucan-Welsch (Eds.), *Metacognition in literacy learning: Theory, assessment, instruction, and professional development* (pp. 215–239). Mahwah, NJ: Erlbaum.

Schumann, J. H. (2010). Applied linguistics and the neurobiology of language. In R. B. Kaplan (Ed.), *The Oxford handbook of applied linguistics* (2nd ed., pp. 244–259). New York: Oxford University Press.

Schwartz, A. L., & Kroll, J. F. (2006). Language processing in bilingual speakers. In M. J. Traxler & M. A. Gernsbacher (Eds.), *Handbook of psycholinguistics* (2nd ed., pp. 967–999). Amsterdam: Elsevier.

Schwartz, B. (2004). *The paradox of choice: Why more is less: How the culture of abundance robs us of satisfaction.* New York: HarperCollins.

Schwartz, B. (2009). Be careful what you wish for: The dark side of freedom. In R. M. Arkin, K. C. Oleson, & P. J. Carroll (Eds.), *Handbook of the uncertain self.* New York: Psychology Press.

Schwartz, B. (2012, January 22). Upside of the downturn. *The Chronicle Review*, pp. B4–B5.

Schwartz, B., et al. (2002). Maximizing versus satisficing: Happiness is a matter of choice. *Journal of Personality and Social Psychology, 83,* 1178–1197.

Schwartz, B. L. (1999). Sparkling at the end of the tongue: The etiology of tip-of-the-tongue phenomenology. *Psychonomic Bulletin & Review, 6,* 379–393.

Schwartz, B. L. (2002). *Tip-of-the-tongue states: Phenomenology, mechanism, and lexical retrieval.* Mahwah, NJ: Erlbaum.

Schwartz, B. L. (2011). *Memory: Foundations and applications.* Thousand Oaks, CA: Sage.

Schwartz, B. L., Benjamin, A. S., & Bjork, R. A. (1997). The inferential and experiential bases of metamemory. *Current Directions in Psychological Science, 6,* 132–137.

Schwartz, B. L., & Metcalfe, J. (2011). Tip-of-the-tongue (TOT) states: Retrieval, behavior, and experience. *Memory & Cognition, 39,* 737–749.

Schwartz, B. L., & Smith, S. M. (1997). The retrieval of related information influences tip-of-the-tongue states. *Journal of Memory and Language, 36,* 68–86.

Schwartz, S. H. (1971). Modes of representation and problem solving: Well evolved is half solved. *Journal of Experimental Psychology, 91,* 347–350.

Schwartz, S. H., & Fattaleh, D. (1972). Representation in deductive problem solving: The matrix. *Journal of Experimental Psychology, 95,* 343–348.

Schwartz, S. H., & Polish, J. (1974). The effect of problem size on representation in deductive problem solving. *Memory & Cognition, 2,* 683–686.

Schwarz, N. (2001). Feelings as information: Implications for affective influences on information processing. In L. L. Martin & G. L. Clore (Eds.), *Theories of mood and cognition* (pp. 159–176). Mahwah, NJ: Erlbaum.

Schwenck, C., Bjorklund, D. F., & Schneider, W. (2009). Developmental and individual differences in young children's use and maintenance of a selective memory strategy. *Developmental Psychology, 45,* 1034–1050.

Schwering, A., Kühnberger, K.-U., & Kokinov, B. (2009). Analogies—Integrating cognitive abilities. *Cognitive Systems Research, 10,* 175–177.

Scott, S. K. (2005). The neurobiology of speech perception. In A. Cutler (Ed.), *Twenty-first century psycholinguistics: Four cornerstones* (pp. 141–156). Mahwah, NJ: Erlbaum.

Scullin, M. K., Bugg, J. M., McDaniel, M. A., & Einstein, G. O. (2011). Prospective memory and aging: Preserved spontaneous retrieval, but impaired deactivation in older adults. *Memory & Cognition, 39,* 1232–1240.

Seabrook, R., Brown, G. D. A., & Solity, J. E. (2005). Distributed and massed practice: From laboratory to classroom. *Applied Cognitive Psychology, 19,* 107–122.

Segal, S. J., & Fusella, V. (1970). Influence of imagined pictures and sounds on detection of visual and auditory signals. *Journal of Experimental Psychology, 83,* 458–464.

Segalowitz, N. (2010). *Cognitive bases of second language fluency.* New York: Routledge.

Seifert, C. M. (1999). Situated cognition and learning. In R. A. Wilson & F. C. Keil (Eds.), *The MIT encyclopedia of the cognitive sciences* (pp. 767–769). Cambridge, MA: MIT Press.

Sell, A. J., & Kaschak, M. P. (2009). Does visual speech information affect word segmentation? *Memory & Cognition, 37,* 889–894.

Semmler, C., & Brewer, N. (2006). Postidentification feedback effects on face recognition confidence: Evidence for metacognitive influences. *Applied Cognitive Psychology, 20,* 895–916.

Serences, J. T., et al. (2005). Coordination of voluntary and stimulus-driven control in human cortex. *Psychological Science, 16,* 114–122.

Sereno, S. C., Brewer, C. C., & O'Donnell, P. J. (2003). Context effects in word recognition: Evidence for early interactive processing. *Psychological Science, 14,* 328–333.

Serra, M. J., & Dunlosky, J. (2010). Metacomprehension judgements reflect the belief that diagrams improve learning from text. *Memory, 18,* 698–711.

Seymour, P. H. K., Aro, M., & Erskine, J. M. (2003). Foundation literacy acquisition in European orthographies. *British Journal of Psychology, 143*–174.

Shafir, E. B., & LeBoeuf, R. A. (2002). Rationality. *Annual Review of Psychology, 53,* 491–517.

Shah, A. J., & Oppenheimer, D. M. (2008). Heuristics made easy: An effort-reduction framework. *Psychological Bulletin, 134,* 207–222.

Shake, M. C., Noh, W. R., & Stine-Morrow, E. A. L. (2009). Age differences in learning from text: Evidence for functionally distinct text processing systems. *Applied Cognitive Psychology, 23,* 561–578.

Shapiro, L. (2011). *Embodied cognition.* New York: Routledge.

Share, D. L. (2008). On the Anglocentricities of current reading research and practice: The perils of over-reliance on an "outlier" orthography. *Psychological Bulletin, 134,* 584–615.

Sharps, M. J., & Wertheimer, M. (2000). Gestalt perspectives on cognitive science and on experimental psychology. *Review of General Psychology, 4,* 315–336.

Shatz, M., & Gelman, R. (1973). The development of communication skills: Modifications in the speech of young children as a function of listener. *Monographs of the Society for Research in Child Development, 38* (2, Serial No. 152).

Shelton, A. L. (2004). Putting spatial memories into perspective: Brain and behavioral evidence for representational differences. In G. L. Allen (Ed.), *Human spatial memory: Remembering where* (pp. 309–327). Mahwah, NJ: Erlbaum.

Shelton, A. L., & Gabrieli, J. D. E. (2004). Neural correlates of individual differences in spatial learning strategies. *Neuropsychology, 18,* 442–449.

Shelton, A. L., & McNamara, T. P. (2004). Orientation and perspective dependence in route and survey learning. *Journal of Experimental Psychology: Learning, Memory, and Cognition, 30,* 158–170.

Shelton, A. L., & Yamamoto, N. (2009), Visual memory, spatial representation, and navigation. In J. B. Brockmole (Ed.), *The visual world in memory* (pp. 140–177). New York: Routledge.

Shen, D., Bai, X., Yan, G., & Liversedge, S. P. (2008). Eye movements in Chinese reading. In K. Rayner, D. Shen, X. Bai, & G. Yan (Eds.), *Cognitive and cultural influences on eye movements* (pp. 255–277). Tianjin, China: Tianjin People's Publishing House.

Shepard, R. N., & Chipman, S. (1970). Second-order isomorphism of internal representation: Shapes of states. *Cognitive Psychology, 1,* 1–17.

Shepard, R. N., & Metzler, J. (1971). Mental rotation of three-dimensional objects. *Science, 171,* 701–703.

Shepperd, J. A., & Koch, E. J. (2005). Pitfalls in teaching judgment heuristics. *Teaching of Psychology, 32,* 43–46.

Sherman, J. W., & Bessenoff, G. R. (1999). Stereotypes as source-monitoring cues: On the interaction between episodic and semantic memory. *Psychological Science, 10,* 106–110.

Sherman, M. A. (1976). Adjectival negation and the comprehension of multiply negated sentences. *Journal of Verbal Learning and Verbal Behavior, 15,* 143–157.

Shih, M., Pittinsky, T. L., & Ambady, N. (1999). Stereotype susceptibility: Identity salience and shifts inquantitative performance. *Psychological Science, 10,* 80–83.

Shiraev, E. (2011). *A history of psychology: A global perspective.* Thousand Oaks, CA: Sage.

Sholl, M. J., Kenny, R. J., & Della Porta, K. A. (2006). Allocentric-heading recall and its relation to self-reported sense-of-direction. *Journal of Experimental Psychology: Learning, Memory, and Cognition, 32,* 516–533.

Shomstein, S. (2010). Attention: Effect of breakdown. In E. B. Goldstein (Ed.), *Encyclopedia of perception* (Vol. 1, pp. 87–90). Thousand Oaks, CA: Sage.

Siegal, M. (1996). Conversation and cognition. In R. Gelman & T. K. Au (Eds.), *Perceptual and cognitive development* (pp. 243–282). San Diego: Academic Press.

Siegler, R. S., DeLoache, J., & Eisenberg, N. (2003). *How children develop.* New York: Worth.

Sillito, A. M. (2004). Visual system: Organization. In R. L. Gregory (Ed.), *The Oxford companion to the mind* (2nd ed., pp. 931–936). New York: Oxford University Press.

Silvia, P. J. (2007). *How to write a lot.* Washington, DC: American Psychological Association.

Simon, D., Pham, L. B., Le, Q. A., & Holyoak, K. J. (2001). The emergence of coherence over the course of decision making. *Journal of Experimental Psychology: Learning, Memory, and Cognition, 27,* 1250–1260.

Simon, H. A. (1955). A behavioral model of rational choice. *Quarterly Journal of Economics, 69,* 99–118.

Simon, H. A. (1995). Technology is not the problem. In P. Baumgartner & S. Payr (Eds.), *Speaking minds: Interviews with twenty eminent cognitive scientists* (pp. 231–248). Princeton, NJ: Princeton University Press.

Simon, H. A. (1996). *The sciences of the artificial* (3rd ed.). Cambridge, MA: MIT Press.

Simon, H. A. (1999). Problem solving. In R. A. Wilson & F. C. Keil (Eds.), *The MIT encyclopedia of the cognitive sciences* (pp. 674–676). Cambridge, MA: MIT Press.

Simon, H. A. (2001). Learning to research about learning. In S. M. Carver & D. Klahr (Eds.), *Cognition and instruction: Twenty-five years of progress* (pp. 205–226). Mahwah, NJ: Erlbaum.

Simon, H. A., & Gobet, F. (2000). Expertise effects in memory recall: Comment on Vicente and Wang (1998). *Psychological Review, 107,* 593–600.

Simons, D. J., & Chabris, C. F. (1999). Gorillas in our midst: Sustained inattentional blindness for dynamic events. *Perception, 28,* 1059–1074.

Simons, D. J., Chabris, C. F., Schnur, T., & Levin, D. T. (2002). Evidence for preserved representations in change blindness. *Consciousness and Cognition, 11,* 78–97.

Simons, D. J., & Jensen, M. S. (2009). The effects of individual differences and task difficulty on inattentional blindness. *Psychonomic Bulletin & Review, 16,* 398–403.

Simons, D. J., & Levin, D. T. (1997a). Change blindness. *TRENDS in Cognitive Sciences, 1,* 261–267.

Simons, D. J., & Levin, D. T. (1997b). Failure to detect changes to unattended objects. *Investigative Ophthalmology and Visual Science, 38,* S707.

Simons, D. J., & Levin, D. T. (1998). Failure to detect changes to people during a real-world interaction. *Psychonomic Bulletin & Review, 5,* 644–649.

Simonton, D. K. (2004). Creativity as a constrained stochastic process. In R. J. Sternberg, E. L. Grigorenko, & J. L. Singer (Eds.), *Creativity: From potential to realization* (pp. 83–101). Washington, DC: American Psychological Association.

Simonton, D. K. (2010). Creativity in highly eminent individuals. In J. C. Kaufman & R. J. Sternberg (Eds.), *The Cambridge handbook of creativity* (pp. 174–188). New York: Cambridge University Press.

Sinha, P., Ostrovsky, Y., & Russell, R. (2010). Face perception. In E. B. Goldstein (Ed.) *Encyclopedia of perception* (Vol. 1, pp. 445–448). Thousand Oaks, CA: Sage.

Skinner, B. F. (2004). Behaviorism, B. F. Skinner on. In R. L. Gregory (Ed.), *The Oxford companion to the mind* (2nd ed., pp. 90–92). New York: Oxford University Press.

Slater, A., & Butterworth, G. (1997). Perception of social stimuli: Face perception and imitation. In G. Brenner, A. Slater, & G. Butterworth (Eds.), *Infant development: Recent advances* (pp. 223–245). Hove, UK: Psychology Press.

Sluzenski, J., Newcombe, N., & Ottinger, W. (2004). Changes in reality monitoring and episodic memory in early childhood. *Developmental Science, 7,* 225–245.

Smallwood, J., & Schooler, J. W. (2006). The restless mind. *Psychological Bulletin, 132,* 946–958.

Smilek, D., Carriere, J. S. A., & Cheyne, J. A. (2010). Out of mind, out of sight: Eye blinking as indicator and embodiment of mind-wandering. *Psychological Science, 21,* 786–789.

Smith, A. D., & Cohen, G. (2008). Memory for places: Routes, maps, and object locations. In G. Cohen & M. Conway (Eds.), *Memory in the real world* (3rd ed., pp. 173–206). New York: Psychology Press.

Smith, E. E. (2000). Neural bases of human working memory. *Current Directions in Psychological Science, 9,* 45–49.

Smith, J., & Baltes, P. B. (1999). Life-span perspectives on development. In M. H. Bornstein & M. E. Lamb (Eds.), *Developmental psychology: An advanced textbook* (4th ed., pp. 47–72). Mahwah, NJ: Erlbaum.

Smith, J. L., Samsone, C., & White, P. H. (2007). The stereotyped task engagement process: The role of interest and achievement motivation. *Journal of Educational Psychology, 99,* 99–114.

Smith, N. (2000). Foreword. In N. Chomsky (Ed.), *On nature and language* (pp. 1–44). Cambridge, UK: Cambridge University Press.

Smith, R. E. (2006). Adult age differences in episodic memory: Item-specific, relational, and distinctive processing. In R. R. Hunt & J. B. Worthen (Eds.), *Distinctiveness and memory* (pp. 259–289). New York: Oxford University Press.

Smith, S. M., & Gleaves, D. H. (2007). Recovered memories. In M. P. Toglia, J. D. Read, D. F. Ross, & R. C. L. Lindsay (Eds.), *Handbook of eyewitness psychology* (Vol. 1, pp. 299–320). Mahwah, NJ: Erlbaum.

Smith, S. M., & Ward, T. B. (2012). Cognition and the creation of ideas. In K. J. Holyoak & R. G. Morrison (Eds.), *The Oxford handbook of thinking and reasoning* (pp. 456–474). New York: Oxford University Press.

Smith, S. M., et al. (2003). Eliciting and comparing false and recovered memories: An experimental approach. *Applied Cognitive Psychology, 17,* 251–279.

Smyth, M. M., Collins, A. F., Morris, P. E., & Levy, P. (1994). *Cognition in action* (2nd ed.). Hove, UK: Erlbaum.

Smyth, M. M., Morris, P. E., Levy, P., & Ellis, A. W. (1987). *Cognition in action*. Hillsdale, NJ: Erlbaum.

Snow, C. E. (1999). Social perspectives on the emergence of language. In B. MacWhinney (Ed.), *The emergence of language* (pp. 257–276). Mahwah, NJ: Erlbaum.

Snow, C. E., & Juel, C. (2005). Teaching children to read: What do we know about how to do it? In M. J. Snowling & C. Hulme (Eds.), *The science of reading: A handbook* (pp. 501–520). Malden, MA: Blackwell.

Sobel, C. P. (2001). *The cognitive sciences: An interdisciplinary approach.* Mountain View, CA: Mayfield.

Sodian, B. (2005). Theory of mind—the case for conceptual development. In W. Schneider, R. Schumann-Hengsteler, & B. Sodian (Eds.), *Young children's cognitive development* (pp. 95–130). Mahwah, NJ: Erlbaum.

Son, L. K., & Kornell, N. (2008). Research on the allocation of study time: Key studies from 1890 to the present (and beyond). In J. Dunlosky & R. A. Bjork (Eds.), *Handbook of metamemory and memory* (pp. 333–351). New York: Psychology Press.

Son, L. K., & Metcalfe, J. (2000). Metacognitive and control strategies in study-time allocation. *Journal of Experimental Psychology: Learning, Memory, and Cognition, 26,* 204–221.

Son, L. K., & Schwartz, B. L. (2002). The relation between metacognitive monitoring and control. In T. J. Perfect & B. L. Schwartz (Eds.), *Applied metacognition* (pp. 15–38). Cambridge, UK: Cambridge University Press.

Speer, S., & Blodgett, A. (2006). Prosody. In M. J. Traxler & M. A. Gernsbacher (Eds.), *Handbook of psycholinguistics* (2nd ed., pp. 505–527). Amsterdam: Elsevier.

Spence, I., & Feng, J. (2010). Video games and spatial cognition. *Review of General Psychology, 14,* 92–104.

Sperling, G. (1960). The information available in brief visual presentations. *Psychological Monographs, 74,* 1–29.

Sporer, S. L. (1991). Deep—deeper—deepest? Encoding strategies and the recognition of human faces. *Journal of Experimental Psychology: Learning, Memory, and Cognition, 17,* 323–333.

Sporer, S. L., & Horry, R. (2011). Recognizing faces from ethnic in-groups and out-groups: Importance of outer face features and effects of retention interval. *Applied Cognitive Psychology, 25,* 424–431.

Stanovich, K. E. (1999). *Who is rational? Studies of individual differences in reasoning.* Mahwah, NJ: Erlbaum.

Stanovich, K. E. (2003). The fundamental computational biases of human cognition: Heuristics that (sometimes) impair decision making and problem solving. In J. E. Davidson & R. J. Sternberg (Eds.), *The psychology of problem solving* (pp. 291–342). New York: Cambridge University Press.

Stanovich, K. E. (2009). *What intelligence tests miss: The psychology of rational thought.* New Haven, CT: Yale University Press.

Stanovich, K. E. (2011). *Rationality and the reflective mind.* New York: Oxford University Press.

Stanovich, K. E. (2012). On the distinction between rationality and intelligence: Implications for understanding individual differences in reasoning. In K. J. Holyoak & R. G. Morrison (Eds.), *The Oxford handbook of thinking and reasoning* (pp. 433–455). New York: Oxford University Press.

Stanovich, K. E., & West, R. F. (1981). The effect of sentence processing on ongoing word recognition: Tests of a two-process theory. *Journal of Experimental Psychology: Human Perception and Performance, 7,* 658–672.

Stanovich, K. E., & West, R. F. (1983). On priming by a sentence context. *Journal of Experimental Psychology: General, 112,* 1–36.

Stanovich, K. E., & West, R. F. (1997). Reasoning independently of prior belief and individual differences in actively open-minded thinking. *Journal of Educational Psychology, 89,* 342–357.

Stanovich, K. E., & West, R. F. (1998). Individual differences in rational thought. *Journal of Experimental Psychology: General, 127,* 161–188.

Stanovich, K. E., & West, R. F. (2000). Individual differences in reasoning: Implications for the rationality debate? *Behavioral and Brain Sciences, 23,* 645–726.

Starr, M. S., & Inhoff, A. W. (2004). Attention allocation to the right and left of a fixated word: Use of information from multiple words during reading. In R. Radach, A. Kennedy, & K. Rayner (Eds.), *Eye movements and information processing during reading* (pp. 203–225). Hove, UK: Psychology Press.

Statistics Canada. (2006). *Population by mother tongue, by province and territory* (2006 Census). Retrieved June 21, 2012, from http://www.statcan.gc.ca/tables-tableaux/sum-som/l01/cst01/demo11a-eng.htm

Statistics Canada. (2012a). *Canadians in context-aging population.* Retrieved March 14, 2012, from http://www4.hrsdc.gc.ca/.3ndic.1t.4r@-eng.jsp?iid=33

Statistics Canada. (2012b). *Information about life expectancy and religious services.* Retrieved March 15, 2012, from www.statcan.gc.ca/start-debut-eng.html

Steel, P. (2007). The nature of procrastination: A meta-analytic and theoretical review of quintessential self-regulatory failure. *Psychological Bulletin, 133,* 65–94.

Steele, C. M. (1997). A threat in the air: How stereotypes shape intellectual identity and performance. *American Psychologist, 52,* 613–629.

Steffensen, S. V. (2011). Beyond mind: An extended ecology of languaging. In S. J. Cowley (Ed.), *Distributed language* (pp. 185–210). Amsterdam: John Benjamins Publishing Company.

Sternberg, R. J. (1999). A dialectical basis for understanding the study of cognition. In R. J. Sternberg (Ed.), *The nature of cognition* (pp. 51–78). Cambridge, MA: MIT Press.

Sternberg, R. J., & Ben-Zeev, T. (2001*). Complex cognition: The psychology of human thought.* New York: Oxford University Press.

Sternberg, R. J., & O'Hara, L. A. (1999). Creativity and intelligence. In R. J. Sternberg (Ed.), *Handbook of creativity* (pp. 251–272). New York: Cambridge University Press.

Stevens, A., & Coupe, P. (1978). Distortions in judged spatial relations. *Cognitive Psychology, 10,* 422–437.

Stine-Morrow, E. A. L., Miller, L. M. S., & Hertzog, C. (2006). Aging and self-regulated language processing. *Psychological Bulletin, 132,* 582–606.

Stone, M. (2005). Communicative intentions and conversational processes in human-human and human-computer dialogue. In J. C. Trueswell & M. K. Tanenhaus (Eds.), *Approaches to studying world-situated language use* (pp. 39–69). Cambridge, MA: Bradford.

Strayer, D. L., & Drews, F. A. (2007). Multitasking in the automobile. In A. F. Kramer, D. A. Wiegmann, & A. Kirlik (Eds.), *Attention: From theory to practice* (pp. 121–133). New York: Oxford University Press.

Strayer, D. L., Drews, F. A., & Johnston, W. A. (2003). Cell phone-induced failures of visual attention during simulated driving. *Journal of Experimental Psychology: Applied, 9,* 23–32.

Strömqvist, S., & Verhoeven, L. (2004). Typological and contextual perspectives on narrative development. In S. Strömqvist, & L. Verhoven, *Relating events in narrative* (Vol. 2, pp. 1–4). Mahwah, NJ: Erlbaum.

Stromswold, K. (1999). Cognitive and neural aspects of language acquisition. In E. Lepore & Z. Pylyshyn (Eds.), *What is cognitive science?* (pp. 356–400). Malden, MA: Blackwell.

Stroop, J. R. (1935). Studies of interference in serial verbal reactions. *Journal of Experimental Psychology, 18,* 643–662.

Student Demographics. (2011, August 26). *Chronicle of Higher Education* (Almanac Issue, 2011–2012), pp. 30–40.

Stuss, D. T., Binns, M. A., Murphy, K. J., & Alexander, M. P. (2002). Dissociations within the anterior attentional system: Effects of task complexity and irrelevant information on reaction time speed and accuracy. *Neuropsychology, 16,* 500–513.

Styles, E. A. (2005). *Attention, perception, and memory: An integrated introduction.* Hove, UK: Psychology Press.

Styles, E. A. (2006). *The psychology of attention* (2nd ed.). New York: Psychology Press.

Suh, S., & Trabasso, T. (1993). Inferences during reading: Converging evidence from discourse analysis, talk-aloud protocols, and recognition priming. *Journal of Memory and Language, 32,* 279–300.

Surprenant, A. M., & Neath, I. (2009). *Principles of memory.* New York: Psychology Press.

Suzuki-Slakter, N. S. (1988). Elaboration and metamemory during adolescence. *Contemporary Educational Psychology, 13,* 206–220.

Swanson, H. L. (2005). Working memory, intelligence, and learning disabilities. In O. Wilhelm & R. W. Engle (Eds.), *Handbook of understanding and measuring intelligence* (pp. 409–429). Thousand Oaks, CA: Sage.

Swanson, H. L., Kehler, P., & Jerman, O. (2010). Working memory, strategy knowledge, and strategy instruction in children with reading disabilities. *Journal of Learning Disabilities, 43,* 24–47.

Swets, B., Desmet, T., Clifton, C., Jr., & Ferreira, F. (2008). Underspecification of syntactic ambiguities: Evidence from self-paced reading. *Memory & Cognition, 36,* 201–216.

Swinkels, A. (2003). An effective exercise for teaching cognitive heuristics. *Teaching of Psychology, 30,* 120–122.

Swoyer, C. (2002). Judgment and decision making: Extrapolations and applications. In R. Gowda & J. C. Fox (Eds.), *Judgments, decisions, and public policy* (pp. 9–45). New York: Cambridge University Press.

Symons, C. S., & Johnson, B. T. (1997). The self-reference effect in memory: A meta-analysis. *Psychological Bulletin, 121,* 371–394.

Szpunar, K. K. (2010). Episodic future thought: An emerging concept. *Perspectives on Psychological Science, 5*, 142–162.

Tabor, W., & Hutchins, S. (2004). Evidence for self-organized sentence processing: Digging-in effects. *Journal of Experimental Psychology: Learning, Memory, and Cognition, 30*, 431–450.

Taguchi, T., Magid, M., & Papi, M. (2009). The L2 motivational self system among Japanese, Chinese and Iranian learners of English: A comparative study. In Z. Dörnyei & E. Ushiodi (Eds.), *Motivation, language identity, and the L2 self* (pp. 66–97). Bristol, UK: Multilingual Matters.

Takeda, K., et al. (2010). Reaction time differences between left- and right-handers during mental rotation of hand pictures. *Laterality, 15*, 415–425.

Talarico, J. M., LaBar, K. S., & Rubin, D. C. (2004). Emotional intensity predicts autobiographical memory experience. *Memory & Cognition, 32*, 1118–1132.

Talarico, J. M., & Rubin, D. C. (2003). Confidence, not consistency, characterizes flashbulb memories. *Psychological Science, 14*, 455–461.

Tanaka, J. W., & Farah, M. J. (1993). Parts and wholes in face recognition. *Quarterly Journal of Experimental Psychology, 46A*, 225–245.

Tanenhaus, M. K. (2004). On-line sentence processing: Past, present, and future. In M. Carreiras & C. Clifton, Jr. (Eds.), *The on-line study of sentence comprehension: Eyetracking, ERPs and beyond* (pp. 371–393). New York: Psychology Press.

Tang, Y.-Y., & Posner, M. I. (2009). Attention training and attention state training. *Trends in Cognitive Science, 13*, 222–227.

Tarr, M. J., & Vuong, Q. C. (2002). Visual object recognition. In S. Yantis (Ed.), *Stevens' handbook of experimental psychology* (3rd ed., Vol. 1, pp. 287–314). New York: Wiley.

Tavris, C., & Aronson, E. (2007). *Mistakes were made (but not by me): Why we justify foolish beliefs, bad decisions, and hurtful acts.* Orlando, FL: Harcourt.

Taylor, H. A. (2005). Mapping the understanding of understanding maps. In P. Shah & A. Miyake (Eds.), *The Cambridge handbook of visuospatial thinking* (pp. 295–333). New York: Cambridge University Press.

Taylor, L. M. (2005). *Introducing cognitive development.* New York: Psychology Press.

Taylor, S. E., Phan, L. B., Rivkin, I. D., & Armor, D. A. (1998). Harnessing the imagination: Mental simulation, self-regulation, and coping. *American Psychologist, 53*, 429–439.

Teasdale, J. D., et al. (1995). Stimulus-independent thought depends on central executive resources. *Memory & Cognition, 23*, 551–559.

Teigen, K. H. (2004). Judgment by representativeness. In R. Pohl (Ed.), *Cognitive illusions: Handbook on fallacies and biases in thinking, judgment, and memory* (pp. 165–182). Hove, UK: Psychology Press.

Teigen, K. H., & Jørgensen, M. (2005). When 90% confidence intervals are 50% certainty. *Applied Cognitive Psychology, 19*, 455–475.

Terlecki, M. S., Newcombe, N. S., & Little, M. (2008). Durable and generalized effects of spatial experience on mental rotation: Gender differences in growth patterns. *Applied Cognitive Psychology, 22*, 996–1013.

Thagard, P. (2005). *Mind: Introduction to cognitive science* (2nd ed.). Cambridge, MA: MIT Press.

Thaler, R. H., & Sunstein, C. R. (2008). *Nudge: Improving decisions about health, wealth, and happiness.* New Haven: Yale University Press.

Thiede, K. W., Dunlosky, J., Griffin, T. D., & Wiley, J. (2005). Understanding the delayed-keyword effect on metacomprehension accuracy. *Journal of Experimental Psychology: Learning, Memory, and Cognition, 31*, 1267–1280.

Thierry, K., L., Lamb, M. E., Pipe, M.-E., & Spence, M. J. (2010). The flexibility of source-monitoring training: Reducing young children's source confusions. *Applied Cognitive Psychology, 24*, 626–644.

Thoman, D. B., White, P. H., Yamawaki, N., & Koishi, H. (2008). Variations of gender-math stereotype content affect women's vulnerability to stereotype threat. *Sex Roles, 58*, 702–712.

Thomas, J. C. (1989). Problem solving by human-machine interaction. In K. J. Gilhooly (Ed.), *Human and machine problem solving* (pp. 317–362). New York: Plenum.

Thomas, L. E., & Lleras, A. (2009a). Covert shifts of attention function as an implicit aid to insight. *Cognition, 111*, 168–174,

Thomas, L. E., & Lleras, A. (2009b). Swinging into thought: Directed movement guides insight in problem solving. *Psychonomic Bulletin & Review, 16*, 719–723,

Thomas, R. D. (1998). Learning correlations in categorization tasks using large, ill-defined categories.

Journal of Experimental Psychology: Learning, Memory, and Cognition, 24, 119–143.

Thompson, C. P., Skowronski, J. J., Larsen, S. F., & Betz, A. (1996). *Autobiographical memory: Remembering what and remembering when.* Mahwah, NJ: Erlbaum.

Thompson, R. F., & Madigan, S. A. (2005). *Memory: The key to consciousness.* Washington, DC: Joseph Henry Press.

Thompson, V. A., Newstead, S. E., & Morley, N. J. (2011). Methodological and theoretical issues in belief bias: Implications for dual-process theories. In K. Manktelow, D. Over, & S. Elqayam (Eds.), *The science of reason: A festschrift for Jonathan St B. T. Evans* (pp. 309–338). New York: Psychology Press.

Thorndyke, P. W. (1981). Distance estimation from cognitive maps. *Cognitive Psychology, 13,* 526–550.

Tincoff, R., & Jusczyk, P. W. (1999). Some beginnings of word comprehension in 6-month-olds. *Psychological Science, 10,* 172–175.

Tobias, R. (2009). Changing behavior by memory aids: A social psychological model of prospective memory and habit development tested with dynamic field data. *Psychological Review, 116,* 408–438.

Todd, N. P. M., Lee, C. S., & O'Boyle, D. J. (2006). A sensorimotor theory of speech perception: Implications for learning, organization, and recognition. In S. Greenberg & W. A. Ainsworth (Eds.), *Listening to speech: An auditory perspective* (pp. 351–373). Mahwah, NJ: Erlbaum.

Todd, P. M., & Gigerenzer, G. (2007). Environments that make us smart: Ecological rationality. *Current Directions in Psychological Science, 126,* 167–171.

Tokuhama-Espinosa, T. (2001). *Raising multilingual children: Foreign language acquisition and children.* Westport, CT: Bergin & Garvey.

Tolin, D. A., Abramowitz, J. S., Przeworski, A., & Foa, E. B. (2002). Thought suppression in obsessive-compulsive disorder. *Behaviour Research and Therapy, 40,* 1255–1274.

Tomasello, M. (1998a). Cognitive linguistics. In W. Bechtel & G. Graham (Eds.), *A companion to cognitive science* (pp. 477–487). Malden, MA: Blackwell.

Tomasello, M. (1998b). Introduction: A cognitive-functional perspective on language structure. In M. Tomasello (Ed.), *The new psychology of language: Cognitive and functional approaches to language structure* (pp. vii–xxiii). Mahwah, NJ: Erlbaum.

Tomasello, M. (2003). *Constructing a language: A usage-based theory of language acquisition.* Cambridge, MA: Harvard University Press.

Tomasello, M. (2006). Acquiring linguistic constructions. In D. Kuhn & R. Siegler (Eds.), *Handbook of child psychology* (6th ed., Vol. 2, pp. 255–298). Hoboken, NJ: Wiley.

Tomasello, M. (2008). *Origins of human communication.* Cambridge, MA: Guilford.

Toplak, M. E., & Stanovich, K. E. (2002). The domain specificity and generality of disjunctive reasoning: Searching for a generalizable critical thinking skill. *Journal of Educational Psychology, 94,* 197–209.

Toppino, T. C., & Long, G. M. (2005). Top-down and bottom-up processes in the perception of reversible figures: Toward a hybrid model. In N. Ohta, C. M. MacLeod, & B. Uttl (Eds.), *Dynamic cognitive processes* (pp. 37–58). Tokyo: Springer-Verlag.

Torbeyns, J., Arnaud, L., Lemaire, P., & Verschaffel, L. (2010). Cognitive change as strategy change. In A. Demetriou & A. Raftopoulos (Eds.), *Cognitive developmental change: Theories, models and measurement* (pp. 186–216). New York: Cambridge University Press.

Torcasio, S., & Sweller, J. (2010). The use of illustrations when learning to read: A cognitive load theory approach. *Applied Cognitive Psychology, 24,* 659–672.

Torrance, M., & Jeffery, G. (1999). Writing processes and cognitive demands. In M. Torrance & G. C. Jeffery (Eds.), *The cognitive demands of writing: Processing capacity and working memory in text production* (pp. 1–11). Amsterdam: Amsterdam University Press.

Torrance, M., Thomas, G. V., & Robinson, E. J. (1996). Finding something to write about: Strategic and automatic processes in idea generation. In C. M. Levy & S. Ransdell (Eds.), *The science of writing: Theories, methods, individual differences, and applications* (pp. 189–205). Mahwah, NJ: Erlbaum.

Townsend, C. L., & Heit, E. (2011). Judgments of learning and improvement. *Memory & Cognition, 39,* 204–216.

Trabasso, T., & Suh, S. (1993). Understanding text: Achieving explanatory coherence through on-line inferences and mental operations in working memory. *Discourse Processes, 16,* 3–34.

Trabasso, T., Suh, S., Payton, P., & Jain, R. (1995). Explanatory inferences and other strategies during comprehension and their effect on recall. In R. F.

Lorch & E. J. O'Brien (Eds.), *Sources of coherence in reading* (pp. 219–239). Hillsdale, NJ: Erlbaum.

Trafimow, D., & Wyer, R. S., Jr. (1993). Cognitive representation of mundane social events. *Journal of Personality and Social Psychology, 64*, 365–376.

Traxler, M. J. (2012). *Introduction to psycholinguistics: Understanding language science.* Malden, MA: Wiley-Blackwell.

Treiman, R., & Kessler, B. (2009). Learning to read. In M. G. Gaskell (Ed.), *The Oxford handbook of psycholinguistics* (pp. 771–785). New York: Oxford University Press.

Treiman, R., Clifton, C., Jr., Meyer, A. S., & Wurm, L. H. (2003). Language comprehension and production. In A. F. Healy & R. W. Proctor (Eds.), *Handbook of psychology* (Vol. 4, pp. 527–547). Hoboken, NJ: Wiley.

Treiman, R., & Kessler, B. (2009). Learning to read. In M. G. Gaskell (Ed.), *The Oxford handbook of psycholinguistics* (pp. 771–785). New York: Oxford University Press.

Treisman, A. (1964). Monitoring and storage of irrelevant messages and selective attention. *Journal of Verbal Learning and Verbal Behavior, 3,* 449–459.

Treisman, A. (1986, November). Features and objects in visual processing. *Scientific American, 255* (5), 114B–125B.

Treisman, A. (1990). Visual coding of features and objects: Some evidence from behavioral studies. In National Research Council (Ed.), *Advances in the modularity of vision: Selections from a symposium on frontiers of visual science* (pp. 39–61). Washington, DC: National Academy Press.

Treisman, A. (1993). The perception of features and objects. In A. Baddeley & L. Weiskrantz (Eds.), *Attention: Selection, awareness, and control* (pp. 5–35). Oxford, UK: Clarendon.

Treisman, A. (2006). How the deployment of attention determines what we see. *Visual Cognition, 14,* 411–443.

Treisman, A., & Gelade, G. (1980). A feature-integration theory of attention. *Cognitive Psychology, 12,* 97–136.

Treisman, A., & Schmidt, H. (1982). Illusory conjunction in the perception of objects. *Cognitive Psychology, 14,* 107–141.

Treisman, A., & Souther, J. (1985). Search asymmetry: A diagnostic for preattentive processing of separable features. *Journal of Experimental Psychology: General, 114,* 285–310.

Treisman, A., & Souther, J. (1986). Illusory words: The roles of attention and of top-down constraints in conjoining letters to form words. *Journal of Experimental Psychology: Human Perception and Performance, 12,* 3–17.

Trout, J. D. (2001). The biological basis of speech: What to infer from talking to the animals. *Psychological Review, 108,* 523–549.

Trout, J. D. (2002). Scientific explanation and the sense of understanding. *Philosophy of Science, 69,* 212–233.

Tsang, P. S. (2007). The dynamics of attention and aging. In A. F. Kramer, D. A. Wiegmann, & A. Kirlik (Eds.), *Attention: From theory to practice* (pp. 170–184). New York: Oxford University Press.

Tsang, Y.-K., & Chen, H.-C. (2008). Eye movements in reading Chinese. In K. Rayner, D. Shen, X. Bai, & G. Yan (Eds.), *Cognitive and cultural influences on eye movements* (pp. 235–254). Tianjin, China: Tianjin People's Publishing House.

Tsujii, T., & Watanabe, S. (2009). Neural correlates of dual-task effect on belief-bias syllogistic reasoning: A near-infrared spectroscopy study. *Brain Research, 1287,* 118–125.

Tuckey, M. R., & Brewer, N. (2003). How schemas affect eyewitness memory over repeated retrieval attempts. *Applied Cognitive Psychology, 17,* 855–880.

Tulving, E., & Rosenbaum, S. (2006). What do explanations of the distinctiveness effect need to explain? In R. R. Hunt & J. B. Worthen (Eds.), *Distinctiveness and memory* (pp. 407–423). New York: Oxford University Press.

Turan, B., & Horowitz, L. M. (2007). Can I count on you to be there for me? Individual differences in a knowledge structure. *Journal of Personality and Social Psychology, 93,* 447–465.

Tversky, A., & Kahneman, D. (1971). Belief in the law of small numbers. *Psychological Bulletin, 76,* 105–110.

Tversky, A., & Kahneman, D. (1973). Availability: A heuristic for judging frequency and probability. *Cognitive Psychology, 5,* 207–232.

Tversky, A., & Kahneman, D. (1974). Judgments under uncertainty: Heuristics and biases. *Science, 185,* 1124–1131.

Tversky, A., & Kahneman, D. (1981). The framing of decisions and the psychology of choice. *Science, 211,* 453–458.

Tversky, A., & Kahneman, D. (1982). Judgment under uncertainty: Heuristics and biases. In D. Kahneman, P. Slovic, & A. Tversky (Eds.), *Judgment under uncertainty: Heuristics and biases* (pp. 3–20). New York: Cambridge University Press.

Tversky, A., & Kahneman, D. (1983). Extensional versus intuitive reasoning: The conjunction fallacy in probability judgment. *Psychological Review, 90,* 293–315.

Tversky, B. (1981). Distortions in memory for maps. *Cognitive Psychology, 13,* 407–433.

Tversky, B. (1991). Spatial mental models. *The Psychology of Learning and Motivation, 27,* 109–145.

Tversky, B. (1997). Spatial constructions. In N. L. Stein, P. A. Ornstein, B. Tversky, & C. Brainerd (Eds.), *Memory for everyday and emotional events* (pp. 181–208). Mahwah, NJ: Erlbaum.

Tversky, B. (1998). Three dimensions of spatial cognition. In M. A. Conway, S. E. Gathercole, & C. Cornoldi (Eds.), *Theories of memory* (Vol. 2, pp. 259–275). East Sussex, UK: Psychology Press.

Tversky, B. (1999). Talking about space [Review of the book *Representation and processing of spatial expressions*]. *Contemporary Psychology, 44,* 39–40.

Tversky, B. (2000a). Levels and structure of spatial knowledge. In S. M. Freundschuh & R. Kitchin (Eds.), *Cognitive mapping: Past, present, and future* (pp. 24–43). New York: Routledge.

Tversky, B. (2000b). Remembering spaces. In E. Tulving & F. I. M. Craik (Eds.), *The Oxford handbook of memory* (pp. 363–378). New York: Oxford University Press.

Tversky, B. (2005a). Functional significance of visuospatial representations. In P. Shah & A. Miyake (Eds.), *The Cambridge handbook of visuospatial thinking* (pp. 1–34). New York: Cambridge University Press.

Tversky, B. (2005b). Visuospatial reasoning. In K. J. Holyoak & R. G. Morrison (Eds.), *The Cambridge handbook of thinking and reasoning* (pp. 209–240). New York: Cambridge University Press.

Tversky, B. (2009). Spatial cognition: Embodied and situated. In P. Robbins & M. Aydede (Eds.), *The Cambridge handbook of situated cognition* (pp. 201–216). New York: Cambridge University Press.

Tversky, B., Morrison, J. B., Franklin, N., & Bryant, D. J. (1999). Three spaces of spatial cognition. *Professional Geographer, 51,* 516–524.

Tversky, B., & Schiano, D. J. (1989). Perceptual and conceptual factors in distortions in memory for graphs and maps. *Journal of Experimental Psychology: General, 118,* 387–398.

Twyman, A. D., & Newcombe, N. S. (2010). Five reasons to doubt the existence of a geometric module. *Cognitive Science,* 1315–1356.

U.S. Census Bureau. (2012a). *State and County Quick Facts.* Retrieved March 14, 2012, from http://quickfacts.census.gov/qfd/states/00000.html

U. S. Census Bureau. (2012b). *Statistical abstract of the United States,* Table 6. Resident population by sex, race, and Hispanic-origin status: 2000 to 2009. Retrieved June 12, 2012, from http://www.census.gov/compendia/statab/2012/tables/12 s0006.pdf

U.S. Census Bureau. (2012c). *Statistical abstract of the United States,* Table 53. Languages spoken at home. Retrieved May 17, 2012, from http://www.census.gov/compendia/statab/2012/tables/12 s0053.pdf

Uchanski, R. M. (2005). Clear speech. In D. B. Pisoni & R. E. Remez (Eds.), *The handbook of speech perception* (pp. 207–235). Malden, MA: Blackwell.

Underwood, G., & Batt, V. (1996). *Reading and understanding: An introduction to the psychology of reading.* Cambridge, MA: Blackwell.

Useem, M. (2006). *The go point: When it's time to decide—knowing what to do and when to do it.* New York: Crown Publishing Group.

Uttal, D. H., Friedman, A., Hand, L. L., & Warren, C. (2010). Learning fine-grained and category information in navigable real-world space. *Memory & Cognition, 38,* 1026–1040.

Vandierendonck, A., Liefooghe, B., & Verbruggen, F. (2010). Task switching: Interplay of reconfiguration and interference control. *Psychological Bulletin, 136,* 601–626.

Vandierendonck, A., & Szmalec, A. (2011a). Preface. In A. Vandierendonck & A. Szmalec (Eds.), *Spatial working memory* (pp. vii–xi). New York: Psychology Press.

Vandierendonck, A., & Szmalec, A. (2011b). Progress in spatial working memory research. In A. Vandierendonck & A. Szmalec (Eds.), *Spatial working memory* (pp. 1–18). New York: Psychology Press.

Vandierendonck, A., & Szmalec, A. (Eds.). (2011c). *Spatial working memory.* New York: Psychology Press.

van Hell, J. G., & Dijkstra, T. (2002). Foreign language knowledge can influence native language performance in exclusively native contexts. *Psychonomic Bulletin & Review, 9,* 780–789.

Van Orden, G. C., & Kloos, H. (2005). The question of phonology and reading. In M. J. Snowling &

C. Hulme (Eds.), *The science of reading: A handbook* (pp. 61–78). Malden, MA: Blackwell.

Van Overschelde, J. P., Rawson, K. A., Dunlosky, & Hunt, R. R. (2005). Distinctive processing underlies skilled memory. *Psychological Science, 16*, 358–361.

van Turennout, M., Hagoort, P., & Brown, C. M. (1998). Brain activity during speaking: From syntax to phonology in 40 milliseconds. *Science, 280*, 572–574.

Van Wallendael, L. R., & Kuhn, J. C. (1997). Distinctiveness is in the eye of the beholder: Cross-racial differences in perceptions of faces. *Psychological Reports, 80*, 35–39.

Vartanian, O., & Mandel, D. R. (2011). Introduction. In O. Vartanian & D. R. Mandel (Eds.), *Neuroscience of decision making* (pp. 1–7). New York: Psychology Press.

Vecera, S. P. (1998). Visual object representation: An introduction. *Psychobiology, 26*, 281–308.

Vecera, S. P., & Lee, H. (2010). Vision: Cognitive influences. In E. B. Goldstein (Ed.), *Encyclopedia of perception* (Vol. 2, pp. 1048–1053). Thousand Oaks, CA: Sage.

Velmans, M. (2009). *Understanding consciousness* (2nd ed.). New York: Routledge.

Velmans, M., & Schneider, S. (Eds.). (2007). *The Blackwell companion to consciousness*. Malden, MA: Blackwell.

Vigliocco, G., & Hartsuiker, R. J. (2002). The interplay of meaning, sound, and syntax in sentence production. *Psychological Bulletin, 128*, 442–472.

Viney, W., & King, D. B. (2003). *A history of psychology: Ideas and context* (3rd ed.). Boston: Allyn and Bacon.

Vingerhoets, G., Berckmoes, C., & Stroobant, N. (2003). Cerebral hemodynamics during discrimination of prosodic and semantic emotion in speech studied by transcranial Doppler ultrasonography. *Neuropsychology, 17*, 93–99.

Vojdanoska, M., Cranney, J., & Newell, B. R. (2010). The testing effect: The role of feedback and collaboration in a tertiary classroom setting. *Applied Cognitive Psychology, 24*, 1183–1195.

Volz, K. G., et al. (2006). Why you think Milan is larger than Modena: Neural correlates of the recognition heuristic. *Journal of Cognitive Neuroscience, 18*, 1924–1936.

Voyer, D., Nolan, C., & Voyer, S. (2000). The relation between experience and spatial performance in men and women. *Sex Roles, 43*, 891–915.

Vu, E., & Rich, A. N. (2010). Independent sampling of features enables conscious perception of bound objects. *Psychological Science, 21*, 1168–1175.

Vuong, Q. C. (2010). Object perception. In E. B. Goldstein (Ed.), *Encyclopedia of perception* (Vol. 2, pp. 643–648). Thousand Oaks, CA: Sage.

Vuvan, D. T., & Schmuckler, M. A. (2011). Tonal hierarchy representations in auditory imagery. *Memory & Cognition, 39*, 477–490.

Wade, K. A., Garry, M., Read, J. D., & Lindsay, D. S. (2002). A picture is worth a thousand lies: Using false photographs to create false childhood memories. *Psychonomic Bulletin and Review, 9*, 597–603.

Wagner, M. (2006). *The geometries of visual space*. Mahwah, NJ: Erlbaum.

Wagner, R. K., & Stanovich, K. E. (1996). Expertise in reading. In K. A. Ericsson (Ed.), *The road to excellence: The acquisition of expert performance in the arts and sciences, sports, and games* (pp. 189–225). Mahwah, NJ: Erlbaum.

Walker, I., & Hulme, C. (1999). Concrete words are easier to recall than abstract: Evidence for a semantic contribution to short-term serial recall. *Journal of Experimental Psychology: Learning, Memory, & Cognition, 25*, 1256–1271.

Walker, P. M., & Hewstone, M. (2006). A perceptual discrimination investigation of the own-race effect and intergroup experience. *Applied Cognitive Psychology, 20*, 461–475.

Walker, W. R., Vogl, R. J., & Thompson, C. P. (1997). Autobiographical memory: Unpleasantness fades faster than pleasantness over time. *Applied Cognitive Psychology, 11*, 399–413.

Walker, W. R., et al. (2003). On the emotions that accompany autobiographical memories: Dysphoria disrupts the fading affect bias. *Cognition and Emotion, 17*, 703–724.

Walker-Andrews, A. S. (1986). Intermodal perception of expressive behaviors: Relation of eye and voice? *Developmental Psychology, 22*, 373–377.

Walton, G. M., & Dweck, C. S. (2009). Solving social problems like a psychologist. *Perspectives on Psychological Science, 4*, 101–102.

Wang, G., Tanaka, K., & Tanifuji, M. (1996). Optical imaging of functional organization in the monkey inferotemporal cortex. *Science, 272*, 1665–1668.

Ward, G., & Allport, A. (1997). Planning and problem-solving using the five-disc tower of London task.

Quarterly Journal of Experimental Psychology, 50A, 49–78.

Ward, G., & Kolomyts, Y. (2010). Cognition and creativity. In J. C. Kaufman & R. J. Sternberg (Eds.), *The Cambridge handbook of creativity* (pp. 93–112). New York: Cambridge University Press.

Ward, G., & Morris, R. (2005). Introduction to the psychology of planning. In R. Morris & G. Ward (Eds.), *The cognitive psychology of planning* (pp. 1–34). Hove, UK: Psychology Press.

Ward, G., Avons, S. E., & Melling, L. (2005). Serial position curves in short-term memory: Functional equivalence across modalities. *Memory, 13,* 308–317.

Waring, J. D., & Kensinger, E. A. (2011). How emotion leads to selective memory: Neuroimaging evidence. *Neuropsychologia, 40,* 1831–1842.

Warren, R. M. (2006). The relation of speech perception to the perception of nonverbal auditory patterns. In S. Greenberg & W. A. Ainsworth (Eds.), *Listening to speech: An auditory perspective* (pp. 333–349). Mahwah, NJ: Erlbaum.

Warren, R. M., & Warren, R. P. (1970, December). Auditory illusions and confusions. *Scientific American, 223* (6), 30–36.

Warrington, E. K., & Weiskrantz, L. (1970). Amnesic syndrome: Consolidation or retrieval? *Nature, 228,* 629–630.

Wason, P. C. (1968). Reasoning about a rule. *Quarterly Journal of Experimental Psychology, 20,* 273–281.

Watson, J. B. (1913). Psychology as the behaviorist views it. *Psychological Review, 20,* 158–177.

Waxman, S. R. (2002). Early word-learning and conceptual development: Everything had a name and each name gave birth to a new thought. In U. Goswami (Ed.), *Blackwell handbook of child cognitive development* (pp. 102–126). Malden, MA: Blackwell.

Weaver, C. A., III, Terrell, J. T., Krug, K. S., & Kelemen, W. L. (2008). The delayed JOL effect with very long delays: Evidence from flashbulb memories. In J. Dunlosky & R. A. Bjork (Eds.), *Handbook of metamemory and memory* (pp. 155–172). New York: Psychology Press.

Weber, E. U., & Morris, M. W. (2010). Culture and judgment and decision making: The constructivist turn. *Perspectives on Psychological Science, 5,* 410–419.

Wegner, D. M. (1994). Ironic processes of mental control. *Psychological Review, 101,* 34–52.

Wegner, D. M. (1996). Personal communication.

Wegner, D. M. (1997a). When the antidote is the poison: Ironic mental control processes. *Psychological Science, 8,* 148–153.

Wegner, D. M. (1997b). Why the mind wanders. In J. D. Cohen & J. W. Schooler (Eds.), *Scientific approaches to consciousness* (pp. 295–315). Mahwah, NJ: Erlbaum.

Wegner, D. M. (2002). *The illusion of conscious will.* Cambridge, MA: MIT Press.

Wegner, D. M., Schneider, D. J., Carter, S. R., III, & White, T. L. (1987). Paradoxical effects of thought suppression. *Journal of Personality and Social Psychology, 53,* 5–13.

Weick, M., & Guinote, A. (2010). How long will it take? Power biases time predictions. *Journal of Experimental Social Psychology, 46,* 595–604.

Weierich, M., & Barrett, L. F. (2010). Affect as a source of visual attention. In E. Balcetis & G. D. Lassiter (Eds.), *Social psychology of visual perception.* New York: Psychology Press.

Weinberg, A. (Ed.). (2012). *The psychology of politicians.* New York: Cambridge.

Weisberg, R. W. (1999). Creativity and knowledge: A challenge to theories. In R. J. Sternberg (Ed.), *Handbook of creativity* (pp. 226–250). New York: Cambridge University Press.

Weisberg, R. W. (2006). Modes of expertise in creative thinking: Evidence from case studies. In K. A. Ericsson, N. Charness, P. J. Feltovich, & R. R. Hoffman (Eds.), *The Cambridge handbook on expertise and expert performance* (pp. 761–787). New York: Cambridge University Press.

Weiskrantz, L. (1997). *Consciousness lost and found: A neuropsychological explanation.* New York: Oxford University Press.

Weiskrantz, L. (2000). To have but not to hold. In J. J. Bolhuis (Ed.), *Brain, perception, memory* (pp. 310–325). New York: Oxford University Press.

Weiskrantz, L. (2007). The case of blindsight. In M. Velmans & S. Schneider (Eds.), *The Blackwell companion to consciousness* (pp. 175–180). Malden, MA: Blackwell.

Weist, R. M. (1985). Cross-linguistic perspective on cognitive development. In T. M. Schlechter & M. P. Toglia (Eds.), *New directions in cognitive science* (pp. 191–216). Norwood, NJ: Ablex.

Wellman, H. M. (2000). Early childhood: Cognitive and mental development. In A. E. Kazdin (Ed.), *The encyclopedia of psychology.* New York: Oxford University Press.

Wellman, H. M., & Gelman, S. A. (1992). Cognitive development: Foundational theories of core domains. *Annual Review of Psychology, 43*, 337–375.

Wells, A. (2005). Worry, intrusive thoughts, and generalized anxiety disorder: The metacognitive theory and treatment. In D. A. Clark (Ed.), *Intrusive thoughts in clinical disorders: Theory, research, and treatment* (pp. 119–144). New York: Guilford Press.

Wells, G. L., & Olson, E. A. (2003). Eyewitness testimony. *Annual Review of Psychology, 54*, 277–295.

Wells, G. L., et al. (2000). From the lab to the police station: A successful application of eyewitness research. *American Psychologist, 55*, 581–598.

Wenzel, A. (2005). Autobiographical memory tasks in clinical research. In A. Wenzel & D. C. Rubin (Eds.), *Cognitive methods and their application to clinical research* (pp. 243–264). Washington, DC: American Psychological Association.

Wenzlaff, R. M. (2005). Seeking solace but finding despair: The persistence of intrusive thoughts in depression. In D. A. Clark (Ed.), *Intrusive thoughts in clinical disorders: Theory, research, and treatment* (pp. 55–85). New York: Guilford Press.

Werker, J. F., & Tees, R. C. (1984). Cross-language speech perception: Evidence for perceptual reorganization during the first year of life. *Infant Behavior and Development, 7*, 49–63.

Werker, J. F., & Tees, R. C. (1999). Influences on infant speech processing: Toward a new synthesis. *Annual Review of Psychology, 50*, 509–535.

Wheeler, M. A. (2000). Episodic memory and autonoetic awareness. In E. Tulving & F. I. M. Craik (Eds.), *The Oxford handbook of memory* (pp. 597–608). New York: Oxford University Press.

Wheeler, M. E., & Treisman, A. M. (2002). Binding in short-term visual memory. *Journal of Experimental Psychology: General, 113*, 48–64.

Whitbourne, S. K., & Whitbourne, S. B. (2011). *Adult development and aging: Biopsychosocial perspectives* (4th ed.). Hoboken, NJ: Wiley.

White, J. (2003). Personal communication.

White, K. R., Crites, S. L., Jr., Taylor, J. H., & Coral, G. (2009). Wait, what? Assessing stereotype incongruities using the N400 ERP component. *Social Cognitive and Affective Neuroscience, 4*, 191–198.

White, S. J., & Liversedge, S. P. (2004). Orthographic familiarity influences initial eye fixation positions in reading. In R. Radach, A. Kennedy, & K. Rayner (Eds.), *Eye movements and information processing during reading* (pp. 52–78). Hove, UK: Psychology Press.

Whitley, B. E., Jr., & Kite, M. E. (2010). *The psychology of prejudice and discrimination* (2nd ed.). Belmont, CA: Wadsworth Cengage.

Whitten, S., & Graesser, A. C. (2003). Comprehension of text in problem solving. In J. E. Davidson & R. J. Sternberg (Eds.), *The psychology of problem solving* (pp. 207–229). New York: Cambridge University Press.

Whitten, W. B., II. (2011). Learning from and for tests. In A. S. Benjamin (Ed.), *Successful remembering and successful forgetting: A festschrift in honor of Robert A. Bjork* (pp. 217–234). New York: Psychology Press.

Wickelgren, W. A. (1965). Acoustic similarity and intrusion errors in short-term memory. *Journal of Experimental Psychology, 70*, 102–108.

Wickens, D. D., Dalezman, R. E., & Eggemeier, F. T. (1976). Multiple encoding of word attributes in memory. *Memory & Cognition, 4*, 307–310.

Wiers, R. W., & Stacy, A. W. (Eds.). (2006). *Handbook of implicit cognition and addiction*. Thousand Oaks, CA: Sage.

Wilding, J., & Valentine, E. (1997). *Superior memory*. Hove, UK: Psychology Press.

Wiley, E. W., Bialystok, E., & Hakuta, K. (2005). New approaches to using data to test the critical-period hypothesis for second-language acquisition. *Psychological Science, 16*, 341–343.

Wilford, M. M., & Wells, G. L. (2010). Does facial processing prioritize change detection? Change blindness illustrates costs and benefits of holistic processing. *Psychological Science, 21*, 1611–1615.

Wilhelm, O. (2005). Measuring reasoning ability. In O. Wilhelm & R. W. Engle (Eds.), *Handbook of understanding and measuring intelligence* (pp. 373–392). Thousand Oaks, CA: Sage.

Willcutt, E. G., et al. (2005). Validity of the executive function theory of attention-deficit/hyperactivity disorder: A meta-analytic review. *Biological Psychiatry, 57*, 1336–1346.

Williams, C. C., Perea, M., Pollatsek, A., & Rayner, K. (2006). Previewing the neighborhood: The role of orthographic neighbors as parafoveal previews in reading. *Journal of Experimental Psychology: Human Perception and Performance, 32*, 1072–1082.

Williams, J. D. (2005). *The teacher's grammar book* (2nd ed.). Mahwah, NJ: Erlbaum.

Williams, J. M. G., Mathews, A., & MacLeod, C. (1996). The emotional Stroop task and psychopathology. *Psychological Bulletin, 120*, 3–24.

Willingham, D. T. (2010, Summer). Have technology and multitasking rewired how students learn? *American Educator*, pp. 23–28, 42.

Wilson, B. A. (1995). Management and remediation of memory problems in brain-injured adults. In A. D. Baddeley, B. A. Wilson, & F. N. Watts (Eds.), *Handbook of memory disorders* (pp. 451–479). Chichester, UK: Wiley.

Wilson, C. E., Palermo, R., Schmalzl, L., & Brock, J. (2010). Specificity of impaired facial identity recognition in children with suspected developmental prosopagnosia. *Cognitive Neuropsychology, 27*, 30–45.

Wilson, M. (2002). Six views of embodied cognition. *Psychonomic Bulletin & Review, 9*, 625–636

Wilson, T. D. (1997). The psychology of metapsychology. In J. D. Cohen & J. W. Schooler (Eds.), *Scientific approaches to consciousness* (pp. 317–332). Mahwah, NJ: Erlbaum.

Wilson, T. D. (2009). Know thyself. *Perspectives on Psychological Science, 4*, 384–389.

Wingfield, A. (1993). Sentence processing. In J. B. Gleason & N. Bernstein Ratner (Eds.), *Psycholinguistics* (pp. 199–235). Fort Worth: Harcourt Brace.

Winston, J. S., Strange, B. A., O'Doherty, J., & Dolan, R. J. (2005). Automatic and intentional brain responses during evaluation of trustworthiness of faces. In J. T. Cacioppo & G. G. Berntson (Eds.), *Social neuroscience: Key readings* (pp. 199–210). New York: Psychology Press.

Wise, R. A., Safer, M. A., & Maro, C. M. (2011). What U.S. law enforcement officers know and believe about eyewitness factors, eyewitness interviews and identification procedures. *Applied Cognitive Psychology, 25*, 488–500.

Wisniewski, E. J. (2002). Concepts and categorization. In D. Medin (Ed.), *Stevens' handbook of experimental psychology* (3rd ed., Vol. 2, pp. 467–531). New York: Wiley.

Wolfe, J. M. (2000). Visual attention. In K. K. De Valois (Ed.), *Seeing* (2nd ed., pp. 335–386). San Diego: Academic Press.

Wolfe, J. M. (2001). Asymmetries in visual search: An introduction. *Perception & Psychophysics, 63*, 381–389.

Wolfe, J. M., Horowitz, T. S., & Kenner, N. M. (2005). Rare items often missed in visual searches. *Nature, 435*, 439–440.

Wolfe, J. M., et al. (2009). *Sensation & perception* (2nd ed.). Sunderland, MA: Sinauer.

Wolfe, M. B. W. (2005). Memory for narrative and expository text: Independent influences of semantic associations and text organization. *Journal of Experimental Psychology: Learning, Memory, and Cognition, 31*, 359–364.

Wolfe, M. B. W., & Goldman, S. R. (2005). Relations between adolescents' text processing and reasoning. *Cognition and Instruction, 23*, 467–502.

Wolfe, M. B. W., Magliano, J. P., & Larsen, B. (2005). Causal and semantic relatedness in discourse understanding and representation. *Discourse Processes, 39*, 165–187.

Woll, S. (2002). *Everyday thinking: Memory, reasoning, and judgment in the real world*. Mahwah, NJ: Erlbaum.

Wong, C. K., & Read, J. D. (2011). Positive and negative effects of physical context reinstatement on eyewitness recall and identification. *Applied Cognitive Psychology, 25*, 2–11.

Wood, J. N. (2011). A core knowledge architecture of visual working memory. *Journal of Experimental Psychology: Human Perception and Performance, 37*, 357–381.

Wood, N., & Cowan, N. (1995). The cocktail party phenomenon revisited: How frequent are attention shifts to one's name in an irrelevant auditory channel? *Journal of Experimental Psychology: Learning, Memory, and Cognition, 21*, 255–260.

Woodward, A. L., & Markman, E. M. (1998). Early word learning. In W. Damon (Ed.), *Handbook of child psychology: Cognition, perception, and language* (5th ed., Vol. 2, 371–420). New York: Wiley.

Worthen, J. B. (2006). Resolution of discrepant memory strengths: An explanation of the effects of bizarreness on memory. In R. R. Hunt & J. B. Worthen (Eds.), *Distinctiveness and memory* (pp. 133–156). New York: Oxford University Press.

Worthen, J. B., & Hunt, R. R. (2011). *Mnemonology: Mnemonics for the 21st century*. New York: Psychology Press.

Wraga, M., et al. (2005). Imagined rotations of self versus objects: An fMRI study. *Neuropsychologia, 43*, 1351–1361.

Wright, D. B., Boyd, C. E., & Tredoux, C. G. (2003). Inter-racial contact and the own-race bias for face recognition in South Africa and England. *Applied Cognitive Psychology, 17*, 365–373.

Wright, R. D., & Ward, L. M. (2008). *Orienting of attention*. New York: Oxford University Press.

Wu, J., et al. (2006). Event-related potentials during mental imagery of animal sounds. *Psychophysiology, 43,* 592–597.

Yamauchi, T. (2005). Labeling bias and categorical induction: Generative aspects of category information. *Journal of Experimental Psychology: Learning, Memory, and Cognition, 31,* 538–553.

Yang, L.-X., & Lewandowsky, S. (2004). Knowledge partitioning in categorization: Constraints on exemplar models. *Journal of Experimental Psychology: Learning, Memory and Cognition, 30,* 1045–1064.

Yang, S.-N., & McConkie, G. W. (2004). Saccade generation during reading: Are words necessary? In R. Radach, A. Kennedy, & K. Rayner (Eds.), *Eye movements and information processing during reading* (pp. 226–261). Hove, UK: Psychology Press.

Yates, J. F. (2010). Culture and probability judgment. *Social and Personality Psychology Compass, 4,* 174–188.

Yoder, J. D. (2013). *Women and gender: Making a difference* (4th ed.). Cornwall-on-Hudson, NY: Sloan.

Youn, J. C., et al. (2009). Development of the subjective memory complaints questionnaire. *Dementia and Geriatric Disorders, 2009,* 310–317.

Young, C. A. (2007, July 21). *Scientists endeavor to make humanoid robots more graceful.* Retrieved July 25, 2007, from http://news-service.stanford .edu/news/2007/July11/robots-071107.html

Zacks, J. M., Tversky, B., & Iyer, G. (2001). Perceiving, remembering, and communicating structure in events. *Journal of Experimental Psychology: General, 130,* 29–58.

Zacks, J. M., Vettel, J. M., & Michelon, P. (2003). Imagined viewer and object rotations dissociated with event-related fMRI. *Journal of Cognitive Neuroscience, 15,* 1002–1018.

Zacks, R. T., & Hasher, L. (2006). Aging and long-term memory: Deficits are not inevitable. In E. Bialystok & F. I. M. Craik (Eds.), *Lifespan cognition: Mechanisms of change* (pp. 162–177). New York: Oxford University Press.

Zajac, R., & Hayne, H. (2006). The negative effect of cross-examination style questioning on children's accuracy: Older children are not immune. *Applied Cognitive Psychology, 20,* 3–16.

Zangwill, O. L. (2004a). Ebbinghaus, H. In R. L. Gregory (Ed.), *The Oxford companion to the mind* (2nd ed., p. 276). New York: Oxford University Press.

Zangwill, O. L. (2004b). Wundt, Wilhelm Max. In R. L. Gregory (Ed.), *The Oxford companion to the mind* (2nd ed., pp. 951–952). New York: Oxford University Press.

Zaromb, F. M., & Roediger, H. L., III. (2010). The testing effect in free recall is associated with enhanced organizational processes. *Memory & Cognition, 38,* 995–1008.

Zauberman, G., & Lynch, J. G., Jr. (2005). Resource slack and propensity to discount delayed investments of time versus money. *Journal of Experimental Psychology: General, 134,* 23–37.

Zeman, A. (2004). *Consciousness: A user's guide.* New Haven: Yale University.

Zentella, A. C. (2006). Hablamos Spanish and English. In H. Luria, D. M. Seymour, & T. Smoke (Eds.), *Language and linguistics in context: Readings and applications for teachers* (pp. 85–89). Mahwah, NJ: Erlbaum.

Zhao, Y., et al. (2011). The neural basis of breaking mental set: An event-related potential study. *Experimental Brain Research, 208,* 181–187.

Zhu, B., et al. (2010). Treat and trick: A new way to increase false memory. *Applied Cognitive Psychology, 24,* 1199–1208.

Ziegler, J. C., et al. (2010). Orthographic depth and its impact on universal predictors of reading: A cross-language investigation. *Psychological Science, 21,* 551–559.

Zimmermann, T. D., & Meier, B. (2010). The effect of implementation intentions on prospective memory performance across the lifespan. *Applied Cognitive Psychology, 24,* 645–658.

Zinn, T. E. (2009, October). But I really tried! Helping students link effort and performance. *APS Observer.* Retrieved June 27, 2012, from http://www .psychologicalscience.org/observer/getArticle.cfm? id=2564

Zwaan, R. A., & Rapp, D. N. (2006). Discourse comprehension. In M. J. Traxler & M. A. Gernsbacher (Eds.), *Handbook of psycholinguistics* (2nd ed., pp. 249–283). Amsterdam: Elsevier.

Zwaan, R. A., & Singer, M. (2003). Text comprehension. In A. C. Graesser, M. A. Gernsbacher, & S. R. Goldman (Eds.), *Handbook of discourse processes* (pp. 83–121).

⟲ Name Index

✪ Subject Index